D0933601

THE STATE'S SERVANTS

THE STATE'S
SERVANTS

*The Civil Service of
the English Republic
1649–1660*

G. E. AYLMER

*Professor of History
University of York*

Routledge & Kegan Paul
London and Boston

First published in 1973
by Routledge & Kegan Paul Ltd
Broadway House, 68–74 Carter Lane,
London EC4V 5EL and
9 Park Street
Boston, Mass. 02108, U.S.A.
Printed in Great Britain by
W & J Mackay Limited, Chatham

ISBN 0 7100 7637 1

The same Arts that did gain
A Pow'r must it maintain.
                    (Marvell, 'An Horatian Ode')

History to the defeated
May say Alas but cannot help or pardon.
                    (W. H. Auden, 'Spain, 1937')

CONTENTS

CONTENTS

TABLES AND MAPS

ix

PREFACE AND
ACKNOWLEDGMENTS

I have tried to explain the scope and purpose of this book in the first chapter. A special word should perhaps be said about chapter 4, 'Social biography'. Readers who find even very simple statistical tables repugnant may be well advised to steer clear of sections iii and iv; conversely, those who find large numbers of individual biographical sketches tedious may want to skim rapidly over section v. I can only say that, as is argued more fully in the text, I believe both approaches to be necessary—and the chapter to have a logical coherence.

I wish to acknowledge my thanks to the Comptroller of Crown Copyright for permitting me to reproduce original documents, and to quote from others, in the Public Record Office and in printed calendars of the Historical Manuscripts Commission, and to Messrs R. M. and R. W. Willcocks for permission to quote from documents in their collection. In verbatim quotations I have followed the original except for extending contemporary contractions, discarding the Old English 'thorn' (for 'th'), and occasionally supplying punctuation necessary to the sense; but I have not meddled with seventeenth-century spelling or syntax. Where surnames have variant spellings, I have followed the way in which a man wrote his own name—provided of course that his spelling was consistent even in that! Dates are given in the Old Style unless indicated otherwise, except that the year is taken to begin on 1 January: e.g. Charles I's execution on 30 January 1649, not 9 February 1649 (New Style) or 30 January 1648 (Old Style, with year beginning on 25 March). Since the book does not contain a bibliography, I have tried to give as full a title and description as necessary on the first occasion any printed or MS. work is cited in the Notes, and thereafter a shortened but—I hope—recognisable abbreviation of this.

For reasons of economy, to try to keep the price of this book down as far as possible under present conditions, the Notes have been printed at the end of the text, rather than as footnotes. I hope that this will not inconvenience readers, and that printing the page numbers of the text to which the Notes refer, above them, will help those who wish to refer to the Notes while they are reading the book.

I am happy to acknowledge many obligations and debts of gratitude incurred in the course of its preparation and writing. I wish to thank the Leverhulme Foundation and the British Academy for grants in aid of research expenses, and most particularly the University of York for its generosity in allowing me paid leave-of-absence in 1967–8.

I have been helped by a large number of individuals in answering queries, sending me suggestions and correcting ignorance or misapprehensions on my part. Amongst those to whom I am grateful are the following: Professor W. H. G. Armytage, Dr Peter Aston, Professor Thomas G. Barnes, Mr Bernard Barr, Dr E. G. W. Bill and the staff of Lambeth Palace Library, Mr W. W. S. Breem (the Honorary Librarian of the Inner Temple), Mr R. W. Clayton, Mr J. P. Cooper, Mrs Mary Cotterell, Dr M. Claire Cross, Mr J. P. Ferris, Mrs Norah Gurney, Professor H. J. Habakkuk, Dr Christopher Hill, Dr A. E. J. Hollaender and the staff of the Guildhall Library, Miss Meryl Jancey, Dr D. W. Jones, Mr R. A. Malyn, Miss Lesley Montgomery, Mr E. L. C. Mullins, Dr Valerie Pearl, Mr D. H. Pennington, Miss Felicity Ranger and the other staff at the National Register of Archives, Miss V. A. Rowe, Dr Ailwyn Ruddock, Mr Conrad Russell, Mr J. C. Sainty, Miss Ruth Spalding, Professor Lawrence Stone, Dr A. A. Tait, Mr Keith Thomas, Mr Christopher Thompson, Mr Kenneth Timings, Mrs Joan Varley, Mr C. Webster, Professor Gwyn A. Williams, Professor Mark Williamson. I am grateful to the Archivists of the following authorities and institutions for answering questions about materials in their charge: Bedfordshire, Berkshire, Bristol, Buckinghamshire, Cambridgeshire and the Isle of Ely, the University of Cambridge, Cheshire, Cumberland, Westmorland and Carlisle, Devon, Dorset, Durham, County Durham, Epsom and Ewell, Essex, Gloucestershire, Herefordshire, Hertfordshire, Huntingdonshire, Kent, Leeds, Leicestershire, Lincolnshire, Greater London (County Hall) and Greater London (Middlesex Records), Monmouthshire, Norfolk and Norwich, Northamptonshire, Northumberland, Plymouth, Sheffield, Shropshire, Somerset, Staffordshire, East Suffolk, West Suffolk, Surrey, East Sussex, West Sussex, Warwickshire, Wiltshire, the East Riding of Yorkshire, the North Riding of Yorkshire, the Yorkshire Archaeological Society. I am grateful to the following Livery Companies of the City of London, either for allowing me to work in their archives or for answering queries about these, and to their respective Archivists or Clerks for their help: the Drapers, the Glaziers, the Goldsmiths, the Haberdashers, the Ironmongers, the Mercers, the Merchant Taylors and the Vintners. In common with other historians, I am under an immense obligation to many editors, compilers, cataloguers, archivists, librarians, collectors and others—both past and present—who have preserved the original materials for English seventeenth-century history and helped to make these more easily accessible: in particular, Mrs M. A. E. Green and the other nineteenth-century editors of the various series of Calendars of the State Papers, G. K. Fortescue and the other British Museum staff who produced the Catalogue of the Thomason Tracts early in this century, successive editors of the British Records Society's volumes of Calendars of Wills proved in the Prerogative Court of Canterbury (and elsewhere), and Mr E. L. C. Mullins for his invaluable *Texts and Calendars*. I am also grateful to the History of Parliament Trust for allowing me to look at unpublished biographies of MPs from the years 1660–90 and to use references contained in these.

I have been greatly helped by the staffs of numerous libraries and record offices, in some cases when their own working conditions were far from easy. And in particular I would like to thank the staffs of the following for their patience, courtesy and co-operation: the Bodleian Library (notably in the 'Duke Humphrey' section of the Old Library), the British Museum (and especially those in the North Library and the Manuscripts Department), the Institute of Historical Research in the University of London, the Brotherton Library in the University of Leeds, the London Library, the City, University and John Rylands Libraries in Manchester, the Public Record Office, and the Borthwick Institute, the City Reference, Minster and the J. B. Morrell University Libraries in York. I am grateful to the two institutions which have employed me since I began the research on which this book is based— the Universities of Manchester and York—and to the stimulus of many colleagues, pupils and others whom I have failed to mention by name.

I am likewise grateful to various secretaries and typists for coping with successive versions of the text and the notes: in particular, Mrs A.-M. Maney, Mrs M. Farrow and Miss A. Cooper.

I should also like to thank all those reviewers and correspondents who have pointed out mistakes or failings in my earlier book, *The King's Servants: the Civil Service of Charles I 1625–1642* (1961). In the forthcoming revised edition, I shall try to incorporate as many of these corrections as possible, though one cannot re-write a book for critics and readers who disliked it root and branch. Equally important I hope that some of the lessons drawn from that have been learnt and will be reflected in its successor.

I have again been very fortunate in prevailing on the kindness of my friends Donald Pennington and John Cooper to read the typescript at successive stages; I am immensely grateful to each of them for their perceptive comments and suggestions for improvement. Naturally, as the author, I alone am responsible for the errors and deficiencies which remain.

Finally, I am grateful beyond what can be expressed in words to my wife, not only for all her help and encouragement at every stage, but for having made it possible for me to do the work and to get the book written.   G. E. AYLMER

CHAPTER 1

INTRODUCTION

R. H. Tawney used to say that all the really important things in history could be reduced either to theology or to economics. If we take these to mean what people think and how they live, the statement may seem unexceptionable. But I believe that he meant something rather more specific, namely to claim a kind of primacy for economic, over social, political or constitutional history; and for the history of human ideas and beliefs as sharing that primacy. To Tawney, a lifelong anglican as well as a socialist, man was not a creature who could live by bread alone, although lacking it he could not live at all. Without wishing to seem ungrateful, as one who owes much to that great and good man, I would suggest that the machinery and composition of human institutions are somewhat more important than this dictum allows. It is with that conviction, hopefully a hypothesis rather than a dogma, that this book has been written. It is meant to be a contribution both to the history of seventeenth-century England and to that of the development of modern bureaucracy. It is my further contention that institutional pressures and practices can operate causally upon the economy of a country, as well as on people's ideas about government and about society. In short, the Marxian metaphor of sub- and super-structure, implying only a one-way causal relationship, that economic processes influence politics and administration but not vice versa, is untenable and must be discarded. Exactly how these interactions operate is, of course, another matter; but a better understanding of that problem may result from studies such as this one.

Over the last ten or fifteen years conservatives and radicals alike in the Western world have shown an increasing awareness that larger plans for the improvement of our society are inseparable from the mechanics of government and from the personnel and methods of administration. This is an academic as well as a 'political' point. In relating the dry-as-dust details of administration and civil servants to wider political and social issues, at least for the seventeenth century, I hope that my work may have played some small part in this growing awareness.

This book will probably be taken by most of its readers as a sequel to one published over a decade ago.[1] In my own mind, however, the present work has a certain logical priority. For the earlier study of administration and officials under Charles I was seen rather as a necessary prologue to examining the same topics during the Interregnum (also known as the Great Rebellion, and as the English Revolution). The relationship between government and society, between administration and wider social, political and intellectual changes during a period of violent upheaval—whether or not it merits the name of a revolution—has always seemed to me a neglected theme, among both historians and political scientists. That then was the original idea in 1949–51, to relate the larger long-term development of English central administration (on more or less 'Toutian' lines)[2] to the history of the Civil War, Commonwealth and Protectorate. It was the lack of an adequate framework of reference, for what administration had been like before the Civil War, which turned my study towards the reign of Charles I. Of course the question does not look the same now as it did twenty years ago. One cannot research and write unaware of the advances in historical knowledge and understanding, or of the changing fashions in historical interpretation. Other people's work, both published and in progress, has profoundly affected what I have tried to do and how I have gone about it. For instance, my decision to omit, except as background, the years from the outbreak of the Civil War to the eve of the King's execution (1642–8), was taken primarily because of the work which other historians were doing on administration in these years. Mrs Glow's work on the Long Parliament's committees,[3] Mr Kennedy's on the navy,[4] Dr Roy's on royalist administration,[5] studies of individual counties by Professor Everitt and others,[6] and above all that of Mr Pennington on committees both central and local,[7] influenced that decision. By contrast, until very recently there seemed to be less work in progress on the 1650s. For the central administration under the Protectorate, there was an excellent short section in Mr Maurice Ashley's first book;[8] since my study has been in progress there have been several important articles, notably by Mr Habakkuk[9] and Dr Farnell.[10] Other work, known to be in progress or now published, will certainly render parts of the present book obsolete, or at least call for its revision.[11]

Equally important are the questions which have been asked by other historians who have not themselves worked on the administrative history of these years. For Professor Sir John Neale, as early as 1948, the English Civil War was to be seen partly as the outcome of 'a putrefying political system', which he traced to the malaise—partly administrative in character—of the years from 1588 to 1603 as well as to the subsequent breakdown under James.[12] For Professor Hugh Trevor-Roper, writing first in 1953 and repeated since, the Independents, the real victors of the Civil War, were back-bench decentralisers with an essentially oppositionist mentality, who had little idea of what to do with State power when they got it, except to decentralise. Cromwell in particular failed with all the Parliaments with which he had dealings, because he did not understand the necessity, or master the techniques, of parliamentary management. So he failed either to lead a Court party in the Commons, or to support those who tried to build one up for him, retaining as he did the essentially 'Country' political attitudes of his earlier days.[13] In 1953 Professor G. R. Elton saw a profound continuity in the development of English central government, with few really big changes between those of the sixteenth and of the nineteenth centuries.[14] By contrast, Dr Christopher Hill has always seen the English Civil War and its aftermath, still to him the English Revolution, as marking a profound change in our national life even if its nature was more complex than he had argued in his early writings. Moreover he has continued to emphasise the importance of the republican administrators and others who survived the Restoration in 1660, and so brought the policies and methods of the Commonwealth and the Protectorate on into the service of the restored monarchy.[15] Mr Habakkuk, on the other hand, has seen little by way of difference between the members of the landowning class on the two sides in the Civil War except that the royalists were proportionately more heavily in debt than their parliamentarian opponents; he and Mrs Joan Thirsk have set our understanding of the Long Parliament's and Commonwealth's land sales on an altogether surer basis than they were before.[16] Meanwhile, Professor Charles Wilson has revived a traditional but neglected viewpoint, by suggesting that the level of taxation is one of the crucial factors in a country's economic development; he has applied this to a comparison of the cases of England and the Netherlands in the seventeenth and eighteenth centuries.[17] Out of the aftermath of the celebrated controversy about the fortunes of the gentry and their political significance,[18] has come important new work on the men in power after December 1648, notably by Professor David Underdown.[19] Likewise, but with a very different perspective partly resulting from his massive study of the peerage, Professor Lawrence Stone has suggested that increasing pressure for upward social mobility, the causes of which were both demographic and educational, in conflict with the values and structure of a rigidly hierarchical society, was a major source of tension in early Stuart England. He has related this to the upheavals of the mid-century, and sees the falling-off in this unsatisfied pressure for upward mobility as an element in the greater political and social stability after 1660.[20] Professor J. H. Plumb's study of political stability has a later chronological emphasis, but his implied background of volatility, not to say chronic insecurity, in early and mid-seventeenth-century England is certainly relevant for the study of administration in the mid-century.[21] In his authoritative new collection of documents for undergraduate study,

Professor J. P. Kenyon has expressed the belief that, from 1641 to 1660, 'in a sense the constitution just marked time'.[22] On a broader canvas, Dame Veronica Wedgwood's writings on the 1640s[23] and Mr Ashley's on the 1650s[24] have raised many points of general relevance for my subject. Indeed, even without direct collaborators, one can hardly complain of working in isolation, or of lacking the stimulus of fellow students and authors in related areas of history.[25]

Nor has the historical treatment of bureaucracy stood still. Over the last decade the approach of sociologists and political scientists has tended to become historically more sophisticated, and hence more relevant for my purpose. Among the classic authorities on bureaucracy, for all the criticisms which are brought against them, Weber, Mosca and Michels continue to claim our attention; Max Weber indeed remains the indispensable starting-point for all further inquiry. Of contemporary non-academic authors, Milovan Djilas's *The New Class* is a major document of our time, even though it has been largely superseded by a dense specialist literature on bureaucracy in eastern Europe and the Soviet Union.[26] On the subject of the British civil service in the nineteenth and twentieth centuries, there has been a kind of merger—and it would seem to the outsider a fruitful one—between historians and political scientists.[27] Among other recent treatments by sociologists, I have found Eisenstadt's *Political Systems of Empires*[28] difficult to relate to historical facts, despite its generous references to my own work. The little book by Blau is a useful guide;[29] so, in briefer compass, is the article by Bendix on bureaucracy in the new *International Encyclopaedia of the Social Sciences*.[30] Much the most valuable introduction for a historian interested in bureaucracy is now the short volume by Dr Albrow in the new 'Key Concepts' series.[31] Here at last is a cool appraisal of nineteenth- and twentieth-century ideas on the subject by someone with a training in both history and sociology. No historian should be too narrow to learn from scholars in related disciplines. But history is an art and a science in its own right, as well as being one of the social or human sciences. And while he should be aware of the work of people with related interests in other subjects, the historian cannot expect them to do his work for him.[32] Anthropologists, for example, have been interested in the phenomenon of bureaucracy in pre-industrial societies. This might be relevant for some aspects of social history, concerned with the village or parish community. But it is hard to see how Weber's ideal-type bureaucracy, or any conceivable variant derived from it (or in total opposition to it) can have any relevance for the study of non-literate societies.[33] In this sense the England of Charles I or Oliver Cromwell, classical China and the modern industrialised states of the nineteenth and twentieth centuries must all have more in common with each other, and even with the eleventh-century papacy or the twelfth-century feudal monarchies of western Europe and the Byzantine empire, than any of them can have with most of pre-colonial Africa. Historians of witchcraft in Tudor and Stuart England have recently exemplified a fruitful and exciting interchange with social anthropology.[34] Subject to correction, I doubt if the same possibilities are open to the student of administration and the civil service. If one were examining the impact of political and governmental action on the English village community, then an anthropological approach might be more rewarding.[35]

Whether by bureaucracy the historian should mean simply government administered by and through officials, organised formally and hierarchically in departments, or something more evaluative—either for better or for worse—I do not profess to know. Since the date of my own previous publication, bureaucracy has become a very dirty word indeed with the extreme Left, as it always has been (when applied to government and not to 'private' enterprise) among sections of the Right. Here self-styled Maoists and Anarchists appear to make common cause with the cartoonists of the *Daily Express* and the commentators and pundits who campaign to 'set the people free'. Anti-bureaucracy has indeed been one of the motive forces of direct action in the universities of the world over the last few years. Maybe the ideal historical scholar should pursue his course in complete detachment from such distractions, though I believe that it is neither possible nor desirable to do so.[36] In the face of militant students, attempting to overthrow academic bureaucracy, when they are themselves maintained by the taxpayer through the governmental bureaucracy, and enjoying the services of (on the whole efficient and sometimes dedicated) university administrators, the middle-aged, middle-class, middle-of-the-road historian needs above all to keep his sense of humour and of proportion. It is in the nature of the human animal sometimes to be ridiculous; we have all been not only absurd but contemptible in some measure at some time in our lives. It is to be hoped that neither the historical apologist for bureaucracy, nor the student revolutionary anti-bureaucrat is, or appears to the other, wholly contemptible all the time.

Is it pretentious to suggest that a detailed, down-to-earth, perhaps humdrum examination of bureaucracy in its political and social context, may do a little to illuminate these great issues? That is for the reader to judge, but such certainly is my hope. This is a study of the interaction between administration and politics, of the relationship between bureaucracy and social structure. There are four main chapters, each concerned with a major aspect of the subject. Chapter 2 surveys the framework of institutions within which the republican administrators of 1649–60 operated. It tries to take particular account of the changes which resulted from the effects of the Civil War and its aftermath, effects which were still being strongly felt in 1649 and after. The construction of this chapter is therefore partly chronological, spanning as it does an eighteen-year period of very marked changes (1642–60), and partly topical, concerned with describing different branches or aspects of the central government.

Chapter 3 is likely to seem the driest to the non-specialist. It is unavoidably the most technical, though an attempt has been made wherever possible to enliven the rather arid topic of 'terms of service' with illustrative examples and short case-histories. Here the topics covered are treated more analytically according to the different ways in which they affected men in the public service: their appointment and entry into office, promotion, tenure, daily routine, other conditions of work, remuneration, and so on. Special attention has been paid to the question whether office was systematically misused for private advantage, judged either by seventeenth-century standards of probity and propriety or by those of today. Dishonesty and corruption among republican functionaries, and as a possible function of the very system itself, has been as closely scrutinised as the evidence permits. This chapter thus spans the subject-matter covered in chapters 3 and 4 of *The King's Servants*.

For chapter 4 the title 'Social Biography' has been used, to indicate the approach adopted. This represents an attempt, however imperfect, to combine quantitative treatment of the men concerned as a group, with studies of individual lives and careers. The officials' political allegiances and religious affiliations have been at least as much the objects of investigation as their social background, family connections, wealth and status. So, in a sense, this chapter tries to combine the functions of most of chapters 5 and 6 in *The King's Servants*. The tables are fewer, simpler, and—it is hoped—a little less naïve, statistically speaking!

Chapter 5, on 'The Impact of the Regime' has no direct counterpart in my previous book. It represents a modest attempt to look at the administration from the outside, from the viewpoint of those being governed and administered. The social and economic assessment in its last section, of the burden of government on society and the relation of office-holding to social structure, corresponds to the last sections in chapters 4 and 5 of *The King's Servants*. In this way it is hoped that rather more coherence may have been given to this problem, than would have been by separating its economic and its social aspects. Logically, moreover it seems to belong with the Impact of the Regime more than with Terms of Service or with Social Biography.

Finally the brief Conclusion (chapter 6) tries to draw some of the threads together. I fear that the serious student of social science will be irritated by the brevity, if not levity, with which important theoretical problems are treated. At the same time, my more traditionally-minded historical colleagues and other readers may be irked to meet them again at all. Finally, some possible directions are suggested for further research, this conclusion marking my farewell, for the time being, to seventeenth-century administrative history.

A word of explanation may seem to be in order about the title of this book. When King and Parliament went to war with each other in 1642, the parliamentarians claimed to be fighting in the King's name and against only the King's enemies, just as much as their royalist opponents did. This idea, for it would be wrong to call it a pretence, became increasingly hollow as time passed. But it was not wholly discarded until the King himself was charged with treason for having waged war against his parliament and people in January 1649. Meanwhile many of those in the Parliament's service were coming more and more to think of some corporate identity as the embodiment of their new loyalty. Some time before the formal establishment of the Commonwealth, reference was being made to 'the State' in this way. Like much else in the English Revolution, this was more a matter of practical convenience than of ideology. The State's ships, or the State's service, provided a useful shorthand, without too specific or partisan a commitment.

The reader will not find the phrase 'The State's Servants' used in contemporary literature, at least not as easily as he could find 'The King's Servants' applied to royal officials before 1642 and after 1660 (or to royalist ones even during these years). But because of the successive changes of regime (and thus of formal allegiance which accompanied these) from 1648 to 1660, any more exact description would be intolerably cumbrous. Even after 1653, although many officials were appointed by Cromwell as Lord Protector, few outside his immediate household circle were known as 'The Protector's Servants'. The term Commonwealth continued to be used to describe the country under the Protectorate; the fleet, for instance, was described in official documents as 'the Commonwealth's ships' throughout the 1650s. So officials would have to be called Servants of Parliament, Commonwealth and Protector; bearing in mind that in 1659–60 England was again proclaimed to be a Commonwealth, this would produce a title fit for a seventeenth-century tract by the time every such qualification had been allowed for. The reader is therefore asked to bear with 'The State's Servants', in the hope that it will justify itself, even if it lacks the support of common contemporary usage.

CHAPTER 2

THE INSTITUTIONAL STRUCTURE

i THE POLITICAL SETTING

The English republic lasted from February 1649 to May 1660.[1] But as far as the administrative system and the officials are concerned, the period with which we are concerned begins with Pride's Purge on 6 December 1648 and ends with the re-admission of the Secluded Members by General Monck on 21 February 1660. Naturally there was a time-lag after both these events; nor was there uniformity or lack of change between these dates. The events of the winter of 1648–9 were the outcome of the uncertainty and deadlock which had followed the King's military defeat in 1645–6: they constituted the only settlement there was to be, but not the 'settlement' for which men had hoped.[2] The removal of the monarchist parliamentarians from the Commons, the abolition of House of Lords as well as monarchy, the declaration of England and its dominions as a commonwealth and its people as a 'free state' and the subsequent imposition of ideological tests and loyalty oaths to enforce support for the infant republic—all these changes were reflected at the administrative level, by the men who remained in office and those who were appointed to office from 1649 on. There were likewise some institutional changes to correspond with the new political order. As will be seen, these were considerably less radical and far-reaching than might have been expected and reflect the peculiar basis of political compromise on which the Commonwealth rested: a regicide republic, yet made and sustained by conservative revolutionaries and (at a deeper level) by a most reluctant military dictator and a highly legalistic, constitutionalist civilian and military establishment.

Some monarchists certainly remained in office under the republic. Yet from the autumn of 1649 they had to subscribe their loyalty to the Commonwealth, as it was then constituted without King or House of Lords.[3] Passive acceptance of a republic and readiness to subscribe are, of course, very different from being a positive republican, and probably only a few officials can be so described.[4] Likewise, despite the rapid changes of appointment which followed the return of the MPs purged in December 1648,[5] many republicans remained in office after February 1660, indeed after the King's return in May. By March 1660 officials were serving a transitional government which was no longer republican save by lip-service, while from May they were once more 'the King's Servants' (as they or their predecessors had been before 1642). That is, they had to accept the assumptions and allegiances and fit themselves into the structure of a monarchical state where the King still ruled as well as reigned until well into the following century. The span of English (and then of British) history from Charles II to George III is truly that of 'mixed monarchy'.

Just as the administrative pattern of the years after 1648–9 had been largely determined by the impact of the Civil War, so, within the period 1649–60, the main administrative developments were to arise from the political changes of 1653.

ii THE CIVIL WAR AND ITS AFTERMATH: RULE BY COMMITTEE

The effect of the Civil War was to remove the head of state and many of his servants from the seat of government. Parliament, which had been encroaching on the executive[1] since the summer of 1641, now had to improvise for itself an administration without the King and his supporters. In part this simply meant new appointments, mainly from 1643 onwards, in place of those officials who were either self-evident royalists or who refused to return to the capital when summoned. Speaker Lenthall's appointment as Master of the Rolls set the tone; others followed. But it meant more than this.

In order to carry on the business of government and to fight the war, let alone win it, Parliament had to create new, or adapt old institutions. Most strikingly, the use of committees—already well tried within the parliamentary context of investigation and legislation[2]—was now extended to other areas of government. The Committee of Safety, succeeded in 1644–7 by the Committee of Both Kingdoms and in 1648 by the Derby House Committee, was the nearest thing that Parliament had to a supreme war council, or to a replacement for the King and the Privy Council at the head of the central executive. Even so, relations with foreign states largely remained under the direct charge of Parliament and various *ad hoc* committees, at least until 1644–5.[3] The first change of name in 1644 reflected both the Scottish alliance and greater delegated powers; the Committee of Both Kingdoms was meant to be a supreme executive body, as well as a war council. The second change of name, in the winter of 1647–8, signified no more than Parliament's breach with the Scots, by then in secret alliance with Charles I. The new committee, in which there also was a marginal shift towards the Commons and away from the Lords, was rather unenterprisingly now called the Derby House Committee, after the place where it normally met.

But the balance between MPs who were to be purged in December

9

1648 (or at any rate did not sit from then until February 1660), and those who took part in the Rump, was significantly different in the Committee from that in the House; this was partly because of the eleven leaders of the Presbyterian party who had been forcibly excluded by the army in the summer of 1647 and were absent until August 1648.

Some of the parliamentary committees of the Civil War years are already well-known because their proceedings have been calendared, or their workings described by modern authors. Others remain obscure. Originally in charge of raising supplies for the army, the committee meeting at Haberdashers' Hall came to be known as the Committee for the Advance of Monies; it was responsible for levying semi-penal taxation on neutrals and passive royalists and on anyone else who had not given or voluntarily lent money or supplies towards the cost of Parliament's forces. Later, the system of penal taxation proper on active royalists became the business of the Compounding Committee at Goldsmiths' Hall.[4] The confiscated estates of royalists who were not allowed to compound, or were unable to do so, came under the control of the Sequestration Committee.[5] The Plundered Ministers' Committee dealt with compensation for puritan clergy who had suffered from the royalists. With the Scandalous Ministers' Committee we move into the world of 'double think' and 'newspeak',[6] since its scope was not limited to moral delinquents, or even psychiatric cases. It was also responsible for purging non-puritan Episcopalian clergymen and imposing tests on all others; these were often replaced by previously 'plundered' puritan ministers.[7] One of the Long Parliament's earliest offshoots to assume executive powers was the Committee for the Navy, although by the later 1640s its precise role in relation to other branches of naval administration was far from self-evident.[8] There were committees, too, for various other traditional branches of the administration, such as the Mint, Ordnance, Posts and Tower of London.

Other aspects of Parliament's war effort, and in particular the new forms of taxation instituted by Pym and his successors, entailed new standing committees with executive powers. A word of caution is needed here. Much of Parliament's war effort was organised on a local, and more specifically on a county and a regional basis, and many of the committees brought into being were not committees of Parliament but mixed ones, composed of MPs and other local supporters to do particular work in particular localities. Thus there were a parliamentary excise committee and a parliamentary customs committee, but for the assessment, the regular direct tax which developed out of the weekly pay and was imposed on friend, foe and neutral alike to maintain the parliamentary armies,[9] there was no central committee but one for each county and city.[10] Likewise for the local armed forces there were non-parliamentary county militia committees. The groupings of several counties into regions for purposes of military organisation, however, were managed by parliamentary committees, of which the one for the Eastern Association is the best known; there were also committees for the Northern and Southern associated counties.[11] Sequestrations, too, were normally organised on a county basis; sometimes the same body acted in several different capacities in a county and is simply referred to as 'the Committee'.[12]

From 1644 appeared yet another species: the committee appointed by and answerable to Parliament with nationwide tasks but composed of non-MPs. The self-denying Ordinance of April 1645 had its consequences in the civil as well as the military administration, since most places of profit under the State were in theory made incompatible with membership of either House.[13] The first, and for a long time the only, major institution to be affected by this was the Committee for taking the Accounts of the Kingdom (1644, reconstituted in 1647).[14]

Post-war reconstruction brought its own problems and with them its own characteristic crop of committees. The taking and passing of accounts was a continuous part of the clearing-up operations. The sale of lands was extended; the first to go under the hammer were those of bishops, in 1646. This time the Ordinance appointed two separate bodies of Contractors and Trustees; the Contractors were in charge of the actual sales. The Trustees, who were often called the commissioners or the Committee,[15] were to keep the property in trust and answer for the money collected, through their Treasurers.

The mention of commissioners is another reminder of continuity as well as innovation. Royal government in England under the Tudors and early Stuarts had been distinguished by its frequent, and growing, use of royal commissions: panels of men, normally part-time and unpaid, to carry out this or that task, investigate such and such a problem.[16] The county commissions of the peace are the best known, but many counties had commissions of sewers in charge of irrigation, also land drainage and river navigation; some also had commissions of swans, to oversee and protect these royal birds, although swans may seem a far cry from sequestered estates, or from assessing and levying taxation. The militia had not come under any commission but under the Lords Lieutenant (and in practice the Deputy Lieutenants) of each county before 1640.[17] The use of committees set up by Parliament and given powers by ordinance, as happened on such an immense scale from 1642–3 on, is not so different from the previous practice of monarchs in issuing commissions, normally under the Great Seal. The essence of both is collective responsibility, the use of part-time amateurs, and revocability, so that the growth of a professional, irremovable bureaucracy is restricted. Looked at another way round, the Tudor and early Stuart sovereigns and then the Long Parliament had to use commissions and committees for so many purposes precisely because England lacked an adequate professional civil service at the local level. It cannot be proved how much the Long Parliament's elaborate system of committees owed to Stuart example, how much to the precedent of earlier Parliaments, particularly that of 1621, and how much to sheer inventiveness. The parliamentary leader John Pym was a great pragmatist—a practical reformer who had himself been a minor revenue official as well as an MP.[18] Moreover, the King followed Parliament in creating machinery for the raising of money by penal taxation and from confiscated estates, and by instituting an excise tax, in the regions which he controlled during the years 1643 to 1646.[19] Probably, given the sheer practical necessity, Parliament (which means the parliamentarian leadership in the Commons) did what it felt it had to do, in the way which seemed most natural.

Still, it was a strange system to survive into a period of even nominal peace. Other post-war policies besides the taking of accounts produced yet more committees. Further land sales were entrusted to bodies of Trustees and Contractors on the model used for bishops' lands. This affected Crown lands (1649), the fee-farm rents of the Crown (1650), the lands of deans and chapters of cathedrals (1649), and the lands of royalists sequestered for treason (1651–3). As with episcopal lands, these various bodies of Trustees were in practice much like committees or bodies of commissioners, those for Crown lands and fee-farm rents being the same individuals. There was less overlap between the two sets of Trustees for church lands because of the political changes which had supervened; several of the 1646–7 Trustees and Contractors were inactive by 1649, but most of the episcopal property had by then been sold. Various obstacles to sales arose—rival claims to titles of ownership and tenancy, concealments and so on—and delayed completion of the business. Accordingly Parliament (by then the Rump House of Commons) set up an Obstructions Committee to clear these away and to hasten the remaining sales. The sale of the late King's and the rest of the royal family's movable goods saw a similar pattern repeated; this time a body of commissioners was in charge (1649). In all these cases, except that of Obstructions, Parliament went outside its own ranks in appointing Trustees and Contractors.

Other changes followed in the sphere of penal taxation. The independent county sequestration committees were wound up and replaced by county commissioners under the direct control of the central parliamentary Committee for Compounding.[20] The separate committee at Haberdashers' Hall for the Advancement of Money (extra taxes of a fifth on personal and a twentieth on real property) had already had its scope limited to convicted delinquents, after they had compounded.[21] The former change, early in 1650, seems to have reflected a collision between local and central interests among the Commonwealth's adherents. The chairman of the Compounding Committee, John Ashe MP, a wealthy Somerset clothier, was apparently in alliance with more conservative elements in his county but based his main power on his position at Goldsmiths' Hall in London. Colonel John Pyne MP was less powerful in London and Westminster but more strongly based in Somerset and stood for more radical policies.[22] Ashe suffered a serious defeat in the spring of 1650 when the Rump decided to wind up its own compounding committee altogether and hand over the whole business of compositions with royalists, advance of money (the one-fifth and one-twentieth) and sequestration to a full-time professional commission. This led to the appointment of the men who came to be nicknamed 'the seven great compounders' or 'sequestrators', whom we shall meet again in this and another capacity. It is not certain whether this change was a delayed recognition of the self-denying principle or—as was said at the time and seems more likely—was to enable the depleted membership of the Commons to give more time to the business of the House while letting full-time outsiders get on with the heavy administrative business of such committees. At any rate, principle or expedient, it was subsequently extended to other committees. The Obstructions Committee of Parliament was replaced by seven full-time Commissioners in 1652; or rather, when we say full-time we mean salaried non-MPs. One of them, Josias Berners, was also a Compounding Commissioner and he was soon in trouble with his colleagues at Goldsmiths' Hall for neglecting their business.[23] The other Obstruction Commissioners, like the Compounders, were drawn from the ranks of committed parliamentarian supporters outside the House, and were mostly men with previous experience of public business. In ecclesiastical administration the Plundered Ministers Committee was eventually replaced by the extra-parliamentary and salaried Maintenance Trustees with wider and more clearly defined powers.[24]

Meanwhile a widespread and vociferous demand had arisen, largely from the ranks of the parliamentary armies, for indemnification against normal liability at civil and criminal law for what had been done in Parliament's service during the Civil War. In 1647 this demand was one element in the breach between the 'Presbyterian'-controlled Commons and the 'Independent'-led New Model Army. But here the parliamentary majority was prepared to meet the Army, half-way at least. Indemnity was, after all, considerably cheaper than paying all their arrears to officers and soldiers before demobilisation; and it raised less thorny issues than deciding which units of the Army were to go to reconquer Ireland, and under whose command. The first, and principal, Indemnity Ordinance was passed on 21 May 1647, and the parliamentary Committee then appointed began work on 5 June.[25] Under the terms of the Ordinance, indemnity could also be claimed by officials and other civilian supporters of Parliament as well as by members of the Army. Unlike most of Parliament's other administrative committees, this one had judicial powers, to halt and require the annulment of proceedings in the ordinary courts of law. This was distinctly less true of the Compounding Committee's powers in cases of disputed ownership and tenancy and in adjudging degrees of royalist delinquency, but both were, in effect, judicial tribunals outside the ordinary legal structure.

In 1652 the principle which had already been applied to compounding and sequestration, and now to obstructions, was extended to indemnity. Interestingly, the new Indemnity Commissioners were to be the seven Compounding Commissioners meeting in another place and—as they themselves decided—on different days of the week. Functionally there was much to be said for this; many items, including some of the most contentious cases, came under their purview in both capacities. But it gave these particular men an unhealthy amount of power over a great many other people—and provided no regular appeal procedure against their decisions.

Some commissions were deliberately made up of a mixture of MPs and others. Such was true of the Excise from 1650.[26] In December 1652, the Commonwealth's defeats in the opening phase of the Dutch War and the desire to concentrate authority and responsibility for naval policy and administration led to the appointment of six 'Admiralty and Navy Commissioners' with wide powers; two were to be MPs on the Council of State, two MPs not on the Council (or, in modern parlance, backbenchers), and two from outside Parliament.[27]

Instances of overlapping committees and conflicting jurisdictions are so easy to multiply that it is tempting to imagine a conscious design of 'checks and balances'. Besides those already mentioned, the 1649–50 Council Committee 'to confer with the Lord General and officers of the Army' would seem to have conflicted with Parliament's Army Committee, itself one of the most active parliamentary committees of the 1640s. In 1650–1 the Council Committees on Irish and Scottish Affairs and on the Ordnance must have produced similar overlaps. During 1651, under the third Council of State of the Commonwealth, the Irish and Scottish Affairs Committee grew into something very like an all-purpose committee in charge of disposing of funds for military and other contingencies.[28] Meanwhile the Committee to confer with the Lord General and the officers had faded out, perhaps being unnecessary when Fairfax (whose council membership was nominal) was succeeded by Cromwell (an active councillor after absence on campaigns during his first one-and-a-quarter years as Lord General), or when Fleetwood and Harrison were also councillors (which Ireton never had been). Likewise in 1651 the Examinations Committee very nearly became one of general state security; during the invasion scare of August-September, there was a short-lived Council Committee of Safety. The third Council had *ad hoc* committees to confer with the Ambassadors and Agents of particular foreign States, but no general standing Foreign Affairs Committee until late summer 1651 (when the full minutes are missing but its existence can be clearly inferred).[29] Under the fourth Council the Foreign Affairs Committee took over the direction of the Dutch War from the Admiralty Committee in August-September 1652 (perhaps because of Vane's long absence on sick leave).[30] By then the Irish and Scottish Committee had almost become a general military-cum-finance committee; with the removal of any immediate royalist menace after September 1651 the Examinations Committee declined in importance. This may also have been due to Bradshaw's ceasing to be permanent President of the Council in December; it had been very much his Committee. In general, committees showed a chronic tendency to encroach on each other's spheres and to exceed their original terms of reference. Often, too, they became associated with the political ambitions of individuals or cliques. This remained at least as true after 1648–9 as it had been before.

At a more routine administrative level, conflicts were numerous. When Compounding had been handed over to full-time Commissioners but before the same men also had charge of Indemnity, there was a collision over an arrest by a deputy Sergeant-at-Arms of someone who should have been privileged.[31] Not long after their appointment, Sir Arthur Hesilrige had warned his cousin Edward Winslow, one of the seven, against the danger of the Compounding Commissioners challenging or reversing the previous decisions of the parliamentary committee for Advance of Monies (at Haberdashers' Hall)—on a case involving £1,700 worth of 'discoveries' in Cumberland.[32] Then there was the vexed question of whether the Commissioners' powers superseded those granted to the special regional Compounding Committee for the four northern counties (of which Hesilrige and the younger Sir Henry Vane were active members).[33] In Essex there was a conflict between the county Sequestration Commissioners and the county Militia Committee.[34] In Lancashire the county Sequestration Commissioners came into collision with the naval Prize Commissioners over royalist vessels seized in the ports there.[35] During the relatively short life of the Rump's four-man Treasury Inspections and Revenue Commission, the Compounding Commissioners more than once felt their lash descend; the same thing recurred with the Barebones' Treasuries Committee.[36] The Protectorate Treasury Commissioners[37] achieved a firmer grip and had the by then much-reduced Sequestration Commissioners altogether more under their control.[38] Whereas in 1653 the duty of sequestering defaulting excise farmers and sub-commissioners had been specifically entrusted to the Compounding Commissioners by the Treasuries Committee,[39] in 1656 the new Excise Appeals Commissioners (themselves by then largely the same men as the Obstructions Commissioners) told the Sequestration Commissioners to nominate subordinate officers of the Excise to execute these powers.[40]

Sometimes what began as a measure of reform could lead to further dispute between rival authorities. In mid-January 1649 the Rump appointed a strong committee of London merchants, together with the Commissioners of the Navy, to 'regulate' all the officers of the navy and the Customs. The terms of this Committee's appointment clearly authorised them to conduct a purge on grounds of administrative probity and moral fitness, as well as those of political reliability. They were empowered to abolish, or recommend the abolition, of 'unuseful' and superfluous offices, and to provide higher salaries for the holders of those which remained, in order to prevent the taking of bribes and fees: interestingly, these are bracketed together. A recent article on this body, 'The Regulators' as they became known, makes admirable use of a newly recovered Minute Book of their proceedings.[41] While one may agree with the author that the Rump got an excellent bargain, by obtaining the part-time services of some of the ablest men in London virtually for free, there is perhaps a slight risk of underplaying the further conflicts to which the Regulators' activities gave rise. Despite the inclusion of the Navy Commissioners (who were themselves salaried executives) among their membership, their work seems to have aroused jealousy and resentment, possibly from Parliament's own Navy Committee which had been largely eclipsed. On 19 March 1649 the Regulators' powers over naval appointments were taken away, and then two days later restored again. As opposed to this, on 7 May the House added the new Customs Commissioners to the Committee, but two days after that removed the Regulators' powers over customs appointments and vested them instead in these very Commissioners! A year later there was another dispute, and their powers were taken away as regards the Ordnance, Armoury and Stores Offices, leaving them with responsibility for the Navy only. Although their historian refers to two years' service, it is clear that the great part of the Regulators' work was done by the spring of 1650. And, as we shall see when we come to look at the quality of administration in the Customs, Navy and Ordnance, their success was hardly lasting or complete.

If we set aside the self-denying Ordinance and the separation of powers, it is hard to see how any theory of checks and balances can fit the disorderly facts. The pattern which emerges is much more one of competing authorities, each jealous of its own powers and territory and free from effective centralised control. The Councils of State of 1649–53 were a great advance in this respect on anything seen in 1642–8. But the Rump's continued use of administrative committees and the failure to subordinate all non-parliamentary committees and commissions to the

Council left the chaotic growth of previous years still only half under control. The wonder is not that there was a good deal of trouble and dispute, but that business got despatched as effectively as it did; even so we must not assume that a tidy disciplined hierarchy would have been more efficient.

The members of these numerous committees were not of course acting in an administrative void. In the first place, all had subordinate staffs. This was true the whole way from the Committee of Both Kingdoms at the top down to the pettiest committee for a sub-division of a county at the bottom. Naturally the size of the staff and the complexity of the tasks allotted to them varied widely, but the very existence of committees and commissions of part-time amateurs necessarily entailed the use of professionals below them. In many cases these men are too obscure, and have left too little trace in the surviving records, for us to know more than their names, and sometimes not even that. Others can be traced, sometimes because they made more mark at the time. The senior and more prominent of them are therefore included within the scope of this study, both in their administrative capacities and as individuals for purposes of social biography. Hence the total number of men classified as officials is proportionately a good deal larger for the eleven years 1649–60 than it was for the seventeen years 1625–42.[42] In delineating the institutional pattern of republican administration it is more important to remember that this whole system of committees and commissions had been overlaid on top of an existing structure of office-holders, law courts and departments.

iii THE CENTRAL EXECUTIVE

As might be expected, the part of the administration which was nearest to the nerve-centres of political power in the State, the central executive,[1] was most affected by the political changes of the 1640s. The removal of King, Privy Council and Secretaries of State from the scene left a gap which the Long Parliament was slow to set about filling. Until the Committee of Both Kingdoms was created in 1644, their place was only filled either by Parliament itself acting executively, or more often by *ad hoc* committees usually of both Houses. The Derby House Committee of 1648 had the same powers as the Committee of Both Kingdoms; indeed it was the same body without the Scottish members. It appears, from surviving records, to have been strictly a committee of the two Houses and not to have appointed its own standing sub-committees.[2]

The establishment of a unicameral Republic saw a real change in the organisation of government and so in administration. Almost at once after the execution of the King, before the abolition of the House of Lords, let alone the formal institution of the 'Commonwealth', the Rump

House of Commons decided to replace the Derby House Committee by a Council of State. The powers delegated to this body were extremely wide; moreover, they were later to be increased after practical experience of its needs. It is tempting to suggest that the new Council of State was to the House of Commons as the old Privy Council had been to the Monarch. But this would be misleading. Although ultimately the Council of State was answerable to the House, its powers were executive rather than advisory. Except for the raising and issuing of money, it could initiate and carry through an almost unlimited range of business. It could give orders to the armies and navies of the State, carry on relations with foreign countries, and take measures for national security. Later it was given the powers of the Lord Admiral and these were in turn entrusted to its Admiralty Committee; thus the Admiralty could be said to have been placed in commission without the formal appointment of commissioners. The Admiralty Committee was dominated by the younger Sir Henry Vane, probably the ablest as well as the oddest of the Commonwealth's civilian leaders, who was also Treasurer of the Navy until the end of 1650. The Navy Commissioners[3] were answerable to this Committee; its relation to the Navy Committee of the House itself is less clear. The preparation of estimates for Parliament and of schemes for financing the navy was probably that committee's main role.

Likewise with the army. The Council of State did not have a military committee as such, although in 1649–50 it had one to confer with the senior officers—a useful liaison between the mainly civilian councillors and the generals and Council of Officers. It was Parliament's Army Committee which had charge of financial provision for the land forces, prepared estimates and hammered out establishments with the generals, and authorised the issue of money.[4] The work of these two bodies and of the Indemnity and Compounding Committees of the House indicates Parliament's continuing executive-cum-administrative role after 1648. Otherwise the biggest single change from the previous executive bodies created in the 1640s is the sudden, luxuriant proliferation of council committees. The royal Privy Council had used committees at least since the later years of James I. In the 1630s there had normally been about five standing committees although most of the routine work was in fact done by the few councillors who attended regularly.[5] The first Council of State (February 1649–February 1650) had about six standing committees; its successor (February 1650–February 1651) had five or six. This pattern was continued through the three remaining councils of the Commonwealth (third: February–November 1651; fourth: December 1651–December 1652; fifth: December 1652–April 1653). But it was not the existence of standing committees only which marked a break with the immediate past. With forty-one members, about two-thirds of whom were reasonably regular attenders, the Council of State almost immediately began to develop the use of numerous temporary *ad hoc* committees. The number of councillors appointed to them varied in number from two or three to eight, ten or more, but they were normally smaller than the standing committees. Soon it becomes almost an arithmetical exercise to keep track of them; nor were most of great importance. But they were certainly not, in the vast majority of cases, a stalling device, to postpone distasteful decisions or to get rid of inconvenient items. Almost all seem to have concluded whatever their business was and to have reported back to the Council itself. The least successful, in settling the business entrusted to it, was one which eventually became a standing committee, that on the Posts.

The subordinate staffs of the Privy Council and Secretaries of State had largely been dispersed as a result of the war itself and their own predominantly royalist allegiances. The elderly Latin Secretary and German language interpreter, Georg Rudolf Weckherlin, continued to act, as did another ideological refugee, René Augier, the King's and then Parliament's Agent in Paris.[6] The mechanism of issuing orders and other instruments under the royal sign manual, signet seal, privy seal and great seal broke down.[7] Parliament had its own great seal made for its commissioners to keep and use, normally on orders from the two Houses; the Speakers of both Houses had seals. But there was nothing equivalent to the formal pre-war hierarchy of the different seals. The nucleus of a new central secretariat began to emerge with the Committee of Safety; someone had to keep its minutes, fair-copy its orders and so on, and it was not to be expected that any of the peers or MPs on it would do so. By the time that this body was replaced by the Committee of Both Kingdoms in 1644, such a secretariat had taken definite shape.[8] The crucial appointment was that of Walter (normally written as Gualter) Frost senior as Secretary to the Committee; he had been involved in supplying the Protestant forces in Ireland during 1641–2. Frost continued to hold this post until his death in 1652. He had marked nepotistic tendencies, or shall we say a strong sense of family connection.[9] A Secretary of State not being available, Ambassadors and Agents abroad in Parliament's service corresponded with the Speaker or later with the Committee of Both Kingdoms.[10] The Master of Ceremonies, Sir Oliver Fleming, one-time Agent of Charles I to Savoy, acted under the direct orders of the Parliament and its Committees to meet, entertain and negotiate with particular foreign envoys.[11] The Post Office, a source of constant contention between rival claimants, was likewise at the immediate disposal of Parliament, in practice of the Commons.[12] The issue was enlivened by the possibility of a constitutional collision between the two Houses, when the Lords tried to assert the claims of one of their own number, that great puritan entrepreneur the earl of Warwick, against the Commons' candidate, Edmund Prideaux, MP.[13] As one would expect, by

1644 the Commons' candidate was left in possession of the field, although the last had not by any means been heard of Warwick's claims.

Apart from Prideaux's work as Postmaster and the various Scout-master-Generals with the armies in the field, responsibility for intelligence too was unfixed. This led to a most unsatisfactory pattern of secret 'revelations' and accusations being made to peers and MPs, often against their own colleagues, and bandied about on the floor of either House. Pym had used this device to good political advantage. But it confused, by its very nature, two quite different matters: public political warfare and secret intelligence and espionage. What was said in the House could not be kept secret, either from the royal court at Oxford or from foreign envoys in the capital. Symptomatic of this, the trade of intelligencer often overlapped with that of journalist during and after the Civil War.[14] The Council of State showed marked reluctance to settle the conflicting claims to the offices of Postmaster-General and Master of the Foreign Posts, or to award compensation to the unsuccessful candidates whose claims none the less had some validity. Perhaps owing to inertia, perhaps because the House or the Council wanted it that way, Prideaux remained effectively in control until the summer of 1653. But his tenure can hardly be called settled or secure.[15]

This illustrates at a routine level a point of wider political importance. Although on paper the Council's powers—and thus those remaining with the House itself—were clearly defined in the Act of February 1649, in practice each tended to refer certain types of business to the other. Was this merely a convenient technique of procrastination? We must remember that all but a very few of the Council's members were also MPs;[16] several were among the most active figures in the House. The frequency with which individual councillors attended varied widely, virtually from nil to 100 per cent. Assuming that the records were equally well kept over the four years concerned, attendances can be seen to have improved appreciably after the first year (see Table 1); not that

TABLE I   *Attendances at the Councils of State, 1649–53**

Council	Total no. of meetings recorded	Average no. of attendances per member	Median no. of attendances	Median no. as % of total no.	Average no. of councillors at each meeting
1st, 1649–50	319	103	100	31	13
2nd, 1650–1	295	125	127	43	18
3rd, 1651	249	120	120	48	19
4th, 1651–2	330	129	133	40	16
5th, 1652–3	121	57	57	47	19

* From *Cal.S.P.Dom.*, Prefaces. The totals and percentages are my arithmetic, not Mrs Green's.

a high level of attendance makes an effective institution, although it may tell one something about the attitude of those involved.

Is it then more sensible to think of the Council as a kind of all-purpose standing committee of the House itself? Almost, but not quite; the relations between the two bodies remain obscure, but neither was a mere appendage of the other. At any given time between 1649 and 1653 there were between 34 and 39 MPs on the Council, leaving something like 30 to 50 non-councillors who were reasonably regular attenders in the House.[17] For the elections to the Council (by secret ballot from 1651 onwards)[18] there were up to 120 voters (and in theory as many candidates), for 41 places. This does not mean that 120 was the normal level of attendance in the Rump. The key vote in November 1651 to set an end to the present parliament was carried by 49–47: with tellers and the Speaker, an attendance of 101.[19]

The Council's staff soon became much more elaborate than that of its predecessor at Derby House. In this respect it was certainly comparable to the old Privy Council. But instead of four clerks, it had a secretary (Frost), two clerks, and from two to five under-clerks. There were also a Sergeant at Arms, eight (later twelve) Deputy Sergeants, and twelve Messengers, plus a House-keeper, two Porters and cleaning staff. The Council also had directly under it the staffs of the other ex-royal, now public buildings in and around London (but excluding the Parliament buildings themselves and the rest of the palace of Westminster), and the central secretariat for diplomacy and foreign relations. In this capacity John Milton as Latin Secretary came under them; likewise the other political warfare experts and news-writers. There was still no Secretary of State, and under the first two Councils there was only a standing committee on treaties with foreign states. From the summer of 1651 the latter body was subsumed in a new committee on Trade and Foreign Relations. But intelligence had already been separated from diplomacy and propaganda alike. Its management was entrusted to Thomas Scot, MP, a dedicated commonwealthsman and one of the more disinterested Rumpers. The reasons for the choice of Scot can only be inferred; presumably he was acceptable to the dominant councillors. On the home front he was ably assisted by Captain George Bishop, a west-country republican and future Quaker. The credit for Cromwell's intelligence service under the Protectorate is often given to Thurloe; this is fair, but he built on foundations well laid by Scot and Bishop. Scot was also assisted intermittently by a small committee, and later (in 1650–1) by a larger standing committee on Examinations (i.e. for hearing secret evidence against people and cross-examining witnesses and suspects) whose chairman was the Council's President (1649–51), its most important non-MP, John Bradshaw.[20]

Bradshaw's original election was a testimony to his role as President of the High Court of Justice for the King's trial. His previous administrative experience was slight and his knowledge of high politics *nil*.[21] Bradshaw was not at first elected President; indeed initially the Council was allowed no provision for a regular chairman, so far did the Rump's 'anti-monarchism' extend.[22] Appropriately, its greatest member, 'the Lieutenant-General' (Oliver Cromwell, MP), acted as chairman for the first week of the Council's existence. But Cromwell, we may suppose, had no relish for such duties. Mutual jealousies among the other leading councillors and the sheer convenience of having one person always in attendance for routine business (signing letters and orders, etc.) may have pointed to the solution. Bradshaw, a humourless mediocrity but honest and no fool, seems to have regarded the Lord Presidency of the Council as his due. He did not attend at all until his appointment; from then on, he scarcely missed a meeting.[23] Prolific records survive of the Council's activities but none, practically speaking, of its deliberations; there are rough and fair-copy order books, but no minutes in the modern sense.[24]

For the election of the third Council (February 1651) the House decided to introduce a principle of rotation in office. Out of 41 councillors, 21 were to be re-elected and 20 elected from those who had not been on the previous Council.[25] It would be fanciful to see in this anything which one could dignify with the description of a 'back-bench revolt'. It was more of a sop to the self-denying principle, and perhaps a recognition of Leveller demands for rotation together with the neo-classical influence of some ardent republicans in the Rump itself,[26] plus no doubt an element of 'Buggins' turn next'. Still it prevented the Council, unlike the Rump, from trying to turn itself into a self-perpetuating oligarchy. More serious from the procedural point of view was the decision, made ten months later, that no committee of the House or of the Council, nor the Council as such, could have a standing chairman (or president) for more than a lunar month at a time. This led to the dethronement of Bradshaw, whose attendance dropped only slightly, whereas that of the seventeen presidents who followed him (January 1652–April 1653) improved markedly during their respective terms.

The machinery at the Council's disposal changed little between 1649 and 1653. Its tasks naturally did. From preoccupation with internal security, Ireland, the Scots and Charles II, its concerns were partly switched to the Dutch War in 1652–3. If security, military, naval and diplomatic business continued to predominate, the volume of routine items and the use of *ad hoc* committees did not slacken. Individual cases were increasingly dealt with *en bloc* by the use of a standing committee on petitioners, or by the first councillors to come in for any given meeting before a quorum was present for Council business to begin. The Council's impact on economic regulation and social policy is hard to assess. The first Council of State appointed a small Trade Committee; the second made Trade and Plantations the business of all its members, through a Committee of the whole Council. Then in August 1650 Parliament set up a separate Trade Council, or Commission, which acted until the end of 1651. None the less the third Council of State (February–November 1651) appears to have had its own Trade Committee, this time combined with Foreign Affairs; in this they were followed by the fourth Council, the fifth also combining Plantations business in the same Committee. The failure to go the whole way, and appoint a permanent non-parliamentary Trade Commission is an exception to the general trend noticed in 1650–2.[27]

How far the mercantile arguments for and against the Dutch War were hammered out in the Council, as opposed to Parliament, can only be conjectured. Certainly the month when Sir Arthur Hesilrige was President (end of December 1651–late January 1652) saw a stiffening of the terms put to the Dutch envoys in London. Vane's Presidency (June 1652) and then his long absence (apparently on sick leave, July–September 1652) seem to have made less difference either way, but by then the die was cast. Probably, like Cromwell, Vane was against the war to begin with but saw that once started it must be won, at least to the extent of England getting on top, though not of destroying the Dutch as the extreme mercantilists would have liked.[28]

Milton's growing blindness and consequent disablement from public business is of greater significance in the history of English literature than of republican administration. But there was one change of great importance in the Council's staff between 1649 and 1653. The death of the elder Gualter Frost in late March 1652 required the choice of a new Secretary. Apparently without hesitation the Council recommended, and Parliament confirmed, the appointment of John Thurloe, who had not previously been in the central secretariat at all. He had, however, gone to the Netherlands with his master Oliver St John in the summer of 1651; he had been sent back before St John and his fellow ambassador Walter Strickland to make an interim report, and this must have impressed councillors and other MPs.[29] Thus he was brought in over the heads of the assistant secretary, Georg Rudolf Weckherlin, and of Frost's son, Gualter junior, who was Assistant Clerk and acting Treasurer for Council Contingencies. The young Gualter Frost was at once confirmed as Treasurer for Contingencies, as well as other provision being authorised for the dependants of the deceased secretary.[30] Thurloe's greatest importance came later under the Protectorate, but he provided continuity at a higher than merely clerical level from the last year of the Rump and the changes of 1653 into the Cromwellian period which followed.[31]

One of the questions which we must try to answer is, how far the end of the Rump with its many committees meant the end of 'committee rule' in the central government and the country at large. But this is best postponed until we have completed our survey of central administration during the Commonwealth.

iv   REVENUE AND FINANCE

The most marked feature of the revenue system under the Long Parliament and then the Commonwealth is its lack of centralisation. Control over all branches of the revenue was nominally in Parliament's hands.[1] But at the administrative level there was an extraordinary proliferation of separate funds and treasuries. As with the committees and commissions of the years 1649–53, it is necessary here too to go back to the early years of the Civil War in order to understand what had happened.

A larger proportion of revenue officials were parliamentarian or neutral in sympathy (at least not actively royalist) than was true in the royal household, or even in the central executive.[2] It did not, however, follow that the Exchequer retained its importance as an institution. This was partly because much of the traditional revenue of the Crown ceased to be available to Parliament, such as customs duties and land revenues from areas not under its control. The Port of London customs were much the largest single item of traditional, pre-1640 revenues which remained to it. Collection of the various subsidies and poll-taxes voted in 1641–2 continued, but with grave interruptions. Precisely why the new sources of revenue devised from 1642 onwards were not ordered to be collected and audited within the traditional Exchequer framework is unclear. The City's insistence in having them under its immediate hand, as security for loans, has been suggested;[3] a general suspicion of the Exchequer and its ways may also be assumed.[4] Although the senior official of the Receipt, the Auditor Sir Robert Pye, was an active, if only marginally parliamentarian, member of the Long Parliament, there is no sign that the Lower Exchequer was treated more indulgently than the Upper Exchequer of Audit. There, although both Remembrancers were royalists, the Clerk of the Pipe was a canny neutral and seven out of nine Auditors of the Revenues and the Prests (moneys advanced on account) were parliamentarian or neutral.[5] Pye was often employed by the Commons as a messenger to the Lords, an indication at least of his acceptability among the parliamentarian peers.

The collection of voluntary donations of silver plate, horses, arms and ready money was entrusted to the Treasurers-at-War and centred on Guildhall. This soon became a precedent, followed in turn with the weekly pay and later the monthly assessment.[6] The first collection of money from royalist compounders arose out of Parliament's commitment to its Scottish allies; at first the Scottish and the Compounding Committees were the same body. Soon the two diverged, and compounding became based on Goldsmiths' Hall, with the compulsory Advance of Monies also separately constituted at Haberdashers' Hall.

The institution of the Excise in 1643 (and its subsequent renewals and extensions, 1644–7) provided a different precedent. Eventually the accounts of the Excise commissioners, like those of the Treasurers for Compounding and the War Treasurers, were audited in the Upper Exchequer, although some of them not until after the Restoration. But the Excise had its headquarters in the City, in Broad Street, and its largest centre of operations (for taxable imported goods) was at the London Customs House. Like the Customs Commissioners, those of the Excise were effectively independent of the Exchequer, and answerable direct to Parliament.

By 1649 the proliferation of minor funds and treasuries had reached extravagant proportions. Mrs Green mentioned several,[7] but her list can be supplemented (see Table 2). The amount of money in these different funds varied enormously. Moreover, the relationship between those which were only revenue collecting, those which were only revenue disbursing, and those which were both, and the sequence of authorisation for out-payments in different branches, left much to be desired. In the early 1640s even the Navy Treasurer was authorised to receive part of the excise direct; so there was no major spending agent who was not also a revenue-receiver. The decision to raise money from land sales, in 1646 and again from 1649 on, increased this awkwardness and complexity. It was to become a constant refrain under the Rump—as indeed under the following regimes of the 1650s—that the revenues must be made to flow 'through one channel'.[8] How far this was achieved will be seen later.[9] At first the Rump, like the Commons before December 1648, tried to keep control through its own Revenue Committee. This body seems to have spent most of its time signing warrants and issuing orders to individual officials, and to have had little grip on financial policy. The demands which had to be met came in relentlessly from the armed forces, via the spokesmen from the Army and Navy Committees. In so far as there was a policy of how to meet or curb them, it was worked out in the House, or on occasion by the House in a Committee of the Whole (or 'Grand Committee' as it was still more often known). By the end of 1652 the Dutch War had necessitated a vastly increased naval budget just when it seemed that military expenditure might at last legitimately be restrained with the agreement of Cromwell and the other generals. These pressures and general dissatisfaction with the existing procedure led to a new departure in December 1652/January 1653. This was comparable to the appointment of the six new Admiralty and Navy Commissioners. There were to be four new Commissioners for Inspecting the Treasuries, with powers to reorganise them as they saw fit. All of these Commissioners, however,

TABLE 2   *The public revenues, 1642–53*

Type or branch of revenue	In whose charge	Where received in and paid out	Where audited
Customs	Commissioners	Their own Treasury; some via Receipt of Exchequer	Upper Exchequer again, as from 1649
Excise	Commissioners	Treasury in Broad Street	Upper Exchequer—one or two accounts in 1650s, others in 1660s
Subsidies and Poll-taxes (voted 1641–2)	Commissioners named in the Acts, for the counties and cities	Lower Exchequer (*or* the Receiver-General there)	Upper Exchequer but much interrupted
Weekly pay, later Monthly Assessment	Army Committee and War Treasurers (later also called Receivers-General) at centre; committees in counties and cities	Own Treasury in Guildhall	Not until after 1660 except by Accounts Committee
All other established revenues, not named separately, for 1643–4	Thomas Fauconberge, Receiver-General	By Thomas Fauconberge, but perhaps at the Lower Exchequer	Accounts Committee
Loans to Parliament on security of Irish, later of bishops' lands and of the excise	Parliamentary Committee	Treasurers at Weavers' Hall	Accounts Committee
Advance (1/5 and 1/20)	Parliamentary Committee	Treasurers at Haberdashers' Hall	No separate account taken before 1653–4 (in 1655); perhaps for earlier years by Accounts Committee
Compositions	Parliamentary Committee	Treasurers at Goldsmiths' Hall	Upper Exchequer (in 1656 and April 1660)
Profits of sequestered lands	Normally as for compositions but via local committees		

26

Type or branch of revenue	In whose charge	Where received in and paid out	Where audited
Land sales	Trustees	Their own Treasurers	In Upper Exchequer, but only the account for episcopal lands passed pre-1660
Wardship and Livery	Court of Wards	Fauconberge for 1643–4	As usual till 1646 (Court abolished)
Crown land revenues	Receivers and Auditors (till sold)	Fauconberge for 1643–4	In Upper Exchequer
Duchy of Lancaster	Court of Duchy	Fauconberge for 1643–4	As usual but incomplete
Alienations	Alienations Office	Fauconberge for 1643–4	In Upper Exchequer
Mint	Master and Warden	Fauconberge for 1643–4	In Upper Exchequer
Hanaper	Clerk of Hanaper	Fauconberge for 1643–4	In Upper Exchequer
Prize ships and goods	Commissioners	Their own Treasurers	By Accounts Committee 1640s (?); some taken in Upper Exchequer 1654

were also MPs. They included one survivor from the 1630s, Cornelius Holland, ex-Clerk of Green Cloth to the Prince of Wales; two were also on the Council.[10] They were soon authorised to order the issue of money as well as to direct the course of receipts. Since the Rump kept its previous Revenue Committee in being, there was a good deal of overlapping in the period which followed. Both bodies appear to have survived Cromwell's dissolution of the Rump and the Council of State on 20 April 1653; the Treasury Inspection Commissioners were the first to be replaced.[11]

By 1652–3 little effective reunification of the revenues had yet occurred. Some branches had been amalgamated: sequestrations, compositions and advances by the appointment of the seven Commissioners in 1650. Some funds had come to a (more or less) natural end: such as money for relief of the distressed Irish Protestants. Full-time administrators had replaced London aldermen and MPs as War Treasurers; a merchant administrator had succeeded a leading politician as Navy Treasurer. Land sales were more or less complete. The last Act for the sale of delinquents' lands forfeited for treason was in train. But for the most part these were never sold, and the owners were allowed to buy

27

back their own confiscated property, in effect to compound for it, though at a stiff rate; so this gave a last fillip to the compounding revenue later in 1653. Advance of Monies was virtually a thing of the past; sequestration was a continuing, minor source of supply. The sale of ex-royal forests, previously reserved for the navy's timber supplies, was in process, but raised virtually no additional revenue. Increasingly the three great pillars of public finance were the Assessment, the Excise and the Customs. On the efficient collection and use of these depended the regime's solvency, and its ability to defend itself. Subsequent changes in financial administration resulted from the political changes of 1653; but practical convenience might well have led to something similar if the Commonwealth had lasted a few years longer than it did.

The various revenue funds, treasuries and disbursing agencies entailed the usual array of junior staffs. The central bureaucracy for the assessment was very small: a deputy treasurer until 1652, two more deputies for the army in Scotland and Ireland, a few cashiers, and an agent to hasten collection in each country. But the spadework was done by county commissioners reappointed in each successive Act. Much of the money never in fact came in to the Guildhall in London but was 'assigned' and paid out direct to garrisons and units of the field army in the localities.[12] In 1653 some of the assessment was diverted to the use of the navy, but normally it all went to the land forces; the Customs revenue and much of the Excise were assigned to the use of the navy. Salaries, fees, pensions and other expenses of the civil government were met out of the minor revenues, unless they were assigned or defalked from the Customs or Excise. Many minor individual payments, notably those authorised by the Rump to its own members, were made out of composition fines or from the profits of sequestered estates. The servicing of the public debt—in its various forms—was easily the largest single item after the upkeep of the armed forces. Most of the money from land sales in fact went in this way, to satisfy the Long Parliament's creditors and not to swell its actual cash resources.[13]

Modern historians have been almost as sharply divided as contemporaries were, if less bitterly so, on how well or ill the Rump managed the nation's finances.[14] Vast sums were raised and spent, not only on paper but, if we set aside the special case of land sales, in fact too. The anti-Cromwellian republicans provided one stereotyped version of how things stood in April 1653; Cromwell himself provided another: in the one case, coffers were bulging with treasure, in the other, they were rattling with emptiness. It is easier to assess the Rump's achievement in administrative terms, and to ask whether the lower levels of the bureaucracy multiplied out of proportion to the tasks in hand and whether an excessive proportion of the gross revenues went on administrative overheads (salaries and wages, plus extra allowances).

For the Assessment an answer has already been suggested. In the Customs there were undoubtedly increases in staffing after 1640; the effects of war on the economy, almost continuous from 1642 to 1654, make a direct comparison very difficult. As between London and the outports, some measurement of comparative costs can be made. For what such yardsticks are worth, in 1652–3 London yielded 71·7 per cent of the main customs revenues, whereas the customs officials in London received only 59·7 per cent of the total amount spent on salaries. Administration was thus more costly in the outports; the total volume of trade carried on there was proportionately smaller, compared with that of London, than were the customs staffs employed in them.[15] As against that, the most sensational scandals which came to light involved the London customs. This could be explained in more ways than one: the greater distance of the outports from the eye of inquiring reformers, the greater honesty of provincials, or the greater temptations to which men were exposed from the very scale of operations in the capital.[16] For all that, unless the rate of loss from evasion was immense,[17] the amount of the gross revenue taken up in overheads was by no means excessive.

The Excise saw an entirely new corps of functionaries brought into being. Because of the way in which the different branches of its administration were kept separate, reflecting the various ordinances and Acts which had extended or altered its scope and rates, the staff seems unnecessarily numerous, especially in London. But disregarding for the present the very different question of its popular acceptance in the country as well as that of the officials' honesty, here again the overall percentage going in the administrative costs of collection was not excessive.[18]

v   THE LAW AND THE COURTS

As we have already seen, three main influences helped to form the administrative system of the republican period. These were the traditional systems, inherited from 1642; the practical necessities of wartime adaptation and innovation (mainly 1643–7); and the conscious creation of a new parliamentarian (and later a republican) structure. The three influences operated to varying extents in the different branches of government.

The traditional system was least disturbed in the law courts. After the successful attacks on Star Chamber and High Commission and the other 'prerogative' and conciliar courts in 1641, and the effective collapse of the other ecclesiastical courts by 1642, the only further change was the delayed abolition of the Court of Wards and Liveries in 1646. This is not to say that all parliamentarians accepted the legal system as it then stood. Far from it. The different schemes for further changes reflected the whole range of opinion on Parliament's side, and 'law reform' was one of the loudest and most constant demands among pamphleteers and others all the way from 1641 to 1659.[1] Several distinct viewpoints are discernible. Some conservatives, perhaps mainly among the so-called Presbyterians or moderate Parliamentarians, who held the ascendancy in Parliament in 1646–7 and again in 1648, were broadly content with the achievements of 1641–6. Apart from a few minor procedural improvements they were satisfied both with the law courts which then existed and with the way in which these operated and were staffed. The politically more radical but socially conservative Independents, especially in the army, wanted fairly sweeping procedural changes aimed at simplification and decentralisation. Cromwell's letters to the Speaker in 1650–1, and passages in some of his later speeches, express his viewpoint with characteristic vigour—and equally characteristic lack of clarity on organisational details. Henry Robinson, fertile pamphleteer, projector, excise administrator and accounts committee member, had a more precise approach.[2] A few lawyers, mostly connected with the regime, wrote in favour of effective, practical reforms within the existing legal system. Among the most prominent of them were William Sheppard, originally a Gloucestershire lawyer and magistrate,[3] and John Cook, Solicitor at the King's Trial and then Chief Justice of Munster, who was executed in 1660.[4]

Then there were the revolutionary law reformers who wanted the law altered out of recognition, or even abolished. The Diggers, in so far as they can be identified with the writings of Gerrard Winstanley, saw the whole system as an outgrowth of private property and the profit motive.[5] The Levellers and their sympathisers generally viewed the existing land law as a part of the 'Norman Yoke' imposed on the free people of England in 1066.[6] Some radical Independents,[7] and millenarian[8] sectaries demanded similar changes but as a part of the temporal reign of the Saints upon Earth, preliminary to the Second Coming of Christ and the general resurrection. Any attempt to construct a single spectrum to measure degrees of conservatism and radicalism among the Commonwealth's adherents breaks down on law reform as much as on religion. Thus Sir Arthur Hesilrige was one of the leaders of the political Independents in the Rump, and so was the younger Sir Henry Vane. Just as in religion Hesilrige was said by Clarendon to be a Presbyterian,[9] whereas Vane was a Congregationalist who became a Seeker with a strong millenarian tinge, so Sir Arthur never gave evidence of serious dissatisfaction with the existing system of law and property relations, while Sir Henry, though as tenacious of his property rights as any reactionary, made threatening noises aimed at the whole existing temporal order.[10] Both became staunch republican opponents of Cromwell's Protectorate, which had a better record in law reform than the parliamentary oligarchy which had controlled the Rump. Remembering this undercurrent of pressure for reform, we may make more sense of the legal system, as it existed in 1648 and continued under the republic.

Some of the ablest common lawyers had in fact been royalists in the Civil War, and they and others would continue to serve the Stuart kings loyally until the Revolution of 1688.[11] None the less, the common law as a whole had been an ally of Parliament in its resistance to James and Charles I. It is therefore not surprising that Parliament's victory produced least disturbance in this area. The customary half-yearly assizes by the Judges in the counties were interrupted but only at the height of the military conflict. The business of the Courts of King's Bench, Common Pleas, and the legal side of the Exchequer continued with little break. True there were changes in personnel but less than in most other branches of government.[12] The legal business of the Exchequer was reduced in volume as a consequence of the changes in the revenue system and in financial administration,[13] and the subsequent appointment of the Accounts Committee. The volume and type of business coming to all three courts was affected by the dislocation of the war in ways which we should more easily be able to delineate if their records had been more fully calendared and so more used by historians.[14] In 1649 there were further staff changes, particularly among the Judges (and Barons of Exchequer). Out of the twelve who had been appointed (and as far as we know were functioning) before December 1648, six were prepared to continue to act under the republic, although—as was to appear in the years which followed—with varying degrees of political (and perhaps moral) reservation about what they would or would not do on the regime's behalf.[15] The Judges may have been 'Lions under the Throne' in the days of Coke and Bacon. This is certainly a very inapt description of them in the time of the Rump and Oliver; sulky tigers off-stage would be nearer the mark.

As a result of the abolition of kingship, King's Bench became Upper Bench. The most sensitive political cases were entrusted to specially empanelled 'High Courts of Justice'—on the model of that used against the King.[16] Hence the Crown, now the 'Commonwealth' side of Upper Bench was probably less important than that of King's Bench before 1640 and after 1660. On the other hand, the Upper Exchequer (of Audit) regained some business in passing accounts, long before the cash side of the revenue system was brought back under the Lower Exchequer (of Receipt). The abolition of Star Chamber, the collapse of the two regional Councils and the effective suspension of the church courts (other than the Prerogative Court of Canterbury), may well have increased the pressure on Chancery and the two Benches. Apart from the minority of actions brought by the Crown which gained it such political notoriety, Star Chamber had continued to be sought after by litigants, for its relative speed and cheapness, up to the eve of its demise.[17] During the

31

previous hundred years or so, Common Pleas had been losing business, for technical reasons, both to Chancery and to King's Bench.[18] As regards private actions, the effect of the political upheavals from 1640 on was thus to hasten the redistribution of legal business, as between the various courts, and at some points to alter the direction of its flow. These shifts of litigation may help to explain the relative unpopularity of different courts. Chancery was regarded as the slowest of all, and as the most costly. Yet the three common law courts were in some ways more capricious in that the law which they administered was more out-dated. They lacked the flexibility of the Chancellor's 'equity', which had enabled Chancery to change more with the times in the previous century, as it would again after the Restoration.[19]

Although Chancery was the foremost object of the law reformers' attacks, it was not touched until 1653, and only with any practical effect from 1655 to 1658.[20] Its senior judges continued to be the Lords Commissioners of the Great Seal, whom Parliament had put in to replace a single Lord Chancellor or Lord Keeper. How much should be read into this putting of the Great Seal into commission? It was not new. After Lord Chancellor Bacon's disgrace in 1621, the Great Seal had been briefly in commission before the appointment of Bishop Williams as Lord Keeper.[21] As with other important committees and commissions of the 1640s, the peers dropped out when their House was abolished in February 1649. In the case of one Lord Commissioner, Bulstrode White-locke, we have his own lengthy justification of why he decided to stay in office despite his disapproval of the regicide and his lack of republican sympathies.[22]

Below the Commissioners was the Master of the Rolls (still the ubiquitous William Lenthall, whose brother was the hated Keeper of the Upper Bench Prison, the Marshalsea, and whose son, also an MP, was one of the six Clerks of Chancery). Then came the Masters of Chancery, the judges for more routine cases. Before the Civil War there had normally been twelve Masters in ordinary and an unspecified number of Masters extraordinary. Parliament does not seem to have kept these numbers up; they were distinctly depleted by 1649. Otherwise the Court of Chancery seems to have continued as before, although the storm which was later almost to destroy it was already blowing at near-gale force.

The civil law had been regarded by many parliamentarians as somehow akin to the prerogative and thus contrary to England's constitutional traditions. Common lawyers of course had their own bread-and-butter reasons for disliking it. But whereas the prerogative courts and one equity court (Requests) had disappeared in the reforms of 1641, and the ecclesiastical courts (largely staffed with civil lawyers) had been shorn of their powers, the civil law with its limited but indispensable role proved surprisingly tenacious, whatever the views of Parliament's more ardent radical supporters. There was no disruption of Admiralty jurisdiction over the winter of 1648–9, and before long some additional judges were appointed.[23] Although the chain of command had been different while there was a parliamentarian Lord Admiral (the Earl of Warwick, 1642–5 and 1648–early 1649), there does not seem to have been any break in continuity; indeed the maritime consequences of the Civil War and changes in relations with different foreign states must have made it as necessary as ever.[24] Only the business of prizes and in particular their financial disposal to the best advantage of the State was taken wholly out of the hands of the Admiralty and put under specially appointed commissioners. In 1648–52 this meant royalist and French prizes; in 1652–4 chiefly Dutch ones, for which separate Commissioners were appointed; and in 1655–60 Spanish ones under (as far as can be seen) the same (1654) commission reconstituted.[25]

The legal business of wills, probate and administration, could not conceivably be dispensed with in a society so conscious of inherited property rights and of the family as an economic unit. Yet this had formerly been in the hands of the hated church courts. Indeed the principal probate institution for most of the country, the Prerogative Court of Canterbury, had come directly under Archbishop Laud and then his successor William Juxon. But since Laud's Vicar-General, Sir Nathaniel Brent, was a strong parliamentarian who acted as sole Judge of the court from 1644 to his death (December 1652), in effect Parliament took the Court over and secularised it.[26] Under the Commonwealth its new Registrars were to be Michael Oldisworth MP, the Earl of Pembroke's secretary, and Henry Parker, one of Parliament's ablest propagandists and a member of the army secretariat.[27] Their tenure was later to be disputed,[28] and there were to be further changes in 1653–4;[29] meanwhile the work of the court went on.

It would, however, be misleading to over-stress the continuity with the pre-war, or at least the pre-1640 legal system. The following courts had gone for ever: Star Chamber, Privy Council acting as a court of first instance between parties, High Commission, Council in the North, and Wards and Liveries. The following did not act during 1642–60: Council in Marches of Wales, Courts of the Marshal (Palace and Verge), Court of Chivalry, and all other church courts except the Prerogative Court for probate and administration. At the local level there was less change. County committees did little to reduce the legal scope of JPs in Quarter Sessions; surviving records show a few interruptions caused by the ebb and flow of war (1642–6, 1648) but continuity otherwise, alike as to institutional forms and the justice dispensed.[30]

vi IRELAND AND SCOTLAND

In one important respect the Commonwealth realised an ambition which had eluded even the most powerful and aggressive of English kings. Edward I and Henry VIII had tried to bring the whole or greatest part of the British Isles under direct English rule. The successors of both these monarchs had seen their grandiose plans shattered on the rock of Scottish 'national' feeling. In 1603 when the crowns of England and Scotland were peaceably united under James VI and I, what seemed likely to be the last serious native Irish resistance to English rule collapsed. Both James and Charles I did therefore genuinely rule over three kingdoms but not as a single political unit.

The Irish central government was a viceroyalty. At the lower levels the Irish administration was staffed by a mixture of men drawn from the older-established Anglo-Irish families, or 'old English' as they are better called, and from the more recent settlers (of Tudor and early Stuart vintage), the 'new English'. The recent arrivals (first-generation settlers) among them were therefore included with the English central officials in the predecessor to this study.[1] Yet, as a viceregal establishment, the Dublin administration had a certain life of its own; it was not a mere appendage or extension of Whitehall and Westminster. As a result of the Irish War of 1641–52 and the eventual total defeat of both royalist English and Catholic Irish forces by the Cromwellian armies, a virtually new civil administration had to be created from scratch. This was extended over the whole country from Dublin outwards in the wake of the English armies. In 1649–50, in his capacity as Lord Lieutenant, as well as Commander-in-Chief of the Army, Oliver Cromwell was the *de jure* as well as *de facto* ruler of at least such areas of Ireland as were under English control. With his return and the appointment, by agreement between him and the Council of State and Parliament at home, of his son-in-law Henry Ireton as Lord Deputy, the situation changed. A Lord Deputy's powers were in theory somewhat less than a Lord Lieutenant's anyway, though in practice a strong Lord Deputy had all the power he needed.[2] Ireton, however, was regarded with some suspicion by his fellow Rumpers.[3] In 1647 he had designed a new constitution involving regular elections for a reformed Parliament; he was perhaps the strongest opponent on theoretical as well as practical grounds of the Rump as a permanent self-co-optive Parliament. This may explain the appointment of four Parliamentary Commissioners to supervise the return to normal civil government in Ireland, made in 1650. These men—Edmund Ludlow, Miles Corbett, John Jones and John Weaver— were more than Ireton's councillors. They were to act with him but possessed authority in their own right. Already there were Treasurers of the various garrison 'precincts' between which the English military leaders had divided the country.[4] Gradually a civil government with courts of law, revenue administration and executive instruments was re-created in Dublin, distinct from the army headquarters. The continued progress of reconquest and pacification and then Ireton's death of fever (November 1651) much increased the Commissioners' power. Crom-well's own commission as Lord Lieutenant had been for three years, so that the Rump could still appoint, by agreement with him, another Lord Deputy, at once, without having to face the question of whether to extend Cromwell's own tenure. Meanwhile the Scottish campaigns had been fought and won, and Charles II's invasion ended at Worcester. Cromwell himself had no mind to return to Ireland. The man designated for Ireton's place was ironically the very one who had helped him to draft the army's constitution of 1647 (the Heads of Proposals), a York-shire gentleman with a brilliant military record, John Lambert. He was not immediately available, since Parliament had already sent him off to Scotland again as one of three joint commanders-in-chief and as one of eight commissioners plenipotentiary to impose a political settlement on the defeated Scots.[5] By the time that he returned and he and his wife began to outfit themselves—over-lavishly, as some contemporaries maliciously remarked—the Rump's civilian leaders had decided, for economy's sake, not to renew Cromwell's commission as Lord Lieu-tenant nor to appoint a Lord Deputy but simply to have a military commander-in-chief, who was also to be a civil Commissioner, but in this capacity only *primus inter pares*. Since Lambert, unlike the existing Irish Commissioners, was not an MP and lacked the closeness of Ireton's personal links with Cromwell, he would thus have been in an exposed position, and not surprisingly he refused the command. How much this was due to pique at the cuts in income and status involved, how much it was a shrewd political calculation of his vulnerability, is hard to tell. Hostile witnesses emphasised the former; on the latter score he had a fair case. So the Commissioners soldiered on, with Ludlow as acting commander-in-chief until a way out was found. Charles Fleetwood, who had come up fast in the military hierarchy during the previous two years, a man of very different character and views from Ireton or Lambert, was proposed instead. As part of a 'package deal', since he had just married Cromwell's widowed daughter Bridget Ireton, he was able to take over his predecessor's furnishings in Dublin; moreover he was prepared to accept appointment as commander-in-chief and senior Commissioner. Since Fleetwood remained lieutenant-general of the army and colonel of a horse regiment, this was not exactly penury.[6] It was not until after Cromwell's own elevation to the Protectorate that his son-in-law's status in Ireland was raised by his being made Lord Deputy. By 1652-3 the English reconquest was virtually complete, and the great task before the

Commissioners was now that of planning and carrying out the huge transfers of land ownership and population on which the Long Parliament had resolved. The motive behind this ruthless piece of 'colonialist' expropriation was threefold: to punish the Irish for the rebellion of 1641 and the long war which had followed, to make any repetition impossible, and to satisfy the Commonwealth's creditors. The latter were of two kinds, who themselves became acute competitors for the best lands: the 'Adventurers' who had lent money for the suppression of the rebellion on the security of Irish lands from 1641–2 onwards,[7] and the officers and soldiers of the army whose pay arrears were to be liquidated by Irish land grants. An elaborate, temporary machinery of allocation and distribution was required with special committees and commissions in London, Dublin, and various other parts of Ireland. Rival claims had to be determined, to decide which Adventurers and which army units were to be satisfied, at what values per acre out of which Irish counties, also which Irish landowners—and others—were liable to the provisions of the Settlement Act (of August 1652), the legal basis for the policy of forcible transplantation.[8] At the same time as this vast undertaking was in hand, the administration of law and finance was settling back into something like a normal peacetime pattern. A few pre-1642 office-holders survived, having switched allegiance from King to Parliament at the right moment; a few existing new-English lawyers and Dublin merchants (and other civilians) were acceptable to the new rulers. But a large proportion of the men appointed were completely fresh to Ireland and represented the civilian element of the new 'Cromwellian' ruling class. In this way, and through the Commissioners' responsibility to Parliament and the Council of State, the Irish government of the years 1652–3 can fairly be thought of as an extension of the English central administration. In a sense this was the fulfilment of earlier policies, notably of James I's Attorney-General, Sir John Davies, who had advocated uniform law and government on both sides of the Irish Sea.[9]

In Scotland, the change from an independent to a subject status was more abrupt and dramatic. Having given the lead in revolt against Charles I (1638–40), the Scots had enjoyed *de facto* independence during the 1640s. The King had had his supporters within the Scottish government, though his high hopes from them were scarcely compatible with his simultaneous encouragement of Montrose.[10] The Scots parliamentary alliance of 1643 led to reasonably close relations (e.g. the Committee of Both Kingdoms) from then until 1647, but the relationship had been increasingly uneasy, culminating in the Scots' alliance with Charles I late in 1647 and the disastrous Hamiltonian invasion of 1648. The aftermath of the Preston campaign took Cromwell and Lambert to Edinburgh, if nominally as allies of the anti-Hamiltonians, the Argyll faction among the old Covenanters of 1638–47.[11] And the English forces soon withdrew, leaving only frontier garrisons. Even England's ex-allies, the radical Covenanters deplored the regicide which more than undid the English generals' diplomacy (especially Lambert's tactful conduct) in the previous autumn. Relations in 1649 can only be described as a 'cold war'. This culminated in the alliance of 1650 (which reflected no credit on either party) between Charles II and the Scottish Presbyterians. The Commonwealth government rightly took this as a direct threat; more dubiously they used it to justify a preventive war. It was on this issue that Fairfax resigned as Lord General and Commander-in-Chief, to be succeeded by Cromwell. And so on to Dunbar, the capture of Edinburgh and Stirling, the bloody victories won by Lambert and Monck, Worcester —'the crowning mercy'—and the later conquest of the Highlands: all this, the military and political history of 1651–4, we must take as read. Its constitutional and administrative effects are our concern here.

The prolonged and eventually widespread Scottish resistance to the English invaders and to the process of conquest led to the complete disintegration of civil government. Nor were there enough reputable Scots of sufficient standing to form a client regime. Even that equivocal character, the 8th Earl and 1st Marquis of Argyll, if politically a potential Pétain, was not a Laval; there was to be no Vichy at Inveraray. Hence by the winter of 1651–2 most of Lowland Scotland was under direct English rule. At the same time the English Commissioners wanted legally binding Scottish consent to the proposed union, which had—as far as the record shows—been decided upon late in 1651.[12] Hence the farce of representatives from the shires and burghs being canvassed for their acceptance, and later having to elect delegates to go to England, not to negotiate as equals but to accept the details of the merger. Parallel to this constitutional union went the partial re-creation of a civil administration. A second set of Commissioners was appointed, this time with limited but specific powers to reconstruct the judicial and financial systems. Then in 1652 Commissioners for the administration of justice followed: from this beginning civil government and law were gradually extended.[13] The new English taxes of the 1640s were imposed on Scotland, as on Ireland. An attempt was also made to impose the English pattern of JPs and sessions at the county level. Only in the Exchequer and Chancery and the civil law did a distinctively Scottish element of procedure and personnel survive this drastic reconstruction.[14] Again, as in Ireland, the Englishmen posted to Scotland after 1651 can fairly be included among the members of the 'British' central government (Table 3). Likewise, too, further institutional changes followed the replacement of the Long Parliament by the Protector.

TABLE 3   *The rulers of Scotland, 1651–60*

Oliver Cromwell	Lord General, invades August 1650, leaves in pursuit of Charles II August 1651.
George Monck	Lieutenant-General, left in sole, temporary, command August 1651.
John Lambert, Richard Deane and Monck	Major-Generals in joint charge December 1651–February 1652. (Monck goes on indefinite sick leave January 1652.)
Lambert and Deane	Major-Generals, January–March 1652 (Lambert home to prepare for Ireland).
Deane	Major-General, March 1652–March 1653 (Deane then recalled to take up naval command).
Robert Lilburne	Colonel, and acting commander-in-chief only, March 1653–April 1654.
Monck	Captain-General and Commander-in-Chief April 1654–December 1659, with a Council from August 1655. (Broghill served as its Lord President, 1655–6.)
Thomas Morgan	Major-General and acting Commander-in-Chief, December 1659–May 1660.

vii   THE ARMED FORCES AND OTHER DEPARTMENTS

The biggest difference between the apparatus of government in the 1650s and that in the 1630s was due to the existence of large regular armed forces. Charles I had raised land armies for his abortive amphibious operations of 1625–8, and again in attempting to subdue the Scots in 1638–40. But the administrative machinery to act—in modern jargon—as the logistical infrastructure for these forces was minimal. In the later 1620s there was indeed a Paymaster of the Forces, with a deputy and a clerk under him.[1] But the finance for the so-called Bishops' Wars of 1639 and 1640 was under the charge of Sir William Uvedale, who was both Treasurer-at-War and Treasurer of the Chamber, and his underlings:[2] a good illustration of the point that the armed forces were the last branch of central government to be fully detached from the royal household.[3] A distinct civilian administration to serve the military machine began to take shape only on the eve of civil war in 1642—and on both sides at about the same time.[4] On the parliamentarian side, the nature of army finance goes far to explain the shape which this took. The key figures were the Treasurers-at-War who were later also designated Receivers-General of the Assessment. There were several civilians attached to the army who seem more properly to be thought of as civil officials than as army officers: such were the Judge Advocate, the Muster-Master General, the Physicians and Surgeons, the Victuallers or 'Providores', the deputy Treasurers-at-War and lesser Paymasters. The Provost-Marshal (or, in modern terms, chief of military police) is a borderline case. In deciding who was an official of the central government, a few arbitrary decisions are inevitable and these are explained below in the chapter which attempts a 'social biography' of republican officials. The staff of the Tower—as a state prison-cum-fortress—have been included with the military administrators, but members of ordinary military garrisons in other forts and castles have not.

The Ordnance Office was no new feature on the administrative scene. The object of close scrutiny in the early 1650s, as it had been in the early 1630s,[5] it managed to survive with little change except that the office of Lieutenant of the Ordnance was abolished in 1652.[6] Under the Rump there was a parliamentary committee for Ordnance and Stores, and a Council of State committee for the Ordnance. The other senior and middle-ranking Ordnance officers remained the same as before: Surveyor, Clerk, Clerk of Deliveries, Master Gunner, Proofmaster. Contractors for cannon, powder and shot worked very closely with this sub-department. John Browne, though no longer a monopolist, was still supplying cannon and shot until his death in 1652, when his son-in-law Thomas Foley and his son George Browne took over; the Browne-Foley marriage represented a merger between the wealden (Kent–Sussex) iron industry and that of the west midlands and Forest of Dean. The centre of the industry was to shift away from the Weald in the following generation. Although Browne and Foley, and for brass guns the Pitt brothers, remained regular contractors, the post of Gunmaker with its attendant monopolistic privileges disappeared. No single cannon-maker would ever again rival the position of John Browne in the 1630s and early 1640s.[7] The supply of gunpowder for the forces' needs through the Ordnance Office became, if anything, even more diffused than that of cannon and shot. There was no one Powder-Maker, comparable to Evelyn or Cordwell earlier,[8] but rather a syndicate of contractors on an *ad hoc* basis, to supply so much powder at a particular price. Some of these men were also connected with the regime in other ways, one or two were indeed officials, but as powder-suppliers they were not on the Ordnance Office staff.

The great controversy about that department was whether it should continue to supply weapons and munitions for the navy as well as the army. After a deadlock between two subordinate bodies, the Rump directed the Council of State itself to consider this.[9] No final decision appears to have been taken before April 1653.[10] The implication was that it would be more efficient to keep the Ordnance simply as a military supply department, and for the naval administration to provide its own munitions. That the Council of State took two years to make its recommendations may point to the intractability of the problem as well as being testimony to its own preoccupations.[11]

This brings us to the navy's own administration, its structure and quality. Although the Navy Office was old-established, its size and scope were much changed. The posts both of Lord Admiral and of the 'principal officers' of the navy had been 'in commission' before; the former for nearly ten years from Buckingham's death to 1638, and the latter during the investigations and reforms late in James's and early in Charles's reigns (1618–30).[12] But the situation in 1649–53 was not really comparable. The 'commission' for the Lord Admiral's office was, legally speaking, vested in the Council of State, most of its powers being delegated to its own Admiralty Committee and some in turn to the Judges of the Court of Admiralty.[13] Certain 'principal offices' were filled, notably those of Treasurer and until 1652/3 Surveyor. There was no Comptroller, and instead of a Clerk of the Acts or Ships, there was a Chief Clerk to the Navy Office. There was a separate Secretary to the Admiralty Committee, as there had been earlier to the Lord High Admiral or Lords Commissioners. The Navy Office was run by a group of Commissioners including the Surveyor; normally about four or five of them directed business in London. Other Commissioners were in charge at certain ports and naval dockyards, with authority over the other senior officers there: the Masters-Attendant and the Master Shipwrights. In the main ports used by the fleet, naval officers seconded to shore service (or men of comparable maritime experience) were in charge, with the rank of Commissioner at Chatham, Harwich and Portsmouth but not at Plymouth.[14]

Much has been written on the naval administration of the Commonwealth,[15] and differing views have been expressed as to its efficiency. For the present purpose it is enough to say that expansion of the 'regular' navy was accompanied by some growth in the numbers and cost of civilian personnel ashore and attached to the fleets, but this was hardly of 'Parkinsonian' dimensions.[16] Looking at the naval budgets of the years 1649–60 one must remember that the English republic was engaged in naval warfare against someone somewhere continuously except for a few months in 1651–2 and 1654. The proportion of total naval expenditure on 'administration', as opposed to building, equipping and supplying the fleets and paying the officers and men, does not seem excessive. Almost certainly the use of Commissioners, or men of comparable standing, in the various dockyards and other ports where revictualling and repairs were carried out, was money well spent. The appointment of the new Admiralty and Navy Commissioners in December 1652[17] concentrated a wide range of activities, all to do with the waging of naval war, in fewer hands; the general impression from the records is one of purposeful activity,[18] and in so far as the proof of the pudding is in the eating, England did win the first Anglo-Dutch war.[19] At a more routine level, the men who mattered most were the Treasurer, the Navy Commissioners, their Clerk, the Admiralty Committee's and later the Admiralty and Navy Commissioners' Secretaries, the Deputy Paymasters of the Fleet, the Master Shipwrights and Masters Attendant in the yards, and the Victuallers. Although navy victualling was on a contract basis, like the supply of powder and military equipment, the regular Victuallers and the victualling agents in some of the ports were in practice members of the naval administration.[20] Ship building was carried on as a direct state enterprise in the naval dockyards although the supply of timber and naval stores was largely managed through private contractors.[21] A particularly interesting experiment in nationalised industry existed in the Forest of Dean, where both the building of frigates on the shore and the exploitation of the iron works further inland was in charge of Major John Wade, who was given his head as a kind of State manager, and seems to have made a good job of it.[22] In naval administration, too, some further changes followed from the political events of 1653.

The other traditional departments of the central government counted for less and are easier to describe. The Office of Works had been a sub-department of the Chamber;[23] it now came directly under the Council of State, as the body responsible for the upkeep of public buildings—that is, mainly the one-time royal palaces and other residences. Apart from the control exercised over it, the Works' staff and activities changed little. It no longer had a great architect and designer at its head; instead Inigo Jones turned to private patronage in his last years,[24] and the Works had to make do with someone of merely average talent.[25] Since its activities were limited to maintenance and repairs, this mattered less than if a major building programme had been in progress. The demolition, or conversion, of some or all cathedrals was more than once discussed. Happily, except in the case of Carlisle and bits of Peterborough and Lichfield, the more drastic suggestions were never implemented. Many puritans saw a religious use for these buildings; a few may even have appreciated their beauty.

The Mint continued to be responsible for the coinage under the authority of Parliament, largely delegated to the Council of State. Its designers were also responsible for medals and for the matrices of seals. So military and naval campaigns, and changes of regime, brought them more work and extra payments. There was a thorough overhaul of the Mint's personnel in 1649. An unusually high proportion of men on its staff, who had been at least passive parliamentarians in the years 1642–8, either could not accept the regicide republic or were felt to be unreliable. As before, the curious dual authority of Warden and Master was continued, despite one or two more radical proposals. Like the Ordnance Office, there is evidence in the 1650s as in the 1630s of continuing internal dissension.[26]

Another obvious difference from the central administration of 1625–42 is, of course, the total absence of a royal household. Those of the late king's children who remained in Parliament's charge (two in 1648–50; one in 1650–2) were committed to the care of a succession of governesses, tutors and governors. These were upper-class supporters of the Commonwealth who were paid on a salary-plus-expenses basis, and cannot by any stretch be likened to the household officers of the king's children before 1642. The Commonwealth met the very modest living expenses incurred by Charles I in his last months as well as the cost of the last abortive peace negotiations with him in the autumn of 1648. They also attempted to satisfy the pre-war financial claims of those among his ex-servants who had not later been active royalists, and of his servants from 1646–8/9 who had acted with Parliament's authority.[27] But for a 'household' as a regular part of the central administration again we must await the years of the Protectorate.

viii   1653: THE ENTR'ACTE

In some ways government, or rather administration, by committees was giving way to that by full-time salaried commissioners during the latter years of the Rump's rule. This was even extended to areas where there had not previously been committees. In the spring of 1653, all fifteen members of the non-parliamentary Law Reform Committee which had been appointed the year before under Matthew Hale (then a sergeant-at-law, not yet a judge)[1] were made Judges for the Probate of Wills and for Administrations, on an unpaid basis.[2] It would be tempting to say that the downfall of the Rump (and its committees) in April 1653 meant the end of committee rule in a more general sense. In the long run this may have been true, but in the short run it is very misleading.

Cromwell's dissolution of the Rump left a constitutional void. He himself continued to act as Lord General, or more accurately as Captain-General and Commander-in-Chief under his commission of June 1650, issued by the very body whose existence he had now terminated. The Council of Officers, all of whose commissions depended either directly on the late Parliament or on Parliament's Lord General, then proceeded to choose a small Council of State to act as an interim civil executive. Apart from the late Parliament and Council of State and their respective committees, all individual appointments and commissions were continued. The courts were ordered to continue functioning, as if nothing had happened. While the new military rulers of the country and their few civilian allies debated what form a constitutional settlement should take, the normal tasks of administration, justice and finance had to be carried on. The army leaders were anxious not to appear as the sole governors for longer than was unavoidable.

The new Council of State, which co-opted additional members during the following weeks, included some members who had been on one or more of the five councils appointed by the Rump between February 1649 and December 1652. Others had experience of civil administration or military command. Granted its unconstitutional origin, the government of May to July 1653 compares reputably with its immediate predecessors and successors. Part of the army's case against the Rump was the latter's dilatoriness and lack of will in carrying reforms through to a successful conclusion. Not surprisingly, therefore, the new men showed themselves more active at first than those they had replaced. The use of committees and commissions was if anything extended. Exactly a month after the forced dissolution of the Rump, the new Council ordered that all who had signed a London petition to Cromwell as Lord General, in favour of restoring the late Parliament or calling a new one speedily, should be summarily dismissed from all their employments. And on the same day a small committee, including Major-Generals Lambert and Disbrowe, was appointed to confer with all other (non-conciliar) committees and commissions about recruiting their numbers and their future management.[3] Fresh commissioners for inspecting treasuries and for taking accounts, a new commission (replacing a half-hearted and lapsed Rump committee) on officers and offices and how to reduce their charge, and a new Army Committee (the previous one having been a parliamentary body) may be distinguished from mere replacements of individuals, due to voluntary retirement or dismissal.[4] There were no other structural changes beyond the absence of a sitting Parliament after nearly twelve-and-a-half years, for eleven of which it had exercised executive as well as legislative power. This in itself meant that the new Council had a wider range of responsibilities than its predecessor. But its members regarded themselves essentially as caretakers; they were divided only over what body should replace them. The outcome was a compromise between those who wanted a larger Council and no Parliament, those who favoured a new Parliament chosen on something like the army's 1647 scheme, and those who preferred a constitutional convention to frame a new government and then summon its first Parliament. It has been effectively argued that Cromwell and his colleagues intended from the first that the body for which writs were issued on 6 June and whose members assembled in Westminster on 6 July 1653 should assume the style and powers of a Parliament;[5] but even this may assume a greater unity of purpose than existed. The Barebones, as it has become known to history,[6] immediately declared itself to be a Parliament. The decision to do so was carried by a vote of 65 to 46; the Tellers both for the Ayes and the unsuccessful Noes each included one member of the future Protectorate Council of State.[7]

Once the style of Parliament had been assumed, the new legislature assumed all the additional executive and judicial powers enjoyed—or abused—by its predecessor. Elections were held to make up the size of the Council to the same number as it had been under the Rump. Other changes followed: revisions in or additions to the appointments made by the Officers and the interim Council since 20 April. The old-fashioned view that under the Barebones England was temporarily at the mercy of a bunch of crack-pot fanatics has long since been exploded. Modern historians disagree about the extent to which the elections and subsequent parliamentary business were manipulated by Major-General Thomas Harrison and the other millenarian leaders.[8] But there was nothing other-worldly about, for example, the Barebones' attitude towards the Dutch War. Were its attempts at more strictly administrative reforms charac-terised by millenarian (alias 'Utopian') fantasies, the work of ideologues and dreamers?

The largest single undertaking in this respect was the attack on Chancery, beginning with the resolution of 5 August 'To take away the Court of Chancery', and culminating in the vote of 15 October to suspend its proceedings for a month.[9] The final Bill for the replacement of Chancery had still not appeared at the demise of the Barebones in December. The abolition of the Duchy of Lancaster jurisdiction and of the Alienations Office, which did take temporary effect, should not be overlooked. All this must be seen as part of the wider, long-term cam-paign for law reform;[10] several of the non-parliamentary reform com-mittee of 1652–3 in fact sat as elected or co-opted members.[11] It is unfair to judge the Barebones by its uncompleted work in this field. Whether it would have been any more successful than the Rump which preceded, or the Protectorate which followed it, in establishing effective county courts and local registries for property transactions, as well as in simpli-fying the procedure, reducing the expense, and expediting the business of the common law courts, while doing without a central equity court even for appeals and so on, must remain non-proven. Relief for im-poverished prisoners for debt was a more modest target towards which the Long Parliament had already taken steps.[12] One of the most dramatic —and for several years most effective—measures of the Barebones was the Marriages Act, really an Act to compel the registration of marriages, births and burials regardless of denomination; its secular character is a useful corrective to any stereotype of narrow fanatical 'Saints'.[13]

If there had been time to implement them, the Barebones' attacks on tithes and advowsons would have entailed comparably important admin-istrative changes. Ecclesiastical administration had passed out of the hands of the Plundered Ministers' Committee, which had ceased to exist with its parent body, the Long Parliament. This had meant more power for the Maintenance Trustees, who administered those church revenues reserved for educational and charitable purposes, and 'augmented' the incomes of deserving clergy and teachers from confiscated tithes and other miscellaneous sources of income (such as any unsold glebe lands).

The complete abolition of tithes would have put a heavy burden on the Trustees, assuming that they had been responsible for administering alternative funds for clerical stipends. Perhaps here the split did show between moderate reforming puritans who none the less wanted a salaried ministry for a state church, and those who believed that the minister should either have a secular occupation by which to support himself or depend on the free-will offerings of his congregation. It was not that the 'moderates', men of Congregational beliefs like many of the Cromwellian inner circle, positively favoured compulsory tithes, but that they drew back from the logical consequences of their abolition: the end of a paid and, as they believed, of a preaching ministry unless an alternative source of revenue could be found. The fall of the Barebones in December 1653 left these measures incomplete; the next steps in ecclesiastical organisation and financial control had to await the new government. Meanwhile those prototypes of the modern Church Commissioners of the Church of England,[14] the Maintenance Trustees, continued their work.

A new Council of State was elected by the Barebones in November. Why these elections went as they did when the law and the ministry were apparently in such grave and immediate peril, is a mystery which facile party labelling into two categories, moderates (or conservatives) and radicals,[15] cannot resolve. By any standard the new councillors were more conservative than those chosen in July. At least five leading radicals were dropped; at least eight staunch Cromwellians were voted in. Cromwell came easily top of the poll, with 119 votes; no 'radical' exceeded 70. If the Barebones were really divided into two parties, the likeliest explanation is that the moderates took the trouble to turn out in strength for these elections but did not bother to attend in defence of tithes, advowsons, or the Court of Chancery. The effect of this new Council on administration is purely hypothetical, since it met only for five or six weeks. It did, however, get rid of one or two radicals from committees and commissions.[16]

The carefully engineered coup by which the Barebones Parliament's existence was ended[17] left many questions unanswered. But the nature of the new political order was soon to have its effect at the administrative level.

ix ADMINISTRATION UNDER THE PROTECTORATE

Oliver Cromwell ruled as Lord Protector under the Instrument of Government (often, to contemporaries, simply 'the Instrument'), from December 1653 to June 1657. Under this constitution he enjoyed supreme executive power as head of state, though in many areas he had to act with the consent of his Council. A Parliament chosen on a reformed basis was to sit for a minimum of five months every three years. Except on the death of the Lord Protector, its executive powers were limited to approving his choice of great officers of state and judges.[1]

In a wider sense than the merely administrative, the Protectorate has been seen as a partial return towards the traditional order, a conservative 'reaction', another major step towards the now inevitable restoration.[2] It can also be thought of as the long-delayed and grossly overdue return to normality after the protracted but essentially temporary expedients of a wartime and then post-war regime.

The Protectorate did not liquidate government by committees, but their part in the administrative system was sharply reduced as a result of changes during the following eight or nine months, from late December 1653 to the beginning of September 1654. The Compounding Commissioners were virtually restricted to managing the few remaining estates under sequestration, and were told to make drastic cuts in their central and local staffs. They continued in being, but had very little to do from the summer of 1654 until 1659.[3] As Indemnity Commissioners they continued to operate until 1655, when the last of the Acts on which their authority was based had expired.[4] Other county committees continued for the specific purposes of supervising the levy and collection of the assessment and control of the militia. Additional county committees resulted from changes in the ecclesiastical system. The so-called 'Tryers', properly known as the Approbation Commissioners, were a new committee with nationwide powers, complementing for clerical appointments the financial role of the Maintenance Trustees.[5] But the Ejectors, or Ejection Commissioners, for getting rid of unsatisfactory ministers on grounds of misconduct or non-subscription to the prescribed minimum of Protestant belief,[6] were appointed as separate bodies for each county.[7] This is a warning against sweeping generalisations about the Protectorate having seen the end of the committees.[8] Changes in the membership of existing bodies were less drastic than might have been expected, perhaps because the November 1653 Council of State had in some respects anticipated the constitutional changes of mid-December.[9]

The new Council of State itself can be seen as an innovation. It was much smaller than any except the interim Council of the previous May–June. The size prescribed by the Instrument was between 12 and 16; during most of the 'first' Protectorate (end of 1653 to summer 1657) there were about 14 members, excluding the Lord Protector himself, whose sittings in Council were markedly infrequent. It was thus comparable in size to the Elizabethan Privy Council. Thurloe sat at the Board but was not yet technically a Councillor. Committees both standing and *ad hoc* were used at least as much as before, but, reflecting the size of the parent body, they were mostly small. Although some petitions were dealt with by Cromwell, through his Masters of Requests, the Council continued to handle a mass of individual cases, often of trivial importance. At the other extreme, more than under the Commonwealth, high issues of foreign policy were believed to be settled by the Protector, his Secretary of State and three or four other intimate confidants, some of whom were not even members of the Council. Not all the witnesses to this tendency are equally reliable. Most of them refer to Cromwell's last years (1657–8), after the reconstitution of his Council and the alteration of its powers in 1657 which was accompanied by Lambert's withdrawal from public life. Gardiner believed that, at least in 1654, the Council's share in foreign policy was one of substance, not merely of form.[10]

Some of the Barebones' reforms were undone by the Protector and his Council; others were confirmed and even extended. A major attempt was made to reform Chancery.[11] Among the great series of reforming ordinances passed from January to September 1654, one restored the Duchy of Lancaster jurisdiction. Another reconstituted the Exchequer and, more effectively than had been attempted by the Rump, interim Council or Barebones, re-centralised the revenue system; the structure was topped off by the appointment of Treasury Commissioners with their own Secretary, very much on the model of 1635–6.[12] A marked, if unsensational change resulted from the restoration of the Signet and Privy Seals,[13] and the Protector's use of his authority to issue instructions under the various seals and—above all—to make individual appointments by letters patent. The Patent Rolls themselves are virtually non-existent for the 1650s,[14] but enough other records have survived to give us a good idea of what they would have contained by way of appointments.[15]

With the Protectorate there was once more a 'court' in the narrower technical, as well as the broader political sense. The Protector's Household was a modest affair compared with that of James and Charles I.[16] As Lord General, Cromwell had already become a rich man with great estates and a very large income. He already had a steward, a cofferer and a personal secretary, as well as ordinary domestics; now the whole thing became larger and more formal. The Steward and the Cofferer were the key men. Subsequently, under the so-called 'Second' Protectorate of Oliver (1657–8) and that of Richard Cromwell (1658–9), there were also a Lord Chamberlain and a Master of the Horse. The Household's annual allocation out of the civil list went up from £60,000 to £100,000. Unlike the Stuart royal household, however, despite the superficially comparable proliferation of posts and the same ritualistic-looking hierarchy, there was quite a simple financial structure. The Steward's and Cofferer's department was the only one for the receipt and issue of money. The sole exception to this was the Protector's equivalent of the royal Privy Purse, the Treasurer for his Contingencies. This operated parallel to the Council of State's Contingencies fund, and may likewise be thought of as more nearly a part of the central executive than of the Household in the strict sense. This process, whereby the Protector's Household expanded and the whole machinery of central government became more like a court once again, was inevitably affected by further political developments.

The first Protectorate Parliament (September 1654 to January 1655) spent most of its time trying to replace the Instrument by a new Constitutional Bill of its own.[17] Since this was never passed, its possible consequences at the administrative level need not concern us, although in certain respects they anticipate what was to happen in 1657. An important committee investigated the financial position, and its report—made by Colonel John Birch, who had been purged in December 1648 and was to be active again in the 1660s–80s[18]—shows how precarious the republic's financial position was, even during the brief interval of peace between the Anglo-Dutch and Anglo-Spanish Wars.[19] It was on the issue of providing for the army and controlling it that the Protector broke with this Parliament, dissolving it on the first day statutorily possible.[20] The tenor of administration in 1655 might well have been much like that of 1654, but for the renewed royalist conspiracy. And despite that, in some respects it was so: as witness the renewed campaign to enforce the Chancery ordinance.

But the demands of internal security and the decision to maintain a standing force of militia by means of a new penal tax on royalists led to the one great innovation of the Protectorate: the so-called rule of the Major-Generals (October 1655 to January 1657). Merely having a senior military commander in charge of a particular region was not new. Sir Arthur Hesilrige had commanded the far north-eastern garrisons in 1648–53; Lambert had been in charge in Yorkshire in 1647–50 and Robert Lilburne since 1654; Disbrowe had charge of the south-west of England intermittently from 1649 to 1651, and he was there again from the spring of 1655. Neither the assignment of revenue raised in a particular county to pay for forces stationed there, nor the imposition of penal levies on political enemies, was in itself a novel procedure. But the combination of responsibilities allocated to the Major-Generals in the second commission, issued in October 1655,[21] did constitute something new in kind as well as in degree. Indeed when the Major-Generals (thanks to the pressure exercised by some of them on the central authorities) got themselves put on the commission of the peace for each of the counties in their respective districts, they represented an infusion of central authority into the localities which was not to be exceeded until the two world wars of this century. The caricature view of them as military satraps and kill-joy puritans purveyed by anglican-royalist propaganda, and accepted by many historians at least until the 1890s,[22] will not do. Most were extremely careful not to act outside due process of law; apart from raising the

Decimation tax and mustering the new militia, their duties were all within the scope of existing laws.[23] Yet they were agents of the central government with power over their localities: comparable to intendants or commissaries on special mission; and some of them did activate 'moral' reform, using existing legal powers in a way that had no precedent. The Somerset JPs of the 1620s and 30s had, for example, set about closing unlicensed alehouses with a certain zeal;[24] but, as we shall see,[25] this was small beer indeed compared with one or two of the Major-Generals. And their ultimate sanction, like that of the Protectorate as a whole, was the sword; so, propaganda and popular myth apart, the militarist, kill-joy image has some slight plausibility. The instinct of the British people to dislike soldiers in politics may even have a sound sub-stratum of historical folk-memory. Yet when we examine the correspondence of these men, and the evidence of their activities in other records, this is not the dominant impression which emerges. From the government's and the Major-Generals' own viewpoint, the interlocking security and fiscal problem was always uppermost. There is no evidence that the 'blue laws' of the Rump, e.g. the death penalty for adulteresses, were more strictly enforced in 1655–6 than either earlier or later during the republican decade.[26]

The tendencies already inherent in the Protectorate constitution, deflected in 1655, were accelerated during and after the second so-called Protectorate Parliament, particularly during the first half of 1657. The inability of the Major-Generals to influence the elections of August 1656 more effectively in the government's favour has been seen by historians as proof of their general futility.[27] Be this as it may, the civilianising of the regime was the dominant theme of the Parliament's work. The new constitution, by which it was intended to make Cromwell king, even when modified to meet his refusal of the crown, pointed strongly in that direction. Compared with the Instrument, the net effect of the Humble Petition and Advice, as the 'Remonstrance' eventually became known, was slightly to augment the powers of Protector and of Parliament and significantly to reduce those of the Council. Since the Council contained a solid bloc of senior officers,[28] it had given institutional form to the political power of the army. When that power was reduced, the likelihood of the army's resorting to direct physical action was paradoxically increased. In the event the new advisory 'Privy Council', as it came to be known, had almost the same composition as its predecessor. Only Lambert, the ablest of the generals, refused to accept the new constitution. Contemporaries and some subsequent historians have ascribed this to disappointed ambition: that he assumed the Humble Petition, which gave the existing Lord Protector power to nominate his successor, to mean hereditary succession: Richard Cromwell and not John Lambert. As his biographers have suggested,[29] this needs a second look. Twice, in

49

December 1653 and the autumn of 1654, Lambert himself had been prepared to have Cromwell offered the crown, or at least to help make the protectorate hereditary. If he had been aiming at the succession all along, this is inexplicable. He may well have come to do so, some time during 1655–6; but he probably saw, more clearly than the politically unperceptive Fleetwood and Disbrowe, that it was not so much the alteration in the Protector's position under the revised 1657 constitution but the people who were promoting it, which spelt the army's doom— and with the army's that of the Good Old Cause itself.[30]

Besides these constitutional and political developments, 1657 saw a striking change in the army's financial position. The assessment in England was cut to the all-time low of only £35,000 a month;[31] the peak level had been £120,000 a month, even latterly it had been £60,000 a month.[32] Added to this overall reduction was the difficult question of how far the revenues of Ireland and Scotland, including the assessments there, would support the English armies in those two countries and how far they required to be subsidised out of the assessment in England and Wales. Since the Protectorate was by then committed to a land war in Flanders as well as a naval and colonial conflict with Spain, this drastic cut was a heavy price to pay for the seal of constitutional respectability. It meant that in its last years the Protectorate was dogged by acute financial crisis.[33] Perhaps again Lambert may have had a shrewder idea than most of his colleagues of what was coming to them, though Montague and Sydenham were Treasury Commissioners and certainly should have known.

One minor fiscal innovation, the tax on unlicensed building in London, entailed its own personnel, though the commissioners were part-time and unpaid. The Protectorate Trade Committee, which originated in 1655, was by this time extremely large and contained several merchants who were to be active under the Restoration. Its role and achievement are hard to compare with those of its 1650–1 predecessor, the Commonwealth's Trade Council. Although its permanent staff were members of the central administration, the Trade Committee itself was an advisory rather than an executive body.

The Protectorate saw further changes in those branches of the central government responsible for ruling Ireland and Scotland. In 1654 the Protector raised his son-in-law Fleetwood from the status of commander-in-chief in Ireland to that of Lord Deputy. The ex-parliamentary Commissioners saw their powers reduced by their being made Councillors. Oliver sent his younger son, Henry Cromwell, on a special mission to Ireland in 1654. Perhaps Fleetwood's easy tolerance of Baptists and other army radicals there was already alarming the Protector and his inner circle of advisers, but how far this was due to lack of grasp and how far to ideological sympathy is hard to tell. Fleetwood has been severely judged by historians, and his later, unpublished correspondence shows him to better advantage than the letters which have been in print since the eighteenth century and on which the hostile verdicts have been partly based.[34] In 1655 Henry Cromwell returned to Ireland as Major-General of the Forces and Councillor; later that year Fleetwood was recalled, ostensibly because he was needed at home, to serve as a Councillor and as Major-General for the home counties and East Anglia. Like Lambert, he acted in the latter capacity *in absentia*, so the excuse was a thin one. On the other hand, Henry Cromwell succeeded him as Deputy only when Fleetwood's three-year commission expired in 1657. This lack of formal authority weakened his position *vis à vis* the Irish Council, on which he believed that his opponents, and Fleetwood's secret allies, had a majority. Also there were too few members of this Council so that the quorum of councillors needed for business was often lacking. Despite constant appeals, the authorities at home were very slow to do anything about this: deliberate sabotage by Fleetwood and Lambert (each with his own resentments about Ireland)[35] cannot be ruled out. Not being Deputy also made it harder generally for Henry Cromwell to govern Ireland, harder for him to win obedience from English settlers, soldiers and officials and compliance from the country's inhabitants at large. Once promoted, he cheerfully acted the part. Contemporary critics (of republican as well as puritan sympathies) professed themselves shocked at the viceregal state which he kept; this was accentuated when his brother made him Lord Lieutenant in October 1658.[36] Reading Henry Cromwell's correspondence, especially for the years 1657-9 when he no longer even notionally had to refer things back to his brother-in-law the Lord Deputy in England, one is struck by a strong sense of *déjà-vu*. Despite the immense changes which had supervened (in Ireland even more, perhaps, than in England) a forcible comparison presents itself with Wentworth's correspondence in the 1630s.[37] Some of the problems for the Dublin Castle government were the same; even more striking, Ireland was still regarded as an out-relief centre for the less hopeful and worse-qualified members of the English governing class.

In Scotland things were different. The top man continued to be the military commander-in-chief, General George Monck.[38] But in 1655 an attempt was made to give English rule a more civilian character. A Council was appointed, consisting predominantly of English officials, under the presidency of Roger Boyle, Lord Broghill (second son of the first and 'great' earl of Cork).[39] Broghill has often been cited as the archetype of ex-royalist, anti-republican supporter of the Protectorate, who symbolises and indeed helps to explain the 'swing to the right' which characterises the years from 1654 on. Certainly he was prepared to accept, indeed in Ireland to promote, the restoration of the Stuarts by late 1659-early 1660; by then Broghill preferred the prospects of Charles

II to whatever regime the republic could offer—renewed military dictatorship under Lambert or Fleetwood, in effect. Socially he was as conservative as any of the Cromwellians, but in matters of government he was a reformer and more insistent on high standards of honesty and efficiency than many republicans. In 1655–6 he sent in a long series of reports and recommendations on administrative reform in Scotland, some of which were acted upon. He left there to take part in the second Protectorate Parliament, in which he was one of the chief promoters of the new constitution, and did not return to Scotland. Ireland seems always to have had the first call on his affections. Before he left Edinburgh, Broghill repeatedly had cause to make exactly the same complaint that Henry Cromwell was making from Dublin: there were not enough councillors for the Council to function properly. This was particularly true when several were elected MPs for Scottish seats in the 1656 Parliament and no quorum was left in Edinburgh. It was not Broghill's fault if the English government in Scotland remained, at bottom, a military occupation. He had ambitious plans for bringing more Scotsmen in, though he saw the difficulties—as Henry Cromwell and his advisers did with broadening the base of government in Ireland, at least to include more pre-Cromwellian settlers, or 'new English' whose families' residence dated from the 1560s–1630s. Both these experiments were cut off prematurely—the Irish one by the fall of the Protectorate and Henry Cromwell's consequent recall in 1659, the Scottish one by Broghill's early departure. There is little evidence that Monck's administrative interests in Scotland ever extended beyond the minimum requirements: internal security, money for the army, a decent standard of law and order. He seems not to have looked beyond the immediate satisfaction of these needs, whereas Broghill had appreciated that to make them lasting, and to cement the Union, wider and more enthusiastic Scottish participation was essential.[40]

In England the transition from Oliver to Richard Cromwell in September 1658 had little immediate impact on the administration. With a Protector who was no longer the effective head of the army, Richard's rule—if it were continued—pointed towards a further civilianising of the republican regime. But this was not to be. Richard Cromwell's government, which lasted just under eight months, was in effect a continuation of that in his father's last years. The Parliament called in December, which sat from January to April 1659, initiated investigations by committee into ways and means, much like its two predecessors. It also attacked one of the ex-Major-Generals for abusing his powers by extorting property from royalist families.[41] Far more serious was its collision with the army which reached a climax between 15 and 20 April. No detailed study of this Parliament has been published.[42] It included an inner group of government supporters, 'Protectorians', 'Cromwellians', or 'Courtiers'. The republican opposition was led by Hesilrige and Scot with Vane joining in on the flank; it mainly consisted of ex-Rumpers and other irreconcilable enemies of the Protectorate. There was also a much larger body of more or less independent country gentlemen, not tied to the government but ready to support it against both the army and the republicans; they included ex-Cavaliers or their sons, ex-'Presbyterians' of 1642–8 who had been in opposition under the Commonwealth, neutrals and also some conservative Cromwellians. Most of the army leaders, having accepted ennoblement from Oliver, sat in the 'Other House', whose recognition was one of the main issues between courtiers and republicans. The Commons had been elected from the old (pre-1653) franchise and constituencies, because of doubts about the validity of the electoral clauses of the Instrument in relation to the Humble Petition. This made the inclusion of members for Scotland and Ireland, on the 1654–6 basis, legally indefensible. None the less, the government won recognition of the Other House as a House of Parliament, and of the members for Scotland and Ireland as MPs in the Commons.

In Richard Cromwell's Parliament all the ablest parliamentarians, the most experienced debaters and the political leaders, except for a few lawyers, were on the republican side. Yet for almost all purposes the government, with its non-republican, 'country' support, had a comfortable majority. Moreover, the device of getting the Speaker to accept a motion 'that the question be now put' acted as an *ad hoc* guillotine. There was scarcely a 'government party', although there were court or administration spokesmen such as Thurloe. But for the Protectorians' fatal error in supporting the crypto-royalist attack on the army (18–20 April), there seems no reason why the Parliament should not have continued satisfactorily. The 'court–country' divisions in it seem to anticipate those under the later Stuarts, and even under the Hanoverians.

Lambert had refused to accept the civilianising policy of 1657 because of those who advocated and supported it; now it was the policy itself which brought matters to breaking point. By 19–20 April the army leaders, under pressure from their own regimental officers, felt that the Protector must be compelled to dissolve the Parliament. Whether they originally intended to remove Richard or to keep him as a puppet ruler— if he were willing to act the part—is less clear. It may well have been the secret connections between Lambert (still out of both military and civil office) and the republican leaders, together with the wishes of the junior field officers, which led Fleetwood and Disbrowe to take their next step. This 'twilight' of the Protectorate, a period of no effective government, was ended on 7 May with the restoration of the Rump.

How are we to characterise the Protectorate's administrative system? It would be premature at this stage in our inquiry to assess whether it was more or less onerous, honest and effective than those of the regimes which preceded and followed it. (Something will be said of this in chapters 5 and 6, below.) But rather more can already be said of its institutional structure. This clearly differed less from that under the monarchy (whether of the 1620s–30s or of the 1660s–80s) than did the administrative structure under the Long Parliament and then the Commonwealth (c. 1643–53). But in trying to estimate whether the Cromwellian administration was more like that of the Rump or that of Charles I and II, we must be careful not to confuse qualitative with quantitative measurement. For the bulk of the traditional English governing class, Cromwell's rule was just as much of a usurpation, of a puritan–republican–military tyranny, as was that of the Rump. Measured more technically, by the typical features of royal administration, not nearly as many of the posts that really mattered were filled by patentees. And, despite the restrictions on the scope of committees after 1653, correspondingly more administration continued to be carried on by salaried Commissioners. As we shall see,[43] there were other respects, too, in which the Protectorate maintained, even if with some modifications, the Long Parliament's tentative and limited steps away from the Old Administrative System towards a more modern idea of the public service. In terms of individual administrators, too, we shall find[44] that the changes of personnel at the middle and lower levels, from Commonwealth to Protectorate in 1653–4 and back again to Commonwealth in 1659, though appreciable, were by no means massive or overwhelming. So the 'monarchical', and in other respects more conservative features of Cromwellian rule should not blind us to the underlying continuity throughout the 'Interregnum' of 1642–60.

X FROM RESTORED COMMONWEALTH TO RESTORED MONARCHY (1659–60)

The restored Commonwealth was ruled by the survivors of 1649–53 between May and October 1659, and again, though on a very different basis, for a few weeks from the end of December 1659 until 21 February 1660. The administrative consequences, though short-lived, were dramatic. The Rump House of Commons showed a marked tendency to behave as though everything that had happened since 20 April 1653, if not positively illegal, was invalid unless approved by Parliament. Some republicans, it seems, would have extended this to all appointments. Tension arose here because the men who had actually overthrown Richard and buried the Protectorate—the army leaders—had been themselves in military office throughout the period 1653–9[1] and in many cases members of the civil administration too.[2] In 1652–3 several of them had been more strongly against the Rump than were Oliver Cromwell and the men who later advised his son. A compromise was reached by the familiar means of an Indemnity Act, safeguarding those who had acted under the *de facto* governing powers since 20 April 1653. This did not protect them as individuals if they had abused their trust. Impeachment proceedings were in fact initiated against Colonel Philip Jones, a South Walian who had ended up as Comptroller of the Protectoral Household. By any standards, the grounds were legally slender, whether or not they were well-founded in morality and fact. Jones was accused of abuses and exactions on the grounds of having risen from being worth 'not £5 a year' to great wealth, and by 'common fame' of having lived latterly at a higher rate than he could have done out of his various salaries.[3] Presumably this was done out of spite, because Jones had backed Richard Cromwell firmly in the April crisis. The kind of abuses of which Boteler had been accused in the preceding Parliament may also have been committed by Jones several years earlier;[4] but nothing specific was ever adduced against him.[5]

At a more routine level, the restored Commonwealth made more changes in the army[6] than in the civil administration. But there were many dismissals and appointments (or re-appointments) in both. The Indemnity Act covered what men had done since 1653 but was not held to validate their appointments. A great many individual posts therefore became automatically vacant; and some of them (e.g. Signet and Privy Seal Clerkships) were not filled. There was a partial return to the earlier system of parliamentary committees and non-parliamentary commissions. But as we have seen, there had never been a total abandonment of administrative committees even at the height of Protectoral rule when parliamentary committees were only occasional and temporary. The abortive royalist rising under the Presbyterian Sir George Booth in Cheshire (July–August 1659), and the fear of more widespread conspiracy, saw a last revival of compounding and sequestration under the Commissioners.[7] But the new Indemnity Act itself[8] was to be administered through the law courts and not by commissioners, as had been true since 1655 of the previous legislation on this subject. Since the indemnity records show that it was often against the normal 'due process' of the courts that those who had acted in Parliament's and then the State's name sought protection, this would hardly seem satisfactory. But it was not to be put to the test.

The army's renewed breach with the Rump arose out of Lambert's victory over Booth, and the officers' desire for more generals to be appointed. Whether in the first instance this campaign was promoted by Lambert himself is not known, but it culminated in a parliamentary counter-attack on him and other senior officers who had sponsored the request, more penal than anything Richard Cromwell's parliament had contemplated, let alone voted for, in the previous April. Indeed at this point it becomes difficult to separate an account of the political background to the institutional changes from the nemesis which began to overtake the whole puritan-republican cause. The army officers and the Rump MPs were racing each other towards the abyss, competing in Gadarene political insanity. The second forced dissolution of the Rump on 12 October 1659 was followed by two-and-a-half months of as near anarchy as anything England had yet experienced. There was very little lawlessness or bloodshed, but the lack of even a *de facto* power commanding general respect and assent produced a vacuum in some areas of government.

The new, temporary supreme executive was the Committee of Safety. This represented an alliance of the army leaders and such of the Rump politicians as could be persuaded to work with them.[9] It controlled the administration in so far as one existed. The Navy and War treasurers were later in severe trouble for having issued money on its authority. But what else could they have done, short of leaving office altogether?[10] Although no judges went on assize after February 1659 (the summer 1659 assizes were postponed because of the threat of a general Cavalier rising and an invasion), the Westminster courts appear to have continued to function. Taxes were still—on the whole—collected. Foreign relations, of a sort, were conducted by the Committee of Safety. But this body never looked like commanding the assent which Cromwell and his Council had done from May 1653 on. Enough was enough: more than enough was exceedingly too much. Of all the regimes of the period this one shows least by way of an administrative pattern. The second-time-restored Rump which met again on 31 December 1659 once more took up where its previous sittings in October had left off, with the added stimulus of having more enemies to proscribe, including some of its own luminaries. But there was one huge difference. The rule of the generals and the Committee of Safety had collapsed from its own weakness, and the Rump's supporters had themselves won back the allegiance of the armed forces sufficiently to regain Portsmouth, the Tower and the fleet. But the salient fact was Lambert's failure to halt Monck's march south. On the day of the Rump's re-assembly Monck's advance guard was at Coldstream in Northumberland; despite assurances from Parliament and the rapidly re-elected Council of State, he showed no signs of stopping. He was greeted by delegations of MPs and Councillors near Leicester in the last week of January, and then at Barnet on 2 February; on the 3rd he entered London. The flurry of appointments continued, purging the disloyal military and civil officers, who had acted from mid-October to late December, and replacing them by others who had been loyal to the Parliament. By this time, however, some of these were not supporters of the Commonwealth at all, but crypto-royalists who regarded the Rump's return as a mere prologue to other changes. The last weeks of republican rule seem like those of men living in a dream-world.

56

It is scarcely credible that Hesilrige, Scot and the rest should have thought that Monck (and their other new allies) would allow the Rump to meander on, setting its own terms for its dissolution and the election of its successor,[11] in the face of widespread and mounting demands for a 'free Parliament'. By then this could only mean one with a non-republican majority. After the Rump's last fatal error of setting Monck at odds with the City of London in mid-February 1660, the General took the obvious first step in that direction, by compelling the House to readmit the secluded Members—the survivors of those kept out since 6 December 1648 (not, be it noted, those royalist MPs who had been excluded earlier). Even then it does not seem as if more than 80 'Presbyterian' or anti-republican MPs re-entered. If the Rumpers had hung together, they need not have hanged separately,[12] or at least they might have delayed the hour of reckoning and made things more difficult for their enemies. But by this time demoralisation had gone too far. Control of the House passed at once to the men of 1648, as the elections to the new Council of State and other appointments show. These men, with Monck and other ex-Cromwellians who had followed his lead as a result of their disillusionment in 1659, ruled the country from the Long Parliament's self-dissolution on 15 March to the restoration of the traditional constitution by the new Convention Parliament in May.

From our point of view, the whole period from April 1659 to February 1660 has the character of an extended—and disjointed—postscript. No pattern had time to take shape. Individual appointments and the membership of committees and commissions are of interest, mainly for what they tell us about some of the men who had acted between 1649 and 1659. This is particularly true after February and remains so after May 1660. It is highly relevant for the social biography of republican officials to see who did and did not continue to hold office or to play any part in public life after the fall of the republic. This also raises the more difficult underlying problem of the impact made by the republic on our national life.[13] But except as an aspect of the general political disintegration, the institutions of 1659–60 do not offer much basis for close study. That the Rump took up schemes for law reform, control of fees and cuts in superfluous offices during the summer of 1659 suggests that some of its members had learnt something from the failures and procrastinations of 1649–53.[14] But when so much has to be set on the other side of the scales, the best we can say of these men is that they had learnt only a little and forgotten very little indeed. Yet we cannot consign the republic's administrative system and personnel to the scrap-heap of history because of the final débâcle and the political suicide of its military and parliamentary masters.

CHAPTER 3

THE TERMS OF SERVICE

i ENTRY AND APPOINTMENT

One way to consider the conditions of service and forms of remuneration of the officials in republican England would be by comparison with the situation under Charles I. We might try to assess whether more and greater changes took place in the office-holding system between 1640 and 1660 than during any other twenty years or so in the century: more change, for example, than from 1600 to 1620 or from 1660 to 1680. An alternative approach would be to compare England with continental European countries, e.g. France or Sweden, first from 1625 to 1640 then from 1649 to 1660, and see what likenesses and contrasts appeared.[1] Either way we must first have some idea of what conditions were like in England during these years; and in this respect it is possible to build up a general picture only by collecting individual case-histories, or illustrations, and then by considering how far these are representative.

As to how men entered the public service and the form of appointments, we have a great deal of evidence of a limited kind. The printed and manuscript sources for the period are rich in letters, petitions and testimonials, either soliciting office for the writer or by third parties recommending a candidate for office.

To begin at the top, on 28 October 1648 Lieutenant-General Oliver Cromwell wrote to the Speaker from his quarters at Boroughbridge on the Great North Road soliciting a favour for Lieutenant-Colonel Cholmondeley, whose eldest son had fought well—as a major—against the Scots at Berwick, but had since died. Major Cholmondeley had been, as Cromwell puts it, 'Customs-Master', meaning head officer or Collector of the Customs at Carlisle, and his father now wanted the place for a younger son; an 'under-tenant' of the place (presumably this means a deputy) was trying to obtain it through the Navy Committee of Parliament which controlled customs appointments, but the grant had been stayed in the House, and Cromwell asked the Speaker's support for the other Cholmondeley son, whose case Colonel Morgan could report more fully to him.[2] But it seems to have been the father who was, in fact, appointed and held office until his death in 1656.[3]

Naturally the persons to be approached were either those who had the right to appoint to the office in question, or such as could bring influence to bear on them. Some trustees, commissioners and other senior officials were given authority to appoint their own subordinates in the ordinances by which they were themselves appointed. For the sale of bishops' lands (October–November 1646) the Contractors, Trustees, Registrar, Registrar-Accountant and Comptroller were named in the ordinance, while the Trustees were instructed to nominate Surveyors; the appointment of under-clerks, porters and cleaning staff was also, by implication, left to those named in the ordinance.[4] This implies a two-stage process: first, recommendations to the House or the lobbying of MPs by and on behalf of persons who wished to be named to the posts covered in the ordinance itself. For example, the man chosen to be Registrar-Accountant for these episcopal land sales had risen to become one of the colonels of the London militia regiments by the end of the Civil War and was apparently acceptable to both the main factions in the House.[5] The Comptroller for Crown Lands, whose duty was to cross-check the accounts of those responsible for the sales, was already employed at the Excise; some of the loans secured on that now being transferred to the security of bishops' lands.[6] This looks like a form of functional pluralism.[7]

Sometimes applications must have been made to the Trustees, or Commissioners, as the case might be, for the lesser posts in their gift. In the principal Act[8] for the sale of Crown lands (July 1649), a Registrar was named and was given power to appoint his own clerk; the Trustees also named in the Act were to appoint the Registrar of Debentures, who was to take in the credit notes for army pay arrears cashable in the form of land grants.[9] In the end this turned out to be a multiple appointment. The same Trustees were given responsibility for the sale of fee-farm rents the following spring,[10] and their Registrar in that capacity was one of the few known Levellers to be employed in civil administration under the Commonwealth, Samuel Chidley. Who had recommended him to the Trustees, when his friends had been in prison and one, Lilburne, had gone on trial for his life? He was certainly not bought off by office; although his unofficial position as co-treasurer for the Levellers disappeared with the general collapse of the movement's organisation, he continued to collect signatures for petitions on Lilburne's behalf.[11]

This practice of sharing the right of appointment between Parliament itself and the senior officials appointed by its legislation, went on throughout the Commonwealth.[12] The net effect was comparable to the old situation whereby, within a law court or department of government, the rights of appointment were shared between the Crown and the judges or 'great officers of state'.[13] And it gave Westminster—the House of Commons and those within its orbit—something of the character of a 'court' in the sense of having political patronage to dispense. Apart from

Parliament's own assumption of direct executive (as well as sole legislative and occasional judicial) powers, it gave MPs power as patrons, or persons with collective rights of appointment, much like those of the top courtiers and officers around Charles I. How much this power was abused it is impossible to tell. Here the evidence is very thin; although we have scattered letters to and from several politicians who were active in the Rump, few complete collections of correspondence survive. How far they made recommendations for appointments—privately, in committees, or on the floor of the House—improperly in return for money or as part of some other kind of deal, can only be surmised. Such transactions would normally have been by word of mouth, and so have left little trace.[14]

We have much more evidence in cases where Parliament was not itself the appointing body, when Members or others put their recommendations in writing to those who were responsible for making appointments. This can be illustrated from the printed records of the Committee, and later the Commissioners for Compounding. Colonel Thomas Birch, recruiter MP for Liverpool,[15] recommended to the central committee an Agent for the Lancashire sequestration commission, presumably a local connection of his own.[16] No sooner had the new salaried non-parliamentary Compounding Commissioners been appointed than Speaker Lenthall urged a treasurer on them.[17] The Commissioners accepted the nominations of Colonel Venn, one of the City Members,[18] for membership of a new London sequestration commission, but insisted that one of those concerned should give up his place as Overseer of houses granted to the poor (under the London corporation for relief of the poor),[19] presumably because his obligations in these two capacities might have conflicted.[20] And we have already seen evidence of rivalry, indeed collision, between two rival groups of would-be patrons at the county level. In April 1650 Colonels Pyne and Popham, MPs, objected to the new commissioners who had been appointed for Somerset by the old parliamentary committee back in February, when their fellow-member Mr John Ashe MP had been in the chair.[21] This marked the beginning of that long campaign of mutual obloquy and denunciation between the appointees of Ashe and those of Pyne which must have all but disrupted the business of sequestration and composition in Somerset over the next year or so. In other counties there was perhaps something nearer to 'monofactional' control. Lord President Bradshaw and Sir William Brereton MP recommended a faithful and deserving person to be on the Staffordshire sequestration committee;[22] Sir John Bourchier MP twice supported an applicant for the post of Agent to the Yorkshire committee;[23] but in a county so extensive as this there were bound to be varied influences if not conflicts of interest, and the Recorder of York, Sir Thomas Widdrington MP, had another candidate for the same job.[24]

In Berkshire we find an alliance of Hugh Peter, the well-known puritan minister, and John Dove MP recommending an agent, and Henry Marten MP the radical republican and Colonel John Barkstead, Lieutenant of the Tower, urging the claims of two people as commissioners the following year[25]—successfully in both cases. When a county was riven by faction, MPs like others were bound sometimes to be unsuccessful. Colonel Thomas Birch MP in collaboration with Thomas Fell, the palatinate judge and husband of George Fox's protectress Margaret, proposed a new Lancashire sequestration commissioner, who was not appointed.[26] But then Birch, despite his privileged position as a Member, had his own troubles in Lancashire.[27] At least once, the central Commissioners had to take the initiative. They invited Denis Bond MP, Dorchester draper and one of the arch committee-men of the Long Parliament, to comment on a candidate for the Dorset sequestration commission or else to propose an alternative of his own.[28]

On what grounds were men put forward as candidates, and what did those making appointments look for in them? The cynic might retort that human nature being what it is, and the office-holding system and social values of the period having been what they were, the answer is simple. Namely that appointments were made in return for cash or other favours, and as a reflection of political influence and through ties of clientage or kinship. And thus that the familiar unholy trio, of the three Ps—Patrimony, Patronage and Purchase—will explain all we need to know about appointment and entry to office now as earlier, even if the outward mechanisms and the idiom differ a little from those prevalent under the monarchy a generation before. On the basis of negative evidence it would be rash to deny this outright. Nor, save for the case of purchase, is there a total lack of positive evidence. Family connections and what we may for the moment still call patronage continued to be of great importance: in an age before public advertisement and competitive examination, how could this have been otherwise? But unless very many of those concerned were consummate hypocrites and self-deceivers, it is equally clear that such links were hardly ever enough in themselves; they were usually a necessary but seldom a sufficient cause for someone getting into the public service or advancing within it. It was not merely for form's sake, or for the record with posterity, when Francis Rous, the elderly puritan MP wrote on behalf of his nephew, Major Rous:[29] 'my/desire herein is only that he may be truly knowne, & then/that the busines may be resolved according to true weight &/worth, & not according to earnest, & empty sollicitations.'

The Commonwealth was a revolutionary regime. It had come to power through civil war and military force, and its legality was not universally recognised in the country. This put a premium on political or ideological reliability, and meant that loyalty to the government was something which patrons needed to stress, and appointing bodies to satisfy themselves about. It also led to a formidable battery of tests and oaths. This in itself was not new. The monarchy had used oaths—in theory at least—to exclude Papists from the King's service.[30] The Long Parliament had imposed its own test, the 'Protestation', in 1641–2.[31] As a result of the Scottish alliance, this had been followed by the Solemn League and Covenant (1643–8).[32] The Covenant's successor was the Commonwealth's 'Engagement', the loyalty oath of 1649–53.[33] But this too was a negative qualification: men who would not take it were not to enter or remain in office after the winter of 1649–50. In the Mint this seems to have led to several withdrawals or resignations.[34] Elsewhere, open opponents of the Commonwealth were already out of office before then. Oliver Cromwell himself was in Ireland when the various Acts to do with the Engagement were passed. And a distinct note of disapproval is evident in a letter which he wrote a year or so later, from Scotland, about its effects—in his new-found capacity as Chancellor of the University of Oxford:[35]

> It's thought Dctr. Reynolds Dctr Wilkinson Mr Cunnett and others whoe are outed about not takinge the engagement, and yett are usefull & Godly and willinge to give satisfaction if meanes could be used to keepe them in, it would heere well. I pray speake with Mr Owen but especially Sir H.V. wth. both freely about itt and if any good may be done lett me heere from you wherein I may be att all Instrumentall.

Although these were academic appointments, for Cromwell the question whether officials had what he considered to be the root of the matter in them would always have mattered more than their readiness to subscribe particular tests or oaths. Not that subscription was enough in itself to secure entry to office; surviving documents emphasise more positive qualities of loyalty. Godliness (of life and conversation) and good affection (to the present government) are the points, often the very words, which recur repeatedly. But even these recommendations are seldom unaccompanied by others of a more technical nature. Over and above loyalty and morality, we find emphasis on men's actual fitness for the work in question. It could mean a particular skill in writing, accounting or foreign languages, or a more all-round ability.

This can be illustrated many times over, but perhaps most aptly from the papers of the Accounts Committee, where political reliability, personal honesty and (in some posts) a measure of technical skill were all involved. Moreover, because this body was a non-parliamentary committee,[36] Rump MPs are found along with others as patrons or sponsors of applications; indeed the names of its correspondents read like a roll call of the Commonwealth 'establishment'—Cromwell and Vane alone being notable by their absence. When Colonel Thomas Harrison MP, the millenarian republican and regicide, wrote supporting one Mr Munck, a petitioner for a messenger's place under the Committee, he stressed the man's honesty and his poverty—due partly to earlier military service in Colonel Whalley's regiment; he was sure that Munck would be faithful and as to his capacity 'full to that ymployment'.[37] Whether as a result of his own intensifying religious fervour or because he suited his phraseology to the occasion, three years later Harrison wrote more extravagantly, on hearing of a forthcoming vacancy; the more important post of Registrar-Accountant was being given up by its present holder, Mr Robert Jeffreys:[38]

And as I desire, soe I am Perswaded of you, that in order to the discharge of your duty to the Lord, and the Publique, you are willing to Incourage and Entertayne men feareing God, And the Bearer hereof Mr Thomas Jefferson, being Commended to mee, by those, whom I doe verey much Creditt, that hee is such a one as feareth God, who hath been a Marchant, And is Esteemed to bee qualified and fitted for such an Imployment, My Request therefore is, that if you part with Mr Jefferes, that then you wilbee Pleased to Entertayne this Gentleman for a tryall, to bee Imployed as your Register Accoumptant and as you shall fynd him quallified for that bussines, soe to Continue him in it, which wilbe Esteemed a favour by him that is Yor Loving friend & desireous to serve you . . .

Notice the deliberate juxtaposition of Jefferson's godliness and his expertise, and the proposed probationary period. Here, Harrison does not claim to know the candidate personally; he is acting for others who do know and support Jefferson. This raises the question whether he can be called the candidate's patron or Jefferson his client. Interestingly, the existing holder, Mr Robert Jeffreys, had been recommended to one of the Committee in October 1649 by Edward Winslow, future Compounding Commissioner (1650–5), as being well versed in accounts, faithful, and positively desiring of employment by the Committee. Like Winslow himself, he was 'a new England gent'.[39] Jeffreys also had a certificate from four MPs as to his proficiency as a merchant and an accountant.[40] The historical compiler, John Rushworth, himself an official, wrote to two of the Committee apologising for troubling them on behalf of someone who was also supported by Major-General John Lambert:[41]

Yet in respect the bearer hereof is knowne to mee for a godly honest man I could not but testify as much. his name is Mr Tendy. his desire is to serve under you by his penn. hee will relate himselfe wherein he may be usefull. I pray you looke uppon him, as honest & faithfull in what hee undertakes. & you will much engage Your most humble Servant.

63

Colonel John Lambert, as befitted a man who was to rise to the top himself a few years later, wrote with a certain trenchancy on Tendy, alias Tandy's behalf:[42]

> Gentlemen, This bearer hath bin long knowne to mee, hee hath suffered much in Ireland, by the insurrection, in England for his Conscience. I am bold to recommend him for some place in yor service, as advantageous as you can, for his charge is great, and his performances I assure myselfe, will deserve a comfortable subsistence. If I were not assured of his trust and fidelity, I should not present him with that affection, which I doe: Gentlemen, what favour you are pleased to doe him, shall truely Engage, Yor assured Lovinge freind to serve you . . .

Lambert indeed understood about patronage, and Rushworth was probably correct in supposing that his own letter was unnecessary. Be this as it may, Philip Tandy seems only to have enjoyed a minor post until 1652–3 when he blossomed into happy pluralism—as co-Registrar Accountant to the Trustees for sale of lands forfeited for treason, Registrar to the Accounts Committee itself, and later briefly as an actual Commissioner for taking the accounts of the Commonwealth; he was also Auditor to the Obstructions Commissioners. But alas he was later accused of having been involved in the notorious 1650–2 traffic in forged debentures; he was removed for incapacity in 1655 and was said to be temporarily out of his mind. He spent much of the following two or three years petitioning for arrears of salary—real or imagined. In 1658 he was paid a lump sum and posted off to Ireland again, where he became a lay preacher. Perhaps Lambert's judgment was fallible or else he did not know his man as well as he made out.[43]

Sometimes what is known in the advertising world of today as the 'soft sell' was felt to be the most suitable line of approach. Six MPs wrote as follows to the Committee in January 1650:[44]

> Gentlemen. Although we beleive you are pressed with suitors for imployment Under you, much beyond the number of those you will have occasion to imploye, yet soe confident are wee that you will regard the abilitie & integritie of any person; more than the force of any Recomendation. That we shall offer to yor favourable Consideration this Bearer Mr Jeoffrey Corbett of whose faithfulnes we are sufficiently assured, And that by his diligent service and attendance, both upon you and yor buisines as a Messenger or otherwise, he will not only doe good service to the Publique. but deserve your particuler favor, as well as this Recomendation from Gentlemen Yor assured Freinds . . .

64

It could also be the 'old boy ticket', as when Lord President Bradshaw wrote to them:[45]

> Gentlemen: The Bearer my old fryend & Schoolefellow seekes (as he tells me) a Messengers place amongst you. He hath done & suffered for the parlyament so much as I could wysh to meete with an opportunyty to helpe him in a larger measure to a subsystence than by troubling you with this Recommendation. But his present desyres being for this place of a Messenger I willingly for him make it my Request to you he may find yor favor herein which I should not doe If I had not the Confidence of his diligence & fidelytie in performance of the Trust you shall Committ to him in the Advancement of the service you have in hand. So with my heartiest salutations I rest and will be Yor friend ready to serve you . . .

Whether his old friend Mr Hugh Middleton was successful, the Committee's records do not show. If he was the Lord President's exact contemporary, he would have been in his late forties; they had come a long way from Marple and the local grammar school.[46]

Sometimes it was for a near and dear one that such letters were written. Samuel Chidley wrote to his two friends on the Committee in support of his brother-in-law:

> a very honest Conscientious man, and ingenuous, and a good Accountant, and is out of employment, my ernest desier unto you is, That so far as it is in your power, you would help him to a Clerks place to the Committee of Accounts . . .

He added, as a postscript: 'my brother's name is Thomas Grace-dieu, a man of a proved integritie, and so Mr Moor,[47] Captain Chilington,[48] & Mr Freeman,[49] or any of their people, and our people, etc. can testifie for him'.[50] The picture implied is one of a close-knit social group, perhaps a sectarian congregation.

A Kentish gentleman who rejoiced in the name of Hercules Langrish had no such advantages. He had to write 'out of the blue':[51]

> Right worthy, and much honored gentlemen, Though I have not the honor to be know[n]e unto all of you, nor to have done any of you such important services as may call for any of you the least favour or respect, yet so confident am I of your affabilities that I have presumed to trouble you with these few lines, and by them to intreate you to bestowe a Clarkes place on my sonne Lucullus who is one that truely feares god, and hath receaved so many wounds in the parliaments service, that he is now disabled thereby to endure hardship, and therefore, I must humbly beseech you to

bestowe this place on him, and the rather because there are great arreares due unto him for his aforesaide services, and hereby you shall not onely oblige him for ever to your services, but Your most humble servant.

There is no trace of the ex-soldier Lucullus Langrish in the Committee's service.

Many of the recommendations, especially by groups of MPs, must, however, have been on the model of Harrison's quoted support for Mr Jefferson, made on the basis of recent acquaintance or even hearsay from others. Hesilrige may well have known Richard Kellam who hoped to be a messenger under the Committee, as he had served for six years in Sir Arthur's cavalry regiment; he was recommended tersely as an honest and godly man.[52] Major John Wildman, ex-Leveller turned solicitor and dealer in land sales,[53] recommended an unnamed bearer to be a solicitor before the Committee, or for some other employment under them. This would be acceptable to God, serviceable to them and to the State, and would oblige the writer; according to the contemporary annotation, Wildman may have been writing on behalf of himself![54]

Other prominent administrators took advantage of the additional posts created under the Accounts Committee. Gualter Frost, Secretary of the Council of State, wrote to two friends on the Committee, on behalf of the brother of one of his own messengers, a man whose praises he could truthfully sing. As to the candidate, however, he could only say 'if hee prove like his Brother (as I hope hee will) You will not repent of giving him an Entertainement . . .' which hardly suggests close personal knowledge.[55] By contrast, Henry Middleton, Sergeant-at-Arms to the Commissioners of the Great Seal, was able to claim that he had been for fifteen years 'familiarly acquainted' with Mr Edward Johnson, whom he and his fellow-sergeant Edward Birkhead were backing for a place. Johnson 'hath bin allweyes a servant to the Parliament; he is well affected to the present government. . . . If I had a mynd to doe him an iniury, I cannot say otherwise than that he is a very Civill honest Conscientious man.'[56] Speaker Lenthall, by contrast, admitted that he wrote on the basis of someone else's recommendation in support of John Jenifer junior's application to be a messenger.[57] Whereas Viscount Monson, Sir James Harrington, Sir Henry Mildmay and Messrs Holland and Trenchard, all MPs, had simply recommended Ambrose Rowland to be the Committee's Clerk; in a postscript President Bradshaw and Thomas Scot MP made it clear that they did so by repute only.[58]

In other cases we can only guess at the closeness of the connection between sponsor and applicant. How far the 'round-robin' kind of testimonial could go can be illustrated from other areas of government. John Canne, the baptist minister, wanted some kind of regular stipendiary employment; he got one testimonial from eight leading congregational divines and another from six senior army officers.[59] He obtained the post of chaplain to the garrison of Hull. Similarly testimonials were submitted on behalf of a would-be naval store-keeper in Chatham dockyard. But in this case the Council's Admiralty Committee instructed the Navy Commissioners to test or assess the candidate's qualifications;[60] apparently the outcome was successful for this applicant was employed there two or three years later.[61] In at least one such case a sponsor asked for his support to be formally cancelled and withdrawn.[62]

Qualifications could be negative or positive. In some cases disqualification, real or alleged, is the better documented of the two. Often this involves tenure more than appointment: that is to say, the conditions under which someone could be removed from office, rather than the grounds which made them suitable to enter it.[63]

Sometimes one office was sought as compensation for the loss of another. Christopher Vyne, Court-Keeper of the Exchequer, petitioned the Committee for regulating the navy and customs ('the Regulators') on the grounds of his own long and faithful services to Parliament in attending committees in the Exchequer and Exchequer Chamber, and his necessities with a wife and ten children. More particularly, however, he had some years earlier (presumably before 1642) invested in the purchase of two messengers' places for himself and his eldest son, to be employed carrying customs record books between the Exchequer and the various ports. The salary (or income) of these places had been over £40 per annum. But subsequent changes in the organisation and accounting system of the customs had taken away the work and hence the value of these posts. Vyne, therefore, asked for a post for his son—at their recommendation—under the Trustees for the sale of deans' and chapters' lands. In another petition, he referred to his nine years' service, and begged for a place as doorkeeper to the Regulators themselves for his son, if the present holder were to die[64]—in substance, though not in name, a 'reversion'.[65] Whether or not Vyne's son obtained a new place,[66] it is worth considering the approximate numbers of appointments involved. The Regulators presumably only had one doorkeeper and a total staff of six or seven;[67] the Trustees for capitular lands, with powers of appointment similar to the other Trustees for episcopal and Crown lands,[68] were a very different matter. They employed no less than 127 surveyors, 35 clerks and 31 messengers in the field; and 3 learned counsel, 2 solicitors and a secretarial and house staff of 15 at headquarters.[69] Of course this was not permanent employment, and its temporary nature helps to explain the high turnover of posts among the same men. Some of them were employed, for example, successively on episcopal and capitular lands; others on Crown lands and fee-farm rents; some on one or other of these and then on royalist delinquents' lands forfeited for treason (sales extending from 1651 to 1653). The amount of work involved in making accurate surveys was considerable, but it seems unlikely that these numerous 'surveyors' were all technically qualified.[70]

Returning to the mode of entry, under the Long Parliament and the Commonwealth we find three main types of written application or submission: a letter or petition from the applicant himself to those making the appointment, or to other people who might bring influence to bear on them; a personal letter, normally by one other person on his behalf, often to one of those on the appointing body, sometimes to them collectively; and finally the collective testimonial signed by any number of people, affirming the candidate's fitness.[71] Is patronage, as the term has been used for the relationship between patron and client in the later sixteenth and earlier seventeenth centuries, the right word to describe the support given to candidates by those who wrote on their behalf? In some instances at least, the concept of 'sponsorship', already familiar to students of another civilisation,[72] is perhaps more helpful.

One of the most important single appointments, at the administrative level, was that of Thurloe as Secretary to the Council of State, in succession to the elder Frost.[73] Was it the result of patronage, in the sense of Edward Nicholas's advancement in the 1620s or Samuel Pepys's in the early 1660s?[74] Thurloe already had a minor office in the Chancery, but this was hardly relevant. He had been in the service of Oliver St John for some years, and accompanied him (and his co-ambassador Strickland) to The Hague in 1651. He returned home ahead of them to make a provisional report on their mission, and as we have already seen, this must presumably have impressed his hearers.[75] Then comes an interval of silence, and after his appointment at the end of March 1652 a wry, ambiguous letter from St John to Thurloe; not at all what one would expect from a patron who had successfully effected his protégé's promotion to a key position.[76] One explanation lies in the fundamental ambiguity of St John's own attitude towards the Commonwealth and his increasing 'disengagement' from active political leadership. Another clue lies in the fact that Thurloe had been acting as a solicitor on behalf of Oliver Cromwell and his family in 1650–1.[77] Presumably he had been recommended to Cromwell by St John, but had commended himself to the Lord General by his efficient despatch of the business in question, mostly over disputed land titles arising from the various grants made by a grateful Parliament to their victorious commander. We cannot prove that this explains Thurloe's promotion in 1652. Of the two decisive council meetings immediately after Frost's death was reported, St John and not Cromwell was present at the first, Cromwell not St John at the second. Another pointer is the fact of Thurloe's later promotion to be Secretary of State under the Protectorate, when St John apparently refused membership of Oliver's Council and deliberately restricted himself to his judicial duties, no longer meddling in politics. He continued to correspond with Thurloe but more on the basis of equals—personal friends—than of master and servant, or patron and client.

Here, as in other respects, the months from Cromwell's dissolution of the Rump to his becoming Lord Protector form an interregnum within the Interregnum. Rights of appointment enjoyed by the Parliament were exercised by the Council from May to July, and then from July to December by the Barebones Parliament. The pattern of application and recommendation was much as before. When sale of the remaining royal forests was being considered by the Barebones, William Ryley, senior, clerk of the records in the Tower, wrote that he:[78]

> humbly offers his best skill and service (having lived in the said Office 28 yeares) conceaving, that if it shall please the Supreame Authority to conferr the Office of Surveyour Generall or Register of the said Forests upon him, he shall be able (through the knowledge and trust he hath of all those Records) to serve them faithfully therein upon such sallary & allowances as have bene usuall in that kynd.

Members of the Accounts Committee received much the same sort of appeals which they had before, if (as far as surviving material shows) at a somewhat lower level. Giles Calvert the radical printer and publisher wrote to William Maddison (son of Sir Ralph, the authority on trade) on behalf of a poor man: 'because of his great necessity, and my selfe being conscious (by that former aquayntance I had with you) of your redynesse to doe good to the helplesse'.[79] Another appeal to Maddison recommended its bearer to be 'A messenger or the like . . . for hee can both wright and caste accounte Redely'.[80]

The Barebones' legislation provided also the same mixture, of direct appointment by Parliament and delegation of the right to appoint, as had the Rump's.[81] Historians differ about the extent to which Harrison and his millenarian allies tried to pack—and then to dominate—the Barebones Parliament,[82] but there is certainly a little evidence of radical puritan pressure at the administrative level. The Welsh preacher, Walter Cradock, wrote direct to Cromwell, as Lord General, recommending 'that renowned ancient saint Mr Rice Williams of Newport, being one who hath served the State in many places, but not gained a penny therefrom . . .', for the Registrarship of deeds in Monmouth or Glamorgan (under an abortive proposal of the law reformers for land registry offices in every county); he added in a postscript, perhaps more revealingly than he knew:[83]

Richard Creed (late servant to Major General Harrison) is also commended unto you by the godly for the registering of wills, the rather because his sufficiency in clerkship might make up what is wanting (as to that) in Mr Williams, they joining together, being men of one heart, will, through God, carry on that work sweetly together.

It is tempting to identify Cradock's two candidates: Rice Williams with one of the new Compounding Commissioners, appointed to make up for those who retired or were purged after 20 April 1653, Richard Creed with the Paymaster of the Fleet and Secretary to the Generals-at-sea. Unfortunately the 1650s saw at least two (possibly three) men of both these names, and the identifications remain probable, not definite.[84]

In the history of the Barebones period, Welsh affairs are of special importance. The Rump's refusal to renew the Commission for the Propagation of the Gospel in Wales (appointed for three years in February 1650) and the consequent frustration of the radicals is one side of the picture; sharp criticisms directed at this commission, for wasting resources and for dishonest management of ex-church revenues by its agents, the other.[85] The interval between Rump and Barebones saw a particularly bitter and complicated wrangle over conflicting rights to the office of Prothonotary of south-west Wales, in dispute between Robert Coytmor, another radical puritan active in naval administration under the Commonwealth, who seems to have retired in 1654, and George Billinghurst, allegedly an ex-royalist. Three years later Coytmor wrote a long rambling account of the affair, 'that you may understand that I have been a great loser rather than a gainer by this unfortunate office'.[86]

Whether or not Harrison and his allies got the better of Cromwell and the more moderate puritans in Parliament,[87] there seems no doubt that 1653 saw stronger emphasis on religious zeal among administrators, though too much should not be made of it. While Lambert sulked in opposition during the Barebones, several future Protectorate Councillors were already in position, and some of the most radical appointments in fact antedated 1653.[88] It has recently been suggested that a powerful group of London-based baptist radicals was in existence from 1649 to 1650.[89] We shall look more closely at the political and religious affiliations of some of these men in presenting their social biography.[90]

The coming of the Protectorate and the institutional changes which followed it[91] altered the pattern of appointments appreciably. Direct appointment by Parliament virtually disappeared between December 1653 and May 1659. A brisk and interesting debate took place during the second Protectorate Parliament in 1657, as to whether the staff for the new London buildings' tax should be appointed in the Act granting this revenue.[92] In the event the Lord Protector was left with authority to appoint the Commissioners, Registrars and Receiver.[93]

Some committees and commissions themselves originally appointed by Parliament, but now by the Protector, continued to make their own subordinate appointments. For naval administration the records on this remain at least as copious as before. The restoration of the Exchequer and the Protector's appointment of salaried Treasury Commissioners with their own rights of appointment opened up a considerable new area; the re-creation of Signet, Privy Seal and Requests' staff another; the renewed existence of a Household provided a third. If a provisional distinction may be made at this stage, administrative correspondence (of the kind quoted and cited above) becomes distinctly thinner—the navy apart; on the other hand, there is a good deal more political correspondence bearing on entry to office. This mostly relates to posts in the gift of the Protector himself, the Lord Deputy of Ireland or (to a lesser extent) the Council in Scotland. And we are heavily dependent on the survival of particular documents in Thurloe's papers and the correspondence of Henry Cromwell.

Dr Ralph Cudworth, the well-known Cambridge Platonist, at this time Master of Christ's College, placed special emphasis on the practical abilities of young men with an academic background. Of a Dr Cumming, he wrote to Thurloe in 1655:[94]

He hath been recommended to his highnes the lord protector by Sir John Reinolds and coll. Goffe, in order to a place now possessed by coll. White in the Tower,[95] upon supposition of his surrender. His highnes was by those gentlemen sufficiently assured of his fidelity, only required some further satisfaction concerning his fitnes for such a civill employment, he having been bred a scholar. Now the gentleman being so well knowen to me to be a person of extraordinary worth and ingenuity (he having been formerly my pupill and since that, my acquaintance in London) I shall make bold to signify thus much to you; that though he have the degree and title of doctor in physick, yet he is one, that is far from being a meer scholar, or one that hath conversed only with books, but as he hath naturally a singular genius and dexterity *in rebus agendis*, and the management of externall and civill affaires, so his education has been such in travaile abroad, as might not make his onely an accomplisht gentleman, but allso afford him much experience of the world, and dispose him for any civill employment. And since his returne from forrain parts he hath been chiefly employed and exercised that way. And I doubt not but his highnes, upon sight of him, and a little speech with him, would sufficiently be satisfied concerning his fitnes for a civill employment.

Sir, I shall therefore make bold humbly to request this favour of you, that if you find him such as I have described him (as I am confident you will) that you would please to present him to his highnes, that he may again desire his highnes favour, which if vouchsafed him, I doubt not but he will hereafter well deserve. And since your employments are so many and weighty, and his highnes not at all times accessible, if at the present time of the delivery of these it be unseasonable and unsuteable to your occasions to waite upon his highnes, if you will please to command this gentleman at any other time, which you conceve most opportune, to waite upon you; and you will then present him to his highnes, and promote his busines for the obtaining of his highnes favour, you will not only exceedingly engage this gentleman, but also deeply oblige, Sir, your most humbly devoted servant. . . .

And again the year after, on behalf of another aspirant—no particular office being mentioned:[96]

I have now, according to that engagement which you were pleased to lay upon me, more particularly and scrupulously informed my selfe concerning Mr Leigh. . . . Hee was the last and the youngest of all those, which I named to you; . . . In a word, sir, I beleeve he will proove a very fitt instrument for you in any way you shall thinke good to employ him in . . . if you should resolve to make use of him, he will make it his busines to accommodate his stile to such a mode and garb as you should desire, as to be lesse scholastick, and more easy, facil and popular.

Thurloe was normally the recipient of requests; but not always. He had a feckless or else very unlucky relative by marriage, Colonel Leonard Lidcott (or Lytcott),[97] who had lost his regiment and was left stranded at the mercy of his creditors in Scotland. Apparently the Secretary went rather too far, for he received a friendly but unmistakable rebuke from his friend Broghill, then President of the Scottish Council, in 1655:[98]

For my respects to col. Lidcott upon your command, you give me expressions, which more rellish of Whitehall 15 yeers past, then now; but in earnest, sir, I shall faithfully endevour to serve him upon your accounte, as much as any man's . . .

Broghill undertook to see whether Lidcott could be proposed to the Scottish Council for an Excise and Customs Commissionership expected to fall vacant shortly. Somewhat different in tone was Broghill's own letter to Thurloe on behalf of Mr Richard[99] Saltonstall.[100]

When mr Saltonstall went from hence, I tooke the confidence to accompany him with a letter of myne unto you; by which he wrote me worde he received much of your favour, and tho' I cannot have the vanity to creddit, that such a production had only that cause, but that his piety only procured your respect towards him; yet since in meere honesty and in affection to the publike he has layd downe his employment heere, rather then any longer by his absence about his privat affaires receive a sallary, for which he did not the duty of the place, I could not but (haveing first humbly acknowledged with much thankfulness what you have alredy proposed for him) humbly beg you to perfect what you have begun; and this I am the rather forced into, because I know both his principle and practice will make him declyne seekeing for himselfe; and therefore unless another doe appeare for him, his vertue may proove his prejudice, if not his ruin; from which I am confident he wil be preserved, if you undertake his business; . . .

Saltonstall, who had been serving as a Commissioner of Justice in Scotland since 1651, became Commissioner for Customs, Excise and Sequestrations there in September 1655, and was promoted to the important post of Customs Commissioner for England early in the following year. Meanwhile, Colonel Thomas Cooper, Saltonstall's brother-in-law, also wrote to the Secretary on his behalf, from his command in Ulster, sending thanks for the help shown:[101]

to my brother Saltonstall, since his comeinge into England. At my taking leave of his highness it was his desire you would put him in mynde of him. Did you know him soe well as his highness doth, I shoold say nothinge of him, and what I doe say, did I not know to whoe I speake, it might bee judged I speake because of relation; but I can say it's not any inducement to mee; and wear hee not related to mee, I shoold say as much as I doe of him. And I cannot but say, hee is one of the exactest christians I know at this day. For his faithfullnes to man, let the experience made of him speake, which is the best witness.

As always, Ireland was a happy hunting ground for the unemployable —likewise for the needy and unfortunate. One approach by Thurloe to Henry Cromwell (still only Major-General and acting Commander-in-Chief, Ireland) was distinctly shamefaced, and reads a little oddly after his earlier appeal which had led to Broghill's rebuke.[102]

There is a nephew of mine, captain Ewer, and nephew to colonel Ewer, who it seems fell within the last reducement of Ireland, and by that means is without any ymployment. Indeed, my Lord, I hear that he is a very sober younge man, and valiant, and otherwise

capable of trust; upon which account only it is, that I am bold to
recommend hym to your lordship's favour and consideration. And
I take upon me this boldnes the rather, because he is the only
person of my kindred, that I have ever moved for in any case. And
I was brought to doe it now with some difficultie; but he being a
younge man, and haveinge lost his father's brother, I meane
colonel Ewer, who brought hym into Ireland, and upon whom he
did relye, I was the readier to appeare in it, espetially to your
lordship, who, as I knowe, wil be pleased to give a good
construction upon any requests of mine, although they should not
be agreeable to your lordship's owne intentions, which I doe assure
your lordship I doe not knowe, that this is, he being a person (as I
am assured) who will not be any dishonour to you in what your
lordship shall please to owne him in . . .

And a month or so later on 25 June 1656, with still more feigned diffi-
dence, he wrote to Henry Cromwell:[103]

I have beene prevayled with much importunitie to trouble your
lordship with a suite on the behalfe of one Mr Fluellin, who is now
in Ireland, who much desires to be sergeant at armes to carry the
mace before the chancellour. I knowe not the man myselfe, but am
assured by an honest freind, that he is very fitt for the imployment
(though I confess that freind is mother in lawe to hym.) I leave
hym to your lordship's favour, as you shall finde hym of desert and
merit. . . .

But more often it was others who approached Thurloe. Examples could
be multiplied both from his published and his unprinted correspondence.[104] Monck took the added precaution of writing to ask Broghill to
'use your interest with Mr Secretary Thurloe' as well as writing direct,
when he sought a commissionership of the navy for his brother-in-law,
Dr Thomas Clarges:[105] 'Though hee is not versed in sea-affaires, yet hee
is well exercised in accompts, which is a great part of the busines of the
commissioners of the navy, and for that perhaps hee will doe as well as
any; and for his honesty I shall oblige'. Something went wrong. According to a later letter from Monck, Clarges unwisely criticised the management of the Post Office in Parliament without realising that Thurloe was
now Postmaster-General![106] Even a letter direct to the Protector was to
no avail:[107]

But I should not trouble your highnes upon that account, if I were
not certainly knoweing, that he is not only faithful to the interest
of these nations, and a true lover of your highnes person and
family, but one of much industry and diligence in busines and very
capable to serve your highnes in this or any other imployment.

Varied and remarkable as Clarges' career was to be, he did not become a navy commissioner under the Protectorate.[108]

Anyone in charge of Ireland was bound to receive more requests and solicitations than he could possibly satisfy, that is without creating new offices as had been done in France and Castile. And Henry Cromwell was no exception. How far some of the appeals to him for help had any direct political significance is hard to tell. The Protector's younger son had a distinctive political standpoint; he was, and was regarded as, an ally of Thurloe, Broghill, Montague and the other conservative 'protectorians', all strong supporters of the proposed monarchical settlement of 1657 and enemies of swordsmen and religious zealots. Yet, as with Broghill in Scotland, this was compatible with a more constructive interest in the quality of administration than was shown by many radical Saints or committed republicans. As with Thurloe, the approaches made, for which evidence has survived, varied widely in character. In March 1657 Gualter Frost, son of Thurloe's predecessor and himself a Clerk of the Council, thanked Henry Cromwell effusively for having made his brother John Frost a deputy clerk of the Irish Council; this showed gratitude to the dead 'who in their life tyme were faithfull to the interest of Your family', and would help to secure yet more firmly the affections of the living.[109] The absentee Lord Deputy sent many requests over, some perfunctory, others elaborate, a few phrased with real warmth.[110] Others who wrote to Dublin were as varied as Thurloe's own correspondents;[111] they included his elder brother, the future Lord Protector Richard, whose own ability to do favours remained virtually nil, except on a reversionary basis, because he lacked either a specific command in the armed forces or a post in the civil government.[112] More of the appeals were either for places in the Irish army or, especially from 1657, in the new Lord Deputy's Lifeguard, or for grants of Irish lands; as in Scotland, the civil establishment in Ireland was modest and the scope for getting into it therefore limited.

Surprisingly few surviving items relate to direct patronage within or arising from the Protector's Household. This may be because the men most concerned, Maidstone, Waterhouse and Malyn,[113] were too prudent to allow their correspondence to survive the Restoration. Martin Noell, the financier, is found passing on a request from Maidstone, the Protector's Steward, on behalf of the head cook's son.[114] Noell himself, who needed help over a debt owed by someone else for which he had become answerable, was described by Richard to Henry Cromwell as 'our very good friend'; because he was 'the great Salt Master of England', a grant at the fishing centre of Wexford would be particularly appropriate; 'and I desire you to take the Patronage of it', wrote Richard, so that Noell's grant should go through smoothly.[115]

A number of men whom the rulers of both Commonwealth and

75

Protectorate would have liked to 'engage' by persuading them to accept office, refused. A strange case is that of John Cook, the regicide lawyer, who refused high office as a disappointed reformer, not as an alienated conservative or radical. Cook had gone over to Ireland in the wake of the conquering English armies and held office under Cromwell and Ireton as Chief Justice of Munster. In the re-organisation of the Irish courts carried out by Fleetwood and then Henry Cromwell in 1654–6, he was offered a place as Judge of the Upper Bench in Dublin. In August 1655 he wrote at great length to Fleetwood, explaining the grounds of his refusal. In effect he said that he could not in conscience act as a judge while the Irish courts and the law remained in their present unreformed state. He gave detailed examples of the excessive costs, delays, and other inadequacies of the Irish legal system. It might be argued that Cook was a disaffected republican who did not want to hold office at all under the Protectorate, and that this letter is just window-dressing to excuse his refusal to serve. It does not read like that.[116] Disillusioned ex-republicans —as opposed to the political opposition led by Hesilrige, Vane and others—certainly existed. Under Richard's Protectorate, Captain Francis Cranwell, an out-of-work sea commander, wrote disgustedly to the Admiralty Commissioners: 'I see it is neither desert nor ability, but favour which carries the game, when old standards are left out who have borne the heat of the day, and the cold of the night.'[117]

There are two separate, if related, questions in attempting any comparison here between the Commonwealth and the Protectorate.[118] Firstly, were the means of obtaining entry to civil office markedly different? And secondly, did a significantly different type of person obtain entry? The second question belongs more to the social biography of the officials under the Republic and is discussed later in chapter 4, sections iii–v, except in so far as it is answered by the first.

The formal powers of appointment did shift—massively—away from Parliament (and Council of State) to the new 'single person' as chief executive. Many more posts were filled by patent under the Great Seal instead of parliamentary Act or conciliar directive.[119] While government by committee was drastically reduced after 1653, commissions continued to be much used as an administrative instrument. The restoration of something appreciably nearer to the old constitution except in name and dynasty from 1657, accompanied as it was by a further 'civilianisation' of the regime, brought additional changes along existing lines. The succession of a Protector because he was his father's eldest son and not because he was a great commander of men would no doubt have brought more changes still had he reigned for longer.[120] As to the qualities and qualifications sought in successful candidates, loyalty or 'good affection' was by definition now something different, although some candidates for office commended themselves by having supported every successive regime, on the anti-Stuart side, since 1642. This could lead simple men into difficulties of expression, as when John Blundell petitioned the Admiralty Commissioners for a place as a Gunner:[121]

> That your petitioner hath served this Commonwealth and former Governments of this Nation for above 20ty yeares as Gunners Mate, and Gunner, in divers of the Navy Shipps, during which time he hath beene a parishioner of Greenwich where he yet dwells with his familie of many small Children. And in all these changes and revolutions, the petitioner hath continued with and reteyned a faithfull affection to former Parliaments and the now present established Government honestlie and orderlie demeaning himselfe liveing without scandall or offence. . . .

Round-robin 'open' testimonials continued too.[122] But the crucial question is whether the kind of patronage or sponsorship, and family connection, which secured appointment, shows any marked change. The Protector himself sometimes wrote, on behalf of fairly remote relatives, in a way that he would not have done as Lord Lieutenant of Ireland or as Lord General (1649–53).[123] Both men in office and those seeking entry tried to commend themselves by making presents to Oliver or his sons. Of course, more of this may have gone on under the Rump without the evidence surviving.[124] Perhaps the idiom was suited to the recipient, but more often it seems that it was the writer who set the tone. Many letters of recommendation to Thurloe[125] are indistinguishable in tone and in the qualities which they emphasise from others written in 1649–53. This will become clearer when we consider the impetus for administrative reform under the two principal republican governments, and the place of reformers in relation to the system of administration.[126]

The revival, from 1654, of posts which had been dormant since 1642 led one or two applicants to base their claims on reversions granted under the monarchy. Sidney Bere, a one-time client of the earls of Pembroke and personal assistant to the elder Vane, applied for one of the re-created Signet Clerkships in this way.[127] And there were complicated disputes over some offices in Chancery and elsewhere which involved reversionary claims.[128] On the whole, however, reversions made in the 1640s and earlier were not accepted as valid; nor did the Lord Protector grant reversions for the offices in his gift.

The extent of pressure on places inevitably affects the tone of applications and recommendations. There is evidence that, in some sectors at least—unlike Ireland—a 'sellers' market' obtained. Under the much reduced Commissioners for managing estates under sequestration, the 1654 successors of the formidable Compounding Commissioners of 1650–3, it was at first planned, for the sake of economy, that there should be only one local sequestration commissioner per county. This led to both legal and practical complications and it was decided to add a second in most cases. From Cheshire the existing Commissioner wrote about the extreme difficulty of finding anyone who was both qualified and willing to act and did not live too far away from the writer to collaborate effectively with him. He suggested a pre-1649 Commissioner, whom he guaranteed to be both 'honest and rational'; the reason why such a paragon had been out of office during the intervening years does not appear. At any rate he was acceptable to the central Commissioners in London.[129]

One last question involves the third of the three Ps: Purchase. Can anything be said about venality of offices under either the Commonwealth or the Protectorate? It is important to remember the legal position and the practical reality in this respect before 1642. Sale and purchase of judicial and revenue offices had been illegal since 1552. The Crown had trafficked in offices widely during James I's reign and the first few years of Charles's; there had been a definite campaign against such venality from 1629 to 1639, which had to some extent reappeared under the spur of growing financial desperation in 1638-40. Meanwhile, quite distinct from the Crown's use of sale as a revenue device, there was the right of existing office-holders to sell outright, or to make some compensatory arrangement with their successors; over and above this again, there was the rake-off taken by great officers with rights of appointment, and by courtiers and other middlemen, from new entrants. There was also venality in reversions at least as much as in immediate appointments.[130] Contemporary pamphleteers certainly believed that some traffic in offices continued in the 1640s, and they demanded more stringent and sweeping legislation against it. The Long Parliament extended the scope of the Edward VI Act by an Ordinance in 1645. But despite a Bill drafted by the non-parliamentary law reform Committee of 1652-3, neither Rump nor Barebones went any further towards total prohibition. Both discussed the question of venality, usually in connection with excessive fees or bribery; if anything, the Barebones seems to have got nearer to legislation than its predecessor.[131] Amongst innumerable charges of corruption brought against the republicans after 1660 by royalist authors was included trafficking in offices, although it is often hard to distinguish accusations of venality from those of bribery and peculation.

As one would expect, the surviving evidence is both exiguous and uneven. Some leading figures under the Rump indisputably received compensation for loss of office, when they surrendered their position or when it was abolished. In 1650 the younger Sir Henry Vane was voted to be replaced by his own one-time client and business manager, Richard Hutchinson. The House voted Vane £1,200 a year in lands by way of compensation.[132] Whether he actually received property of this value is unclear, and for our present purposes irrelevant. The point is whether Vane 'sold' the office: not, almost certainly, to Hutchinson and not, voluntarily at least, to the State. Compensation for compulsory purchase seems a more apt description, without implying that it was an admirable way of doing things, especially by high-minded puritans. In 1652 Parliament decided, on the Council of State's recommendation, to abolish the post of Lieutenant of the Ordnance, held since 1650 by Major-General Harrison, who was thereupon voted delinquents' lands worth £500 per annum to make up for the loss of this office.[133] Again it would be absurd to speak of his having sold it.

A lesser figure, Colonel John Downes, had been Auditor of the Duchy of Cornwall—a pre-1642 office-holder who had survived by being an active parliamentarian. The post ceased to exist, or anyway to be worth anything, with the Crown land sales of 1649–50, and Downes was duly compensated.[134] A royalist claimant in 1660 turned this into an assertion that he had sold his office to the government.[135] Another compensation case was that of the elder Salwey whose executors were to receive regular payments for several years out of the profits of his Remembrancer's Office in the Upper Exchequer; improper or not, this was a form of pension, not a sale.[136]

There are one or two other cases of would-be or actual venality under the Protectorate. A Captain Rance petitioned that his aged father-in-law, Roger Pollard, who had long before bought the two offices of Gunner and Warder in the Tower and had already lost the former of them, might have leave to sell (or assign) the latter 'to some person of approved fidelyty, whereby he may not become altogether a Sufferer'.[137] More complicated was the case of the Smithesby family, related by marriage to the Cromwells. Thomas Smithesby had bought the Housekeepership of Hampton Court for £700 from the Marquis of Hamilton in January 1641, to hold for their joint lives; the King had granted it to Smithesby alone for his life the following April (luckily for any claim in the 1650s, since Hamilton went to the block a month or so after his sovereign). Smithesby's tenure had been recognised and his stipendiary fee and allowances paid by the Revenue Committee of Parliament (?1643–53), and then by successive individual occupants of Hampton—the two Lord Generals, Fairfax and Cromwell. The Protector had promised him £500 for the Housekeepership, 'he leaving the same in H.H.'s free disposal'; he had now assigned it 'for a valuable consideration' to Major Hezekiah Haynes[138] who wanted the Protector to allow him the £500 to recoup himself for his purchase from Smithesby. It is not clear whether Haynes got his money or whether in effect it remained a private transaction between the two parties.[139]

Other claims at the Restoration were supported by similar allegations, most of them untestable. Some seem more plausible than others. Elia

Palmer who had succeeded to the Surveyorship of the Ordnance in 1656, having long been deputy to the previous Surveyor, petitioned in 1660 to be continued in the office, on the grounds that he had paid £730 for it, which was more than he had yet made, his wages being a full year in arrears; more material to Palmer's prospects, his request was backed by the most powerful man in England, General Monck.[140] More vaguely and less circumstantially, a Commissionership of Alienations was alleged to have been bought from the Lord Protector.[141] Most of the other evidence of venality comes from the common law courts: notably Exchequer, Common Pleas, and the Welsh circuits. Again it would be extravagant to describe as venality the compensation which the Long Parliament ordered for officers of the abolished Court of Wards and Liveries in 1647—the royalists excluded, of course.[142] Emphasis on the legal side of government is supported by another witness—at the opposite end of the political spectrum from royalist vilifiers of the Saints—an out-and-out adherent of the Good Old Cause. Writing his *Memoirs* in embittered exile, Edmund Ludlow (Rump MP, acting commander-in-chief Ireland 1651–2, in opposition 1654–9) accused Oliver St John of having trafficked in subordinate offices as Chief Justice of Common Pleas (1649–60), and of having been at special pains to secure a clause protecting himself on this score in the Indemnity Act which was passed by the restored Rump in the summer of 1659.[143] Some independent evidence supports this. Several senior Protectorate officer-holders were reported to be worried about the implication that, if all appointments made since 20 April 1653 were unconstitutional and invalid, then all the profits of office during the intervening six years might have to be restored. Some of the more militant parliamentary republicans, like Scot, Hesilrige, Ludlow, Vane and the lesser men who had in some cases done well for themselves until 1653 but had taken no part in public affairs since then, apparently argued this way. Others who served under Oliver Cromwell but had then helped to overthrow Richard Cromwell's Parliament and to restore the Rump felt very differently.[144] The Act, in fact, invalidated all appointments made since 20 April 1653 but indemnified their holders as to their receipts and activities (provided these were not criminal in the normal sense of the word).[145] On the other hand, St John had been made Chief Justice by the Rump itself, so the validity of his 1653–9 tenure was not in question. Nor does any of the evidence about the profits of office (salaries, fees, perquisites) from April 1653 to May 1659 being in peril specify gains from venality. St John himself having prudently left no papers which bear on this, we might seem obliged—as so often in this area—to return a verdict of 'non-proven'. There is, however, a little more to suggest that offices in Common Pleas were bought and sold, whether or not the Chief Justice gained directly from it. One of the Filazers of the Court, petitioning in 1660 to be allowed to remain in office, asserted that he had bought his place in about 1654.[146] At a slightly more senior level, the Masham family appear to have sold the Pleas office after the premature death of the eldest son, William Masham, heir to Sir William.[147] In the end we are left with no more than a balance of probabilities. Cordially as he disliked St John for having worked under Cromwell and then, as he believed, having helped to promote the Restoration, would Ludlow have gratuitously invented this allegation? The 1552 Act had specifically reserved the rights of the two Chief Justices to profit from changes in subordinate posts, while the lawyers resisted reform more tenaciously and, on the whole, successfully than those in any other field of public life during the 1640s and 50s. This is not proof; but it puts the burden of probability on St John having done what any sixteenth- or seventeenth-century Chief Justice assumed was his right and proper due, at least to receive a substantial sum when an office in his gift changed hands.

Outside the Common Pleas, there is more retrospective evidence about one of the Welsh Prothonotaryships, and a claim in 1660 that the reversion had been bought in 1654.[148] Independent evidence exists to show that the senior Remembrancership in the Upper Exchequer was bought by a Somerset gentleman, John Dodington, in 1658.[149] More was heard about this particular instance because Dodington's fitness to execute and so to hold the office was called in question.[150]

Even if we refuse the benefit of the doubt to republican judges and politicians, purchase does not seem to have been nearly as widespread or important a mode of entry as it had been before, and was to become again. The decisive question is the balance between sponsorship, for family, 'old boy', old-fashioned clientage, or even corrupt reasons, and sponsorship on the grounds of genuine qualifications—ability, skill, honesty and loyalty. It is of course an equation for which we can never work out an exact result. How often, moreover, did ideological fitness operate against the other qualifications? This might work in more ways than one. Men obtained offices if they were parliamentary republicans from 1649 to 1653, militant radical puritan republicans in 1653, 'moderates', 'courtiers' or 'protectorians' from 1654 to 1659, and parliamentary republicans again in 1659. In all such cases ideological opponents would say that their political commitment explains why they were appointed, implying that they should not have been. In weighing the importance of loyalty and allegiance in appointment to office, we must beware of confusing a necessary with a sufficient cause.

That the wrong men sometimes got in, was not denied by some who supported the successive governments of 1642–60. Violent criticism of colleagues can be found without accusations of disloyalty, but merely on grounds of incapacity.[151] Cromwell himself had begun his career as an army commander with a firm belief in careers open to talent, provided men had 'the root of the matter' in them—that is, a minimum puritan conviction and honesty of purpose.[152] Perhaps it was less that he consciously changed his beliefs on becoming Lord Protector, rather that the successive disillusionments of the years of power, especially 1653–8, must have induced a certain weary cynicism. A head of state could not operate with the same freedom and directness as could a commander in the field under seventeenth-century conditions. Generally speaking, the bigger the institution, the less the man at the top really decides.

ii TENURE

Under the old system of royal administration, offices could be held on three main kinds of tenure: for life, during good behaviour, or during pleasure. There were exceptions and refinements, but these three covered the vast majority of cases.[1] Predictably, the political events of the 1640s brought about changes here, as in the actual appointments which were made. In arrogating to itself much of the Crown's previous powers of appointment, Parliament made many office-holders dependent upon its own pleasure, often until they legislated or ordered otherwise. Whether this was more secure than royal pleasure might depend more upon political developments than upon the holder's performance in office. Many other appointments were made subject to good behaviour; this had a certain ideological, even moral appeal to parliamentarians who could still remember the 1610s–30s; a few had themselves experienced royal use of tenure during pleasure to oust inconvenient judges and ministers. A variant of good behaviour was to appoint for a fixed period of time. Sometimes this was a matter of psychological warfare, to portray parliamentary control of the executive as a temporary expedient until the monarch came to his senses again. It helped to emphasise the correctness of their temporary and 'provisional' appointments—and Parliament's general reluctance to usurp the royal prerogatives. After the regicide and the abolition of monarchy, such a restraint ceased to operate. Yet the Rump's admittedly dilatory and half-hearted but not wholly insincere attempts to work out a more permanent constitutional settlement set a further premium on a pretence of temporariness. Rather surprisingly, the two Prest Auditors of the Upper Exchequer were reappointed for three years in April 1652.[2] As for the mass of subordinate clerkships and other minor offices to which Parliament did not itself appoint, they were mostly held during the pleasure of the appointing committee, commission, or trustees, or for the duration of that parent body. Some of the Rump's legislation shows the same distinction with tenure as with appointment. The seven Compounding Commissioners were initially appointed from April 1650 to January 1652.[3] In the Excise Act of six months later, the sub-commissioners (in the localities) and most other subordinate staff were to hold office until the Commissioners (appointed by Parliament for the duration of the Act) should order otherwise.[4] There were exceptions to this pattern. The Admiralty Committee of the Council could appoint to minor naval offices as the Lord Admiral had previously done, on the more traditional tenures.

From the autumn of 1649 willingness to subscribe the Engagement became an additional requirement for continued enjoyment of state office, whatever the tenure might be. This raised the fundamental issue, whether parliamentary enactment could override grants by patent. One of the Rump's first actions was to confirm the judges and others in their posts; for the most part Parliament was keener to keep men in its service than to get rid of them. But there were exceptions.

As early as 1645, the Long Parliament had threatened to punish any persons who refused employment as sub-commissioners and treasurers of sub-committees for taking accounts, or for refusing to subscribe the Covenant on entering such employment.[5] This was threatening men to come in and warning them to stay out in the same breath. That the Engagement was invoked against individual office-holders can be seen in many cases which came before the Indemnity Committee and Commissioners (especially in the years 1650–3).[6] There were other 'disqualifying' Ordinances and Acts which they had also to see were enforced. Those of September–October 1647 were meant to exclude all royalists from electing to, or holding, a wide range of local offices.[7] That of December 1647 referred particularly to municipal offices in London, and was aimed at those who had supported the presbyterian 'forcing of parliament' in July–August 1647 (before the army's occupation of the capital and its first purge of the Commons). It also disqualified all who had promulgated, distributed, or subscribed the Leveller 'Agreement of the People' of October.[8] The next 'disqualifying' laws were the Engagement Acts of 1649–50; the last—as late as the autumn of 1652—was aimed at excluding those who had aided and abetted the royalist-Scottish invasion of 1651, notwithstanding the generous terms of the General Pardon and Oblivion Act (February 1652).[9] Subscription of the Engagement as a condition of holding office was abolished by conciliar ordinance within the first month of the Protectorate.[10] When something comparable was reintroduced in 1659 its enforcement was left to the ordinary legal machinery of the courts, rather than being in charge of specially appointed commissioners.[11]

Despite the Rump's assumption of almost unlimited authority, the differences between the various forms of tenure continued to affect appointments more often than dismissals. Only those who argued, on the basis of an original contract, that in a revolution all power reverted to the hands of the people, wished—or were logically able—to maintain that all offices were automatically at the disposal of the sovereign people—or of their delegated 'Representative'.[12] Realities under the Commonwealth were different, and the issues were fought out on narrower, more prosaic, grounds.

Officials at all levels of the administration could be affected. Three men who could sign their names and two others who were illiterate, serving in Woolwich dockyard, prefaced ten articles against Thomas Bartrum, Master of the Ropeyard there, as follows:[13]

> That whereas there is an Act of Parliament, against all such, as shall, or have acted, or abetted any against the Parliament, or their proceedings since the year 1641. shalbe incapable of bearing office in any place belonging to the NAVY [sic], Wee think it our duties to discover to such as are in Authoritie the Carriages of any that we know to be Enemies to the State.

As well as abuses in his office, they charged Bartrum with denying and denigrating Parliament's authority, and with having encouraged the 1648 Kent rising; he was also alleged to have exacted bribes as a condition of getting them a wage-rise and to have made them spend time with him in an alehouse as a condition of employment! No doubt some dock workers' leaders of more recent times could have taught him a few tricks; no doubt, as with them, there was another side to the story. Sometimes the story of abuses by subordinate naval officers is so long (and so tall!) that if even half were true, it seems amazing that such men had ever been tolerated in office. Thus the carpenter of the *Swiftsure* had been discharged by Colonel Willoughby, Navy Commissioner at Portsmouth, for a combination of drunkenness, idleness, irresponsibility and dishonesty which reflected gravely on his captain for having let things reach such a pass.[14] Likewise with the warrant officers (bos'n, carpenter, gunner and purser) of the *Duchess*, as reported by their captain a few years later.[15] Despite the praise which has rightly been accorded them, the 'Regulators' of 1649–50 had apparently left more than a few stones unturned and skeletons rattling in naval cupboards.[16]

Sometimes it was in claims for pay arrears that evidence was cited about the acquisition and tenure of an office. Two men called George Vaux were successively Housekeepers of Whitehall. Under Charles I, the elder had paid £500 to Sir John Wentworth and £1,000 to Mr Leach, Gentlemen Ushers, assigned to the earl of Pembroke and the King;[17] the salary had then been £200 a year payable by privy seal warrant out of the Exchequer, presumably also to cover cleaning expenses. The father had received another £108 to cover incidental costs for the thirteen months, November 1648 to December 1649. His son, the younger Vaux, held office by patent under Parliament's Great Seal of 4 July 1650; he was only asking for 10s. a day (£182. 10s. 0d. p.a.) plus £20 or so expenses for the six-and-a-half months, June 1650 to February 1651. With some exaggeration, he stated that this was only half what his father had been getting (actually £182. 10s. 0d.+£20 = £202. 10s. 0d., as against £308). He set out the duties of the office, which included employing chimney sweeps, weeders, and cleaners to remove coal dust, close-stool filth and other rubbish.[18] In 1660 the elder George Vaux tried to recover the office for another son, John, alleging that his own replacement by the younger George had been a political usurpation.[19]

The restoration of appointment by patent from 1654 produced several disputes between rival claimants. Before that, the replacement of the Rump by the Lord General and the new Council of State led to changes of a different kind. After the Rump's forced dissolution, it was at first simply taken for granted that all judges, officials and non-parliamentary commissioners would carry on as before.[20] But within a few weeks a newsletter-writer listed several senior officials, including navy, excise and customs commissioners, who were being put out for refusing to act under, or to own, the new regime;[21] many of these appointments would have been at Parliament's pleasure anyway. However, refusal to recognise the authority of a government or serve under it would presumably be cause for dismissal whatever the terms on which a man held his place. Some junior officials had always been on a precarious tenure, politics apart. In January 1651, the Council of State had simply decided to pay off some of the redundant staff under its own Sergeant-at-Arms.[22] What we have here is the rather different distinction between established and supernumerary staff, the latter naturally enjoying little security. The more familiar seventeenth-century distinction, between officers 'in ordinary' and 'extraordinary', is analogous but not quite the same thing. Holders of 'innovated offices' had been the objects of attack under Charles I,[23] albeit without much effect, and the notion of reducing the number of superfluous officials was a familiar one. The Rump had at least one committee on offices, inherited from the Long Parliament before Pride's Purge, and revived at successive intervals.[24] At the beginning of 1652, the reduction of office staffs in departments was handed over to the Council of State, but only temporarily it seems.[25] In June 1653 the new Council duly set up its own Committee on the inspection and improvement of public offices; two out of its five members had also been on Hale's law reform committee. Those entrusted with this challenging task were directed to confer with a senior lawyer also on the Hale Committee (somewhat paradoxically an ex-royalist) and with whomever else he cared to bring along, and then to report back on ways and means to the Council itself.[26] But this was overtaken by the assembly of the Barebones Parliament, with its own somewhat different approach to administrative reform. Apart from a revival of appointments by Parliament, it is hard to discern any pattern in the tenure of offices granted from July to December 1653.

It should not be supposed that the coming of the Protectorate meant a wholesale shift back to the forms of tenure enjoyed by office-holders under the monarchy. But the restoration of the traditional sequence for issuing grants—sign manual to signet to privy seal to great seal—tended, as one would expect, to be accompanied by a partial shift back to the traditional forms and terminology. A paper was presented to show how it had been done. Significantly, perhaps, the specimen grant in this draft was for life,[27] but only a small minority of the Protector's appointments were in fact made on this, normally the most secure of all tenures;[28] still less was the government prepared to admit claims based on grants for life made by the King before 1649.

At the very top there was least difference from the procedure under the Commonwealth. In July 1654 Oliver's son-in-law Fleetwood was appointed Lord Deputy of Ireland for three years, but commander-in-chief of the forces in Ireland during pleasure.[29] In 1655 Broghill and his colleagues were appointed to the Scottish Council for what was presumably meant to be three years, but by the time the grant had gone through was for more like two years, ten months.[30] In November 1657 Cromwell appointed his son Henry Lord Deputy and commander-in-chief Ireland, on the same terms as Henry's brother-in-law three years before. At a slightly lower level of political importance, Edmund Prideaux was re-appointed Attorney-General during his good behaviour, but his fellow law officer, the Solicitor-General, was given tenure during (the Lord Protector's) pleasure.[31] In the restored Exchequer the Treasury Commissioners themselves (Councillors-of-State or men of comparable standing) held during pleasure; most of the other officers were appointed during good behaviour. Life tenure was accorded to the Clerk of the Parliaments, the Clerks of the Privy Seal and of the Signet (but not to the Keeper of the Privy Seal or the Secretary of State), to the Chief Graver of coins and medals in the Mint (but not to most of his colleagues), to Norroy King of Arms (but not to the Heralds and Pursuivants in the Office of Arms).[32] At the level where courtiers and great men were rewarded with local offices as minor perquisites of protectoral favour, Disbrowe was made Keeper of St Briavel's Castle in Monmouthshire during pleasure, whereas Claypole became Master of Whittleswood Forest, Northants, for life.[33] It is hard to see any rhyme or reason in this, except that generally the more 'formal' an office the likelier that the tenure would be for life, the more 'political' the likelier that it would be during pleasure or for a term of years, leaving good behaviour as the main residual category in between. To generalise on slender evidence, there were more good behaviour appointments than had been made by Parliament since 1649, indeed since 1642; there were fewer life appointments than there had been before 1640/42, and were to be initially after 1660.[34]

Conflicting claims to offices during the Protectorate often tell us more about tenure in earlier royal grants—and about other conditions of employment—than they do about the current position. Edward Basse, an ex-Receiver-General of land revenues, and unsuccessful claimant for the same office again, lamented that:

> The saddest, and most unkind heart-breaking loss is in that an
> Office under the Great Seal of England worth 250 li. *per Annum de
> Claro* for his own Life, and the adding of another which cost above
> 1,000 li. 20 yeares since, The Profits of which for 16 yeares past,
> and the 2 Lives to come amounts to—£6,500.

He pleaded at least for compensation, if not for the office, and claimed precedents for this, but it would seem to no avail.[35]

The Searchership of the Customs at Sandwich had been the subject of a celebrated dispute under the Personal Rule,[36] and an echo of this is heard in 1656. The three 1637 holders recited the terms of their grant from the King—for their joint lives; in January 1654 two of them had transferred it to the third for the remainder of their lives and the life of the longest lived of them. All three had now surrendered it to the Protector and apparently sought either compensation or a fresh grant.[37] It is not clear by whose authority the January 1654 transfer was made; if it was a purely private transaction in an office held by patent, its validity would be doubtful. On the other hand, searcherships were not normally granted direct from the Crown; there is no trace of them in the docquets, etc., of the Protector's patents.[38]

Characteristically, Chancery offices were to cause the bitterest and most complicated disputes during these years. In some of them the question of tenure was inseparable from that of allegiance since 1642. Thomas Willys (or Willis) esquire found himself disputing his title to the Clerkship of the Commonwealth (alias the Crown) with his own one-time deputy, John Bolles, gent. Willis explained in his petition that he had got leave from the late House of Lords to go to his Hampshire residence in August 1643; he had then been captured by royalist troops and forced to go to Oxford; his requests to the King that he should be allowed to return to London being refused, he had left Oxford as soon as he could— a full year before its surrender in 1646—and had rendered himself up to Parliament's authority eight years and five months ago. Again with the Lords' permission, he had left Bolles behind, sworn to serve as acting Clerk in his absence (December 1643), and this was the latter's only title to the office, whatever he might plead to the contrary. He claimed that in 1648 Bolles had supplicated to the Long Parliament's Petitions'

Committee for a fee of £60 per annum and other allowances, which were denied him 'because they well knewe that hee was not absolute Clarke of the Crowne nor had any Grant or Patent thereof'. Willis denied voluntary desertion of his post (as a ground for forfeiture). He also claimed, less plausibly, that Bolles's grant as acting Clerk was ended by the dissolution of the Parliament which had appointed him, although the fact that the late Parliament had never questioned his own patent was another reason for its being valid. Heads he won, tails his opponent lost! Lastly, neither he nor his son and heir being a delinquent whose estate was forfeit, he begged the Protector to restore him to his office—and to allow him to receive his arrears of fees and allowances 'for the payment of his debts and creditors and for his future subsistence without which hee and his sonne wilbee utterly undone and perish . . .' The case was heard by an *ad hoc* committee of two Councillors on 11 and 14 April 1654. Willis had eight witnesses, none very weighty; Bolles mustered twenty-two, including several senior Chancery officials.[39] The immediate outcome can only be inferred; Bolles may have continued to hold the office for the next few months. In 1655, however, the clerkship was granted away from both of them to Nathaniel Taylor, a radical puritan lawyer, who held it on good behaviour. With the restoration of the Rump in 1659, both Bolles and Willis renewed their attacks, being united only in wishing to dispossess Taylor, who none the less managed to retain the office until after the Restoration.[40]

Much more complicated was the case of the Register's (or Registrar's) Office. This produced a veritable literature—printed pamphlets, law reports, etc.—and we must summarise boldly. The office of Registrar, or a reversion to it, had been granted by the King to Sir Thomas Jermyn, a leading courtier and a privy councillor, sometime before his death in 1645.[41] His widow claimed the office on the grounds that this grant had never been invalidated; she strenuously denied that he had been a royalist: 'Sir *Thomas* was never a Delinquent, but lived quietly at home, and payed Taxes, and there is due to him upon the publique Faith 1,000 l. and upwards.' The office was her own and her younger children's[42] only remaining livelihood, for she had had to dispose of all Sir Thomas's personal estate in order to get out of prison where she had been thrown by his creditors. The only one of the co-patentees who was a delinquent, namely her son Thomas, had compounded and her own case was covered by the February 1652 Oblivion Act.[43] Unfortunately for Lady Jermyn, the Long Parliament had chosen to treat Sir Thomas as a delinquent *qua* holder of this office, and as early as 1643 it had been granted to Walter Long, MP for Ludgershall, Wiltshire, who in turn becoming *persona ingrata* after December 1648, was replaced by Miles Corbet (a regicide MP) and Robert Goodwin (another active member of the Rump). She argued that Long's grant was already terminated by that to Corbet and

Goodwin; as to theirs, she seems to have relied on the fact that it had been made on a misapprehension, namely that the office was forfeit for Sir Thomas's delinquency, which she denied, and therefore that it should be inoperative. The position was further complicated by the self-denying Ordinance. Since April 1645 no MP should have held such an office at all unless he had (like for example Cromwell as Lieutenant-General in 1645–6) an indemnifying ordinance to excuse his doing so. Hence deputies to MPs often became 'acting' holders of offices, at least for a few years (c. 1645–8);[44] in effect this was true here. That consideration ceased to apply after April 1653, but it was arguable that grants made contrary to the Ordinance had already been invalidated before then.

The Parliaments of 1656–7 and 1659 failed to reach a decision on the case, and the restored Rump, in which Corbet and Goodwin both sat,[45] referred it to the Commissioners of the Great Seal. They deliberated on the three-cornered conflict on 19 October 1659; technically they considered the case brought by Long against Mr Jasper Edwards and the other deputies and clerks of the office. They ordered Long to be admitted to act as Registrar until further order, but to be accountable for all the profits received, and to give security for these and the records of the office to one of the Masters; nor was this order to prejudice the claims of Lady Jermyn, or of Corbet and Goodwin.[46] Why Bradshaw and his colleagues found for the Presbyterian anti-Rumper Long is not clear, but it is tempting to speculate; another of the Commissioners was that same John Fountaine whose royalist past had been so suspect to the Rump in 1652, and this time, too, his had been the only contested appointment to the Great Seal.[47] (The third was Thomas Terrill, or Tyrrell, who had served in the parliamentary army until 1644–5 but whose later political record was one of apparent neutrality.)[48] The following spring the restored Secluded Members, Long amongst them, got Parliament to refer the dispute once again to the Commissioners; Bradshaw was now dead and it was Whitelocke's friend, the Recorder and historian of York, Sir Thomas Widdrington, who sat with Fountaine and Terrill. In the event, Long was merely ordered to return some books and papers which he had taken away from the office; otherwise things were to be carried on as directed the previous October.[49] But the Long Parliament had by this time ceased to exist and England was a republic or commonwealth in name only; the Convention Parliament was about to assemble. The sands were running out for men like Corbet and Goodwin. Indeed, all the Long Parliament's appointments since early 1642 were in peril unless their holders had commended themselves to the returning King. Early in 1660 yet another claimant or interested party made a last desperate attempt to keep Long out of the Registrarship. The well-known republican administrator, Henry Scobell,[50] appealed to his friend, the Secretary of the Admiralty Office, Robert Blackburne, 'understanding that it is referred to the Comrs. of the Admty. & Navy to employ ministerial Offices [*sic*] for the publique.' Scobell put the case for the actual working deputies, as opposed to the Registrar regardless of who held that office. His own name was to be concealed, presumably for political reasons (though perhaps also because of his age and growing infirmity). He enclosed a paper outlining the history of the Registrarship from the 1637–8 reversionary grant to the Jermyns down to the order of January 1660 diverting the profits of the office to the public revenue. He concluded: 'For 19 years past the work hath been wholly done by the Deputy Registers, they who went away with the profits as Masters of the Office having never done for it one shillingsworth of service either to the State or Client.'[51]

Somewhat different were the disputes which resulted from the Protector's Chancery Ordinance of 22 August 1654 and its enforcement the following year.[52] Not that the Registrar's Office was exempted from its scope. Section LIV stated that this post was not to be executed by deputy and named as four co-Registers those who had earlier been deputies to the various MPs, the future defendants in Long's 1659 suit.

The Ordinance was a statesmanlike compromise between the Barebones Parliament's preference for total abolition and the lawyers who believed that only a few marginal improvements were needed. It signified the Protector's keen personal interest in moderate law reform, and the Hale Committee experience of two men then on his Council (Ashley Cooper and Disbrowe). Even so, it nearly foundered on the entrenched opposition of the senior equity judges, whose own reforming orders of October 1649 were procedural only and did not touch the structure of the Court and its personnel.[53] A further order by Lenthall in March 1654, as Master of the Rolls, related only to the better keeping of records in the Six Clerks' Office; this was substantially repeated three months later.[54] Implementation of the Ordinance was postponed until after the first Protectorate Parliament (September 1654–January 1655), but then it was pushed through. In the end, two out of three Lords Commissioners (Whitelocke and Widdrington) resigned, whereas Lenthall—after a great deal of huffing and puffing and refusing to sit as a judge for some weeks—gave way and continued at the Rolls. Apart from procedural changes, the Ordinance altered the composition of Chancery radically. It also affected the tenure of existing and future office-holders. The Lord Chancellor, Lord Keeper or Lords Commissioners (as the case might be), the Master of the Rolls, and any other officers of the Court who enjoyed rights of appointment were forbidden to take any money for the nomination or admission of anyone to any such place, on pain of losing their own offices as well as paying a fine of twice what they had received. The biggest change of personnel resulting from the Ordinance arose from its abolition of the notorious Six Clerks' Office and its replacement of the six by three co-equal Chief Clerks, with their under-clerks limited strictly to sixty, instead of the previous multitude.[55] This raised the fundamental question of whether an Ordinance made by the Protector and his Council could override grants of office by royal patent or otherwise, unless these were enjoyed only on pleasure tenure, which was certainly not the case with the Six Clerks or the Registrars.

The Lords Commissioners and Master of the Rolls were heard before the Council on 23 April 1655; Lenthall's objections included his own impending loss of profit and 'the taking away all the offices which are in his gift and giving them to other men'.[56] Neither here, nor in the long, rambling, self-justificatory account of the affair given by Bulstrode Whitelocke is there any evidence that the judges would concede, or could even grasp the wider issues which were at stake. With a show of altruism Whitelocke pointed out that[57] 'The Commissioners and Master of the Rolles are by this Act of Regulation made instrumentall to deprive several persons of their Freehold without Offence or Legall Tryall. . . .' But corporate solidarity does not seem to have extended very far. For some the Ordinance was a bread-and-butter question. The Lenthall family was deeply involved, because William's son John (also a Rump MP) had been made one of the Six Clerks by the Long Parliament and was not one of the three Chief Clerks named in the Ordinance. Against this loss of an office held on life tenure, John Lenthall waxed eloquently indignant:

> Your Petitioner humbly offereth to your Highnes consideration,
> That the propertie of your petitioner (and the people in their
> freeholds, and Estates) is not onely warranted, and taken care for
> by the Lawe of God himselfe, written twice over with his owne
> finger, but by our Magna Charta thirtie times over confirmed by
> severall Acts of Parliament attended by the common-Law, and many
> other Statutes of this Nation, the Armies Protestations, and your
> Highnes oath and promise made upon the takeing of the
> Governement upon you.

A second petition, after the Ordinance had gone through, accepted his loss of office but begged for compensation instead.[58]

The 1654–5 Parliament was too busy challenging and trying to revise the Instrument of Government to scrutinise all the preceding protectoral and conciliar Ordinances, but that of 1656–7, as well as bringing in a new constitution, also sifted this non-parliamentary legislation at least with superficial thoroughness. The result was an Act passed in June 1657 validating most of the Ordinances of January to September 1654, confirming one or two only for the duration of the existing parliament, and abrogating those not listed under either of these two headings.[59] The Chancery Ordinance was among the very few reserved to the middle category. This presumably reflected divisions in both government and parliamentary circles between the lawyers and the administrative reformers, which would have cut across the main political split in the Parliament between supporters and opponents of the Humble Petition. It meant that the Ordinance lapsed when Cromwell angrily dissolved his last parliament in February 1658, the government having lost control of the Commons in the short second session. Moreover, under the second Protectorate constitution the chief executive and his Council had lost the right to legislate even temporarily during the intervals between parliaments.

This in turn imperilled those in Chancery who had held office under the 1654–5 ordinance. Signs of a counter-attack by the ex-Six Clerks are visible as early as mid-February,[60] but the dispute came before Lords Commissioners Nathaniel Fiennes and John Lisle on 4 March 1658. As a compromise they ordered that the Sixty (the attorneys or under-clerks) should be allowed to continue to act in the causes for which they were already being retained and employed; they were therefore to have access to the records of the Court, to receive back their commissions from the Lords Commissioners and to acknowledge receipt of certain payments to them *qua* attorneys.[61]

> Their Lordships nevertheles leaving the said six clarks to their remedy at common law for any fees or dutyes of right belonging to them or detayned from them by the said sixty attorneys as they shalbe advised.

So far from taking up this suggestion of a private suit at common law, the Six resorted to direct action. When nine of the attorneys brought an action in Chancery against the Six (John Lenthall included) the following July, their counsel unfolded a tale of violent defiance of the earlier order and disturbance of their clients in prosecuting the causes before them. The Six, they said:

> Have in the night time taken away their seates in the publique office together with all their settles, desks, bookes, papers, letters of directions and writeings, in the same seates, desks, and settles, and not onely soe but have alsoe posted upp a publique declaration and prohibition under their hands thereby declareing the plaintiffs, or most of them, to bee forejudged the Court and prohibiting all others from joyneing with them in the way of practice and proceedings in clyents causes as by the said declaration or prohibition nowe produced appeared . . .

An injunction was accordingly granted, protecting the attorneys' position until into the Michaelmas term.[62] At the end of October, despairing of an amicable settlement and unable to get their own house in order, the

Commissioners told both parties to apply to Parliament instead, or to take such other course as they should be advised.[63] Since writs for Richard Cromwell's Parliament had not yet been issued, this was somewhat hypothetical. The last Protectorate Parliament came and went; the second Protector went too. After the Rump's return we find the same dispute being heard before the father of one of the defendants—Speaker William Lenthall in his capacity as temporary Keeper of the Great Seal! The emphasis now was on the earlier interruption of the 'ancient course and Orders of this Court'; all bills filed since 4 February 1658 (when the Protector's ordinance had lapsed), and all records kept by anyone outside the Court since then, were to be brought into the Six Clerks' Office to be filed forthwith. The under-clerks' powers of independent action were further reduced by two additional orders made by Lenthall later the same month.[64] The Restoration orders issued by Lord Chancellor Clarendon and Lenthall's successor at the Rolls, Sir Harbottle Grimston, in 1661, reaffirmed that the Six Clerks were the sole Attorneys of the Court.[65]

The Chancery Ordinance left its mark on other offices besides those of Registrar and Six Clerks. The established number of Masters was changed and their seniority (by date of appointment) interrupted. Two of the Long Parliament's Masters in Chancery, Edwyn Rich and Edward Eltonhead, complained of having been put out and of having thereby lost their seniority. In 1660 it was ordered that all changes of personnel made since 1648 should be negatived, not only those of 1654–8; Rich and Eltonhead were to be restored. This was the work of the Convention Parliament, not of Clarendon as Charles II's Lord Chancellor.[66]

What does all this tell us about the forms of tenure? Clearly, if an office could be abolished by statute, let alone by conciliar ordinance, then the practical difference between the three normal tenures would diminish, if not disappear. The Chancery judges' opposition to the Ordinance is a pointer to what might have happened if more extensive law reform had been seriously attempted, whether under Rump, Barebones or Protector.

At a lower level than Masters, Six Clerks and Registrars of Chancery, however, men could sometimes lose their places by simple executive action. In Ireland, a regional official who had married a papist 'whereby he hath made himself incapable of continuing in his said employment', was summarily dismissed and replaced.[67] In the spring of 1658 the Admiralty Commissioners directed as follows:[68]

Upon consideration had of the numerousness of the Clerkes attending on the Comm[rs] of the Navy, and conceiving the number and charge of them may very well admit of an abatement. It is ordered that all the Clerkes (excepting Mr Turner their Clerk

Generall) be discharged from their respective imploymts. from & after the first day of April next inclusive, and their Salaries taken off And that there be only Six Clerkes settled for the future to attend the carrying on of the affaires of the Navy Office. And it is hereby referred to the said Com^{rs} of the Navy to consider of fit and able persons, and of competent salaries to be allowed unto them, for that service. And to propound their names & Salaries unto us by Tuesday next, To the end a settlement may be made thereof.

Shortly after this there was a vacancy, owing to the death of Mr Rabbinett, one of the Masters-Attendant 'of the States yard' at Chatham:[69]

[The Commissioners] finding that the business relating to the said office formerly transacted by 2 psns. may for the future be carried on by one hand, And that in effect it hath been so for several years past; the said Mr Rabbinett having been (as we are informed) through age & other infirmities a long time disabled from acting. It is ordered that the place of Master Attendant formerly enjoyed by the said Mr Rabbinett be henceforth taken away & made void together with the salary appertaining thereunto. Whereof the Comrs. of the Navy are to take notice.

The Navy Commissioner resident at Chatham, Peter Pett, had in fact suggested two possible candidates a few days earlier: 'I mean such a person whose abilities diligence & integrity may be such as may be as well fit to serve yo^u abroad as at home.' He claimed that one of the names which he was putting forward also had the support of Admiral Montague.[70] Suppression of an office in this way on the incumbent's death prevented a fresh appointment rather than terminated an existing one.

Resignation or removal from office could produce an awkward situation for the new, incoming holder. When the Chief Justice of the Upper Bench, Henry Rolle, agreed to retire after his clash with the government on Coney's case,[71] his successor-designate, the ex-Presbyterian lawyer and MP John Glynne, wrote apprehensively to Thurloe:[72]

I have considered that the delivering of the writ to my Lord Rolle is not a sufficient surrendering of his place without the same be donne in Court and entered of record. And my Ld. Rolle with whom I have been, concurrs with me in opinion and will be ready to do it. And therefore if there be haste, yo^u please, to send a direction to Justice Aske, to goe to my lord and take his acknowledgment. it is donne suddenly, you may please to send the writ to justice Aske, that my lo. Rolle may deliver it, in his presence. This is necessy, to be donne, before yo^u seale a newe writ. W^{ch} I thought my duty to informe And submit it to you . . .

The question of whether a judge who would not sit in a 'political' case or treason trial should forfeit his place for incapacity had wider implications than these quibbling technicalities might suggest. But incapacity could be hard to define elsewhere, too. The Masters-Attendant in the naval dockyards (from 1653 Deptford, Woolwich, Chatham and Portsmouth) were on the borderline between the administrative and technical staff of the yards and the seagoing naval officers. They were usually men who had already been sea captains and who might expect to be so again. In 1657 there was trouble with one of them because he was unwilling to go to sea, apparently regarding the post as a permanent shore 'billet'. Did this make him liable to dismissal?[73]

An equally wide issue was raised by lack of qualifications. When John Dodington came to be admitted as First Remembrancer of the Exchequer at Michaelmas 1658, the Court told him 'that not having Experience himself, he must find an able Deputy to execute it. And that the grant of an office to an unskilful person is void', one Elizabethan case and one passage in Coke's *Institutes* being cited in support of this. Dodington's admission was therefore respited for two days, 'but at last after the admonition he was admitted, the Court telling him they had many precedents of denying Admission to such Officers for want of Skill'.[74]

Of more direct political significance was the case of the Lord Protector versus the Town of Colchester in 1655, ordering the bailiffs of the town to restore Arthur Barnardiston to the Recordership there.[75] Their grounds for removing and refusing to restore him amounted, broadly, to neglect and misconduct, including his employment, at a stipend of £40 per annum, of a deputy recorder who was not even a qualified barrister. Chief Justice Rolle, in one of his last judgments, held that the key point was the failure of the municipality even to hear Barnardiston before they removed him, 'and it is very hard to deprive one of his freehold without hearing him make his defence'. As counsel, Glynne accepted that Barnardiston had been wrongly absent but emphasised the failure to send for and hear him; the Court ordered his restoration unless cause was shown the following day—a successful minor blow at Colchester's independence.[76]

The restoration of the Rump and so of the 'Commonwealth' in May 1659, as we have seen, called in question all appointments made on whatever tenure since 20 April 1653. More relevant here, the Long Parliament's reappearance meant a revival of appointments by Acts of Parliament and on tenures specified in such Acts. This continued until the final Act of voluntary dissolution on 15 March 1660. It would be tempting to see the Protectorate, with its appointments for life, as a kind of proto-Restoration. But, comparing the range of offices tenable for life in 1654-9 with the equivalent range in the 1630s or the early 1660s, this would be highly misleading. Moreover it is artificial and misconceived to isolate a single aspect of office-holding, however vital it was to those involved at the time.

iii DEPUTIES, PLURALISTS AND ABSENTEES

Permission to perform one's official duties by deputy was commonplace in the seventeenth century. A clause allowing the appointee to nominate and act by a 'sufficient' (that is an able, or qualified) deputy was a normal part of most patents under the early Stuarts.[1] Only at the top, with judgeships and great offices of state, was this unusual. The virtual lapse of patent appointments from 1642 to 1653 meant a corresponding shrinkage in the number of such deputations. However, some parliamentary ordinances, acts and orders allowed the use of deputies; deputies also continued from before 1642, or else acted by virtue of authority other than that of Parliament.[2]

Some MPs had made their deputies into the nominal holders of the offices concerned when the enforcement of the self-denying Ordinance compelled their own withdrawal from such posts in 1645.[3] Sir William Allanson, MP for York, was allowed to act as Keeper or Clerk of the Hanaper in Chancery[4] again from 1647. In May 1649 he was reduced to litigation against the relative and heir of his late deputy John Reynolds who had made off with the ready cash, books, papers and notes from the office! Allanson now sued Henry Reynolds, a London pewterer, hoping that he would be compelled either to account for the money—allegedly £2,000—in his possession, or to pay it back forthwith and to swear to what he had in bonds, bills, etc. The outcome is unclear, but it looks as if Allanson got what he wanted; he presumably also appointed a new deputy, for which he claimed authority by his own terms of appointment back in 1644.[5]

Sometimes deputies were in effect subordinate officials rather than substitutes. This was true of the deputy War-Treasurers with the armies in Ireland (from 1649) and in Scotland (from 1650); and to an extent from 1649 to 1652 with John Blackwell at Guildhall when the Treasurers were the same small group of London aldermen who were the Receivers-General for the monthly Assessment. In 1652 the Aldermen were dropped, and Blackwell became co-Treasurer himself. Sir Adam Loftus, a survivor from the pre-1641 Irish regime who had remained loyal to Parliament, still held the dual offices of Vice-Treasurer and Treasurer-at-Wars in Ireland, to which somewhat ironically he had been appointed by Wentworth after the fall of Lord Mountnorris.[6] Although by the late 1640s and early 1650s his only real job was in England as treasurer and accountant for various Irish relief funds, his son Nicholas was his deputy in 1646 and one Henry Aldritch in the early 1650s.[7] Likewise the Chief Clerk, or Secretary attending the Generals-at-Sea was normally the Paymaster and deputy Navy Treasurer for the whole fleet or part of it.[8] Again Richard Hutchinson, who succeeded Vane as Navy Treasurer at the end of 1650, had been his deputy for some time before that. At the highest level, Ireton was Lord Deputy (1650–1) while Cromwell was still Lord Lieutenant of Ireland. But when Fleetwood was made Lord Deputy under the Protectorate (in 1654) he had already been Commander-in-Chief and Parliamentary Commissioner for two years without a Lord Lieutenant. From 1655 to 1657 Henry Cromwell was—in effect— Lord Deputy Fleetwood's deputy in charge of Ireland, but his title was only Major-General of the Forces there. Succeeding his brother-in-law as Lord Deputy in 1657, Henry was in turn made Lord Lieutenant by his brother Richard at the end of 1658, but there was not to be another Cromwellian Lord Deputy. Also under the Protectorate, two of the Major-Generals of 1655–6 had special leave to act by deputy. Fleetwood, who was recalled from Ireland on the pretext that he was needed for this service and on the Protector's council, had three deputies for the home and East Anglian counties. Lambert, at this time the second man in the government of the country and the probable inceptor of the whole scheme, had two: Robert Lilburne for Yorkshire and Durham, and Charles Howard for the other three northernmost counties of England. Howard, later earl of Carlisle and grandfather of the builder of Castle Howard, reported direct to the Protector[9]—or to Secretary Thurloe as the case might be; Lilburne's relation to Lambert seems to have been a slightly more dependent one. Fleetwood's deputies, too, were responsible direct to the central authorities. In this case the Protector's two principal lieutenants were absentees acting by proxy.

At humbler and more routine levels the use of deputies continued in the traditional way. That same aged Warder of the Tower whose son-in-law petitioned for the Protector's permission to sell the office also wanted leave to continue performing by deputy.[10] A complicated and lengthy dispute about the office of Garbler of Spices[11] to the City of London involved the question of whether the Lord Mayor or the holder could appoint a deputy garbler. It was finally discovered that the first grant did include a deputation clause whereas the second did not. The real issue here was one of tenure and the jury's view was, apparently, 'no forfeiture without precise notice'.[12]

The revival of patent appointments under the Protectorate may have meant that more offices were executed by Deputy. There were deputation clauses in most of the Exchequer appointments of 1654–5;[13] at least two of the Clerks of the Privy Seal were acting by deputy in the late 1650s.[14] But even under the Commonwealth a good deal of this must have gone on quietly, especially in the law courts, that sector of government least affected by the political changes of the 1640s.[15] Robert Henley continued to act as Chief Clerk of King's Bench[16] through his deputy

Samuel Wightwick until he was sequestered from it, when Wightwick succeeded him. William Drake MP almost certainly performed by deputy as Custos Brevium of the Common Pleas; likewise his eventual successor in this office appointed by the Commons in 1659, John Trevor MP, the future Secretary of State.[17] Nor does it seem likely that the Mashams (father and son, both William, both Rump MPs, knight and esquire, who died in 1656 and 1655 respectively) executed in person the Mastership of the Pleas office in that court.[18] Moreover, although his scope had been much reduced by the altered fiscal system after 1642, the now ageing Sir Henry Croke of Chequers continued as Clerk of the Pipe in the Upper Exchequer until his death in 1659. Although he was sufficiently involved to testify to the fees taken in his office, he, too, acted largely by deputy.[19] The same may also have been true of the Essex parliamentarian Colonel Thomas Coke, who from 1652 doubled up the Second Remembrancership of Exchequer with his duties as Trustee for various Crown land sales.[20] In Chancery we have already seen that the controversial Registrar's office was executed by deputies until the 1654 Ordinance was put into operation the following year. And instead of the Six Clerks, largely acting through a horde of deputies and under-clerks, the Ordinance prescribed three Chief Clerks (with no deputation clause) and sixty under-clerks only.[21] The tendency towards Parkinsonian proliferation of officials in a downward direction was to be halted, as much as the creation of superfluous senior posts. So if the Protectorate spelt some increase of deputies at the Seals and in the Exchequer, it also saw an attempt to reduce them in the Court of Chancery. With the Registrarship of Chancery, as we have seen, two different kinds of deputy appear. Early in 1652 Henry Scobell, then Clerk of the Parliament and later Clerk of the Council, was acting as personal deputy for Miles Corbet MP during his absence on the public service as parliamentary Commissioner in Ireland; in addition there were four Deputy Registrars, two of whom attended court (in Westminster Hall) and two of whom worked at the Rolls (in Chancery Lane). What Scobell did, beyond safeguarding Corbet's interests against the four Deputies, is far from clear.[22]

At the lower, secretarial, levels one man's relations with his employers illustrates how absence was not always the only reason for acting by deputy. Here we see it rather as the pretext for seeking leave to do so. Tracy Pauncefote, the second son of a minor Caroline official and patentee, Grimbald Pauncefote, of Gloucestershire origins, was serving an important Rump committee in March 1649 and in this capacity was sent to the then Accounts Committee with a message. Sometime during the following twelve months he became Secretary or Registrar to the new (October 1649) Accounts Committee, but apparently without severing his former connection. In April 1650 he excused his absence to the Accounts chairman on the grounds of illness—the ague, as fashionable an explanation in the seventeenth century as influenza is today. In July he was asking for leave to act by deputy; in September his absence was again being excused, by his friend Sergeant Birkhead, on the grounds of his other employment taking priority.[23] Sickness could, of course, be a cause of prolonged absence without any other complications. Such was the case with Clement Baker, Secretary to the fee-farm Trustees, who could get no relief for a sprained and poisoned finger from London physicians and so went off to consult a wise woman in the country.[24]

Pluralism, or the holding of more than one post by the same person, is more complicated. It raises the question of which offices were—measured in a practical, commonsense way—full-time and which were part-time; we must also consider to what extent duties in different offices were linked together or necessarily overlapped, so that the same man holding two or more of them could be a kind of 'functional' pluralist. Thus under the Commonwealth William Jessop, the earl of Warwick's man of business,[25] was co-Secretary (with Robert Coytmor) to the Admiralty Committee of the Council (as he had previously been to the Lord Admiral), and a member of the special Army Accounts Committee; from 1653 he was Clerk of the Council and (1655-9) Treasurer for the Lord Protector's Contingencies. Robert Blackburne was Secretary first to the Navy Committee of Parliament, then from December 1652 to the new Admiralty and Navy Commissioners, and at the same time Secretary to the Customs Commissioners. One of Professor W. K. Jordan's 'Men of Substance', Henry Robinson, as well as being a pamphleteer and projector, was first of all Auditor of the Excise and then Secretary to the Excise Commissioners until this post was suppressed as superfluous in 1653; he was a leading member of the Accounts Committee (1649-59) and from 1649 also Comptroller (that is, employed to check the treasurers' accounts) for the sale of Crown lands. Henry Broad, his colleague on the Accounts Committee, was also an Exchequer Auditor. Equally of a functional nature was the doubling by John Blackwell junior and Richard Deane (cousin of his namesake the admiral who was killed in action in 1653) of the Treasurership-at-War with the Receiver-Generalship of the Assessment; likewise by the notorious John Jackson of the Excise Treasurership with the position of Agent-General for the new forces raised (to relieve Ireland) since 1646;[26] and from 1654 by Sir William Roberts of posts in numerous financial Commissions with the Auditor-ship of the Receipt.[27] A natural transition, or promotion, with a short overlap, was Richard Sherwyn's treasurership of Goldsmiths' Hall in 1652-5 and then his secretaryship to the Treasury Commissioners (1654-60). More on the margin of functionalism was Captain Edward Horseman, salaried member of the Army Committee (1654-9) and Teller of the Exchequer, who also became a Customs Commissioner in 1656.

This was even more true of George Downing who, having ceased to be Scoutmaster-General to the Field Army, became a Teller of the Exchequer and Envoy to the United Provinces. In 1659/60 Pepys was acting as his deputy in the Teller's office, and it may well be generally true that the four Tellerships of the Receipt were performed *in absentia* by deputies.

When one of the two Chamberlains' offices in the Exchequer was re-granted at the end of 1655 the usual deputation clause was included. But here again there seems to have been a distinction between a potential deputy to the Chamberlain and the (regular) Deputy Chamberlain in the Lower Exchequer. A contemporary note states 'that Edward Fawconberge the other Deputy Chamberlaine was made Chamberlain by the same authority and the same date'; but a further 'memorandum' added that 'the use to be made of this patent is that, if Sr. S. Stuart says that the Chamberlain may do the business of the Deputies, answer he could not without a patent and particular authority as appears by this patent'. This suggests that they were then reputed to be distinct offices.[28]

Despite the existence of deputies, absentees and pluralists, some departments suffered from having too few officers rather than too many. The Compounding Commissioners twice proposed to the Army Committee that an office of 'travelling surveyor-generall' should be created under them. The holder was to supervise the county sequestration committees. At one stage a provisional appointment was made, but then it was disallowed. The Commissioners argued that thousands of pounds would thereby be saved—a severe reflection on the efficiency if not the honesty of the local commissioners.[29] No such office was, in fact, created and in 1653–4 the personnel engaged in composition and sequestration were sharply reduced.

The amount of absenteeism, other than that due to illness and to permitted deputation, was probably small. This was largely because the number of sinecure posts outside the law courts had been drastically cut, compared with pre-1642 or post-1660, despite the restoration of exchequer and seals in 1654–5. And there is evidence for contemporary disapproval of absentees as well as sinecurists.[30]

As has already been emphasised, many members of committees and commissions served on a part-time basis. But this was often because the same men belonged to more than one such body, or were employed in some other public office as well. This should not therefore be confused with absentee office-holding, still less with sinecurism. As a special kind of practical pluralism, it was fully compatible with the more modern, professional civil service which was taking shape during these years.

iv CONDITIONS OF WORK AND EMPLOYMENT

Some terms of employment for officials were bound up with the various tests and loyalty oaths which were a condition of their appointment and continued tenure. This went far down the scale. In April 1647 the new City Surgeon of York was given eight days in which to take 'The Nationall Covenant', or else he was to 'be displaced'.[1] Under the Ordinance for the Northern Association, all members of the York Committee had to take not only the Covenant but also 'the several other protestations agreed upon by the Parliament'.[2] But some of the undertakings were technical, in the sense of being related to the nature of the work concerned, rather than ideological. As under the monarchy, Receivers-General of Crown and other public land revenues had to give security and get 'sureties' to do the same on their behalf when they entered office.[3] When three Treasurers for Prize Goods were appointed by Parliament in April 1649, it was specified that they must enter into recognizances for £2,000 each.[4] The Excise Act of that summer included various penalty clauses for misconduct. More positively, the officers who were to be appointed to taste and view allegedly decayed wines and tobacco were to have a special oath administered to them.[5]

The apparently comprehensive *Book of Oaths*, published in February 1649, was either a piece of antiquarian research or else deliberately put out in the royalist interest. It ranges from the oaths to be taken by Privy Councillors and others of the King's great officers of state, to those which bishops' chancellors are to administer to midwives! It goes as far back in time as to take in the Treasurership of Calais and even the Stewardship of Gascony! And it comes down to the 1641 Protestation and the 1643 Covenant. But many posts of great practical importance in Parliament's administration are not mentioned in it at all.[6] As is true earlier, most oaths prescribed for entry to particular offices are wordy and tautologous, and tell us little about the actual business and routine involved.

Sometimes a more general responsibility was put on those in charge of a particular department. This was especially so after the lapse of the 'Regulators', the moral-cum-administrative reform committee of 1649–50 for the customs and navy. In 1650 the Customs Commissioners published a detailed *Collection of . . . Orders and Rules,* for the joint benefit of their subordinate staffs in London and the outports and of the merchants and shippers, both native and foreign, who were involved in paying customs.[7] Whether this experiment led to greater efficiency is less clear. Since the booklet is not arranged by offices but by functions, it is not strictly comparable with the evidence obtainable from oaths and other conditions of admission. A Protectorate ordinance put responsibility for the suppression of drunkenness and swearing among their subordinates firmly on to the Customs Commissioners.[8] Without an elaborate system of tale-bearing and informers, the news of casual profanity in the remoter outports would seem unlikely to have reached the Commissioners in London. Even for those on the Thames, the practicality of this may be doubted when out of earshot of the head office in the Customs House! Perhaps in partial recognition of such limitations, the powers given to senior officials over their juniors were sometimes—deliberately—both vague and sweeping. Thus the Treasury Commissioners were given power to 'quicken' all Exchequer and revenue officers and commissioners who came under them, to call any such to account and to dismiss unnecessary ones:[9] another condition of employment which would appear to have reduced security of tenure.

Other acts and ordinances, by contrast, laid down in some detail the actual work-routine of those concerned. The head Excise Office in Broad Street was to operate from 8 a.m. to 12 noon and from 2 to 6 p.m.—presumably six days a week. Ships' goods liable for excise were to be delivered there during the hours of daylight, or between 7 a.m. and 5 p.m. from September to March inclusive.[10] Under the Chancery ordinance, so vexatious to the senior judges there, the Commissioners of the Great Seal were to sit five-and-a-half days a week (during the law terms).[11] The Commissioners of the Great Seal and the Master of the Rolls had themselves issued a codification of previous 'orders in Chancery' in the first year of the Commonwealth. This may have been intended to prevent more radical reform being imposed on them from outside, or as a genuine attempt at limited improvement, or both. But in any case it dealt with legal and administrative procedure rather than with work routine for particular offices or officials.[12]

The common law judges[13] issued *Rules and orders* for their respective courts in December 1654. Again it is unclear whether these represented genuine, if strictly limited measures of reform or were merely palliatives to keep the reformers off. Be that as it may, as with Chancery five years earlier these publications are almost exclusively concerned with procedure and the additional vexed question of the qualifications of attorneys entitled to practise there. They tell us virtually nothing about the duties or work routine of the officers and clerks, although they may be under-rated as contributions to the history of law reform in the 1640s and 50s.[14] By contrast, the Postage Ordinance of 1654 prescribed the exact speeds at which letter-posts were to travel on the main road-routes, in summer and in winter—a more out-of-doors condition of service![15]

Information about hours of work, holidays and daily routine is often incidental to the original purpose of the documents from which it comes. Because of a dispute inside the Accounts Committee in 1659 we know that its then chairman, Henry Broad, was living in Chiswick and commuting, and that he was by then on bad terms with his colleague, the illustrious Henry Robinson.[16] Earlier, when Mathias, son of Benjamin Valentine MP (who had been in prison for most of the 1630s after his part in the 1629 session) was called away at short notice to accompany the army on its northward march in July 1650, he apologised elaborately to the rest of the committee for not having been able to take formal leave of them or ask their permission to be absent.[17] Then, as now, officials could stand narrowly on points of protocol when it suited them to do so, and stretch other powers and rights correspondingly widely on different occasions. The co-Treasurers of Accounts took grave objection to an order transmitted and signed by the Committee's clerk, to produce their accounts; such a directive should have come direct from the Committee itself.[18] Several committees and commissions drew up minutes for their own procedure when they first met or soon after. Again the Accounts committee is well-documented on this. On 19 November 1649, with nine out of their eleven members present, they resolved as follows:

1 To follow the letter of the Act appointing them and to apply themselves primarily to receiving, examining and determining the accounts of treasurers, receivers and collectors of money, plate or goods.

2 If any officer or soldier should offer an account for determination, already provided for by any other order or ordinance, to refuse it and leave the party to take it to those persons properly appointed for the same.

3 If anyone present any account for which no provision has been made in any Act, Ordinance or order, this is to be received but to take its turn.

4 The 42-day time limit for accounts to do with London and Westminster to be reckoned from Monday 15 October last, when the Act was published, to 27 November next inclusive.

5 All accounts of money, etc. raised by pretence of the authority of the late King or of anyone acting under him, to be kept apart from the rest in separate books.[19]

As to the second point, from 23 November 1649 the Committee for Army Accounts consisted of the same men plus two others, sitting in a different place and with a separate staff.[20] Parliament's directive of November 1651, forbidding committees from having permanent chairmen, brought consequential changes lower down. The Compounding Commissioners resolved that James Russell should take the chair for one month in place of Samuel Moyer, chairman from April 1650 to January 1652.[21] The fullest of these procedural orders are those for the Council of State itself and its subordinate staff.[22]

Some innovations of the early 1650s affected clerks and others at a junior level more than members of committees or commissioners themselves. Such was the Act prescribing the use of English instead of Latin and law French in legal documents, and the use of ordinary hand-writing (i.e. cursive script, either secretary hand, or italic) instead of 'court-hands' in all official papers.[23] Considering that Lord President Bradshaw's own archaic handwriting[24] certainly derived from a legal court-hand and not from any sixteenth-century cursive script, this has its ironical side. Potentially more important, because it threatened the livelihood of copying-clerks and those whose income from fees depended on how much they transcribed for members of the public, was the use of printing for official documents. This, like the use of arabic instead of roman numerals in accounts and other papers, was never the subject of legislation,[25] but it was undoubtedly on the increase especially on the fiscal side of government.[26] It is indeed likely that the use of printed forms was already making economies in manpower possible. The Treasurers-at-War may well have been able to manage with a more modest staff of subordinates—relative to the scope of their respon-sibilities—than would have been possible if every routine item had been hand-written. The same may have applied to the Treasurer of the Navy's office, and perhaps to some of the commissioners and trustees in charge of land sales. That legal costs were cut by reducing the writing fees seems less likely; then as now, conveyancing was probably the crucial issue. The whole topic requires fuller investigation, and over a longer span of time.

As in almost all revolutions, bureaucracy increased in England during the 1640s, and its inevitable accompaniment was a growth in form-filling. But many more of the forms were now printed.

Evidence about the physical location of courts, departments, commit-tees and commissioners is relatively plentiful, if—on the whole—un-revealing. The Long Parliament's special ties with the City went back at least to the winter of 1641–2, when the Five Members took refuge there from the King's attempt on them. The nature of Pym's new fiscal system led to this being carried much further, with the various funds and taxes having their treasuries in the halls of different London companies, elsewhere in the City, or beside the river between there and West-minster.[27] By 1649 the diversification of the revenue system had come to entail the geographical dispersal of its separate parts all over the capital, and any successful campaign to make the revenues once more flow into and through 'one channel'[28] would imply a reduction in the number of these locations. It would be tedious to list the seat of every known branch of the central government; the general effect is what matters. Particularly from 1643 to 1653 there was a major shift away from White-hall (the palace being largely used as lodgings for politicians and others, including some officials) to the City of London. But the City here includes that vital strip along the north bank of the Thames from old Scotland

Yard to the Fleet, where many of the ecclesiastical and secular magnates of the Tudor period had had their town mansions. Others, such as Freeman House and Gurney House, were named after the more recent civic dignitaries who had built or embellished them.

One of these, Worcester House, was the subject of an acrimonious dispute due to parliamentary carelessness or ineptitude. The original non-parliamentary Accounts Committee of 1644–8 had sat at Freeman House, one-time residence of the London courtier of the 1630s, Sir Ralph Freeman. This committee was largely composed of 'presbyterian' supporters and virtually collapsed in the period following Pride's Purge.[29] Its successors were not fully established until the Acts of October and November 1649;[30] the new accounts committee, which was then constituted, had as its nucleus four out of the five members appointed for one year only, to take special charge of the army's accounts, in August 1648.[31] The new Committee of October 1649 for civil accounts was allocated Worcester House as its headquarters, but this had already been occupied by the Crown land-sale Trustees appointed in July,[32] so the Accounts Committee set up their quarters at the Duchy (of Lancaster) House in the Strand instead, and here apparently at least some of their offices remained until 1658. In March 1650 the Trustees for the sale of fee-farm rents (largely the same body as those for the sale of other Crown lands) succeeded to Worcester House. By the summer of 1652 some of the accounts offices including that of the Treasurers had been transferred there, and it seems as if the largely identical Army Accounts Committee (of November 1649) may have met there too. And by 1659 they may all have transferred to Worcester House.[33] In 1650 the Committee thought it worth while drafting a Bill for an additional Act for taking accounts, explaining that they were having to use Duchy instead of Worcester House, and giving accountants who had so far failed to bring in their accounts one more week within which to do so and offering the usual rewards to informers who helped to bring in such defaulters.[34] This was not taken up by Parliament, and the Committee had to make do with their existing powers. No tardy accountant appears in fact to have pleaded that he had taken his papers to the wrong house and failed to find where they were sitting.

Meanwhile Worcester House was the subject of another clash in November 1653. The Accounts and Public Debts Commissioners of the Barebones[35] decided to establish themselves there, and were promptly evicted by the fee-farm Trustees, who drafted[36] a long reply to the complaint by the Debts and Accounts Commissioners' Secretary. The fee-farm Trustees explained that they had offered the use of several rooms but *not* of one particular large room which they needed for their own business. Notwithstanding this and the fact that the Debts and Accounts Commissioners had an order to use the Duchy House instead (like their predecessors the civil Accounts Committee), the Commissioners had returned to the attack. The Trustees suggested that the Obstructions Commissioners (who had in 1652 succeeded the Rump's Committee for removing obstacles in the way of land sales)[37] might be persuaded to move instead; if Obstructions would vacate their large room for Fee-Farm, then Fee-Farm would surrender theirs to Debts and Accounts. But a provisional agreement with Obstructions broke down when the Commissioners went back on their word and re-occupied the room which they had undertaken to give up. An alternative arrangement, to share their own room with the Debts and Accounts Commissioners on alternate days, also broke down with mutual acrimony, lockings-out, etc.[38] The outcome can only be surmised, but the Barebones' Commissioners were soon to be superseded, and the old (1649) Accounts Committee came back into action despite the restoration of the Upper Exchequer the following year, while Crown lands and fee-farm business continued to trickle on during the mid- and later 1650s.[39] But it was not only the Accounts Committee who were in trouble over Worcester House. On 6 February 1651 the fee-farm Trustees demanded their rooms there back from the Sequestration Commissioners.[40] Since the Compounding, Advance and Sequestration Commissioners operated from Goldsmiths' and Haberdashers' Halls in the City, it seems that this must have been a hangover, either from the parliamentary Sequestration Appeals Committee of the late 1640s, or from the Westminster and Middlesex Committee which had been very active earlier in the Civil War years.[41] Finally in the last Protectorate Parliament it was decided that the whole house should be restored to the Dowager Countess of Worcester and that all government committees should find alternative accommodation—a victory presumably for the crypto-royalists and the 'country' party in the House.[42]

Generally the Protectorate saw a limited return of government departments to Westminster and Whitehall. But not entirely so, compared again with the position before 1640 or after 1660. Before the days of the telephone there must have been great practical advantages in geographical concentration. But, as with the use of handwriting instead of print, there were those with a vested interest the other way: the Messengers who formed an inevitable part of the junior staff under every court, committee, commission or other department.

V OFFICERS' PAY

Among the most obvious features of seventeenth-century officials' remuneration is its sheer variety.[1] This is only slightly less true for the 1650s than for the 1630s. Once more, it is difficult to give a general impression of what things were like except by individual examples.

Salaries

On the whole, the lesson of the earlier seventeenth century was well learnt: that, within limits, it pays to pay people well. This involved what were still often called fees,[2] i.e. stipendiary payments by the government to its officials, but were coming to be known increasingly as salaries or (further down the scale) as wages. These were generally a good deal higher than they had been before 1640–2 and had certainly been increased more than any mere cost-of-living increase since then would have justified. Whether their real value was greater than, say, in Henry VII's or early in Henry VIII's reign is another matter—and more diffi-cult to estimate. When twelve Navy Commissioners were appointed by Parliament in September 1642, four non-MPs among them were ordered to receive £100 a year each; one was to receive the stipend and fees due to the former Surveyor of the Navy, one (a ship designer and builder) the allowance (not stated in the Ordinance) which he formerly had from the King. One of the MPs (the younger Vanc) was already the Treasurer of the Navy and well remunerated as such, and nothing was said about a salary for him or for the other five MPs on the Commission. The Admiralty Secretary was to have £200 a year; presumably his was meant to be a full-time appointment, which those of the Commissioners were not.[3] The establishment for admiralty and naval affairs was to change a good deal between then and the early 1650s, but the precedent of higher salaries was continued.

The same was true in other areas of administration. In the first land-sale Ordinance—for episcopal estates in November 1646—the Registrar-Accountant was to have £200 a year plus salaries for his under-clerks—the Comptroller also £200.[4] When additional responsibilities were laid on some of these officials by securing the loan of £200,000 on the bishops' lands in the following spring, the Registrar-Accountant was awarded another £200 a year.[5] If anything, the trend was upward during the years 1642–3 and then levelled out, while in the early 1650s there were some attempts to cut salaries as well as to reduce the number of officials, for example in the Excise.[6] But in the later 1640s the story was one of additional posts with larger salaries, rather than of significant reductions in either. The special Army Accounts Committee's five members appointed for one year (August 1648) were to receive £300 each, plus £100 for staff and expenses, provided that neither they nor their under-clerks took any fees or gratuities.[7]

The Regulators (January 1649) were allocated no salary or other pay-ment for themselves, but were given power to increase the salaries of necessary naval offices as well as to abolish superfluous posts.[8] Some-times an award of salary went with an injunction against taking fees;[9] some posts carried a fixed stipend plus a sliding scale of allowances. The deputy Sergeant-at-Arms appointed to bring defaulting sequestrators before the Accounts Committee (August 1648) was to have £40 a year plus 'riding charges'.[10] The Register for the sale of capitular lands (April 1649) was to have £100 a year stipendiary fee plus other fees as fixed in November 1648 for episcopal lands;[11] the same went for the Crown land-sale Register in July. Here the Surveyor-General got £150 a year for himself and his clerks—no fees being mentioned; the Comptroller had the large salary of £300.[12] The Excise Act of August 1649 said that Parliament would fix the Commissioners' salaries; they in turn were to set the wages for all the staff whom they appointed.[13] When the new Army Accounts Committee was named in November, the members' salaries were left to the Crown land-sale Trustees, with the approval of Parliament's Obstructions Committee; likewise for their clerks and assistant Surveyor-General—except that a ceiling of £80 a year for two years was set for him.[14] The Trade Commissioners of August 1650 were not themselves to be paid, but were allowed £200 a year for their secretary and up to £300 for the rest of their staff.[15] It is not always easy to tell whether an additional Act augments or replaces an existing salary awarded in a previous Act or Ordinance. The original fee-farm measures of March and August 1650 had, in effect, re-named the staff already in operation for other Crown land sales, presumably at their existing salaries since none was specified in these Acts.[16] The additional fee-farm Act of February 1651 allowed the Registrar-Accountant £200 a year, and the second Additional Act of August 1652 gave him another £100 (once-for-all, not annually)—but was the £200 per annum still in force?[17] In the Rump's third and last Act for the sale of royalists' lands forfeited for treason, the Registrar-Accountant's salary was raised to the astronomical figure of £600 per annum, but this was because the redoubtable Colonel Robert Mainwaring, who had held this post for all land sales since 1646, was now dead and was being replaced by a troika of lesser lights.[18] In the Barebones' additional fee-farm sales Act it was directed that the salaries (query, as in previous fee-farm Acts) should end after six months—before April 1654.[19]

Equivalent Protectorate salaries were perhaps marginally lower than those of the Commonwealth. The Maintenance Trustees (or church commissioners of their day) were only to have £100 per annum each (September 1654).[20] By contrast, the twice-restored Rump of February 1660—almost in its expiring breath before the return of the Secluded Members—voted its revived Sequestration Commissioners £300 a year each, though the flowing tide of counter-revolution meant that they probably never received a penny of this.[21] By contrast, the almost moribund (civil) Accounts Committee had been reduced to employing first three new clerks, and then a fourth, in April 1658, on the strict understanding that they should expect no salary at all, but—by then like the committee members themselves—await what came in through their combined efforts. According to how much was raised, they were to receive up to a maximum of £60 a year each. They were free to quit and take up other work, but undertook not to complain against the Committee either while in its employment or afterwards.[22] As we shall see, this was only an enfeebled version of the payment-by-results system, which was extremely widespread.[23]

On the basis of this and much other evidence about the profits of civil and military offices,[24] it is tempting to conclude with the Commonwealth's contemporary critics that the new republican 'establishment' did itself very well. Had the country merely exchanged one kind of 'spoils system' for another? At this stage we can hardly give a general verdict on the nature or quality of republican government. However, on salaries it is worth remembering that the Long Parliament's apparent self-indulgence with the public purse arose partly out of the very restraints to which its members subjected themselves. Members' wages from their constituencies were all but extinct by 1640.[25] With civil war and then a parliament of indefinite duration, many members were cut off from their ordinary sources of income from lands, offices, trades and professions—a very different situation from sessions of a few weeks or months as in the 1620s or earlier. It was especially serious for those parliamentarian MPs whose own estates were in royalist-controlled areas and where the payment of rents was interrupted during the Civil War (1642–6). Failing to vote themselves a regular allowance out of the public purse, it is not surprising that members instead appointed each other to numerous offices—some more lucrative than others. Against this background arose the popular clamour of 1644 directed against a 'broken-backed' war and those believed to have a vested interest in its indefinite continuance. This, coupled with the war party's wish to oust the existing army commanders from their positions, helps to explain the self-denying Ordinance, first moved in December 1644, finally accepted by the Lords in April 1645.[26] The immediate effect of this was to put some MPs in an even worse plight, by removing at a stroke the official incomes on which they had been living. And shortly afterwards Parliament did vote its members, who could show that they were not receiving their normal income from land and other sources, a weekly allowance of £4. Curiously, this was mainly taken up by the moderates or peace-party members, who had—on the whole—not been office-holders before April 1645; some had held military commands briefly back in 1642–3, a few still did so until the Ordinance and the concurrent reorganisation of the army according to the 'New Model'. From 1647 several members secured private ordinances allowing them to hold civil office, as had already happened with Cromwell and two or three other favoured military commanders. But this still left many without any direct, legitimate income from office.

The same remained true of the Commons after the removal of the conservatives in December 1648 and the establishment of the republic the following February. As we have seen, the Rump created a new and effective executive body, in the shape of the Council of State. But the Councillors (whether deliberately following the precedent of the royal Privy Council, or that of the Committee of Both Kingdoms in 1644–7) did not have salaries; they were unpaid, while the parliamentary allowance of 1645–7 also appears to have lapsed. Oddly, the lesson about adequate pay helping to make people less dishonest was thus applied by the Commonwealth's rulers to everyone except themselves. This was far from the case with the generals and other military and naval commanders. The officers of the armed forces are only our concern here in so far as some of them were also, *qua* MPs or commissioners, among the civil rulers of the republic. But as regards salaries and income from office, a sharp distinction must be drawn. Army and naval officers' pay, like that of other officials, was often in arrears,[27] although—on the whole—less so after 1649. With that proviso, the level of military remuneration was generous. Some of the civilian salaries already cited appear in a different perspective if we remind ourselves that around 1650 the Lord General received £3,650 a year, a Major-General of Foot and a Lieutenant-General of Horse £365, a Colonel of Horse or of Foot £218. 8s. 0d., a Captain of Horse £182. 10s. 0d. and even a Captain of Foot £146. 0s. 0d. The Commander-in-Chief, Scotland, was paid at the rate of £2,190 per annum in the absence of the Lord General (that is, from August 1651 on).[28] In estimating the total pay of the military leaders it is important to remember that all generals were normally also colonels of regiments (the Lord General of two, a horse and a foot regiment), while all colonels were in turn company or troop commanders, and so were also paid as captains of foot or horse as the case might be.[29] In the navy, a full admiral was paid at the rate of £1,095 a year and a vice-admiral normally at £547. 10s. 0d.; captains ranged from £273 for a first-rate to £91 a year for a sixth-rate. Payments were usually for irregular periods of sea service, often less, occasionally more than a year at a time.[30] Considering the degree of independent responsibility likely to be involved, naval pay rates appear relatively modest beside those of army officers. But the military pay rates were even more favourable measured against those of civil administrators, let alone compared to the position of MPs not holding office.

This can be related to the growing tension between the Rump and the army (1651–3). Among its members Cromwell (Lord General), Fleetwood (Lieutenant-General), Harrison (Major-General), Blake (Admiral), even garrison colonels like Sir Arthur Hesilrige, Sir William Constable, Valentine Wauton, William Sydenham, Philip Jones, Thomas Mackworth, and Thomas Birch, were in very different circumstances from the mere civilians. The wonder perhaps is less that some members of the Rump were not wholly honest, but that more of them were not more dishonest.[31]

After 1653 this particular problem did not recur, at least not in the same form. From 17 September 1656 to 26 June 1657 was the longest parliamentary session,[32] and MPs as such no longer formed part of the executive. But in one respect the Protectorate recognised the problem, as it had existed up to 1653. The members of the Protector's Council were paid, at the handsome rate of £1,000 a year each, regardless of their other emoluments. Of those who sat from December 1653 to April 1659, this would seem to have provided the following with their only official income, for some or all of the time: Sir Gilbert Pickering,[33] Walter Strickland, Henry Lawrence, the earl of Mulgrave, Viscount Lisle, Sir Charles Wolseley,[34] Edward Montague,[35] Sir Anthony Ashley Cooper, and Richard Major. For the more aristocratic and civilian elements in the Council it was therefore important; for the military men—Lambert, Fleetwood, Disbrowe, Skippon and Sydenham—as later for Montague and for Secretary Thurloe, it was supplementary to other sources. Who thought of this, we cannot tell; it is not specified in the Instrument of Government's clauses on the Council. Lambert, a man of good, if expensive tastes seems a likely originator of the scheme.[36] In 1659–60 the restored Rump saw a return to an unpaid Council. The MPs of 1659–60 were considerably stricter with themselves than they had been in 1649–53. The Councillors of State voted each other and some of their staff venison from the State forests and parks, but that was about all.[37] Again, the military and naval men were much better provided for than the rest. Even in the absence of a Captain-General the three Commanders-in-chief were to receive £3,650 a year for England and Ireland, and £2,190 for Scotland—not a differential which one can imagine George Monck and his wife having relished.[38]

Poundage

Payment on a percentage or 'poundage' basis was already well known before the Civil War.[39] It was particularly favoured for the remuneration of receivers and paymasters. There was an apparent failure to grasp that the right incentive for an official receiving revenue was of exactly the wrong sort for one on the disbursing side, although in 1659 Sir Arthur Hesilrige was to extol the merits of poundage as against fixed salaries, without making this distinction.[40] The higher the level of state spending, the greater such a man's remuneration would be. Sometimes it was not precisely poundage but a sliding-scale salary according to turnover. Thus after Richard Hutchinson had threatened to resign as Navy Treasurer in the winter of 1653–4, he was mollified by a new salary award; the flat rate was to be £2,500 a year, and for every £100,000 spent on his account yearly over £1,300,000 he was to receive another £100.[41] More often the arrangement was so much in the pound. And exactly how much could vary in a way which it is hard to relate to any fixed principle. The Treasurers for the £90,000 a month assessment of April 1649 were to receive 1½d. in the pound;[42] that is, if the assessment continued at this rate for twelve months the Treasurers-at-War and their deputies would get 1/160 of £1,080,000, or £6,750. *Per contra* the three Prize Goods' Treasurers of the same month were allowed 12d. in the pound, or 5 per cent, to cover their own expenses and the payment of their deputies and clerks.[43] But prizes were, of course, chancy and could vary from zero to hundreds of thousands of pounds—or so men always hoped—in a single windfall. In fact at this date the ships being taken were royalist or French and were unlikely to be worth much unless money was captured on its way to or from the 'King of Scots', as the republicans called Charles II.

In some of the land-sale Acts there was quite a complex tariff of poundage. Thus on capitular estates, the Contractors were to have 3d. and the Treasurers 2d. in the pound.[44] For the sale of the late King's and the royal family's goods (as opposed to lands), including pictures and furniture, the Trustees and their agents were to have 7d., the Contractors 5d., and the two Treasurers 2d. in the pound.[45] On Crown lands, the Contractors and Trustees got 3d. each, and the Treasurers 1d.[46] The county Sequestration Commissioners appointed by the parliamentary Compounding Committee in January 1650 were allowed 12d. in the pound;[47] in October, the Treasurers for the sale of glebe lands belonging to rectories 2d.[48] The assessment Act for £120,000 a month in November 1650 allowed 1d. in the pound to collectors and sub-collectors, 1d. to the various county commissioners' clerks and a maximum of 1d. to the Receiver-General for each county, a total of 3d. apart from the Treasurers, who are not mentioned but presumably were still to have 1½d.[49] For the fee-farm rents and royalist lands forfeited for treason the Trustees were simply allowed 2d.[50] In the case of the former we know how it was divided. An elaborate scheme was proposed by the Trustees and submitted to Parliament's Obstructions Committee for their approval, as the third share-out of poundage money on 30 May 1651. The total sum available was to be divided into thirty parts, of which the twenty-four Trustees and Contractors were to have 24/30 (or 1/30 each), the four Treasurers 4/30, the Register and his clerks 1/30 and the Comptroller 1/30. The running total of sales recorded two days later was £90,978, so at 2d. in the pound one-thirtieth of the total poundage due to date came to just over £25.[51] Whether this was a fair return obviously depended on how much work had been put in,[52] but it was hardly wealth, even by seventeenth-century money values. Nor can £117 each for the best part of a year's effort be thought immodest.[53]

The Barebones Parliament allowed the Judges and the Messenger for the despatch of poor prisoners' cases 6d., and in London 2d., in the pound.[54] Under the Protectorate, the Sequestration Commissioners still got 12*d*. in the pound, but now on the profits of sequestered estates only, composition having been ended.[55] The Protector and his Council fixed the Excise Commissioners' rate at 2*d*., but for some reason left that of the Customs Commissioners to be set by the special Committee for regulating the Customs, or by others whom they should appoint. The accounts show that they received 4*d*. in the pound.[56] The second Protectorate Parliament allowed a total of 6*d*. on every pound collected from fines and compositions on London buildings, of which the commissioners were to have 3*d*., the three Registrars 1*d*., the Receiver or his deputy $\frac{1}{2}$*d*. and the Clerks 1$\frac{1}{2}$*d*.[57] The last abortive treason land-sale Act of the Rump allowed the newly-appointed Treasurers-General 2*d*. and the Committee (or Commissioners) 1*s*. 6*d*. in the pound, apart from the payment of informers and 'discoverers' of concealments—the highest rate recorded.[58] The collectors of assessment arrears in Hertfordshire were allowed 2*s*. or 10 per cent in 1654.[59] But this was a very different matter; discovering arrears was more like a speculation.

Sometimes this type of payment resembled a capitation levy, which was always unpopular. The minister of religion in Portsmouth dockyard begged for a stipend of £50 a year in lieu of dependence on a groat (4*d*.) from every seaman on the books there every month.[60] The position of officials who were paid on contract was different again, but these were virtually limited to Victuallers, Commissaries and others who supplied clothing, equipment, arms and munitions, on a regular basis.[61]

Revenue-farming involved a different relationship. Parts of the excise were farmed throughout these years and rather more of it under the Protectorate than earlier. But an ambitious scheme to lease the whole of the customs and excise to a big syndicate in 1657 came to nothing.[62] The profits of the excise farmers, as opposed to the commissioners, can only be guessed at, but the position of Martin Noell in the years 1655–9 would seem comparable to that of the Jacobean and Caroline customs farmers, whose role as government creditors has been so clearly explained by Professor Ashton.[63] Very much like the royal customs farmers in 1641–2, the Protector's excise farmers were called to book by Parliament in 1659.[64] An assessment of the effectiveness of republican financial administration is attempted later in this book.[65] Revenue farmers, like Contractors, were a small element among republican officials; this form of remuneration, therefore, affected very few people.

Fees

Fees paid to officials by members of the public and by other officials had been a grievance long before 1642. Several members of the Long Parliament must have had first-hand experience of it, as one-time sheriffs and accountants, or simply as litigants and grantees who had to pay fees.[66] And there is some evidence that when the parliamentarians came to construct their own machinery of government, they tried to restrict fee-taking and may even have toyed with the idea of its abolition. Some of the larger salaries paid were indeed made conditional on those concerned taking no fees at all or drastically restricted ones.[67] But Parliament did not go far enough in this direction to satisfy its own radical supporters. Few comparable topics except law reform provoked more pamphleteers so bitterly; with how much justice is another matter.[68] If investigation and legislation could restrain exactions, the Rump deserves some credit here. Its critics said—in effect—that merely having some of the right intentions was not enough: draconian measures, abolition not reform, were the only answer. Sometimes the details were written into the Ordinances and Acts, as in the prescription of 2d. a mile riding-charges which the accounts Messengers could demand from those whom they attached for the Committee, and the 3d. per sheet of every examination or account written out for anyone found by the committee to be in arrears, and 12d. for every order written out for every such person;[69] or in limiting the Register for the sale of capitular lands to the same fees as for episcopal lands, 2d. for every fifteen-line sheet of writing.[70] Some-times the senior commissioners or other officers concerned were left to fix their subordinates' fees, like the Commissioners of June 1649 for giving relief to those who had surrendered on Articles.[71] In September 1650 the Compounding Commissioners exercised their powers to fix the fees (as well as salaries) of their Registrars and Examiners and the Clerks to their learned Counsel.[72] The two patterns persisted. An Act of Novem-ber 1650 prescribed the exact fees to be taken in the Upper Exchequer for passing the accounts of lords of manors and liberties, or their bailiffs on ex-church lands. But the main Exchequer Ordinance of June 1654 said that fees were to be prescribed in the letters patent appointing officials, while the Protector's Ordinance earlier that month, reviving the Duchy of Lancaster's court at Westminster, went even further, allowing fees and perquisites simply as they had been before its suppression.[73] An Act against recusant Catholics in 1657 left the Auditors' fees for taking the accounts of minors' guardians to be fixed by the Treasury Commis-sioners—or by the Lord Treasurer and Chancellor of the Exchequer if these posts were filled.[74]

There is, however, a little evidence that the fees actually taken in some branches of government may have been more substantial than would be gathered merely from perusing legislation and other formal pronounce-ments. One of the officials at Gurney House wrote to 'his very loving brother,[75] Mr Clement Baker', secretary to the fee-farm Trustees at Worcester House, listing the fees involved in a purchase of church lands, presumably so that Baker knew what to charge the buyers of fee-farm rents; there was also a separate schedule, prescribed by the Trustees themselves, of charges for the particulars provided by the land-revenue Auditors for prospective buyers.[76] In general, with these and the fees for orders and contracts for purchases, the amount to be paid varied with the value of the property or rent in question. Fees for the granting of military commissions do not appear in any Act or Ordinance,[77] but they must have represented a very worthwhile source of income for the Lord General's staff and have been quite an appreciable burden on self-made officers. Since the amounts recorded (for the years 1647–50) vary considerably, they may have been gratuities, that is tips, rather than prescribed fees as these were known in the law courts and elsewhere. Generally the tariff was higher for cavalry than infantry commissions, and practically none are recorded for the Lord and Lieutenant-Generals' own regiments.[78]

While the Long Parliament failed to abolish fees, the attempts to restrict them and to stamp out exactions were almost continuous. Indeed scepticism arises from the very multiplicity of those involved in this campaign. As early as August 1644 the Revenue Committee of Parliament was investigating local complaints against exactions by Messengers.[79] The Revenue Committee's Messengers were being complained of in another county seven years later when the local Sequestration Commissioners took it up with the Compounding Commissioners, who in turn passed the allegations back to the parliamentary Revenue Committee.[80] The Long Parliament had more than once appointed a special committee to reduce fees, sometimes in conjunction with abolishing unnecessary offices and attacking bribery. The last of these was set up by the Rump in October 1650. Then in January 1651 the Obstructions Committee of the House was given a general responsibility for investigating excessive fees.[81] Almost immediately they required the Indemnity Committee to certify the fees of their officers and clerks.[82] In April it was the turn of the Compounding Commissioners—with the added rider that the fees taken by their staff were alleged to be excessive; the answer was a flat denial of exaction and an assertion that only Registers, Examiners and Counsels' clerks received fees at all and that these were posted up on the office door for everyone to see.[83] Parliament itself prescribed triple forfeiture for those taking excessive fees or gratuities on the sale of glebe lands (October 1650);[84] the Protector and his Council were to go further and prescribe loss of office for exactions in the Exchequer.[85]

Numerous schedules of the fees which could properly be taken in various offices have survived, and many are dated. One batch, from early November 1650, presumably represents the activity of the Rump's previous committee on offices and fees; it covers several Exchequer offices.[86] The achievement of the Obstructions Committee in this field appears, to say the least, somewhat slender. In January 1652 the new law reform committee under Matthew Hale, now in charge of fees, ordered a general return from all courts and departments. The surviving items are for Exchequer and Chancery, and it may be significant that those from the former on the whole complement and do not repeat the returns made to the parliamentary committee a year and a quarter earlier.[87] Even the previous investigators were now investigated. There is a return from the Usher in the Court of Wards 'where the Commitie of Parliament sitts for the removing of Obstructions', acknowledging that he took a fee of 4d. per affidavit.[88] The height of self-denial might seem to have been reached a year later when the twenty (unpaid) members of the law reform committee were themselves appointed temporarily as judges for the probate of wills, and the fees from the Probate Court (formerly the Prerogative Court of Canterbury) were ordered to be wholly at the disposal of the Treasury Inspection Commissioners. But alas for such good intentions! Only a week later the House, presumably on the Commissioners' recommendation, ordered that the fees normally taken by the judges and officers of the Probate Court should continue until further notice.[89] Fortunately some other documents surviving from the Protectorate give us an idea of what was involved in this. The fees due on the valuations of estates were tabulated according as they were due to 1) the Commonwealth, 2) the Register or Actuary (the post which had been the subject of so much controversy since 1649), 3) the Clerk, 4) the Receiver and Sealer, 5) the Examiner, and 6) the Messenger. The probate fees on a will of an estate worth under £20 came to 5s. 6d., on one of £20 to £100, 8s. 0d., and for every £100's worth above that another 6d. (No. 5 is a blank here—the Examiner got no probate fee.) On the Quietus Est—that is at the end of it all when the executors could go ahead, legally in the clear—the fees on an estate of under £40 were 10s. 4d., on one over £100, £1. 4s. 4d.; for a definitive sentence, read out in court, the total fees were 25s. 8d.; for copies of a will 8d. per sheet of twenty lines. Looked at another way round, the number of individual fees payable to the Commonwealth was 49, ranging from 26s. 8d. to 2d.; to the Registrar 52, from 5s. to 2d.; to the Clerk 34, from 5s. to 2d.; to the Receiver 32, from 1s. 8d. to 2d.; to the Examiner 3, from 2s. to 2d.; and to the Messenger 7 or 8, from 1s. to 1d.[90]

As with earlier tables of fees, which resulted from enquiries in the 1590s, 1610s and 1620s–30s, this is of only limited use unless we can discover how many wills of what value went through the Court annually. The number can be estimated,[91] but not the value of the many thousands of estates involved. Even computer-aided research would not really provide us with the answer which we need here. An anonymous 'Proposall' of January 1656 gives a little more evidence. It refers back to a new fee schedule for the staff approved by the Council of State in June (1653), just after the April 1653 Act.[92]

Which fees to the Register are worth, (as it is conceived) about 2,000[ll] yearly and the Clerkes fees are very large. Tis thought that the Actuaries place as Actuary is worth about 300 li yearely, but yet hee assuming the title of Register swallowes All those other great fees which might bee saved. Tis obvious likewise, that lesse than halfe the Nomber of Clerkes and Ministeriall Officers might execute that office, to which if they were reduced, as much more might bee saved.

Control should therefore be vested in 'some well meriting persons', in order 'That the Third part of the fees, now allowed for Executing the said Office goe for the future to his Highnes over and above what his Highnes now hath . . .' Further proposals for the organisation of the Probate Court followed. This paper followed the retrospective appointment of salaried judges in August 1654, two of whom had been among the twenty unpaid ones of 1653–4, one of them being a civil lawyer with a definite interest in reform.[93] As much as £8–9,000 a year was said to be involved, apart from the one-third increase which might be hoped for.[94] The scheme looks like an anticipation of the late-eighteenth- to early-nineteenth-century idea of a 'fee-fund' for each court or department, out of which the officers and clerks should be paid a stipend, the residue being left as revenue for the State. This was the penultimate stage before fee payments to officials were, for practical purposes, abolished and replaced by wages and salaries.[95]

The Probate Office was not unique in officials being forbidden to take fees, but in other instances this was related to particular transactions. On 1 October 1651 Parliament ordered that £28,330 should be paid out of the Treasury of the Grand Excise to the War Treasurers and that the latter should repay it, without fees, by the end of the following January.[96] The pension of John Lilburne, the ex-Leveller leader, was ordered to be paid without fees while he was a political prisoner; this had to be repeated by the Council before the Exchequer would obey.[97]

The revival of the exchequer and the seals in 1654–6 produced a fresh crop of fee schedules, and more complaints about the inadequacy of income from fees to support the holders of certain posts. But this was preceded by the most elaborate and ambitious attempt of the whole decade to regulate fees by government action: the Chancery Ordinance of 21 August 1654, enforced from the summer of 1655 to February 1658.[98] Several of its clauses relate to fees and include a schedule or appendix of those allowed in the main offices of the Court.[99] It is instructive to compare this table with the returns made to the Hale Committee in February 1652.[100] The Master of the Rolls' fees appear identical in the two except that on every Sheriff's patent, out of the Six Clerks' Office, for the *dedimus potestatem*,[101] he was to receive 6s. 8d. (1654) instead of 8s. 8d.

(1652); otherwise, the Ordinance specifies a longer list of permitted fees than his own return. Unfortunately, of the six offices whose fees are scheduled by the Ordinance, there are returns for only two in 1652, and the second of these, the Registrar's, is woefully incomplete as regards fees though informative about the structure of the office.[102] In all, there were returns from about twenty-six offices (held by one or more individuals) and from twelve attorneys collectively, most of which are scarcely touched in the Ordinance and which—one might therefore presume—were allowed to remain as they had been. It was the Six Clerks whose fees had been so thorny a topic in the 1620s and 30s; their return (if they made one) in 1652 has not survived. And they were the most harshly treated in 1654–5; their whole office was remodelled with three Chief Clerks, whose schedule of fees, though lengthy, was certainly more restricted than those taken by the Six.

The purpose of the Protectorate's fee schedules of 1655–6 was fundamentally different from that of the returns made in the years 1650–2. The object was now to establish from earlier precedent what should be allowed when officers were being appointed by patent, often after a lengthy vacancy in the office concerned. These schedules relate almost exclusively to the Exchequer, and for some posts there it was not felt to be by any means a formality. Denis Bond, one of the inner circle of Rump committee-men and member of all five Commonwealth Councils of State, had apparently abandoned political ambitions and accepted the semi-sinecure office of Clerk of the Pells and Treasurer's Clerk in the Lower Exchequer (31 August 1654). In July 1655 he wrote anxiously to Thurloe, having heard that the fees of Exchequer offices were about to be prescribed and would pass the Great Seal later that week. He reminded the Secretary, so that his own business 'may be speedily despatched . . . for I apprehend that if this opportunity should bee lett slip, it will prove a matter of no smale difficulty to certify any thinge for the future', and he accordingly asked for help on the following day.[103] In fact the fee schedules at the Great Seal for Bond's offices are only dated 27 September by the Clerk of the Privy Seal who signed them, so it is not clear that things were as urgent as Bond purported to believe.[104] Since this office had been vacant under the Commonwealth, there is no earlier return of the Clerk of the Pells' fees against which to measure the 1655 schedule, short of going back to the 1630s. Sometimes marginal reductions can be seen to have been imposed. In the case of the Chamberlains there is some overlap between the two tables and little change can be seen.[105] Outside the Exchequer, the Sergeant-at-Arms attending the Lords Commissioners of the Great Seal had a generous scale of allowances for making arrests, fetching people and then keeping them in custody. In 1652 the ceiling had been £20 for the arrest of an earl or above; in a re-grant of this office, made in December 1656, the maximum was £20 for a baron or above;

the daily custody of a knight was cut from £1 to 10s., likewise for an esquire; the arrest fee for a gentleman and below ('a common person') was cut from £3. 6s. 8d. to £1. 6s. 8d., and the custody fee likewise to 10s. daily.[106]

The other revived offices whose holders had anciently depended on fees, some of them exclusively so, were at the Signet and the Privy Seal. In September 1655 they petitioned the Protector in somewhat flowery terms:[107]

> Sheweth That the greatest part of such Businesse as did formerly passe under the Signet and Privy Seale (from which the said Clerks derived their cheifest benefitt) is now wholly taken away, and on the other side the Businesse of the Publique (for which they receive no fees) is much increased, Whereby it comes to passe, that the labor of yor petrs in discharge of their duty, in order to yor Highnes Service is made farr greater, and the profitts so much lessened, that the same wth modesty enough, may be termed inconsiderable. In consideration whereof, May it please yor Highnes to appoint such competent Salaries for them as yor Highnes shall in yor gratious mind thinke fitt . . .

This was referred via Thurloe to the Council, and then passed on to a small committee.[108] Its report proposed a reasonable compromise:[109]

> We are humbly of opinion that the 4 Clerks belonginge to these said offices respectively have each of them 100 l. p. ann. a piece for their settled sallary and that they have also liberty to take and receive the fees usually taken heretofore accordinge to the particulars thereof mentioned in the paper annexed And we doe further humbly offer That in Case the said sallary and fees shall hereafter appear not to amount in the whole to 200 li per Ann for each of the said officers that then further Consideration thereof be had to make up the yearly profitts to their imployments to and to the said somme of 200 li per ann to each of them . . .

There was either a misconception as to what the ancient salaries of these posts had been or else deliberate deceit. Before 1642 the Clerks of the Signet had received no fee but £50 board wages a year each; those of the Privy Seal a £5 annual fee only. But in the fee schedules recommended by the Council Committee, the Privy Seal Clerks' salaries were stated to be £150 apiece,[110] unless this was what was now estimated to be needed to bring the total emoluments of the office up to the proposed £200 a year for each holder. We know that the value of these clerkships varied directly with the number of grants passing through them; as a deputy Privy Seal Clerk in 1660–1, Pepys has some relevant information on this.[111] In all probability, after the initial burst of appointments in 1654 and re-appointments with fee schedules annexed in 1655, the Protector's grant-making machinery was less used than that of his royal predecessors. Even if the Cromwellian patent rolls had survived, their contents might be something of an anticlimax.[112]

It is not, therefore, surprising that the radical pamphleteers of 1659 took up where those of 1653 had left off. They demanded that the (restored) Commonwealth should abolish fees, and institute a really effective self-denying Ordinance (or separation of powers) and, in substance if not in name, a salaried civil service.[113] It was not to be. The restored Rump did make one or two bows in the direction of administrative reform,[114] but other concerns supervened. Little pattern can be discerned in the matter of fees from May to October 1659 or from the end of December 1659 to 20 February 1660. The short-lived military regime of October to December perhaps showed more interest and had a greater impetus towards achieving such reforms, but this time the price of military dictatorship was felt to be excessive—even to achieve the rule of the Saints on Earth. The task of regulating fees in the face of 'country', or consumer criticism awaited the restored King and his ministers.

Gratuities

The income which some officials received in gratuities is not easily measured. Whereas fees were fixed and public, presents and tips normally rested on an informal basis. As we shall see later, a further problem arises from the need to distinguish them from bribes, that is gifts improperly or corruptly given and received.[115] As to their importance as a source of income, it is often hard to be sure what kind of officials took gratuities, or accepted presents.[116] When the discontented mathematician turned diplomat, John Pell, wrote grumbling to his wife that her last letter had taken three weeks to reach him in Switzerland, he went on:[117]

> If you would have the messengers of Whitehall careful to bring
> you your letters, you must give them something for their labour;
> and young Mr. Hartlib[118] would have more mind of your business,
> if he did not think he wrought for nothing; . . .

A suitor or client might offer a present to an important official but, as in more modern times, regular 'tipping' was commoner at the lower end of the hierarchy, among ushers, doorkeepers, porters, messengers and the like. Some of the parliamentary legislation which regulated fees also forbade gratuities.[119] By contrast a gratuity could occasionally achieve almost formal status, as between one government department and another. In October 1652 the Compounding Commissioners ordered the payment of a £5 gratuity to the officers of the Post Office, for having taken their letters to and fro for three years without any extra payment.[120]

Those best placed to exploit their official positions in order to gain additional, informal, but not necessarily illicit or corrupt remuneration of this kind, would have been the Council Secretaries, Frost and then Thurloe, and subsequently Thurloe as Secretary of State, and their respective staffs. Negative evidence is always dangerous, but not invariably misleading. There is certainly less complaint or other evidence about gratuities for these years than has survived from before 1642.

vi ARREARS

Claims for more pay seem to have been as familiar a part of the seventeenth-century as they are of the twentieth-century scene. Our concern here is not, however, with the economic question of monetary in relation to real earnings, but with the more mundane matter of when—and whether—officials actually were paid. The men at the top were usually in the best position to press for prompt payment, while those concerned with out-payments and receipts normally saw to their own reimbursement out of the moneys for which they were responsible. But nearness to the centre of affairs did not always suffice. When the elder Gualter Frost, Secretary successively to the Committee of Both Kingdoms and that at Derby House and then to the Council of State, died in 1652, he left behind him a morass of debts dating from 1641–2 when he had been a commissary for the Protestant forces in Ireland. The State, his heirs and executors alleged and his political masters tacitly agreed, owed him several thousand pounds which he (and then his estate) in turn owed to various creditors, mainly those who had provided the supplies for which he had been the agent or middleman. This remained unsettled more than a year after his death.[1] And in February 1656 his eldest son petitioned the Protector's Council for £75 to cover certain extra disbursements, and for an increase of salary to meet his own expenses as Treasurer for the Council's contingencies (he was also one of its Clerks). He requested consideration, his charge being great. The item is docketed, cryptically: 'Remember it another time'.[2]

Changes of government, too, could leave a trail of unmet commitments, which involved officials. The ushers, messengers and doorkeepers who had attended the various committees of the Barebones Parliament petitioned the Protector in February 1654. He passed it on to the Council who called in Henry Scobell, Clerk of the Parliaments and Council Clerk; his report made on 12 April was read and received on the 27th. Certain payments were agreed to be owing, and some were in due course made, though Scobell's recommendations diverged from the figures given by the petitioners themselves.[3] The officers attending the Council of State purported to be in a like plight, the messengers' salaries all being over twelve months in arrears 'which hath bene mainly occasioned by the uncertainty of the times through the many Revolutions of government . . .'[4] Sometimes the accounts of the various treasurers and commissioners show that out-payments were made in one year for salaries due to officials for the year before, or even longer ago than that.[5] Even men once so privileged and influential as the Commissioners for Sequestration and Advance (alias the Compounding Commissioners) were over a year in arrears when the Treasury Commissioners reported on their case in 1656, likewise their entire staff. Payments totalling over £3,400 were advised to be due and were recommended for issue.[6] It was another thing for such substantial payments to be made, especially at a time when money was short thanks to the war with Spain and tax-cuts at home. The widow of a Receiver-General of land revenues claimed in 1657 that her husband had spent £90 in obtaining his patent and commission, paying fees and expenses, maintaining a clerk and travelling to London, and that she was also being charged with £180 arrears allegedly owed by him to the State.[7]

The families of officials who died at the wrong moment, financially speaking, had a particularly difficult time. Such was perhaps the case with Alice, widow of Thomas Smith, a Navy Commissioner of the 1640s and 50s and pre-Civil War secretary to the earl of Northumberland as Admiral of the Fleet and acting Lord High Admiral of England. Her petition was referred by the Council to the Admiralty and Navy Commissioners in April 1658. They found that Smith was owed £3,140. 12s. 11d. for expenditure on freight charges in the years 1643–51; as to the other debts which she claimed were owing to him, £2,501. 8s. 5d. (out of £2,824. 13s. 5d. claimed) had been assigned to him in Public Faith Bills 'of which the said commissioners can make no judgement in regard they know not how to trace the certainty of such kinds of debts'. A note signed by his fellow Navy Commissioners showed that out of the £3,140, £2,286 represented Smith's advances and £854 other people's which he had bought up at 12s. in the pound: that is, he had been speculating in unpaid debts owed by the State to other individuals. Mrs Smith had asked the Protector for £3,000 out of the total of £6,000 which her husband had been owed. It is not clear how much she finally received.[8]

Some of these 'hard-luck' stories should be taken with a certain scepticism. And without further evidence to provide a cross-check, it is often difficult to tell the genuine from the bogus. One Samuel Richardson wrote to the Secretary of State from Islington in May 1656, requesting various payments owing to him, or else that he might be allowed to buy a large quantity of fee-farm rents at Worcester House instead. He claimed to have lost a ship to the enemy eight or nine years before, and to have got nothing back on a purchase of soldiers' pay arrears made in December 1647. He also added in the margin of this, 'having served in a publik place 3 yeares without any allowance for the same being thirto appointed by the honerable the counsell of state that now is'.[9] Certainty of payments depended on the general buoyancy of the revenues as well as on influence. It could also depend on the state of a particular branch of the revenue if the payment had been assigned, such as the assignment of the Judges' salaries out of the customs. If this practice became too widespread, or if a particular revenue got overburdened, it defeated its own purpose; priorities then had to be worked out—or competed for—within different categories of revenue. Sometimes the delay lay with an official's own superiors, sometimes with those who received the warrant but could or would not obey it, as can be seen in a letter addressed to the Crown lands and fee-farms Trustees in the latter part of 1653:[10]

> Honoured Gent' It hath pleased you in your serious vein to consider of the allowance and Continuance of Salaries; yet fearing myselfe to be forgotten or retrencht (because I have not been importunate as (perhaps) some have, I thought it now a part of my duty to crave a warrant under yor hands for the two last Quarters of Lady Day and Midsomer I having obteined none since the 25th of December. 1652 although my hourely attendance hath been the same as in the very heat of the Businesse For which I shall etc.
> [in a different hand] who am your meniall Servant Robt. Greene.[10]

The most elaborate system of assignment was for the payment of different units of the army out of the assessment raised from particular areas. Civilian officials administered this locally, but the staff of the War Treasury were themselves affected by it.[11] When one county got overloaded, an assignment could be transferred to another.[12] From 1649 to 1659 the pay of the army in England did not get into such serious arrears as those which had bedevilled politics back in 1646-7. But the back pay for the troops who had served in the Civil Wars, and later for those stationed in Ireland and Scotland, was not all made good in cash. The army's arrears were largely met from English Crown lands and confiscated Irish property. Individual soldiers, or even whole units, who could not wait for their share or who preferred cash frequently sold their 'debentures' (tickets of arrears) at a discount, to dealers like the Mr Richardson mentioned above.[13] Many civilian creditors, including some officials, were allowed to have their debts owing from Parliament settled on the condition that they 'doubled', that is, lent as much again as they already had done and so received lands worth £2x where £x was the original debt.[14]

Arrears due to the one-time servants of Charles I and their possible settlement by the republican government, are another story. To summarise a complicated business at the danger of distortion, those who could make their case for having been loyal to the Parliament since 1642 could at least submit claims both from before 1642 and from the years of conflict (1642-8), and some of them were actually paid.[15] But this did not always work out to their satisfaction. Someone as close to the Cromwell family as William Smithesby, Keeper of the standing wardrobe and privy lodgings at Hampton Court, petitioned the Protector for a total of £13,110 due to him in the form of grants, unpaid annuities, board-wages, liveries and stipendiary fees, and expenses in the upkeep of Hampton. Of this no less than £10,000 represented ten years of a £1,000 annuity which he had bought (presumably as a speculative investment) for £6,250. He also gave evidence of his loyalty to the parliamentary cause; he asked to be allowed to collect the money which he was owed, out of arrears of revenues owing to the late king and the royal family and from debts still due to them; alternatively he asked for a yearly allowance to replace the £1,000 a year lost from the Petty Customs' account.[16] This presumably preceded the paper already cited in which Thomas Smithesby was said to have been promised £500 in lieu of all further claims on the house-keepership which had—in effect—been bought by his brother-in-law, the deputy Major-General for East Anglia, Major Hezekiah Haynes.[17]

Arrears could have quite different implications. In January 1657 three referees, appointed by the Protector, reported to him on a dispute between the county assessment Commissioners for Shropshire and John Llewellin petitioner and others concerned. They found that Llewellin had been a surety for one William Jewkes, late Receiver of Shropshire assessments, whose arrears owing to the State were £1,600; this spelt ruin for his surety. They found:[18]

> that the receaver hath imbezzeled the said moneys and converted
> it to his own use and with parte thereof bought an estate which the
> said Commissioners say they are of opinion that the Act of
> Parliament touching Assessments doth not warrant them to make
> sale of.

The other two sureties being themselves insolvent, it fell very hard on the petitioner whose loyalty they certified. So they recommended an order to levy part at least of the arrears on Jewkes's own estate. That was the other side of the picture. The settlement of pay arrears properly owing to officials, and the enjoyment by them of other material advantages, can be separated only very artificially from the question of favour and influence. Favours illicitly done, or influence improperly exerted in turn involve the misuse of office and misconduct by officials. And this raises the whole question of official probity and corruption.[19]

In concluding this discussion of pay and arrears, it is worth asking whether any differences emerge either between different levels of seniority, in different branches of the administration, or at different dates within the eleven years of republican rule. Generally, those worst placed were junior officers dependent on salaries which were not adequately secured on particular revenues, and who did not have powerful and benevolent masters, or 'friends at court'. It would be tempting to suggest that the Rump set a general tone of greater laxity and indulgence, and that officials were more likely to do well under the Commonwealth than under the Protectorate, with its increased financial stringency—and perhaps its more rigorous standards. But, for the moment, let us leave this as an unproven hypothesis, if one worth re-examining later in the light of other evidence. The main disposal of church, Crown and royalist lands took place between 1646 and 1652, while the great share-out in Ireland fell somewhat later (1652–5). Although there was a campaign in 1656–7 for 'discoveries', to hunt out lands and goods belonging to the state or the Protector, and improperly concealed by private persons,[20] by then little remained to be distributed. Together with the reduction of the assessment to an unprecedentedly low level by Parliament, this may have meant that from 1657 to 1659 the less influential salaried officer had a poorer prospect of prompt payment than at any time since the end of the Civil War. Standards of conduct apart, resources were scarcer in relation to commitments.

vii THE VALUE OF OFFICES

It would be naïve to calculate the value of offices to their holders from the various forms of official remuneration alone. Even in cases where the salary and the fees or poundage, if any, are known, there remains the problem of additional gains, whether licit or illicit. In some cases there were recognised perquisites, which had not been abolished under the Long Parliament or Commonwealth; such were the rights to dispose of chippings, shavings and sawdust in the naval timber yards, the one 'dead pay' allowed per ship's company and (probably) also for each troop of horse in the army, and gratuities where these were allowed in addition to fees, or as an alternative. It is much more difficult to assess the monetary value of the ability to do and to obtain favours, and of other comparable advantages gained through holding office. All this is before we begin to consider whether dishonesty and corruption were widespread, and whether they added significantly to the value of offices. Nor are we yet attempting to answer the question of whether office-holders were prospering more or less than members of other social groups and professions. This too needs to be considered in relation to their commitments, the expenditure which was economically or psychologically necessary for them in keeping up the positions which they held.[1]

For the reigns of James and Charles I, there are numerous contemporary estimates of the annual values of various offices. Some are in addition to separate calculations of their different component elements, such as salaries, diet and fees.[2] Have we anything comparable for the Commonwealth and the Protectorate? The answer is, very little; and some of the figures which we do have are suspect for one reason or another. In 1660 the annual value of the Second (or Treasurer's) Remembrancership in the Upper Exchequer was said to have fallen over the previous twenty years from £1,500–£2,000 to only £300 because of the abolition of wardship and other feudal incidents. But this was put forward as part of a claim for compensation.[3] When the pre-Civil War royalist holder's family were petitioning to recover the Custos Brevium office in Common Pleas from the Herbert family, they valued it at £2,000 a year.[4] In 1657 Monck thought that Johnston of Warriston's place as Clerk Register of Scotland was worth £2,000 a year; and in this case the holder's own estimate of his fees received from subordinate officials in 1656–7 was £2,214.[5] A junior post under the Scottish Council was, by contrast, said to be 'not worth 25 L. yearly' by Broghill in 1657.[6] Samuel Morland, who was to become a crypto-royalist in 1659 and a chronic projector and petitioner for pensions after the Restoration, complained in 1658 that his fees as a Signet Clerk had come to only £8 in the previous quarter, scarcely enough to pay for a writing clerk and the cost of parchment. Of the £150 a year salary, he wrote: 'I would willingly lose 1/3 to be freed from the trouble of soliciting and writing for the rest.'[7] This is a revealing commentary on the Signet Office emoluments discussed in the previous section of this chapter, and a reminder that salary payments were often far in arrears. On the other hand, it seems that Thurloe and Morland received half of Marchamont Nedham's profits from his position as official news-editor and newspaper-publisher. For the two-and-a-quarter years May 1656 to August 1658, this half-share came to £636. 6s. 6d., of which Nedham said that he had paid Thurloe £300 and Morland £72, the arrears still due to them according to Morland thus being £267. 16s. 6d., plus what had fallen due since 26 August.[8] Also from the last years of the Protectorate, Monck's brother-in-law, the future Restoration MP Dr Clarges, received various salaries totalling £250 p.a. as Agent in London for the armies in Ireland and Scotland. This was not always paid promptly; on the other hand the Agent was in a position to do many favours and perhaps to receive hidden benefits.[9]

Sometimes letters requesting help from Thurloe in obtaining offices for friends or relatives give a figure for their worth. Major-General Goffe wrote to the Secretary from his headquarters at Winchester in April 1656, on behalf of Nathaniel, son of the reverend Mr Whitfield, a returned New Englander. He suggested a customs waiter's place worth, he said, £100 a year, as an improvement on Whitfield's present employment as clerk under the Navy Commissioners, a clue to relative incomes perhaps.[10] Sometimes rumour could inflate. Philip Nye, the well-known congregationalist divine, assured Thurloe that the place of Registrar to the Ejection Commissioners (for purging unsatisfactory clergy), held by his son John, was not worth over £400 a year even while the ejection ordinance was in force, and would soon fall far below this. For technical reasons, he explained, 'the revenue of this place is open and as visible as any office his highnes hath to bestow'; over and above the established fees, 'I know the Registrer dares not in Conscience take a shilling'; yet the place had been 'a seasonable and happie providence' to him and his family, and 'it were a greate unthankfulnes, to the lord (& to the hand by which he conveied it) in me, if I should deminish it lessen it.'[11] A paper presented on behalf of the officers of the Lower Exchequer in 1655 purported to show, by comparing old and new receipts from fees, how particular offices had fallen in value, and so was meant to support a case for salary increases. This is worth looking at more closely (Table 4).

There are a few instances where the receipts in a particular office are measured against the expenses incurred by its holder. A rare instance survives in Thurloe's papers, of a note submitted by or on behalf of a major-general who was also on the Protector's Council. His salary as major-general was £6 a day, or £2,190 a year; as Councillor £1,000 a year; and he received from the regiments (of which, presumably, he was an officer) another £400, making a total of £3,590. On the outgoings side, his household expenses were £50 a week, or £2,600 a year, which seems fairly lavish; on stables and 'necessaries belonging', he spent £500, on servants' wages £700; his casual expenses were £500. The total was £4,300 a year, and he adds pithily: 'Wants 710. 0s. 0d.'—his income being overspent by nearly 20 per cent.[12] Whoever this was, he either had no landed (or other non-official) income or deliberately kept this and any expenditure arising from it completely distinct.

Some further evidence here relates to the republic's diplomatic agents serving abroad, although for a number of reasons they may not be typical of other officials. Mr Edward Rolt's total expenses for his embassy (strictly, his agency) to Sweden in 1655–6 came to £2,152. 14s. 1d.; his total receipts were £1,881. 9s. 1d.; the amount remaining unpaid and due to Rolt was therefore £271. 5s. 0d.[13] Major-General Jephson, who was appointed to go to Sweden in 1656, proposed to do things on an altogether grander scale, and set his charge for equipping himself and his train, and for embarking, alone at £1,170. Jephson fell ill and died on his return journey, almost certainly before his full, and somewhat outrageous claim had been met, for a dry comment has been added to the foot of the account: 'Post mortem nulla voluptas'.[14] A short mission to Paris, possibly one of those made by George Downing, in 1655, cost £249. 16s. 3d., leaving a net profit of £50. 3s. 9d., since £300 had been received.[15] The most copious, if not in all respects the most informative material of this kind relates to the nephew of the Commonwealth's Lord President, Richard Bradshaw, who was agent at Hamburg from 1649 to 1660. He was a prolific correspondent on money matters as on other topics.[16] In April 1657 he was sent on a special mission to Moscow, to

TABLE 4 Values of some Exchequer offices*

Office	Auditor of Receipt	Clerk of Pells	Teller	Chamberlain	Talley Cutter	Sergeant-at-Arms	Usher	Messenger
	£ s. d.	£ s. d.	£ s. d.	£	£ s. d.	£	£	£ s. d.
Former salary	316 13 4	333 15 0	31 13 4	57	6 0 0	—	6	6 16 10½
Former fees	1183 6 8	416 5 0	468 6 8	93	60 13 4	?	144	93 3 1½
Total	1500 0 0	750 0 0	500 0 0	150	66 13 4	100	150	100 0 0
Estimated fees in 1655	200 0 0	150 0 0	50 0 0	50	20 0 0	?	? or —	—
Suggested salary	600 0 0	300 0 0	350 0 0	50	40 0 0	?	50	25 0 0
For clerks	200 (for 4)	150 (for 3)	100 (for 2)	—	—			
Total	1000 0 0	600 0 0	500 0 0	100	60 0 0	(?)	(50)	(25)

* PRO, S.P. 18/97/58i, referred 10 April 1655, report by (?)Edward Fauconberge, 22 May. He suggested starting the new salaries as from Michaelmas 1654 'in regard the fees have been nothinge not a penny hithertoo'. Edward was one of the chamberlains; his better-known brother, Thomas Fauconberge, was the co-Auditor, but died some time between early May and mid-July (Will, P.C.C., 187 Aylett).

128

negotiate with the Tsar (the 'Great Duke', as Bradshaw calls him), and he got back to north Germany just over a year later. He claimed to have spent in all £2,906. 18s. 0d. on this agency. His expenses and receipts for the Hamburg post are hopelessly confused with the accounts for his activities as a buyer of powder, masts and other naval stores for the State; as Resident in north Germany and also—intermittently—in Denmark, he claimed to have received in all £11,112. 2s. 0d., and to have spent of his own £13,300. 2s. 10d., by October 1658. After rather more than nine years' employment he was thus owed £2,188. On his naval stores account, however, at least according to the Exchequer's reckoning, Bradshaw was £3,461. 5s. 10d. in pocket.[17] If—and it may be too big an assumption—we can take both these totals at their face value, he had thus netted £1,273 in nine years or so, which seems extraordinarily modest.

For every piece of solid evidence about the total value of offices, or the complete incomings and outgoings of office-holders, there are numerous references to individual items of payment. Taken in isolation, these are tedious and do not add up to anything coherent. Nor is it really possible to separate the question of valuation from those to which we must now turn: the legitimate exploitation of office-holding, and finally the dubious and improper gains made from it.

viii THE USE AND MISUSE OF OFFICE
FOR THE ADVANTAGE OF OFFICIALS

It is impossible to calculate what seventeenth-century civil servants made out of their positions over and above their direct gains as officials. But it would be a mistake to exclude the exploitation of office for private advantage because it cannot be quantified.[1] More difficult and interesting is to try to draw any kind of line between fair and reasonable behaviour, of men helping themselves and each other within the limits of the permissible, and conduct which, even by seventeenth-century standards, shades off into the impermissible. Again we can only generalise by means of particular instances. And, while we are—as always—at the mercy of the surviving evidence, what is available covers a remarkably wide range.

Sometimes it was no more than a matter of what we should call having 'contacts' in the right places. In June 1656 Griffith Bodurda, a minor official who was to be a back-bench MP in the next parliament, wrote to Mr John Powell 'att the Committee Chamber for the Admiralty' about a meeting which he was trying to arrange between one of Powell's superiors, Admiralty Commissioner Colonel John Clerke, and Chief Justice Glynne, a fellow Welshman for whom Bodurda was acting. The subject of the desired meeting is not clear, and the sheer problem of getting hold of people whom one wanted is perhaps all that is to be inferred.[2] John Rushworth, the compiler of historical records, wrote to 'his kind freind Mr. Hall att the Exchequer office in the Temple':[3]

> Sr. I have beene troubled with an Ague. else I had waited on you;
> I am in present want of the decree, for Impropriations: & the
> Information & plea, of James Maulever about Kthood business:
> It was in the yeare 1631: or thereabouts. I pray you spare noe Cost
> for a searche of them. & lett this bearer, receive them att yo[r]
> hands. whoe will Convey them to mee to Battersey; The Clerks
> whoe transcribe them, shall have what you please to direct this
> Bearer to give; For other fees & yo[r] paines I shall put them on the
> publique scoare: I am Sr. yr. very humble servt. Jo: Rushworth.

Later that year he wrote to 'his much respected friend', the influential William Jessop, on business of a different order:[4]

> I was engaged in a Journey tomorrow, into Essex, to meete the
> Warden of New Colledge about renewing of a Lease of some
> Concernemt. to my selfe: otherwise, I had given my personall
> Attendance; But Mr Greene my partner, in Col. Thorpes business;
> will Attend the Councell, & give them Information, as much as I
> Can in that business: wee have neither of us any advantage, but
> greate trouble, & vexations: only, wee interpose, with o[r] endevo[rs].,
> to see the publique satisfied, next, his Credito[rs]., & lastly, to gett
> o[r] selves a Discharge, for o[r] future securitie. I referre all to Mr
> Greene, (whoe hath laid out many thousand pounds in this business)
> what Answeare to returne to this [or their] Councell. bee pleased,
> Sr. to present my Excuse. and you will much engage y[r] very
> humble servt. Jo. Rushworth.

The Colonel Thorpe in question was a bankrupt whose affairs Rushworth and Greene had taken over;[5] he had been in prison since November 1653 on suspicion of forging 'double bills', for the purchase of confiscated royalist lands—a variant of the great 'forged debentures' scandal.[6]

In 1649 Viscount Monson MP petitioned the Council of State for the payment of his pension. In fact it was one granted long before to his wife, the widow of the Armada hero Lord Howard of Effingham, later created Earl of Nottingham. Monson who, like Sir Henry Mildmay, was one of those unattractive ex-courtiers and servants of Charles I who sat in judgment on their royal master, clearly felt that his case was a shaky one. He distinguished between:[7]

> ancient pensions warily graunted upon good considerations, and
> those of latter time, which were fraudulently requested, and as
> inconsiderately graunted, to the depressinge of the Crowne and
> exhaustion of the subject.

Again at the level of the titular peerage, in 1650 the Countess of Monmouth begged an Exchequer Auditor for the loan of one of his books for a few days, to help set her affairs in order. No reward is mentioned beyond ardent proffers of her gratitude and good will.[8] As one would expect, the Accounts Committee's papers contain several requests for favour—usually for speedy audit of the accounts concerned. But Thomas St Nicholas, a Kentish gentleman who had held financial posts in Lancashire and Yorkshire during the 1640s and was in difficulties through being separated from many of his papers, asked for more time: the accounts were largely in York and he was now back in Kent—or London.[9] More typically, in 1652, three MPs wrote to the Committee requesting speedy despatch for the accounts of the Treasurers for maimed soldiers and widows.[10] Parliament's victualling Agent at Carlisle, who was also the Customs Collector of the port there, asked for leave to keep a sizeable amount of money in hand, explaining the special difficulties of providing supplies at short notice in a region so barren of wealth and human resources.[11] Since the prolonged use of credit balances by treasurers, receivers and paymasters for their own profit had been notorious as a means of supplementing some official incomes before the Civil Wars[12] and was now being attacked by the Accounts Committee, there was more to this than might appear.

Two days before the battle of Worcester, the Admiralty Committee's secretary, Robert Coytmor, wrote to the Navy Commissioners in a way which implies the stretching of favour to its fullest legitimate limits. The problem arose from Major-General Harrison's interest in Mary-le-bone Park, the timber from which had earlier been reserved for the use of the navy. He was sending Harrison's agent on to them, having himself assured him:[13]

> That all the Commissioners would be ready to doe the Major
> Generall all the Civill respects and courtesyes that is meet for you,
> to doe, considering the great and weighty employment he is upon
> at present abroad, and that you would not suffer him to receive any
> damage att home if it lay in your power to prevent it.

Timber in an ex-royal forest provided the subject of a comparable appeal a few years later, as can be seen when a protectorate Navy Commissioner is found writing to one of his colleagues as follows:

> Sr. There came this day Mr. George Cooper Brother to Sr.
> Anthony Ashly Cooper, to Or Office, and was importunately
> urgent with my self (there being noe other of oʳ Bretherin in
> towne) to write unto you concerning some tymber trees in
> Clarendon Parke; which as hee affirmes, hee bought of the
> Contractors at Worcester House; though now they are challenged

by the State as reserved for the use of the Navy, and his earnest re[quest is that][14] you would forbear sale of them at this present turne; That hee may have a little liberty to cleere his Interest in them, or have Opportunity to purchase them upon equall termes with others, he lookeing upon the alienation of them from him as very prejudiciall in severall respects. This Gent^m being a freinde of mine, and a Fellow Trustee for Ministers maintenance I could not but recommend his desires to you with this addition from myself theat you will favo^r him in anything consistent with the publiq' good and the trust comitted to you, which shalbe acknowledged as a favo^r to yor affectionate freind & servant, . . .

A postscript adds:

Hee doth not intend the trees that are already felled, but such as are yet standing, hee also engageth to take noe advantage by the lapse of tyme if they be not taken away according to the tenor of the Act.[15]

The case evidently dragged on. Almost exactly three years later, after a written petition on the same matter had been referred to them by their Treasury colleagues, the Admiralty Commissioners had remarked in reply: 'We do a little wonder he should insist upon any right in this business, the State of the case being cleerly thus; . . .' They went on to explain that the trees in question had been unequivocally reserved for the navy's use in the Act of Sale; so from their point of view there could be no question of accepting Cooper's request.[16] Once more, the outcome is unclear. Ashley Cooper was no longer, even by the earlier date, a member of the Protector's Council; so the need to afford special favour to his brother was correspondingly less urgent. But George Cooper was a minor official himself, and it was this which seems to have given him some moral advantage in his encounter with Edward Hopkins, a returned New Englander who had originated in Shrewsbury.[17] Equally on the borderline was the request contained in a letter from Charles Longland, the Agent at Leghorn, to Thurloe in April 1657:[18]

I hav latly bauht a smale ship's lading of Seragusa [sic] wynes, & sent it hom to mr. Edward Goodwin, marchant, to sel for me. I had som thohts to have implored your honor's recommendations to his hynes or his councel, that the customs and excys mygt hav bin eas'd, this beinge a new sort of wyn, which I now send hom to try experiment of its acceptation and vent in Ingland [sic]; and in such cases favour is shewed all the world over for marchants incouragement in any new commerce or desygn; but herein I wil not pres any thing upon your honor, knowing your natural disposition to extend your favours and goodnes to your servant. I hav sent hom by the sayd ship a Barbary grey mare, not so young as I could wish her, but young enuf, I hoep, to breed a couple of colts at lest, as I am wel informed. If she wer but fyv year ould, I should think her worth his hihnes acceptance. She wil be braught unto your honor by mr. Goodwin, and presented you fre of al charges for his hyhnes I have not seen a Barbary horse soe tal as this, but a mare never soe: she wil be the fitter to breed; she was never shod til she cam hether, which made her lam; so I puld off her shooes again. She is not for the sadel, but for breed, if she proves to his hyhnes liking.

During the Protectorate a number of prominent republicans, his own one-time employers under the Commonwealth, are found appealing to Thurloe. It is not always clear which tale is a genuine hard-luck story and which a request for special favour. In August 1655 Sir Henry Vane wrote for help in winding up his father's estate, which included a miniature private armoury:[19]

> Sr. This Bearer who is Administrator of my Fathers personall estate and upon his comming downe to this place to apprayse and make sale of such goods as are appertaining unto him here, I have advised him to apply himself unto you, to obtaine the Lord Protector's or Councell's pleasure concerning the Armes that are in this Castle; that by such orders as shalbe thought fit to be given therein, the Administrator may know how to behave himself in what concerns him in such part of them as he shalbe able to prove my Fathers property in; as to their appraisement or Sale; and for what Concernes the State, there may be some course taken if it shalbe soe thought fitt, for their removall to New Castle or what other place shalbe judged meete; My purpose being if God please to prepare and dispose all things here for the residence of my Wife and Family the next Spring, and (if I may have leave) to make the Castle rather for pleasure than strength and fit it only for a dwelling house; for which purpose if I may have so great an obligation from you as to move on my behalf and procure an order to that effect and the removall of the guarrison, I shalbe ready on all occasions to acknowledge it, and esteeme it an addition of your favers and Civilitys unto him who is your ancient freind and very humble servant H. Vane.

At this time, it must be remembered, Vane was not yet regarded by the Protectorate authorities as an irreconcilable opponent. He had withdrawn from public affairs in May 1653 but had not yet taken much part in opposition. Very different was the situation by the time a report was made to the Protector, on a reference from Thurloe, about Vane's claim to the

Forest of Teesdale. In 1628 the Crown had sold various properties there to four London citizens, reserving certain forests, chases, parks and castles. The elder Vane had bought part of these lands with the forest from the citizens for £9,094. 11s. 3d. in 1634; in 1635 he had got a grant from the King of the reversion to the Master and Keepership of Barnard Castle forest after the death of the then holder, William Bowes, and the Keepership of Teesdale Forest, etc. The first grant was said to have excepted the forest, the second to have granted only the office of Bow-bearer; it is not clear on what grounds. For the past fourteen years (that is, by implication, since 1643 or so) Vane had been taking all the rents, issues and profits of the parks, forests and chases reserved originally to the Crown, which now belonged by right to the Commonwealth, and had generally behaved as if he owned the freehold.[20] On the face of it, this was a tale of abuse and chicanery; if so, it should presumably have been dealt with by the Obstructions Commissioners, or in 1656–7 by those for Discoveries (alias Concealments).

Thomas Scot, chief of Intelligence for the Rump and its Councils, had acquired some of the archiepiscopal estate at Lambeth, on part of which the State's barge-houses had been built. In December 1655 he begged Thurloe to procure him a rent for the same, or alternatively a lump sum composition to cover both the arrears and his whole interest in it. In October 1656, being about to leave Lambeth and settle in the country, he wrote a reminder to Thurloe, enclosing a letter to the Protector, in which he assessed his total claim at £5 per annum rent for six years plus 14 years' purchase (£70), a total of £100; or else the arrears could be counted as less but the price raised to $14\frac{1}{2}$ or 15 years.[21]

Hesilrige, like Vane, had important interests in the north-east, except that his were of more recent acquisition.[22] In Thurloe's papers is a memorandum from him that one Christopher Mickleton had been proved to be a delinquent back in January 1649, having acted as a 'providore' (or commissary) for the Earl of Newcastle's army during the first Civil War, for which he had duly been deprived of office and for-bidden to hold any public place (this would be according to the Ordinances of September and October 1647, whose enforcement fell within the Indemnity Committee's purview). But, alas, Mickleton was now made Prothonotary of the Court of Common Pleas at Durham and Deputy Register of the Chancery there. Not merely was this wrong because he was a convicted delinquent, but—o tempora, o mores—he would act revengefully against Hesilrige, especially as he would have charge of the records which concerned Sir Arthur's estates in county Durham.[23]

Vane's friend Richard Salwey had also acquired interests in forests. As late as November 1658 he wrote to the Secretary of State from Wychwood, on behalf of the borderers there who were being forced to contribute timber for the building of a wall, 'wherto we are sorely prest, by the great prejudice we continue to sustayn in relacŏn to the Lord Lenthal'. He begged for the new Protector's aid, it 'being the pleisure of poore men to dig, and the borderers to carry stone'. Only illness had kept him from waiting on Richard Cromwell himself; he had also approached Fleetwood, who had accepted the post of Lieutenant of Wychwood Forest at the entreaty of Lady Danvers, on behalf of her son, an infant.[24] Was this a genuine case where the rights of small men and local interests were being upheld against the mighty and influential (i.e. William Lenthall, the Master of the Rolls), as with Oliver Cromwell himself and the fen-men in the 1630s? Or was Salwey's appeal simply a rationalisation of the fact that his own interests were being damaged by the collection of material for the wall—whatever this was?

An exceedingly complicated dispute involved the allegedly wrongful sequestration of a wealthy Devon royalist, Sir John Stawell, or Stowell, K.B. There is some evidence that he was felt to have been harshly treated by both Rump and Barebones.[25] But any reversal would have threatened the purchasers of his various estates; one of these was the Dorset parliamentarian (and future pro-divorce pamphleteer of the Exclusion Crisis) William Lawrence of Wraxall. In November 1654 he issued a printed petition, addressed to the referees appointed by the Protector's Council, from Edinburgh, where he was acting as Commissioner for the administration of justice, to defend his title during his enforced absence on government service.[26] Was Lawrence asking for an improper favour? Even if one accepts that the sequestration of Stowell's estates was an abuse, this hardly implicates those who had bought them from the State. Publishing a printed petition, rather than relying on personal contacts, scarcely implies improper use of office or influence. A similar appeal but addressed to Parliament, this time against the loss of an estate which he had bought, was made by the poet, George Wither, who was also a minor official. Although Thomason has annotated 'Juggler' against Wither's name, the same point about reliance on open appeal rather than secret influence applies here too.[27]

Our last case is one of favour being used improperly, or at least of an accusation to this effect. In January 1652 one Edward Chappell wrote to John Bradshaw, who had just ceased to be permanent President of the Council but continued to be known as 'Lord'. He attacked the malicious behaviour of one Richard Floyde (alias Lloyd), who pretended—as a kinsman of Bradshaw—that his influence was necessary to get business done before the Council of State; Floyde refused to return Chappell's papers to him without a £50 payment, and threatened to burn them otherwise; he then had Chappell arrested on an action for alleged debts of £500. Chappell begged Bradshaw's help in this, and in stopping Floyde from taking his name in vain. This particular story can be taken a little further. On 21 April the Council's Admiralty Committee considered a reference made to it by order of the 9th, of an information by Richard Lloyd [sic] against Edmund [sic] Chappell. It concerned malicious words allegedly spoken by Chappell (as Lloyd later admitted) in the hearing of Lloyd's brother and not of himself; but a letter from his brother in the country was not found to contain the words alleged. Denis Bond was to report this to the Council. According to the letter, Chappell said that he had suffered heavy losses from the King's Party (as an Exeter merchant) and that Parliament should make good his ship and its equipment. Lloyd then produced a further answer to Chappell's charge against him. The previous October Chappell had asked him to present a petition to the Council about nineteen pieces of iron ordnance taken from him in 1641, for which he had allegedly been offered only a quarter of the value; accordingly he had had the matter referred to the Admiralty Committee. On the Committee's report and a certificate from Colonel Bennett (presumably as to the truth of the claim) it was then passed on to the Irish Affairs Committee of the Council plus Bennett. Chappell had achieved this, though Lloyd had wanted to present it direct to the Council and so to finish the business. Chappell said he could now do it for himself, without Lloyd's help, and refused to give any satisfaction or reward for the latter's efforts.[28]

> But said My Lord President was put downe to the lower end of the table, and not fitt to be ymployed any more in the businesse, And that this second Order from the Councell was good for nothing but to wipe his tayle, with much more to that purpose . . .

Lloyd claimed that he had devoted two months to this affair and begged for consideration. He added a vicious postscript: when asked why he had waited so long to claim for his guns, Chappell had said that he hoped the King would have won the war and then he would have got more satisfaction than he could expect from the Parliament. The truth of all this is hard to seek. It seems unlikely that Chappell would have appealed to Bradshaw personally if he had also been abusing him to other people, unless the alleged abuse followed the January appeal and this had had no result.

It would be wrong to imply that accusations were made only against eminent republicans, or that dubious appeals for help were made only by them. Cromwell's secretary (as Lord General and later as Protector) William Malyn was attacked in print, for obstructing petitions and other approaches, in a way which reflected on members of the inner circle of protectorians and army leaders. Again the reliability of a witness with an acute sense of grievance is a little suspect. The presence of a paranoid element in some of the attacks made on leading men does not prove them to be false; it is, however, a caution against accepting them too readily.

In 1657 a Captain John Bernard appealed against those who had conspired and poisoned Cromwell's mind against him since 1649. He alleged that he had spent £500 proving that Speaker Lenthall and 100 others were guilty of serving the Pope's interest, and that lands worth £200,000 a year were wrongly detained from the Commonwealth. This had all been suppressed by Major-Generals Whalley and Goffe, Colonels White and Grosvenor, the Muster-Master-General Dr Stanes, and the Judge Advocate Henry Whalley. In 1650 he had unearthed a Cavalier-Leveller plot, a discovery which Scot's assistant Captain Bishop and the Judge-Advocate for Lambert's forces in the north, Thomas Margetts, had suppressed. In 1651 he had been attacked by one Stephen Sprat, 'a Jesuited leveller'; at the High Court of Justice (which one is not clear) the Leveller leaders could prove nothing against him. Then he had been posted to Lytcott's regiment and had been trapped by his Colonel, other officers in the regiment and Margetts with accusations of making false muster returns when the regiment was in Fife. He was cleared of this and returned to Westminster in September 1651, only to be denounced before a local JP there as a cheat. In November, Malyn read his petition and the certificate clearing him from the false musters' charge:[29]

> Mr. Malyn being then impowred to read Petitions and Papers relating to the Army, and report the state thereof. But Master Malyn chose rather to sin against God, and his own soul in having respect to my great enemies, and also to ly against the truth, than to take that opportunity for doing good . . .

So he again prevented Bernard's business from reaching the Lord General. A further appeal did get through, and a Committee was set up, including Colonel Winthrop (Stephen, brother of John Winthrop II of Massachusetts), Lieutenant-Colonel Worsley (the future Major-General) and the ubiquitous Margetts. But a conspiracy by Lytcott and his Major and Judge-Advocate Whalley led to their report in turn being hushed up, and to Bernard again being condemned. Once more he had appealed to Cromwell; once more it was blocked by Malyn. But this time his case was referred to Major-Generals Whalley and Goffe—the latter was said to have admitted that Bernard was innocent and was being framed. Now Winthrop weighed in against him, threatening him with the debtors' prison for £600 which he had spent on the public good. Bernard's arrears were now referred to War Treasurer Blackwell who did nothing, being a crony of Malyn. He had only been saved since then by his neighbour Colonel Mill putting him on to his muster-roll, at 4s. 6d. a week, for the last two years. In 1656 yet another approach to Malyn got nowhere.

> Moreover being told by a friend, how Maj. Gen. Berry was as a father to Mr. Malyn, and the chief instrument to prefer him to

your Highnesse; I did thereupon state the foregoing particulars in an abstract 13 February 1656, and Maj. Gen. Berry promised Mr. Malyn should do me right. But Mr. Malyn and his confederates so surprised him, that after two months delay he justified Mr. Malyn in his manifest wickedness: moreover Col. Mill being a member of the same gathered Church with Mr. Malyn did on a sudden lay aside his engagement into the rest of the Referees to silence the clamors of my creditors, and declared to one of them that I have nothing due from the Commonwealth, nor no Estate, and that he would not give 3d. for any Estate I should recover, . . .

Mill then stood aside, to allow Bernard's creditor to arrest him. Another supplication to Mill failed. He then tried a Dr Wells on the Popish plot line: 'to make your Highness odious, in order to their laying your Honour in the dust'. Wells took his letter about it to the Protector:

And they came to my house about it, at which time I discovered some part of the conspiracy to him in general terms, and told him it was very dangerous to proceed in laying it open until the aforementioned Officers and members of the Army were either undeceived, or removed.

An appeal for a confrontation with his accusers before the Protector was refused by their influence. And his accusation coming to Malyn's hands, 'he being Agent for them all', another frame-up had been contrived. Bernard was now in prison on a charge of felony and burglary, being falsely accused of having broken into Winthrop's Westminster house with two fellow criminals. It was this which had finally driven him to appeal in print to the Protector, for justice as between him and his enemies, notably Winthrop:

And I presse you the more for a speedy strict examination, which may be done in 24 houres; and so prevent the further laying open the nakedness of your Officers, which hath been your secret enemies design to force me unto all along, especially ever since 29 July 1651, . . .

One of those accused with Bernard had since cleared himself and Winthrop had had to drop the charges against him, but maliciously maintained them against Bernard. And so on . . . Who noticed this when even George Thomason, the assiduous collector of tracts, seems to have missed it, and whether there is anything there besides the wanderings of a sick mind, we shall probably never know.

John Bernard was certainly not alone in using the printed word to demonstrate his acute sense of grievance. Towards the opposite end of the political spectrum (since he was pro-Leveller whereas for Bernard the Levellers were part of the Popish plot), the appropriately named James Frese, Freize or Freeze, an unsuccessful Muscovy merchant, kept up a long barrage of complaints. He spent most of the years 1646–9 in the Fleet Prison for debt, and like many radical pamphleteers he attacked the whole system of indefinite imprisonment for debt and—above all—the prison staffs who made their profits out of the prisoners' miseries.[30] One of these prison officers was a particularly frequent target, and even became the subject of a parliamentary investigation. This was the Speaker's brother, Sir John Lenthall, Warden of the King's Bench prison. In 1647 Frese published a petition to Parliament explaining that, back in 1645, he and two others had discovered secret pro-royalist treasons by Lenthall, and had reported this to Parliament's examinations committee, via the committee at Salters' Hall. But Laurence Whitaker, the examinations chairman, had reported to the House clearing Lenthall and inculpating them. Frese had since suffered fourteen months in the Fleet by the indirect practices of Lenthall and with the compliance of its Warden, Henry Hopkins—this was after a peregrination through the prison of King's Bench itself and that of the White Lion in Southwark. His inability to pay the gaoler's fees meant that he was kept a close prisoner, while Lenthall and Whitaker had his papers rifled in order to destroy incriminating evidence—of the former's treason and the latter's perjury. Frese said that he had made his whole estate over to a Mr John Baker of Coleman Street, his leading creditor, and others as far back as 1637. Even the radical MP Henry Marten was accused of keeping a report about this, from the Committee on poor prisoners for debt, in his pocket for five years. Altogether it was a sorry tale of chicanery and malpractice.[31] And one might suspect Frese at least of an element of Mr Micawber if not of mild persecution mania, were it not for the other evidence which we have against Lenthall.[32]

ix CORRUPTION

No civilisation has yet existed in which the boundary between the permissible and the impermissible has been clear and precise at every point. Moreover, setting aside some of the very primitive societies studied by anthropologists and others postulated by pre-historians, it is a condition of the human situation that this should be so. But the alignment of that border and the particular areas of doubt and ambiguity along it vary greatly with time and place. The tests of what constituted abuse of official position, dishonesty and corruption in mid-seventeenth-century England are obviously not those which we should apply in public life today. Indeed it is tempting to agree with Professor Hurstfield that all pre-nineteenth-century systems of government lacked some of the basic prerequisites for proper standards of conduct. On this view, patronage, venality, payment by fees and gratuities, use of influence, are all part of a larger whole; and a good deal of what today would be regarded as impermissible and even dishonest was a necessary part of it. No doubt some individuals were, even by such pre-modern standards, less honest than others. Perhaps some whole eras were characterised by greater laxity—usually spreading from the top downwards. But it was mainly a matter of degree, and we should not expect to find great differences between one pre-modern administration and another.[1] As against this another modern historian, Mrs M. Prestwich, writes of the 'cancer of corruption' spreading through the court and government of Jacobean England, by contrast with the situation under Elizabeth I or in Colbertian France:[2] a far cry from Gibbon's description of corruption as 'the most infallible symptom of constitutional liberty'.[3] It is not necessary here to adjudicate between recent authorities where they disagree about the reign of James I, only to differentiate between their respective approaches to the problem of corruption. One hypothesis which we must keep in mind is that there can be little to choose between e.g. the 1620s, the 1650s, the 1680s, because of the limits imposed by the underlying nature of the system. In the face of this institutional determinism, it may be suggested that there are, on the contrary, marked differences between the 1620s and the 1630s, and that logically there is no reason why there should not be at least equally marked contrasts between the 1650s and the 1660s, or even between 1649–53 and 1654–9.

In trying to assess the quality of republican government, whether under the Commonwealth or the Protectorate, there is an immediate problem about the evidence. As will shortly be seen, there is a good deal of this, and it relates to a wide range of malpractices, real or alleged. Does this represent no more than the tip of the iceberg breaking surface, and so signify a thoroughly corrupt system? Alternatively does it indicate a fairly rigorous attempt to clean things up and to enforce higher standards? It would be a mistake to answer this question here and now; we shall return to it after our review of the cases for which there is record.

Corruption can take many forms, and we must distinguish several distinct kinds of dishonesty and abuse involving officials in republican England. Often, however, the story of a single man's activities involves more than one of them. Put bluntly, these are forgery, fraudulent accounting, peculation and malversation (that is, misuse of public money or supplies), extortion, improper pressure to secure improper advantages out of government action, and bribery for the same ends. Some are more characteristic than others of different branches of government or different types of official.

Parliamentary legislation showed an awareness of the dangers. The Excise Act of 1649 prescribed severe penalties for anyone who attempted to corrupt an excise officer, and for any officers who were so suborned.[4]

Perhaps the fact that this was written into the provisions for the excise administration more specifically than elsewhere indicates that it was felt to be a more acute danger there. There was a great deal of resistance to the collection of excise; whether there was more attempted or actual bribery to evade payment is less sure.

Forgery

Reference has already been made to Crown lands and rents being used to meet the army's pay arrears. The machinery for this involved the issue, by the War Treasurers' office, of 'debentures', or certificates as to the amounts owing to the individuals and units concerned. 'False', or forged, debentures had first come to Parliament's notice as early as February 1650. The Army Committee reported on the matter the following April; at this stage it was ex-Crown lands which were being used to meet the army's pay arrears. A certain Abraham Granger had been caught and sentenced together with several accomplices. Then on 11 June 1651, after most of the Crown lands and fee-farm rents had been sold, the Worcester House Trustees (who were in charge of fee-farm sales) were sent an anonymous letter. The author alleged great abuses to the State and the soldiery, through this traffic; he named several participants including Lieutenant-Colonel John Jackson, who was Treasurer of the Excise and Agent for the new forces raised for Ireland in the later 1640s. In the latter capacity Jackson was responsible for transmitting sums earmarked on the excise which totalled £750,000. The informer proposed cross-examination of some of those concerned and wanted his own name withheld until they were safely convicted, as he had got his story from them 'in their iollity'. Granger and company may by then have served their year in prison and been released, or else it may be that—for some reason which our sources do not explain—he and the others had never, in fact, been committed. Renewed activity is evident in 1652. At the end of May the second ringleader, Joshua Fugill, and various others were lodged in Newgate Prison, and a search warrant was out for the rest, including Granger. A paper dated 13 August named twelve people already under arrest, fifteen for whom there were warrants out and against whom there was detailed information, nine others for whom there was much evidence but as yet no warrants, while there was a further 'pending' category including the entire staffs of both Worcester and Drury Houses (the latter being the seat of the so-called 'Treason Trustees', responsible for the sale of ex-royalist lands). Jackson was again named, in the second category. Oddly, or maybe not so oddly, back in 1650 he had sought and been granted indemnity against prosecution by someone else whom he was himself prosecuting, not at law but before the Army Committee, over forged debentures! Meanwhile Fugill gave a bond for £2,000 and his two sureties bonds for £200 each, for his appearance the following October. And in that Michaelmas term a civil action in one of the courts tells of a would-be purchaser, the influential Alderman John Fowke, himself the Comptroller for the sale of church lands, having had counterfeit debentures sold him by the defendant—a case, perhaps, of the biter bit. Yet in June 1653 George Bishop, the late government's counter-intelligence expert (who worked immediately under Thomas Scot, the regicide MP), expounding in a memo for the new Council his own part in the investigations, referred back to 1652 but wrote as if the entire gang were still out on bail. Nemesis did not finally overtake them until the latter part of 1654, whether or not this was another instance of the Protectorate finally bringing to completion what the Commonwealth could not, or would not do. Those swept into the net now included an Assistant Cashier of the naval Prize Office, as well as the inevitable Fugill and Granger. Once again Colonel Jackson was incriminated but not arrested, though he was not employed in financial administration after 1653. Colonel John White (Clerk of the Ordnance as well as a Contractor and Trustee for land sales), Edward Greene (co-registrar Accountant to the fee-farm and Treason Trustees), and Philip Tandy (another official at Drury House) were also again named.

It is the republican officials involved with whom we are concerned here. Of those named, Jackson went on Cromwell's West Indian expedition of 1654–5, despite the protests of the army commander, General Venables. Afterwards Venables condemned both Jackson's past record as a forger and perjurer, and his conduct in the Caribbean, where according to Venables he had compounded bigamy at home with adultery and drunkenness in the Barbados and cowardice in the face of the enemy on Hispaniola. It was a strange choice for Cromwell to have made as Adjutant-General, particularly if Venables was himself speaking the truth when he said that he had tried to warn the Protector about Jackson; he invoked an independent witness to this.[5] Jackson apparently survived, but remained out of employment until 1659, when on his re-entry to office he was to be described by a hostile writer as 'A seeker, lay preacher, Exciseman';[6] for some this would have been enough in itself to damn him without any taint of corruption. White, by contrast, became a political opponent of the Protectorate, and was removed from the Clerkship of the Ordnance in 1656; he was even arrested on suspicion of treason in 1658. He resumed office as a republican under the restored Commonwealth of 1659 and acted under the military regime of that autumn, following which he was described—from the Right—as 'a man of strange opinions'.[7] Greene we have already met, involved in business with John Rushworth in 1655, but his official employment at Drury House had come to an end before that.[8] Tandy, something of a minor pluralist, was removed for temporary mental incapacity in April of that year, but was sufficiently recovered—and in favour—to be paid his arrears so that he could go over to Ireland in 1658, where he became a lay preacher—to provide the ideological superstructure, no doubt, for his earlier land speculations there.[9] It is notable that we have only Granger's testimony for their involvement, and from other evidence he was a resourceful scoundrel, to whom bearing false witness would not have come hard. As it is, among the officials whom he implicated in the conspiracy the score might read something like this: one sincere republican (White) not guilty of fraud, one junior bureaucrat (Syddall of the Prize Office) probably guilty, and one senior one (Jackson) certainly so, one probable case of mental unbalance (Tandy), and one non-proven (Greene).[10]

The Cromwellian authorities were bedevilled by a strangely similar scandal in 1657–8 which again had first blown up in 1653. When ships of the navy came back to port after long cruises or missions abroad, there was seldom enough ready money in hand to pay the crews all that they were owed in arrears of pay. Accordingly tickets were issued giving the amounts still due; as with soldiers' debentures, these were sometimes bought at a discount by dealers. This in itself was not illegal. But it was also alleged that forged tickets were in circulation, and that tickets were being made up from the ships' books for men who had deserted, from which the purser or others would subsequently take the profits.[11] As early as April 1653, when Richard Hutchinson was looking for an excuse to resign from his office as Navy Treasurer, he had criticised the system of payment by tickets:[12]

> I am apprehensive what the danger and hazard of such payment will unavoydablie be, & must professe in those confusions I would not continue my employmt. for more then I will speake of . . .

He complained, too, of duplicate and counterfeit tickets. This was borne out by a report made a few months later by himself and two other Navy Commissioners:[13]

> Wee find many frauds and imbezelmts. Counterfeiting of tickets and other abuses referring to the Navall affaires, which in case there bee not power given to some persons appointed to that purpose, otherwise then to prosecute the ordinary course of law wee see little remedy likely to bee, for that there is a tendernesse to take away the lives of men, and many times want of cleare proof as to the Condemning persons though proof sufficient for inferior punishmts. if some were impowered to inflict other punishmts. upon the finding out such abuses, which wee conceive will bee much better then now it is, and bee a meanes to prevent many abuses wch. now are acted

An interesting point, though one not immediately relevant here, is that the Commissioners felt the death penalty for forgery to be a disincentive to conviction, and so an inefficient deterrent. In 1657, in the face of similar complaints, it was ordered that henceforth all such tickets should be made out on a standard printed form, with only the names, dates, amounts and signatures to be added by hand.[14] Presumably printed forgery was felt to be more difficult, or at least a more elaborate undertaking. Shortly after this came an order forbidding the issue of tickets to men on ships in home, that is British, waters.[15] But this clearly proved unenforceable. Unlike the forged debentures' case, the counterfeiting of seamen's tickets appears to have been a chronic problem, widely diffused on a small scale, rather than a conspiracy master-minded by professional criminals.

Dishonest treasurers and accountants

The opportunity to make illicit gains through fraudulent accounting was open to only relatively few officials, and on a grand scale to a mere handful. Moreover the dual checks of the Exchequer Auditors and the two (army and civil) accounts committees would seem likely to have inhibited those so tempted. Much of the Accounts Committee's routine business involved sums of money unaccounted for from years before—often from the time of the Civil War (1642–6).[16] Often there was no implication of dishonesty, although appeals to the Indemnity Committee (and later the Commissioners) from the Accounts Committee show that some accountants felt the need to invoke protection. The main legislation (passed from 1647 on) covered men for what they had done on Parliament's orders, or on those of authorities acting under it, but specifically excluded those whose accounts were held to be unsatisfactory or suspicious. However, it proved impossible to keep these categories distinct, hence such contradictions between different parts of the Indemnity Ordinances.[17] Sometimes an element of political prejudice may have been involved. In the autumn of 1648 the House of Commons, in which the moderates or so-called 'Presbyterians' then had a majority, went out of its way to approve the accounts of Sir John Clotworthy, who had been active in the Irish campaigns since 1641. We must not, of course, credit Sir John and his friends with foreknowledge of Pride's Purge, but it turned out to have been then or never: at least then or not until February–March 1660! The Rump re-opened the matter, and the whole dossier concerning Clotworthy and his fellow accountants was passed first to the Council of State, in September 1649, and then the following winter to the Accounts Committee. They were still wrestling with it well into 1650. Clotworthy and his associates do not seem to have had to make good any arrears, and the matter was left unsettled—for another ten years.[18]

As for the Treasurers-at-war and their staffs, whatever suspicions might attach to those who made large personal fortunes while in this service,[19] the only overt scandal concerned George Bilton, Deputy Treasurer for the forces in Scotland. The evidence is characteristically ambiguous and incomplete. Bilton had held this important post since the winter of 1651–2 and that of Receiver-General of the assessment in Scotland from 1653 or 1654; he obviously enjoyed the close confidence of successive commanders-in-chief. On 20 November 1655 Monck wrote to Thurloe excusing the Deputy Treasurer for his misfortune in having lent £5,000 of the State's money to a merchant, one Captain Bressil,[20] who had then unluckily gone bankrupt. There is no hint at this stage of Bilton being more than unlucky. The storm broke in late February 1658, when Monck reported that £30,000 was involved in the Deputy Treasurer's misuse of public money; two days later he mentioned another £16,000— Bilton by then being in the notorious Tolbooth prison. A lengthy investigation involving the close co-operation of the War Treasurers in London was then set on foot. Bilton's estate at Kinneill in the Lothians was sequestered—barring certain incumbrances on it, including debts to Monck himself and two of the Scottish judges. By the end of Oliver Cromwell's lifetime, the sum to be recovered out of the culprit's estate had been agreed at £16,500. But no conclusion appears to have been reached before the summer of 1659, when the new Commonwealth Council of State took it up, and Bilton petitioned Monck for limited freedom within Edinburgh Castle after sixteen months' close arrest. He died in 1660. Presumably his lands and the coalmines and saltworks established on them then reverted to their original owners as part of the general Scottish Restoration settlement. Whether George Bilton was calculatingly dishonest, or merely careless and unlucky as well as self-interested, remains non-proven, though in his case the burden points towards guilt.[21]

Suspicion of 'fiddling' their accounts has also attached to two of the Rump's most prominent leaders. In 1647 the original (that is, Presbyterian appointed and dominated) Accounts Committee reported to Parliament's Navy Committee that the payment of arrears due to navy personnel was at a stand, and that the blockage was with the younger Sir Henry Vane, the Navy Treasurer.[22] There is further evidence to suggest that Vane, although not personally dishonest in the conventional sense, behaved—as Clarendon wrote of him—like a man 'loosed from ordinances', a Saint or 'superman' above the ordinary rules. Over half a century ago, C. H. Firth and the naval historian Oppenheim concluded that Vane's contemporary biographer George Sikes had exaggerated his pecuniary disinterestedness. When he was confirmed as Navy Treasurer by a special measure of July 1645, contrary to the self-denying Ordinance of that spring, Vane's tenure (during good behaviour) was made conditional on his paying in to the Receiver of the (ex-Crown) Revenues, half the clear net profits of the office. And Sikes says that he did just this.[23] But those who have examined the surviving naval accounts, for 1645–50, have not found any evidence of this repayment, and have concluded that Vane simply flouted this proviso and kept the lot.[24] This is not quite conclusive because he might possibly have made the repayment separately, direct to Fauconberge, the Receiver-General, not as a part of his navy accounting; and only fragments of Fauconberge's receipts and accounts have survived.[25]

The other point on which modern historians differ sharply from his first biographer—who may indeed better be called a hagiographer—concerns Vane's leaving the Treasurership at the end of 1650, which we have already discussed. According to Sikes:[26]

In the beginning of that expensive War, (as unwilling to make a prey of his Countries necessities) he resigned his Treasurership for the Navy, causing the customary dues of that Office to be converted into a Salary of a thousand pounds per annum. The bare poundage of all expense that way, which in times of peace came to about three thousand, would have amounted to neer twenty thousand by the year during the war with Holland. Were his personal circumstances and the condition of his Family-affaires at that season and since, well known, it would render this piece of self-denial the more memorable. Some inconsiderable matter, without his seeking, was allotted to him by the Parliament in lieu thereof.

But the Dutch War did not begin until 1652, and even Vane's role in the Commonwealth's foreign relations would hardly have enabled him to foresee it in 1650. So, chronologically speaking, this will not do. It is also less than the whole truth on the financial side. Before Vane's surrender was in question, Parliament had voted that the Treasurer should have a fixed salary of £1,000 p.a. in lieu of all existing fees, dues and perquisites. In so far as the scale of naval operations was if anything contracting at that time, with the defeat of Rupert's royalist squadron, this guaranteed a minimum stipend; in fact, however, there were still very considerable fleets at sea with the expedition to the West Indies and Virginia under Ayscue, blockade of the royalist-presbyterians in Scotland and further assaults on the Scillies and Channel Islands still in progress. So the £1,000 p.a. probably represented, and was meant to represent, a cut and the setting of a ceiling.[27] We may agree[28] that it is not Vane's ability or his honesty which is in question, but acceptance of Sikes's version of these transactions. On his personal probity, we can probably accept the more favourable verdict of his biographer:[29]

As for the keeping of his hands free from all manner of Bribes, or what ever might be so interpreted, all the while he was engaged in publick action, I refer you to his own solemn appeal on the Scaffold. . . . He openly challenged all men, to shew wherein he had defiled his hands with any mans blood or estate, or that he had sought himself in any publick place or capacity. . . . Many hundreds per annum, have been offered to some about him, in case they could but prevail with him, only not to appear against a proposal. On the least intimation of such a thing to him, he would conclude it to be some corrupt self-interested design, and set himself more vigilantly and industriously to oppose and quash it.

Before returning to the problem of corruption in naval administration, we must review the evidence against another Commonwealth leader, Sir Arthur Hesilrige, Bart. The case against Hesilrige is twofold, general and particular. In general he is held to have misused his position as Governor of the far north-eastern garrisons, especially that of Newcastle-on-Tyne, which he held from 1648 to 1654, in order to amass a great personal fortune, by acquiring one-time properties of the Bishop of Durham, either gratis or at outrageously cheap rates, and of using Scottish prisoners-of-war as a private subsidised labour force to exploit the coalmines there. The latest historian of Newcastle takes this as a fact, accepting the evidence adduced by earlier historians.[30] Short of an exhaustive examination both of local sources and of the records for dealings in episcopal and royalist lands, it is difficult to offer an opinion. Probably Hesilrige's apparently large-scale purchases did not represent cash transactions at all, but were payments to him, for earlier pay arrears and for his expenses in raising and equipping his own regiment (1642–4) and later as a garrison commander.[31] This may have been undesirable and it may not show the highest standards of self-denial in a revolutionary leader, but it is no more 'corrupt' than the acceptance by Fairfax and Cromwell of lands voted to them by Parliament for their services. Moreover if Sir Arthur was dishonestly misusing his position as Governor for personal gain, he was an audacious liar, a consummate hypocrite, or both. On 16 November 1649 he wrote to the Accounts Committee in London:[32]

Gent' I doe Intreat you that there may be a sub-Committee of Accompts in the County of Durham with as large powers as your ordinances grant; I beleive the State hath beene exceedeingly abused by Receivors of moneys and Goods in those partes, and that there are also moneyes in Collectors and Treasurers hands that were gathered for the Earle of New-Castles forces, I shall further assist you in this as you shall direct, It is resolved that Maior Mayer should goe into Ireland with all possible speed. I heare his Accompts are before you. I pray you grant him your dispatch that

so he may have noe excuse of delay, amongst us, and so with my
best respects to yor selves; I rest Gent' yo^{ur} affectionate servant.

After his fall from power and withdrawal into private life, he wrote more
defensively to their successors, on 23 November 1653:[33]

> Gent' I believe it is Notoriously knowne that I was sent downe
> by the Gen' Fairfax who had the Consent of parliament w^{ith}out
> which I could not have gone from parliament to take Care of
> Newcastle Gateside Tinemouth Castle and those parts. And that
> after Duke Hamiltons defeate att Preston the now Lord General
> Commanded me to attend him to the takeings in of Barwicke And
> Carlisle which I did and those two townes beinge unfurnished of
> all manner of provisions when they were given up to the General.
> He not knowinge How to provide better for them on the sudden
> made me the Gover^{nor} of both And by that I was impowered to
> dispose of monyes and all other necessarie provisions for there
> preservation And upon all occasions both parliament and the
> Counsel of State sent me lett^{ers} Commandinge me to take Care of
> the Counties and the Garrisons which I observed to the uttmost
> that lay in my power And I Nether spared monies nor any thinge
> else that I thought might preserve the whole or any part And Yet I
> disposed Not six-pence of the CommonWealths monyes But I
> should have done the like had it bin from my owne Purse and I
> Blesse the Lord the monyes were spent to good purpose For God
> keept both Counties and Garrisons. I hope I may very well justifie
> what I appointed to bee payed and if any perticuler sticke w^{ith}
> you if you please to require it I shall give you the reasons and
> grounds I went upon. My desire was to keepe the states mony
> what I could And I conceive it was the greatest frugalitie not to
> spare from Necessaries. My Writeings and powers are most in the
> North and Cannot in a short time bee produced. I hope you will
> find noe just Cause to delay the account And I intreate that y^{ou}
> will not stand strictly to observe formes where simple Plaine and
> honest dealinge appeares I shall endeavour to give you any
> satisfaction I am Gent' Your affectionate Servant

This is not, of course, specifically to do with church lands or the use of
prisoner-of-war labour; nor indeed did Hesilrige deny that he had come
to hold a large part of the former episcopal estates. When justifying his
refusal to take his seat in the Cromwellian 'Other' (or Upper) House, he
remarked jocularly:[34]

> I thought not to have troubled you, but now I am up, I will tell
> you truly why I will not take the Bishops' seat; because I know
> not how long after I shall keep the Bishops' lands. For no King no
> Bishop, no Bishop no King; we know the rule.

Blustering and high-handed, self-interested and self-important Sir Arthur certainly was. The general gravamen of dishonesty, however, seems to remain an open question.

One specific charge against him involves a *cause célèbre* of the period, his bitter personal collision with the Leveller leader John Lilburne. Again Newcastle's historian assumes Hesilrige's guilt, but Lilburne's latest and most authoritative biographer is more reserved.[35] The case involved Harraton colliery near Chester-le-Street in county Durham, which had belonged to a royalist delinquent. The Lilburne family (but not John himself) had an interest in it, and one Joseph Primate had the main stake as tenant. Primate claimed to have a lease from an earlier grantee and—not himself being a delinquent—sought to be left in possession. Hesilrige apparently claimed to hold it by lease from the Sequestration Committee for the north-east counties, a tenure which overrode the supposed rights of Primate and his fellow tenant, George Lilburne. The case blew up in November 1651 when John Lilburne publicly attacked Sir Arthur on behalf of Primate and his own relative. The matter of Harraton colliery was referred to the Commissioners for Compounding who devoted a series of meetings to it, from 6 November to 12 December. Lilburne rashly claimed that the Commissioners had been overawed by Hesilrige, who had used improper pressure to secure a wrong verdict, against the wishes (as he later alleged) of their radical chairman, Samuel Moyer. The House of Commons, possibly instigated not by Hesilrige but by Cromwell, who may have seen a golden opportunity to settle once and for all with a chronic and dangerous troublemaker, reacted violently to this attack on Sir Arthur and their appointees —the Compounding Commissioners (whom Lilburne had named as having been suborned). They treated it as a gross breach of privilege, and proceeded with ferocious zeal against Lilburne, imposing penal fines and banishment on pain of death if he returned.[36] Neither the editor of the Compounding Commissioners' papers nor any of the historians who have commented on the affair appear to have consulted the original record for the Commissioners' role. The fair-copy order book cited by Mrs Green was made up from the original rough minute-book, which shows at least nine meetings being devoted to Harraton. It is remarkable that amongst the entries for 13 November and p.m. 25 November there are some heavy crossings out.[37] At the final meeting on 12 December all seven commissioners were present and no vote is recorded as having been taken. The commissioners found that the whole colliery had been sequestered from Colonel Thomas Wrey since 1644, and no part of it discharged from sequestration as was alleged by John Lilburne (who appeared before them as Primate's solicitor). They saw no cause to take off the sequestration or any part of it, and formally resolved that all parties claiming any interest in it be left to take their course by law, by which means the right of present possession was to be established. They added —whether naïvely, gratuitously or corruptly, we can only guess:[38]

> And whereas it hath bin often publiquely alledged before us since this cause was depending that Sr Arthur Hezelrig was interested in the case & had not don according to Justice in seizeing upon the said Colliery Wee do declare that wee do not find by any thing that appeares to us that hee hath any interest at all in the said Coliery.

Either Hesilrige had a bad conscience about these proceedings against Lilburne, or else he possessed more compassion than he is sometimes credited with. At the height of his influence, in June 1659, the restored Rump reversed the January 1652 sentence, albeit posthumously as far as Lilburne himself was concerned.[39] That the Lilburne family had continued to regard Hesilrige with disfavour during the intervening years is not surprising. The Leveller's elder brother, Colonel Robert Lilburne, deputy Major-General for Lambert in Yorkshire 1655–6 and military commander at York for most of the period 1654–9, wrote sourly to Thurloe about Hesilrige's acquisition and tenure of Durham lands.[40] Again, this is evidence of disapproval, and a pointer to Sir Arthur's high-handedness and self-interest; it is not proof of dishonesty.

Bribery

With rare catholicity the Rump expelled one of its members for blasphemy (in effect unitarianism), one for adultery,[41] and a third for corruption. This was the Yorkshire peer who had got in on a by-election, Lord Howard of Escrick. Unlike Hesilrige and Harraton colliery, or Vane's tenure of the Treasurership of the Navy, his case is straightforward and the facts are agreed. In June 1650 Howard was accused in the House, probably by the millenarian General Thomas Harrison, of having accepted bribes from royalists in order to get them off the full penalties of sequestration and composition; and an investigation was under way by September. In 1649, Howard had been chairman of Parliament's Sequestrations Committee, although since April 1650 this business had been transferred to the Barons of the Exchequer (as appeals judges) and to the seven non-parliamentary Compounding Commissioners. And at one stage in 1644 he was chairman of the Committee for the Advancement of Money which met at Haberdashers' Hall. The only mystery is the length of time which the House took to have the evidence assembled for the committee which was appointed and then for its report to be made and acted upon. Were there other members who feared a thorough investigation of the whole compounding and sequestration machinery? We cannot know, but it seems at least possible. Nine months after the original charges against Howard, the parliamentary committee of inquiry sent an order to the Compounding Commissioners, that all persons—in the Commissioners' employment or otherwise—giving evidence as witnesses against Howard were to be indemnified against any counter-action. For if Howard had been exonerated, the fearful penalties for contempt of Parliament and breach of members' privileges might otherwise have been set in motion against them. Three months after this, in June 1651, the House found Howard guilty, and proceeded to punishment. The immense fine imposed and his imprisonment were soon remitted on his pleading poverty, old age and ill-health: actually he was only in his fifties and lived—albeit in great obscurity—for another twenty years! But the punishment of expulsion from the House and perpetual exclusion from membership of Parliament and public office remained as a salutary warning.[42]

The House could also be sensitive about allegations against officials whom it had appointed. In July 1651 one of the Trustees named to take charge of royalist lands forfeited for treason and to be sold for the public good was accused of trying to take money as a broker from candidates for subordinate places. The Trustee, a Mr Samuel Gookin, was said to have asked £50 as the price of procuring a surveyorship under the Act for sale. However, the information against him seems to have been dismissed, his election as a Trustee was confirmed, and he continued to act for the rest of the decade.[43] As against this, in its last months before the Cromwellian dissolution, the Rump again had a committee investigating abuses by trustees, contractors, officers and clerks acting under the authority of the House or any of its committees. This appears to have involved another of the Treason Trustees, Arthur Samwell, and the regicide MP for Reading, Daniel Blagrave.[44] The whole business of penal taxation and confiscation of estates for political reasons—of its very nature—offered peculiar scope for abuse and temptations to those engaged in its administration. A comparison may be made with the persecution of recusant Papists from the latter years of Elizabeth I to the Personal Rule of Charles I, and—more loosely—with other ideologically-motivated campaigns against minority groups and defeated opponents, in sixteenth- and seventeenth-century Europe and in our own times. The informer, the blackmailer, the perjurer, the briber, the bully and the cheat are all, alas, at a premium under such conditions. Perhaps what is most remarkable about the penal taxation and confiscations of the 1640s and 50s in England is not the fact of a few scoundrels being at work—and a number of abuses occurring—but that things were not far worse. Unfortunately the very density and volume of the composition records, the comparative inadequacy of other sources, such as those on sequestration, and—as always—the fortuitous survival of private letters and papers, makes it difficult to offer more than a few impressions. The printed *Calendar* alone shows that there was an immense number of petty disputes between the various men concerned with composition and sequestration at the local level, many of which involved denunciations—often mutual—for one kind of alleged malpractice or another. Thus a certain Mr Cheesman, ex-Cornet of Horse and later Agent for the Berkshire county sequestration commissioners, flits through its pages as both the object of attack and the instigator of complaints. In one collision with the Compounding Commissioners in London, his counsel was his erstwhile troop commander, Captain Bray, a leading Leveller sympathiser whom Cheesman had himself supported against the Generals.[45] The denunciation of five ex-sequestration commissioners in South Wales was also of political significance because this reflected on Colonel Philip Jones, future Cromwellian courtier and privy councillor, whose 'creatures' they were said to be. This anticipates the attempt to impeach Jones in the restored Rump of 1659, on grounds of common fame against a man who had risen to great wealth from such humble beginnings.[46] The long and bitter quarrel in Somerset between the supporters of Ashe and those of Pyne has already been cited. Disputes involving charges of corruption, mostly of showing undue favour to royalists, or engrossing lands and fines for private gain, are also recorded from the counties of Cambridge, Devon, Hereford, Lancaster, Nottingham and York.[47]

One specific case involving charges of bribery is more fully documented than most, although even here the dossier is incomplete. This concerned a Worcestershire landowner, Sir Edward Seabright, Bart., and his wife Elizabeth, who had extensive parliamentarian connections, being a daughter of Sir Richard Knightly of Fawsley. The case broke on 7 November 1650 when Daniel Cox, the Compounding Commissioners' Registrar, asked for a copy of the information against him of miscarriage in Seabright's case, being confident of clearing himself. An informer named Fowle alleged that Seabright had bribed Cox to have his case reheard after the witnesses had been suborned so that no delinquency would appear and the case for Sir Edward's having to compound or else be sequestered would thereby disappear and be deleted from the record. In the early months of 1651 another witness, or informer, named Collett enters the story. The Commissioners at this stage found no proof of Cox having been bribed, but evidence of his negligence in allowing records to be embezzled (i.e. wrongfully removed) and so of his unfitness to continue in office. On the other hand one John Stirt of Worcester was ordered to be arrested for bribing the witnesses in Seabright's case. Subsequently the Commissioners decided that, after all, Sir Edward had procured the incriminating depositions against himself by bribery, and had substituted others based on perjured evidence. All his estates, in several different counties, were therefore ordered to be re-sequestered (25 February 1651). And two weeks later the Worcestershire county commissioners were ordered to examine fresh matter against him. In April Seabright asked to know what the charges against him were in order to vindicate himself. He now denied having been a royalist at all, asserted that he had lent £1,000 to Parliament on the Public Faith, and had relieved various parliamentarian garrisons; yet he was wrongly accused before the Commissioners for the Advance of Money (the same men sitting in Haberdashers' Hall at different times during the week) of having sent horses to the King's army and of having accepted the King's grant of a commission of array. He had been acquitted of all this once, and expressed amazement at his re-sequestration. The next day he changed his tack and begged to be allowed to compound. Various references to the Commissioners' learned counsel followed. In June, Seabright again begged to be allowed to clear himself of the two charges—of delinquency and bribery; he was willing to pay a fine and offered to advance half of it before he was allowed to disprove the charges laid against himself; if he succeeded in this, the half should be repaid, otherwise he would pay the rest. On 16 June 1651 his fine was set at £3,618, estimated as one-sixth of the capital, or three times the annual value of his estates of inheritance. He was given three months to make good his accusations concerning the bribery charges, but the fine was to be paid with the usual time-limit. Cox then came back into the picture, wanting copies of the charges against himself. He admitted the miscarriage of certain documents in the case but counter-attacked by alleging that the main witness now called against him, one Robert Wakeman, had himself changed his evidence and was an interested party. The Worcester campaign of August–September 1651 caused remarkably little interruption to these proceedings. In October, the Commissioners' Counsel asked for instructions. They found that Lady Seabright had indeed given £400 to an intermediary, who had paid Wakeman £200, he in turn telling Cox and the Committee's then Messenger, Stephen Kirke, that there would be £50 for each of them; Stirt was also to have £80, and various payments were earmarked for the witnesses who were to withdraw their previous evidence and give it differently. In December, Seabright begged to be allowed to meet the bribery charges in the open; having paid half the fine, he was meanwhile to receive his rents from his Worcestershire tenants, i.e. his estate was not to be treated as if sequestered. The bribery hearing took place in January 1652. A report was ordered to be made to Parliament and Seabright's payment of the second half of his fine was to be respited until the House had given its decision on this. In March the onus in getting a decision from the House was placed on Seabright; he was given two months in which to do so, failing which he was to pay the rest of the fine. But in May 1652 he was given a further two months. In July the Commissioners agreed to hear more details about the value of Sir Edward's estate and the charges on it, which would affect assessment of the correct fine at one-sixth, but they refused to re-open the questions of principle as to delinquency and bribery. In September the Commissioners decided that no more time could be allowed for the other half-payment (we must remember that they were under constant pressure from the Revenue Committee and other bodies to produce ready cash); as a *quid pro quo* they offered not to report to Parliament the fact of Seabright's delinquency but only the matter of bribery. On 12 October 1652 he petitioned the House direct; he rehearsed his whole case afresh, starting with his having been framed for alleged delinquency before the Worcestershire county commissioners back in 1646. Again he offered to make the half-fine (£1,809) a free gift to Parliament: the most he conceded was having acted for the King before the battle of Edgehill (presumably between June[48] and October 1642). Parliament thereupon ordered the Compounding Commissioners to inquire into the bribery and delinquency charges and to stay all proceedings against Sir Edward meanwhile. At last, late in November, they agreed to hear both the main charges together, having repeatedly refused to do so before. Earlier witnesses and parties—Collett and others—reappeared, wanting a speedy hearing of what affected them. In March 1653, five weeks more were allowed, and the Worcestershire commissioners were ordered to send up all the relevant papers in their possession. The final hearing was to take place within two weeks of this. But about nine weeks later Seabright complained that the Worcestershire Committee were holding back some information favourable to his case, and the order to them, to send up everything relevant, was repeated. A hearing was ordered on 17 July, but so that he could have no possible grounds for saying that he had not been able to get his witnesses together in time, Seabright was given yet another six weeks' grace. Hearings took place on and off all that autumn. On 30 December 1653, after two changes of government and a more than 50 per cent change in the membership of the Compounding Commission,[49] the re-hearing verdict was at last given.

Seabright was then cleared of the charges of both bribery and delinquency, and discharged from sequestration. Payment of the second £1,809 was remitted shortly after this. In April 1654 he is found thanking the (then) Commissioners (by now with much reduced powers) and asking for restitution of the first half of the fine and for various rents in Worcestershire and Staffordshire wrongly received by the County Committees in question while his estates were sequestered. On 25 April the Commissioners resolved that Sir Edward had voluntarily offered to compound and had paid his half-fine freely in the normal manner of a delinquent and they had no authority, from Parliament or otherwise, to order its re-payment. Here the story peters out.[50] What does it tell us? That Lady Seabright did bribe, or try to bribe, witnesses; that Daniel Cox, the Commissioners' Registrar, was guilty of gross negligence for which he forfeited his office; that the whole machinery of composition and sequestration offered remarkable scope for procrastination by royalist delinquents as well as by the authorities; but also that a charge of bribery could be successfully rebutted given sufficient stamina—and perhaps influence.

If bribery and extortion were likely to find their fullest scope in the areas of compounding, advance and sequestration, such phenomena were far from unknown elsewhere. One of Rushworth's assistants in the Army Secretariat from 1648, Robert Spavin, was acting as Cromwell's secretary by 1649. In June of that year he was dismissed and disgraced for having been caught counterfeiting the Lieutenant-General's hand and seal in issuing 'protections' (against proceedings for debt, or to royalists) in his name, presumably for money. One letter-writer thought that Spavin would escape any severe punishment, because of his connections in high places.[51] If the allegations against his successor Malyn have any foundation, Cromwell—to say the least—made some dubious choices.

The army

There were scandals, too, involving army officers. Garrison commanders seem to have been the most prone to temptation—or else merely more likely to be found out. Keeping dead men's names on the books and drawing their pay (a long-standing abuse in the navy, from the sixteenth century to the eighteenth), or misusing funds allocated for repairing forts and castles or replenishing arms and munitions brought several to grief. William Clarke noted at the end of June 1651:[52]

> I thinke its a climacktericall yeare with our army officers, you and others reporte and [sic] divers amongst them that have suffered eclipses. . . . I have at this [time] articles against (I thinke) at least halfe a dozen officers. Col. Whichcot Governor of Windsor, Captain Harrison Gov. of Upnor, Captain Scrope Gov. of Harwich Lt. Foy, Lt. of a troop of horse others which I cannot for the present remember.

Earlier that summer there had been a court martial, in Scotland, of the Leveller ex-trooper who had risen to be a Lieutenant-Colonel, Edward Sexby. There is no evidence that this was a political 'frame-up'; nor indeed that Sexby was regarded as a Leveller or an opponent of the Rump or the Army High Command at this date. He had been acting as Governor of Portland, Dorset, in 1650, and had received orders to prepare part of this regiment for Ireland. This was then countermanded and he was ordered to take them up to Scotland. Only two of the articles brought against him at the court martial were really serious: one, that he had had a soldier executed at Morpeth, Northumberland, on the regiment's way north, without due process, the other that he had mustered some men (i.e. reported their presence and himself drawn their pay) who were absent. As to the first, Sexby was cleared, thanks to his own convincing defence and a supporting letter from Sir Arthur Hesilrige within whose command the execution had occurred. The second day's proceedings saw seven or eight hours of debate by the members of the court martial on the second article. Finally it was decided that Sexby must lose his commission for having detained the pay of seven or eight soldiers from his Portland force, 'Who would not goe with him for Ireland which (although as to his own intentions he did for the advancemente of the publiq. Service) yet now proves to bee the greatest crime coming under an Article of Warre'—as William Clarke recorded in conclusion.[53] There does not even seem to be proof, at least according to Clarke, that Sexby had held back the seven or eight men's pay for his personal gain rather than as a disciplinary measure. Politically it was a costly decision. Although he still had ahead of him a brief career in 1652 as a secret diplomatic emissary from the Council of State (or perhaps from Vane and Cromwell personally) to the *Frondeurs* of Bordeaux, Sexby soon returned to his old Leveller allegiance and became a dedicated and dangerous enemy of Cromwell and the Protectorate. No wonder that a week later Clarke recorded, 'There being some Articles Intended against Lt. Col. Crooke of Coll. [Charles] Fairefax's Regt. he hereupon laid downe his Comassion [*sic*]'.[54] Again, as with evidence of abuses and dishonesty in the civil administration, two quite contrary explanations are both—so far—compatible with the facts: that these cases show either how bad things were, or how effectively stricter standards were being enforced.

The navy

For much of the time under both Commonwealth and Protectorate, the navy constituted as large a branch of public expenditure as the army, or even exceeded it. Hence the performance of naval administrators was of great importance—and our interpretation of the evidence about them is crucial to any assessment of republican government as a whole. As to seagoing officers, Oppenheim, who generally extolled the probity and efficiency of the republican navy, provides a formidable list of delinquents. Out of forty-one cases of captains investigated for serious offences between 1652 and 1660, no less than twenty-four involved pecuniary dishonesty of one kind or another, and the vast majority of these dated from 1654–9;[55] while in the naval service ashore, accusations of petty embezzlement and misuse of stores and equipment appear to have been chronic. But the largest single body of evidence points to what those making the accusations portrayed as a major conspiracy to defraud the state—by the well-known shipbuilding and administrative family, the Petts of Chatham, and their allies. In the early 1650s, one Pett was Master Shipwright at Deptford, another the same at Woolwich, a third was a Navy Commissioner, and a fourth Clerk of the Cheque at Chatham; their clients and dependants were said to occupy numerous other posts. Vague and unspecific charges made by the Carpenter of Chatham dockyard late in 1651 to two shipwrights referred darkly to 'the kindred' and 'that knott' which if 'broke, it would tumble all out of itself'.[56] A Mr Adderley, the chaplain of the dockyard, joined in, inveighing that[57] 'wee did see by sad experience, it is not for the States Advantage to have a generation of brothers, Cosins, and Kindred, pack't together in one place of publique trust and service . . .' A vigorous counter-attack on Adderley, for failing to preach as the duty of his place required, is signed by four Petts. As a result of these charges and counter-charges, although the nature of the alleged abuses remained unclear, some action was taken. But once again we can see the weakness of multiple, overlapping authorities. In mid-December 1651 the Council directed its Admiralty Committee to consider appointing special commissioners to investigate the Pett-Adderley dispute, and two days later these commissioners received their instructions. They were to report back by the end of January. But in the middle of that month, as if in ignorance of the Council's action, Parliament referred the whole controversy about the running of Chatham dockyard to its Navy Committee. And some of the items which are described in the *Calendar* as proceedings before the special commissioners are, in fact, depositions taken before members of that Committee, although most seem to have been made to the commissioners.[58] John Taylor, Master Shipwright at Chatham, and George Maplesdon, an under-officer there, defended Joseph Pett and a colleague from the charge of having made faked entries in the books belonging to the Storekeeper's office; at worst they had made mistakes, and their alterations of the record were not to deceive, or to conceal illicit private gains.[59] Articles for and against a Captain John Browne (Governor of Upnor Castle on the Medway) show the lesser administrative staff of the yard deeply and evenly divided. Browne was defended by Adderley and other anti-Pett men; the Petts' supporters attacked him—for disloyalty, neglect and absenteeism, as well as fraud and embezzlement. These charges were spelt out in some detail.[60] Then it was the turn of Richard Holborne, Master Mastmaker and cousin to the resident commissioner (Peter Pett): disloyalty and embezzlement of timber were the main charges against him, and were likewise denied.[61] Joseph Pett, Assistant to the Master Shipwright (Peter Pett senior) admitted signing one of the pro-royalist Kentish petitions of 1648 but utterly denied the charge of embezzlement.[62] A longer document contains notes of examinations taken on oath before Colonels Thomson and Feilder and Mr Aldworth, MPs and members of the Navy Committee, from 'Witnesses to prove the charge presented against Commissioner Pett'. Some of the charges—of disloyalty, obstructing reform and deceiving the Regulators[63]—were vague and general; others, such as the embezzlement of nails and timber, misappropriation of a dwelling-house, false musters, more specific.[64] Then follows the case against Peter Pett's brother Phineas, Clerk of the Cheque at Chatham. Again false musters stand out from looser charges of abuse and appointing the wrong sort of man. Article 7 is characteristic:[65]

> That the sayd Clerke of the Checke hath Corruptly used the Power which the State hath intrusted him with for their service in his place, in that he doth therewith so much advance his own Punktillios, revenge private discontents and reward private Courtiers.

One or two of the articles against Joseph Pett, Assistant to the Master Shipwright and the Commissioner's cousin, were a little more down to earth than this,[66] which is hardly more than to say: 'he operates the patronage system to my [the deponent's] disadvantage'. There are further details about the charges against 'C' (either Christopher or Captain) Pett and Phineas and Joseph and against John Browne about the timber meant for Upnor Castle.[67] Peter Pett counter-attacked with a vigorous charge against Adderley the Minister, William Thomson the Master Caulker, and Thomas Colpott the Bos'n of the Yard. Misuse of supplies for his private gain, as well as general unfitness and absenteeism, were laid against the latter; neglect of preaching and slander against Adderley; 42 witnesses were allegedly ready to support these charges.[68] Further proofs against and rebuttals by the three accompanied this.[69] On 29 January Captain Phineas Pett replied to the charges of making false musters,[70] and then—in a way which is so typical of our sources—the evidence simply peters out. Whether because of mounting preparations for the naval war with the Dutch which was now looming near, or for less creditable reasons, the inquiry was never followed up. Thus by implication Commissioner Pett and his relatives and dependants were exonerated. At least they remained in office unpunished.

A slightly different perspective on Chatham dockyard is provided by a long letter to Thurloe from Captain John Taylor, the Master Shipwright there, early in the Protectorate. He referred to a petition on behalf of a 'companie of Cristians at Chatham' for a preaching minister to act with Adderley. Contrary to his earlier line as a Pett supporter, Taylor regretted Adderley's temporary suspension:

> if Through mistakes the Counsell should lay aside Mr. Adderley itt would be a thing of the sadest consequences amongst us, beyond what you can thinke of, he being a man knowen . . . to be sound in

doctrine unblamable in life and one who is tender to all in whom he sees the least apearans of God, never was such a man laid aside from preaching since the daies of the bishops power . . .

He knew that the real ground for action against Adderley was:

A distast taken against him by Commissioner Pett and the greate ground is because he said Mr. Pett did countenance ungodly men and did discountenance thos who feared God . . .

This should be no grounds for loss of place, and the right appointment of 'an Impartiall man' would heal this breach to the public advantage. 'Sir I know your principles and frendship alalonge to Sts: which makes me bould to laye this case breefly before you . . .' He begged for Thurloe's influence in effecting a reconciliation and ended with a further encomium on Adderley.[71] Taylor, whose role in the 1651–2 disputes appears relatively detached, seems to have occupied a neutral 'middle-ground' between the Petts and their opponents. In the conflict between Adderley and Pett he put the emphasis on moral-cum-doctrinal issues, rather than on the question of honesty and corruption. However, a kind of 'private empire' created by one family in a state dockyard seems—to say the least—administratively unhealthy.

Whatever the truth about this, some lesser cases are open to no reasonable doubt. When Captain Nehemiah Bourne was at Dover for the Admiralty and Navy Commissioners during the Dutch War, he was disgusted by the embezzlement of cables, hawsers, sails, and other materials which was going on there; these were being stolen from prizes taken into Dover and then sold privately. He perorated with righteous indignation:[72]

I cannot be silent in such cases where I see such great disapoyment [sic] of the cleare intentions of the state; which is to give an incouragemt. to all that serve you faytfully: I hope my freedome used in such cases as these will find a good acceptation with your Honours; (I having no other designe but to render myselfe faythfull to my trust and to prevent unavoidable inconveniences that will follow upon such disorderly and proposterous courses) . . .

Even here a trace of hyperbole may be suspected. Other letters from Bourne (one of the many returned New Englanders in the administration) show considerable touchiness about the respect due to him and to his authority, both before and after he became a Commissioner of the Navy himself in December 1652. Dover was not a regular naval base or a state dockyard, and the loyalty of the officials there is suspect on other grounds.[73] There had been a long and bitter wrangle over the appointment of a Foot-Post there back in 1649.[74] In 1650 came a collision between the army authorities and the Governor, Colonel Algernon Sidney, leading to his removal from the command. This also produced an unresolved deadlock as to whether the proceedings of a court martial, or of the General Council of Officers, were independent of (and co-equal in authority with) the jurisdiction of Parliament and the privilege of its members.[75]

Minor embezzlement cases can be found under the Protectorate, too, in the years 1655–7.[76] More serious in its implications was the case against John Ackworth, Store-keeper at Woolwich in 1658. He was suspended following charges of having misappropriated naval stores. Just over a month later he was readmitted, having paid an £80 fine, and given a bond of £1,500 for the faithful discharge of his duties in future. His son, who had removed cordage from the Yard, was merely suspended.[77] Soon after this, it was Chatham's turn again. The Master Caulker and two foremen were ordered to be dismissed for gross neglect which had led to the burning of the frigate *Happy Entrance*. But the Master Caulker had to be allowed back because the Navy Commissioners could not find a suitable replacement! He was one of the three men accused by Commissioner Pett in 1652.[78] At Portsmouth, the Master Joiner was dismissed for negligence about the same date, but his superior the Master Shipwright there testified on his behalf.[79] Periodically something of a clean-up seems to have been undertaken; perhaps in 1651–2 and 1653–4, with another in 1658. If we add the matter of Vane's profits and the forged seamen's tickets, then inefficiency and maldistribution of scarce resources (rewarding some people too well and others not enough) seems a weightier indictment than large-scale corruption.

Customs and Excise

In the customs administration, the likeliest type of offence was the bribing of junior officials in order to evade payment of duties on cargoes of imports. This might well be more convenient, and perhaps also cheaper, than smuggling.[80] One such case involved a Waiter and Searcher at Topsham, a creek (or sub-division) of the port of Exeter. He had been put out by the Customs Commissioners for 'undue carriage and unfaithfulness'; one of the witnesses against him subsequently appealed for indemnity.[81] In 1658 a case was brought in the Exchequer by the State against a merchant named Mico for having evaded payment by corrupting two under-officers—in the Port of London. The outcome of the suit is unclear, after Mico's counsel had succeeded in pleading a demurrer against forced self-incrimination.[82]

On the other hand, investigation of what looks on the surface like the biggest scandal of all was never pressed to a conclusion. Alternatively, this story may merely illustrate the extreme difficulties of accountants who were managers of a major revenue on a commission basis and at the same time government creditors. The central figure was Colonel Edmund Harvey, citizen and draper of London and recruiter MP for Great Bedwin in Wiltshire, who had been a regular attender as a Commissioner of Justice at the King's trial but was not a regicide (in that he did not sign the death warrant). When the customs establishment was remodelled by the Rump in April 1649, Harvey was named first among the new commissioners, and he continued in this capacity until November 1655. Then, only a week after he had entertained the Protector 'most magnificently' in Fulham Palace, which he had acquired as part of the bishop of London's erstwhile estates, he was arrested and sent to the Tower, charged with having cheated the State of £30,000 or more. Together with his brother-in-law, Captain Henry Langham, who occupied the strategic post of Cashier-General in the Treasury of the Customs, and others un-named, Harvey was said to have managed the customs completely for some years. Three weeks later, he and Langham were alleged to owe over £54,000 on a year and a quarter's account (from June 1654 to September 1655). On Boxing Day, after various pleas of ill-health etc. by himself and his wife, Harvey was released on bail. Regular extensions of this, parallel with repeated examinations of his accounts, followed during 1656. Consultations about possible legal proceedings against him were never followed up; eventually the debt which he and his fellow commissioners were held to owe was settled at £22,000 (reduced from £23,000); another £57,722 was definitely taken off their charge. The customs' accounts for these years show that this latter sum was in fact written off that for 1652–3, which was declared and passed in the Exchequer at the height of the investigations, in January 1656. The 1653–4 account was not declared until June 1657, but strangely it shows the £57,722 still being carried over from the previous one; this left the accountants still indebted to the State for almost exactly the same amount (£57,188). Their penultimate account, for June 1654 to Michaelmas 1655, was declared on the same day, and shows them owing a notional £50,384. Their last account of all, for the six months September 1655 to March 1656, which was passed along with its two immediate predecessors, reveals that the almost derisory sum of £326. 6s. 8d. had actually been levied on Harvey's goods and chattels by the sheriffs of London towards the original debt of £57,722, in order to produce the final consequence, namely that the accountants were at last 'Even and Quitt'.

It is a tangled skein. The importance of the London financial community to the Protectorate, indeed to any government, as potential creditors, needs no emphasis; and this may well have mitigated the severity of proceedings against Harvey and Langham. Whatever the truth of the matter, it is also possible that charges of fraud, as opposed to careless accounting or mismanagement, could not have been made to stick. The sweeping changes of customs personnel in 1655–6 suggest, at the very least, grave disquiet. But £326 seems a poor return for so much bother—and public scandal.[83]

Another apparently serious case which did reach the courts turns out on closer examination to be a mare's nest. This involved the regicide Lord Mayor, Sir Robert Tichborne, who was also a Customs Commissioner (1649–56), and an alleged seizure of smuggled gold bars. But the charges of misappropriating either the gold or the penal fine of £2,000 imposed on its importers dissolved in a cloud of contradictory witnesses. The surviving documents are more revealing about the internal structure of the London customs service, showing the close-knit family connection of the Langhams, to whom John Jackson was probably also related and whose honesty we know was suspect. But it tells us nothing about administrative corruption except on the old adage, 'no smoke without fire'. Were Tichborne and his associates in this case parties to Edmund Harvey's and Henry Langham's much bigger frauds? It seems unlikely that we shall ever know.[84]

The collection of the excise was open to the same type of malpractice as that of the customs. In practice most of the evidence relates to alleged abuses by collectors and resistance to payment rather than to accusations of bribery.[85] This is not to say that everyone in the excise was wholly honest; there was much contemporary discussion and controversy about how it should be administered, notably in 1649 and again in 1657–8.

Prisons and the law

Extortion was the commonest charge brought against the officers and clerks of the law courts and, above all, those involved in running the prisons. Without re-opening the large topics of law reform and fees, there is evidence (from Chancery orders issued both before the Protectorate Ordinance and after the Restoration) of abuses in that court and attempts to remedy them.[86] The various attacks on the Warden of the Upper Bench prison, and similar complaints against Henry Hopkins, Warden of the Fleet, should no doubt be treated with suspicion—as with present-day complaints by convicted criminals against prison officers. However, neither in the 1650s nor today does this prove all such complaints to be wholly unfounded. In the seventeenth century the law relating to debt meant that many otherwise perfectly respectable people spent time in prison, often spells of long duration.[87]

The way in which prisons were run, with the prisoners having to pay fees to their gaolers and for their own maintenance, had long been known to give scope for abuse.[88] In the 1640s several pamphlets and broadsides took up the refrain;[89] in October 1650 the Rump recognised the problem to the extent of appointing a committee on abuses by prison-keepers.[90] Nothing appears to have come of this. By the beginning of 1653 the Council of State had received so much evidence against one senior prison officer that it submitted the whole dossier to Parliament. This was a matter of some delicacy, for the accused was the Speaker's own brother, Sir John Lenthall, Marshal of the Upper Bench and Keeper of the Marshalsea. Even the Rump could not pass over the Council's submission in complete silence, but not surprisingly there was little inclination to pursue the matter, and the Rump referred it to the court of Upper Bench—the very body of which one branch was under attack.[91] Seven months later, the Barebones (in which the ex-Speaker did not sit) showed no such inhibitions. They ordered Sir John Lenthall's arrest and entrusted the management of the Marshalsea to Edward Dendy, the Council of State's Sergeant-at-Arms and a trusted republican. In August 1653 reports were made on the Upper Bench prison and its suspended Keeper. But the Barebones too, even in its short career, saw such minor reforms and remedial actions overtaken by the press of greater events, and no conclusion appears to have been reached.[92] Moreover, Parliament had again been anticipated by the Council. According to a hostile (royalist) newsletter-writer, they had been spending a lot of time on Sir John's case because one of the new Councillors himself wanted Lenthall's job! The endless sequence of investigations was resumed yet again by the Protector's Council early in 1654; the year after that Lenthall was trying to recover both his office and his 'book' (presumably a list of prisoners and what they owed) from Sergeant Dendy.[93]

In this instance we are fortunate in having a variety of evidence from different sources.[94] Unusually, too, we have Lenthall's own published defence, as well as the attacks on him. The general basis of his case was to argue that the very nature of his work, which involved mediating between imprisoned debtors and their creditors, meant that he made enemies. But he denied the charges of conniving in escapes by prisoners, or of accepting money for their improper release, and he even counter-attacked against the Hale law reform Committee who seem to have cross-examined him, alleging that their own chairman, the lawyer John Fountaine, was an ex-royalist who had taken part in a conspiracy against him back in 1643. As well as defending himself against other detailed accusations, Lenthall said with a rhetorical flourish that he would prefer to be in prison (his own prison?) rather than remain in the Messenger's custody; he took particular exception to Dendy lecturing him on how to observe Parliament's authority; finally he appealed to the Barebones, which was then sitting, for justice tempered with mercy. In the course of his defence he strongly implied that he had bought his office when he was granted it by patent from the King back in the 1630s; unspoken, perhaps, was a tacit assumption that this gave him a right to recover his outlay by running the Marshalsea at a profit.[95]

As in so many other cases we are left with a feeling of uncertainty. Was it the system which was at fault or the man; should we not, in Lenthall's case, agree that the evidence suggests something of both?

Some charges of corruption and investigations of abuses have an element at least of the political post-mortem about them. This applies to the Committee appointed by the Protector's Council in November 1655 on supposed abuses in the sale of Dean and Chapter lands, and the consequent losses to the State from false returns made by corrupt surveyors.[96] It is also true of the parliamentary committee of October 1656 on the alleged scandals associated with the Trustees for the sale of royalist lands forfeited for treason at Drury House. In this case it was decided after about ten weeks that the ex-doorkeeper to the Trustees had had a grievance and had been slandering them deliberately; they were exonerated and their accuser imprisoned.[97] But abuses against the State through the under-valuation of delinquents' estates were again cited when Commissioners were appointed to enforce the new Act on Catholic recusants' estates in September 1657.[98] So there seems to have been a continuing suspicion here, over and above the slanderous doorkeeper.

The attacks on Major-General Boteler and on Colonel Barkstead, the Governor of the Tower, in Richard Cromwell's Parliament,[99] and on Colonel Philip Jones in the restored Rump, certainly have something of this retaliatory character. This is cause for a certain wariness towards such charges, but not for their complete dismissal.

Some cases of apparent dishonesty may, on the contrary, indicate secret royalist sympathies.[100] This could be true of Thomas Beauchamp, Clerk-Register to the Trustees for the sale of the late king's and the rest of the royal family's goods. In January 1653 a Commons committee was appointed to investigate various charges of bribery and extortion against him. Nothing had been achieved by the fall of the Rump three months later, and in 1654 the inquiry was reactivated by the Protector's Council. But in 1660 Beauchamp pleaded very strongly that he had helped to save some items of the late king's possessions (pictures included) and to keep checks on the whereabouts of many others; he asked to be paid for this, which would have been remarkable effrontery if he were merely a corrupt republican functionary.[101]

Diplomatic agents abroad were particularly vulnerable to the offer of presents which could come very near to being bribes. Their pay and allowances were often heavily in arrears, and in seventeenth-century Europe generally it seems to have been assumed that visiting ambassadors and lesser envoys could expect presents from the governments of their host countries. How often this led them to send home deliberately misleading information, or to give advice in the interest of a foreign power rather than of their own, is hard to estimate. The evidence about one case under the Protectorate illustrates some of the complications. According to a modern Swedish historian, accepted by the foremost British authority on seventeenth-century Sweden and Anglo-Swedish relations, Cromwell's envoy sent to mediate in the Dano–Swedish conflict of 1657–8, Philip Meadowes, was bribed by the king of Sweden to the tune of 10,000 riksdaler (rixdollars).[102] No doubt this was more to the point than the Order of the Elephant which was bestowed upon him by the impecunious king of Denmark,[103] but there is no evidence that Meadowes allowed his judgment or his reports to be influenced by it. Moreover, the fact of the gift was soon known in London, for on 27 May 1658 Samuel Hartlib wrote to John Pell:[104]

> Of domestic news I told y[ou that] the kg. of Sweden has bestowed upon Mr. Mead[owes . . .] gen. the sum of 9000 rix-dollars, who hath [received in]structions to go, instead of resident Bradshaw [to the] Duke of Muscovia.

A fortnight later he reported that this last order had been counter-manded, and that Meadowes was going to the king of Sweden and not to 'the Muscovite'.[105] Apart from the discrepancy between 9,000 and 10,000, it seems a very public kind of bribe. For if Hartlib knew about it, the presumption must be that Meadowes's chief, Thurloe, did so too.[106]

It could be argued that in this respect the Protectorate's standards were lower than those of the Commonwealth. Having referred the general topic of bribes to *ad hoc* and then to standing committees in December 1648 and April, August and September 1650,[107] the following year the Rump had discussed a measure to prohibit the acceptance of any gift by a Minister of the Commonwealth abroad from any foreign state or prince. A bill to this effect was committed after a second reading; then, like so many of the Rump's other good intentions, it disappears from view.[108] In 1652, when the diplomatic crisis with the Dutch was developing into open war, the House was more concerned with preventing improper approaches being made by foreign envoys in this country to Members of Parliament and others.[109]

Thurloe

One last topic remains to be considered in relation to the Protectorate: the probity of John Thurloe himself. There is no adequate biography of Cromwell's Secretary of State,[110] and although he bequeathed a massive collection of papers for the benefit of posterity, Thurloe had ample opportunity to winnow incriminating items out of these in the years between his retirement from the public service and his death in 1668.

There seem to be four possible counts against him. The first is the suggestion that the East India Company offered him a valuable pearl (for his wife) in connection with the renewal and extension of their charter. The known facts are that one Richard Wylde, who wanted a three-year appointment as Consul at Surat and *carte blanche* to make what profit he could out of it, offered him a share in the pearl fisheries there and £500 a year, together with a 'fair jewel' for Mrs Thurloe. This was to be on condition that he, Wylde, was allowed to carry on a 'free and open trade' there with all the added advantages of being Consul. If the East India Company's patent was restored and he was sent instead as their president there, then 'the jewel only shall be presented as before with such other vanities out of India, as shall manifest the said Richard Wylde's thankfulness for Mr. Secretarys favour and assistance herein'. Wylde also appears to have petitioned the Protector about the Dutch at Pulo Run in the East Indies and their abuse of the 1654 treaty earlier that summer; there is no evidence that he had been in charge at Surat for over twenty years, although he was on the Company's committee in the early 1650s. His only subsequent posting was as a Writer to the Company's court at Surat in 1658. Vanities out of India indeed![111]

The second and third charges were brought up in 1659. During Richard Cromwell's Parliament it was rumoured that Thurloe had accepted an annual bribe of £1,000 from the farmers of the ale and beer excise for London and the area, to keep them free of all legal proceedings by their enemies the brewers, but that when the brewers threatened parliamentary action he went back on this.[112] On 28 July 1657 Thurloe had written to Henry Cromwell apparently strongly endorsing a plan for a single giant Customs and Excise farm for everything except the duties on ale and beer, and another unified farm for these. In this way it was hoped to raise £800,000 and £200,000 a year respectively, or at least £100,000 a year more than the current yield on the Customs and the Excise combined; 'and yet', the Secretary added, 'I believe we had very honest gents to be commissioners, and careful men too'.[113] But neither plan went through. The ale and beer excise for the London region (the City and suburbs, Westminster, Southwark, Middlesex and Surrey) was leased for three years at £128,400, or £42,800 per annum; other farms for counties or groups of counties followed.[114] And when Richard Cromwell's Parliament debated the excise in March–April 1659, it was the farmers and not the brewers who got into trouble, the latter being allowed the privilege of presenting their case against the former at the bar of the House. But there was no recorded mention of improper influence on the Secretary by either group.[115]

After his dismissal from the Secretaryship under the restored Commonwealth, Thurloe was accused of having made excessive profits in his capacity as Postmaster-General (1655–9). This charge is rather better documented because Thurloe had full statements of the Post Office accounts prepared, at least for 1659, to use in his own defence.[116] How far this was simply a piece of political retaliation by his erstwhile masters in the Rump or by friends of the last Postmaster-General but one, Attorney-General Edmund Prideaux MP (who died late in 1659), can only be surmised. When Thurloe was restored as co-Secretary of State briefly from March to May 1660, the Posts were kept out of his hands, but there were no further proceedings against him over this. Efficient management and personal profit went together under the system of farming. The point at which a high return became an excessive one must have been a matter of subjective judgment, then as now.

The last case is of a different character. Thurloe preserved several letters (some anonymous and some not addressed to him, but all clearly identifiable) from the well-known double agent, the ex-royalist Colonel Joseph Bampfield. He proposed a deal, whereby Thurloe was to assume the pre-emption of tin from the Cornish mines on a profit-sharing basis. The gain which Bampfield offered, initially at least, was to be 'of such a nature as you may lawfully receive it'. The main reason for supposing that Thurloe was at least prepared to consider this particular proposition comes from the sheer number of the Colonel's approaches to him about it, and from one or two remarks in the letters. But Bampfield, whose own position was to say the least equivocal, may well have wanted to trap Thurloe into some kind of indiscretion, which would then give him a hold over the Secretary. At one stage he appears to offer a guaranteed minimum of £5,000 a year: 'as to the objection you once made, that you did not desire to have to doe with Marchands accounts, I shall looke soe carefully after it, that you shall neither suffer, nor be troubled in it'.[117] Without trying to claim too much for a man who may plausibly be seen as the archetypal pliant bureaucrat, this still seems a slender basis for any general charge of corruption against Thurloe. That he made what he reasonably, and by his lights properly, could out of his offices, is not to be doubted. But the amassing of a vast fortune comparable to that of Robert Cecil in the 1600s, Strafford in the 1630s, or even Sunderland in the 1680s, was not within the ken of this prudent, useful but essentially limited man.[118]

The subject of corruption has a certain fascination for some historians, as for some political journalists and fiction-writers of today. But we must keep a sense of proportion, and—as R. H. Tawney once warned me[119]— avoid writing the pathology rather than the history of administration. Yet its importance in any general judgment of the system is undoubted, and the bland assumption that all sixteenth- and seventeenth-century administrators were corrupt in that their standards were far different from ours, while true, is unhelpful. We shall be better able, perhaps, to take the measure of this problem when we have looked at some of the men engaged in administration during these years and considered the economic role of office-holding in republican England.[120]

CHAPTER 4

SOCIAL BIOGRAPHY

i PURPOSE AND METHOD

The subject of this chapter is, quite simply, the men who staffed the institutions described in chapter 2, and who worked under the conditions discussed in chapter 3. But to say that is a little too easy. As with any body of people having certain attributes in common, whether they be astronauts, professional footballers, disc jockeys or academic historians, there are difficulties of definition. For this purpose I have included anyone who held a civil office between the Regicide (January 1649) and the return of the Secluded Members (February 1660). I have defined office here to include administrative posts, though not field or seagoing commands, connected with the army and navy. Commissioners and members of committees have been included where these were salaried posts, whether or not they were 'full-time'. I have taken the English central administration to include any holders of offices in the localities who came directly under the orders of the central authorities, e.g. customs staff in the outports as well as in London, excise personnel[1] in the towns and counties as well as in London. The members of the Irish government after the reconquest (from *c.* 1652) have also been included, as have those in Scotland under the forced 'union' (of 1652–60). Army officers are included if they also held civil offices; among these are the 'Major-Generals' of 1655–6, but not normally regional or garrison commanders, unless, like Sir Arthur Hesilrige at Newcastle in 1648–53, they had major non-military responsibilities. By these criteria the Protector and his Councillors are included, but MPs of the Rump[2] as such are not. Nor are the Councillors of State of 1649–53, for it was only under the Protectorate that this became a salaried position. Similarly, commissioners of the navy are in but not—as such—members of the Admiralty committee of the Council of State, or of the Navy committee of the Rump. I have not used a minimum salary as the criterion of whom to include at the lower level because of the marked variations here from one sector of administration to another; I have included clerks, secretaries, even under-clerks if they seem to have had any scope for administrative initiative, cashiers, paymasters, deputy receivers and so on, and the marshals and doorkeepers of important bodies (the Council itself, and

major commissions and committees). I have excluded, no doubt arbi-
trarily and without achieving complete uniformity, menials—cleaners,
copying clerks and messengers unless they had a definite administrative
role. Gaps in the records as well as my own fallibility have certainly led
to omissions; wrong identifications[3] may have resulted in mistakes either
way. Give or take whatever seems a fair margin of error, nearly 1,200
names have been recorded using these criteria.

The purpose of what is here called social biography is to establish the
presence and absence of possible characteristics in the group of people
with whom one is concerned. So much has been written recently about
so-called Namierisation in history, some of it by historians of the highest
standing,[4] that it is perhaps only fair to the reader to say a little more here
about its connection with group biography.[5] I am happy to acknowledge
an intellectual debt to the late Sir Lewis Namier, having first read his two
great books[6] as an undergraduate over twenty years ago; re-reading parts
of them from time to time as I do for teaching purposes and general
interest, I see no reason to revise my youthful opinion. If history is a
professional discipline at all and not only a branch of literature (I hope
it is both!), then Namier's work seems as substantial a contribution to
its development as anything produced in this country since F. W. Maitland's at the turn of the century. Indeed it is hard to read the opening
chapters of the *Structure of Politics* with an open mind and not feel that
1929 marks some kind of watershed in English historiography—perhaps
more so in general than in our understanding of the mid-eighteenth-
century political system. As to any more personal influence, I was never
a student or a colleague of Namier, and met him to talk to at length on
only one occasion. So whether this intellectual and professional admira-
tion, not uncritical however, makes me a 'Namierite' must be left to the
reader to decide.

Namier's method of studying eighteenth-century British politics
included, but was not confined to, the group biography of MPs.[7] The
charges against Namierisation are perhaps reducible to three: that the
method, if carried to extremes, causes excessive concentration on the
mechanics of politics to the neglect of issues and principles; that excessive concentration on the family and political connections, the genealo-
gies, the estates, the investments, and the other material interests of
those under examination (eighteenth-century MPs with Namier;
seventeenth-century officials here and in *The King's Servants*) implies
that men's political actions are determined by considerations of this
order together with their unspoken, even unconscious assumptions,
rather than by ideas, beliefs and long-term ambitions not geared to
short-run interests; and finally that the combined effect of these two
fundamental errors is to embody in Namierite history a 'right-wing' bias,
in favour of the establishment and the governing class and against radical

theories and popular forces and, as it has been expressed, to 'take the mind out of history'. Whether or not Namier, or other supposed Namier-ite historians such as Dr J. B. Owen, Mr J. Brooke or Professor Ian Christie, are guilty of these sins it is not for me to say. It is certainly true that Namier admired the British political system and the English governing class and expressed contempt for ideologists and revolu-tionaries—of the Right as well as the Left.[8] That group biography inevitably entails these convictions seems so implausible a notion that it is surprising how people of such intellectual distinction as Professors Butterfield and Hobsbawm[9] can ever have wished to maintain it. The charge of taking the mind out of history, of neglecting the social and political (and come to that, the economic) influence of ideas—Tawney's 'theology'[10]—is a more serious one but also more easily, because demon-strably, rebutted. As in my previous study of Charles I's officials (1625– 42) but *a fortiori* when discussing an age of ideological conflict and of upheaval in society arising partly from this clash of ideas, I have where-ever possible included men's beliefs and ideological connections in my examination of their background and careers. Would that more such material could be brought to light about more of them. Whether we shall emerge from this chapter indoctrinated with a mindless, elemental conservatism, I must therefore again leave reader and critic to judge.

One further problem of method remains to be briefly discussed. Ideally, as in the official *History of Parliament*,[11] or in Mrs Keeler's dic-tionary of the original members of the Long Parliament,[12] group biog-raphy should include an equally thorough study of all those comprised in the group. Failing this, the investigator can adopt one of two methods, or a combination of both: to select a few interesting cases and treat them at length, in the hope that they are more or less typical examples of the rest, or to select from the whole group a sample of more manageable size and investigate its members as thoroughly as possible. The larger the total group and the more limited the researcher's resources the more necessary it is to fall back on the well-tried method of sampling. To revert to our light-hearted comparison at the beginning of this chapter: astronauts would not—at present, that is—need to be sampled, profes-sional historians and footballers surely would. The danger of the sampling method is obvious: that author and reader will be deadened by an inter-minable series of numerical tables, which are both dull and possibly statistically meaningless. Since there will be a certain number of tables in the subsequent sections of this chapter, it may be as well to issue this warning about them now. While retaining an unrepentant belief that the historian should present his material in quantitative form where this is appropriate, I have tried to confine my use of tables to two areas: either where the material can be presented more clearly and palatably than in an extended passage of text, dotted with figures, i.e. as a superior descriptive exposition; or where a point can be made, or at least a hypothesis proffered, on the basis of quantitative evidence presented in tabular form and verified mathematically.[13] Historians should not be criticised for using figures and borrowing from the statistical methods of the natural and social sciences, but rather for getting their figures wrong, or inflating their importance by dubious or faulty statistics.[14]

A more serious objection to the sampling method arises from the heterogeneity of the group from whom the sample is being taken. Where, as in this case, the variation in importance—and hence in the amount of information available about them—is extremely wide, it becomes impossible to achieve comparability for the purposes of statistical analysis. If we postulate that there are twenty distinct pieces of information about the members of our sample in which we are interested, and on average we manage to establish evidence on fifteen or sixteen of them for each person, there may still be very wide variation on either side of this average. Thus, for several members of the sample all twenty items will be firm, specific, perhaps even detailed, but for others only perhaps three or four items out of the twenty will rest on this amount of evidence. I can see no means of totally overcoming this difficulty, although I have tried to achieve as even an average level of information as possible, and I do not believe that it invalidates the sample which I have taken.

The danger of the other approach, of taking a few individuals and writing them up as examples, should be obvious. The very survival of material in quantity about any historical personage below the first rank makes him exceptional. The fact that this was a defeated regime, which collapsed and disappeared in 1660, means that primary sources for many of our men are even scantier than they would be for officials of corresponding importance before and after. Moreover, as will be argued below, the significantly different social origins and family histories of these men, compared with those of the 1625–42 officials, again reduces the likelihood of some kinds of evidence being as readily available. None the less, more is known about some than about others. Most, of course, is known about Oliver Cromwell himself and, among functionaries of middling rank, John Milton. There would be no point in swelling this chapter out with little biographies of Cromwell and Milton, or indeed of any others for whom there are adequate biographies. But below the top level of the ruling élite (Cromwell, the Younger Sir Henry Vane, Thomas Harrison, John Lambert), this is mainly true of those who were eminent in some other capacity—as poets, medical doctors, artists or virtuosi. Outside the ranks of politicians (defined mainly as MPs, at least for 1649–53) and of military and naval leaders, not many of these men are even in the *Dictionary of National Biography*. Of some who are in that great and indispensable work of reference, it is possible to say a little more, while there are others not in it who seem sufficiently interesting and about whom enough is known for short, biographical sketches to be reward-ing.[15]

At the other extreme many remain obstinately obscure. Apart from evidence of their appointment or performance of their duties some have left no traces behind them; others are unidentifiable in the sense that there are two or more men of the same name who are known to have been around at approximately the right dates, but it is not possible to decide which of them is the official of that name. With the very obscure, or those with the commonest names, identification often comes from some apparently almost incidental piece of information which acts like a 'cross-bearing' to give a 'fix' in navigation. However, it is a poor historian who spends too long blaming the inadequacy of his sources for what may well be his own shortcomings. Certainly in one sense there has been no lack of materials for establishing whom this chapter is meant to be about.

ii SOURCES AND CHOICE OF SAMPLE

Most of the names come from the same administrative records which have been drawn upon for the two preceding chapters of this book. These include the various series of State Papers and their respective printed *Calendars*,[1] the declared accounts in the Exchequer records, the legis-lation of successive governments from the eve of the Civil War to the Restoration,[2] the official Parliamentary Journals,[3] other parliamentary materials such as private diaries,[4] and further collections of state papers and letters either in the British Museum or the Bodleian Library—some of the most important of which are printed.[5] Foremost among other sources are the Thomason Tracts, now in the British Museum.

The membership of the administration once established, serial num-bers were allocated to all concerned and a sample of 200 drawn from the whole, 1,175–1,180 on the statistically recommended 'random numbers' system.[6] It is to be hoped that this has thereby avoided biases arising from alphabetical sequence as such, for which the 1625–42 sample was open to criticism.[7] This is, therefore, an objective sample of just over one-sixth of the total of all concerned. Within a sample of 200 some oddities are naturally liable to appear. The total number of national figures—political and military leaders—in the 1,175 being relatively few, such a small sub-group will not be 'represented' in a balanced way within the sample. Thus the 200 happen to include Oliver Cromwell and his son-in-law Henry Ireton, but not Sir Arthur Hesilrige, his ally Thomas Scot or the Younger Sir Henry Vane.[8] Not as a control on the validity of the sample but to concentrate attention away from those at the very top and the bottom, a selection[9] of 100 important administrators of the middle rank has also been made. These include sixteen members of the 200 sample. For example, of the 'Seven Great Compounders' of 1650–3,[10] only Josias Berners is in the 200 sample, but he and the other six are all included in the 100 selection. Only two or three under-clerks to the successive Councils of State of 1649–60 are in the sample; all the principal Secretaries and Clerks are in the selected hundred.[11] The same kind of difference between the composition of the two groups applies to other sectors of the administration: finance, the navy, etc. In the two sections which follow an attempt has been made to apply methods of collective biographical research first to the 200 sample and then to the 100 selection, and to suggest some comparisons between the two groups. The kind of materials used here are varied; some will be obvious to all students of early modern English history, others less so. The basic sources include admissions records of the Universities and Inns of Court,[12] apprenticeship and other records of the London livery companies, county histories—from those of the seventeenth and eighteenth centuries to the massive *Victoria County History* which is still far from complete[13]—Heralds' Visitations and other collections of pedigrees both contemporary and modern.[14] Miscellaneous printed and manuscript materials have thrown up a lot of incidental information; wills, notably from the Prerogative Court of Canterbury collections,[15] have been amongst the most rewarding type of source; alas, private letters, autobiographies and journals are largely lacking, though there must certainly be some which I have failed to trace. Among the 200, there are about thirty whose identification remains uncertain or about whom virtually nothing has been discovered. Of the 100, only about eight or nine remain in this historical limbo. Further genealogical research would undoubtedly bring a few more to light, but after all men did not live and die 300 years ago for our convenience today; and genealogical investigation, while fascinating in its own right, should not be invested with undue historical significance. More such research might well not have produced much significant additional information about these men.

Nor should it be supposed for a moment that the 200 sample and the 100 selection (between them 284 men) exhaust all the interesting individuals. There are eminent men who did not happen to be in the random sample, nor quite to earn a place in the selection of key administrators. Samuel Cooper, the greatest of English miniature painters,[16] is included in the sample, but not the selection; Thomas Sydenham, one of the greatest of pre-nineteenth-century clinical physicians,[17] is not in either. John Rushworth, the historical compiler,[18] is in the selection; William Petty, virtuoso and later a founder of 'political arithmetic' (alias economics) is not in either. Of the three great English poets who walked together in Oliver Cromwell's funeral procession, Dryden[19] is not in the sample, though his father is; Marvell and Milton are (I hope fairly) in the selection of 100. But because all three were eminent poets—present or future—in the service of Cromwell's Protectorate, one should not·

assume that they had much else in common. Their fathers were respectively a London scrivener, a Hull parson, and a Northamptonshire squire. Their formal educations were, it is true, above average in duration and quality.[20] As to their place in the State's service, Milton obtained office as a reward for his pamphleteering in 1649 and because his excellent Latin qualified him for drafting diplomatic documents; Marvell was recommended via the Fairfax family and began as a private tutor to a ward of Cromwell's; Dryden's entry seems to owe more to family connections with the Pickerings and the Montagues—the chief protectoral families of Northamptonshire. These differences are perhaps in turn reflected in their loyalties. Only Milton can be shown to have had any real commitment to the republican cause, and even his loyalty to the Commonwealth and then to the Protectorate was far from uncritical. He alone, however, continued to argue for a republic in 1659–60, and he alone was in any danger of suffering at the hands of the restored monarchy in 1660.[21] Marvell served the Protectorate loyally and—so far as the record goes—the restored Commonwealth of 1659 also, but his ideological commitment was altogether more qualified, indeed equivocal is not too strong a word. Marvell was a patriot but not a puritan or a republican. Only in the 1670s did he become an implacable critic of Charles II's government and its ways. He was not a time-server, but he was in Mr Quentin Skinner's sense, a '*de factoist*'.[22] As for Dryden, to have been a minor Protectorate functionary only reinforces the contradictions so evident in his career and his writings. If he could versify in honour of Oliver's memory, why should he not have served in Oliver's administration? To make a great problem out of Dryden's political principles and ideological commitment at this time seems unreal; perhaps, unlike Milton and Marvell, he developed late, but he was also a good deal younger. (Milton was 30 before the end of Charles I's personal rule, Marvell when he was tutor to Fairfax's daughter, Dryden only in 1660). It would be easy to say that he was a time-server, but the more spectacular change came later with Dryden's conversion to Rome and deviation from the cause of high-Tory, divine-right legitimacy, to his disastrous support for James II.[23]

iii SOCIAL ANALYSIS: THE SAMPLE OF 200

These men range from the great to the unknown. As a random selection of high and low alike, they are fairly typical, except, as has been explained, within the top élite. Thirty-five are in the *DNB*, and two more, only half-identified, may be; the fathers, brothers or sons of nineteen more are in it. There are other biographies or biographical accounts of about forty of them.[1] Apart from wills and official documents, only about twenty-five of them left what can be called personal materials—letters, diaries, other papers or published works. An extraordinary variety of backgrounds is to be found among them, and the social as well as individual variations in the population of Stuart England are certainly conveyed by considering these 200 men.[2]

Most of them had been born in the seventeenth century, many around the decades 1600–30 (Table 5).

TABLE 5 *Sample of officials: date of birth*

pre-1590	c. 1590	1590–1599	c. 1600	1600–1609	c. 1610	1610–1619	c. 1620	1620–1629	c. 1630	post-1630	Un-known
9	5	12	6	28	5	34	12	23	4	2	60

There may be a slight bias here in that the better known and better connected were likely to appear on the public scene younger; probably the 'unknowns' here would include more older men. Most had therefore grown up in the later years of James I or early years of Charles I; most were already adult before the great upheavals of the 1640s. Their median age in 1649 was around 38 (Table 6).

TABLE 6 *Sample of officials: approximate ages in 1649*

Age	60+	50s	40s	30s	20s	20 –	
number	14	18	33	46	27	2	Total 140
%	10·0	12·9	23·6	32·9	19·3	1·4	To nearest 1% = 100

For many, life during their thirties must have been dominated by the years of Civil War (1642–6 and 1648). As will be seen,[3] for a large minority their activities during these years can be reasonably well documented: in military or civil employment, and for those born much after 1620 in completing their education or other training. What they had been doing before that, and more particularly during the Personal Rule of Charles I (1629–40) is for many of them more obscure, but generally speaking they were leading private lives in the station to which it had pleased God to call them. Only ten were in office under the Crown before 1642. Turning to their family background, and their places in their respective families (Table 7), both are significantly different from those of the 1625–42 officials.

This is not to say, as Professor Lawrence Stone has recently come near to suggesting,[4] that the Civil War and accompanying upheavals resulted from the upward pressures of those trying to make their way in the world, under conditions of population growth, educational expansion and relative social rigidity. It does, however, look as if there may be something in the hypothesis which—after all—is only a development of

TABLE 7   *Sample of officials: place in family*

	1st or only son (including 1st surviving)	% of known cases	2nd or younger sons	Known	Unknown	
1649–60	46	48·4%	49 51·6%	95	105	=200
1625–42*	76	57%	57 43%	133	61	=194

* *King's Servants*, Table 14, p. 259.

the much older, traditional interpretation of the Great Rebellion as a
revolt against patriarchal authority, in which heads of families were more
likely to identify with *pater patriae*, the monarch, and younger brothers
and sons with those opposing him.[5] On the other hand, the very facts of
population growth—larger families and more sons reaching maturity—
would tend to mean that there were simply more younger sons around
and available to be officials—or anything else—in 1649 than in 1625. It
would be necessary to produce a rather elaborate 'control' sample from
the population at large to demonstrate whether or not this were so. It
may well be that the demographic historians of Cambridge[6] and elsewhere have it in their power to produce such a sample and give the
answer. I do not. Still, we should not make too little of our evidence any
more than too much. My figures cannot in themselves be taken to validate Stone's hypothesis, but an eight per cent swing from first to younger
sons between the 1625–42 and 1649–60 samples certainly does not argue
against him. Proportionately more younger sons may have been in office
under the Republic than had been under Charles I.

There is also a possible social-class bias in these figures. The family
trees of gentry are more likely to be known than those of non-gentry, and
the younger sons might be fewer among the non-gentry who are in turn
proportionately more numerous among those whose place in the family is
unknown. More evidence as to the likelihood of this will emerge from the
figures in Table 8.

TABLE 8   *Sample of officials: fathers' status* (Total=200)

Peer or	Baronet or Knight	Esquire or equiva-lent	Esq./ Gent. border-line	Gentle-man	Gent./ Mr border-line	Citizen or mer-chant	Yeo-man	Other Ple-beian	Clergy	Un-known
1	15	22	10	38	13	14	4	20	6	57

* See note 7.

Here a social bias in the 'unknowns' can be taken as a fact. A few
esquires or other borderline armigerous gentry may have slipped through
the net,[7] but virtually all the 57 unknown fathers must have been on the

Gentleman/Mr borderline or below, so that the total number below Gentleman would be substantially larger than that among the known cases. Can anything now be done to cross-check on a possible social bias as between elder and younger sons? Table 9 demonstrates the expected connection between obscurity of social origin and place in the family being unknown. So much is obvious enough. A further table may clinch this and tests a possible connection between younger sons and their social status (see Table 10).

TABLE 9   *Sample of officials: fathers' status and place in family*

Father	First or only son	Younger son	Unknown which son	Total
Peer	1	0	0	1
Baronet/Knight	5	9	1	15
Esquire or equivalent	11	8	3	22
Esquire/Gentleman borderline	3	3	4	10
Gentleman	17	13	8	38
Gentleman/non-Gentleman borderline and 'Mr'	5	3	5	13
Merchant/Citizen	2	6	6	14
Yeoman	0	1	3	4
Other Plebeian	1	3	16	20
Clergy and Medical	1	3	2	6
Unknown	0	0	57	57
Totals	46	49	105	200

TABLE 10   *Sample of officials: family position and social status* (1)

	Father's rank Esquire/Gentleman borderline, and above	All cases where father's status is known
First sons	20	46
Younger sons	20	49
Unknown sons	8	48
First as % of known total	50	48·4
Younger as % of known total	50	51·6
Unknown as % of total	16·7	33·6

Thus, contrary to our expectation, there is no evidence that lowly social origins, while linked to unknown familial structure, are in turn related to the elder-younger son distribution. This strengthens the significance of an $8\frac{1}{2}$ per cent overall shift from elder to younger sons as between 1625–42 and 1649–60, as a change in its own right.

How does the family background of these men, measured by their fathers' status, compare with that of the 1625–42 officials? Table 11 shows that there was a massive reduction in the number of republican officials whose fathers ranked as Esquire or above, compared with Charles's officials. If we include all office-holders whose fathers' status was equivalent to Gentleman or above as well as these, the reduction was still considerable. What does this indicate? We must remember that a definition by status is not necessarily the same as one by wealth or landownership. Even so, it suggests a major shift within the gentry class, and—if to a lesser extent—away from that class altogether.

TABLE 11   *Sample of officials: family position and social status (2)*

	1625–42*	1649–60	% change
Sons of Esquires and above			
the whole sample	45·9	19·0	−26·9
known cases	56·0	26·6	−29·4
Sons of Gentlemen, or the equivalent, and above			
the whole sample	65·5	43·1	−22·4
known cases	80·0	60·1	−19·9

* *King's Servants*, Table 15 and p. 263.

It would be facile to leap to any far-ranging conclusions from this, that the Civil War was, after all, a class struggle by the bourgeoisie against the landed classes or, more imprecisely but by the same token also more credibly, of the middling against the upper levels of society. That it did in some measure have this aspect, I believe no impartial student of the period can doubt. The trouble is that in emancipating themselves from Marxian dialectic and the rigid schema of class conflict too many historians have also abandoned the massive evidence for an element of class division in the struggle.[8] The views of Clarendon and other contemporaries, of Guizot and Gardiner, should not be lightly discarded. But how are we to define the middling and the upper levels of seventeenth-century society? In terms of local government and control over the villages and hamlets of what was still an overwhelmingly rural society for the nine-tenths of the population outside London and the other major towns, the upper or ruling class might be equated with the landowners—men of the rank of Gentleman and above. But this leaves us with one or two awkward problems. Apart from London and the other cities and larger boroughs which were certainly not controlled by landed gentry *qua* landowners, what are we to make of non-landowning gentlemen, even of men equivalent in rank to esquires but without any substantial estates? A distinction has recently been suggested by Professor Alan Everitt, and accepted by Professor Lawrence Stone, between

'county gentry' and 'parochial gentry'.[9] Because of what Stone has elsewhere described as the 'inflation of honours',[10] in particular the reckless
creation of baronets and knights by James I, this would not correspond
exactly to differences of rank. Nor would it invariably be correlated with
wealth, the size of a man's estate or his income. By county gentry are
meant, by and large, those from whom the JPs and other royal commissioners (for subsidy assessment, sewers, i.e. land drainage, etc.)
would be drawn, and from whom most MPs came. The parochial gentry
would be escheators, receivers of Crown rents, high constables of hundreds, lathes or rapes, and grand jurors, although local officials of this
level would often be of yeoman status. Within their own parishes such
gentry would be great men—unless the parish happened to contain a
peer or member of the county gentry; even then they would be figures of
substance, in relation to the farmers, craftsmen, peasants and labourers
of the rural populace at large. But at the county level they would not,
except collectively as grand jurors or parliamentary electors, count for
much compared with the county gentry. No doubt this distinction, based
on a *de facto* notion of standing and influence, could be faulted in individual instances. There must have been some men on the borderline, or
hard to place either side of it, but that does not invalidate the definition.
By and large it probably did correspond to a distinction between esquires
and above (that is baronets and knights) on the one hand, and gentlemen
on the other. Likewise it probably corresponded to a rough-and-ready
difference of wealth which some historians would argue was the more
fundamental. The richest families with the largest estates formed the
greater or county gentry; those with smaller holdings often of only one
or two manors, or even less than a whole manor, and often holding
tenancies from other landowners, made up the lesser or parochial gentry.
The biggest and most serious qualification to be made[11] is to emphasise
regional variations. It is clear from sources such as taxation returns (not
relying on heralds' visitation records) that the distribution of gentry
varied markedly from one county to another. Some counties, such as
Devonshire,[12] Herefordshire,[13] west (but not east) Dorset,[14] perhaps the
upland parts of Yorkshire,[15] and Kent[16] abounded in lesser gentry.
These same counties might, of course, as in Kent and Yorkshire, also
have their share of greater gentry. The contrast is rather with counties
such as Lincolnshire, parts of the east midlands and East Anglia, where
there were relatively more well-to-do yeomen, and tenant farmers of
indeterminate rank,[17] and where many of these yeomen were as wealthy
—and perhaps at the parish level as influential—as the lesser, or parochial gentry of other areas.[18]

As an added complication, rigid distinctions of rank were breaking
down, or becoming increasingly eroded during the very period with
which we are concerned. The gap between the theories of the heralds and

the classification of armigerous gentry based upon these, and the descriptions used by those concerned, their neighbours and even in official records, continued to widen. Especially in urban sources, but also in the tax records for some counties, there is the ambiguous designation 'Mr'. It is ambiguous in that it is hard, often impossible, to be sure whether it signifies Master, a term applied only to esquires and gentlemen, or Mister, which already had some kind of non-armigerous, if not positively plebeian, connotation.[19] Hence the rather unsatisfactory category, in tables 8 and 9 above, of 'Gentleman/Mr borderline' to take in men so designated. For the late seventeenth century Professor Everitt has coined the term pseudo-gentry to embrace such types, notably in the towns.[20]

Returning to the status of our officials' fathers, when allowance has been made for all these difficulties of classification, there is a marked shift away from the greater or county gentry, compared with the civil service of Charles I. And there is a smaller but still appreciable shift away from gentry defined as widely as possible—the whole armigerous or would-be armigerous and landowning[21] class. Why should this have been so? One answer is that proportionately more gentry, especially greater gentry, were royalists in the Civil War than was true of the population as a whole; more were therefore in opposition and ineligible for office under the republic. Of the peers and baronets this is demonstrably so. But for esquires and *a fortiori* gentlemen it remains open to debate, and in need of further, quantitative research on more counties and regions of England and Wales. For instance, Everitt's work shows that in Kent most of the county gentry of 1642 were either royalist or neutral, or such moderate or lukewarm parliamentarians that they disappeared from county government,[22] and were largely replaced either by outsiders to the county altogether or by members of the parochial gentry.[23] He suggests a similar process elsewhere.[24] By contrast, in a county such as Suffolk, most of the county gentry were themselves puritan parliamentarians, and continued substantially in control right through the 1640s and 50s.[25] This variation seems to have arisen partly from what one might call the social geography and human ecology of a county. By and large, the up-country areas of the north and west were the most prolific of small gentry and these same areas were predominantly, though not universally, royalist. The more royalist a county's governing group in 1642–5 and the later it was conquered by Parliament's military forces, the more thoroughly and (on the whole) the more radically the government of such a county was transformed; more new men came in and more of them were from relatively humbler social backgrounds. Can the same hypothesis be applied to the national administration? We shall be better able to answer this question when more information about the sample has been presented and discussed.

Whatever the arguments about the social class of pre-Civil War officials, and whether they belonged to the rising or the declining gentry, both or neither, one undoubted fact was the improvement in their own rank or status which they achieved, during and probably largely as a consequence of their official careers.[26] The same is true of the 1649–60 officials, but to a less marked extent (Tables 12 and 13).

TABLE 12   *Sample of officials: status achieved by 1660s* (Total = 200)*

Peer	Baronet or Knight	Esq.	Armi-gerous (Esq./ Gent.)	Gent.	Border-line Mr/ Gent.	Alder-man, Citizen, Merchant	Yeo-man	Ple-beian	Clerical and Medical	Un-known
4†	18	61	5	39	29	18	1	0	6	19

* Including immediate promotion by Charles II but excluding the results of 1660 attainders.
† Including one by inheritance and one (anomalously) Lord Protector!

TABLE 13   *Sample of officials: extent of rise in social status*

Rose by 3 degrees or more	9 (including gradations within the peerage)
Rose by 2 degrees	18
Rose by 1 degree	43
Remained stationary	50
Declined from father's rank*	18 (including younger sons who themselves stayed level)
Total of known cases	138
Unknown	43 + 19

* Attainders and convictions for treason are not included here.

The upward movement can also be measured in another way. Thus of the known cases 50·7 per cent rose by one degree or more, compared with 59·7 per cent of the known cases among the 1625–42 officials,[27] and 19·6 per cent rose by two or more compared with 30·9 per cent[28] in the earlier group—a rather marked falling off. This may mean that status was coming to count for less, so that people were less concerned where they ended up and what they called themselves or what they were styled by others. Some of the downward tendencies also reflect the larger percentage of younger sons, who if their fathers were esquires themselves had to rise by one degree (gent. to esq.) to break even. Moreover, the defeat of the republican cause in 1660 again operates here, as we shall find it doing elsewhere. This produced a quite different outcome from what would have been the case if more men in the sample had died before the collapse of the regime which they were serving.

England, even with Wales and its minor dependencies, such as the Channel Islands, was a relatively compact, unified and homogeneous country by the mid-seventeenth century. We should therefore, expect a

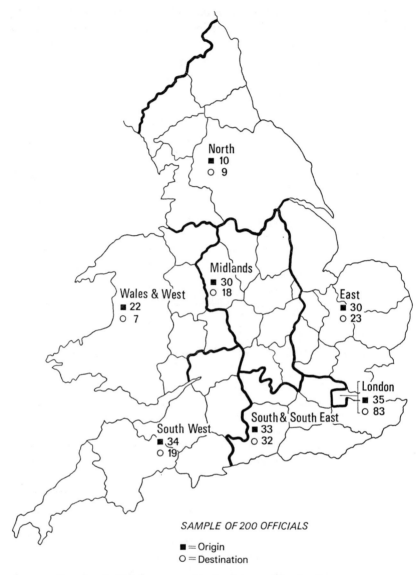

SAMPLE OF 200 OFFICIALS

■ = Origin
O = Destination

MAP I   *Sample of officials: geographical origins and destinations*

sample of officials to show a wide distribution of geographical origins. By and large this was so (Table 14 and Map 1).

Where a man's family had definite roots in more than one region, he has been counted more than once here. There are thirty-nine such instances, counted in this way. I am not referring here to a single outlying manor held by a great landowning family, but to second residences, cases where family origins span regional (as well as county) boundaries, and families with London (or other urban) residences as well as country seats and estates.

TABLE 14   *Sample of officials: geographical origins* (1)

The North (Cumberland, Durham, Lancashire, Northumberland, Westmorland, Yorkshire)	10
The Midlands (Buckinghamshire, Derbyshire, Leicestershire, Northamptonshire, Nottinghamshire, Oxfordshire, Rutland, Staffordshire, Warwickshire)	30
The East (Bedfordshire, Cambridgeshire, Essex, Hertfordshire, Huntingdonshire, Lincolnshire, Norfolk, Suffolk)	30
The South and South-East (Berkshire, Hampshire, Kent, Middlesex without the London suburbs, Surrey, Sussex)	33
The South-West (Cornwall, Devon, Dorset, Gloucestershire, Somerset, Wiltshire	34
Wales and the West (Cheshire, Herefordshire, Monmouth, Shropshire and Worcestershire)	22
London, including Westminster, Southwark and the suburbs	35
Scotland	4
Ireland	4
The Channel Islands	2
Foreign	1
Total of known instances	205
Total of known individuals	166
Unknowns	34
Multiple origins	39

It has seemed more sensible to group the English counties rather than to tabulate them individually, if the numbers with which one is dealing are not to become too small to be meaningful. To know that one man came from county Durham and one from Cumberland out of the 166 whose origins are known can tell us little, and it would be unwise to start constructing an argument on this basis. But that only ten in all had roots in the six northern counties compared with around thirty in each of four other regions, does begin to signify. Are there any surprises or features of particular note in this table? One or two obvious, if negative points emerge. The 34 from the South-West remind us that the parliamentarian–republican cause did not find its supporters overwhelmingly, let alone exclusively, in London and the south-eastern half of England. In proportion to total population, especially of educated young men, it is far from clear that the eastern and south-eastern regions are over-represented in relation to the rest.[29] The following individual counties show six or more men with origins in them: Cheshire, Devon, Dorset, Essex, Kent, Middlesex, Northants, Somerset (including Bristol), and Wiltshire. The preponderance of London and Westminster over any single group of counties is noteworthy, but not very surprising. The influences involved in entry to office will help to explain some of these 'clusters' from particular areas,[30] and perhaps negatively the thin showing of others. One minor surprise is the lack of colonial Americans, notably New Englanders. This is by way of such marked contrast to the 100 selected administrators[31] that it suggests failure on the research side.[32] Apart from this there is no reason to suppose that the 34 unknowns would be distributed in any particular way, with one possible exception. Since non-gentry are harder to trace, and since proportionately more of the known Londoners are non-gentry, the unknowns might be expected to add proportionately more to the London figure than to the rest. As against this, men from provincial towns are harder to trace than Londoners, because of London apprenticeship records. Even if the London total were nearer 50 than 40, this would still be only 25 per cent of the total. Moreover, the fact that these figures for origins are of instances, not individuals, operates with peculiar force in the case of London. Twenty men's families had interests and/or residences in London as well as in some other part of the country, far more proportionately than had such connections in two regions other than London. No doubt it would be much tidier if each man had originated indisputably in one location only, but such was not the case. At any rate the percentages of known cases (for we cannot risk, statistically, a hypothetical distribution of the unknowns) are as shown in Table 15.

TABLE 15   *Sample of officials: geographical origins (2)*

	North	Mid-lands	East	South and South-East	South-West	Wales and West	Lon-don	Other	Totals
1649–60 %	4·9	14·6	14·6	16·1	16·6	10·7	17·1	5·4	100
1625–42 known instances	9	36	37	34	20	19	33	17	205*
%	4·4	17·6	18·0	16·6	9·8	9·3	16·1	8·3	100·1

* *King's Servants*, pp. 267–8, Table 19, counties etc. regrouped as for 1649–60. The large number of Others is accounted for by 12 from Scotland, 3 from the Continent, and 1 each from Ireland and the Channel Islands.

Thus the biggest changes are away from the Midlands and the East, and towards the South-West and Wales. Within 'Wales and the West', however, another marked change is concealed. In 1625–42 all but two instances (seventeen) were from the English border counties; in 1649–60 eight were from Wales. Amongst individual counties in different regions, Devon was up (from three to seven instances), so were Dorset (from four to eight), Middlesex (from four to nine), Northants (from four to eight), Somerset and Bristol (from three to eight), Wiltshire (from two to six), and Yorkshire (from three to five); Herts was down (from eight to three), so were Oxfordshire (from eight to two), Surrey (from six to four), Warwickshire (from seven to one) and Worcestershire (from eight to one).[33] Apart from the West Midlands (mainly royalist in 1642–5) and parts of the South-West (largely parliamentarian initially in 1642–3) it is hard to correlate any of this with regional differences in the Civil War. Again the circumstances of patronage, family connection, and for 1649–60 religious links too,[34] as they affected individuals and small groups in particular districts, probably afford a sounder explanation. Nor must we forget that though the overall proportions from other regions (notably the South and South-East) and the numbers from some individual counties are similar in the two groups, these may have been composed of very different kinds of individuals. The nine men from Suffolk in 1625–42 and the five in 1649–60 are a case in point.

How far did office affect geographical, as distinct from social, mobility? Since the great majority of posts in the central administration were located in Westminster or London, their holders needed some kind of residence there during their tenure of such offices. And because relatively few of them under the republic were part-time officials or served in rotation, as some had under the monarchy, most of those working in the capital probably had residences there—as opposed to lodgings. Again, the sudden ending of the government's existence in 1660 meant that very many of those in its service had their tenure interrupted. Far fewer died in office, or were succeeded in their posts by sons or other near relatives. So again the effects of being office-holders were, for many of them, altogether more temporary than for those of 1625–42, despite the earlier period having been followed by the Civil War itself. None the less a marked geographical shift did occur (Tables 16 and 17).

A slightly different method of counting multiple or secondary estates and other interests has been followed for the 1649–60 men;[35] so an exact comparison must not be pressed too far. Even so, it is clear that office-holding under the republic was associated with a somewhat different pattern of geographical mobility than it was under Charles I. The shift away from the South-West was a little more pronounced than with the earlier men, and there was no shift to the South and South-East (excluding London) as there had been before. Again we must bear in mind that

TABLE 16   *Sample of officials: geographical destinations (1)*

Region	The same instances as for origins	Different instances from those of origins	Unknown in relation to origins	Totals	Multiple instances
North	5	4	0	9	7
Midlands	15	3	0	18	11
East	20	2	1	23	11
South and South-East	15	13	4	32	12
South-West	18	1	0	19	4
Wales and West	5	2	0	7	3
London	25	47	11	83	35
Scotland	3	1	0	4	0
Ireland	3	6	1	10	5
Channel Islands	2	0	0	2	1
New England	0	2	0	2	1
West Indies	0	1	0	1	0
Foreign territories	0	8	0	8	4
All known instances	111	90	17	218	94

Men for whom destinations unknown	38
Known men	162
Men with multiple destinations	56

TABLE 17   *Sample of officials: geographical destinations (2)*

	North	Midlands	East	South and South-East	South-West	Wales and West	London	Other	Totals
1649–60									
Number of instances	9	18	23	32	19	7	83	27	218
% of known total	4·1	8·3	10·5	14·7	8·7	3·2	38·1	12·4	100
Change from % of origins	−0·8	−6·3	−4·1	−1·4	−7·9	−7·5	+21	+7	
1625–42									
Number of instances	5	30	48	55	12	7	83	20	260*
% of known total	1·9	11·5	18·5	21·1	4·6	2·7	31·9	7·7	99·9
Change from % of origins	−2·5	−6·1	+0·5	+4·5	−5·2	−6·6	+15·8	−0·6	

* *King's Servants*, pp. 267–8, Table 19, counties regrouped as before. 'Others' now include 11 to Ireland.

although in both these eras normal administrative tenure was interrupted, the effects were more dramatic for the officials of 1649–60. For one thing, many more of the older men of 1625–42 had been in office before Charles's accession in 1625 and more of the younger ones re-appeared in 1660 than was true of those of 1649–60 being in office either before 1649 or after 1660.[36] However, this may not be the whole story. Politics apart, the King may have recruited more of his servants from the areas further from London and more of them may have acquired property in the 'home counties', that is the whole south-east corner of the country, as well as having London residences.[37] By contrast more of the servants of the Commonwealth and Protectorate may have kept their provincial roots where they originated, for reasons distinct from the effects of 1660, great as these were. One test of this hypothesis is to see whether more of those who died in office before the Restoration had shifted their main properties and residences than was the case amongst the sample as a whole (Table 18).

TABLE 18   *Sample of officials: date of death and geographical shift*

	Shifted location or principal residence	No shift of location or main residence	Unknown	Totals
Dead by May 1660	11	13	1	25
Died after May 1660	57	57	16	130
Date of death unknown	1	8	36	45
Totals	69	78	53	200

Thus, discounting the unknown cases, there is very little difference to be seen. Moreover, the reasons for men having moved could be so varied that little seems to emerge here. (Note that because men, not instances, have been counted in Table 18, no direct comparison with Table 16 is possible.)

Next, what sort of education or other training had these officials had? Unfortunately, admissions registers of schools are so irregular in their coverage of the seventeenth century that it is not worth trying to do anything systematic for this stage.[38] There are plenty of pitfalls, too, in using the published admissions records of the two ancient English universities.[39] And it may be that my failures of identification are more numerous than they would be if it had been possible for me to work direct from the manuscript registers of matriculations and the surviving records of colleges and halls.[40] Some of the same cautions apply to the legal institutions of higher education or further training. The records of the smaller Chancery Inns are virtually non-existent; as to the four Inns of Court, the Middle Temple register is the most recently published and reliable, the Inner Temple typescript copy appears to be meticulously accurate,[41] the registers of Lincoln's and Gray's Inns are older and less reliable.[42] As to other forms of training, the bindings to apprenticeship and freedom books for some London Companies are available, in print or manuscript, for the relevant years, and I have consulted only the most important of these.[43] The figures for apprenticeship are therefore minimum ones, whereas for the Universities and the Inns of Court there may be some mistakes, but few omissions (Tables 19 and 20).

TABLE 19   *Sample of officials: further education—university or legal*

Father's status	Oxford	Cambridge	Other Univs	Total	Gray's Inn	Lincoln's Inn	Inner Temple	Middle Temple	Other legal	Total
Esquire or equivalent and above	11	9	1	21	6	10	3	5	3	27
Gent./Mr	13	10	3*	26 (24)	7	3	4*	11*	4*	29 (27)
Citizen/ Plebeian etc.	1	7	0	8	3*	0	2	2	1*	8 (5)
Unknown	1	0	0	1	0	0	0	0	0	0
Total	26	26	4	56 54 men	16	13	9	18	8	64 59 men

* Denotes multiple instances, of men at more than one institution. Totals in brackets are those of men, not instances.

TABLE 20   *Sample of officials: further training—apprentices*

Gentleman or above	19
Below Gentleman	19
Unknown	9
Total	47

At first sight it seems surprising that only 27 per cent received university education, and 29·5 per cent common law training. For the 1625–42 officials the university total was 78, or 40·2 per cent, and the legal education figure 68, or 35 per cent. But in both cases the striking difference is at the upper end of the social scale, sons of esquires and above providing 43 of those at universities and 32 of those at the Inns in 1625–42, as opposed to 21 and 27 for the 1649–60 officials. The fact that sons of the upper classes were more likely to go to university is the explanation for the total difference between 1625–42 and 1649–60 regardless of social origins.[44] It would be going too far to say that the republic's office-holders were 'worse educated' than their predecessors under the monarchy. Still, whether we regard the generality of the State's servants from 1649–60 as ruthless opportunists and interloping usurpers or as a fairly representative collection of men, many of whom were, no doubt, both able and ambitious, it remains surprising that so few from the lower ranks of society had got beyond—presumably—the grammar or writing-school stage of education.[45] Indeed, if the records were available, we might well find proportionately fewer grammar school alumni and more old boys of writing-schools—the 'secondary technicals' of their day—than among the civil servants of Charles I. But this is only conjecture. There are certainly far more ex-apprentices of London Companies among the 1649–60 officials. Looking at the University and Inns of Court figures more closely, the sample corrects a qualitative impression gained earlier[46] of a Cambridge and Gray's Inn predominance. In relation to the size of the two universities, Oxford, the smaller, produced proportionately more republican functionaries. Likewise among the inns, the totals here are not markedly out of proportion to the total size of the four. The apprenticeship records show a marked social difference from those of the universities and the inns, though probably not more than might be expected. It might be argued that the economic dislocation caused by the Civil War, and blighted commercial and industrial prospects drove men out of business and into government service in the 1640s to a greater extent than at other times. But this remains a guess, and the figures available at this stage cannot be used to demonstrate its truth.

The more practical, realistic way of looking at it, is to remember the Long Parliament's piecemeal improvisation of an administration from 1642 on.[47] Men had to be found to staff these institutions, to operate the system. And the question can be seen as one of supply and demand, even if—put in these crude but decisive terms—it cannot be answered. What was the pressure on places? Were the Long Parliament and its subordinate committees and departments, *qua* employers, in a position to pick and choose, to turn men away on grounds of unsuitability as well as disloyalty or immorality? Or were they hunting for young—or not so young—men who were both qualified and loyal? The close ties between parliamentarian financial administration and the Livery Halls of the City is perhaps in itself sufficient explanation for the entry of some men already free of the London Companies and employed by their members. One might ask the same about the successive republican administrations of 1649–59. What were the 'terms of trade' as regards recruitment? Some differences can be discerned. Several men who had been in the service of the Long Parliament between 1642 and 1648 either withdrew or dis-qualified themselves from office in 1649[48] and a considerable number of new recruits were needed. Some of them came from the army which, despite the Irish and Scottish wars, was on the whole being steadily reduced. The consequences of the further political changes in 1653 on recruitment, seem to be reasonably clear. Subscription to a uni-cameral commonwealth without King or House of Lords, implying tacit approval of the events of December 1648 to February 1649, was no longer required under the Protectorate. And the disgruntled republicans who withdrew were counter-balanced by the ex-royalists, ex-neutrals, ex-presbyterians (or moderate parliamentarians of 1642–8) and younger less politically committed types who came in. The year 1659 saw further changes: zealous protectorians went out; doctrinaire republicans came back. From May 1659 to March 1660 the atmosphere was so nearly one of continuous purge and counter-purge as to destroy any semblance of a normal recruiting pattern, at least in the upper and middle ranks. No doubt lower down things went on with less interruption. Recruitment must have been least affected by political changes, on the part of both employer and employed, at the humbler, more routine levels, usually filled by men of obscure origins. Not that this is quite the whole story, and some further figures may be used to supplement and amend it.

The problems of entry and appointment to office have already been discussed in their own right.[49] Here we are concerned with them from a different point of view, in relation to the men who staffed the adminis-tration (Table 21).

Some of these categories are more objectively defined than others. Despite my earlier work on Charles I's officials, I may have failed to notice one or two who were in office before 1642. Still, the classification is clear: either a man was in office before the King left London early in 1642 or he was not.[50] The category of active parliamentarians is also tolerably clear, although there are inevitably more omissions here: there are no complete lists of the junior officers, let alone the rank and file, of all Parliament's armed forces; others employed as clerks under committees and in departments may also have been overlooked. 'Active', of course, is a more subjective definition. It might have involved anything from being in the vanguard of the victorious armies or at the nerve-centre of parliamentary taxation, to merely keeping a routine office 'ticking over' under wartime conditions without being expelled. Moreover, for men who are classified as active in the localities rather than in the army or in civil office at the centre, there is the further problem of whether being named to com-mittees is evidence of active membership. On the whole I have assumed, in the absence of evidence to the contrary, that constant and repeated appointment to committees and commissions, persisting after 1642/3 does indicate, if not strenuous participation, at least a degree of support

TABLE 21 *Sample of officials: factors in entry to office*

	Number of instances		Total number
	Sole evidence	Part of evidence	of officials involved
i Pre-1642 office-holders who survived into 1649 or later	5	5	10
ii Active (civil or military) parliamentarians, 1642–8	23	36	59
iii Patrimony	2	6	8
iv Patronage	13	50	63
v Purchase*	0	3	3
vi Religious connections	0	25	25
vii Entry 1648/9–53 (in lieu of other evidence as to why)	38	12	50
viii Entry 1653 (ditto)	7	3	10
ix Entry 1654–8 (ditto)	16	6	22
x Entry 1659 (ditto)	1	2	3
xi Professional qualifications	2	35	37
xii Ex-royalist	0	3	3
xiii Totals	107	186	293
Number of officials for whom there is more than one kind of evidence			93

* Pre-1642 and therefore included in category i.

for Parliament's cause. Particularly, once Parliament was quite clearly winning the war, by the summer of 1645, it had no need to try to win over more adherents or to compromise more waverers by enrolling them in its service, as had perhaps been the case in 1642–3 and even into 1644.[51] Patrimony has been defined as involving the transmission of an office from someone to his son, son-in-law or brother, or entry into an office procured by paternal or fraternal influence. Any family influences less immediate than that have been included under the wider, more important category of Patronage. A few cases of patrimony may have been missed, but not many, unless a lot of marriage relationships which have not been brought to light could be linked up with particular appointments. Otherwise the same family name in the same or a related office is usually the clue here. As for purchase, it tended to be kept out of sight at all times, and this was particularly so during the 1640s and 50s. There were instances of venality during these years, mainly in the law courts;[52] and it may be that the sample is unrepresentative here of a particular sub-group within the total body of people from whom it is taken. About 25 members of the sample held offices in the courts;[53] it would certainly not be surprising if a few more beyond the two known pre-1640 instances of purchase occurred.

Patronage is an altogether different matter. A complete knowledge of all the human and institutional inter-relationships of the 1640s—a knowledge beyond the grasp and capacity perhaps of any historian, not merely of the present author—would enable many gaps to be filled in here. This and the religious category are the ones where incomplete evidence and research must have taken their heaviest toll. Interpolation, alias 'informed guesswork', is a hazardous business, but it would not be surprising if the total cases of patronage in entry to office were in reality double what they appear as here. The same is true, to a lesser extent and for slightly different reasons, of religious connections. I have included an instance here only if it appears that a man's membership of a particular gathered church or congregation, or his religious affiliations in general, were connected with his entry to office. The mere fact of apparently puritan or Calvinist beliefs without such a link is not enough. If there were membership lists of more Presbyterian classes and Independent and Baptist congregations, this total too would be considerably swollen. Political, as opposed to religious connections are here included under Patronage, which thus has a slightly more 'ideological' character than it had as a factor in entry to office for the men of 1625–42.[54] Entries at different dates during the eleven years of republican government (Table 21, vii–x), constitute both a residual category and a reminder of the rate of turnover in offices; in some cases youth, in others mortality, explains these changes. About a quarter of the sample may still have been under age or only just grown-up around the end of the first Civil War (c. 1646),[55] and this accounts for some of the entrants after 1649 of whose previous activities we have no trace. Likewise some of the appointments of the 1650s were simply to replace men who died in office, rather than representing any kind of political change. With detailed information about more of the individuals concerned it might be possible to make some comparison between factors in entry under the Commonwealth (1649–53) and those under the Protectorate (1653–9). But the small numbers of definitely new entrants in each case about whom enough is known makes any quantitative assessment impossible. As will be seen,[56] however, it is possible to suggest an impressionistic contrast between the Rump's civil servants and the Protector's.

'Professional qualifications' (category xi) is likewise an arbitrary one imposed on the material, not arising directly from it. I have included such elements as whether men in legal office had been called to the bar, whether those in revenue posts had prior experience in commerce or finance, whether those on the secretarial-diplomatic side had linguistic skills or training in drafting documents; the previous tenure of offices entailing comparable skills and responsibilities has been allowed to count. This is an amorphous category which might well be swollen further with more evidence. But it would be inadmissible to argue from this tentative figure how well-trained and qualified the republican civil service was. Lastly, royalism (xii) is self-explanatory, being defined by conviction and payment of penal taxes. One pardon came as early as 1649, the other two followed the demise of the Rump in 1653.

Once in office, many stayed there until death or political cataclysm removed them. Others moved on, some upward, some laterally, in the administration. With the system of committees and commissions inherited from the 1640s, a new kind of pluralism had grown up, of a functional nature. Others, however, were pluralists in the more traditional sense, and some were absentees too. There was markedly less multiple office-holding and performance by deputy under the republic than there had been under the monarchy (and was to be again from 1660 to the early nineteenth century), in large part because there were fewer sinecures, less venality, and fewer offices held on life tenure and with semi-heritable reversions. The extent of mobility in office (Table 22) is harder to define if one eliminates pluralism.

TABLE 22   *Sample of officials: promotions, transfers, pluralism, deputation*

Changed office once, 1649–60	32
Changed office twice or more, 1649–60	9
Returned to a different office after an interval out of office	4
Returned to the same office after an interval	7
Held two or more offices at once	33
Absentee and/or performer by deputy, all or part of time	6
Deputy office-holder all or part of the time	10

(First four categories bracketed: 52)

One salient point emerges here. By adding the first four categories together and subtracting them from the total in the sample we are left with 148, or 74 per cent, who remained in one office throughout their term of service within the period 1649–60. Correspondingly, whatever well-known instances spring to mind—Cromwell as Lord Lieutenant of Ireland with Henry Ireton as his Lord Deputy (1650–1)—the phenomena of absenteeism and deputation were hardly widespread.

Whether the men entering and holding office from 1649–60 came from a new social class or from a different stratum of the same class as those of 1625–42, has already been considered briefly.[57] How far, once in office, did they consolidate their position in terms not of status[58] but of land and wealth (Table 23)?

This is a meagre total which the discovery of more inventories and family papers might do something to augment. The nature of the Restoration Settlement is probably responsible not only for the relative poverty of these 200 men but also for the paucity of the evidence about their properties and personal finances. I cannot pretend to have worked through all the records of land sales (church, crown and royalist) in the period,[59] and my knowledge of individual interests in Ireland is derived from printed sources only.[60] Some of the losses of property were due to attainders and treason trials, others to indebtedness, bankruptcy, degeneration or sheer bad luck; other evidence of wealth comes mainly from wills. Perhaps the 100 selected administrators of middle rank will show up differently from these men, who may be biased towards juniority and thus obscurity, as well as being untypical at the very top. Or perhaps officials at any level are the wrong people on whom to base an assessment of the evidence for the alleged emergence of a new landed class during the Interregnum.[61]

TABLE 23   *Sample of officials: land and wealth*

Known to have bought land, c. 1640–60*	44
Interests in Irish lands	15
Known to have lost lands again and/or to have died poor	10
Known to have died rich, and richer than they began*	59

* Most of those in the first category are also in the fourth; the total number for whom there is information here is not above 75.

Frequent reference has already been made to the political changes within the years 1649–60 and to the effects of the Restoration. It is worth trying to put this on a firmer basis (Tables 24 and 25).

TABLE 24   *Sample of officials: effects of political change, 1649–59*

Not in office 1649–53 or 1659; in office only under the Protectorate between Dec. 1653 and May 1659	Not in office 1654–May 1659; in office only under the Commonwealth 1649–53 or 1659	Date of death unknown in relation to Dec. 1653	In service under Commonwealth and Protectorate
31*	38†	3	128

* Of whom 5 were dead before the Commonwealth was restored, May 1659.
† Of whom 3 died before Dec. 1653.

TABLE 25   *Sample of officials: effects of political change, 1660 and after*

Dead by May 1660	Executed	Died in exile	Other pains and penalties, including died in prison	Lost office or withdrew into private life	Retained office or resumed it after May 1660	Unknown
25	1	2	4	83	37*	48

* Of these, 2 held local office only, and 2 resumed office only after 1688.

As to Table 24, of the 31 in the first column, some were undoubtedly non-republicans who would not serve under the Commonwealth, while others include those whom it would not employ but who were acceptable to the Cromwellian Protectorate. Likewise, of the 38 in the second column some were committed republicans whose opposition to monarchy extended to a single person as Lord Protector, while others were prepared to accept Cromwell's dissolution of the Rump and his rule as Lord General before and during the Barebones (April–December 1653) and left office only after he became Protector. One or two, rather oddly, went out temporarily in 1653 and then returned in 1654. But some cases in both these categories are explicable on non-political grounds, such as illness or old age, youth or the attractions of an alternative career. Only men who were clearly eligible for office (i.e. adult and in the country) at both dates (December 1653 and May 1659) and made the switch either way—in-out-in again, or out-in-out again—were definitely motivated by political principles. Some of the protectorians were ex-presbyterians or moderate parliamentarians of the 1640s and even ex-neutrals from Civil War days; some were of a markedly higher social status than those quitting office in 1653–4. There seems to be a phenomenon of socially upward patronage operating under the Protectorate; unaristocratic as Cromwell's government was by pre-twentieth-century standards,[62] he seems to have cultivated members of the old peerage deliberately. In the sample there are Charles Howard, grandson of a peer and a future earl, and Viscount Lisle, heir to the earldom of Leicester. There are others outside it, such as Mulgrave, Fiennes, Fauconberg and Rich. Many men of similar social background were in office under both Commonwealth and Protectorate. But religious and republican zealots are more characteristic of the former, other more courtly, conservative types of the latter. There was far from being an abrupt or massive shift, but a slight 'swing to the Right' under the Protectorate is clearly discernible among the officials.[63]

The figures in relation to 1660 are more interesting and require fuller discussion. $12\frac{1}{2}$ per cent are known to have been dead by May 1660, most of them having died in office, and a few more of the Unknowns may belong in this category. The number who suffered more than loss of place (including permanent disablement from holding office) was very small. The crucial question is how those in the Unknown category would divide between those who lost, or withdrew from office, and those who remained in, or returned to the service of the Crown. I have made only a general survey of the personnel of Charles II's administration and some junior officials in it may have been overlooked.[64] A few more may have died before May 1660 than has been established, but the great majority of the Unknowns are certainly men who withdrew, or were expelled from their posts, or whose offices—in consequence of the

Restoration—actually ceased to exist: e.g. parts of the Excise administration (on commodities other than alcohol and soft drinks), the machinery of compounding and sequestration, the regular monthly Assessment, and (as early as 1659) the Lord Protector's Household. One qualification to be made is that more than the few noted must have kept or later obtained local offices, as against central offices in the localities. More may have re-entered office temporarily during James II's attempted conciliation of the Protestant dissenters under his suspension of the Test Act (1687–8), and one or two more than have been noted, who resisted these blandishments, may have reaped their reward by re-entering office after 1688 during the reign of William and Mary. As always in such classifications, there are a few awkward borderline cases. Major-General Philip Skippon, for example, is usually said to have died on the eve of the Restoration. And there is no doubt that he was living in total retirement, elderly and ailing by then, but his will contains a note of two oral codicils on 24 and 26 June 1660, with two men of some substance as witnesses which makes them unlikely to be a forgery.[65] But such instances are marginal. If we set aside the Unknowns altogether, on the assumption that they would divide in the same proportions as the Knowns, the significant figures are as shown in Table 26.

TABLE 26   *Sample of officials: position after 1660*

Known to have been alive in May 1660	127
Held office under Crown	37 = 29·1%
Never in office under Crown	90 = 70·9%

The question is whether this lends quantitative support to the view that the Restoration was less sweeping at the administrative than at the political level, with important consequences in later Stuart government.[66] There is the technical statistical point of how firmly we can argue from the sample to the whole body of republican officials with a total of just over three-quarters of known cases.[67] If we felt able to do this, allowing for around $12\frac{1}{2}$ per cent who were already dead, this would leave about 1,000 to be divided in the proportions shown in Table 26. That is to say, about 290 men who had been in office under the Commonwealth or Protectorate would—on this hypothesis—have been in office at some stage between the 1660s and the 1690s. This is a substantial number and surely sufficient to affect the royal administration as a whole; we shall find an instructive comparison here with the 100 selected administrators.[68]

Generally, however, the predominant impression is of withdrawal into private life. Many who had been prominent figures in Cromwellian England simply disappear from view. Occasional traces in denominational or local records and perhaps the evidence of their wills is all that survives as evidence of another ten, twenty or thirty years of such men's lives.

Some must have lived in real poverty and hardship, deprived of the financial benefits of office and without other assets or earning-power; others simply resumed their earlier careers as landowners, lawyers, doctors and merchants or traders. No doubt some throve in these capacities, some marked time, and some declined. Occasionally a will, made long after the period of a man's official service, sheds retrospective light on his career then and during the intervening years, but many of these documents are brief, formal and unrevealing.[69]

iv SOCIAL ANALYSIS: THE 100 SELECTED OFFICIALS

As has already been emphasised, the group with which we are now concerned is not a sample but a deliberate selection. Because these men are on the whole less obscure, and were more important than the majority of those in the 200 sample, we might expect them to be more committed supporters of the regime and to show, in some respects, more positive characteristics than those exhibited by the 200. Not that all of them were more prominent than all members of the sample. Sixteen of the sample 200 are amongst the selected 100, while another seventeen of the sample are in a sense too prominent to be in the selection.[1] Twenty-four of the selected 100 are in the *DNB* (with entries for close relatives of nine more); there are other lives or biographical accounts of about seventeen more. Several are mentioned in either general or specialist histories of the period, and the names of many others will be familiar to anyone who has browsed among the printed sources.[2] In some respects (Table 27) they turn out to be not so different from the sample, which suggests that the random inclusion of people from the very top and the bottom of the republic's government among the 200 has not produced serious distortion.

TABLE 27 *Selected officials: date of birth*

	pre-1590	*c. 1590*	*1590–9*	*c. 1600*	*1600–9*	*c. 1610*	*1610–19*	*c. 1620*	*1620–30*	*c. 1630*	*Total known*	*Unknown*	*Total*
Age in 1649	4	1	7	2	17	2	20	4	13	1	71	29	100
	60s		50s		40s		30s		20s				

Thus, as with the 200, the median age of those known was around 39–40 in 1649; qualitatively, however, there seems to be a difference. Several very young men are noticeable among the most active and prominent; equally so were a few much older men, born around 1600 or before. Again, this means relatively little until we have built up a fuller composite picture of the group and can relate this to other information about them (Table 28).

TABLE 28   *Selected officials: place in family*

First or only sons	Younger sons	Unknown	Total
30	18	52	100

With over half being unknown, and remembering our earlier discussion about the possible biases associated with obscurity and lack of information, too much should not be made of this. Even so, the difference from the sample is very striking. These busy, often pushful men who rose to positions of some importance if not eminence under the republic include a much higher proportion of elder to younger sons than was true of the 200 sample. The significance of this is hard to assess but it may become clearer if it can be correlated with other characteristics of the group (Table 29).

The shift away from the traditional upper or ruling class is even more marked here than with the sample. Only nine definitely came from the level of Esquires or above, although 45 were still from gentry and equivalent levels (including clergy and borderline 'Mr's). The change is clearly away from aristocracy and greater gentry but to lesser, or parochial and urban, gentry as much as to non-gentry. It now becomes decisive, if we are to take this point any further, whether people styled 'Gent.' or 'Mr' but not classified as armigerous by the Heralds, or necessarily endowed with hereditary estates, are to be thought of as having belonged to 'the Gentry' in the sense of the traditional upper class of landowners. Alternatively, should we see them as having constituted a segment—numerically small but perhaps disproportionately significant—of what Clarendon was to call 'the middling sort', and which—on common sense grounds—we would call 'the middle classes', if we were not bedevilled by arguments for and against the Marxian historical doctrine? Be this as it may, these men still cared sufficiently about status to achieve a massive improvement on that of their fathers, unless they were merely borne upward on a kind of socio-economic tide—and a continued 'inflation of status' if not 'of honours' (Table 30).

We have now a total of 61 on the Esquire/Gentleman borderline or above and 80 (or 86 per cent of the known cases) as the equivalent of Gentleman of some kind or other. We have to remember the increasing erosion of meaning from the title of Gent. and the growing use of the ambiguous Mr, as well as the partially restored distinction between them following the Restoration. At the Esquire level, despite some tightening up when heraldic visitations were revived in the 1660s and again in the 1680s, any objective test of armigerous status was weakening, other than how a man was esteemed by his neighbours if not by society at large.[3]

TABLE 29 *Selected officials: fathers' status and place in family*

Fathers	Peer	Knight and baronet	Esquire	Esquire/ gentleman	Gentleman	Gentleman/Mr borderline	Yeoman	Merchant, citizen	Other plebeian	Clerical and medical	Total known	Unknown	Total
Sons	0	1 first; 2 younger	4 first; 2 younger	4 first; 1 younger; 1 unknown	10 first; 6 younger; 5 unknown	3 first; 1 younger; 1 unknown	1 younger; 1 unknown	3 first; 2 younger; 7 unknown	2 first; 2 younger; 14 unknown	3 first; 1 younger	30 first; 18 younger; 29 unknown	23 unknown	100
Total	0	3	6	6	21	5	2	12	18	4	77	23	100

TABLE 30 *Selected officials: status achieved*

Peer	Knight, baronet	Esquire	Esquire/ Gentleman borderline	Gentleman	Gentleman/ Mr borderline	Alderman, citizen, merchant	Other plebeian	Clerical and medical	Total known	Unknown	Total
0	11	42	8	10	8	12	1	1	93	7	100

199

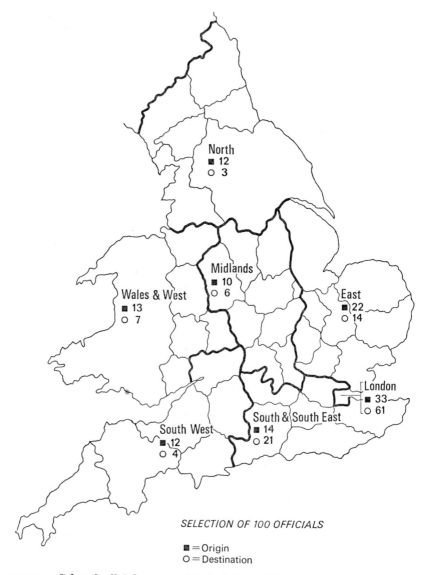

SELECTION OF 100 OFFICIALS

■ = Origin
○ = Destination

MAP 2   *Selected officials: geographical origins and destinations*

Still, it remains clear that these 100 men were more successful than the 200 drawn from the administration at large in ending their days significantly higher in the social scale than they had begun (Table 31).

TABLE 31   *Selected officials: extent of rise in social status*

Rose three degrees or more	7	72·2% of known cases as
Rose two degrees	9	= compared with 50·7% in the
Rose one degree	36	sample of officials (Table 13)
Unchanged	17	
Declined from father's rank	3	
Total known	72	
Unknown in relation to fathers	21	

At least one man in this group[4] is known to have disapproved of titles. And there may have been other political and religious radicals who did so too. But, short of indicating a wish not to be made a peer[5] and perhaps avoiding a knighthood or baronetcy, it is not clear how much a man could do. Modern 'honours' can be, and sometimes are, refused. Style is more difficult to part with. But in so far as Esquire and Gentleman had become more subjective measures of self-esteem in the social scale and less a matter of heraldic or other official authorisation, what men called themselves may be more of a pointer than it had been earlier in the century. Some radicals of the 1650s omitted any style in making their wills; others, whose families were not armigerous, called themselves Esquire or Gentleman. Lawrence Stone's thesis about alternative avenues of social advancement being more easily available and more acceptable by the late than in the early seventeenth century, is obviously relevant here.[6] But this still leaves open the question of whether style mattered less to people generally after 1660 than it had done before 1640, or whether on the contrary there were now more ways of attaining a higher status about which people still felt strongly.

The extent of geographical mobility is scarcely less dramatic than that of social mobility (Tables 32–4 and Map 2).

Expressed in percentages these changes are still more striking and well worth setting beside those for the 200 sample, and for the earlier sample of Charles I's officials (Table 33).

Granted that some of the total numbers in the different categories (see Tables 32 and 34) are too small for the changes to be statistically significant, the trend is unmistakable. And, as before, the figures for some individual counties are perhaps more interesting than those of the regions to which they have been allocated. Thus the number in Suffolk fell from six to one, in Yorkshire from nine to three; in Kent it rose from two to seven and in Middlesex from four to nine. If we put Essex, Kent and Middlesex with London, no less than 59·1 per cent of the known

TABLE 32   *Selected officials: geographical destinations*

Region	The same instances as for origins	Different instances from those of origins	Unknown in relation to origins	Totals	Multiple instances
North	3	0	0	3	1
Midlands	2	4	0	6	1
East	11	2	1	14	10
South and South-East	8	11	2	21	10
South-West	3	1	0	4	2
Wales and West	3	4	0	7	3
London	30	30	1	61	25
Scotland	1	0	1	2	0
Ireland	0	5	2	7	5
New England	3	4	0	7	7
West Indies	0	3	0	3	3
Foreign	0	2	0	2	0
Totals	64	66	7	137	67
Known men				94	
Men with multiple destinations				43	

destinations are found there (4+7+9+61 out of 137). Here, by contrast
with the sample of 200, the New Englanders come into their own; and
Professor Sachse's emphasis on the importance of these returned exiles
is amply upheld.[7] The effects of the Restoration on the careers of a large
proportion must have altered the pattern from what it would have been
if more had remained in office to the end of their lives.

TABLE 33   *Selected officials: extent of shift, in residence and property*

Region	Origins as % of known instances	Destinations as % of known instances	Change between columns 2 and 3	Comparable % change for 200 sample	The same % for 1625–42 sample
North	9·8	2·2	−7·6	−0·8	−2·5
Midlands	8·1	4·4	−3·7	−6·3	−6·1
East	17·9	10·2	−7·7	−4·1	+0·5
South and South-East	11·4	15·3	+3·9	−1·4	+4·5
South-West	9·8	2·9	−6·9	−7·9	−5·2
Wales and West	10·6	5·1	−5·5	−7·5	−6·6
London	26·8	44·5	+17·7	+21	+15·8
Other	5·7	15·3	+9·6	+7	−0·6
Total	100·1	99·9			

TABLE 34 Selected officials: geographical origins and destinations

Region	North	Midlands	East	South and South-East	South-West	Wales and West	London etc.	Other	Total known (men, not instances)	Unknown	Total instances	Multiple instances
Origins	12	10	22	14	12	13	33	7	93	7	123	30
Destinations	3	6	14	21	4	7	61	21	94	6	137	43

TABLE 35 Selected officials: higher education and further training

Father's status	Oxford	Cambridge	Other universities	Total	Gray's Inn	Lincoln's Inn	Inner Temple	Middle Temple	Other legal	Total	Apprentices
Esquire or above	1	2		3	2	1		1		4	} 5
Gentleman/Mr	2*	4	3*	9 (8)	4	2				6	
Citizen/plebeian		5		5	1*		2	1*	1	5 (4)	16
Unknown											7
Total	3	11	3	17 (16 men)	7	3	2	2	1	15 (14 men)	28

* Allow for multiple instances.

Again, their formal higher education was surprisingly limited, but their commercial and industrial bias shows up clearly (Table 35).

Small as these sets of figures are, the predominance of Cambridge and Gray's Inn is striking, in contrast to their absence in the 200 sample, noted earlier. As with the New England element, perhaps this is another aspect of the more ideologically 'committed' character of this group as opposed to the sample. The small total numbers of those who had been to a university or one of the inns is related to the small number of upper-class recruits and also to the excellent openings during the 1640s for men of talent, without much formal training or higher education, of whom there were no less than 33 out of the selected 100.[8] How far was this reflected in their appointment and entry to office (Table 36)?

TABLE 36   *Selected officials: factors in entry and appointment*

	Number of Instances		
	Sole evidence	*Part evidence*	*Total instances*
Pre-1642 office-holders surviving	0	5	5
Active parliamentarians, 1642–8	23	51	74
Patrimony	1	8	9
Patronage	1	33	34
Purchase	0	1	1
Religious connections	0	22	22
Entry 1648/9–1653 (little other evidence)	4	5	9
Entry 1653 (little other evidence)	0	3	3
Entry 1653/4–58/9 (little other evidence)	1	2	3
Professional qualifications	0	19	19
Total	30	149	179
Officials for whom there is multiple evidence			70

As before, we must remember that some of these categories are more objective and clear-cut than others, and that in some the probable omissions are inevitably more numerous. It is surprising, unless it is merely a predictable commentary on the surviving evidence, that more religious and political (patronage) connections have not been established, although they may be shrewdly suspected in several more instances. Easily the commonest reason for a man in this group being in office between 1649 and 1660 is that he had been a civil or military adherent of Parliament in the years from 1642 to 1648. But, as with the sample 200, this is only a restatement of the problem. Why were such men active parliamentarians during and after the Civil War; or rather, how did they come to be employed in Parliament's wartime and post-war administration? Perhaps it will help to establish how many of them were in completely or substantially new posts, and how many occupied pre-Civil

War offices (as distinct from continuing to occupy them). The best way to do this is by adopting a rough-and-ready functional classification, according to the branch of the administration or type of work and responsibility involved (Table 37).

TABLE 37   *Selected officials: old and new offices*

Branch or aspect of administration	*In estab-lished pre-1642 posts*	*In newly established posts*	*Total*
Ecclesiastical	0	1	1
Mint	2	0	2
Post Office	2	1	3
Central executive*	9	4	13
Revenue and finance	6	14	20
Diplomatic	5	0	5
Legal	1	0	1
Works and (later) household	1	3	4
Military (including ordnance)	1	11	12
Naval	7	14	21
Scotland and Ireland	1	5	6
Land sales	0	11	11
Compounding, sequestration, advance and indemnity	0	17	17
Accounts	0	7	7
Total	35	88	123†

* Including Clerks of the parliament etc.
† Includes 19 men counted twice and 2 counted three times.

Some of these headings are more artificial than others. Thus the separation of land sales from other revenue and finance, including customs and excise, is arbitrary. So is the inclusion of deputy Treasurers-at-War and Receivers-General of the Assessment under military and not under revenue or Scotland and Ireland as the case might be. Some men occupied old-established offices in one capacity, new ones in another; others held more than one position but exclusively of the old or the new variety. In some cases it is the newness or otherwise of the place which is doubtful. Some posts in the central executive under the Council of State and its committees are different in name only from the pre-1642 Clerkships of the Privy Council etc., and so have not been counted as new; the Treasurership for Council Contingencies and the Secretaryship to the Intelligence Committee were genuinely new.

It is clear at once[9] that most of the important new posts were connected with the fiscal and revenue system in the widest sense, and with the armed forces, or lay in areas where standing commissions operated as both legal tribunals and administrative departments. Some of the

officials connected with finance and land sales may not have been particularly committed or conscientious, while others in apparently less sensitive
areas were in practice more zealous supporters of the regime and had
higher standards of probity.[10] It is perhaps surprising that any lukewarm
supporters whose loyalty was suspect or whose honesty was open to
doubt should have been tolerated in the central executive itself or at the
heart of the financial system. The answer may be simply that until (at
the earliest) the summer of 1659 neither George Downing nor Samuel
Morland, nor any of the others in this group who were to bridge the
great divide of May 1660 successfully, was in fact 'disloyal' to the
Commonwealth; nor had they been disloyal to the Protectorate from
1653/4 to 1658/9. In this, after all, they were no different from the
greater men who bridged it at the highest political levels: Monck,
Montague, Broghill. As to personal and financial rather than political
reliability, only three were demonstrably less than wholly honest.[11] The
distinction between old and new offices obviously does not correspond
exactly to that between old and new men, but the two phenomena are
clearly connected. This will become clearer as we complete our attempt
at a quantitative group portrait of the selected 100.

Having entered office, how does their mobility in it compare with that
of the sample (Table 38)?

TABLE 38   *Selected officials: promotions, transfers, pluralism, deputation*

Changed office twice or more times	3	
Changed office once	29	= 36 (Sample 26%)
Returned after a break out of office	4	
Held two or more offices etc. at once	39	(Sample 16·5%)
Absentee and/or performer by deputy	2	
Deputy office-holder	6	
One (principal) office only in 1649–60	52	(Sample 74%)
In one office throughout 1649–60	15	(Sample 13%)*

* This is a minimum figure; some of the most obscure men in the 200 sample
may also belong here, bringing the total up to more than 30.

The impression here is one of men thrusting themselves forward and
being called on to act in varied capacities, either in succession or simul-
taneously. Our elimination of political and military leaders and judges
at the top and of minor functionaries at the bottom, as contrasted with
the sample, would predictably have this effect, given the general character
of the administrative system.

What use did these office-holders make of their position (Table 39)?

As with the sample, some of these figures are surely too low. More
than 16 must have bought lands; with sufficient labour, more such
information might be found, whereas evidence about their total wealth
at the end of their lives compared to what they began with, is—for many

of them—irretrievably lost. The fact that over half should have died well off is a reminder that the Restoration, whatever its effects on their careers in the public service, cannot have been universally catastrophic for their fortunes.

TABLE 39   *Selected officials: property and wealth*

Bought lands 1640s–50s	16
Interests in Ireland	8
Died rich, or richer than they began	54
Lost lands again and/or died poor	8
Multiple instances in first 4 categories	19
No evidence of change in wealth	33

Simply by virtue of being more important than most of their fellow administrators, we might expect their careers to have been more affected by the changes of regime within the period 1649–60. This does not seem to have been so (Table 40).

TABLE 40   *Selected officials: effects of political change, 1649–59*

	Not in office 1649–53 or 1659; in office only 1653/4–58/9	Not in office 1653/4–58/9; in office only 1649–53/4 or 1659	Tenure not affected by changes of 1653 and 1659	Date of death unknown in relation to Dec. 1653
Number	6	21*	73	—
Sample 200†	15·5%	19%	64%	1·5%

* Includes 6 who died before December 1653.
† See above, Table 24.

Whether because of their indispensability to whatever government was in power, or their greater commitment to the republic as such, or the absence of political leaders from the selection, the selected 100 thus show greater durability in office than the sample 200. It remains to be seen how the Restoration affected them; again we might expect it to have done so more positively (Table 41).

The difference here may, of course, be due to the larger total of unknowns in the sample. If, as is strongly suspected, most of these belong in the category of losing or quitting office in 1660, then of those still alive in May 1660 a slightly larger proportion of the selection would have survived the Restoration successfully or subsequently have re-established themselves in the public, or royal service than was true of the sample. Once more the question is, what importance to attach to the 20 per cent element of continuity in, or resumption of, office, from republic to monarchy. Within this category, only six or seven can be said to have held

TABLE 41 *Selected officials: effects of political change, 1660 and after*

	Already dead by May 1660	Executed	Died in exile	Died in prison; other pains and penalties	In prison temporarily	Lost office or withdrew into private life	Remained in office under Crown, or later resumed it*	Pension from Crown but no office	Unknown
Number %	17	0	1	2	3†	52	20	1†	8
Sample %	12·5			55		45	18·5	—	24

* In two cases only after 1688; local offices such as JP have not been counted here.
† Overlaps with those in column 6; therefore excluded from totals.

208

equally or more responsible posts after 1660. There is an overlap, but certainly no statistically significant correlation, between them and those known to have died rich. Some of our selected 100 probably did better for themselves financially in private life than they would have done by continuing to serve their country—or monarch—according to how they saw it.

Here, as with the sample 200, much remains to be said. On some of the most interesting aspects we do not have sufficient and comparable information about enough of them to make a quantitative assessment possible. It is time now to look at some of those from both groups as individuals; as such they may be typical of numerous others or else characteristic of no one but themselves.

v   SOME CASE HISTORIES

A historian wants to know the characters in his story in as many different ways as possible. He needs to see the men who served in some public capacity, for instance, in close-up, both at work and at home. Otherwise they will remain like figures passing in a street, people one sees every day but about whom, as individuals, one rarely ever learns anything.[1] Ideally he also wants to see a man (or woman) in history both as others saw him and as he saw himself. But, alas, this is almost all a matter of empty theory as far as our men are concerned. Apart from their wills, often made many years later and sometimes under conditions of severe illness or senescence, we have virtually no autobiographical or first-hand biographical materials about any of them, or materials only of the most fragmentary and limited nature. Moreover, as landowners and business or professional men, surprisingly few have left voluminous records behind them. This is by contrast with Charles I's officials—patchy as personal source-materials are for them too;[2] it also contrasts with the more plentiful evidence surviving for later Stuart officials.[3] Considering the number of puritan apologias, histories, accounts of conversions, funeral sermons and so on,[4] it is remarkable for how few Commonwealth and Protectorate officials anything even of this sort has survived.

The two leading figures of the time who wrote their Memoirs or Memorials at greatest length are Edmund Ludlow[5] and Bulstrode Whitelocke.[6] Although best known as a Lieutenant-General of Horse and a republican opponent of the Protectorate, Ludlow was also a Commissioner for the civil government of Ireland from 1650 to 1655 and in that capacity within the scope of this study. Whitelocke was a Commissioner for the Great Seal from 1649 to 1655 and again in 1659, and a Treasury Commissioner from 1655 to 1659/60. Thanks to the zeal and ingenuity of his latest biographer,[7] Whitelocke's personal journal for his early career before the Civil Wars is now in the British Museum.[8] From this

Whitelocke emerges as a distinctly more human figure, less self-righteous and self-exculpatory than in his published *Memorials*. Milton wrote no formal autobiography, but a whole volume of writings 'on Himself' has recently been published.[9] We have many of Marvell's letters after 1660, very few before, and not much else.[10] The elder Sir Henry Vane left a brief autobiographical fragment;[11] Hugh Peter wrote a short self-justification for his family on the eve of his execution in 1660.[12] Sir Anthony Ashley Cooper, the future Earl of Shaftesbury, a member of the Protector's Council in 1653–4, also left a fragment of apologetical memoirs, which tells us nothing whatever about the period when he was in office, emphasising instead his innocence of regicide (which was true) and his important role in effecting the Restoration (which was grossly exaggerated).[13] Then there is the appallingly critical account of another Cromwellian councillor, Philip Sidney, Viscount Lisle, by his father the Earl of Leicester.[14] Together with other materials in the Sidney Papers and Lisle's will (made when he was himself Earl of Leicester in 1697),[15] this does tell us more about Lisle as a person. Proud, touchy, quarrelsome, with an irregular private life,[16] one wonders why and how he was tolerated in the Council of State, on which he sat from 1649 to 1659, with only a short break in 1653. It is another reminder of the desire under Commonwealth and Protectorate alike, but especially the latter, to conciliate the old peerage if they would give even a modicum of support to the republican regime.

When we turn to the middle ranks of the administration, the lack of such private materials becomes a much more severe handicap. Perhaps the best way to convey a more human impression of the men with whom we have been concerned quantitatively in the previous two sections of this chapter will be to look at some of them according to their place in the machinery of government and their personal characteristics.

Compounders and other commissioners

Of the seven men appointed in 1650 to manage the system of penal taxation, Josias Berners was the nearest to being a politician in his own right. He was born in the 1600s into a London family of minor gentry, with both legal and civic connections. As with many others who acted under the Commonwealth, a humbler social origin was ascribed to him in the eighteenth century, when he was described as 'originally a serving man', but this is misleading. Berners went to Gray's Inn in 1620, where his uncle, Robert Berners Esquire, was a Counsellor at Law. Although he does not seem to have been called to the bar, he may well have practised as an attorney or solicitor during the later 1620s and the 1630s. He seems to have lived in what was the Middlesex commuters' village of Clerkenwell all his adult life. His first public appearance was as an assessment commissioner for Westminster in 1643. Whether his positive anti-monarchist leanings or merely his domicile and profession in the London area made Berners a parliamentarian remains surmise. In 1647–8 he was more regularly named to commissions for Middlesex and Westminster. By January 1649 he was sufficiently reliable to be named as a commissioner of the High Court of Justice, to try the King, but there is no evidence that he ever acted in this capacity. Not that Berners objected on principle to prerogative jurisdiction, that is trial by special legislatively appointed commissioners, rather than by judges and jurors, for he served as Registrar to a subsequent High Court of Justice, which proceeded against royalist conspirators in 1651–2. According to his eighteenth-century biographer, it was his wife's influence which prevented him from acting either in 1649 or against the royalist conspirators in 1658 when he was again named to a High Court. His refusal, or anyway failure to act against the King did not halt the flow of minor appointments, mainly of a local nature. But his first major position was as one of the seven commissioners appointed in April 1650 to execute all the powers formerly residing in the various parliamentary and other committees for compounding, sequestration and the advance of monies. He was by then styled Esquire and named first among his colleagues,[17] although he did not act as chairman of the committee once it began to function. The annual salary of each commissioner was £300. Berners was already a Contractor for the sale of Dean and Chapter lands but this was not a stipendiary post. In 1652 the seven Compounders were also given charge of all Indemnity business, replacing the previous parliamentary committee. Berners had already been appointed to the body curiously known as the Obstructions Committee or Commission, which was set up to inquire into and overcome the various legal and other obstacles which had prevented the successful completion of the various land sales (episcopal, royal, capitular, etc.) ordered since 1646. His colleagues on this body were also non-MPs, if somewhat different types, but he appears to have felt that as the only trained lawyer he must give priority to Obstructions business. On these grounds, he excused his absence to his fellow Compounders; as to the Indemnity Commission, he scarcely sat at all during most of 1652–3. At the beginning of 1652 he was also appointed to the Hale Committee on law reform, but this was designedly part-time—and unpaid. For Obstructions he received another £300 a year; there is no evidence that he forfeited his Compounding-cum-Indemnity salary because of non-attendance. In the spring of 1653 the Law Reform Committee members were made temporary Judges for the Probate of Wills, without stipends but with the right to take the usual fees.

Berners accepted the dissolution of the Rump, in that he did not join in the protest against it as did three of his six colleagues, who lost their jobs in consequence. Presumably his attitude in 1653 was that of a radical republican who had become disillusioned with the failings of the Parliament and its members. He was not in the Barebones Parliament, but this can hardly be taken as a pointer to his convictions. Although reappointed as a Compounding Commissioner at the fall of the Bare- bones and the inception of the Protectorate in December 1653, it is clear that he would not accept this second coup or counter-revolution. He received one or two other minor appointments to do with forests, land drainage and river navigation (in 1654–7) and he was actually reappointed to the then moribund Compounding Commission at the accession of Richard Cromwell in September 1658. But there is no evidence of his taking any significant part in public affairs or central administration from December 1653 until the fall of the Protectorate and the reinstitution of the Rump in May 1659. During the Protectorate, Berners corresponded from London with another political opponent of the Cromwellian regime, John Hobart of Norwich, from which his sincerely parliamentarian atti- tude is clear. His opposition was to the rule of a single person instead of a properly elected legislature. And despite his acceptance of its demise in April 1653, the Rump's restoration in 1659 saw Berners emerge for the first time as a political figure. Having helped to present an anti-Protec- torate London petition to Richard Cromwell's parliament the previous February, he was now rewarded by being named as one of ten non-MPs elected to the restored Council of State in May. He served actively in this capacity until October, and sided strongly with the Rump against the army leaders, when they again interrupted its sittings and then tried to govern through a committee of safety. Berners acted as an ally of Hesil- rige and Scot against Fleetwood and Lambert; he helped to secure the Tower in December 1659 and on the second restoration of the Rump he was re-elected to the Council. But, like Hesilrige and the other republi- cans who had put their faith in Monck as a counterweight to Lambert, Berners was abruptly removed from public life with the return of the secluded members on 21 February 1660. Although he could easily demonstrate that he was not a regicide, he was obviously a marked man. He was not dismissed from his offices; they simply ceased to exist. According to the eighteenth-century author, the Rev. Mark Noble, who never gave his sources, Berners was refused a pardon by the Restoration government as too dangerous, but remained unpunished thanks to the King's clemency. He appears to have died very early in 1661. Berners was still a man of substance at his death, with lands in Hertfordshire as well as Middlesex and shares in London's water supply, the New River Company (of which he was also the Secretary). He provided generously for his near relatives and servants, making Christ's Hospital his ultimate residual heir; he cared sufficiently for his books and papers to leave them specifically to his only son who inherited most of his other property. The male line of the family died out in the next century. It is remarkable that Berners is not in the *DNB*, considering his importance from 1649 to 1660.[18]

Captain William Molins, alias Molyns or Mullins, was also a Londoner but of definitely non-gentry origins. He was probably a cordwainer and upholsterer, of whom nothing is known before his emergence as an active parliamentarian in the City from 1644 on. He was Comptroller of the Ordnance (or artillery) for the City's forces from 1645 to 1647. What part he took in the clash between the City and the army in that year is unclear. He was acting as a Sequestration Commissioner for London by 1649–50 and would appear to have had no difficulty about accepting the new government. In September 1649 he 'bought' nearly £1,000 worth of episcopal lands in Kent; this was presumably in large part a credit transaction for money owing to him by the State over the preceding eight or nine years. It can only have been his London sequestration work which qualified him for his April 1650 appointment as a Compounding Commissioner. He acted very regularly in that capacity, and from 1652 as an Indemnity Commissioner. But he was one of the thirty-six prominent Londoners who in May 1653 petitioned Cromwell either to restore the Rump or to call another parliament forthwith; and he was accordingly removed from all his salaried posts and employments. Molins was reappointed in 1659 and appears to have acted again until early 1660, even during the Committee of Safety's regime of October–December 1659. He was insufficiently militant, or notorious, to suffer at the Restoration, which he survived, returning to the London business world from which he had emerged twenty years earlier. A more obscure figure than Berners, he too was evidently some kind of parliamentarian republican, but may have been a presbyterian in religion. He or his father acted as an elder of St Margaret's, Fish Street, in the later 1640s, and one or other of them uttered conventionally Calvinist sentiments in his will (made and proved in 1662).[19]

Richard Moore's background was somewhat different. His grandfather, also Richard, was an active west-country parliamentarian MP until his death in 1643; his father Samuel (1594–1662) was on numerous county committees for Monmouth, Herefordshire and above all Shropshire, the family's county of origin, right through from 1642/3 to 1660, but never held office at the national level; presumably Samuel remained at home and operated regionally from there. Our Richard was at Gray's Inn during the Civil War and after. He had held no previous office when he was appointed to the Compounding Commission in April 1650, aged about 23, an example of family or connectional patronage at its most effective—and potentially damaging. Whatever his ability or integrity—

on the eve of the Restoration Moore was to be described as a 'time-server'—he attended regularly, also for Indemnity business from 1652; he was re-appointed at each renewal of the commission in 1653–4 and again in 1658–9; he was a London militia commissioner under the restored Rump (winter 1659–60), and then vanishes from public view, until he re-appears in Shropshire years later. Moore is the most colourless of the original seven 'great compounders'; indeed the adjective hardly seems apt in his case save for the power which he helped to wield.[20]

Samuel Moyer (c. 1609–1682/3) was the wealthiest and perhaps the most powerful of the seven. Born in Essex but apparently raised on the Surrey shore of the lower Thames, he was an established London merchant by the 1640s, and first appears as one of the important managers of the London 'Sea Adventure' to Ireland, speculating in the naval side of the projected re-conquest, in June 1642. His next entry on the public scene, and his first official appointment, was as a commissioner to deal with ex-royalists who came in from the King's quarters (November 1645); he was then named as one of several non-MPs to be added to the parliamentary Compounding Committee (February 1647); he was appointed to various London commissions and committees in 1647–8; in January 1649 he became a member of the special commission to 'regulate' the offices of the Navy and Customs, while in February 1649 he was named to the second High Court of Justice, to try the Duke of Hamilton, the Earl of Holland and other royalist leaders held responsible for the bloodshed of the second Civil War in 1648. Moyer had bought, or been allocated to pay debts owing to him, nearly £9,000 worth of episcopal lands, and had £600 invested as an Irish Adventurer. He was no stranger to the business of penal taxation when appointed a Compounding Commissioner in April 1650, for he had been serving under the Haberdashers' and Gold-smiths' Hall committees as early as 1643–4. Perhaps in recognition of this or of his standing in the City, Moyer was chosen by his colleagues to act as chairman, until at the end of 1651 chairmanship of all committees was ordered by Parliament to rotate monthly or oftener.

Moyer was one of the wealthiest and most influential lay members of the Baptist churches. When he became a Baptist is not clear, but this may well account for the slowness of his advancement from 1643 to 1646. He is very conspicuously not an elder of any of the London Presbyterian classes, although several known Congregationalists were so appointed. By 1653 he appears to have been a political ally of Major-General Thomas Harrison. According to Lilburne he had held out for the truth against Sir Arthur Hesilrige's pressure in the Harraton Colliery case of 1651, but had been voted down by his more pliant, less honest colleagues. His other offices in the early 1650s included the post of Check Inwards at the London Customs, also salaried at £300 per annum but presumably not requiring lengthy personal attendance. For an export-import merchant to hold such a position seems open to precisely the objections which the radicals were then bringing against the Rump and its members. He was also a Law Reform Commissioner and hence became a Probate Judge. Moyer would seem to have followed Harrison and the leading Baptists in their approval of the April 1653 dissolution. He was obviously regarded as an influential ally by the new government, and was nominated to the Barebones Parliament, which in turn elected him to the Council of State. The complexity of divisions within the Barebones is signified by Moyer's failure to obtain re-election to the Council in November 1653, although he has been rightly regarded by historians from Gardiner to Trevor-Roper as one of the radical leaders in that assembly. Re-appointed to the Compounding Commission in December 1653, his opposition to the Protectorate was none the less as unqualified as Harrison's; he lost his Customs post in January and ceased to act as a Commissioner in February 1654. Like Berners, but through a different kind of opposition to the Protectorate, Moyer re-emerged as a radical republican leader in 1659, and was re-appointed to his Commissionership and as Probate Judge by the Rump in May 1659. He was acting in sequestration or composition business as late as the winter of 1659–60 but withdrew totally into private life after 21 February. Unlike the Lambertian Independents and the militant Fifth Monarchists, there is no evidence that the Baptists projected any opposition by force to the King's return, although like others of his faith Moyer was imprisoned lengthily in the early 1660s and had to pay £500 for his release. He remained a wealthy and well-connected man, living in London but with a country estate in Essex, and representing his company (the Mercers) on the Gresham College committee as late as 1673; he died, full of years, in the early 1680s. His eldest son inherited and became a landed gentleman in Essex, high sheriff of his county and a baronet, but on his dying without male issue the family failed in this line. Moyer provided carefully for both his soul and his worldly goods. His mercantile connections were extensive, with £3,200 invested in the East India Company and £400 in the Royal African Company and shares in at least four ships. He did not forget to dispose of his best Persian carpet and sought hard to avoid family quarrels over his property. Moyer also remembered the bluecoat children of Christ's Hospital and the Mercers' Company, his 'dear Pastor', Mr John Collins, and the poor of Collins's congregation. Either he had been reconverted in old age from Baptist to Congregationalist beliefs, or he was an ecumenical kind of puritan, for he directed that money left for the relief of poor and needy ministers should be distributed jointly by Collins and the Congregationalist leader (an ex-Cromwellian) Dr John Owen. Characteristically, Moyer set a ceiling for the cost of his own funeral, but it was as high as £300. A decent measure of affluence, even luxury—and a fitting state—were evidently fully compatible with his ardent religious faith. If an 'extremist' in one sense, Moyer was no crackpot; one could call him a 'fanatic' only by misusing that word and applying it to anyone with strong views, opposed or unsympathetic to one's own.[21]

With James Russell (*c.* 1610–1655), another Londoner on the Commission, we return to a more obscure level, except for his having kept links with his provincial place of origin at the same time as he became a man of standing in the City. While nominally he was apprenticed in the Drapers' Company (1626), as the orphaned son of a non-armigerous gentleman, in reality Russell's master was a merchant adventurer and member of the East India Company, and he had clearly become a merchant of some standing himself by 1642, when he was elected to the Common Council of London. Apart from those connected with the City, Russell's early appointments were mainly in the Customs. He visited Flanders, combining business with a political mission, in 1644. He was appointed as a Tryer for the Seventh London classis, at St Stephen's, Coleman Street, the parish from which the great radical Independent John Goodwin had been evicted by the Long Parliament. Russell was a Contractor for the sale of bishops' lands, and subsequently acquired over £4,800 worth of them. Like other future Compounders, he was a Regulator in January 1648/9, and a Contractor for Dean and Chapter lands later that year. As well as being a Commissioner, from 1650 he was Check or Cheque-General for the Outports. His Hereford connections are underlined by a reference to his making a journey to that county early in 1652 when his fellow Compounding Commissioners asked him to investigate the local commissioners and, if necessary, take action against them. Russell joined in the London petition against the demise of the Rump and lost all his offices in consequence. He was, however, offered a role in the Anglo-Danish negotiations during the summer of 1654 and may have gone over to Denmark then. He died intestate, in London, the next year. Presumably a Congregationalist puritan in religion and a parliamentary republican in politics, Russell's importance was by virtue of the posts which he held, notably as Compounding and Indemnity Commissioner, although his most responsible position was briefly as an Admiralty and Navy Commissioner (from December 1652 to May 1653).[22]

Arthur Squibb the younger (d. 1680) came of a minor Dorset gentry family. His namesake Arthur the elder (1578–1650), Teller of the Exchequer and latterly also Clarenceux King-of-Arms, was his first cousin once removed and—on the maternal side—his uncle by marriage. Although Arthur senior was a parliamentarian, it is far from clear that this was a decisive influence on the younger Arthur, whose brother

Lawrence was a royalist Teller of the Receipt and man of business to Francis Lord Cottington, Charles I's Chancellor of the Exchequer and Master of the Wards. The younger Arthur appears to have had no formal higher education, but in the early 1640s he was employed by Sir Edward Powell, Master of Requests, a Herefordshire landowner with interests in the iron industry. Powell was to be a neutral, or 'side-changer' during the Civil War. By 1646 Squibb was employed officially as collector of the sequestered revenues of the Archbishop of Canterbury, mainly in Kent. He was probably also a sequestrator under the Compounding Committee, and he was named to various London committees and commissions in the late 1640s. He had acquired a reversion to a tellership at the same time as his brother's appointnent in 1640, and he invested £300 in the promise of Irish lands.

His appointment as Commissioner for Compounding in April 1650 was Squibb's first major position. It recognised his experience in sequestration work and his commitment to the puritan Commonwealth. It is not clear whether or not he was yet a member of the small but vociferous (and in 1653–4 temporarily influential) Fifth-Monarchy sect. He was constantly late for committee meetings; perhaps he was waiting for the Second Coming, or at least for the rule of the Saints upon Earth. Squibb followed Moyer in accepting the dissolution of the Rump, and he too was nominated to the Barebones Parliament in July 1653. Professor Trevor-Roper has shown that Squibb's house in Westminster was used as a meeting-place by the radical leaders in the Barebones. But we should not exaggerate his importance; unlike Moyer he was not elected to the Council of State. And there must have been plenty of members who were ready enough to go along with Moyer and Squibb in voting down the Court of Chancery, or in abolishing tithes and advowsons, without committing themselves to Squibb's more extravagant beliefs—or to his executive leadership. Unlike Moyer he was dropped from the Compounding-cum-Indemnity Commission immediately on the institution of the Protectorate; his relatives' claims to the tellership, which he had apparently sold, were likewise turned down when the Exchequer was re-established later in 1654. Although not arrested during the Protectorate, Squibb was regarded as a potential Fifth-Monarchist and republican conspirator against the regime. Like others of the same complexion, he was restored to his commissionership in 1659 and acted in compounding business into the winter of 1659–60. Although not actively engaged in resistance to the Restoration or in Venner's Fifth-Monarchy rising of the following winter, Squibb was equally an object of suspicion to the monarchy. Once more his claim to the tellership was rejected. He died at Chertsey in Surrey where he had latterly lived; what he lived on after 1659 is unclear. That he had contrived to retain some of the land in which he had invested during the Interregnum seems probable, but remains unproven. He bequeathed property in Essex and Ireland as well as legacies. But these were small (£30 per annum to his wife), and his total wealth was probably modest. Squibb thanked God for his health and property but made no specific mention of his soul: there is no evidence either way as to his persistence in extreme millenarian beliefs. Squibb belongs to the same broad category as Moyer, but he was more radical in religion, less wealthy and influential, and—even in 1653—considerably less important. He was the only Compounding Commissioner for whom the adjectives extremist or fanatical might seem appropriate.[23]

Lastly among the original seven Compounders was Edward Winslow (1595–1655), the only one to be noted in the *DNB* and to be the subject of a modern biography. These honours have been accorded him more as one of the Pilgrim Fathers and leaders of the infant colony of New Plymouth than as an official under the Commonwealth and Protectorate. Winslow came from a Gloucestershire–Worcestershire family at the lower end of the gentry class bordering on that of yeoman; the Winslows were certainly not within the scope of the Heralds when they visited these counties. He served as Assistant Governor to the redoubtable William Bradford in New Plymouth almost continuously from 1624 to 1647 with terms as Governor when Bradford stood down, in 1633, 1636 and 1644. He was back in England by 1649 when—described as Gentleman and Citizen—he was appointed one of the Trustees for the sale of the goods (that is, movable possessions) of the late king and the rest of the royal family. Winslow had no other administrative experience in this country before his appointment to the Compounding Commission in 1650. Whether or not for the same kind of reasons as Molins and Russell did so, he too joined in the petition against the forced dissolution of 20 April 1653 and was consequently dropped from all his employments in May. Presumably he remained in opposition to the rule of Cromwell and the new Council and then of the Barebones.

Surprisingly, and alone among the original seven, he was re-appointed to office at the beginning of the Protectorate and served actively throughout 1654. Near the end of that year he sailed for the Spanish Main as one of the civilian commissioners appointed by the Protector and his Council to accompany Admiral Penn and General Venables on the ill-fated 'Western Design', which after failing disgracefully in the attempt on Hispaniola led instead to the English conquest of Jamaica. But Winslow was spared the shame and ignominy, and the squalor of the campaigns on the greater Antilles; he died at sea between Barbados and Hispaniola in May 1655. His will, composed at the beginning of the voyage, disposed of property whose extent and value is unclear, in both New and old England. He omitted any religious prologue. Unless most of his land was already settled on his son, the impression is one of rather modest wealth.

What Winslow had lived on in London is problematic—his official salary only, it may be, in which case office must have been a near necessity to him. Winslow cannot be said to typify returned New Englanders, most of whom came from Massachusetts Bay and not New Plymouth; he is also unusual in having been prepared to serve both Rump and Protector while rejecting the first of the two revolutions in 1653. His own religious position, presumably one of separatist congregationalism, may have made him suspicious of the Baptists' prominence in 1653. But this is speculation. Winslow was an experienced administrator, but in the utterly different circumstances of a new country with an ideologically committed settler population.[24]

Edward Carey (c. 1620–1657) was the second son of an Esquire from the strongly puritan county of Huntingdon. His father is not named in the 1613 visitation there; either the family moved to Epperton, alias Everton, only between then and the late 1630s, or else the Careys were not genuinely armigerous. He entered Clare College, Cambridge, in 1636, matriculating at the university in 1637; in 1641 he went on to the Middle Temple. He was a law student in London throughout the Civil War, as far as the record shows, being called to the bar in 1648. He was evidently a supporter of the new Commonwealth, and became a commissioner to take the accounts of the army in November 1649. In May 1650 the newly appointed Compounding Commissioners made him their Examiner; he had already acted as counsel to the Committee for the Advance of Monies and in 1651 he served similarly with the Indemnity Committee. His annual salary as Examiner was £160; in 1652 this post was extended to cover the Commissioners' new responsibility for Indemnity business too. When the Rump's adherents were removed and the vacancies needed to be filled, his was a logical appointment to the Compounding-cum-Indemnity Commission (in July 1653). Having accepted the dissolution of the Rump, Carey appears equally to have gone along with the forced transition from the Barebones to the Protectorate, and he apparently continued to serve until his death in 1657. He was regarded with sufficient favour to be appointed to a judicial post in Ireland, as Baron of the Exchequer, but he seems not to have taken it up; he sat in the Second Protectorate Parliament and was then Deputy High Steward of Westminster. Compounding and Indemnity business having virtually ceased by 1655, in 1656 he was appointed to the new Commission on Concealments or 'Discoveries', to seek out titles to land etc. which were the Protector's or the State's by right but had been wrongly kept in private hands. He also acted as a judge in London. He died during the summer vacation of 1657, leaving property in his county and at Marylebone, whither he had recently moved from Westminster. His main Everton estate seems to have been worth only £100 p.a. Carey represents the type of not very affluent younger son of a minor gentry family, who must have been almost wholly dependent on his earnings as a lawyer and then as an official. His prominence in the public service at a relatively early age may be variously ascribed to positive enthusiasm for the puritan republic, his ability and professional qualifications or—more tentatively but not implausibly—to a Huntingdonshire connection between his family and the Cromwells or other parliamentarian leaders, although neither his father nor his brother was named to any committees. The only mystery about Carey concerns his Irish appointment and his failure to go over and take it up. No wonder successive governors of Ireland were always complaining about the shortage of judges and councillors.[25]

John Upton (*c.* 1618–1689/90) had a family background superficially similar to that of Richard Moore. His father, also John of Lucton in Devonshire, married Dorothy, daughter of Sir Anthony Rous and half-sister of both Francis Rous and John Pym. Upton senior went to the Inner Temple; our John had no formal higher education, but in 1612 he was apprenticed to a Citizen and Haberdasher of London who was also a Merchant Adventurer and member of the East India Company, and became free as a Haberdasher in 1641. He was related by marriage to John Thurloe, and by 1653 this may have counted for as much as the Rous and Pym connections through his father. His first employment had been as a commissioner for the sale of captured Prize Goods in 1649; next he became co-Victualler of the Navy (November 1650), a position arguing business experience and credit-worthiness. He was evidently no devotee of the Rump and was added to the Compounding and Indemnity Commission in July 1653, being re-appointed after the fall of the Bare-bones in December and again early in 1654; he also served on the Irish and Scottish Affairs Committee under the temporary Council of State in the summer of 1653 and in 1655 became a Commissioner for Accounts, to compensate for the now inoperative Compounding-Indemnity post. More important, and symbolic of his mercantile standing, in 1655 Upton became a Commissioner of the Customs, one of a small syndicate who managed this major branch of the public revenue on a percentage basis. He remained in this post until 1659; he was re-appointed a Sequestration and Compounding Commissioner by Richard Cromwell in 1658, but the restored Rump evidently regarded him as unacceptable, being a committed Cromwellian; probably this arose through the Thurloe rather than the Rous connection. He held no office, and (as far as can be seen) took no part in public affairs from the fall of the Protectorate until well into the reign of Charles II, when rather surprisingly he again became Commissioner for the Customs under the Treasury Commission of 1667–72, this time at the enviable salary of £2,000 a year. Upton lived to see the Revolution of 1688, having apparently remarried in 1673. He provided for a considerable number of children and other relatives including his sister-in-law, Secretary Thurloe's widow. From the nature of his testamentary dispositions, it seems that Upton died a wealthy man, although how much of this was due to his nine years' service under the republic is unknown. He should perhaps be thought of primarily as a merchant for whom navy victualling and customs management were natural extensions of interest, while the business of Compounding and Indemnity was outside his normal range.[26]

The other additional Compounding Commissioner appointed in 1653 was an elderly South Walian, Rice Williams (?pre-1580–?post-1659), a radical puritan without many other apparent qualifications. He is to be distinguished from his namesake Rice, alias Rees, Williams, a London mercer, who had been a supplier of the royal household before the Civil War. Moreover, like many Welsh names, his is an extremely usual one; probably he was of minor gentry stock from the Glamorgan-Monmouth region, and went to Oxford in the reign of James I. What he did between then and the later 1640s is an almost total blank. He was named to local committees from 1647 and 1648 on. In 1652, as we have seen, he was recommended for office solely on religious grounds. It is tempting to see Williams's appointment to the Compounding and Indemnity Commission in July 1653 as part of the Harrison-Moyer-Squibb take-over bid from within the Cromwellian regime. On the other hand, when the final parting of the ways came between the Cromwellians and the Harrisonians in December 1653, Williams stayed with the former; he remained in office until 1655 and resumed it again when the Compounding and Sequestration Commission was revived in 1658–9. His last public appearance was in 1659, and he may have died intestate in that year, no will being extant. There is no evidence that Rice Williams had any means of support in London besides his income from office; how he managed from 1655 to 1658 is not clear, unless he withdrew to his modest patrimony in Monmouthshire. Religious connections seem to explain his entry to office. Early in 1654 an itinerant radical preacher in Monmouthshire was accused of having taught that 'Christ was as old as old Rice Williams of Newport, one of the Propagation Commissioners, and had a large grey beard'. What made him a Protectorian, and not—as might have been predicted—a Harrisonian republican, we cannot tell; conceivably the long-delayed fruits of office were one element in his decision.[27]

Just as the Compounding and Indemnity Commissioners of the 1650s had often qualified themselves in some kind of official service during the 1640s, so the same is broadly true of the members of the various Accounts Committees.

Nicholas Bond (d. 1673) was of obscure, certainly non-gentry origins. He was acting as a commissary, or supply official, for the parliamentary armies by 1643–4, and in 1645 he was serving in the Household of the King's children, who were Parliament's prisoners. He was presumably a London businessman, conceivably of Surrey origins; although he was later designated Esquire, he was not of a gentry family. He seems to have had no connection with the well-known parliamentarian politician and committee-man, Denis Bond of Dorchester, extensive as were the latter's family ramifications. Nicholas Bond became an Auditor and member of the Committee for taking the accounts of the officers and soldiers of the army in July 1648; and, like his colleagues on that body, he was named to the new Accounts Committee in October 1649, and remained on it until the end of its career in 1659. He collected other offices too. In 1649 he became a Contractor for the sale of Crown lands; he was Keeper of the garden at Nonsuch House, and briefly in the mid-1650s co-Farmer of the excise on Timber. His most onerous post was as Steward in charge of the entertainment of foreign envoys, which he undertook in 1652 and was trying to resign, on grounds of ill-health, in 1657. Bond was unaffected by the various changes of government, and appears as a 'mere' functionary, prepared to serve Long Parliament, Commonwealth, Lord General and Barebones, Protectorate, and re-stored Commonwealth by turns. He bought (or, more likely, was repaid with) over £1,600 worth of episcopal lands which he presumably had to disgorge in 1660. Yet he managed to retain at least the tenancies, for he disposed of these very same properties in his will over a decade later. His cash legacies totalled over £4,400, plus annuities and portions to be raised out of lands. Bond clearly had puritan sympathies, for he left £200 to 'the poor and such as are in necessity and want especially Prisoners that suffer for conscience sake . . .' As with Upton, it looks as if most of Bond's wealth must have come from trade or other business interests; public office appears a lengthy but incidental break in his career. As for his beliefs, he was simply a puritan to whom the political niceties of Commonwealth or Protectorate meant little.[28]

Henry Broad's background is, if anything, even more obscure than Nicholas Bond's, but his career during the Civil War was somewhat different. He was acting as an Auditor for the accounts of the parliamentary armies as early as November 1642; in April 1643 he audited the expense account of the committee sent to Oxford to negotiate a peace settlement with the King the previous winter; during 1644 he acted as co-auditor mainly for the army of the Eastern Association with a certain Richard Wilcox, with whom he was to be associated for the next fifteen years. In November Wilcox brought a very serious charge against Broad of falsifying accounts, presumably for his personal advantage, and a lively controversy arose with both men enlisting influential supporters. Eventually the case died down, Wilcox having apparently failed to make good his allegations. At any rate, both continued in Parliament's service, although one would not have expected them to make the most harmonious of colleagues after such a collision. Broad also acted as Secretary to Parliament's Committee for the associated counties of the Eastern Association. He was not on the non-parliamentary Committee for the Accounts of the Kingdom (of 1644 to 1648/9). But along with Bond and Wilcox he was appointed to the important Committee of Auditors for taking the accounts of the army in July 1648—the embryo of the Commonwealth Accounts Committee of October 1649, of which he was inevitably a member. Moreover on the restoration of the Exchequer under the Protectorate he became an Auditor of the Revenues in it. He was still acting there and on the Accounts Committee in 1658–9; thereafter he fades back into the obscurity from which he had emerged. We do know that in 1650 he lived in Westminster, while by 1654–5 he had moved out to Chiswick. He was still there in 1659 when he was fiercely critical of the delays due to the inaction of Henry Robinson, the Accounts Committee's best-known member. Broad may still have been alive in 1665 if it was his son who went to Oxford in that year and not the son of some other Henry Broad of London, Gent. He was made a grant of arms as an Esquire in the mid-1650s when Yorkshire origins were ascribed to him; he got this grant confirmed in 1661. Unless this is completely bogus, he cannot therefore be the Henry Broad of Worcestershire, Gent., born about 1582 and educated at Brasenose College, Oxford, Clement's Inn and the Inner Temple; nor can he have originated in the eastern counties as one might suppose from his military auditing work. Presumably Broad had a patron or connection in the army, the Exchequer or Parliament in the early 1640s; if it were known who this was, much else about his career would fall into place. As it is, we can only suppose that he was at least a negative parliamentarian and subsequently a republican of both Commonwealth and Protectorate varieties. Broad was a specialist in accounting, unlike some of his fellow committee members, but whether he was self-taught or had some earlier training in handling accounts remains unclear.[29]

The future chairman of the 1650s Accounts Committee, John Greensmith (d. 1665), was another London businessman. He was living in the City in 1638, and is found helping to collect signatures against the bishops in December 1641, when he is described as a tobacconist. He may have been the John Greensmith who helped to publish the semi-official newspaper, the *Weekly Accompt*, in 1643 and acted as a collector of intelligence or informer for the Committee of Both Kingdoms in 1645; later in that year he was put on the committee to deal with royalists who came to

London from the King's quarters without having compounded. As a merchant of London he invested £300 in the future distribution of re-conquered Irish lands. Although he received no further official appoint-ment until the setting up of the new Accounts Committee in October 1649, he was considered to have done so much extra work—whether as an auditor or in some other capacity—during the years 1649–52 that he was then recommended to receive an extra £500, as well as the £200 per annum owing him as a member of the Accounts Committee which was to be paid in Irish or Scottish lands. In fact he seems to have received £200 in 1653. In that year the Lord General and Council of Officers put him on a committee to choose a new Accounts Committee (30 April), and from June to October there was an intermediate Committee for Accounts without Greensmith. But in the latter month this body was in turn replaced by another new Committee, of which he was the chairman and which was to operate—albeit latterly on a part-time and largely unpaid basis—until the eve of the Restoration. He was evidently as acceptable to the restored Rump of 1659 as to previous regimes, for he was promoted to join Arthur Squibb and Company on the reconstituted Sequestration and Compounding Commission of 1659–60. Then the curtain falls. In Greensmith's will, made and proved in the plague year of 1665, he describes himself as being of Bethnal Green, Stepney. In 1695 his widow had moved back into the City, although not to the same parish where he had lived long before; presumably she was a good deal younger. He disposed of considerable sums to her and other relatives, and a wharf or quay at Newhaven in Sussex. Apart from a conventionally Calvinist prologue, Greensmith's will tells us nothing of his beliefs or other con-nections except that he apparently belonged to the nonconformist con-gregation of a certain Mr Pamma and one of the overseers whom he named was a Mr John Jackson, conceivably one of the ex-republicans of that name. A London businessman of strongly puritan and parliamen-tarian leanings is about as far as it seems safe to go in describing Green-smith.[30]

Richard Wilcox, who was Broad's colleague and then his accuser in 1644, was another specialist in military accounts and their auditing. He may have come from a minor Leicestershire gentry family, and, as the younger son of a younger son, have moved to seek a better future in London. He is described as being of Kensington, Gent., in 1647 when he acknowledged having received back £276 which he had formerly advanced for invest-ment in an American colonial project. He also invested modestly (£50) in the Irish lands adventure of the 1640s. Either Wilcox was a fairly large-scale lender to Parliament or his salary as an Auditor had fallen into hopeless arrears, for in 1647/8 he was awarded £1,000 to be paid out of the revenues of the Committee for Advance, at Haberdashers' Hall.

But in 1651 he had still only received £200 of this. Seven years later he was ordered to be paid £600, or three years' arrears as a member of the Accounts Committee. Unlike Greensmith, Wilcox was on the Army Accounts Committee of July 1648; like Greensmith and Broad, he was on the Commonwealth Committee of October 1649, and then like Broad but again unlike Greensmith on the interim Committee of June to September 1653. The Barebones Parliament evidently regarded Wilcox with suspicion as someone who was owed money by the State and so ought not to be on the Accounts Committee, and they refused to name him to it. It is not quite clear what happened, for Wilcox resumed his membership and went on acting as an Auditor under the Protectorate, although no subsequent Ordinance was passed to vary the composition of the Committee after the Barebones. He was also appointed to other minor auditing and investigatory committees in 1656 and 1657, but fades into obscurity in 1659–60. It was possibly his grandfather who died at a very great age indeed (he must have been well over 100) in 1662; more likely this was Wilcox himself, if he had by then returned to Leicestershire and can be imagined to have described himself as 'very aged' by his 69th or 70th year. If so, he was able to leave £150 to a younger son, and £300 for his daughter's marriage portion, with a bride-cart worth £30. His legacies etc. totalled nearly £600, plus landed property left to his elder, and the residue of his personal estate to his younger son. Wilcox's religious views were again orthodox Calvinist. There is no other clue, and perhaps it was the onset of old age which caused him to fade from the scene before the Restoration. As for his quarrel with Broad, the rights and wrongs are impossible to discover, but conceivably the charges had political implications if the two auditors had rival patrons in the high command of the army.[31]

Apart from Henry Robinson (1605–73), whose biography has already been written by Professor W. K. Jordan, it will be clear that the members of the various Accounts Committees of 1648 to 1659 were less prominent men than their colleagues involved in Compounding and Indemnity business. And as Jordan's excellent account of his connections and career shows, Robinson was only rather incidentally an Accounts Committee member. Of a Staffordshire and London gentry-cum-mercantile family, he went to St John's, Cambridge, but left to enter the Mercers' Company and subsequently traded in Italy. He was one of the leading radical but anti-Leveller pamphleteers of the 1640s and 50s, writing in favour of free trade and against monopolies, for moderate law reform, for religious toleration, and on numerous other topics. His first major post was as Auditor of the Excise in the mid-1640s. Possibly his views on ecclesiastical matters delayed his preferment until the Independents' victory over the Presbyterians in December 1648. In 1649 he became Comptroller for the sale of Crown lands and was later put on to the Accounts Committee. In 1650 he became Secretary to the Excise Commissioners. He also tried to get control of the Post Office, to which he had a rather dubious indirect claim.

Robinson was an extremely talented man. What Professor Jordan's account does not quite bring out is that the price of his versatility was over-extension. Robinson's fault as an administrator was to try to do too many things at once, and in consequence to neglect some of them. He lost his Excise Secretaryship in October 1653 partly because of remissness in attendance; in 1659 he was criticised by Henry Broad for being 'troublesome and wilfull' on the Accounts Committee. Perhaps he was more at home under the Rump than the Barebones or the Protectorate. In August 1659 he was appointed as the third Register-Accountant in a new land sales scheme, which never had time to take effect and would in any case have been something of a come-down for the one-time Comptroller. The Restoration ended Robinson's administrative career, and his last years are very obscure. Professor Jordan was right to make him one of the leading non-ecclesiastical theorists of Independency. His views and qualifications explain his career as an official, in which despite his talents he was not particularly successful.[32]

Under-officers of commissions and committees

Many of the committees and commissions of the 1640s and 50s were staffed on a part-time basis, by men who were pursuing other careers or had other employments in the public service. It is therefore obvious that the permanent secretaries, clerks, registrars, solicitors, accountants, even the head messengers who acted under them were vital to their effective functioning. To go in quest of such men is to enter an administrative underworld, most of whose workings, and the lives of whose participants, are lost for ever to the historian. In a few cases, however, the accidental survival of personal materials, or chance references in other documents, enables us to reconstruct something of their careers.

Martyn Dallison (or Martin Dallyson, *c.* 1617–1658) was apprenticed to a member of the Scriveners' Company in 1633. He presumably became free of the Company in 1640 and eventually rose to become its Warden in 1654 and 1655. He was of non-gentry origins and for most of his career lived at Harringay, then a residential village out in the Middlesex countryside; later he moved to Hammersmith where he died. The machinery of penal taxation had scarcely been set up when Dallison is found employed by the Committee for the Advance of Monies; in 1644 he was also acting as Clerk to Parliament's Committee for the Army; in November he became Accountant to the Haberdashers' Hall Committee.

In 1650 he became Registrar to the Commissioners for Compounding, Sequestration and Advance, and in 1652 held the same posts under them for Indemnity business. In 1649 Dallison had nearly left the public service. During the summer, the Committee for Advance ordered their Treasurer to pay his arrears; whether because these were not forthcoming, or through dislike of the Engagement, or, as he said at the time, for reasons of health and his business career, in October Dallison asked to be relieved of his duties and to be allowed to resign in favour of his own clerk, one Daniel Cox. Unless he was really planning to sell his position in some disguised fashion (like the younger Sir Henry Vane as Navy Treasurer), this indicates a fairly strong inclination. Yet, the request having been refused, he remained in office and even held a more responsible post from 1650 on, although by 1655 he must have been freer to return to his scrivener's business, for the work of composition and indemnity came virtually to an end. Most of what we know about Dallison as a person comes from his will, which is unusually full and informative. After acknowledging the universal fact of human mortality, he defended a man's divine right to his individual property 'in such outward Estate, as by industrie in a lawfull Calling, God hath blessed him with all'; then he affirmed his faith in God's Election of himself as one of the redeemed. The whole religious prologue is quite different from the common form of conventional Calvinism. It is much longer and its tone is altogether more intense. Dallison next provided small legacies for numerous relatives, the aged poor of Hammersmith, his favourite divine, the elder Edmund Calamy, and two or three other ministers. The Scriveners' Company was to receive an inscribed plate worth £3. 6s. 8d., with the testator's name, coat of arms, date of death and the words 'ut fratres diligete'. To his eldest son went all his books and manuscripts, as also his gold signet, best sword and belt, best horse-pistols, and rose-diamond ring—a reminder that even the most fervent puritans could also care for some good things of this world. Dallison was also concerned about the future of his son, who was then still an infant. Besides providing for his inheritance of property he showed an intense concern over the boy's choice of a career. He was either to go to the university, or be apprenticed 'to some trade he shall most incline to (except Marchandizing unlesse my Wife and freinds advise him thereto . . .)'. The younger Martyn was severely admonished as to his future conduct whether as student or apprentice. The will ends with a series of additional ethical and religious admonitions to the testator's son, wife and his other children. It was made four days after the death of the greatest of all puritan men of action and proved two months later, on the eve of the late Protector's funeral. The younger Martyn Dallison duly became a freeman of the Scriveners' Company by patrimony, in 1674. However easily caricatured, as Zeal-of-the-land-busy or what Ben Jonson was fond of calling a 'religious caterpillar', such men as this may well have made reliable servants compared with most minor functionaries employed by seventeenth-century governments.[33]

Ralph Darnell (1600s–1660s) was unusual among republican administrators in that he was already in office under the monarchy before 1642, albeit in a very minor capacity. Born as the sixth son of a family on the gentry/plebeian borderline, he came from Hertfordshire and was educated at Christ's College, Cambridge. He appears to have gone on to Gray's Inn after a rather lengthy interval, although without having taken a degree; he then transferred to the Middle Temple in the mid-1630s, by which time his father was dead and he was living in London. While not called to the bar, Darnell was clearly a practising lawyer, and in this capacity he became one of the four attorneys in the Court of Wards.[34]

Apparently a parliamentarian from the beginning, Darnell served in the Court of Wards in London, not in the King's at Oxford, until its abolition in 1646. Various schemes were then mooted to compensate him for the loss of this place, including appointment to a sinecure office in Chancery (found already to be promised to someone else) and a lump sum of money (almost certainly never forthcoming). In the end he was made Assistant-Clerk to the Parliament, first under Henry Elsyng and then under Henry Scobell. This ceased to be a regular post in 1653 although he resumed it during the three Protectorate Parliaments (1654–5, 1656–8, 1659). Meanwhile Darnell entered the service of the Trustees for the sale of Crown lands, becoming counsel for them in 1649, and for the Trustees in charge of the sale of the fee-farm rents in 1650; in 1651 he obtained the post of Registrar for the sale of royalists' lands forfeited for treason, under the so-called 'Treason Trustees'. The bulk of the work entrusted to these various sets of trustees was over by 1653–4, but Darnell apparently continued to act for them until at least 1657; much the same was true of his work *qua* counsel for the Indemnity Commissioners. He was involved in a sharp dispute at the reassembly of the second Protectorate Parliament for its short-lived second session in January 1658, and was reprimanded for assuming that he was still Clerk Assistant. He had his revenge on some of his erstwhile republican masters by testifying as a Crown witness against the Regicides in the autumn of 1660; this was his last public appearance. He had acquired property in Herefordshire and probably retired there. His son John had a successful legal career, becoming a King's Sergeant and a knight, before his death in 1707. Ralph Darnell had died long before, having left his memorial in the form of a subscription to his old college's building fund, but his will has not been located. His views and outlook remain an enigma, though his role in 1660 suggests less than ardent support for the republican cause.[35]

James Glisson (b. 1608–9) was the seventh son of an obscure Dorset gentry family of Bristol origins. His brother Francis became a well-known physician, holding a medical chair at Cambridge for over forty years (1636–77)! It may have been through the patronage of his brother's patients, who in 1654 included the young Ashley Cooper, that James Glisson entered government service. On the other hand, there was a tightly-knit group of Dorset parliamentarian gentry, some from the same district, who seemed to have formed a county connection at the national level. Glisson had seen local military service in the 1640s and was styled Captain in a friend's will in 1656. By 1652 he was serving under the Accounts Committee as their Registrar, and in the mid-1650s apparently combined this with a Clerk's place under the Crown land-sale Trustees. In April 1658 the Accounts Committee formally appointed him as one of their three Clerks, on the clear understanding that the £60 annual salary could not be guaranteed unless the Committee made enough money (presumably out of fees, rewards from the State and discoveries) for any of its members or staff to get anything—an odd arrangement by all accounts. Then Glisson disappears again into total obscurity, although his brother weathered the great climacteric of 1660 quite successfully. The physician's latest biographer notices James but errs in stating that he died young in 1621.[36]

By his latter years Humphrey Jones (c. 1615–1690) was a more substantial man. His elder brother the well-known John Jones, regicide MP and republican brother-in-law of Oliver Cromwell, was executed in 1660. As a younger son of a lesser gentry family from North Wales, Humphrey had his way to make in the world. In 1641 he was acting as Receiver of Crown revenues in Cheshire, but during that decade he established himself as a merchant in London via the Mercers' Company, of which he had become free in 1638. In 1649 he became co-Treasurer to the Trustees for the sale of the King's (and the rest of the royal family's) goods, and continued to serve in this capacity until 1657. Meanwhile Jones also acted as financial agent and London correspondent for his elder brother John and probably for other North Walians in Parliament's and then the Commonwealth's service. Whether he shared John's anti-Protectorate views is unclear. Humphrey survived the Restoration except for the presumed loss of nearly £2,450 worth of episcopal lands of which he was the joint recipient in 1648 and 1652. He had an active career in London municipal politics as common councillor and alderman's deputy, though he did not make the aldermanic bench in his own right. His brother John's son, John, was his own eventual male heir, to whom he left his mid- and north Wales property, subject to various legacies and annuities. The impression conveyed is one of modest wealth and conventional piety, but this was over thirty years after Jones had been in the State's service, and his official career in the 1650s seems little more than an interpolation. Presumably he obtained office through his brother, and although he must have taken the Engagement, there is no evidence of positive republican commitment in his, as opposed to John's case.[37]

Clement Oxenbridge (*c.* 1620–1696) was altogether more of a factotum than Jones or even Dallison. His grandfather, John, was a puritan divine in the time of Elizabeth and James I; his father, Daniel, was a doctor of medicine, who first practised in Northamptonshire and by 1638 had moved to London where he died in 1642. There is no evidence of Clement having had any formal higher education. Family connection and native ability appear to explain his advancement. His eldest brother John was a puritan minister, friend of Marvell and other well-known contemporaries; one of his sisters was Major-General Philip Skippon's second wife (by her third marriage) while another married Oliver St John. As early as 1644 Oxenbridge appears in the papers of committees as an undertaker or contractor for confiscated church and royalist lands, and when capitular lands were ordered to be sold by legislation in 1649, he was formally named as a Contractor. In 1652 he became Comptroller or Cheque-Master to the Commissioners for the sale of prize goods—an important post during the naval war with the Dutch; he was also a Commissioner on the Articles of War (to deal with royalists claiming indemnity under various surrender agreements) from 1652 or 1653.

His most mysterious—and possibly most significant—office was in connection with the Post Office. He is described by one authority as having been the chief under-officer below the Postmaster-General until 1653. According to another historian of the British postal services, Oxenbridge was the leader, or moving spirit, of the free-enterprise interlopers who tried to undercut the official posts around 1652 to 1654, during Captain John Manley's contract, itself a kind of interregnum between the overall management of Edmund Prideaux and that of Thurloe. Oxenbridge seems to have been excluded from the Posts from 1654 to 1658, and to have contrived re-entry in 1659–60; perhaps an early Restoration description of him as an 'anabaptist' is a sufficient explanation of this. He was not finally ousted until the winter of 1660–1. According to one source he was briefly employed in naval business during the second Dutch war. Whether as a well-known nonconformist who had resisted the blandishments of James II or for other unexplained reasons, Oxenbridge began a second official career, again in the Post Office and in the Household of Queen Mary, after 1688, when he must have been well into his sixties, if not nearer seventy. He died in 1696; no will has been found. Oxenbridge's various activities seem to cohere in a pattern, although it would help to solve a complex puzzle if we knew whose man he was during the long struggle for control of the Post Office.[38]

Tracy Pauncefote, or Pansfoote, was the younger son of a minor Gloucestershire gentry family. During the Personal Rule his father Grimbald was joint holder of the unpopular patent for measuring and scrutinising iron; he was also a revenue Receiver for the Duchy of Lancaster. He married Anne Tracy, sister of a baronet. How and why the younger Pauncefote became a minor parliamentarian official is unclear, except that his father was appointed to the Gloucester county sequestration committee in June 1643. Tracy was admitted to Gray's Inn in 1645, and by 1648-9 was employed by the Committee of Officers concerned with providing money for the Army, a liaison body between the Council of Officers and the House of Commons, in which Ireton was the leading figure. In 1649-50 he was the Registrar of the Accounts Committee, but more than once he had to excuse his poor attendance on the score of his other commitments with the Committee of Officers. In 1651 he petitioned the Council of State; since it was referred by them to Parliament's Trade Council, his petition may have been to do with his father's iron patent. He also acted as co-Clerk to the High Court of Justice set up at Norwich that winter (1650-1) to try royalist conspirators in East Anglia, and was Clerk to the Council's own Examinations Committee under its efficient Secretary, the future Quaker and Bristol merchant, Captain George Bishop. In 1654 he was serving as Registrar to the Commissioners on royalist claims to indemnity under the surrender articles. In the early 1650s Pauncefote was living in Petty France, Westminster. Besides the relatively modest stipends from his various posts, he can hardly have had other means of support in the capital, where he died intestate in 1659, being described as Esquire of Gray's Inn. He must still have been in his thirties, so ill-health as well as other duties may genuinely have caused him to worry about his poor attendance at meetings. Beyond that, it is impossible to say anything of Pauncefote as an individual. He was an official for whom £3 a week meant a modest competence, but it would be unwise to say that this was his only reason for serving the Commonwealth.[39]

Although he features more frequently in the State Papers than Pauncefote, Philip Tandy is a more elusive figure. He may have gone to Gloucester Hall, Oxford, in 1632; if so, no style or place of origin is recorded for him. To judge from subsequent references, he may have been an English settler in Ireland or, since John Lambert was his patron, a Yorkshireman with Irish interests. Certainly he 'adventured' £400 in Irish lands—a considerable sum for a person of such apparent obscurity. In 1646 he was denounced by the Presbyterian divine Thomas Edwards as 'a great Sectary' who had been active in the north and at York, and was quoted to show his Baptist sympathies. He was recommended to the Accounts Committee by John Rushworth, himself a north-countryman, as well as by Lambert. Tandy appears to have obtained a place as Examiner under the Treason Trustees (in 1651 or 1652); either he was promoted, or this post was re-established under a different name, and he became co-Registrar Accountant for forfeited land sales in 1652; by then he was also Registrar to the Accounts Committee and by 1653 Auditor to the Obstructions Commissioners as well. It seems to have been an ill-advised piece of pluralism for the body responsible for auditing accounts to have employed someone who was also in the service of a revenue-raising body (in charge of land sales) and another potentially so (Obstructions). At any rate, in 1655 Tandy ran into serious trouble. In January he was cited in connection with the Fugill-Granger forged debentures scandal, and in April removed from his Registrarship for incapacity. According to one source he was temporarily 'out of his mind' and the trouble may have been mental illness as well as corruption. No legal proceedings were taken against him, but in 1656–7 he was paid his arrears for his Obstructions' work and in effect pensioned off. Meanwhile in October 1653 he had actually been promoted from being Registrar to full membership of the Account and Public Debts Commission. Considering that in the preceding January Tandy had himself been under investigation after allegations that he was taking rewards, bribes and excessive fees in his land sales capacity, this was a remarkable appointment. One accusation of dishonesty might be mistaken, but unless someone was pursuing a vendetta against Tandy, two such charges (in 1653 and 1655) can scarcely be so. Yet he continued to receive grants of money, or at least orders and warrants for such payments, to cover his various arrears, into 1658. He then went or perhaps returned to Ireland, where he performed as a lay-preacher. And there he disappears from the historical record, except for an apparent re-appointment, in connection with the abortive resumption of forfeited land sales, in August 1659. His last recorded activity was investigating a faith-healer in 1665. It is possible that he was an ancestor of the nationalist hero and conspirator of the 1790s, Napper Tandy, but unfortunately I have not been able to trace any such connection. In Philip Tandy's administrative career, a certain busy-ness together with influential backers seems to have partially counteracted other good reasons against his continued employment. His honesty, to say the least, remains open to grave suspicion.[40]

All-rounders

It is characteristic of seventeenth-century administration that some of the most active officials are impossible to classify or categorise. They served on committees and commissions, but also held other posts connected with the revenue and taxation machinery or the central executive; some were also minor politicians.

Adam Baynes (1622–70) is in many ways one of the best-documented secondary figures of the republican era. Born near Leeds, the eldest son of a Yorkshire family on the minor (non-armigerous) gentry-yeoman borderline, he had the drive and capacity to have become a great captain of industry had he lived 100 or 200 years later. Without any formal higher education, Baynes entered the parliamentary army in the north and by 1648, with the good luck so characteristic of the successful entrepreneur, obtained a company under the rising star, Colonel John Lambert. In the early years of the republic his only civil appointments were at the local level. A crucial stage in Baynes's fortunes came when he was selected to be the northern brigade's Agent in the capital; and he remained in London when the army moved north to invade Scotland in the late summer of 1650. From then on his surviving correspondence becomes voluminous; it is largely triangular, between Baynes in the south and his relatives and connections in Yorkshire and his military colleagues in Scotland. Lambert appointed him as one of four attorneys to manage the land purchases for the Brigade out of the debentures for pay arrears. And it was from this base that he began his own large-scale purchases, the most spectacular of which was the royal manor and estate of Holdenby or Holmby, in Northants, for £22,299. 10s. 6d. It is hardly conceivable that Baynes paid the Crown land-sale Contractors anything approaching this sum. He had, it is true, just made a financially and socially advantageous marriage into the Dawsons, a gentry family of Heworth, just outside York. But even allowing for whatever portion was brought by his wife, Martha Dawson, and for his own pay arrears (at most a few hundred pounds), a vast shortfall remains to be accounted for. The Baynes correspondence, as we should perhaps expect, gives us no clue. But the owner and part-occupant of Holmby and a figure in Northamptonshire ruling circles Adam Baynes duly became, and remained so until the Restoration.

Meanwhile his other employments began to multiply. With the ascendancy of Lambert during the early years of the Protectorate, his ex-protégé was appointed to the Army Committee (February 1653/4), then as a Commissioner successively for the preservation (=improvement) of the Customs, to enforce the prohibition on the planting of tobacco in England and Wales, and for hearing appeals connected with the collection and administration of the Excise; in November 1655 he also became an Agent for the granting of wine licences. His income from office must by then have been considerable. The Army Committee's members received £100 a year each and the Excise Appeals Commissioners £300 each; the Wine Licence Agency may have been worth some hundreds of pounds in fees; then there was his captaincy, for he remained on the payroll of Lambert's regiment. Baynes sat in the Protectorate parliaments of 1654 and 1656; he was a JP for his county (Northamptonshire, not

Yorkshire, that is). He had 'arrived' as a member of the Cromwellian establishment. Yet he had already been noted by the Quakers as more sympathetic to them than most local magistrates, and like his patron and commanding officer he grew increasingly out of sympathy with Cromwell's second parliament in its religious intolerance, neo-monarchism, and encroachment on the army's privileges. Lambert withdrew from public life in the summer of 1657; Baynes's fall was not as dramatic, but he was dropped from the Army Committee in February 1657/8, and he received no further preferment until Lambert's return to power in May 1659. He was then made one of the Commissioners in charge of arrears due to the Customs, the Excise and the revenue from prize goods and ships. Although not involved in Lambert's last-ditch rising against the Restoration in April 1660, Baynes was regarded with grave suspicion by the authorities as a loyal, indeed devoted, adherent of the republican general. Naturally he lost Holmby; he had already demolished most of the mansion and converted it into a smaller, more manageable house. He had at least one spell of several months in prison (1666–7) and took no further part in public life. Even so, Baynes contrived to retain some of his acquisitions; and although he had raised part of the purchase price on the Holmby estate by pulling down the house and selling the materials and fittings, he was apparently not made to pay damages to the Crown for this, despite an action brought against him.

Baynes's will omitted any religious prologue. He disposed mainly of recently acquired Yorkshire property, including a large colliery just outside Leeds, which was carefully apportioned between his wife, his brother and his ten children. He had received a grant of arms from the Commonwealth herald Ryley in 1650, but this was not confirmed after the Restoration, and it is debatable whether technically he had succeeded in rising into the armigerous gentry or not. Be that as it may, he had shown an energy and versatility of which his official career was only a part, besides a commendable freedom from sectarian bigotry. If Baynes had played a prominent part in it, a hypothetical Lambertian Protectorate would have been efficiently and not illiberally served.[41]

The career of William Jessop (c. 1603–1674/5) provides a notable instance of dual employment: both by the State and by an aristocratic patron. Moreover, despite his modest origins as the son of a Stafford townsman, Jessop is a substantial historical figure about whom a good deal of evidence survives. Although not formally admitted to Gray's Inn until the 1660s, when it must have been an honorific entry, Jessop was attached to, and probably employed by, the Inn from an early age. By 1630 he was in the employment of Robert Rich, second earl of Warwick, and in this way became clerk and later secretary to the Providence Island Company and the Trustees of the abortive Say-Brook Plantation scheme.

Warwick was a leader of the moderate, but firmly committed parliamentarian peers. In 1642 Jessop was acting as one of the deputies to Parliament's Treasurers-at-War, and from then until 1645 he served as Warwick's Admiralty secretary. When his patron ceased to be Lord Admiral as a result of the self-denying Ordinance in 1645, Jessop remained in office and became Secretary to Parliament's Admiralty Commissioners, a post which he was to hold—with minor variations of title—until 1653. He was thus at the centre of the Long Parliament's and then the Commonwealth's naval administration. Meanwhile, perhaps through his service with the Army Treasurers, he also became man of business to Robert Devereux, third earl of Essex, Parliament's Lord-General (1642–5), and was Essex's most active executor after his death in 1646. Jessop continued to act for the Rich family, not only for the earl, and became a partner in some of their ventures including the voyages of the notorious freelance privateer, *The Constant Warwick*. Although the House of Lords was not directly involved in Pride's Purge, Warwick was among the peers who rejected the Rump's ordinance for the King's trial and thus helped to precipitate the Commons' assumption of sole legislative power. He remained in opposition, though not engaged in royalist conspiracy, throughout the years of republican rule until his death in 1658, after a partial reconciliation with Cromwell when his grandson married the Protector's youngest daughter. Whether the execution of his brother, the notorious side-changer Henry Rich, earl of Holland, in March 1649 (after the use of the Speaker's casting vote) affected Warwick's attitude can only be surmised. If the Rump had wished to conciliate Warwick, let alone win him over to the infant Commonwealth, it would have been prudent to spare the egregious Holland—whose responsibility for part of the bloodshed in the second Civil War of 1648 was palpable and direct.

The imposition of the Engagement seems to have posed a sharper dilemma for Jessop than did continuing in public office after the Regicide. His papers include a series of personal notes about whether he ought to subscribe; although undated, these must belong to the autumn of 1649 or the following winter, and are therefore an integral, if personal and unpublished part of what Mr Skinner and others have called 'the Engagement Controversy'. Jessop had been named as a Tryer for the twelfth London classis, covering Holborn where he then lived, in 1645, 1646 and 1648. And, unlike many of those named in the Long Parliament's ecclesiastical ordinances, he seems to have taken the presbyterian-inspired Solemn League and Covenant very seriously. It was with Article 3 of that document, expressing loyalty to the King, that he found the Engagement least compatible. He sought to justify subscription, in his own mind, by intelligent '*de factoist*' arguments: the removal of the King's person, which Jessop had been powerless to prevent, had ended his obligation to the King; likewise the violation of Parliament's rights and privileges was not his doing; moreover forty MPs constituted a quorum, and since the House had not declared its own privileges to have been violated by Pride's Purge, who was he to say that they had been? The next points were whether the King's death automatically dissolved the Covenant as far as it referred to Parliament, and whether a true parliament must consist of two Houses:

> If the parlemt. be in the members of both houses whether admitted to sitt or not; what advantage bring I to their priviledges by standing out? . . . What service do I do therein to God. & whether doth my Covenant so restraine to a parliamentary govermt. in the sense intended But [*sic*? that] I must not at all declyne it?

He went on to justify his submission to those then in power on providential grounds:

> And the submission I am to declare is in relation to the Commonwealth as established with 2 qualifications.

These were the absence of a king, on which he felt justified even allowing for the position of the late king's son, and of a House of Lords, about which he remained undecided. He interpreted loyalty to the Commonwealth, on these conditions, as 'no more then a Conformity which I intend however to give them'. He could then still decline to carry out unlawful actions in their service. Jessop went on to reflect on the undoubted godliness of many now in power, and used this as another argument for his serving them, while his standing out might contribute to 'new Broyles' and even—worst of all—to a successful royalist comeback. Above all, subscription would not entail approval of past acts of violence; as for the future, his obligations as a Christian and as an Englishman would still be binding even if he swore allegiance to this, or to any other government; finally if they were not acting in His interest, God would soon remove those now in power anyway and the problem would solve itself. He ended on a strongly biblical note.

Whether Jessop was happier under the Protectorate when the Engagement was repealed is not known, but it may be supposed so. From 1649 to 1653 he had to share his Admiralty duties and responsibilities with a more positive supporter of the Republic, Robert Coytmor, one of the radical Welshmen in the Commonwealth's service. And in 1653 Jessop was transferred to the central executive, becoming Assistant Secretary to the Council in 1653 and its Clerk in 1654, as well as Treasurer for the Lord Protector's Contingencies—an enhanced version of the old Keeper of the (royal) Privy Purse—in 1655. He must have been a busy man, for he was also on the various Accounts Committees of 1649, 1653 and 1655 and on that for the Public Faith in 1657-9. In 1657 he was briefly reinvolved in Admiralty business; he also saw to the Thames Ballastage patent on Warwick's behalf (*c.* 1648–57); he was Warden and Supervisor of Chatham Hospital, and Receiver of payments for the draining of Bedford Level in the Fens (from 1650/1). As well as all this, he continued to act privately for the Rich and Devereux families, and probably for other aristocratic houses. In May 1659 he was regarded as a sufficiently positive Cromwellian, or sufficiently dubious in his loyalty to a Commonwealth, to be dropped from the Council staff. This break in his official career, plus his aristocratic connections, served Jessop in very good stead the next year. He was restored as Council Clerk after the Rump's second restoration at New Year 1659/60 and so continued until the Restoration in May following, thus acting under the non-regicidal, non-republican regime of February–May 1660. Under the Convention he was appointed Assistant Clerk of the Parliaments (for the House of Commons), and consolidated his position by testifying against the Regicides in the autumn.

Because he had a struggle in his own mind over whether or not to subscribe the Engagement, it does not follow that Jessop was a lukewarm or ineffectual servant of the English republic. Indeed all the available evidence suggests that he was a man of great energy, despatch, conscientiousness, and considerable ability; and it was unavoidable in the circumstances that he failed to make good his patron's claim to the Post Office in the early 1650s. Apart from his notes about the Engagement, almost all of Jessop's surviving personal papers relate to the last phase of his career, after the Restoration. We know that back in the 1630s he had married the daughter and heiress of a London citizen and member of the Fishmongers' Company. By this marriage he had a daughter—his only child. In the early 1650s he was a widower, and in 1655/6 he was remarried to a widow of Hertfordshire origins, the sister-in-law of the parliamentarian colonel and conqueror of Guernsey, Alban Cox. In the winter of 1660–1 his second wife died. Whether owing to this bereavement, his own advancing years, or his now being politically unacceptable, Jessop held no important office from 1661 to 1668. He was temporarily re-employed by the Navy Commissioners, which put him in an inferior position to his own successors at the Admiralty office. Pepys remarked of Jessop coming 'cap in hand' from the Commissioners, adding 'though indeed he is a man of great estate and of good report'. Meanwhile his personal circumstances had again changed. In 1656 his daughter Anne had married William Hilton or Hylton, alias Hulton, head of a well-to-do Lancashire gentry family. In his latter years Jessop was to get most personal satisfaction out of his connection with the Rich family, where from his humble beginnings as a servant he had now become an intimate friend, and from the family life of his daughter and son-in-law. More than one of his grandchildren came to stay with him in his bachelor quarters in Holborn and Gray's Inn; he was a fond but not, it seems, an over-indulgent grandparent; he took inordinate pleasure in placing his grandson at an exclusive boarding school in Essex which was patronised by various noble families.

In 1668 Jessop grumbled at having to resume office. He was persuaded by Lord Brereton (the chairman) and others to accept the post of Clerk-cum-Secretary to the newly formed Public Accounts Committee or Commission. From his correspondence one can see why Jessop was trusted and why his services were so much sought after. Even in his letters to his own daughter he instinctively lapsed into shorthand when he was referring to the affairs of the various families for whom he acted. The grandfatherly role which he clearly so much enjoyed may seem far from the storm and stress of West Indian privateering plans or the Interregnum Admiralty. Such consistency as there was in Jessop's public career owed much but not all to Warwick's patronage. His notes on the Engagement are conspicuous for omitting any mention of his master, though they are notable for his being apparently more concerned about the disappearance of the Lords than of the monarchy. His papers convey an impression of his character. Jessop was indeed the kind of man by whose patient work in the background empires are built, great fortunes sustained, fleets and armies kept at sea or in the field; yet £310 adventured in Irish lands was perhaps his own greatest gamble. Content to serve with loyalty and efficiency, he was not a man himself to play for the highest stakes.[42]

Less versatile and less important men than Jessop still had their part to play. Richard Lucy (c. 1619–78) was the third son of a knight and the nephew of Sir Richard Lucy, Bart., recruiter MP for Old Sarum. A local commissioner in Warwickshire in 1647–8, Lucy was admitted to Gray's Inn as late as 1652, aged over 30. This was unusual. Had he no means, and a career still to seek? Whatever the explanation, his rise after that was rapid. He sat in the Barebones, where he was definitely not a member of the militant reforming group. He was appointed to the Army Committee the following winter and remained on it throughout the Protectorate. He was a Probate Judge from 1654 to 1659, an Excise Arrears Commissioner briefly in 1653–4, and a special magistrate in Middlesex (1654); he was also named as a Tryer and to at least one High Court of Justice. Whether he lost all these positions in 1659 is uncertain, but he was re-appointed to the Army Committee in February 1659/60. After the Restoration, his two elder brothers having died (one without issue, the other leaving a daughter), he retired to his Warwickshire inheritance. When he made his will at the time of the Popish Plot, Lucy left everything to his son and nothing to his wife, although she was named as co-Executor. Otherwise there is nothing of personal interest and nothing to remind us of the Barebones Parliament and the Army Committee. Lucy belonged to the existing upper class but he remains a more shadowy figure than many officials of humbler social origins.[43]

William Robinson (1611–66) was Henry Robinson's younger brother (see pp. 225–6 and n. 32 above). Unlike Henry he seems to have gone straight into trade, not via the University, and in the early 1630s he was in Italy following a commercial career. According to Professor Jordan's account of Henry, William became a trader in pepper during the 1640s and 50s. In 1651 he was made a Trustee for the sale of lands forfeited for treason. Apart from this work, which was virtually completed by 1654, Robinson held no office during the middle 1650s, perhaps returning to private trade. At the same time a namesake, who was almost certainly a relative, served in the army in Staffordshire as a captain (1643–5) and eventually rose, apparently always in local forces or militias rather than in the regular field army, to the rank of major. By 1649 this William Robinson was in serious financial straits because of his own pay arrears and other people's claims against him, possibly for requisitions which he had made in Staffordshire. Whether through family influence or otherwise, he was appointed Secretary to the Generals-at-Sea and in particular to Edward Popham. But this was only a temporary post; Major Robinson was also involved in making up accounts under the Council of State's direction early in 1651, as a special budgetary assistant. Rather surprisingly, in view of the highly responsible nature of this work, he received no official appointment. During 1650–1 he was again on Popham's staff but acting as the Admiral's agent in London rather than accompanying him to sea; Popham died in 1651. Whether because Robinson was known as a loyal supporter of the Commonwealth or because he had a wide circle of acquaintances in Rump circles, he was appointed to the central executive in 1659, becoming a Council Clerk extra-ordinary in July, and an established Clerk in September. Moreover he continued to act under the Committee of Safety after the military coup in mid-October—a fact which was to cause him the loss of office when the Rump again reappeared at the end of December and a new Council of State was elected in January 1660.

Our main personal knowledge of Major William Robinson comes from a short series of letters to his wife, written during his tour of duty as Admiral's secretary in the summer of 1649. The tone of this correspondence is religious, without being lugubriously pious, and warmly affectionate. Major Robinson refers to large numbers of in-laws and influential friends including Colonel (the future General) Charles Fleetwood, Colonel Valentine Wauton MP and Speaker Lenthall; but his connections also included the wealthy royalist financier Sir Nicholas Crispe and his family. Yet to get his business effected in the House of Commons he seems to have depended in part on the efforts of his wife, Anne, in conjunction with the Staffordshire county committee, in whose service he had been when the expenses in question were incurred. On 2 June he wrote from the *Admiral* in Milford Haven to ask 'Whether the successe have bin worth thy paines . . .?', being confident that 'I did not scruple serving them to or beyond the uttermost of my power'; and on 6 June from the *Triumph* at Lundy Island 'I am sure I have deserved a favor from them, what I shall find I know not'. By 26 June, writing from the *Leopard* off Kinsala, he had learnt that Parliament had referred his accounts to the Army Committee 'whoe I hope will deale well with mee'. Referring to letters which his wife had forwarded to the Speaker and to Valentine Wauton, he approved of her scheme 'to buy some pretty present for Col. Wauton, both for gratitude for what is past and quickening him for whats to come: though I take him to bee a gentleman of as unselfish a spiritt, and unbyassed courtesy as any in the Parliament'. At this stage he was hoping for a grant of £200 a year out of the revenues of Dean and Chapter lands: 'But lett Col. Fleetwood presse to gett 200 li a yeare assigned either out of Kings or Deane and Chapters lands'. But on 3 July, having heard from her again, he wrote more gloomily from the *Charles* in Plymouth Sound:

> for a probable opportunity once lost is most commonly remedilesse;
> And I know I should not long be absent if Sollicitation would
> dispatch; but I see the House is of the old Temper still, and (as all
> other great bodyes doe) it moves slowly . . .

And on the 5th, having heard of a scheme to hold by-elections to recruit the Commons, he told her to find out whether Mr Isay Thomas (recruiter MP for Bishop's Castle) or Mr George Devereux (recruiter MP for Montgomery) would be re-admitted to the House. If not, there would be vacancies in their constituencies, and 'for either of those I believe I might bee chosen for, some whoe are very powerfull to elect in each place having long since motioned both places to mee'. Yet because Devereux's was a Welsh seat, he judged that Thomas's was the likelier of the two. The scheme for further piecemeal elections then lapsed, but it is far from clear that Robinson's £1,008. 19s. 0d. arrears, accepted in principle by Parliament on 12 June 1649, were ever made good.

William Robinson is a confusingly common name, and there are several difficulties of identification concerned with these letters. The Admiral's secretary, ex-Staffordshire Major and future Council Clerk, is to be distinguished from the pepper merchant, free of the Mercers' Company, who was the younger brother of the well-known Henry. With his tender and constant concern for his 'dearest Nancie', and his nagging worries over the pay arrears, notwithstanding his influential friends and relations, Admiral Popham's secretary, Major Robinson, emerges as a more attractive and human figure than some puritan husbands. He may have died in 1673 according to the Rev. John Owen, Oliver Cromwell's sometime chaplain, but his activities after 1660 are utterly obscure.[44]

John Stone (d. 1678) was a more specifically civic type than most of those described so far. He was either the son of a prominent Londoner, or of another London businessman of the same name. Described as Gentleman of the Ordnance (i.e. the artillery) under Fairfax in 1649 and as Captain during the following decade, Stone's active military service, if any, during the 1640s had probably been with the City's forces. His most responsible post was as Receiver-General for the monthly assessment in London, in which capacity he was answerable direct to the Treasurers-at-War. In 1653 Stone became more prominent. A London representative in the Barebones Parliament, he was put on the Committee for the Inspection of the public Treasuries (September), in November he was elected to the short-lived seventh Council of State and in December he became briefly an Admiralty and Navy Commissioner. This eminence was not quite sustained under the Protectorate when Stone's responsibilities were of a more routine nature. He was on various Committees concerned with the Customs and Excise and Prize Goods; in 1655 he became both an Accounts Commissioner and a member of the large new Trade Committee. In September 1654 his regular employment and income were assured by appointment as a Teller of the Exchequer, at £400 a year without fees. As an Excise Appeals Commissioner he had another £300; he was also a Wine Licence Agent. Stone sat for Cirencester in the three parliaments of 1654–9; no other connection with Gloucestershire has been traced, though possibly he had acquired more land there. His career after the spring of 1659 is obscure. He or another John Stone is found assisting in the recovery of Charles I's possessions in May 1660. His will, made and proved in 1678, suggests a fairly strong theological interest, one biblical commentary being bequeathed with his Bible to his eldest son. The legacies are substantial, but no property further afield than the Essex and Surrey suburbs is mentioned. The importance of Stone's official career in his business and personal life is hard to gauge. Evidently a protectorian as much as a republican Londoner, his accumulation of offices and commissions suggests a narrow basis for the Protectorate. Able and well-affected businessmen prepared to serve the State were perhaps at something of a premium after 1653.[45]

Fiscal types

Several of those whose careers have already been sketched had connections with the revenue and taxation system. Some held regular posts on the financial side of the central administration. But those discussed so far did not make their main official careers in the field of tax collection, revenue disbursement, or budgetary administration. As elsewhere, there is no guarantee that the most significant members of the administration are the ones about whom most can be discovered as individuals, or vice versa.

Like many others in the 1640s, Samuel Bartlett found employment in the new Excise administration. By 1647 he was Grand Cashier, and Clerk to the Treasury of the general office for the excise on salt. In 1649 he became Assay Master of the Mint following the purge of non-subscribers to the Engagement in the Mint. In 1653 he succeeded to the very responsible office of Comptroller of all Excise raised in London. This and the Mint office he held concurrently until 1660, when he was put out of both. Elias Ashmole, in petitioning for the Comptrollership of the Excise, said that Bartlett had been active against the King's interests, while a claimant to his Mint position alleged that he was 'a violent fanatic' who had been put in by the regicide President Bradshaw's influence. Whatever the extent of Bartlett's ideological commitment may have been, there is another reason why he would have been a valuable man to have in such financial positions. His father was an Exeter goldsmith, and in 1632 Samuel was apprenticed to the London goldsmith Thomas Vyner (or Viner) who was a major government creditor under the Long Parliament, Protectorate and restored monarchy alike. Vyner was knighted by Cromwell when he was Lord Mayor in 1653–4. Bartlett would have completed his apprenticeship in 1640, a hopeful moment for a man of talent with these connections. In 1648 John Rushworth, the future historical compiler then an under-Clerk to the Parliament and Secretary to the Lord General, appointed him to receive £50 which he, Rushworth, had just been awarded by Parliament. Bartlett's principal office was worth £750 a year (plus a Mint salary of £66. 13s. 4d. and allowances); he was styled Esquire in the later 1650s, but in 1660 he reverted to plain Mr. He may have been the Samuel Bartlett of St Giles, Cripplegate, London, Gent., who died in 1671, leaving cash legacies totalling about £1,150. If so, the religious prologue to his will was fuller and more fervid than the common run—and this would fit in with the 'violent fanatic'. Otherwise the Vyner connection best explains his prominence.[46]

John Blackwell junior (1624–1701) is an altogether better-documented man. Indeed as with Jessop, Berners and Moyer, it is surprising that the sources for his career do not include the *DNB*.

His father, John Blackwell senior, was a well-to-do London grocer who had helped to supply the royal household, under one of the purveyance agreements, before the Civil War. He also lived the life of a Surrey gentleman up the river at Mortlake, then a village in open country. The elder Blackwell was an active parliamentarian; he invested heavily in the Irish adventure and later in bishops' lands. He was a Contractor (1646–7 and 1649) for the sale of these and capitular lands. He sat on the second High Court of Justice, of February–March 1649 (to decide on the fate of Hamilton, Holland and Company). In 1651 he became an alderman, and later that year was chosen Sheriff but managed to avoid acting as such. Because he was a creditor to the State from 1641–2 on (and was owed nearly £2,800 by the King from before 1642 too), Blackwell senior seems to have fallen heavily into debt. A paper dated 1656, just over a year before his death, lists debts totalling £35,768. 15s. 3d.—a vast sum for a private individual. No wonder he was said to be the author of a pamphlet in favour of securing all Parliament's debts on the Public Faith, back in 1644, when Thomason described him as a 'scrivener he was at that tyme mad and put into Bedlam, but about a yeare after came again to his senses'. Certainly in his will, made orally on the eve of his death, the elder Blackwell refers to debts, and leaves his wife £100 a year over and above her jointure, empowering his eldest son to raise portions for his other children as well as to pay his debts out of the residue of his estate.

The younger John Blackwell entered the parliamentary army at an early age, and by 1645 had the good fortune or perspicacity to be a captain in Cromwell's own regiment. The late Professor Godfrey Davies, who edited C. H. Firth's notes on the regiments and their officers for publication as *The Regimental History of Cromwell's Army*, evidently felt that there was something discreditable about Blackwell's transfer from service in the field to the Treasurers-at-War's department, which he believed to have taken place in 1648. On the contrary, Blackwell was serving as a Deputy War Treasurer by March 1645/6, if not September 1645, and continued to do so without a break from then on. It seems likely, to judge from other pamphlet references, that both Blackwells were counted among the Independent minority in City of London politics, and this would fit well with his Cromwellian ties. It may also explain the slowness of his promotion after this very early start. Until 1645 the post of Treasurer-at-War had been held by an MP. From then on it was held jointly by a group of wealthy Londoners, mostly aldermen, who were often known as the Treasurers at Guildhall; they were also, in effect, the central Receivers-General and accountants for the weekly pay, which later became the monthly assessment.[47] By 1648–9 Blackwell had become the senior Deputy Treasurer, but in view of his later reputation this may not have been due solely to Cromwell's backing. In that year he was proposed as an additional War Treasurer himself, but the proposal was defeated by 23 to 21—a thin House even for the Rump. It would be rash to read too much into this. The vote could have represented objections by civilian Rumpers to having one of Cromwell's men in such a post. It could have been a status question: hitherto the

War Treasurers had been knights, aldermen or at least men of consider-able substance—and thus of personal creditworthiness. In 1652, when the last aldermanic Treasurers appointed in the 1640s withdrew, Black-well became co-Treasurer with William Leman, an obscure back-bench recruiter MP. Leman, in fact, is one of the few Members whom it is fair to classify as primarily a middle-level administrator, in the sense that he was more significant in this capacity than he was politically. After the dissolution of 20 April 1653 he ceased to act, and Blackwell was joined by another army type, Captain Richard Deane, a cousin of his older name-sake, Colonel and then Admiral Deane, who had also begun his Civil War career as a captain in the army. The military now had their own men controlling their own purse-strings, and this partnership continued until 1659. Then Deane, who seems to have been the more positive republican of the two, became a Council Clerk and confidant of Fleetwood and the military Junto, while Blackwell—the more specifically Cromwellian of them, but by then a member of the Fleetwood 'Wallingford House party'—remained as War Treasurer.

In 1647 he had married Elizabeth Smithesby, a cousin of his step-mother, who was also related to the Cromwells. The Smithesbys were one-time royal and later protectoral wardrobe officials and housekeepers. Not that Blackwell was the kind of Cromwellian who was a monarchist in the making. He was evidently regarded both by the restored Rump (of late December 1659–February 1660) and by Monck and the interim government of February–May 1660 as unreliable for having acted under the Committee of Safety in the autumn of 1659, and he was not re-appointed. Indeed in the Restoration settlement he and Deane were singled out, being among the few administrators who were disqualified in perpetuity from holding any public office under the Crown. Blackwell had been elected Alderman of London in 1659 but had paid his fine to avoid acting. Possibly (as in the later 1640s) it was partly his radicalism in a London context which was held against him politically in 1660. He was among the numerous ex-officials of the Commonwealth who were called as prosecution witnesses against the Regicides in the autumn of 1660. The purchaser of some of Blackwell's Irish lands, Lord Kingston—himself an ex-Cromwellian—seems to have become his protector in the mid-1660s. He employed Blackwell as a land surveyor in Cheshire, emphasised his repentance for the events of the 1640s and 50s, and de-fended his Irish acquisitions against royalist attempts to have them for-feited without compensation. Thwarted in his career as a public official, Blackwell developed his New England trading interests; his first wife died in 1669, and in 1672 he married secondly the youngest daughter of General Lambert, then languishing as a state prisoner on St Nicholas Island in Plymouth Sound. Blackwell evidently became well-known in Anglo-American colonial circles, and in 1688 William Penn appointed him as his Lieutenant-Governor for the new colony of Pennsylvania. Unhappily he was ground between the upper and nether millstones of a touchy, unpractical proprietor, and an irascible, unmanageable Assembly of settlers. Blackwell found his task a hopeless one, and soon abandoned it, resigning with Penn's approval in 1690; but the grounds which Penn gives for having originally appointed him are more interesting for our purpose. The founder of Pennsylvania wrote that Blackwell was:

> I suppose independent in judgement . . . of high repute as a wise and virtuous man; and yet, though Treasurer in the Commonwealths time, to the Army in England, Scotland and Ireland, a place in which he might have gained many thousands by the year, he was remarkably just and refused all perquisites and a great place in King Charles's and King James's time in Ireland, because it depended upon them; besides, he was pregnant and experienced and had formerly commanded men.

It was an added advantage from Penn's viewpoint that he was not a Friend.

This was John Blackwell's last appearance on the public scene. But his son and heir Lambert became Esquire Harbinger to William and Mary, and subsequently Envoy to Genoa and Tuscany. He was knighted in 1697, became a Norfolk landowner, and—a sad commentary on the heritability of financial acumen—a Director of the South Sea Company. It seems likely that while Blackwell lost his own and his father's church lands at the Restoration, something at least of his Irish investments was salvaged.

William Penn may have viewed the administration of the republican period through a romantic haze. But except for the scandalous case of George Bilton, the War Treasurers and their Deputies did handle millions of pounds with exemplary honesty. That they took advantage of their influential position to get priority for the settlement of their own just claims for arrears, is true; but it would have been unnatural if they had not done so. Thurloe's letter to Henry Cromwell on behalf of Blackwell when he was setting out for Ireland in 1656, to try to straighten out his own and his father's interests there, conveys the flavour of this very well:

> Captain Blackwell's occasions drawing him to Ireland for the final settlement of his lands there, according to such orders, as he hath obtained from His Highness and Council here, I was willing to take the boldness of accompanying him to your Lordship with this letter, and therin to recommend him to your favour, as a person who deserves very well of the state, and is of great use daily in the things, which relate to his trust. I suppose a speedy despatch of

what he shall have an occasion to address your Lordship and the Council in, will be a great conveniency to him, as it will to the public service here, which will soon be sensible of his absence. In both which respects I do earnestly desire your Lordship's favour on his behalf . . .

Fortunate the regime which can command such servants as this, even if after an interval of thirty years the grass seemed unduly greener on the hills of yesterday.[48]

Edward Cosen[49] (1602–89) is a more obscure man, more strictly a revenue official and nothing else. He belonged to the small minority of republican officials whose fathers had previously been in royal service. Edward Cosen senior was Clerk of the Carriages to James I and then Charles I; whatever his origins—which were non-armigerous—he lived at Croydon where he died in 1636. Presumably through his father's connections with the Household, the younger Edward Cosen entered the service of the elder Sir Henry Vane.[50] During the Civil War Cosen acted as Westminster correspondent for Vane when he was away from the capital. At the same time he became Clerk to Parliament's revenue committee, of which Vane was a prominent member. With the institution of the Commonwealth in 1649, this became the Committee for the Public Revenue, on which the younger (but no longer the elder) Vane still sat; Cosen was then sometimes described by the more dignified title of Secretary rather than Clerk. A hostile pamphleteer said that in the mid-1640s his office was worth £1,500–£2,000 a year. The official stipend was 6s. 8d. a day plus expenses for himself and his clerks; in the early 1650s he also held the semi-sinecure office of Comptroller of the Pipe, in the largely moribund Upper Exchequer of Account, at an annual fee of £40. Unless one assumes that he made an enormous amount from gratuities, if not corruption, the figure given in the royalist source seems excessive; but it is not impossible.

Cosen was clearly on the upgrade. He obtained a grant of arms in 1651; he bought a Gloucestershire estate and, at some stage—for it was not inherited—another in Leicestershire. There is no record of his serving the Commonwealth in England after the summer of 1653, and it is possible that he followed the elder Vane (d. 1655) into retirement or the younger Vane into opposition. An Edward Couzens was, however, an official of the Scottish Exchequer in 1659; this may well be our man, and may explain his absence from the English scene in 1659 when so many ex-republican functionaries of 1649–53 re-appear in the administration. In May 1660 Cosen prudently obtained a royal pardon and in 1661 a confirmation of his now invalid grant of arms. He was then described as being of Hillsley, Glos.; but when he came to make his will, as a very old man, in 1688, he was of Charley, Leics. He had outlived all his children; his heir general was a granddaughter; his heirs male were remote cousins, also named Edward Cosen, in Wrexham and Kent, and a nephew, son of his brother Richard who had been his subordinate in the Exchequer thirty-five years earlier. The legacies and annuities prescribed in the will are modest, but the value of the two main properties is not stated. Probably Cosen's years in the public service (at least twelve, or twenty if he moved on to Scotland after 1654) had contributed substantially to his modest fortunes. As to his views, he was perhaps a client of the elder Vane rather than a parliamentarian, let alone a republican by conviction. The religious sentiments expressed in his will are conventionally Calvinist, and contain the added preference for a private evening funeral by torchlight. Unusual perhaps only in his longevity, Cosen was among those in the middle ranks upon whom the Long Parliament and then the Rump depended for the successful implementation of their policies. More we cannot say, except that these policies failed in 1653 and again in 1659–60 for political reasons and not because of administrative incompetence.[51]

Richard Hutchinson (1597–1669/70) is a less well-documented figure than Blackwell but arguably even more important. The third or fourth son of a Lincolnshire mercer (himself the younger son of a wool merchant and one-time Mayor of Lincoln), Hutchinson emigrated to Massachusetts Bay in 1633–4 along with his elderly mother, at least two of his brothers and a married sister, Mrs Wheelwright; his eldest brother William was already in his forties with a grown-up family by the time they were leaving England. Presumably religious convictions had a good deal to do with their decision to emigrate. Once in New England the Hutchinsons soon became living witnesses to the 'dissidence of dissent'. Three of the brothers joined in protest against the banishment of their sister's husband, the Rev. John Wheelwright, for heterodoxy in religion. Then, more notoriously, they became involved in the case mounted by the Rev. John Cotton and other leading Massachusetts divines against William's wife Ann. After the defeat of the Hutchinson-Wheelwright party—and, by the same token, of the youthful Governor Sir Henry Vane the younger (ruling during a brief interval in John Winthrop's long tenure)—the whole family moved on to the newer and less illiberal settlement of Rhode Island in 1638. Richard, however, apparently returned to Massachusetts and was back in England by 1643. Whether or not he had been a London apprentice and then free of his company before he left for America in the early 1630s, Hutchinson is described in documents of the 1640s–50s as Citizen and Ironmonger, and he was probably already a well-to-do merchant. He returned to find his family's erstwhile protector, the younger Vane, a leading parliamentarian and

Parliament's Treasurer of the Navy. Hutchinson was able to supply the mercantile experience and creditworthiness which Vane lacked; he became assistant and then Deputy to the Treasurer. In Whitehall-Westminster circles, it was possible for Hutchinson to be described as a 'menial servant' of Sir Henry Vane, but this was absurd—and seems merely to have been a means of evading the fifth and twentieth taxation. The first office to which he was appointed in his own right was in 1643 as co-Treasurer for the funds to relieve widows and orphans, sick or maimed soldiers, that is, war casualties generally and their dependants—a post which he continued to hold until 1650. He was described as Vane's Deputy by early 1645. And if the self-denying ordinance had been strictly enforced, he might even have become Treasurer in that year. But Vane, on agreeing to forgo half of the profits of his office, was allowed to retain it by special dispensation, so Hutchinson remained Deputy. Considering the extent of Vane's other commitments and activities, most of the routine management of naval finance during the 1640s must have been effectively in Hutchinson's hands. In January 1649 he became a Regulator (one of the special commissioners to purge the officers of the Navy and Customs). In 1650 came Vane's offer to surrender the Treasurership provided he were amply compensated for doing so; and the Rump's subsequent vote that Hutchinson should succeed him at the end of the year, when Vane acted as a Teller against the motion.[52] It is not clear whether these events signified a rift between Hutchinson and his patron: despite his threatening to resign more than once, the new Treasurer showed no sign of following Vane into opposition in 1653-4, and remained in office until 1660, when he retired into private life, becoming once more a successful merchant and investor. He was MP for Rochester in Richard Cromwell's Parliament.

Hutchinson's tenure as Treasurer was by no means all smooth sailing. In early April 1653, just before the Rump was dissolved, he asked leave to resign unless he was allowed more favourable financial terms, and he repeated this threat at almost yearly intervals. The nub of the matter was whether, by being paid a lump sum, he was doing worse than earlier Treasurers had done on the old poundage basis. The answer was, of course, that the greater the navy's annual financial turnover, the more likely that poundage would yield a larger total income to the Treasurer, unless his basic salary were adjusted upwards. After the defeat of the royalists at sea as well as by land (1649-51), the Commonwealth's naval strength and expenditure were briefly cut back. But during 1652 worsening relations with the Dutch, which rapidly escalated into full-scale naval war, saw this process halted and then dramatically reversed, so that expenditure reached a new peak by 1653-4. Then with the return of peace the navy was felt to be excessively large; despite the decision to attack the Spanish Indies (taken June 1654, implemented 1655), reductions were again made. Once more, as relations with Spain in Europe deteriorated to the point of open war (1655–6), the scale of naval expenditure mounted again; and by 1657–8 it was back more or less at its peak level. There was this difference, however: that the Protectorate was markedly less successful than the Commonwealth had been at raising the money to meet its commitments, and expenditure on the navy (for supplies, etc. as well as seamen's wages) fell more and more heavily into arrears (1658–9). Since Hutchinson's salary depended on the size of turnover, calculated on expenditure, not income, he was personally unaffected by this. And for all his repeated complaints, he did not do badly out of his office (Table 42).

TABLE 42   *Richard Hutchinson as Navy Treasurer*

1651–2–3	Basic salary £1,500 p.a.
1653, June	Awarded another £1,000 p.a. for one year only.
1653, Dec.	Says his total salary is £4,000 but could have been £30,000 on the old basis.
1654–5	To have £1,500, plus £100 for every £100,000 handled above £700,000 a year.
1655–6	On the same basis as for 1654–5.
1656–7	Now on £1,500 p.a. plus £200 for every £100,000 over £700,000; requests this be back-dated to cover 1651–4!
1657	£1,500 p.a. plus £200 as above, repeated.
1656	Actual salary for 1¼ years = £1,875 (= £1,500 p.a.).
1658–60	Actual salary for 2½ years = £3,830 (= £1,500 p.a. + £80).

His total profits from office are impossible to calculate.[53] Nor can we be certain that a man of his commercial calibre gained more from his remuneration in the public service than he would have made if he had been able to give his full attention to private business enterprise. According to legend, Hutchinson lost £60,000 worth of property in the Great Fire of London; none the less, his will made just over three years later provides fairly generously for his wife, six sons and other relatives, and gives the impression of considerable wealth; only his Irish lands caused him anxiety.[54] Hutchinson omitted any religious prologue from his will, but it would be absurd to build any elaborate theories about a possible loss of faith on so slender a basis. His descendants included the future earls of Donoughmore in Ireland and the eighteenth-century loyalist Governor of Massachusetts, Thomas Hutchinson. His youngest son and executor, Eliakim (1641–1718), continued the tradition of Massachusetts Bay Company membership and was a benefactor of Harvard College. Perhaps a better understanding of Hutchinson's religious position and his relationship with Vane, on both of which there is little firm evidence, would help us to set his administrative career from 1643 to 1660 in a more meaningful context. As it is, he emerges as the type of able business-man who will render honest and efficient service to government if—and only if—he is adequately rewarded by his own lights. In Pepys's view, 'never was that office better managed, or with more credit or satisfaction to the service'. Again it is remarkable that he is omitted from the *DNB* and from the *Dictionary of American Biography*.[55]

By contrast, Martin Noell (*c.* 1620–65), about whom much more has been written, was first and foremost a financier, to whom government service was an incidental additional means of extending his economic interests. Born of middle-class origins in Stafford, his father moved to London and became a scrivener, Martin being admitted as his apprentice in 1637. Nothing more is heard of him then until 1648 when, described variously as Gent. and Merchant, he appears as a commissioner in London and as a shipowner who had suffered losses in the royalist attack on Scilly. Noell's real breakthrough came in the early 1650s when he obtained the position of co-farmer of the excise on salt, at a rental of £15,000 a year. His own profits from this can only be guessed, in the absence of any private or business papers. But thereafter he never looked back. Noell's secret was to be ready to advance money (in cash) when and where suc-cessive governments wanted it, and to be prepared to wait in order to recoup himself out of the future income of the various revenue farms in which he was involved. He was said to act as personal paymaster, that is broker or money-lender, to the Cromwell family: of this the proof is lacking. But certainly the Protectorate came to depend upon Noell more than it did on any other single man, for ready cash and credit.[56] He was also farmer of the excise on silks, both home-produced and imported, on spirits, soap, glass, iron, salt, lead, etc., on salt produced in Scotland, and on sea-coal exported; in the summer of 1657 he was named as leader of the syndicate for the projected 'super-farm' of the entire Customs and Excise revenues. Meanwhile he was on various committees and commis-sions, particularly for the 'southern expedition', alias the Western Design of 1654–5, of which he was a leading protagonist, having strong commercial interests in the Caribbean. At the same time Noell was consolidating his position both in the City and in his native county. He became Steward of the Scriveners' Company in 1653, Assistant in 1655 and co-Master in 1659. He achieved the aldermanic bench in 1657, and in 1656–8 and 1659 was MP for Stafford, where he founded some alms-houses during the 1650s. In 1657 he was joint Deputy to Thurloe as Postmaster-General. By the late 1650s he was being attacked as a would-be monopolist, and there are signs that with deteriorating government credit he was becoming more acutely concerned to safeguard his own advances by obtaining orders for priority repayments. The transition back from Protectorate to Commonwealth in 1659 cost Noell his post-office place. Nor does he seem to have been as heavily involved financially in 1659–60 as he had been in 1654–8, although this may be a misleading impression given by uneven survival of contracts, memoranda and so on. Whatever the truth of this, Noell made the subsequent transition to royal service successfully. He soon emerged as a creditor of the restored monarchy, and as one of its mercantile-colonial advisers. He was knighted in 1662, by which time he had apparently transferred his main energies and interests temporarily to Ireland, where to help safeguard them he became an MP (1661–5). He died, it is said of the plague, in 1665. His wealth cannot be estimated from his will but the range of his interests and investments is conveyed by it: lands in England, Ireland and Barbados, offices and revenue farms, shares in the Royal Africa Company and in various ships, etc. The religious prologue is of the most cursory, though Calvinist in tone; he left nothing to charity, having already endowed his father's home town, but he provided liberally for his servants. The friends named in it are almost all business and trading associates in the City, with scarcely anything about them to remind posterity of Sir Martin's Cromwellian past. As to religion, his will may have been made under acute pressure when he was struck by the plague, and we have no reason to doubt his conventional piety. Then, as later, this was fully compatible with speculating in forced labour, either white or coloured, in the West Indies, and with exploiting the poor through their need for basic commodities whose prices he controlled as a tax-farmer.[57]

Sir William Roberts (1606–62) seems much more of a treasury and all-round governmental type by contrast. His background, too, was very different from Noell's, his family being well-established Middlesex gentry seated at Willesden; William was born the twin son of Barne or Barnes Roberts, but his father died when he was a small boy and his twin brother died at Eton in 1619, leaving William as the main heir to his grandfather, Francis, who died in 1631. On his mother's side, the family had a mercantile connection too.[58] Educated at Queen's and then Emmanuel College, Cambridge, as a pupil of the great puritan divine, John Preston,[59] he went on to Gray's Inn and was knighted by James I at the age of only 19 (1624). The reasons for this sudden prominence are not clear. Roberts appears to have lived the life of a normal educated country gentleman, participating in local government during the reign of Charles I; and from 1631 he was a wealthy man in his own right. His political allegiances never seem to have been in any doubt. He was appointed a Deputy Lieutenant by Parliament in the first winter of the Civil War, and from the beginning of 1643 he was named to every committee or commission connected with his county. His first national position was as a Contractor for the sale of episcopal lands in 1646. The Contractors, as opposed to

the Trustees, were more like a business syndicate than a body of administrators. He held the same post for Crown and capitular lands and fee-
farm rents (1649–50), but was a Trustee for the sale of lands forfeited for
treason (1651–3); as well as holding local offices and commissions,
Roberts was appointed to the Rump's non-parliamentary law reform
commission under Hale (January 1652), and in the same year he became
a colleague of Josias Berners on the Obstructions Commission. Since
this body was meant to be remedying the failure to complete the sales of
church, Crown and royalist lands, Roberts was virtually being asked to
investigate his own failings.

The political changes of 1653 elevated rather than depressed his fortunes. In November–December he was briefly on the Cromwellian-
dominated Council of State. In the first year of the Protectorate he
became co-Auditor of the Receipt with the ageing Thomas Fauconberge,
and on the latter's death in 1655 sole Auditor, for which he received £500
a year salary and had the use of a rent-free house in Westminster. As an
Obstructions Commissioner his salary was £200. While finally, having
been a temporary commissioner to inspect and investigate the treasuries
and revenues of the Commonwealth in July and December 1653, he
acquired additional positions as a Wine Licence Agent and an Accounts
Commissioner in 1655. He was an MP in 1653 and again in 1656–7; he
then became a life peer in Cromwell's Upper House, where he sat as a
government supporter in the parliaments of 1658 and 1659. Roberts had
been named as a Commissioner of the High Court to try the King back
in 1649, but had prudently not acted. At the Restoration, he lost a £1,077
investment in Northamptonshire bishops' lands, his offices and commissions, and his title as a lord. He did not, however, suffer any additional
penalties, and was evidently a very wealthy man when he made his will
in 1662; his only unmarried daughter was to have a £2,000 portion and
£100 for her trousseau provided that she married with her mother's
consent. He disposed of property in several parts of Middlesex and a
Worcestershire rectory. But his instructions for his wife envisaged that
some of the younger of his five sons might well be placed as clerks or
apprentices, or in some other 'lawfull calling'. His eldest son had been
raised to the baronetage by the restored King. Personal touches are few.
In the summer of 1655 Roberts and one of his sons were set on by thieves
near Tyburn; he was wounded and the boy killed. In 1656 his clerk in
the Receipt was accused of taking fees on the payment of John Lilburne's
pension, which was meant to be free of such burdens; Sir William was
accordingly summoned by a committee of the Protector's Council. Was
Roberts a time-server, whose properties happened to lie within Parliament's quarters; a sincere puritan, parliamentarian, or even republican,
or what? His prominence during the Protectorate perhaps suggests a
preference for a hierarchical society with the traditional institutions

firmly maintained, even if under Cromwellian rather than Stuart rule; more is surmise.[60]

With Samuel Sandford, alias Sandiford (*c.* 1621–99), we return to the Bartlett-Cosens level of revenue officials. Sandford came of a very minor Lancashire gentry family, but seems to have lived in Shropshire. He became connected with the Excise in Lancashire in the mid-1640s but was a local commissioner in Shropshire in 1647–8. He obtained a post in the central Excise administration, as Solicitor for Charges (in charge of vetting claims for expenses), in 1647 at the modest stipend—scarcely more than a retaining fee—of £22. 5s. 6d. a year. However, in 1650 he was promoted to the important post of Surveyor-General Itinerant of the Excise in the provinces, and he seems to have continued in this office, at a salary of £182. 10s. 0d. a year plus travelling expenses, until the fall of the republic. Sandford was back in Lancashire in the 1660s. He typifies the obscure functionary of the middle rank whose work was still of a responsible nature. While there might only need to be one Martin Noell or even William Roberts, many more officials such as Sandford were needed to operate the regime's finances effectively.[61]

Richard Sherwyn or Sherwin (d. 1675) is a less obscure man than Sandford, though his origins are untraceable. By the early 1640s he was serving as a clerk to the Auditor of Receipt, Sir Robert Pye MP, a somewhat lukewarm parliamentarian;[62] he was then styled Gent. In 1650 he became Auditor to the Commissioners for Compounding and Sequestration, at what appears to be the excessively generous salary of £350 a year. And in the summer of 1653, after the purge of pro-Rump officeholders, he became co-Treasurer for Compounding etc. at Goldsmiths' Hall. Strangely, his salary in this office was actually less (£200 increased to £250 a year for each of the two Treasurers) than in the Auditorship. In 1653 he became Clerk to the Assistants to the new Revenue Committee, in effect replacing Edward Cosen; and in 1654, although his old master Sir Robert Pye was excluded from the re-established Exchequer, Sherwyn assumed the key position of Secretary to the Treasury Commissioners. In this capacity he was to receive retrospective praise from Bulstrode Whitelocke who became a Commissioner in 1655 after quitting his Chancery place.

By the later 1650s Sherwyn had become a man of substance. He had a house off the cloisters of Westminster Abbey; Thurloe tried to get him a seat in Richard Cromwell's parliament, where he represented Ludgershall in Wiltshire. He acted as a messenger between the Treasury and the House of Commons. On the fall of the Protectorate and the re-institution of the Rump, Sherwyn apparently continued to act, although he was not one of the officials afterwards accused of serving the illegal

Committee of Safety (October–December 1659). At the Restoration, his original patron Pye was solemnly reinstated as Auditor, although he was by then too old to carry out even nominal duties. Sherwyn himself lost all the important positions he had held during the 1650s. But thanks to Pye's support he was kept on as a Treasury Clerk, later also becoming a Tax Agent. He was living in Covent Garden as a man of considerable wealth when he made his will in 1675, and his affairs were still very much bound up with the Pye family, for whom he seems to have acted as a trustee. His own daughter was to have a portion of £3,000; his other legacies totalled at least another £1,600. There is evidence of connections, perhaps family origins, in Wiltshire and in Somerset. Sherwyn gave £100 for impoverished Ministers of the Gospel who had left their livings, or been ejected for nonconformity, which emphasises to his lasting puritan religious feelings whatever his political position. Nor should he be seen merely as a subservient client of Sir Robert Pye.[63]

Secretaries, good and bad

Some of those whose careers have already been sketched, notably William Jessop, were essentially personal secretaries and confidential men of business, anticipating Charles II's description of Sidney Godolphin—that he was 'never in the way, nor out of the way'. Those to whom we now turn served primarily as secretaries to individuals or institutions, although some were both more and less than mere secretaries.

Gualter (alias Walter) Frost the elder (15??–1652) was a man of obscure and, it may be presumed, humble origins. In 1619 he married a Suffolk girl, Phoebe Seffray, at Chevington. By 1637 he was sufficiently well-to-do or well connected for his eldest son, also Gualter, to enter Emmanuel College, Cambridge, as a pensioner. The elder Frost's first known political employment—we can hardly call it public office!—was in 1639–40 as a secret courier between the English opposition leaders and the Scottish Covenanters. Disguised as a commercial traveller he apparently took secret, if not potentially treasonable letters to and fro, rolled up in a hollowed-out walking stick. He must have been regarded as absolutely trustworthy by those involved. And it is highly probable, though no evidence has been found to support this, that he was already well known to at least one of the leading puritan-parliamentarian opponents of Charles I. On the basis of neighbourhood, the Barnardiston family seems the likeliest.[64]

In 1642, like many other future republicans, Frost switched his interests to the re-conquest of Ireland. And he appears in the records as a Commissary, helping to supply the Protestant forces there. This involved using his own credit on the government's behalf, and left him with a load of debt from which he never escaped. About the time when civil war broke out at home, he returned and became an intelligence agent under Parliament's Committee of Safety (1642–3). When this body was replaced by the Committee of Both Kingdoms in the spring of 1644, Frost became its co-Secretary or Clerk. Again, we can only surmise why he should have been selected for this appointment, but he must have commended himself to those members of the new Committee who had also been on its predecessor. By the late 1640s Frost had become sole Secretary to the Derby House Committee; he was also employed in counter-revolutionary propaganda, as an author and editor against the Levellers. With the establishment of the Commonwealth in 1649, Frost became Secretary to the new Council of State, at the handsome salary of 40s. a day (or £730 a year) plus 2s. 6d. a day for his servant. He continued in this position for just over three years, until his death in March 1652. Frost had already petitioned more than once for the settlement of arrears due from his Irish commissary work back in 1642. And after his death it emerged that his family's affairs were in such a chaotic state that the Council felt obliged to set up a special committee to sort them out, with the help of his heir Gualter the younger. According to their findings, Frost died worth about £5,900, of which about £3,400 represented his earnings in eleven years' service of the State; as against this, he owed no less than £5,000 for Irish provisions. An initial vote of £1,000 was accompanied by a recommendation from the Council to Parliament that further provision should be made for Frost's family—and his creditors. And as late as 1656 one of his ex-partners or creditors from the early 1640s was still petitioning for relief. Moreover the total figure of £5,900 for his estate is rather misleading. Of this, £2,000 had been assigned out of the Excise but was not due to be paid for some years; £2,000 was invested in the East India Company, £1,100 in the Guinea Company and £800 in the Fens. Leaving as he did a widow, four sons, two daughters and seven grandchildren, this was hardly riches. Not surprisingly, perhaps, Frost showed distinct nepotistic tendencies. His eldest son was already Assistant Secretary to the Council at £1 a day and two others were on its subordinate staff; one of them was later to become Clerk of the Crown and Hanaper in the Irish Chancery.

Frost's position was arguably the most responsible one open to any official of middling rank in the entire administration. Not only did he have charge of the Council's books and papers and its agenda, he was commissioned to write state papers both for internal government use and for publication. His anti-Leveller writings have on the whole been dismissed as the productions of a reactionary hack, but his statement of Anglo-Scottish relations was probably more valuable, while in 1650 he and the younger Vane served together on a committee entrusted with preparing a narrative of the affairs of the Commonwealth, to be presented to Parliament by the Council. His loyalty must have been regarded as beyond suspicion, although paradoxically he had a namesake whose estates were ordered to be seized in 1651 for conspiracy against the Commonwealth. It may seem remarkable, but perhaps at this stage will no longer surprise the reader, how little we know of Frost as a man. He died intestate.[65]

The importance of the younger Gualter Frost's being passed over for the Secretaryship of the Council in March 1652, in favour of Thurloe, has already been stressed.[66] Whether or not this was partly due to a reaction against the Frosts' tendency to make the Council's staff into a family 'closed-shop', it was certainly a setback. Walter, or Gualter, the younger had become Manciple of Emmanuel where he had shown particular skill in matters concerned with the College water supply and had proved himself a mathematician of some ability. He had then, presumably during the Civil War, entered the service of the City of London, and became Sword-Bearer to the Lord Mayor. By 1648 he was helping his father in tasks like the examination of prisoners under the Derby House Committee, before becoming Assistant Secretary to the Council of State in 1649. When he was passed over in 1652, he continued in that office and was also—no doubt partly as compensation—made Treasurer for the Council's Contingencies. He continued in the latter post until 1659, although with Jessop's appointment as Treasurer for the Protector's Contingencies in 1653–4 it became markedly less important, the sums which he handled declining steeply. And to mark this, his salary of £400 a year was cut to £300 in 1655. When the Council's staff was reorganised under the Protectorate in 1654, Frost was definitely ranked as junior to Jessop and Scobell, the Clerks, quite apart from Thurloe. On the other hand in 1659 he did better than most of the Cromwellian Council officials, being reappointed Treasurer of Contingencies by the new Commonwealth Council of State, albeit only at £200 a year salary. It appears, too, that he continued to act in some capacity under the Committee of Safety the following autumn. After that he disappears from view, not even his date of death being known. Apart from his integrity of life being praised along with his mathematics, the younger Frost remains almost totally enigmatic. Perhaps the simplest explanation is the correct one; the Councillors may have looked for someone else to take over at his father's death because the younger Gualter was not quite up to becoming their Secretary.[67]

Unlike the Frosts, Jessop and others of comparable importance, Henry Scobell (d. 1660) was included in the *DNB* because of his connection with parliamentary history. Possibly of Norfolk origin, his early years are obscure. By 1643 he was acting as an under-clerk to the Clerk of the Parliaments, and may have become the Under-Clerk soon after that.

When Parliament's Great Seal was put into the hands of Lords Commissioners, Scobell became their Secretary in 1644; during the 1640s, he also established himself as Deputy Registrar of Chancery.[68] A political opponent, the presbyterian Clement Walker described Scobell as 'heretofore a poor under-clerk in Chancery, who writ for 2d. a sheet' and implies that his later Chancery office was in connection with land sales. But Walker is no more reliable than Clarendon on the personal backgrounds of radical parliamentarians and republicans, for whom he had a vitriolic hatred. Possibly Scobell began as a writing clerk in Chancery and transferred to Parliament's staff through Speaker Lenthall's appointment as Master of the Rolls; more we cannot say. By the late 1640s he was evidently recognised as a supporter of the radicals, or Independent party, in the House. After some procedural amendments—and once it was clear that their present Clerk, Henry Elsyng, would not act under them—the Rump appointed Scobell Clerk of the Parliaments at £500 a year plus fees on petitions and private bills.[69] He continued in this capacity until 1653, but got into trouble with the first Protectorate Parliament in 1654 for trying to intrude himself as Clerk rather than waiting to be reappointed by the House, and in January 1658 after a further struggle he failed to establish himself as Clerk to either House. He had become Registrar for the sale of Dean and Chapter lands in 1649 (Walker's reference was clearly to this post) for which he was eventually paid £750 to cover eight years' intermittent work without regard to his gains from fees and gratuities. On the reorganisation of the Council of State's staff in 1653, and presumably in compensation for the Clerkship of Parliament being temporarily in abeyance, Scobell became a Council Clerk at a salary of £1 a day; this was confirmed in 1654. In 1659 he suffered a dual defeat, losing his council post and failing to recover his parliamentary one. Perhaps the truculence which he showed towards the two Protectorate Parliaments was now held against him by the restored Rump; but he may well have been regarded as a committed protectorian. Age or ill health may also have affected him, for he died the year after. In his will, made in July 1660, Scobell disposed of four Norfolk manors, a house in Westminster, and legacies and annuities totalling several hundreds of pounds. His nearest male heirs were nephews. He left the Trustees for the maintenance of poor scholars in London £10 annually for the rest of an eight-year subscription, and £50 for the relief of poor debtors in the London prisons. He praised God for his property and noted finally 'I leave this world and the things of it to goe to my Lord Jesus'. In a codicil added in his own hand he remembered his pastors and teachers, the Congregationalists Mr John Rowe and Mr Seth Wood. A puritan-inclined outlook is unmistakable, even if the pious expressions are less longwinded than in some such cases. Scobell held lucrative offices, and unless he spent prodigally he must have made a considerable amount out of them. His ability and significance as an administrator are harder to assess. He evidently had the gift of commending himself markedly to some people and not at all to others. By 1654–8 his attitude towards the Clerkship of the Parliaments was positively proprietary and he was to suffer for it. His service under the Cromwellian Council was perhaps third in importance, after Thurloe's and Jessop's.[70]

It is tempting to describe John Thurloe (1616–68) himself as the perfect secretary. Certainly he was out of his depth as a political and parliamentary leader, a role into which he was forced under Richard Cromwell in 1658–9. As a political commentator and reporter, the evidence of his many letters to Henry Cromwell and Broghill (1655–9) suggests a clear, informed intelligence, but an inability to see things from the other side's point of view—and so to assess properly their strengths and weaknesses. This may also apply to Thurloe in the fields of security and foreign affairs: that he was an exemplary gatherer and processer of news and intelligence but less good at analysing it and recommending what should be done. That, however, is to judge him by the highest—and perhaps, for the mid-seventeenth century, by over-exacting—standards.

Born the son of an Essex parson with no special advantages of wealth or connection, Thurloe had little higher education. He somehow commended himself to Oliver St John MP and Solicitor General, in whose service he is found at the Uxbridge peace negotiations of 1644. He may have been in St John's employment by the late 1630s. He seems to have been enrolled at one of the small, so-called Chancery Inns, Furnivall's, but only entered Lincoln's Inn in 1646 at the advanced age of 30, and was duly called to the Bar in 1653. Meanwhile, no doubt through St John's influence, he became Receiver or Clerk of the Cursitors' fines (namely fee charges) in Chancery in March 1648, a post valued at £350 a year. 1651 was really the year of Thurloe's breakthrough. He then began to act for Oliver Cromwell as a solicitor over land transactions, and he went to the Netherlands as secretary to the Ambassadors extraordinary, St John and Strickland, reporting on their behalf to Parliament and to the Council. Only these circumstances can explain his appointment as Secretary of the Council in place of the elder Frost, at the end of March 1652.[71] From the republic's, and perhaps also from Cromwell's point of view it was a masterly move. When the Rump Council of State was dissolved in April 1653, there was continuity in the Secretaryship and so in all the Council's business and papers, and the same was true when the Barebones-elected Council was in turn replaced by the protectorate Council in December 1653. Thurloe, now styled Secretary of State, was given a seat on the Council board, ceasing to be merely its senior official. And in July 1657 he finally became a member in his own right of what was now the Protector's Privy Council. As Secretary of

State he was *ex officio* in charge of the postal services, but he did not assume direct control as Postmaster-General until the end of the current two-year lease in 1655, and he became farmer of the postal revenues only in 1657. Thurloe had become so completely identified not only with the Cromwellian regime but with the civilian, and in general more conservative wing of the Protectorate's supporters, that his supersession by the restored Rump of 1659 was a foregone conclusion. Not being the regicidal, radical type of Cromwellian, and having always kept on excellent terms with General Monck, he was acceptable as compromise candidate under the interim government of February–May 1660. Although there was never any serious possibility of his being employed under the restored monarchy, the story that Thurloe would have been brought to trial but for his threat to reveal unpleasing facts about leading royalists from his secret papers is legendary. None the less, at one stage the draft Bill for the general Act of Pardon and Oblivion did contain a clause excepting him from some of its benefits. On 8 August 1660 the House of Lords agreed to delete it. Some individual royalists and their families who had come to grief thanks to Thurloe's intelligence service may have had personal grievances against him, but he had never sat on a High Court of Justice; nor had he acted with the army against Parliament in 1659. Even without Monck's protection, he would probably have been safe; with it, he was perfectly secure.

Thurloe's gains from office are impossible to calculate. There is no evidence that he died a very rich man, although only his very modest investment in church lands was forfeited in 1660, his main purchases having been as a trustee for the St John family. He was accused in 1659 of having made an excessive, if not dishonest profit out of the Post Office, but cleared himself effectively. Almost all the other evidence for his alleged corruption comes from items preserved in his own papers, or from hostile gossip.[72] We need not, however, doubt that he took full advantage of his position. For instance his deputy governorship of the Adventurers for the fen drainage scheme (1656) fitted in well with Thurloe's evident ambition to become a leading man in his chosen locality, the Isle of Ely. His house, built at Wisbech, cannot have been cheap. In February 1658 he became Chancellor of the University of Glasgow, the first Englishman to fill this post, in 1659 MP for Cambridge University, with which he had not previously had any connection. Moreover he clearly exercised patronage in favour of his relatives, and took for granted a situation where people were as dependent on him as he had once been on St John. Thurloe was no radical, let alone revolutionary, but he was a highly efficient and—as far as the evidence goes—honest public servant. Not the least notable feature of the evidence which we have about him relates to his wretched health. He was seriously ill in 1653, 1655, 1657–8 and again in 1658. The nature of these illnesses is not clear, but it is not surprising that he died in his early 50s; it is more remarkable that someone so constantly afflicted should have been able to play such a leading part in public affairs.[73]

The secretaries employed by the Generals individually or by the Army Council collectively were also well placed to advance their own interests. John Rushworth (1612–90) the historian, combined being Fairfax's secretary (1645–50) with the Cursitorship of Chancery for Yorkshire and Westmorland (from 1643), an under-clerkship of the Parliament, and part-time government journalism. When Fairfax resigned in 1650, Rushworth's position apparently lapsed. At any rate he did not go to Scotland with Cromwell; he became a member of the Hale Committee on law reform in 1652, and co-Registrar of the Court of Admiralty in 1654, a place which was worth about £423 a year to its two holders together over the three years 1654–7. Rushworth had dedicated Vol. 1 of his *Historical Collections* to Richard Cromwell, then still Protector in 1659, and he had no part in the affairs of the restored Commonwealth or the army's usurpation. When Fairfax re-emerged briefly in public life as an ally of Monck, Rushworth was restored to favour, and was a Clerk to the Council of State from March to May 1660. What of the following thirty years? As the *DNB* bluntly records, he died a drunkard in a debtor's prison. But before he came to that sad end, Rushworth had completed his invaluable *Collections*, down to 1649, although the latter volumes were not published in his lifetime. He had become an honorary MA of the Queen's College, Oxford, in 1649, but in practice was a student of Lincoln's Inn. His father was an obscure Northumberland gentleman. Rushworth acted as an agent or man of business for several aristocratic families at different stages in his career. Despite his loss of office in 1660, he regained a foothold, serving as Treasury Solicitor, 1661–5. In 1667 he was said to be acting as secretary to the new Lord Keeper, the ex-Cavalier Orlando Bridgman. The decisive point in his career would seem to have been his connection with the Fairfax family, which antedated their emergence as parliamentarian Generals. His appointment as Clerk Assistant to the Clerk of the House of Commons, in 1640, was hardly due to his previous experience as solicitor for the town of Berwick-on-Tweed, his only employment recorded before that date. Rushworthy was a commentator on events as much as a participant in them.[74]

Henry Parker (1604–52), who was Secretary to the General Officers in Ireland from 1649 until his death, is in some respects a puzzling figure. The most original and daring of all Parliament's pamphleteers in grasping the fundamental issue of sovereignty, Parker was rewarded by becoming Secretary to the Army in July 1642, and, according to Mrs Glow, Secretary to the Committee of Safety (1642–3). But he was also well connected: educated at Oxford and Lincoln's Inn, the son and younger brother of knights, his mother a Temple of Stowe, so his early posts at the centre of Parliament's machinery of government may not have been solely due to his *Observations* and other writings.[75] Parker never quite made good the promise of this flying start. He did not become secretary to the Committee of Both Kingdoms in 1644 or later, as might well have been expected; and in 1646, for reasons which his biographer Professor Jordan finds hard to explain, he accepted the much more peripheral post of English Agent in Hamburg, and Secretary to the Merchant Adventurers' Company there. He appears to have stayed at Hamburg for the best part of three years. On his return to republican England in 1649, Parker became co-Registrar for the Prerogative Court of Canterbury jointly with the Earl of Pembroke's man of business, Michael Oldsworth, or Oldisworth, MP; there was to be a good deal of dispute about this office during the years to come, but it brought in an assured income through the labours of the under-clerks or deputies' deputies, who actually did the work. Then when the Irish expedition was being planned, Parker was selected—probably by Ireton—to go there as Secretary to the Generals. As far as is known, he was in Ireland from August 1649 until his premature death in 1652. That Parker was a trenchant and clear-minded writer and an important theorist of radical parliamentarianism is beyond doubt. His place in the intra-parliamentarian conflicts of 1646–9 and in the early Commonwealth is less clear. Probably he remained what he had been from 1643–4, a spokesman and adherent of the gentry Independents: radical in relation to those of more conservative views and interests, but conservative in relation to Levellers, millenarians, or militant Baptists, and even perhaps to some republicans of the Ludlow-Marten variety.[76]

William Clarke (*c.* 1623–66) was the humblest in origins of the principal army secretaries, but thanks to prudence and good fortune rose further than any of the others. He appears to have been born of a plebeian London family, without any inherited advantages, and to have had no formal higher education[77] before he became assistant to Rushworth in the Army secretariat about 1646, and then Secretary to the Army Council in 1647. It was in this capacity that he made shorthand notes of the Putney (October–November 1647) and Whitehall (December 1648–January 1649) debates; he also began to compile his own archive—the collection now known as the Clarke Papers. By 1648–9 he was Fairfax's co-secretary with Rushworth; hence he stayed in England with the Lord General when Parker went off to Ireland with Cromwell and Ireton. In 1650, after Cromwell's return and Fairfax's resignation, Clarke provided the element of continuity, becoming Secretary to the General Officers of the field army for the Scottish campaign. The next crucial shift in his fortunes came in August 1651. When Cromwell turned south in pursuit of Charles II and the invading Scots, Clarke was left as Secretary to the acting commander-in-chief Scotland, Lieutenant-General George Monck. Towards the end of the year, Monck was joined by Major-Generals Deane and Lambert; when he retired on grounds of health, they acted jointly; Deane then became sole commander and was in turn succeeded by Colonel Robert Lilburne. In 1654 the renewal of guerrilla warfare in parts of Scotland combined with the implementation of the political union became too much for Lilburne, and he was succeeded by Monck, now with plenary powers and the rank of full General. Clarke remained through all these changes and was thus at army headquarters in Scotland continuously from 1651 to the winter of 1659–60, when he came south with Monck himself to settle the future of England. Much of the material in the Clarke Papers for these years consists either of routine items connected with the organisation of the army in Scotland, the reports of successive commanders, or copies and originals of news-letters sent to Clarke by his correspondents in London, notably by his brother-in-law, the journalist, censor and supposed Leveller sympathiser Gilbert Mabbott. Clarke was also Treasurer for Army Contingencies in Scotland (1653–7) and temporary Keeper of the Great Seal of Scotland at least once. Like Rushworth, he was empanelled as a witness against the Regicides in the autumn of 1660. In 1661 he reaped his real reward, gaining the Secretaryship-at-War to Charles II and a knighthood. Ironically his elevation and his continued connection with Monck was to cost Clarke his life, for he was mortally wounded on the deck of the Admiral's flagship, in battle with the Dutch (June 1666). Although he had radical political and religious connections, there is no evidence of his holding such views himself. He can be regarded as a lucky oppor-tunist, or a pragmatic adherent of *de facto* authority. William Clarke was certainly an efficient secretary, and as an outstanding document-collector and record-keeper has posterity deeply in his debt.[78]

The career of another less distinguished figure also illustrates the impor-tance of Monck as a patron. In 1650–1 the Clerk to the Irish and Scottish Affairs Committee of the Council was one Mathew Lock (also spelt Matthew and Locke). His origins are quite obscure. In the 1650s another Matthew Locke (*c.* 1620–66/9), who had been trained as a London scrivener, was Customs Collector, first at Portsmouth and then at Hull. The committee clerk is likewise to be distinguished from the well-known musician, Matthew Locke (*c.* 1630–77), although proof that they were three different people can be established only from the evidence of the 1660s.

In 1653 or 1654, Locke was attached to the new English civil adminis-tration in Scotland. From 1655 to 1659 he acted as Clerk Assistant to the

Council there; after Lord Broghill's departure in 1656, Monck was the acting chairman, or *de facto* president of this body. And it was perhaps a natural step for Locke to become his personal secretary, even if a transfer the other way round from private to public service is a more characteristic feature of seventeenth-century bureaucratic careers. Like Clarke, Locke came south with Monck in 1659–60, and remained in his employment after the Restoration. It was entirely due to his patron that he succeeded Clarke as Secretary-at-War in 1666. He remained in this post until his own resignation in favour of another better-known administrative factotum of the late seventeenth century, William Blathwayt, who bought the office from him in 1683. Locke therefore climbed from quite humble republican beginnings to a measure of eminence under the restored monarchy. Once more, practical usefulness plus the good luck of being in the right place at the right time to enjoy really effective patronage, seems to explain his career. Of his origins, circumstances or opinions virtually no trace remains.[79]

Cromwell's personal secretaries are a contrasting pair but do not reflect a judicious choice of men, if we compare them with Thurloe or Clarke. Robert Spavin (1621–50/1) was a Yorkshireman of humble rural origins. He became a London merchant with strong interests in colonial trade and shipping. How and why he entered the Army secretariat is unknown. He was serving as Cromwell's secretary in 1646–7, and by 1648–9 he was Assistant to Rushworth as well as Secretary to the Lieutenant-General. In early November 1648 he wrote to William Clarke from the besieging army's camp around Pontefract:

> I am very glad and so [are] the rest of our friends to hear of a beginning to action with you. I verily think God will break that great idol the Parliament, and that old job-trot form of government of King, Lords and Commons. It is no matter how nor by whom, sure I am it cannot be worse if honest men have the managing of it—and no matter whether they be great or no . . . the Lord is about a great work, and such as will stumble many mean-principled men, and such as I think but few great ones shall be honoured withall.

These are the authentic accents of apocalyptic revolutionism as we might hear them, in their secularised idiom, on the barricades today. Then as now, however, it was sometimes a question who was 'honest' and who 'mean-principled'. For just when his career must have seemed set fair (assuming that he had survived the bogs and fevers of Ireland and the ambushes of nationalist guerrillas), Spavin fell like Lucifer. In the last week of June 1649 a scandal broke: he had been counterfeiting Cromwell's signature and seal to sell protections to ex-royalists and neutrals in the Lieutenant-General's name. A court-martial was held, but it is not clear that Spavin suffered any formal punishment beyond loss of office and disablement from further employment. He returned to private trade and made his will on the eve of a voyage to the East Indies early the following year; he presumably died at sea or in the east. There the matter would rest—that Cromwell had the misfortune to employ a dishonest, as well as fanatical secretary, of whom he had to rid himself—but for the terms of Spavin's will. Not merely does it make clear that he had extremely influential mercantile connections, with such men as Martin Noell, Maurice Thompson, and William Pennoyer, with interests in Africa and the West Indies as well as in the East India Company, but the debts which he listed as then owing to him included £550 from Lord Lieutenant Cromwell, 'which hee most unjustly deteynes from mee'. This was not Spavin's pay arrears, which he noted separately; it may represent the capital and interest on a loan which he had advanced. But it is at least possible that these were the takings on the forged protections which his master had confiscated. Since none of Cromwell's own personal accounts have survived, we do not have the other side of the picture. And it would be grotesque to argue on this evidence that the great puritan hero was himself guilty of less than complete propriety, in retaining his secretary's illicit gains while Spavin took the rap. Still, there is the fact of no positive punishment being meted out (forgery normally carried the death penalty under the ordinary criminal law) and there is the further fact that Spavin—scoundrel, antinomian superman 'loosed from ordinances', or it may be mild paranoiac—clearly felt himself to be the wronged party. Yet he did not forget the poor of his native townships in Yorkshire, and in a curious codicil to his will, contested unsuccessfully by his brother and executor, he left £100 to the wife of his landlord 'for all the kindnesses', and for the first child to be born to her and to survive if he, Spavin, did not return from the Indies, promising more for her if he did. Perhaps we should take this at its face value, simply as the repayment of friendship and hospitality to a man who had become something of an outcast among his own kind; maybe, however, he was loosed from other ordinances besides those forbidding forgery.[80]

Spavin was succeeded by a truly 'faceless' bureaucrat, and one who conspicuously failed to make much of a career while holding a potentially key position. Conceivably of an Essex yeoman family, apprenticed in the Drapers' Company, William Malyn became Cromwell's secretary on his return from Ireland in 1650; he continued in his service when Cromwell became Lord General (1650–3), and then Protector (1653–8). Very confusingly he had a namesake who was a Captain in the Protector's regiment and was one of the dissident, republican-inclined officers dismissed from it in February 1658. A William Malyn or Melyn was serving as an under-officer in the London Customs in the summer of 1650, and this may be the right man. Our William Malyn is occasionally found involved as a political go-between or correspondent, but he was so totally eclipsed by Thurloe that there was never any question of his becoming an important administrative figure. He was criticised by Henry Cromwell for having got an Irish land-grant in his own favour passed under the Protector's personal seal. He visited the extremist Quaker James Naylor in prison and reported to his master in favour of continued severity rather than leniency. In September 1658 Malyn did not take over as Richard Cromwell's secretary but temporarily became Secretary to the Army Council; however, he remained loyal to the Cromwell family. Presumably he gave satisfaction; after Spavin that was perhaps not too difficult. He vanished from public view in 1659, although he was still alive in the early 1660s. Malyn then disappeared into obscurity as complete as that from which he had come.[81]

Of the principal naval secretaries who acted under the various regimes of 1649–60, an account has already been given of William Jessop. His colleague, Robert Coytmor, was a different kind of man. The Coytmor family were small gentry landowners from Caernarvonshire, where Robert the elder was a parliamentary commissioner in the late 1640s. I have not discovered how Coytmor entered the service of the Earl of Warwick, who was employing him by 1644; perhaps there was some link via a patron or relative. He (or his father) is found annotating a document prepared for Parliament's financial business, about the revenues of the Isle of Man, in 1642. From 1645 he was officially co-Secretary to the Admiralty, a place which he held until 1653. If Coytmor was disturbed by the same problems of political allegiance as beset Jessop, we know nothing of it. In November 1649 he was granted another £50 a year salary, on condition that neither he nor his clerk took any fees; this made £150 in all. We also know that he disliked the use of titles such as Worshipful and Esquire: a pointer towards radicalism. More notably, in naval matters Coytmor sometimes expressed judgments and opinions of his own, which were more than mere echoes or reflections of his masters', particularly in communicating with the Navy Commissioners on behalf of the Admiralty Committee. At the same time either he or his father was involved in a protracted series of disputes about the Prothonotaryship of south-west Wales, to which he had obtained a title in 1650. It was a perennial source of trouble. In this connection he is found as a petitioner to the Indemnity Committee (in 1651–2); he (or his father, but probably our Robert) appears as claimant to an ex-royalist's coal mine in north Wales before the Compounding Commissioners (in 1652).

Coytmor's career as a naval functionary received a severe check with the appointment of Robert Blackburne as Secretary to the new Commissioners for the Admiralty and Navy in December 1652. This commission was a kind of inner directorate for the prosecution of the naval war against the Dutch, and its powers overrode those of the existing Admiralty Committee as well as those of the Navy Commissioners. Coytmor continued to act in naval business until—probably—March or April 1653; nor did he initially oppose the dissolution of the Rump and direct rule by the army. By 1654 his naval career was a thing of the past and he was interested only in his Welsh legal office. Coytmor then seems to have reverted to his father's way of life as a lesser squire in north Wales, except for a brief appearance when he was under subpoena as a witness against his former masters in 1660. In 1649–52 he came as near as anyone in his position could to influencing policy as well as merely implementing other people's decisions.[82]

Robert Blackbourne, or Blackburne, is a more substantial figure whose career was correspondingly more successful. Of ambiguous origin geographically speaking, for his certificate of arms implied Yorkshire parentage whereas Blackburne spoke of himself as a native of Plymouth and he may well have been a London apprentice if not a Londoner by birth, he first appears in the service of Parliament's Commissioners for the Navy early in 1643. In the autumn of 1648 he served as co-Secretary to the parliamentary commissioners empowered to negotiate with the King in the Isle of Wight, amongst whom was the younger Vane, the Navy Treasurer. In the early 1650s Blackburne was solicitor to the Commissioners of Customs, as well as being in the service of the Rump's Navy Committee. In 1652 he obtained two important promotions, becoming secretary to the Customs Commissioners and later (in December) to the new Admiralty and Navy Commissioners. He retained these posts until 1660, thus being at the centre both of naval affairs and the customs revenue from near the end of the Commonwealth until the Restoration. He then forfeited his Admiralty post which went initially to William Coventry, as secretary to the new Lord High Admiral, James, Duke of York; but initially he was confirmed as Customs Secretary, and subsequently became secretary to the East India Company.

Blackburne's minimum income from his two offices in 1652–60 was £500 a year. He became involved in something of a wrangle with the Protector's household authorities over his house in Scotland Yard, off Whitehall, which was wanted for the quartering of the Lifeguard. Blackburne argued that he had had to pay considerably more for the new house, which he then had to take as a replacement, than he had received by way of compensation for the one which he had vacated. The outcome is unknown, but he was hardly being reduced to destitution by losing £100 or so on the transaction. He may have lived on in prosperous retirement, for a Robert Blackburne widower was assessed for property worth £600 in the parish of St Andrew Undershaft, London, in 1695. He was not called as a prosecution witness against the regicides; whether this was because his position at the crucial juncture (in January 1649) disabled him, or because he retained some residual loyalty to his one-time republican masters, we cannot tell. Pepys was initially inclined to sneer at him as an ex-puritan now ready to drink people's health with the rest. But by 1663 he was listening to Blackburne with respect on such themes as conditions in the 1650s and liberty of conscience. The Blackburnes may have belonged to that group of nautical-cum-mercantile types from the south-west, several of whom also had New England connections and from whom some of the 1650s Navy Commissioners were also drawn. It may none the less be true that the family originated in Yorkshire: like other heraldic pedigrees, his was probably touched-up but not wholly invented. Blackburne's naval papers leave an impression of business-like activity and he was—from all appearances—a man who merited his place, by whatever means he had originally obtained it.[83]

Lastly, with Thomas Turner (1600s–1681), Clerk-General to the Navy Commissioners 1645–6 to 1660, we return to the level of the efficient office-manager with no executive pretensions. He had been a naval ship's purser in 1642, but by 1643 was seconded for duties ashore, and in February 1646 was finally replaced in his pursership. A Thomas Turner was Clerk of the Statute Office in Chancery, for taking recognisances in 1648–9, but the name is a common one and this was almost certainly another man. Our Thomas Turner lived on Tower Hill. In 1655 he said that he had been a clerk under the Navy Commissioners for thirty years and Clerk-General to them for fifteen; he wanted a rise on his salary of £100 a year. But despite receiving occasional gratuities, such as £60 extra in 1654, he seems to have stuck at £100. Turner was ousted in October 1660, but was allowed to retain the Purveyorship of Petty Provisions. In 1668 he obtained the Storekeepership in Deptford Yard. At first Pepys resolved to get on well with him, though refusing Turner's offer to buy a half-share in his Clerkship of the Acts. Subsequently the diarist formed an extremely unfavourable impression of Turner: 'a very knave', 'that doting foole' and 'the most false fellow that ever was born of woman'. To John Evelyn, however, he was 'my good neighbour Mr Turner'. Whatever the truth about his moral character and his political sympathies, compared with the others whom we have considered here— Jessop, Coytmor and Blackburne—Turner had remarkably little impact on naval affairs.[84]

A mixed garland

Sir John Thoroughgood, or Thorowgood (c. 1595–1675), is one of the forgotten worthies of the seventeenth century. In 1649 the Rump

decided to supplement their own Plundered Ministers' committee by a
non-parliamentary body, the Trustees for the Maintenance of Ministers.[85]
The Trustees were not made responsible for appointing or getting rid of
clergymen and teachers, but for augmenting clerical and educational
stipends out of the funds at their disposal. These were supposed to have
included a large part of the income from cathedrals' dean and chapter
estates. But owing to the Commonwealth's continuous financial difficulties, only a fraction of this wealth was left at their disposal. They were,
however, given control of other funds, partly transferred from the compounding and sequestration authorities. This enabled them to direct
royalist landowners to augment parsons' incomes out of tithes and glebe
lands, which would otherwise have been sequestered, or on which composition would have had to be paid. And for eleven years the Trustees
carried on this work of making up stipends to something like a tolerable
minimum wage, gradually—in the process—superseding the Plundered
Ministers' committee which finally disappeared with the Rump in 1653.
The Trustees were re-appointed with wider powers on the eve of the
first Protectorate Parliament (2 September 1654). No doubt there were
many parish clergy, lecturers, schoolmasters and even dons, who felt
that they should have got more from the Trustees' fund than they did.
And only a fraction of all stipends were augmented at all. Still, it was one
of the Republic's most constructive educational-cum-ecclesiastical
undertakings. And, until Queen Anne's Bounty, without parallel in the
history of the established Church, although the governments of Henry
VIII and Edward VI had professed similar good intentions.

One would expect to find that the men put in charge of this scheme,
which offered scope for applying tests of ideological fitness to potential
recipients, would have been committed, out-and-out supporters of the
regime. Certainly their religious complexion would seem likely to be
vigorously puritan, in the narrowest party sense. It is therefore remarkable to find that the man who usually acted as the senior Maintenance
Trustee was an ecumenical protestant, and only in the most generic
sense a puritan at all. John Thoroughgood was the second son of an
ecclesiastical administrator, Commissary to the Bishop of Norwich
under James I. Possibly through this connection, or else through his
marriage to the daughter of Thomas Meautys, Clerk of the Privy
Council,[86] he secured his entry to court circles. In 1633 he went to
Scotland with the King as one of the Gentlemen Pensioners, and was
knighted there. It is not clear how militant a parliamentarian he was
during the Civil War, although he was named to the Middlesex militia
committee in 1644. His main residence was in what was then the
fashionable if increasingly suburban village of Kensington. He was also
named to the equivalent committee in Norfolk, and again to the Middlesex one, in 1648; in 1649 he became an assessment commissioner for both

Westminster and Middlesex. He was a commissioner of Oyer and Terminer for Middlesex in 1653/4, and held various other minor offices both local and central.[87] But his main administrative work was undoubtedly as the senior Maintenance Trustee.[88] Presumably in recognition of his broad sympathies, no measures were taken against him at the Restoration, which he may well—in a quiet way—have helped to promote. Indeed, although he must have taken the Engagement in 1649–50, there is no evidence that he was a republican by choice. And he was soon appointed Gentleman of the Privy Chamber in extraordinary to the returned monarch. This was an honorific post with only nominal duties, but it gave access to the penultimate sanctum before one reached the royal presence.

In 1665 Thoroughgood published a work of somewhat tedious edification: *The King of Terrors Silenced, by Meditations and Examples of Holy Living and Holy Dying, As the same was Recollected and Recommended . . . To be distributed among his Kindred and his Friends at his Funeral.* In the Preface, addressed to his friends, he says that he had finished the work by about 1 May 1664, on entering his seventieth year.[89] For our purpose the significant point is not the book's more or less orthodox predestinarian theology, or its prolix moralising, but Part V, 'Being Ten Blessed Examples of Holy Persons, relating to a happy passage out of this life into a better'. There is only one famous name among them, but they are well worth listing for what they tell us about the author:

1 The Earl of Hanauw, d. 1612, ex-ambassador from the German protestant princes to the court of St James's.[90]
2 Mr John Meautys, Esq., d. 22 December 1635, secretary to Lord Keeper Finch.[91]
3 Mrs Juxon, wife of Mr John Juxon, citizen, d. aged about 27.[92]
4 The Archbishop of Armagh.[93]
5 Mr Benjamin Rhodes, steward to the Countess of Oxford and the Earl of Elgin, d. 1657.[94]
6 Mrs Anne Rhodes, servant to the same, also d. 1657.[95]
7 Dr Harris (1578–1658) of Campden, Glos, who refused to be made a D.D. by the Earl of Pembroke as Chancellor of the University of Oxford in the late 1640s, d. December 1658.[96]
8 Mrs Scot, daughter of Sir Matthew Howland, who married (i) the son and heir of Sir Walter Roberts of Kent, and (ii) Mr Scot, a Kent JP,[97] d. December 1658.[98]
9 Msr du Moulin, d. aged 90, 10 March 1658/9.[99]
10 Mr Crook (1574–1649), born in Suffolk, fellow of Emmanuel College, Cambridge.[100]

Apart from the ladies, who may have been pious enthusiasts, it is not exactly a list of puritan 'fanatics'.

Thoroughgood's anticipation of his own demise was a trifle premature, for he lived another ten years, to the ripe age of 80. In his will he made provision for the aged, indigent and best-disposed people of his home parish in Norfolk, of his Essex estate and of Kensington, and separately for ministers of the gospel who were in want. He had no direct heir, and after numerous legacies left the residue of his estate to a nephew; the religious tone is Calvinist certainly, puritan not at all. Thoroughgood is hardly a dramatic figure on the Interregnum stage, but his existence is a reminder against seeing religious divisions in too narrowly partisan terms.[101]

So much controversy has already been aroused about the career of 'Doctor' Benjamin Worsley (1617/18–78) that one hesitates before descending into the arena. This is partly because of the obscurity alike of his early and latter years, and partly arises from his quarrel with the famous William Petty. But these are not the reasons why Worsley is notable for our purposes here. He was the son of a non-armigerous family of Kineton (near Edgehill) in Warwickshire, although his maternal grandfather was later described as a Gentleman of Coventry. He is said to have been born and schooled in London. The first authentic fact is his service as a surgeon in the English army in Ireland *c.* 1640–1, for which he must presumably have had some preliminary training if only of the apprenticeship type; the second is his admission to Trinity College, Dublin, in 1643. By 1645 he was back in England, apparently as a prisoner for debt, and during the following years (1646–8) he was involved in trying to get a project, probably for making gunpowder, patented by the House of Lords. He was already known to the influential Boyle family by then, and he may have come to the notice of the Earl of Leicester's heir, Viscount Lisle, when the latter was in Ireland. Worsley's residence in the Netherlands during part of 1648–9 seems to have had a formative influence on his economic ideas; as it did too on his scientific thought, which was alchemical and metaphysical in tone, distinctly reminiscent of what Dr Frances Yates has told us of the 'renaissance magus'.[102] More important for our purpose, in Holland Worsley got to know the younger Vane's sister, Lady Honeywood. Another friend, providing a possible link with the rulers of the Commonwealth, was the veteran Dorset MP John Trenchard. These connections, together with his place in the circle round Samuel Hartlib, seem the likeliest explanation for what is otherwise, on the basis of his career to date, a surprising appointment. In August 1650 the Rump made Worsley Secretary to its new standing Council of Trade, at the very respectable salary of £200 a year. It was in this capacity that he wrote two anonymous pamphlets, strongly mercantilist in tone, and helped to draft the famous Navigation Act of November 1651, which precipitated the first Anglo-Dutch War. The

Trade Council continued to function only until the end of 1651, and by 1653 Worsley was back in Ireland, but then returned to England preparatory to taking up a new post as Secretary to Lord Lisle, ambassador designate to Sweden. In the end Lisle's mission was postponed, and Bulstrode Whitelocke went instead. Late in 1653 Worsley became Secretary to the Commissioners for the government of Ireland. With the elevation of Cromwell's son-in-law Fleetwood from being merely commander-in-chief to the Lord Deputyship of Ireland in 1654, there was a re-shuffle of subordinate posts there. Worsley now became Surveyor-General (of lands) to the Irish government. He was thereby pitchforked into the enormous and hideously complex task of surveying the whole country with a view to completing the forced transplantation of native landowners to the far west, and settling the various English claims to the forfeited lands. Unlike Petty, a more brilliant man whose career runs strangely parallel to his, there is no evidence that Worsley had taught himself the technique of land-surveying. From December 1654 the work was nominally shared between them; in fact it was completed in 1655 by Petty alone, who was to denounce Worsley in no uncertain terms.[103]

Perhaps in his capacity as a friend and client of the Boyles and the Sidneys, Worsley weathered the Restoration successfully. He is indeed said to have succeeded Thurloe in the management of the Post Office in 1659, but like other aspects of his career this is ill-documented. He next appears in the correspondence between John Winthrop the second, the Governor of Massachusetts, and Samuel Hartlib, the ageing reformer, being described by the latter in 1661 as a confidant of the Lord Chancellor (Clarendon) in colonial, or 'plantation' matters. Certainly he presented Lady Clarendon with a brief autobiography. His Irish experience and his work for the Commonwealth in matters of commercial policy were positive assets, but it is not clear from other sources that he was as influential with Clarendon as Hartlib believed. It was at about this time that Worsley began to style himself and be called 'Doctor', although he had never been awarded the degree of doctor of physic or medicine. His medical knowledge, such as it was, may have been involved in his claim to a patent for that familiar Victorian and early-twentieth-century laxative, senna pods, in 1667-8. More important, owing to unknown patronage or recommendations he became a member of the select committee on trade in 1668, assistant to the Secretary of the Trade Council in 1670, and finally himself Secretary and Treasurer to the Trade and Plantations Council of 1672. But he soon resigned as a nonconformist under the Test Act in September 1673, and disappears almost completely from public view. Shortly after his death, his library of over five thousand volumes was auctioned in May 1678. Such are among the known facts of Worsley's life.[104]

Granted that Worsley's is a remarkable biography, can his career be used to support a general argument for the continuing influence of republican men and methods after the Restoration?[105] His importance as an administrator lies in the Irish-colonial-commercial spheres, where the similarity of policies between the 1650s and the 1660s–early 70s is palpable, independent of any thesis of more general administrative continuity. Nor can it be demonstrated from the evidence whether Worsley was an originator of such major legislation as the 1651 and 1660 Navigation Acts, the Enumerated Commodities Act of 1663 and the Plantation Duty Act of 1670.[106] The more aggressively anti-Dutch aspect of Restoration policies and the absence of Worsley's pet nostrum of free ports point more strongly to George Downing's influence than to his. We may agree that his career bridges the Restoration in a most interesting and—if we knew more about him—suggestive way, without necessarily conceding that he, rather than greater political and mercantile figures, was the main author of the English 'Navigation Laws' and all that these were to entail for the history of the British Empire.

The positions which Thurloe combined under the Protectorate were in several different hands during the Commonwealth. Foreign Intelligence was in the charge of Thomas Scot MP; the Post Office was under Edmund Prideaux, who was also Attorney-General; Gualter Frost was Secretary to the Council of State until he was succeeded by Thurloe himself. Domestic Intelligence, while nominally also in Scot's charge was in practice from 1650 in the hands of a capable self-made west-countryman of radical views, Captain George Bishop (d. 1668/9). One George Bishop, the son of a Wiltshire farmer, was apprenticed to Richard Field of the Stationers' Company of London for nine years in 1621, but became free of the Company after just over seven years, in 1628. Another George, who by his age seems the likelier of the two, the son of a deceased Bristol dyer, was apprenticed to a pewterer there in 1634 and became a freeman of Bristol in 1642; he was a merchant venturer of that city by 1650, and he or yet another namesake continued as such into the 1670s–90s. Yet a Mr George Bishop of London was elected a free burgess of the Bristol Merchant Venturers in 1651. And, whatever his previous connections there may have been, this seems to be our man. What had he been doing meanwhile? His means and place of earning his living in the 1630s are unclear. At that time there cannot have been a very good living to be made for all those who were entitled to practise their trade as stationers of London, that is as printers, publishers and booksellers. During the early 1640s one George Bishop was in partnership with Robert White in Warwick Court, off Warwick Lane in the City. White had become free in 1639 and was still in business nearly thirty years later. They were amongst the most active publishers of parliamentarian newsbooks, the forerunners of modern newspapers.

Some of these were official publications; others depended upon private enterprise and presumably had to show a profit.[107] The flow of news-books put out by Bishop and White continues into the winter of 1644–5, and then thins out until Bishop appears in October 1645 as editor of the official *Parliament's Post*. At what stage our George Bishop joined the army, or how he attained the rank of captain, is not known. Yet another was a captain in Edmund Ludlow's regiment in Ireland during the years 1651–3, but unless he was an absentee who drew his pay while staying at home, this cannot have been our man. Captain George Bishop was present at the famous debates in Putney church in the autumn of 1647. He was one of the few officers who spoke strongly on the Leveller side, in favour of drastic action against the King, and opposed the negotiations which Fairfax, Cromwell and Ireton had been trying to conduct with Charles.

Bishop's service under the republican Council of State is evident as early as May 1649, when he reported to them from Bristol. He sent a further report on the damages done in the Forest of Dean the following December. In 1650 he became Secretary to the Council's Committee for Examinations, that is for cross-examining suspects; and in 1651 Secretary to the next Council's[108] 'Close' or secret Committee. In that year he played a leading part in ferreting out possible royalist conspirators, and was allowed considerable sums by way of expenses for this. But by the middle of 1652 his work had diminished with the passing of the Rump's Pardon and Oblivion Act and the decline of organised Cavalier opposition.[109] In September 1653, whether or not because he was out of sympathy with the new government, Bishop asked for his accounts to be settled and for leave to retire. His salary had been £200 a year, but he was awarded another £985 for arrears due on his expenses. According to a later account (a confession, made by a servant of the renegade Leveller, Colonel Edward Sexby, in 1657, and therefore suspect as a source), Bishop had already begun to get involved in republican plots against Cromwell in 1653. This seems unlikely. Apart from disgruntled ex-Rumpers and those who protested at the disappearance of parliamentary rule after the dissolution of the Long Parliament, there was little radical opposition to the Lord General before his breach with Harrison and the Barebones republicans and then his assumption of the Protectorship in December 1653. The next year Bishop was back in Bristol, possibly earning his living as a brewer, and he stood as an 'opposition' candidate in the first Protectorate parliamentary elections during August 1654. Defeated at the polls, he and his fellow candidate petitioned against their successful opponents, alleging electoral malpractices. Whatever the truth of this, he remained a staunch anti-royalist (unlike Sexby, who attempted to promote a Cavalier-Leveller alliance). In the early part of 1655, both before and immediately after the abortive royalist rising, he offered his services and sent unsolicited information to Secretary Thurloe, who by then combined Bishop's old duties with those of Frost and Scot, and soon those of Prideaux too. A rival informant told Thurloe that Bishop was 'turned half a quaker', and a month or so later someone else described him to the Secretary as 'that viper Bishop'. Presumably in a time of incipient crisis he had hoped to be given emergency powers in Bristol and to be allowed to resume his old craft of counter-intelligence. The rising led by Penruddock once safely over, Thurloe dunned him for some lost papers of the late Archbishop Laud; Bishop denied responsibility for them and suggested that he should try Thomas Scot instead. From 1655 Bishop re-appears, or—as the case may be—first appears in print: not this time as a newsbook editor or a printer, but as a Quaker author and publicist. In 1657 he was said to have backed George Fox against James Naylor within the Friends' movement; in 1659, after the fall of the Protectorate, he briefly resumed a political role. But his name was vetoed when he was proposed as a militia commissioner for Bristol, and the restored Rump made no other move to re-employ him. In 1656 he had been accused of having some of Charles I's possessions in his hands, and this accusation was repeated, with more sinister implications, some months after the Restoration. But in spite of all this, and his previous activity as a discoverer of Cavalier conspiracies, Bishop seems to have been unmolested. He continued to publish, condemning with sturdy impartiality King, Parliament and the puritan authorities in New England alike for their persecutions of Quakers. His standing among the Bristol community of Friends evidently grew. By the later 1660s he seems to have been a recognised leader there; and the crowd at his funeral in the Friends' cemetery was said to have been the largest ever seen on such an occasion in Bristol. Notwithstanding the ill-documented gaps in his career, and ambiguity of identification with the stationer and editor, Bishop clearly exemplifies the political militant turned religious radical. If the proof of the pudding is in the eating, his administrative work for the Rump must be accounted highly successful.[110]

'Colonel' Sir Thomas Herbert (1606–82) has been so fully and well written about that only the briefest summary of his bizarre career is called for here. His biographer, Mr N. H. Mackenzie, established the facts of his life in detail some fifteen years ago.[111] Thomas Herbert was the son of a York merchant and grandson of a lord mayor, descended from an illegitimate line of the main aristocratic Herbert family of South Wales. Through the patronage of the third Earl of Pembroke, then head of the family, he was made an Esquire of the Body to Charles I and enabled to marry the daughter of Sir Walter Alexander, Gentleman Usher. The young Thomas's fortune was, however, to be sought more in the tradition of another aristocratic relative, Lord Herbert of Cherbury—in literary endeavour. Before taking up his post at court, he went abroad, and the first edition of his *Description of the Persian Monarchy . . . A Relation of Some Yeares Travaile* appeared in 1634, by which time he had been settled at Westminster for three years or so. In 1640/1 he bought the estate of Tintern in Monmouthshire (including the abbey ruins) from his cousin Richard, the heir to Herbert of Cherbury, perhaps a conventional enough move, although he was never to live there and the value of the property to him is problematic.

His career then began to diverge from what we might call the courtly norm. Like others of his name and lineage in royal service, or who—in Sir Edmund Verney's immortal words—'had eaten the King's salt', he did not support his monarch in the first Civil War. And from 1644, possibly again owing to the influence of Pembroke (the fourth earl this time), he acted as one of Parliament's civilian Commissioners to the Army, at a salary of £1 a day. This employment apparently continued until 1648 when he was allowed to appoint a deputy to act for him there, consequent upon his preferment to be Groom of the Bedchamber to the imprisoned King in the Isle of Wight. He held the latter post from late 1647 to the eve of the King's execution in January 1649, and this formed the entire basis of his later claim to have been a royalist. Although he became warmly attached to Charles I and was to profess his loyalty with some ardour in retrospect, there can be little doubt that Herbert was appointed because he was considered reliable by Parliament, even though he happened also to be acceptable to the King. After 1660 Herbert and his descendants attempted to bury in total oblivion all his other Interregnum appointments. It was Mr Mackenzie's achievement to identify Charles I's faithful attendant with Parliament's army Commissioner. The latter position Herbert resumed from 1649 to 1652, acting mainly in Ireland. This in turn led on to other employments there. He first became Commissioner for the administration of justice, then Secretary to the Commissioners for the civil government of Ireland (in 1653), and finally from 1654 to 1659 Clerk of the Council in Dublin.[112] Meanwhile his only daughter Elizabeth married Colonel Robert Phayre, one of the three officers to whom the warrant for the King's execution had been addressed in 1649. Without the Herbert connection Phayre might well have suffered as a regicide in 1660, like his colleague Hacker and the officer in charge of the guards at the execution, Colonel Axtell. Herbert acquired some Irish property but made no great fortune out of his office, in theory one of the most important in the government under the successive Lord Deputies, Charles Fleetwood and Henry Cromwell.

Although he lost this office at the Restoration, or rather failed to recover it after losing it in 1659, Herbert could not get anything else except a baronetcy by way of compensation, for all that he laboured his services to the restored king's father back in 1647-9. He stayed on in

London until 1665, when in the face of the Plague he retired to York;
then as now, living was cheaper in the north too. By the time that he
made his will and gave directions for his funeral monument, his parliamentarian and protectoral services seem to have been obliterated from
Herbert's mind. He referred to Henry VIII's 'great chess-board'—a gift
from a generous master, if we are to believe him—to a Bible given to his
father-in-law by Prince Henry, and to a silver clock also given by
Charles I. On the other hand, he did not disown his near-regicidal son-
in-law, who duly received a bequest. Herbert's monumental inscription,
now in the parish room of St Crux (being all that remains of the church
building), dwells on his services to the King but is silent as to the rest
of his public career.[113] An element of the time-server or side-changer is
hard to eliminate from the impression which Herbert gives. The phrase
'of Tintern', as he styled himself, was perhaps a symptom of family
esteem, an effort to make good the earlier slur of illegitimacy on his
ancestry.

vi CONCLUSION: A COLLECTIVE PORTRAIT

Professor Sachse of Wisconsin has given us a valuable group portrait of
returned colonial New Englanders in the service of the English Republic.[1] It would be possible to attempt something similar for other groups
which can be distinguished among the officials. Some might be defined
functionally, by the kind of work on which they were engaged. Such
would be the diplomats, a characteristic group, especially under the
Protectorate: Lockhart, Downing, Meadowes, Morland, Pell and
Bendish, ably seconded at the consular level by Longland and others.
The legal types would form another such category, although one would
have to eliminate those who merely bought or otherwise acquired a legal
office, such as John Dodington,[2] and consider the professional lawyers,
whether they were in judicial or other posts. Below the judges, the most
interesting types here are the Commonwealth's and Protector's Counsel,
the legal advisers and 'men of business', such as John Reading, William
Sheppard and Gabriel Beck.[3] John Cook, that epitome of honest Independency and frustrated reforming zeal, remains *sui generis*.

The medical men are a slightly less obvious group. Again we would
have to distinguish those whose service was exclusively medical, such as
John Bathurst, Joseph Waterhouse, Lawrence Wright, and the surgeons
Thomas Trapham father and son.[4] By contrast, there were several who
also acted in some other administrative capacity, or whose public service
was wholly non-medical: Jonathan Goddard, Aaron Gurdon, Lewis du
Moulin, Nicholas Lemprière (from Jersey, to be distinguished from his
better-known brother, Michael), William Parker, William Petty, Thomas
Sydenham, William Stanes, Daniel Whistler and Benjamin Worsley.[5]

This is by no means an exhaustive roll call of medical men in republican service, let alone of all those known to have had radical sympathies in politics or religion. It suggests a more than random association between medicine and the puritan-parliamentarian-republican cause, the reasons for which we can only surmise, unless we are to suppose that doctors were readier to accept a *de facto* situation, and to serve anybody who offered them employment. This might possibly apply to professional practice, but hardly to administrative service in general, let alone pamphleteering and other such activities. Several of those concerned had received at least part of their higher education in Scotland or the Netherlands: a possible common element which may help to explain their sympathies. Alternatively, with professional men as with lesser gentry and urban businessmen, the fact that there were fewer sons of the aristocracy and the greater gentry in the public service meant *ipso facto* that there were more office-holders from other social and occupational backgrounds. Certainly the sudden appearance of numerous ex-London apprentices, who were almost wholly absent in 1625–42 except at the lowest levels or among the Customs Farmers, points this way, or at least underlines the change without establishing the logical sequence of cause and effect. The proportionately greater support which Parliament had from the urban and rural middle classes than from the landed upper class could be the explanation, both for the apprentices and for the medical men too. The reasons for that greater support lie in the nature of the Civil War itself.

Other groups are defined by their members having been singled out after the fall of the regime in 1660. Of those whom we have classified as being primarily officials rather than politicians, Edward Dendy,[6] Andrew Broughton,[7] and John Phelps[8] were attainted with the Regicides in 1660, for having served under the High Court of Justice at the King's trial. While John Blackwell,[9] Richard Deane,[10] Major William Burton,[11] Richard Keeble,[12] and Alderman John Ireton[13] were regarded as sufficiently dangerous—or odious—by the Convention Parliament to be included among the twenty persons banned from holding public office for life, on pain of forfeiting all benefit under the Act of General Pardon and Oblivion.

Then there is the rather different category, the dozen or so ex-officials who testified as prosecution witnesses at the trials of the Regicides in 1660–2. On the face of it, their conduct may seem to epitomise that of the a-political, establishmentarian careerist. But it is important to remember the legal position in this instance. 'Treason' was a plea of the Crown; and, once subpoena'd, a prosecution witness might lay himself open to the penalties of a suit for 'misprision of treason' if he refused to testify, or at the very least to indefinite imprisonment for contempt of court. In the early 1660s, it would have taken a very brave and committed man to have run such a risk.[14] By the letter of the law the case against some of the Regicides and *a fortiori* against the non-regicides tried with them (Hugh Peter, and later Lambert and Vane) rested on shaky foundations, however obvious their guilt may have been as a political fact. And Counsel for the Crown naturally did not want their case to founder on legal technicalities; therefore the more witnesses that they could muster against each defendant the better. So in these circumstances it is unwise to condemn Blackwell, Clarke, Coytmor, Darnell, Jessop, Rushworth and the others in this group as despicable time-servers, if not as so many Judas Iscariots. No doubt it was more unpalatable for some of them than for others to give evidence against their former political masters. Only Blackwell and Coytmor are known, from other sources, to have been republicans by conviction; and Coytmor was the only witness who seems, from the record, to have shown real reluctance to help the prosecution. Among them was an illiterate ex-Messenger, who may have been nursing a grievance ever since he had got into trouble over some debentures several years earlier.[15] Yet all of them, having been in office before 1654, must have taken the Engagement, even if one (Jessop) had agonised over it at considerable length. Whatever one's views about making moral judgments in history, a historian should always err on the side of charity. On the other hand there is no getting away from the fact that Blackwell and Coytmor were in the witness box, Peter, Dendy (*in absentia*) and later Vane in the dock.

If the preceding sections have conveyed an impression of what the servants of the English republic were like, both in the aggregate and as individuals, then this chapter has served its purpose. It would be interesting to be able to compare these men, either the whole 1175–80 or the 200 sample, or the 100 selection, with other groups of men in the seventeenth century, to assess the likenesses and differences. As far as the evidence is comparable, this was attempted in section iv, by looking back to the officials of Charles I from 1625 to 1642. At some points striking differences emerged, while in other respects there was little to tell between the two groups. Ideally we ought to do the same thing for a comparable group of civil office-holders from the Restoration era; perhaps the period of the Cavalier Parliament (1661–79) would serve as well as any other. But this comparison, if it is to be made, must be left to another occasion, and perhaps to another historian. If we give even limited support to Professor Lawrence Stone's hypothesis about changing patterns of social mobility in Stuart society, we should expect to find the gentry re-invading the middle ranks of the administration. Impressionistically, from a reading of secondary works, and from browsing in some primary printed sources, I believe that this was so.[16] However, in the Interregnum (1642–60) a comparison might be attempted with MPs, JPs or members of County Committees, or indeed with army officers, puritan clergy, or practising barristers. Some of these groups—politicians and army officers for instance—would show a stronger political commitment to the republican cause; others, such as the lawyers, would be less politically involved than officials. In terms of social background, the most interesting comparisons might be either with Congregationalist and Baptist ministers, or with the officers of the parliamentarian-Cromwellian armies. Again my ability to make such comparisons rests on partial, unsystematic evidence. In the upper and middle ranks of the army there was a major shift away from upper class (aristocratic and greater gentry) leadership in the years 1644–7, and towards the emergence of relatively more 'self-made' men. I say relatively because there, as in the central administration and in local government, the change was not so much from one social class to another as from one stratum to another within a single class. As to the clergy, there was less of a social but rather more of an educational shift. For although some of the most radical puritans (e.g. John Goodwin or, among the laity, John Milton) were intellectual mandarins to their fingertips, there was an anti-academic, anti-intellectual strain in popular puritanism over and above the actual decline in the number of ministers with university degrees. Yet the insistence on an adequately financed preaching ministry had never been stronger or more genuine.

In the 1640s and 50s the civil administration, like the armed forces, provided an alternative career for the type of men who before and after these decades would have been more likely to pursue careers in other professions—the Church, law and medicine—or in the world of business. Indeed, opportunities elsewhere may have diminished during and immediately after the Civil War. Professor Stone may well be correct in suggesting that the pressures for upward mobility slackened again after 1660. But the short-run effects of the 1640s and 50s must surely have been to increase the opportunities for such upward movement. Perhaps the career market, like the land market, became saturated, and by the late 1650s, if not earlier, there may have been too many offices for the number of suitably qualified—and politically reliable—candidates. The Cromwellian attempts at 'settlement' and reconciliation, which involved a *detente* with a wider section of the old upper class, widened the range of those available for the public service. At the same time, republican leaders who sacrificed glittering prospects, indeed the realities of power and wealth, on grounds of principle, and went out into opposition at different stages between 1653 and 1657, had their administrative counterparts. Even so, the turn-over of officials at the higher and middle levels from 1649 to 1659 is less than one might expect in a time of rapid political change. This may suggest a time-serving attitude or alternatively evidence of a 'non-political' civil service in embryo, according to which way one chooses to look at it.

Huge sums of money changed hands, in taxation, penal levies, forced sales, etc., during these years. Yet, despite the charges brought by disgruntled political opponents, evidence of vast fortunes being accumulated by office-holders is scanty. As already suggested, the countervailing effects of 1660 must be borne in mind; in addition more money was being invested in colonial and other trading ventures rather than being spent on 'conspicuous consumption'. Certainly if we take house-building, suggested by Professor Trevor-Roper as a useful criterion for the distribution of wealth within the peerage and gentry, between office-holders and others, under Elizabeth and James I,[17] there is less to show here. Building of course went on, or rather was resumed after an almost total interruption during the actual years of civil war (1642–8), but on a reduced scale. Of those whose careers have been discussed in this chapter, or who are included in the sample of 200 and the selection of 100, only three are known to have had houses built for themselves. They are Thurloe at Wisbech, Adam Baynes, who pulled down the great house at Holmby and replaced it by a smaller one, and Bennet Hoskins in Herefordshire. Naturally, if we take in all of the 1,180 or so men drawn upon in this study, and other prominent political, military and ecclesiastical figures of the Commonwealth and Protectorate, the total grows considerably. Among those in any way connected with the civil government of the republic, houses were built or substantially enlarged and rebuilt by Oliver St John, the fourth Earl of Pembroke, Hesilrige, the younger Vane, Fairfax, Edmund Prideaux, Chaloner Chute (Speaker, 1659), Sir Henry Blount or Blunt (law reform committee; probate judge, etc.), Sir Gilbert Pickering, Sir Anthony Ashley Cooper, Roger Hill (Baron of the Exchequer, 1657–9, etc.), the reverend Dr Cornelius Burgess, Edmund Waller, John Lisle, John Maynard (Protector's Sergeant-at-Law, 1658), and Edward Cludd (probate judge; Army Committee, etc.). No doubt this list could be lengthened by more exhaustive research.[18] But it will be obvious that many of the leading men, both at the top political level and among important administrators, are conspicuous by their absence. This may have been partly a product of the puritan ethic: a reaction in favour of frugality, against lavish, wasteful expenditure; it may reflect too a general sense of political insecurity and a preference for keeping assets liquid—and anonymous; it may also mean that fewer really spectacular and rapid fortunes were in fact being made. Some of the most notable house-building of the 1650s was actually undertaken by members of royalist families who were excluded from office.

In spite of the continuing activities of the heralds and kings-of-arms, social distinctions counted for less and the use of office as a status-elevator was on a much more modest scale. An heraldic visitation was projected under Richard Cromwell in 1658–9; none in fact took place between 1635 and 1662. Distinctions of rank below that of knight were becoming markedly less clear and less objectively enforceable. A man's self-designated style does, as we have seen, sometimes provide useful evidence about him. The England of the 1650s was still a stratified, hierarchical society, but less so than before 1640–2 or after 1660. The unpopularity of the Exclusionists of 1679–81 in some circles, and again of those Nonconformists unwise enough to swallow James II's ground-bait in 1686–8, and the distinctive upper-class, anti-popular nature of the 1688 revolution and the 1689 settlement—are all part of the heritage of republican England, as it was mediated through the Restoration of 1660. If, as has been argued here, the 1690s in some respects saw a resumption of the policies and methods of the 1650s, the reform of naval administration[19] and the establishment of contributory pensions in the Excise and Customs services[20] lend additional support to such an hypothesis. As against this, it would be wrong to portray the governments of Charles II and James II as having been administratively retrogressive in all respects.[21] The actual management of the customs and excise revenues, which were leased to farmers again at the Restoration, had been brought back under direct administration well before 1688.[22] And although the 1690s were undoubtedly a watershed in the history of public credit, the technique of short-term revenue anticipation, as developed in the Restoration era, survived far into the eighteenth century.[23] By contrast, the Land Tax—as it took shape in the 1690s—owed more to the Assessment of the 1640s and 50s than it did to any intervening type of direct tax.[24] Hence there are difficulties in assessing the influence, either of men or of methods, from the time of the Republic, on the reforms and innovations which are to be found both in the 1660s–80s and after the Revolution of 1688–9.

It is hard to estimate whether their years in office made more difference to the officials of the republic as individuals and to their families than it did to the way in which the country was governed. As with all administrative systems, the impact was a two-way one. More of what this meant for English society as a whole, outside the administration, will be suggested in the next chapter. For many of those with whom we have been concerned in this chapter, 1660 and the aristocratic reaction which followed cast a long shadow across their lives. For many, the Restoration meant that their period in the public service had the character of an extended interlude in the full span of their careers. Good and bad, efficient or incompetent, godly or cynical, patriotic or time-serving, all of them were in the State's service, during a time of revolutionary turmoil and profound disturbance in our national history. And whatever else we do, however we may ultimately assess them, to shrug such men off altogether and simply to neglect them is as inhumane as it is unhistorical.

CHAPTER 5

THE IMPACT OF THE REGIME

i INTRODUCTION

It is a common complaint against administrative history that it tends to be written from the point of view of the governors rather than the governed. And the correlate of this alleged 'establishmentarian' bias is the extreme difficulty of writing genuine 'popular' history at all—for any country—before the eighteenth or even the nineteenth century. To an overwhelming extent, the mass of people, above all individuals from the poorer, more obscure classes, only get into the pages of history when something extraordinary happens, such as the Gordon Riots or the storming of the Bastille, and when they get into trouble. For all the evidence of popular participation in public affairs, notably through the Leveller movement in 1646–9, the England of the Commonwealth and Protectorate is no exception to this. And it is hard to portray the impact of the republican regime on the common man except through the kind of records which show him (or her) in trouble of one kind or another. History written entirely from official records obviously suffers from a danger of one-sidedness; however, the proposition can perhaps be stood on its head as a warning against the contrary danger. History written exclusively by a government's committed enemies presents its problems too. Because of the extent to which the Civil War had been a conflict of class and ideology and not merely a quarrel within the governing minority, the system of penal taxation on royalists has provided historians with a great deal of evidence about the upper classes. For the parliamentarian minority among the peers and gentry, however, let alone for 'the middling sort' in town and country, we have nothing comparable to the records of advance, composition and sequestration. Hence the particular value of the Indemnity Papers.[1] These show us ordinary rank-and-file parliamentarians appealing for help against proceedings in which they were often the defendants in the ordinary law courts. The political and legal establishments were thus potentially in conflict, at least in certain respects.

In general, the wider the variety of different types of source material that are available, the better the historian's chances of giving something like a balanced picture. In this respect we are better placed for the republican period than in many historical situations. First, there are the surviving records of the central government, which themselves range from the parliamentary journals and Oliver Cromwell's speeches and letters to the minute books of committees and commissions and the accounts of treasurers and receivers. Secondly there is the pamphlet literature, representing a remarkably wide range of opinions and attitudes over a huge diversity of topics. Thirdly, for some purposes serving as a kind of cross-check on both these, there are the surviving records of local government, at the county, the city and borough and occasionally even the parish level. Lastly, contemporary private records (letters, diaries, journals, memoirs) afford an additional insight into people's attitudes towards the public issues of the time. Here, just as much as with official documents or published propaganda, a lack of balance can arise in the viewpoints which are represented. For instance, in an area little touched upon in this book, we have John Evelyn's diary entries about the position of Anglican worship under the Protectorate,[2] and we have the autobiographical collections of the ecumenical but presbyterian puritan, Richard Baxter, on some of the same issues.[3] But we do not have anything comparable from any leading Congregationalist, such as Owen, Nye or either of the Goodwins, to give us their view of fanatical episcopalian adherents to the Book of Common Prayer who rejected a flexible, tolerant, decentralised, yet still puritan state church. To take another topic of more direct relevance here, we have much evidence about opposition to taxation by the government's enemies, but very little in defence of the republic's fiscal system, although this was certainly more equitable as well as more onerous than anything England had previously known.

All too often, therefore, the historian is working within the confines of one particular type of evidence. Occasionally, as with social biography, one kind of source gives us a kind of cross-bearing on another, but all too seldom so. The different sections of this chapter are not meant to be mutually exclusive, but they are in practice distinct to a regrettable extent. How far these sources make it possible to present a true picture of the government's impact—in terms of politics, religion, social and economic policies, justice and finance—is the problem, to which this chapter is meant to be a contribution. It will be for the reader to judge the extent of its success.

ii THE PAMPHLET EVIDENCE

Despite the re-imposition of a more effective censorship, more grievances and aspirations were expressed during the 1650s than had been before the Civil War, or were to be again for some time after the Restoration. How far the tighter controls over publishing introduced in 1649, compared to those operative since 1641, affected the kind of topics discussed, is partly guesswork. Certainly the troubles of both individuals and groups continue to find expression. Some of these have a direct bearing on our theme here, illuminating aspects of the administration in operation, or revealing some of its members, in ways which it would not be possible to do from official sources. For instance, the semi-official *Souldiers Catechisme*, which went into numerous editions from 1644 on, included amongst the parliamentarian war aims 'the regulating of our Courts of Justice, which have been made the seats of iniquity and un-righteousness'.[1] This is certainly relevant in explaining the background to the subsequent campaigns for law reform. The list of signatories of the petition published in May 1653 for the restoration of the Rump or the speedy summoning of a new parliament helps to explain why certain officials were dismissed and replaced.[2] As we have already seen, other pamphlets or broadsides suggest possible connections between the political stance of an individual and his experience of official malprac-tices. Further cases will be discussed below.

The reasons why men went into print during these years are almost as varied as historians' explanations of the issues at stake. Only a fraction of the total output of publications bears, even indirectly, on the adminis-trative system or those operating it. Sometimes, points about adminis-tration and officials come up as part of a wider set of demands, complaints or proposals. This is true of the Leveller writings between about 1646 and 1653. In *The Remonstrance of many thousands of the Free-People of England. Together with the Resolves Of the Yong-Men and Apprentices of the City of London, in behalf of themselves, and those Called Levellers* . . . (September 1649), an attack is included on MPs, Commit-teemen, Sequestrators, Excise-men, etc. who have enriched themselves at the country's expense. In every such case the *Remonstrance* demands that two honest men should testify what such a person was worth, in personal estate, and what his debts were, in 1640. All illicit takings since then should be surrendered and put into a kind of war-damages' fund, to compensate 'honest commoners' who have suffered losses from the activities of either King or Parliament. No one should hold office for more than a year at a time; 'and then a new one to be Chosen by the Generality of the People; every one above the Age of Twenty (except Servants, Beggars, or Criminaries) to have a free voice in the Election, and the major part to carry it by voice or signing of hands thereto'. A separation of functions, if not of powers, is assumed in the further demand that no one should practise as a lawyer if he was also an MP.[3] A broadside of similar tenor, three years later, repeated the demand for the annual election of all local officials,[4] while the somewhat curiously named *Anti-Levellers Antidote against The most venomous of the Serpents, The Subtillest Monopolizers. Collected by divers Officers and Soldiers of the Army, and other honest People of this Nation* offered instead an elaborate calculation (Table 43) of how much could be saved annually by various legal and administrative reforms, without such democratic measures as these.

TABLE 43 *Proposed economical reforms, 1652*

1 The elimination of 1,000 wrongful arrests, costing on average £20 each in fees and costs	=	£20,000
2 The frauds of under-sheriffs, bailiffs, etc.	=	£120,000
3 The abolition of 8,000 parish bailiffs making £150 a year each	=	£120,000
4 And of their hangers-on and dependants	=	£40,000
5 Four sergeants in each of 200 corporate towns at £200 each	=	£160,000
6 And of their Yeomen and Assistants	=	£53,333
7 Further savings on the legal costs of creditors and plaintiffs	=	£100,000
8 And of defendants	=	£50,000
9 The extortions of 50 Under-Sheriffs and their deputies at £800 each	=	£40,000
Total		£583,333 (*sic**)
10 Plus half as much again for Wales and Ireland		£290,000
Final total		£873,333

* The total should be £703,333. The text includes both items 2 and 3; the author's total would, however, be correct if either 2 or 3 were counted, but not both.

Further proposals suggested that the abolition of the copying of legal documents would save £96,000 in Chancery, of which £48,000 was in the offices of the Six Clerks and their under-clerks, and as much more in the common law courts. On a different kind of calculation, it was asserted that the average cost of a trial at law was £26. 10s. 0d. of which half could and should be saved; reckoning 16,000 such trials a year and £10 extra expense for each, due to the activities of 'monopolizers' of various legal processes, this would mean another saving of £648,700. On my arithmetic £372,000, but again I may have misread the text. By various stages, some more fanciful than others, the following grand totals were arrived at:

Losses in the estates of private persons prevented	=	£3,157,338
Money extorted and exacted, to be saved	=	£2,611,369
Total savings		£5,768,707

Additional proposals included one that no monopolisers, meaning holders of law clerkships apparently, should practise unless they either had done so for seven years or were accounted able clerks; rewards and bribes were attacked, along with *novi homines*, 'Jacks in Office'. A later marginal entry noted 'Divers Officers have been so impudent that they have not blushed to say, they could not be half-content with their salary, without taking Gratuities'. While ostensibly less radical than the Levellers, the authors' greater naïvety is shown by their belief that these reforms would bring about a return to the good old days—when parliaments were annual and kings were virtuous![5]

Occasionally there are indications of corruption and extortion being stamped on. A journalist reported from Newcastle on 28 December 1649 that:[6]

A Lawyer this weeke for taking excessively of a poore country man, had his gown torne over his ears, in the face of the whole court, and sent to the gaole till he pay 500 M [£366. 13s. 4d.] to the poor man for satisfaction, and to undergoe what penalty the court shall inflict upon him.

On the other hand, another correspondent reporting a little later from the south-west suggested the inefficacy of ideological tests:[7]

Things work very strangely in these parts, for whereas it was thought Cavaliers and Neuters would have been put out of all places of trust in this Commonwealth, and honest men put in their rooms, it appeares to the contrary, some welaffected put out, and Known Cavaliers put in their places; certainly this change proceeds from the domineering of Saturne, or some other evill Planet.

So much, at least in this writer's estimation, for the Engagement. Yet from York it had been reported earlier that 'the well affected are generally satisfied as to that [the Engagement] if there be no other tacite sense, as to perpetuallize the present Parliament . . .'. Yet, the same writer concluded, 'the Parliament have no better way to satisfy the peoples grumblings than taking off their yoaks as much as possibly can be'.[8]

Whatever the calculations of optimistic radicals about the savings to be made from administrative and legal reforms, it was the tax burden which weighed most heavily with ordinary people, almost regardless, it would seem, of class or party. The Hon. Robert Boyle had written to his fellow projector, Benjamin Worsley, some time in 1648:[9]

The plain truth of it is, that (betwixt the injustice of those, that hold the civil sword, and the unruliness of those, that draw the martial) things are carried in so strange a way in the West, that these parts can afford little content or safety to any man, that is not either a soldier, a sequestrator, or a committee-man.

Before accepting this at its face value, we must remember that no one is wholly objective or infallible, not even a founding Fellow of the Royal

Society. Moreover, considerable steps were taken from 1649 on to abolish free quarter by keeping the army's pay more up to date, to reform the abuses of compounding and sequestration, and to curb the powers of local committees.

Some proposals about officials and the administration arose from the debate about the future of the Commonwealth itself, and more particularly the problem of parliamentary reform (including the replacement of the Long Parliament itself). The conservative republican *Severall Proposalls for the Generall Good of the Commonwealth with the Grounds and Reasons thereof* (Feb. 1650/1) came out in favour of the reform of offices and fees, but against annual rotation. And it showed distinct oligarchical tendencies in allowing a self-perpetuating Parliament and Council of State.[10] Moreover, to condemn venality and extortion without the positive corollary of adequate salaries and an enforceable code of official conduct was about as helpful as being against wage demands without curbing inflation. The following summer the millenarian element in the army demanded, *inter alia*, complete accounting for all public moneys received, by all treasurers, committees, etc.; a lifting of oppressions and excessive taxes from the people, 'that so the poor may no longer be insulted over by the rich . . .'; and a reduction in the number of law courts together with restricted numbers of officers and revenues,[11] while the official petition of the Council of Officers, presented to Parliament by six senior field officers in August 1652, called for reform of the Excise by a committee in every county—a strange nostrum, unlikely to appeal to those who believed that one of the country's worst troubles was a superfluity of committees. Besides financial reforms intended to render the revenue system more acceptable by being more efficient, the officers wanted a non-parliamentary committee to consider monopolies, pluralism, superfluous offices, and excessive salaries, and to report to Parliament so that speedy redress could be achieved:[12]

> That in regard to the present great affairs of Parliament, a
> Committee of honest and well affected persons without the House,
> may be appointed and Authorized to consider of the charge, and
> inconvenience to the Common-Wealth, by Monopolies, Pluralities
> of places of profit, unnecessary places, and large Sallaries, and to
> offer the same to the Parliament for redresse to be made therein.

The idea of a non-parliamentary, but carefully selected, committee may well have come from the field of law reform. There the Rump had bowed to military pressure and appointed men of varied legal experience but undisputed reforming zeal at the army's insistence.[13] The form of radicalism for which they stood varied from group to group, one is tempted to suggest from officer to officer, within the army. But it is fair to say that when Cromwell and the officers overthrew the Rump Parliament and its

Council of State in April 1653, they did so with a strong moral commitment to administrative reform. And despite the politically unrepresentative nature of the army, they can be said to have undertaken this
commitment, in part at least, as a response to popular feeling and public
opinion at large.

Subsequent events in 1653 showed that this was easier said than done
and that there was no single radical, reforming party. Yet to represent
Lambert and the other Protectorians as having betrayed the cause of
reform by using the radical republicans to overthrow the Rump, and
then themselves riding to power through the downfall of the Barebones,
is to mistake one aspect for the whole picture. Some of the ordinances
passed by the Protector and his Council during the first nine months of
1654, in which Lambert had an important share, dealt with these very
questions. One spokesman for the radicals in the Barebones indeed
defended the delays over the Assessment Bill, which seemed to threaten
the army's livelihood, on the grounds that they were trying to reform the
tax structure. They wanted a uniform Pound Rate instead of the present
inequality, the Assessment amounting—so it was alleged—to 12 and 13
shillings in the pound in some areas of the country and only 2 or 3
shillings in others.[14] The Rump had more than once addressed itself to
the same problem, but with characteristic lack of decision.[15] And the
successive cuts in the Assessment, from £120,000 to £35,000 a month
during the course of the Protectorate (1654–7), should have done more
to reduce dissatisfaction than any such scheme for re-distribution or re-
rating.[16] That is, if people are objective in their attitude towards taxation,
which is by no means always the case.

With the Protectorate comes a revival of pamphlets expressing the
theme of Court versus Country, reminiscent of the 1620s–30s and anti-
cipatory of the 1670s. It is a feature of this genre that they are almost
invariably pro-Country, anti-Court. No Richard Hooker, no Warden
Sparrow, rose to the defence of the establishment in the mid-seventeenth
century. Or did he? In November 1653 there appeared Στερέωμα: *The
Establishment: or, a Discourse Tending to the settling of the Mindes of
Men, about some of the chiefe Controversies of the Present Times* . . . Like
Ireton in the Whitehall Debates of 1648–9[17] the anonymous author
defended 'the power of the Civill Magistrat in Matters of Religion';
secondly the need for an instituted and fixed ministry, that is clergy for
a State Church; and thirdly, 'the Necessity and Excellency of Humane
Learning'; but not, disappointingly, the need for an effective administration. Then as now, and perhaps with as little justice, the universities
(and even the churches) had more defenders against their critics than the
Civil Service.[18]

The new tone emerges with the first Protectorate Parliament (1654–5).[19]
But, as we saw with the Chancery Ordinance,[20] it would be misleading to

identify the Protectorate government or the Court with narrow vested interests, and the parliamentary opposition or the Country with progress towards administrative reform. No doubt this is the impression which some sections of the opposition wished to convey. Although it does not use the words Court and Country, an electioneering broadside of late June 1654 identifies the malpractices of officials with political divisions in the forthcoming parliament. The tone of *A Memento For the People, about their Elections of Members for the approaching Parliament* is anti-government or 'Country' but not overtly anti-republican. It includes this warning:[21]

> Those that live, and intend to live upon the public purse, are not equally concerned in levying of moneyes upon you, with those that live upon their own estates and trades. Publick Officers, that have great Places and Salaries from the common purse, put in a penny, and take out a pound.

The remedy, on the lines which ought to have followed from the self-denying Ordinance of 1645, was strict separation of the executive and legislative powers.

The more modest, but still largely unfulfilled hopes of government supporters are well summed up in a petition from the North Riding of Yorkshire to the second Protectorate Parliament. Tax cuts are to be made, as far as is compatible with security; the judges are to receive salaries and nothing else; the excise is to be reformed; one or more courts are to be re-established in the north, likewise regional registers for wills, administrations, contracts, conveyances, and suchlike documents. The tone is explicitly anti-royalist, and in favour of 'healing and settling'.[22]

More characteristic of the genre is *An Appeale From the Court to the Country* of October 1656. This is largely to do with the suborning of Parliament's independence as a legislature by the Protector having packed it with officers, placemen and pensioners, and does not deal with administrative reform.[23] The same is true of the better-known retrospective *A Narrative of the Late Parliament* (1657),[24] and its postscript *A Second Narrative* (1658).[25] Yet in the descriptive panegyric by one R. Hawkins, *A Discourse of the Nationall Excellencies of England*, published in the same year, amongst the many points picked out for commendation was that the overheads on the taxes collected were very low, as was the amount wasted on pensioners and favourites.[26] In the republican Slingsby Bethel's account of Richard Cromwell's parliament (January–April 1659) we return to the Court–Country theme of 1656–7.[27]

With the return to a Commonwealth under the restored Rump in May 1659, the demands began again for legal, administrative and fiscal reform which had characterised the years 1650–3.[28] There was the added, more strictly political complication of whether those who had acted under the late usurper (Oliver) should be made to disgorge all that they had received in fees, salaries, wages, rewards, etc. In the end it was decided they should not, in all likelihood because of the equivocal position of the army commanders[29] who acted so prominently in affairs from 1653 to 1658.[30] Still, there were denunciations of pluralism whether by civil or military officers,[31] while one of its radical puritan supporters was quick to remind the restored Rump of earlier disillusionment with them:[32]

> That there was a preferring of unworthy men unto places of greatest trust and profit; Relations and other worldly respects swayed more than due qualifications. . . . As for good men and such as will faithfully serve you and their Country, it is below their Principles to be running after you for places; such a practise sutes not with their spirits, but with a sort of servile mercenarie fellows that will hire out themselves to do anything for their belly.

And there was more in the same vein. The Rump itself made some gestures in the direction of greater probity, and allowed impeachment proceedings to be initiated against Cromwell's ex-Comptroller of the Household, Colonel Philip Jones from South Wales, largely on the grounds of misusing public office.[33] One specific proposal put forward seems not so much against corruption as in favour of republican virtue[34] 'That the chargeable office and officers of the Exchequer, (as to receipts and payments) may be reduced and regulated, as being calculated more for the Meridian of the Court, than fitted for the service of the Common-Wealth'. This was echoed in a petition from 'divers youngmen Inhabiting in and about the borough of Southwark'—a stronghold of popular radicalism, allegedly also of vice—demanding 'That the publick Revenues and Imployments may be contracted into as few hands as maybe, that so the less may be expended in Salaries'.[35] Investigations of the various revenue departments were set on foot, and proceedings speeded against accountants who were in arrears to the State. The government of the restored Commonwealth evidently felt that it had a mandate to clean up the administration, rectify abuses and grievances, in much the same way—paradoxically—as Cromwell and his supporters had felt that they had one six years earlier. It is impossible to tell whether the restored Rump of 1659 would have avoided the unpopularity incurred in its previous incarnation. The members pledged to dissolve themselves by 7 May 1660,[36] but their interruption from mid-October to the end of December and the re-admission of the anti-republicans on 21 February 1660 meant that they had much less than a clear year in which to prove themselves and on which to be judged by public opinion—as expressed in print. Among the most constructive programmes tendered to them was Hugh Peter's *Long-Parliament-Work . . . in XX Proposals*. This included a call for direct management of all revenues and an end to tax-farming; other points involved taking the accounts of all public money received and spent, better salaries for judges and others, and further measures for law reform.[37] It is straining credibility to suppose that the Rump would have got very far with much of this by May 1660, even under the most favourable political conditions, although they may have learnt one lesson from 1649–53. For they did avoid paying compensation and affording other special favours to individual members while so many wider grievances remained unmet. By the autumn of 1659, out-and-out adherents of the Good Old Cause—such as Vane and Milton—were thinking in terms of a self-co-opting perpetual senate in place of any parliament at all. The administrative implications of this are largely guesswork. To say that there would have been a loss of public accountability to the nation through its elected representatives would be to think too much in nineteenth–twentieth-century terms. Such a government could not easily have been less accountable to popular feeling than other seventeenth-century regimes.

Although Lilburne was dead and the other leading Leveller and Digger pamphleteers silent, some of the radical programmes of 1659 went as far as all but Winstanley's of a decade earlier.[38] We even find a spirited—and quite detailed—case being made for a progressive income tax.[39] For many opponents of change, the times never are ripe for such schemes; but this, like parallel demands for a state medical and a state legal service, has a breathtaking quality when seen in the shadow of Monck's advancing army and the imminent return of the old order. It is true that the arguments for and against a land tax and an excise were hammered out in the Convention Parliament, during the autumn of 1660; but the circumstances were so different that the comparison is a little forced. Even those who most ardently opposed giving Charles II the perpetual excise on liquor did not venture to suggest a progressive levy on landed incomes instead! By contrast, the idea of admitting only properly qualified office-holders and of ending venality did survive the Restoration.[40] On both the Rump's and Cromwell's administrations, the ex-royalist Roger Coke may be allowed the final, contemporary comment. Of the Rumpers, he wrote:[41] 'They were a race of men indefatigably industrious in Business, always seeking men fit for it, and never preferring any for Favour, nor by Importunity. . . . They thus excelled in their Management of Civil Affairs.' And on the Protector, he gave the better-known encomium: 'Westminster Hall was never replenished with more learned and upright Judges than by him; nor was Justice either in Law or Equity in Civil Cases more equally distributed, where he was not a Party.'

Many of those who blossomed into print as critics of government, then as now, did so in part because they were at odds with it. The range of grievances varied widely, as did the men involved, but remembering the censorship, particularly from 1649 to 1659, it is surprising what criticisms were publicly ventilated. The motive of personal or collective grievance existed even among some of the most notable, such as John Lilburne himself. His case is different only because he came up against authority so often, but this certainly does not, by crude reductionism, invalidate the principles behind his criticisms. Similarly, to say that Winstanley became a communist because he had failed as a businessman may not be untrue, but it is simply inadequate as an explanation of his writing and his career. We shall concentrate here on expressions of grievance against the administration, including the law and the tax system as well as the operations of central and local government, the enforcement of legislation and the conduct of officials.

Sometimes these publications reveal no more than the divisions within the administration and the conflicts of overlapping jurisdiction already discussed.[42] They can thus hardly be said to exemplify the response of people in society at large to the impact of government upon them. In 1655 Thomas Baker, clerk of the First Fruits Office in the Strand, denounced the Maintenance Trustees for allowing clerical incumbents to evade paying first fruits to him. He saw these not as a relic of episcopalianism and royal supremacy over the Church, but as an established part of the State's revenue which should not be lost; no doubt Baker's own official livelihood depended on their continuance.[43] Likewise the earlier collision between Mr Andrewes Burrell, some time Master Shipwright of the Navy at Woolwich, and the Navy Commissioners was an internal dispute about the efficiency of naval administration at the end of the Civil War. Burrell, who came from Wisbech in the Fens, had previously gone into print on the question of fen drainage, in opposition to the great Dutch engineer, Sir Cornelius Vermuyden. When he proposed to speed up naval shipbuilding by keeping all men-of-war down to one deck of gunports along the ship's side, his opponents, the Commissioners, countered by denying his technical competence. Their critic, they alleged, 'scarce ever saw salt water, and consequently never saw service'; since he subsequently retired from service as a shipwright, the result was presumably a compromise. Burrell seems to have been given a chance to prove his worth in that capacity, and it looks as if he became disillusioned and left the public service in 1651 or 1652.[44]

Some publications reveal a struggle for possession of the same office, as with two 'recruiter' MPs and the Ushership of the Receipt. This position had been held, on a virtually hereditary tenure,[45] by the well-known parliamentarian pamphleteer Clement Walker, who was elected MP for Wells in 1645 and secluded by Colonel Pride along with his ally William Prynne in December 1648. When Walker was imprisoned, illegally and without ever being brought to trial, for his writings against the Independents, his office was apparently sequestered, or at least bestowed by the Revenue Committee of the Rump on Humphrey Edwards, recruiter for Shropshire and a regicide. In a characteristically vigorous counter-attack, written shortly before his death in the Tower, Walker accused Edwards of being a side-changer who had been among the king's followers when he came for the Five Members in January 1642. Moreover since he, Walker, had executed his Ushership by Deputy for forty years—a nice touch—there was no reason why imprisonment should be held to disable him from it; the Revenue Committee had thus disseized him from his freehold without due process at law. The campaign for the Ushership was continued by Walker's son and his deputy against Edwards. Shortly after this Mrs Walker, now a widow, weighed in with the plea that the office had been part of her marriage jointure sixteen years before her late husband's supposed offence. She in turn begged annulment of the Committee's order and asked permission to seek legal compensation for her losses from being deprived of the office.[46]

Implications of corruption rather than of mere high-handedness emerge from other such disputes. At a lower level of administration, but one of more practical importance, William Jervis, Gentleman, a litigant against the Drury House Trustees, attacked their one-time Clerk, John Hodder. Jervis maintained that Hodder had been justly dismissed by the Trustees (who were in charge of the sales of royalist lands confiscated for treason), but that he had then mounted a malicious prosecution against them, using him, Jervis, as his instrument; Hodder was acting in collusion with other discontented under-officers who had also been discharged. Jervis denied thinking ill of the Trustees at all, except over the specific matter for which he was prosecuting them; he now disowned his share in these proceedings, and at the same time strenuously denied having been bribed by the Trustees to do so. Presumably they were in a position to show him more—or less—favour, however, according to his own role in relation to Hodder's attack on them. Perhaps the oddest thing here is why Jervis should have bothered to put all this into print at all.[47]

One of John Lilburne's Leveller allies, Samuel Chidley, in defending his leader against attack from a Scot called David Browne, expounded his own grievances against the Commonwealth. Browne had suggested that he, Chidley, had been justly dismissed by his erstwhile official employers, the Land Sale Trustees at Worcester House, 'for deceitfull dealing and unjust Levelling in Civill matters there, against many both poore and rich, . . .' Chidley admitted that there were numerous complaints against the Trustees; what with their own 'unadvisedness' and the unpaid debts of 'the poorer sort' this was unavoidable. As to his own office, of Receiver of Debentures, 'the time was expired which is limited by the last Act'; therefore his employment had come to a natural end, yet the Trustees were unjustly failing to pay his salary up to date. He emphasised his faithful service to the Commonwealth, and claimed to 'have performed my place without extortion of Bribes, according to the universal disease that is inbred amongst almost all Clerks, that make not the Word of God their rule'. Of the two specific procedural points on which he admitted that fault might have been found with him, one was his use (on debentures) of the saving formula 'Errors excepted'; the other was his wish to write 'in the year of the Lord *Christ* 1650' instead of 'the Lord *God*'.[48] The one-time stocking-seller, Leveller organiser and Independent lay-preacher may not have been designed by nature for a career as a bureaucratic functionary.

Some of the bitterest personal attacks in print were made by men who had suffered imprisonment—often, as they believed, wrongly—against their gaolers or others allegedly responsible. Robert Robins claimed to be languishing in a Southwark prison because of a judgment in the Marshal's Court over a debt of 5s. 6d. He denied that the Court still had proper jurisdiction since the withdrawal of the royal household from London and Parliament's Ordinance against the authority of the Knight Marshal. For our purposes the most interesting aspect of this is not so much Robins's complaint of wrongful imprisonment, to which there are many parallels,[49] as his ability to relate this to wider issues of administrative reform. The Prothonotary of the Court, who had signed the warrant for his arrest, was said to have bought his place for £2,500 and to be aiming to 'pick it up againe by theis writts'. The total illegal takings involved, that is from private individuals caught up in the Marshal's Court and its jurisdiction, were—somewhat wildly—put at £200,000 a year. Since the Knight Marshal's own patent had been voided by sequestration, the Steward of the Court (not, it would seem, himself a royalist) was challenged to a trial at law.[50] At the time when Robins was writing, the exact position of the Marshal's Court is unclear; but a little later the profits of the Knight Marshal's office were in the hands of another recruiter MP and regicide, William Say. When the total abolition of the Court was voted by the Rump in July 1651, Say's gains were specifically safeguarded against the Compounding Commissioners who had been trying to recover £100 a year from him.[51]

The grievance of imprisonment for debt became merged with the wider rights of freeborn Englishmen in the writings of the Leveller supporter James Frese. His campaign, conducted largely from within the King's Bench prison, extended at least from 1645 to 1659. Persistence apart, it cannot be said that the quality of his writings does much for the cause which he had at heart.[52]

John Lilburne's attack on the integrity of the Commissioners for Sequestration and Compounding over the Harraton colliery case has already been discussed.[53] Here it is worth noting that if he and his client Joseph Primate had not printed and published their petition to the Commons attacking Hesilrige and the Commissioners, the Rump would hardly have had even the dubious grounds which it did for the savage sentence of banishment given in January 1652. It is, as his modern biographers have found,[54] extremely difficult to be sure whether Lilburne courted martyrdom strictly as a means of gaining publicity and winning support for his principles and the cause which he had at heart, or sometimes also out of self-advertisement and sheer incorrigibility. A comparison might be ventured with Gerrard Winstanley's pamphlets (of 1649–50) after the Digger colony in Surrey had been broken up, first by local men enforcing a decision in the Courts and then by troopers from Fairfax's regiment.[55] But the parallel is not altogether valid. Lilburne did not, unlike a royalist such as Judge David Jenkins, or a presbyterian ex-parliamentarian such as William Prynne, reject the whole machinery of penal taxation and the legal basis on which it rested. His point was an administrative one against improper pressure and a wrong decision, not a constitutional one against illegal authority. The Digger theorist's position in this respect was nearer to that of Jenkins on the Indemnity Ordinance[56] or of Prynne on the Excise.[57] Winstanley's rejection of the manorial rights of lords over common lands and of the jurisdiction used to uphold these was both economic and theological in its fundamental basis. Interestingly, however, it was also constitutional; for he held that the abolition of kingship and the constitution of England as a 'Commonwealth and free State' automatically rendered manorial authority invalid. And it was largely on these grounds that he advocated support for the infant Commonwealth, to the extent of taking the Engagement himself.[58]

Captain Robert Norwood was no Lilburne or Winstanley, although he was commended by the former[59] and possibly shared some theological tenets with the latter. Whether as a result of malice or of misunderstanding, Norwood found himself charged under the Rump's Blasphemy Act of 1650, apparently being accused of pantheism along with Mr Tany, a Ranter. The nearest he came, at least in print, to anything heretical was to say that the individual human soul was a part of the Divine Essence. For this a parliamentary committee had him indicted by the Upper Bench, in consequence of which he spent six months in prison awaiting trial. He was released and at once resumed his attack on the committee, one of whose members—a clergyman, not an MP (it was a mixed committee)—he said was as guilty as he was. Norwood went on to develop a full-scale critique of any state church and an ordained, officially maintained ministry and to demand complete toleration, under a magistrate who should be neutral in matters of religion. He welcomed the downfall of the Rump and the advent of Cromwell's rule as Lord General followed by the assembly of the Barebones. His constitutional ideas were lifted wholesale from the writings of John Sadler, the republican Town Clerk of London, although they are less indigestible than in their original form.[60] The keynote was that all governments were inferior to those from whom they took their trust; and he warned the Barebones Members against 'that golden apple of unlimitedness'. Norwood's case is a reminder of the quasi-judicial role of the committees set up to administer parliamentary acts and ordinances; by 1651–3 these were sometimes more of a threat to radical supporters of the puritan republic than to politically quietist Anglicans or even Papists.[61]

A certain Captain Nathaniel Burt got at odds with the Probate Court over the administration of his father's will. He alleged a conspiracy against himself by his own younger brother, the officers of the Saddlers' Company of London (to which Burt senior had belonged) and the officers of the Court; this in turn led on to litigation in Chancery. As is evident from the full title of the piece which he published after this, Burt had the same gift, which we have seen in others, of identifying his own cause with the wider issues of overthrowing corruption and doing God's work. Compared with Norwood, or even Lilburne, his tone was distinctly more religious even when the issue was a basically secular one: the jurisdiction of the Probate Court and the reform—or abolition—of Chancery. In the summer of 1653, he published *An Appeal from Chancery, To the Lord General and his Counsel of Officers, As also to the Counsel of State, And to all freeborn Englishmen of honest hearte, who have not forfeited their Liberty, or captivated their Reason . . . who desire . . . that Christ's Kingdom may be advanced; and that of the Beast may be thrown down, with all their covetous, persecuting, lying, partial, extorting, bribing, perjured Officers, Ministers, and Attendants, either that have been corrupt Parliament-men, Committee-men, Judges, such who are in places of Judicature, Justices, Lawyers, called Counsellers, or concealers of our Law, and Registers or Clerks, with every corrupt member thereof, by any name or title whatsoever distinguished, in England or in places called Innes of Court . . . or those in places of Government in Cities, Ports, Guild-Halls, Companies, Corporations, or Fraternities who usurp authority over Englishmen . . .* (including incidentally those who are followers of anti-Christ and allies of the former 'serpentine brood').[62] Exegesis hardly seems called for, but perhaps this kind of effusion does help to make the Barebones' attack on Chancery more comprehensible. Sad to say, Burt was still in the trammels of litigation two years later.[63]

This was not Burt's first brush with authority. In August 1649 he had published a letter addressed to all MPs, attacking the Mayor and other municipal officers of Dover. At the same time he was attempting to invoke the indemnity machinery against them, on the grounds that as ex-delinquents (or royalists), they were holding these offices improperly, indeed illegally. Having given him more time to produce his witnesses, the Indemnity Committee then dismissed Burt's case, and upheld the defendants, two days after his printed appeal to the House.[64]

Accusations of administrative impropriety sometimes merged into the fantasy world of the paranoid. We have aleady met Captain John Bernard who claimed to have spent his time and fortune from the late 1640s to 1657 proving that Speaker Lenthall and a hundred other prominent people were serving the Pope's interests, and that in consequence lands worth £200,000 per annum were wrongly detained from the Commonwealth, being in private hands when they should have been sequestered. He alleged that his complaint had been improperly suppressed—by fellow-travellers like Goffe and Whalley, and then smothered by the Rump's intelligence chief Captain George Bishop and the Judge-Advocate of the army, Margetts. While serving in the regiment of Colonel Lytcott, the Speaker's nephew, he had been wrongly accused of making false muster returns in order to bring about his ruin, he said. But he had eventually been cleared; now it was the Lord Protector's mind which was being poisoned against him.[65] No doubt some lands did go unsequestered because of improper favour shown to friends and relatives of leading parliamentarians; but hardly on this scale and not because Lenthall and others were agents of a popish plot. Significantly, Bernard used a similar phrase to one of Prynne's, another victim of the conspiracy theory, in describing one of those who had attacked him as a 'Jesuitical leveller'.[66]

Our final instance offers a more plausible glimpse of the inner Cromwellian circle. A Mr Tillam was accused of giving out that he had a special licence from the Protector to preach in any church where the living was vacant. Robert Eaton, the author of the account, acting on behalf of people in Colchester who were being taken in by Tillam, knew William Malyn, Cromwell's secretary, and mentioned this in conversation: 'which Mr Malyn hearing of, said, He was very confident he never had any such Instrument granted him by the Protector . . .'. He then asked Cromwell, and reported back to Eaton and others confirming this, adding that an order should issue out to apprehend Tillam. So when Tillam shortly afterwards accused Eaton of saying that his authorisation to preach was counterfeited, Eaton was able to reply by referring him back to Malyn. Publication here would seem to have served partly as a channel of information, partly to clear the author's good name and challenge his opponent to do his worst. It is surprising that Tillam was not shown up locally and dealt with by the magistrates, without resort to Malyn.[67]

A few pamphleteers, however vocal and gifted, do not constitute the people of England, or even—necessarily—a representative sample of public opinion. Are there any other sources which can be used to supplement or assess the value of their writings?

iii THE OFFICIAL RECORD: COMMITTEES AND COURTS OF LAW

The records which a government keeps, for its own use and future reference, are by no means the same as its public showing in print—meant either for contemporaries or for posterity. Even highly respectable governments of the parliamentary type show a tendency to increase the area under the seals of secrecy and to restrict publication if pressure is not brought to bear the other way. Naturally we cannot tell what would have happened to the parliamentarian and republican archives if either the Commonwealth or the Protectorate had succeeded in perpetuating itself. Presumably the records would have been merged with those of the various monarchical institutions, and the papers of statesmen either deposited or left in the private hands of the family and descendants. If a Cromwellian and not a Hanoverian dynasty had been reigning in 1742, it is hard to believe that so catholic and so 'undoctored' a collection of Secretary Thurloe's papers would have been published within less than a century of their compilation and only three generations after their owner's death.[1] A decent edition of Oliver Cromwell's speeches and his official correspondence would surely not have had to await Carlyle in the nineteenth century; but would it have been an honest text? John Rushworth was, of course, at work as a 'contemporary historian' in the 1650s, but he was mainly working on the 1630s and made no attempt then, or after the Restoration, to proceed beyond 1649.[2] So there may be gain as well as loss from delay in publication; Rushworth was a heroic collector and an accurate editor but he was certainly not impartial. As to the papers of those characteristic institutions of the Interregnum, the Committees, an enormous quantity was recovered from their various Clerks and Secretaries by orders of the Restoration government in 1660–1, and deposited in the State Paper Office. Since the State Papers are mainly the archives of the royal Council and the Secretaries of State, this was an arbitrary decision. Incidentally, it has meant that the voluminous records of the various Accounts Committees are described as 'Commonwealth Exchequer Papers', but have a State Paper reference number in the Public Record Office.[3]

The records of the Committees and Commissions for Compounding, Advance of Money and Sequestration reveal the impact of parliamentarian and then republican administration on royalists and—to an extent—neutrals. Occasionally there are hints of abuses by under-officers or misconduct by local sub-committees. What they do not show is the truth of allegations about malpractices at the top—improper pressure, corrupt favours, victimisation and so on—although the heavy deletions in the original minute book during the Harraton colliery case are, to say the least, suggestive.[4]

The Indemnity records and the Accounts Committee's archives are almost alone in showing us how the regime affected its own minor and obscure adherents. But the Indemnity records tell us about even humbler parliamentarian and then republican supporters than do the Accounts. Moreover, because of the nature of the 'indemnity' which was afforded by the various Ordinances and Acts, many of these records show protection being sought against legal proceedings which were in train elsewhere.

In one respect the different sources all agree. In the Thomason Tracts there are more items attacking the excise than any other major branch of the revenues.[5] There is independent evidence of anti-excise riots in 1647 and 1650.[6] And in December 1649, soon after a sequence of orders directing members of the army to keep out of law suits between private parties, Fairfax authorised the use of military units to suppress opposition to the excise and, if necessary, even to help the local sub-commissioners in its collection.[7] The records of at least one local community show strong opposition to the farming of the excise, notably that of the duties on ale and beer.[8] And in the indemnity records themselves, far more cases relate to this than to any other form of taxation. These instances stretch the whole way through the Indemnity Committee's and Commissioners' records, from 1647 to 1654. They cover an extraordinarily large number of different districts over a very wide geographical area. Despite a preponderance of cases from London, followed by Kent, at least twenty-six English counties and one Welsh county are represented, and there are a good many more instances when the location is not made clear. One of the most striking points to emerge here is that the Committee—and later the Commissioners—by no means always upheld the Excise officials who appealed to them for help and protection against proceedings in the courts. This can be taken to illustrate either the strict legalism of the regime, even in its most arbitrary and innovatory aspects, or the old adage that there is no smoke without fire—implying that abuses and high-handedness were commoner in the Excise than elsewhere. As with the areas of administration most subject to charges of corruption, a bit of both is perhaps the likeliest explanation.[9]

One case, trivial in itself, will suggest some of the issues involved. On 29 October 1652, one Alexander Skiffe, an officer under the Excise sub-commissioners in Kent, petitioned the Indemnity Commissioners for relief. He was, he alleged, being sued by one Edward Campion for distraining on the latter's goods by warrant of the sub-commissioners consequent on non-payment of money due for excise. Campion, the plaintiff in whatever court Skiffe was being sued (although he was the defendant here), was cited to attend on 23 November. But—in a fashion which is common with indemnity cases—the hearing did not in fact take place until 21 December. On Skiffe's motion for the stay of the suit against him, and on his giving security that he would meet such costs and damages as might be awarded in Campion's favour, if the Commissioners decided not to relieve him, the suit against him was ordered to be stayed —apparently *sine die* (at least no duration is stated). However, nearly a year after the original petition, on 11 October 1653 the Commissioners wrote about it to the Excise Commissioners. Before proceeding to judgment in the case of Skiffe versus Campion, they recommended that the Kent sub-commissioners' proceedings against Campion be thoroughly scrutinized, to see whether these had been according to the various acts and ordinances for the excise:[10]

> Or whether by colour of that authority they have not oppressed the poore man . . . not doubting but if the poore man appeare to you to have bene wronged by yo[r] Sub Com[rs] he may receive yo[r] direccon for his satisfacson & reparacon from them.

For this was what the evidence now suggested to the Indemnity Commissioners had in fact happened; and they recommended that the business between the parties be settled by agreement or, if this were impossible, that the Excise Commissioners should certify their findings to them. On 20 December, after hearing the evidence and learned counsel for both parties and having read a certificate from the Excise Commissioners, they at last proceeded to judgment. Skiffe was indemnified. Campion was to discharge him and give him a formal release from all the charges. But in view of the Kent Sub-Commissioners' proceedings against Campion, no award was made against him for costs. Whether Skiffe had to meet his own costs or whether his employers paid them does not emerge.

It should not be supposed that the excise was unique in occasioning opposition, resistance and legal proceedings which then led to indemnity suits. There were numerous cases involving sequestered goods and property, notably to do with debts, rents and tithes. In one instance, which may have political significance, the soldiers of Colonel Philip Jones's regiment (whose disbandment has already been ordered back in 1651) petitioned in June 1653 for protection from a suit brought against them for helping the Sequestration Agents to collect rents. This was granted.[11] But direct involvement of the army was unusual.

At least until its successive reductions in 1655–7, the monthly assessment was easily the heaviest tax levied by the republic. If the volume of complaint and counter-measure were proportionate to the weight of the burden, one would expect it to have generated even more indemnity suits than the excise. This was certainly not so, although there were many cases involving the assessment in one way or another. It is clear that the poor as well as the rich resorted to litigation in resisting payment. Some of the cases relate to distraints levied on very small items and on tiny amounts of property: a cloak and a pint-pot. Others are about matters of greater substance: sheep, cattle, a bullock or a mare. Some are really actions of a different kind, against alleged ex-royalists wrongly acting as assessment commissioners or collectors. None the less, the commonest types of case seem to have arisen from disputes about the respective liabilities of landlord and tenant.[12] We must remember too, that although the Army Committee and the Receivers-General had Agents in most counties, much of the actual assessment and collection was in the hands of local committees appointed for the various counties and cities, or other fiscal units. So it may be that the unpopularity of tax officials overlaps here with general resentment at the activities of county committees. Samuel Sheppard's *Committee-Man Curried* (a 'comedy' in verse) of July–August 1647, for example, brackets committee-men, excise-men and those responsible for the sufferings of royalists (presumably the agents of compounding and sequestration).[13] Contemporary reality needs carefully disentangling, too, from subsequent royalist, anti-parliamentarian, anti-republican propaganda.

The third main branch of the revenue system, the customs, directly affected far fewer people than the assessment or the excise. Whether for that reason or because of its being a long-established, if in some respects highly controversial form of taxation, resistance to its collection produced noticeably fewer indemnity suits than did the other two. Eleven out of fourteen cases noted from 1649 to 1653 inclusive cover the London customs. In one of the few provincial instances, from Bristol, the customs officials of the port had their request for indemnity turned down, and were told to face the consequences of the law-suit which was pending against them.[14]

One part of the Long Parliament's indemnity legislation was of particular benefit to members of the army; this involved apprenticeship. Broadly speaking, it specified that ex-soldiers who had begun their apprenticeship before military service need not complete their full term, and could begin to practise their respective trades as freemen as soon as they returned to civilian life. Many cases for relief from prosecution were brought on this basis. Most were successful, but some turned on whether or not a man had been an apprentice, or his father a freeman as he alleged. For example, in 1649 two substantial citizens of Bedford were cited to appear before the Indemnity Committee as a result of a petition from someone lately in the army who maintained that although he was himself an ex-London apprentice, because his father was a freeman of Bedford he had settled himself there but had been molested in his trade by the defendants. It seems highly probable that the individuals concerned were political opponents. Bedford was riven by clashes between the oligarchic and popular factions at this time. The town records state that the matter of the petition touched the liberties and freedom of the corporation: the petitioner (the ex-soldier) was a foreigner, being the younger son of a freeman and therefore not eligible by inheritance, either according to the custom and usage of the corporation, or by the law of the land. The Mayor (a relative of the defendants) was to certify the true state of the case to the Committee; expenses arising out of the plaintiff's petition or from this riposte were to be met out of the town's chamber. As is often the case, the indemnity records themselves fail to make clear what was the eventual outcome, although temporarily the Committee upheld the petitioner's claim.[15]

Some of the difficulties in interpreting the impact of the regime on the 'common man' are due to problems of social and economic definition more than to the nature of the records. When, for instance, we find someone described as a 'labourer' petitioning and winning his case, we may be tempted to suppose that the indemnity machinery was indeed available to, and genuinely used by those at the very bottom of society. But when we read on and discover that this case was over a £10 debt and that the plaintiff also got £25 costs, it becomes clear that the designation labourer must here have been compatible with having at least moderately substantial personal possessions.[16]

It is, however, abundantly clear that office-holders of whatever rank were by no means always successful either as plaintiffs or as defendants. The indemnity laws emphatically did not develop into a general *droit administratif*. In 1652 three of the Navy Commissioners sought indemnity against someone called a 'bricklayer' (presumably in practice a builder), who had sued them for dispossessing him from some premises which adjoined the Navy Office and which they alleged belonged to the navy. After some months' delay, their petition was dismissed and the existing law-suit left to take its course; subsequently the defendant was awarded £20 costs, and five months later the Indemnity Commissioners verified that their naval colleagues had actually paid these.[17] The excise officials who were not upheld when they sought indemnity were therefore more numerous but not different in kind from those in other sectors of the administration. Whether it was the constitutional principle at issue, the economic burden of the tax, or the administrative procedures involved which made the excise the most contentious—and the most vulnerable— remains unclear. Certainly the indemnity machinery, although originally set up in 1647 largely to meet the grievances of the army, did not operate as an instrument of a ruthless or monolithic military despotism.

A few law cases in the printed reports enable us to look at this from the other side, from the point of view of the regular machinery of justice in relation to Commonwealth and then Cromwellian administration.[18] An Exchequer case of 1658 involved the alleged evasion of customs and excise duty by a merchant importing currants who was said to have bribed two under-officers to let him off payment of duty on a cargo of 290 casks. The judges apparently divided 2–2 as to whether the defendant, the importer, could plead self-incrimination as grounds for refusal to answer the English Bill, which was the form of the process against him. This refusal appears to have stood, leaving the two officials thoroughly besmirched in reputation and without the opportunity to defend themselves.[19] Remembering other instances of corruption in the London Customs, perhaps this was just as well.[20] Another kind of case involved the indemnity machinery's powers over persons disqualified from local office on political grounds. An action was brought in the Upper Bench in 1651–2 by a churchwarden of St Clement's, Oxford, for scandalous words allegedly spoken against him—to the effect that he was not qualified to execute the office. The Court held that loss of credit was a greater matter than loss of office. Chief Justice Rolle:[21] 'Officers which have no benefit by their offices have more need to be repaired, if they be scandalised in their Execution of them, and here the scandal is great losse to an honest man.' The office, as such, was a burden, not a profit; the more cause not to be blasted in reputation through executing it. The verdict went in the churchwarden's favour. Not that the Indemnity Committee or Commissioners by any means always upheld informers against those who were holding office, when allegedly disqualified by royalism or on other grounds. Sometimes an element of malice or personal spite was clearly felt to be involved. An interesting minor case in 1655 involved the Protector versus the Master and Fellows of Gonville and Caius College, Cambridge, over the right to appoint a school usher. The issue seems to have been whether or not the State could compel his replacement for unsatisfactory conduct. The Protector's Counsel:[22] 'this is a publique office, and not a private, and tends much to the publique good and is like to the case of an Alderman, or Freeman of a Corporation, or a Fellow of a College.' The other argument was that since this was a private school it was a private post, under the College. In the end the matter was referred to the Assize Judges, one of whom, Oliver St John, happened also to be the Chancellor of the University.

A more serious issue was at stake in the case of the Protector versus the Town of Colchester also in 1655. The State was trying to compel the bailiffs of the town to restore the Cromwellian Nathaniel Barnardiston to the office of Recorder, from which they had removed him on grounds of misconduct and neglect. He had acted by a deputy who was not even a qualified barrister. But the judges decided that Barnardiston should be restored, basically on the grounds that he had not been given a fair chance to defend himself against the charges brought. Rolle: 'it is very hard to deprive one of his freehold without hearing him make his defence'.[23] In a rather different context the judges of what was then still King's Bench in 1647 had upheld, on technical grounds, the claim of the London radical Stephen Estwick to be restored to his place on the Common Council of the City; but here the State had not been a party.[24]

The narrow limits of state power, as interpreted by the judges, can be seen in the case of the Protector versus Streeter in 1655. Captain John Streeter, alias Streater, was a political opponent of the Protectorate who had been committed to prison by order of the 1654–5 Parliament for publishing scandalous pamphlets. The legal question at issue, as with Lilburne's return from banishment in 1653, was whether an order of a dissolved parliament remained in force. Unlike an Act, an order was felt to lapse; and Streeter accordingly got his *habeas corpus* on giving a bail bond for £500, the Attorney-General being left free to proceed against him the following term.[25]

Sometimes the Assize Judges had to deal with cases which were not overtly political in the sense of being brought by the State, but had marked political overtones. At York in 1649 an action for words was brought, the plaintiff alleging that someone had said to him: 'he was a thief and had cousened the State, he being then a Sequestrator . . .' An action was held to lie for the first words; the further words being an additional slander and not merely explanatory of the first ones, but the nicer touch related to the possibility of its being slanderous to say some-one was a Sequestrator![26] Something more like a political verdict was given at York shortly after this when a royalist called Marris who had seized Pontefract Castle for the King in the second Civil War of 1648 was indicted and arraigned for High Treason, for levying war against the King. Judges Thorpe and Puleston found him within the scope of the great treason statute of 25 Edward III and he was executed accordingly.[27] But there was a little more to it than that. Pontefract was seized for the King only after the royalist forces elsewhere had surrendered, and its garrison was believed to include the group of desperate men who had murdered Colonel Rainsborough, the leading army radical, on 29 October 1648, in revenge for the shooting of Sir Charles Lucas and Sir George Lisle after the surrender of Colchester.[28] It is remarkable that the execution of Marris has gone unnoticed, while those of more distinguished royalists, condemned by courts martial or high courts of justice, have excited so much hostile comment.

To return to a more characteristic case; one apparently innocent of any political implications dragged on for several years in the Upper Bench. It involved a keepership of part of what had been a royal manor. The question was whether this office (its value and status are problematic) necessarily passed with the ownership of the land. At one stage it enabled Judge Newdegate, finding for the defendant, to utter the following unexceptionable sentiments (the reader will have to bear with the reporter's law French!):[29] 'Le Prerogative del Roy ne destroiera ne prejudicea le property del Subiect, . . . mes son Prerogative enable luy a protecter ses political childeren ses Subiects.' For the plaintiff, however, it was held by Chief Justice Glynne that, although every office is an employment, not every employment is an office, and judgment was given accordingly. The case was apparently re-heard and the verdict reversed at the assizes in Essex in 1666. On this note of platitudinous homily and syllogistic exercise we may fittingly leave the judges. The published records of the courts and the assizes show remarkably few indications that men were living through a time of civil war and revolution.

iv IN THE LOCALITIES

The overwhelming impression afforded by the records of local government is one of continuity. Naturally, just as the Assizes were interrupted at some junctures during the Civil War and again—briefly—in 1659, so justice and administration at the municipal and county level suffered some short-term dislocation here and there. But if we consider the basic tasks of those engaged in local government, notably of the JPs and those working under them, the changes are often hard to seek; such as there were cannot always be directly related to the political changes at the national level. If there were innovations resulting from outside pressures, they could be a little unexpected, as in one county where the new mathematical technique of logarithms was used to calculate the assessments on hundreds and townships.[1]

The primary task of the local justices was the enforcement of law and preservation of order. There were certainly changes in progress here. Since the 1590s it had been mandatory on the JPs in Quarter Sessions to refer difficult or contentious cases of felony to the Assizes.[2] In several counties this seems to have developed into a convention that only minor felonies, not carrying the death penalty, were to be dealt with at the Sessions and that all major felonies would automatically go on to the Judges. In so far as this had yet become general, it meant that the death penalty was a rarity at the Quarter Sessions and that whippings (for theft, assault and contumacious vagrancy) had become the severest penalty.[3] Exceptions can be found, and more work remains to be done for the counties whose Quarter Sessions records survive but have not been printed. But the tendency is unmistakable, and seems to have been little affected either way by the events of 1640–60. One obvious novelty is the evidence of political offences, sufficiently trivial to be dealt with summarily. Thus in Bedfordshire in 1652 a widow was fined 5s. for opprobrious words against the government and the country's governors, and a gentleman 10s. for false and scandalous words against the forces of the Commonwealth.[4] Yet in the neighbouring county of Hertfordshire, which had been less solidly parliamentarian during the Civil War and whose surviving records have been fully calendared, there are virtually no such cases. There is, however, evidence (from 1654 onwards) of religious militants (perhaps Quakers although they are not so described) disturbing church services and being proceeded against for this.[5]

Middlesex presents a rather different picture. There the Justices had a standing commission, equivalent to Oyer and Terminer, requiring them to try capital cases. For what such figures are worth, the annual average number of executions was slightly higher under the Republic than it had been under Charles I, but considerably lower than under James.[6] There was one execution in 1652 of a woman for adultery, under the Rump's notorious Act, and a large number of acquittals thereafter.[7] Presumably this was due to the humanity or good sense of justices and jurors rather than to an improvement in morals. If there were also more 'political' cases we must remember the greater powers of the Middlesex justices, and that the county then included much of what was already—in effect—part of the 'Greater London' which was rapidly taking shape. In respect of crime, as in so many other ways, the capital and its immediate surroundings were *sui generis* in seventeenth-century England. It was here, for example, that the 'Spirits' were at work in the 1650s, gangs of ruthless and accomplished professional kidnappers, who 'spirited' young men and women of the industrious classes away and had them shipped, sometimes still unconscious, down river on ships bound for the plantations, where white labour and girls of child-bearing age were always at a premium.[8] In Middlesex, too, we find proceedings, initiated by a parliamentarian-puritan against a practising, self-confessed Jewess, which after reference to the Assembly of Divines led to the court ordering her release.[9] Political offences, too, are markedly commoner than in the provinces. In 1648 a victualler, a weaver and a butcher were bound over to appear and answer charges:[10]

> For calling the Parliament and their Committees rogues, and for
> uttering many other invective and railing speeches against them,
> and for threatening to pull downe the house of John Williams, one
> of the members of the Committee of the Tower Hambletts.

Later that year a Porter of Gray's Inn and a Holborn woman were in trouble 'for selling and uttering unlawfull pamphletts'.[11] A rescue of several seamen from the press gang 'by a tumultuous Company' is recorded in a 1654 case. Daring robberies were commoner in an area where so much liquid wealth was concentrated. Speaker Lenthall was robbed of £1,900 in numbered moneys (coins); the thief, a labourer, was sentenced to death.[12] Accusations of scandalous words continue right through the 1650s, under the Protectorate as much as the Commonwealth.[13] Counterfeiting, with possible political, or anyway administrative significance appears too. The issue of a forged order from the Council of State, signed by Thurloe, for an appointment to the position of Surveyor-General for Customs and Excise in Ireland led to charges against the bogus appointee and two others, all styled Gentleman; a confession followed.[14] Another forgery was for simple monetary gain, being an order from the Protector to the farmers of the beer excise in London, Middlesex and Surrey, to pay the bearer £250. The defendant admitted counterfeiting both this order and a note from one of the Tellers of the Exchequer.[15] Sometimes frustration with bad conditions seems the likeliest motive, as with a seaman's wife who assaulted the Captain of the State's frigate *Wexford*, striking him in the face and calling him rogue and horse-turd.[16]

What does all this add up to, in terms of puritan and republican impact at the local level? Apart from the Adultery Act (the more iniquitous for being limited in its capital clauses to women), the nearest thing to a moral tyranny could arise from the wide interpretation and strict enforcement of the Blasphemy Act. In 1653 a man was charged with gross and revolting blasphemy for having written to his girl friend, in a private letter from the East Indies, that he would rather be in bed with her than in heaven with Jesus Christ. He was informed against and when asked about the letter, replied: 'A pox on Jesus Christ'. But having returned from the East, he had become an alehouse-keeper and was said to propagate his blasphemies more easily as a result. He was given six months in Newgate and then twelve months on bail, and forbidden to keep an alehouse for the future.[17]

Whether many more cases of this type would appear, if the records for indictments, trials and sentences were more complete for a wider range of counties, is a matter of opinion. In Norfolk, a fairly puritan county, a man was sentenced to a whipping for cohabitation with his daughter, where by the letter of the law incest ought to have carried the death penalty.[18] Two sentences of three months' imprisonment for fornication turn out on closer inspection to be for bringing unwanted children into the world whose 'settlement' under the Poor Law was the real issue.[19] As for sabbatarianism, this had been a constant source of minor prosecutions before 1640 and was again after 1660, although more so in some counties than others. In Norfolk we find a clergyman being fined £5 for reading an Exchequer order from the pulpit and then (still on Sunday) for delivering a copy of it to someone.[20] The commonest offenders in this respect were alehouse-keepers, for allowing drink to be consumed before church services were safely over. But again there was nothing peculiar to the 1640s and 50s about this. Moreover, even if there were marginally more such cases in some areas during these years than before or after, we have the usual problem about the evidence: was stricter enforcement catching out a higher proportion of offenders, or were there more offenders of whom much the same proportion got caught? In Hertfordshire during the 1650s, we find individuals indicted for disturbing church services; in the 1660s whole droves of people in that county are indicted for not going to church at all. It was, of course, a strongly puritan area in which there were more post-Restoration Nonconformists than there had been Quakers under the republic.

By contrast, are what might be called the endemic problems: drink, sex, violence and the poor. Swearing is perhaps a minor variant of these, except that it usually had a political or religious overtone. In Warwickshire a husbandman was fined £3. 10s. od. for swearing in 1652; with wages of farm workers at something like 1s. 2d. a day this was a lot of money.[21] But it is hardly a unique case. The size of the fine is not given in another Warwickshire case when the objectionable words had a political context: 'Shite upon the States', 'A Turd for the States' and 'I care not for the States', the third of which seems scarcely scandalous save to an over-sensitive government which felt very unsure of itself.[22] Indictments for fornication and sabbath-breaking, however, do seem to disappear, and those for swearing to dwindle after the Restoration. So much residual truth in the traditional view of puritanism, as standing for 'no more cakes and ale', there does seem to be in the case of Shakespeare's home county. In a region with strong Roman Catholic elements, accusations under the Recusancy Laws disappear from the mid-1650s—an undoubted point for Cromwellian tolerance—and re-appear in the mid-1670s—evidence, one can only think, of Anglican-Cavalier intolerance. To take another topic sometimes exclusively associated with puritanism: in no county whose records enable us to be precise, were witchcraft accusations limited to the Interregnum.[23] They were certainly commoner in some parts of the country than in others, as for instance Wiltshire.[24] More characteristic of revolutionary times is an admission of having been bribed to say that someone was engaged in a (royalist) plot, in order to procure the confiscation of their estate;[25] and for the particular kind of intolerance operative then, the indictment of two weavers for atheism and blasphemy.[26] Cases of seditious words against the government, on the other hand, continued briefly in the 1660s. At the opposite end of England, in the North Riding of Yorkshire, there do not seem to have been any particular types of crime or law enforcement peculiar to the 1640s–50s.[27]

Law enforcement is itself an ambiguous term, not relating exclusively to crime. The justices also had a wide-ranging role as local administrators. By far the largest single area of administrative responsibility put on the justices of Elizabethan and early Stuart England arose from the Poor Laws and their enforcement. We must try to see whether the events of 1640–60 and the kind of governments which were in power made much difference. It used to be believed that the code of poor relief was at its most effective under the Personal Rule of Charles I, thanks largely to Laud and Strafford, and thereafter declined dramatically, as a result partly of the disturbance caused by civil war and partly of the changed social values and policies in evidence under the republic and after the

Restoration.[28] More recent studies have led to substantial revision of this view. Thanks to Professor Elton we now know how much the Elizabethan government, in its legislation, owed to earlier Tudor examples and influences dating from the 1530s.[29] Likewise Professor Jordan and others have challenged, or qualified, the somewhat roseate view previously accepted of the 1630s, while Laud and Wentworth, if not debunked, have been substantially demoted from any primacy in this field.[30] More directly relevant to our purpose here, one general study concerned particularly with London and a monograph on one county, published in the early 1930s, have thrown further doubt on the old-fashioned view of poor law administration during the Interregnum.[31] Work done more recently on Warwickshire fully strengthens this revision, although confirming the older view in that more is seen to have depended on local initiative and persistence, less on central direction, than before 1640–2.[32] The enforcement of relief, whether for the impotent or the able-bodied poor, had been uneven from year to year even under Elizabeth and Charles I, reaching a peak normally in years of grain scarcity and trade depression when conditions were at their worst for the mass of the people. It is therefore not surprising to find the Long Parliament and later the Rump most concerned with the problem of poverty during the very bad economic conditions of 1647–9.[33] The notion that the puritan parliamentarians and their republican successors simply abdicated responsibility and abandoned everything to the workings of inexorable economic laws of supply and demand is like a caricature of early-nineteenth-century *laissez-faire*, and must now be discarded as a travesty of the facts. Certainly the downfall of conciliar rule in 1640–1, the disruption caused by civil war, Parliament's own preoccupation with the war and—second only to that—with the church settlement, and the lack of an executive body with supervisory authority, all contributed to a removal of central control. But this does not mean that the justices abdicated and gave up any pretence at implementing relief. Records in print for those years for Hertfordshire, Sussex, Warwickshire, Wiltshire and the North Riding, do not show any dramatic disappearance of items connected with the Poor Laws.[34] The same seems to be broadly true of the towns. If we include free schools (and free places at fee-paying schools and colleges), hospitals, almshouses, workhouses and the apprenticing of poor children as well as outright poor relief, then there is evidence from Dorchester, Exeter, Leicester, Newcastle, Reading, Weymouth and York of continuing concern, and often of effective implementation.[35]

Naturally there are changes in emphasis. The relief of wounded and disabled parliamentarian ex-soldiers and their dependants bulks larger than that of other 'impotent' persons. The problem of the ne'er-do-well, able-bodied vagrant, as opposed to the honest working man hit by unemployment (a distinction which the seventeenth-century official had to draw before 1640 and after 1660 as well), raised particular problems of security. The interruption of trade due to the war and its aftermath made some forms of relief all the more urgent, yet rendered it doubly difficult either to force masters to keep men and women at work uneconomically or to allow subsidised competition against them by public provision of materials for the unemployed to work on. So strongly were the problems felt in London that, under the added spur of harvest failure the preceding summer, an ordinance was passed in December 1647 setting up a corporation for the relief and employment of the poor in the City and its liberties (that is, including some of the suburbs outside the City proper).[36] It is not altogether clear from the late Margaret James's account how effective this was. The measure was substantially re-enacted by the Rump less than seventeen months later, this time giving fuller legal powers to the corporation for punishing those who disobeyed them.[37] More important for our purpose, the earlier ordinance gave all other counties and corporations (that is, cities and boroughs) authority to take like powers and erect similar corporations. It is not clear whether or not that part of the 1649 Act which replaced the ordinance assumed repetition of this particular clause; nor is there evidence of such action being taken elsewhere either in 1648 or in 1649 and after.[38] The Rump debated poor relief more than once. But like so many of its other schemes for domestic reform, this seems to have been perennially swept aside by more urgent business, or perhaps to have been the victim of the Members' dilatoriness and their 'long weekend' habits.[39] Nor did the Council of State, despite its wide-ranging powers compared with those of previous parliamentary executive bodies, have authority over local justices in this specific respect. Although the Barebones had a committee on the Poor,[40] there was no renewed parliamentary action until the second Protectorate Parliament passed a stringent anti-vagrancy Act in 1657 and another against persons living extravagantly without visible means of support; these measures reflect both security considerations and puritan disapproval of voluntary idleness.[41] But they were not grossly out of line with other Tudor and Stuart measures, by no means exceeding the so-called Settlement Act of 1662 in the severity of their implications.

More interesting is the question of local initiative during the 1650s. Besides Mr Beier's work on Warwickshire, evidence from Kent points strongly the same way,[42] while in other counties already cited for the 1640s there was no apparent slackening. For parts of the decade there is additional evidence relating to Norfolk, Northamptonshire, and Surrey.[43] Maimed ex-soldiers and soldiers' widows and orphans continued to feature prominently. Earlier measures, or aspects of policy which were closely related to the Poor Law even if they arose from separate statutes, were also enforced. Such were the 1589 laws that no cottage should be

built with less than four acres of land attached to it, the provisions for
compulsory apprenticeship of bastard and other pauper children, and
attempts to check profiteering in times of scarcity by licensing middlemen—especially in the corn trade. The enforcement of the main apprenticeship clause of the famous 1563 Statute of Artificers takes us away
from the problem of poverty as such. Here, as with cottages, vagrants,
bastards, badgers and higlers,[44] houses of correction, etc., the preoccupations of the justices varied considerably from county to county, possibly
more than they did within the same counties from year to year, or even
from one decade to the next. But in most of these matters their work
seems to have gone on during the 1650s much as it had in the 1620s and
30s, and as it continued to do in the 1660s and 70s. Attempts to control
prices (especially of grain) had earlier been re-inforced by emergency
orders from the royal Privy Council and such orders are less evident
after the early 1630s. None the less, here too regulation continued, at
least in some counties.[45] Attempts to control wages undoubtedly continued. Examples survive from both ends of the country, for Wiltshire,
York and the North Riding, and a large list could certainly be compiled.
As with earlier wage assessments, it is not always easy to be sure whether
the justices were more concerned with fixing maximum or minimum
rates, and some increases on earlier levels do appear in the 1650s.[46] But
as with the enforcement of apprenticeship the impression of continuity—
of interest, if not of identical policies—is very strong.[47] The proper upkeep of highway-roads and bridges was another continuing preoccupation, again with regional variations. If there had been some inevitable
slackening during the 1640s, this would seem to have been fully made
good during the 1650s.

In some counties the justices were particularly concerned with the
way in which local government taxation should be raised. There was no
statute prescribing exactly how the rates for poor relief, road repairs,
etc., should be assessed and levied. But the general consensus moved
towards the modern system of a pound rate rather than levying so much
on each district. In Hertfordshire, the JPs were particularly strong on
this, insisting that those with large personal holdings, i.e. in stock, goods
or cash, must be rated on these 'visible estates' just as others were on
their landed estates. In 1653 one parish was ordered to abandon an 'acre
rate' which it had instituted. It is not always clear whether the rating
assessments refer to local taxation or to the Assessment—the monthly
tax which maintained the army. The parliamentary Assessment was
managed by a separate Committee for each county, whose members
normally included some who were also on the Commission of the Peace.
The militia too, since the collapse of the royal system of Lords and
Deputy Lieutenants, was in the hands of county committees for most of
the time from 1649 to 1660. Indeed, the names of the Assessment and

Militia Committees, together with those of the JPs, are the best way of identifying the leading local administrators during the republic. The exception to this is 1655–6, when in collaboration with special Commissioners for securing the peace of the counties the Major-Generals had charge of a newly constituted militia, paid for by the penal 'Decimation Tax' on royalist landowners.

The original commission to the Major-Generals, in August 1655 stressed the security aspects of their work and did not imply general supervision of local government. This was spelt out more fully in the successive revisions to the instructions of September and October.[48] If there is any point during either Commonwealth or Protectorate when the policies and preoccupations of the central government ought to show up in local records, it is under the Major-Generals.

Here, as in so much else, we are at the mercy of available evidence. For instance, the Major-Generals who corresponded most regularly and fully with Secretary Thurloe were not always operating in counties for which we have Quarter Sessions and other records, at least in usable printed editions. This is true of Whalley, except in the case of Warwickshire, his other counties being Derby, Leicester, Lincoln and Nottingham; of Berry who acted in North Wales, Shropshire, Worcestershire and Herefordshire; of Disbrowe in the six south-western counties, other than Somerset; and of Goffe in Berkshire, Hampshire and Sussex. It is clear, however, that their Commission and Instructions alone were not felt by all of them to be a sufficient authorisation to participate in the Sessions and the other work of the justices. They must be added to the Commission of the Peace for their respective counties, so Whalley told Thurloe.[49] Once this had been achieved, what do the local sources tell us about their impact—that is, outside the specific areas of security, militia and decimation? The abolition of cruel sports and the banning of race meetings—the latter as probable Cavalier gatherings—have become notorious, although despite Macaulay's famous gibe the former seems laudable enough.[50]

A better test case is afforded by the question of drink and alehouses. No one today supposes that the Puritans of Cromwellian England were like nineteenth-century temperance reformers or contemporary 'teetotallers'. Still, some Puritan writers and preachers were particularly strong in their condemnation of excessive drinking, especially arising out of social or pseudo-religious festivities. All later sixteenth- and seventeenth-century governments tried to limit the number of alehouses by licensing them, to control both their numbers and the conditions under which they might operate, to distinguish sharply between alehouses and either inns or taverns, and to proceed against alehouse-keepers who allowed disorder or other improper behaviour on their premises. The question is whether during the rule of the Major-Generals this was done with more vigour, system and effect than at other times. The principle of closing alehouses which were considered superfluous was not new. Nor was it new to regard them as potential centres of subversion, especially if people spent time drinking in them on Sundays when they should have been at church or, after church, engaged in some traditional outdoor sport. Dicing, cards and other games that lent themselves to gambling were particularly suspect. That there was a class element in this, when one thinks of the gambling and drinking at the court of James I, or of what went on in the Whitehall of Charles II, seems undeniable. The point here is the extent of action from the centre.

The Major-General who lays most stress on this aspect of his work, in his reports to Thurloe, is Charles Worsley, who was in charge of Lancashire, Cheshire and Staffordshire. He boasted of having closed 200 alehouses in the hundred of Blackburn (a large area, though poor and remote).[51] Yet just as the principle of sharing the burden of poor relief beyond the districts worst affected was still being effectively applied in Lancashire under the Commonwealth and Protectorate,[52] so the criteria for limiting numbers of alehouses[53] can be traced back at least to the 1580s:[54]

These things shalbe cheflie considered the abilitie and conversacion
of the person, the number of alehouses, that none or ells as fewe
as maye be shalbe allowed to kepe aelehouse in houses which
stande upon or nere mores or places farre distant from hye waies
to markett towenes or churches.

It may have been more of a novelty to impose this ruling, against alehouses off main roads and away from towns, in some counties than in others; likewise the practice of taking recognisances (bonds) for good behaviour when licenses were granted. In Norfolk this system would, if generally enforced, have made it impossible for any poor person to have kept an alehouse at all, for a licensee had to enter a recognisance for £40 and to have two sureties at £20 each who were in turn worth £10 per annum in land or had a personal estate of £200 (the equivalent of the parliamentary franchise, 1654–7).[55] Norfolk and Hertfordshire are two counties where the issuing of general orders about licensing can be related to the presence at the Sessions in question of the two deputy Major-Generals concerned. Both sets of orders insist that the prospective licensee must be 'well affected to the present government' as well as being 'of an honest life'. In Hertfordshire, every alehouse, like a modern public house was to have a sign over its door, while no bailiff or bailiff's under-officer was to be licensed to keep one. The Norfolk orders are more detailed about the means of procuring and issuing licences and also direct that, since there are too many, the total number should be reduced. Both share the desire to limit alehouses to main roads and the neighbourhood of sizeable towns: this suspicion of drinking in remote rural districts is odd, but, as we have seen from Lancashire, not new.[56] Presumably it is explained partly by a fear of robbers and highwaymen or potential conspirators frequenting remote places, or by the unspoken assumption that only bona fide travellers and visitors to market centres should be able to refresh themselves by the wayside.

In turning to assess their achievement we must remember that the rule of the Major-Generals was only in full operation for eleven months (October 1655 to September 1656 inclusive), although in theory their commissions were in force from August 1655 to the beginning of 1657. Apart from the blitzkrieg tactics of Charles Worsley,[57] who died of illness allegedly brought on by exhaustion in the summer following his winter campaign, one would not expect great or lasting results from so short a term of office.

As far as the available evidence enables one to generalise, the effects of republican rule were less marked in matters of policy than in those of personnel. It was the fact of the Major-Generals and the special Commissioners, more than of what they did, which became a folk-memory— an English upper-class bogey comparable to the Münster commune of 1533–5 or that of Paris in 1871. Often it was their social origins, like those of some justices put into the commission of the peace in the 1640s and 50s and of other local officials in these years, which aroused most hostility. Not that sequestration would necessarily have been any pleasanter even if it was carried out by a member of the victim's own social class. Or might it have been? Perhaps more consideration was shown, more evasion allowed in compounding and so on, when the traditional rulers remained in control. Correspondingly, the more strongly royalist that a county had been in the Civil War, the bigger the change of men in its government when Parliament's forces gained the day there; up to a point, too, the more presbyterian a county had been the bigger the change after 1648–9. And what holds for the counties seems, broadly speaking, to be true for cities and towns also.

The governing bodies of towns shared some of the same concerns as the county magistrates. The prevention and punishment of crime, poor relief in its varied aspects, wage assessments and regulation, licensing and control of alehouses were all urban as well as rural problems. Again, setting aside the relaxation of central control from the collapse of the Privy Council in 1641 to the institution of the Major-Generals in 1655, remarkably little seems to have changed under the Long Parliament and then the Republic. As in the counties, there was direct dislocation due to the war followed by post-war re-adjustment, both being of varying consequence in different regions. The items of business which appear in published town records for the first time in these years include complaints against the assessment and the excise and against free quarter taken by units of the army, enforcement of the law on the Engagement and measures against politically subversive 'words', enforcement of the Blasphemy Act, and implementation of orders for the better maintenance of ministers. But even some of these have earlier and later parallels in (e.g.) the Tudor and later Stuart Treason Laws, measures against recusants, conventiclers and Nonconformists, support for municipal lectureships (salaried preaching posts), and the billeting of soldiers—in the south of England 1626-9, in the north 1639-40.

The most distinctive aspect of town governments was perhaps their concern to preserve economic exclusiveness. This could take the form of jealously guarding acquisition of the freedom of the municipality, which could in turn have political implications in so far as freemen of a town were often both its parliamentary and its local government electors. In other instances the main issue was the right to practise certain trades and crafts, and control over entry to these by strict enforcement of the apprenticeship laws. Evidence of this can be found from Bedford, Dorchester, Leicester, Newcastle, Rye, Salisbury, Weymouth and York—a fair geographical spread, how representative of towns in general it is hard to know.[58] The supply of seamen for the navy was not yet in the hands of the 'press-gangs', and responsibility for pressing a specified number of mariners, or other fit men, for sea-service was often put on to the local authorities in the seaports. This and the free-quartering of troops may well have been among the acutest causes of resentment peculiar to townsmen. But the sharpest expression of feelings, although it came from a seaport, arose from the army's alleged infraction of the laws on apprenticeship and the practice of crafts and trades. In November 1657 the Mayor and Jurats of Rye appealed for help to their own MPs and to Colonel Morley, who sat for the nearby borough of Lewes. They said that they had allowed all ex-soldiers who had been born or raised there to set up in their respective trades and callings in the town (whether or not they had served a full apprenticeship), had extended this privilege to ex-soldiers married to Rye women, and had also permitted ex-soldiers and others (not comprehended in these two categories) to remain in employment as journeymen there. Those not included under these three headings had received notice to desist from practising their trades and callings, and to depart from the town. On their refusal to comply, the Mayor and Jurats had called upon the constables to execute these orders. This in turn had been opposed by an army captain, who (egged on by another captain) had rescued one of those arrested on the pretext that the man was enlisted in his unit. This turned out to be bogus, as the captain later admitted; the only one whom he had promised the other captain that he would enlist under him was not the man rescued but a notorious ill-doer and one 'greatly prejudiciall to the poore trades- men of this Town'. As a result of which 'the course of justice is obstructed and the soldiers emboldened to despise and condemne all Government and ministers thereof'. They appealed both for economic aid, in the face of excess population and shortage of work, and for legal (or political?) redress as an 'opprest Corporation'.[59]

This may be contrasted with the firm but extremely courteous tone of the letter sent by a colonel to the corporation of Exeter in 1649 intimating that part of his regiment would have to be quartered there.[60] Certainly between 1649 and 1658 there is no evidence of widespread conflicts and collisions at the local level. Free quarter was very much the exception; it was avoided wherever possible, heavier taxation in one form or another being seen—correctly enough—as altogether preferable. In the 1640s and again in 1659–60 things were different; but even during the years of civil war and its aftermath, there are numerous indemnity cases to remind us that the military certainly could not ride roughshod over the rights of property or the normal procedures of law and local government. That is even if we suppose that more than a small criminal element and a few high-handed extremists in the army had ever wished to do so.

As for the civil arm of republican rule, there was nothing new about friction between agents of the central government and local officials. The misadventures of certain Messengers of the Chamber under Charles I, and the troubles of the Council in the Marches of Wales provide ready instances from before 1642.[61] None of this is to deny that some of the State's servants under both the Commonwealth and the Protector did abuse their powers and their official positions—locally as at the centre. The charges which were later brought against William Boteler, Major-General in Bedfordshire, Huntingdon, Northants and Rutland, may or may not have been well-founded; the available calendar of records does not suggest any clue either way.[62] But one would not expect him, or William Packer (Fleetwood's deputy in Hertfordshire, Oxfordshire and jointly in Buckinghamshire), a militant republican and a strong Baptist lay-preacher, to have been exactly tender to royalists. On the other hand a man of relatively humble origins like the Herefordshire sequestrator Silas Taylor is praised by John Aubrey for the help which he afforded to compounding royalists in that county.[63] Studies of particular areas show the contrasting elements of individual favour and hostility which were inherent in the system of penal composition.[64] To say this is not to imply that everything depended upon the quirks of individuals.

By contrast, how did the localities look, viewed from the centre? The correspondence of the Major-Generals and the special security Commissioners in 1655–6 makes clear what some of the regime's own committed supporters thought of the local officials in its service. Robert Lilburne and his Yorkshire colleagues complained bitterly against ex-cavaliers who misused their positions as lawyers and in local offices to take revenge on honest men—that is, on government supporters.[65] While on the Welsh Marches, James Berry complained of the sheer inadequacy of such local petty functionaries, when he wrote to Thurloe:[66]

> I beseech you be carefull in disposeing powers and places, to put them into good hands, or you undoe us. We have such a pittiful company of officers in state affaires that it is a shame to see it, excisemen, treasurers, clerk [sic] of the peace, pronotaries, stewards, bayliefes and captaines, and broad — — — ministers. I am filled with complaints of them, and when I can have while to serch them out, shall trouble you with an account of them. In the meane time all I beg is, you would be carefull what new ones you make.

It is absolutely right to stress the importance of the local community in seventeenth-century England more than was done by S. R. Gardiner and C. H. Firth writing in the later nineteenth and early twentieth centuries. Yet it would be an extraordinary new kind of historical sentimentalism if this emphasis led us to suppose that justice, honesty, enlightenment and good sense were invariably to be found at the local end among the governors of counties and towns, and never at the centre in the national government and administration when the two were in conflict.[67]

V ADMINISTRATION AND SOCIAL STRUCTURE

Local government and justice may well have affected more people's lives to a greater extent than anything arising from central government and administration. But in so far as some of the policies which were enforced locally arose from decisions taken at the national level, the distinction is an artificial one. This is obviously true of taxation and conscription, of the Major-Generals' rule and of some puritan cultural policies—the bans on stage-plays and cruel sports, for example. But the influence of government on society is by no means limited to the direct effects of its administration.

The 1640s and early 50s saw a ferment of ideas about education. There were many different would-be reformers, ranging from critics of the universities to protagonists of new methods in primary and even infant teaching. In some regions, notably in Wales and the far north of England, there is evidence of constructive work initiated centrally, at the school level,[1] which can be related to the Maintenance Trustees' work in augmenting teachers' stipends. In higher education there was the abortive Cromwellian scheme for a University of Durham.[2] The effect on Oxford and Cambridge of puritan-republican rule is a matter of continuing controversy,[3] but there was certainly a brisk interchange of personnel between Whitehall and the universities in these years. Since education depended largely on private endowment and charitable giving, conflicting views about English philanthropy in this period are also relevant. According to the leading authority, Professor W. K. Jordan, there was a marked decline in philanthropic giving during the Interregnum, and this continued after 1660. This would fit in with the orthodox view that the amount of money raised in local taxation rose steeply in the course of the seventeenth century and was vastly greater by 1700 than it had been before 1640.[4]

The extent of social mobility in English society during the seventeenth century is also in debate. Professor Lawrence Stone's thesis of an upward thrust—demographic, educational, social and cultural in its origins—culminating in civil war, and followed by marked decline in this upward pressure as well as by an actual reduction in educational facilities after 1660, might in turn be related to Dr Christopher Hill's thesis of a revolution which turned in a conservative direction after 1647–49–53 and thus began to head for restoration of the old order. On this view the administrators of the Cromwellian Protectorate in particular would be those who consciously or unconsciously decelerated, even retarded, social change, and prevented English society from transforming itself as fast as it would otherwise have done. In so far as the Protectorate was in some respects less radical than the Commonwealth, there is—in very general terms—something to it. But as with so many other ambitious historical interpretations, it is often difficult to relate precisely to the evidence. Sometimes the same sources may equally well be used to support other, quite contrary hypotheses. The lack of reliable evidence, especially of a quantitative kind, leaves all too much room for hypothesis and interpretation. Yet we should not run away from the evidence which is there. Compared with the system of office-holding under Charles I, that of 1649–60 was less traditional. And as we have seen, the administration itself provided an avenue for social advancement to more people of lower social standing than had been true before. Whether the mobility achieved through office during the 1640s and 50s should be seen as a consequence of other social and economic changes, or as itself a cause of social change, is likely to remain a point of disagreement. On the view put forward here, more weight has been given to the second of these hypotheses: namely that political necessity and administrative innovation contributed to social change, rather than that social and economic revolution brought about consequential changes at the political and administrative levels.

vi GOVERNMENT AND SOCIETY: FISCAL AND ECONOMIC RELATIONS

One crude but effective way of measuring the impact of government on society is by its cost. To make any sense this has to be relative to national income or to the measurement now preferred by economists, gross national product; but here our ignorance is crippling. It is far easier to begin from the government side, starting with the tax burden proper, and to move from that—however tentatively—towards some estimate of government as an economic 'cost' to society.[1]

For taxation under the Protectorate we are well served.[2] If we move back to the Long Parliament and the Commonwealth it becomes more difficult; and as we extend taxation to cover sequestration and land sales as well as compounding and the advance of money, the problem becomes more complicated still. Composition fines and the rents and profits accruing from sequestrated estates clearly belong to the government's income. By the same reasoning they represent, albeit in a special penal form, part of the fiscal burden of government on society. The same can hardly be said of the sale of capital assets, whether for ready cash or in settlement of existing debts. Some of these debts had originated as loans to the Long Parliament and were met out of episcopal and capitular lands, fee-farm rents, royalists' lands forfeited for treason and confiscated Irish lands. Others constituted the army's pay arrears and were settled out of Crown estates and Irish lands. The money raised in ready cash from the forfeited estates, as opposed to Crown and Church lands, is more difficult to categorise; it was hardly part of the government's own capital assets of which they were disposing in order to meet their current needs. However, since only a trifling amount (some £15,000) is at issue, this does not matter very much.[3] It is almost impossible to divide out the money raised by penal taxation on a year-by-year basis except by crude averaging. Over the whole period 1643–55 it yielded, in fines, rents, and the rest, something like £1,834,170.[4] This excludes the money 'advanced' between 1643 and 1652 (in effect, up to 1647) on the fifth and twentieth, for which no account appears to have survived.[5] This would bring it up to around the £2 million mark; the Decimation Tax of 1655–6, for which again we have no complete accounts, might be added in here as a minor part of the penal tax burden. In attempting any calculations, there are three different types of source available to us, each with its own problems and limitations:

1 Various contemporary estimates and statements about the public revenues, some printed in the *Commons Journals*, others still in MS. As one would expect, these are usually in the form of current balance sheets, or estimates for the following year.[6]

2 The accounts rendered in the Exchequer (or to the Accounts Committee) by the treasurers and receivers, for these various funds and sources of revenue. These were sometimes audited and passed quite quickly after the year (or other accounting period) to which they related; others post-date the Restoration, and represent more a calling to account of republican officials than revenue statements;[7] moreover some of them, too, cover periods of more than a single year.[8]

3　From 1654 on, for all branches of revenue other than the Assessment, that is for those which notionally passed through the Lower Exchequer of Receipt, there are in addition the Receipt Books and Declaration Books and other series kept there.[9] Mr Ashley used these to work out his totals of net annual revenue for 1654–8 inclusive;[10] from this it appears that the annual average for these five years was just under £1½ million.[11] He calculated the total yield of sales and compositions at just over £6 million and that of the three main branches of revenue (Assessment, Customs and Excise) at an average of £1·8 million yearly under the Commonwealth. In the first Protectorate Parliament a government spokesman reckoned the total annual revenues at £2¼ million, but this was optimistic.

But our concern here is not quite the same as Mr Ashley's was. For his study of public finance, the net amount of money available to the Cromwellian government was crucial, particularly in order to demonstrate the short-fall between this and its expenditure in relation to the public debt. For our purpose, however, it is the gross tax burden which is significant, and the problem is rather to decide what is a tax and what is not.

As anyone who has worked on seventeenth-century accounts and similar records will realise, each of these categories of document presents its own difficulties of interpretation. In arriving at the figures which are given below (Table 44), I have tried to eliminate items of revenue which are duplicated on different accounts, either through having been transferred—for accounting purposes—from one fund or treasury to another, or through having been carried over from the roll or book used for one accounting-year (or other time-span) to another. In the knotty instance of land sales, I have ventured to depart at one or two points from the illuminating figures given in Mr Habakkuk's article. I have taken the items charged against the various accountants on the Receipts side, under the heading 'Rent and Profits', as a part of government income, or of what the State was taking out of society. As will be seen, when it is averaged out over thirteen years, this makes very little difference to my totals. The big problem is how, for our present purposes, to treat the liquidation of earlier debts and the settlement of the army's pay arrears. In trying to measure the gross fiscal burden, it has seemed on balance more realistic to exclude these, as well as the money raised by the sale of capital assets. Even so, the mysteries of seventeenth-century accounting, together with the complete disappearance of some accounts, leave us with an unavoidably wide margin of error. Subject to all these provisos, my estimates are as shown in Table 44.

What did these totals mean in terms of their contemporary impact? At its maximum (£120,000 a month) the Assessment was running at the rate of something like eighteen pre-war parliamentary subsidies a year!

TABLE 44 *Gross fiscal burden, 1650s*

Assessment	1647–60 = £11,205,545, av. £861,965 p.a.[12]
	or 1652–60 = £6,676,583, av. £834,573 p.a.
Customs	1652–7 = £1,809,049, av. £361,807 p.a.[13]
Excise	1650–8 = £2,765,171, av. £395,024 p.a.[14]
Minor revenues	(prize goods, which are easily the largest in 1653–4 and 1656–7, being excluded)
	1652–9 = £204,453, av. £29,208 p.a.[15]

Advance $\frac{1}{5}$ and $\frac{1}{20}$: no totals before 1652, but little yielded after 1648[16]

Composition and sequestered rents

1643–55 = £1,834,170, av. £152,847 p.a.[17]

Land sales (and sales of the King's goods, pictures, etc.)

in cash = £1,946,555*
doubled = £1,959,585[18]

Rents and profits from Crown, Church and Royalists' lands

= £87,330 from 1646–7 to 1659–60
= £6,718 annual average

Annual average total revenue, excluding capital transactions (Land sales, above)

= *c.* £1·7 million p.a. 1649–54
falling to   *c.* £1·55 million p.a. 1655–9

* Of this figure, however, £1,338,947 represented payments to the army for arrears and demobilisation, leaving only £607,608 as the genuine income in cash from sales, rents, profits, etc.

Even at its eventual minimum (of £35,000 a month) it was equivalent to over five such subsidies. In Bedfordshire the total burden of Ship Money (1634–40) was £9,960; during the years 1642–52, a total of £122,973 is reckoned to have been extracted from this (strongly parliamentarian) county;[19] an average of £11,179 per annum. Across the country in Staffordshire, records preserved for the small township of Hatherton show a striking contrast within the decade of republican rule. From 1650 to 1659 inclusive the total raised there for internal town uses was £59; the comparable figure for taxation by the state, and other compulsory external expenditure, was about £267. No wonder that there is evidence from the same area of complaints against the excessive weight of the assessment and other levies and against the mis-rating both of districts and individuals for these taxes;[20] while at an individual level the astrologer and almanack-writer William Lilly tells us that he paid 22s. [query a year] Ship Money, but in the 1650s was paying about £20 [a year] on no bigger an estate.[21] There can be no doubt that even under the Protectorate the tax burden was heavier than it had been under the monarchy, or than it was to be again—wartime votes of supply apart—until after the Revolution of 1688.

For the 1690s Professor Charles Wilson has published figures from Gregory King's writings, to show the comparative weight of taxation in England, France and the Netherlands. The same objections apply here as in trying to work back by interpolation from King's other tables in order to arrive at estimates for the mid-century. It is, however, relevant that even after all the tax increases of the period (especially those actually introduced during the 1690s), King still reckoned the Dutch to be paying two-and-a-half times as much per head in taxes as the English (£3. 2s. 7d. to £1. 4s. 0d. a year). On the other hand the English and the French he believed were then paying almost the same (£1. 4s. 0d. and £1. 5s. 0d. p.a.), which is very different from the estimated position before 1640 according to the American economic historian, Professor J. U. Nef, who calculated that the French were then paying vastly more. The Interregnum may therefore have contributed towards this comparative as well as absolute increase in the level: whether for better or worse in relation to the national economy or the general well-being is of course quite another matter. High taxation in the seventeenth century was far from signifying the same as it does today, having little in common besides the prominence of military budgets.[22]

We also need to estimate how much was taken by officials and other government servants, such as contractors, over and above the amount levied in taxes. For 1625–42 it was suggested that the cost to the subject from fees and gratuities was equivalent to at least 40 per cent and perhaps nearer two-thirds of Charles I's apparent revenue.[23] How far are the reduction of venality, the restrictions on fee-taking and the disapproval of gratuities likely to have lowered the comparable cost in the years 1649–60? In making detailed comparisons with the years before the Civil War, there is further difficulty. As has been shown in chapter 2, the institutions of government were by no means the same, so we are not able to compare like with like. To recapitulate briefly, the following had gone: the royal household (until the appearance of a protectoral household in 1654), Star Chamber, the High Commissions of Canterbury and York, the Councils of Wales and the North, the Duchy of Lancaster Court (until 1654), the Stannaries, the Court of Wards and Liveries (from 1646), and most of the church courts. The constant elements remaining were: Chancery and the Great Seal, the three Common Law Courts (including Exchequer), the Upper Exchequer of Audit (from 1649), the Lower Exchequer of Receipt (from 1654), the Mint, Navy and Ordnance, and the Signet and Privy Seal Offices (from 1655). The new ones were first and foremost the army, a mass of varied committees, commissions and separate treasuries, and last but not least (until 1653) a standing Parliament. Measured by visible cost the Protector's Household was much more expensive than the Rump Commons. In terms of real costs, including fees, gratuities and other perquisites and favours transferred from society at large to MPs and others, the reverse may well have been true.

What more can be said about invisible costs in estimating the total burden of republican government on society at large? Some under-officers of committees (from secretaries and clerks down to doorkeepers and messengers) no doubt had to be tipped, if the customer wanted satisfaction.[24] But it is hard to believe that anything like as much money changed hands annually in fees, gratuities, presents and bribes as had done before 1640–2. This is not something which can be neatly demonstrated with facts and figures. It remains a strong impression from having studied both the official records and a wide range of other source materials for 1625–42 and for 1649–60. On the other hand, the total salary bill for the government's servants was certainly up—even if we exclude the armed forces of the State. Except in the law courts, the tendency towards higher stipendiary fees was almost universal. Hence there was a shift in the form which the burden took, apart from its weight. That a lot of people were paying heavier taxes is beyond dispute. The Assessment was at least as effective a tax on landed and non-landed wealth as Ship Money, and, as we have seen, much heavier; the Excise affected many people considerably more than the Customs duties can have done, falling as it did on beer, ale, and cider, as well as imported wines and 'strong waters' (spirits); likewise on salt, soap, butter, cloth (until 1654) and leather. Among basic commodities only grain, meat (after 1647) and timber were exempt. By contrast with the wider incidence of taxation, a narrower range of people, largely consisting of officials and of those who had business to do with the government, paid less in fees and gratuities. If we try to calculate an annual average for the republic, even omitting land sales, the tax burden considerably exceeds the annual revenue of Charles I (whether for 1636–9 or for 1631–5) and the estimated amount changing hands annually in fees and gratuities at that time added together. Even if my earlier estimate for the pre-Civil War fee-cum-gratuity burden was too low,[25] the 1649–60 tax level is still likely to be at least equal to this and the total from taxation combined. Are we simply to say, then, that the burden of the central government on society, of the 'Court' upon the 'Country' in Professor Trevor-Roper's use of these terms, had grown heavier? The facts seem undeniable. Yet it would be misleading to leave it at that. The 'Court', if this be the right word for it, the 'establishment' or 'the thing'—the name preferred by Cobbett and Mr A. J. P. Taylor—was very differently composed from its pre-Civil War equivalent. The establishment of both Commonwealth and Crom-wellian England was essentially puritan and military, largely non-aristocratic, and less predominantly of gentry social background. It was not, even in 1657–9, 'courtly' in the sense understood by most people, and as was so before 1640–2 or after 1660. Certainly until 1654 'Court' does seem a misnomer; after that it makes more sense, and in 1656–9 the word was used by contemporaries.

Can we compare the economic significance of office, and the wealth changing hands via the administrative system, in 1649–60 and in 1625–42? This is where middle-aged caution comes in; it no longer seems to me sensible to interpolate back from Gregory King's national income figures for the 1690s, in order to arrive at a hypothetical national income for the 1650s, and then to measure the wealth involved in office as a percentage of this. But I believe that the amount of money transferred through office had grown faster than national income (or gross national product, if we had the means to estimate it), between the 1630s and the 1650s. This is if we include military and naval personnel in both decades; if it were limited to civilians in and connected with the central government, the 1650s total would be much lower and it would also be smaller as a percentage of national income. Moreover, in the republican decade office acted as an agent of distributive justice to a limited extent. Taxation was not progressive, despite at least one demand that it should be. But whereas before the Civil War the existing upper classes had been the greatest beneficiaries, and the wealth transferred via office had been the more significant the higher people were in the social scale, after 1642 and particularly from the later 1640s to 1653 this was not so. If we include compounding and advance (but not confiscation and land sales) in our totals, much of the wealth so transferred was being taken away from the aristocracy and gentry and even from some of the financial-mercantile élite, and was being distributed among slightly wider sections of the population. Particularly in the army, but to a lesser extent in the navy and in civil administration, many men of middling and lesser gentry background and others of non-gentle plebeian origins were being paid salaries which were equivalent to considerable incomes by mid-seventeenth-century standards. Even the horse troopers and common foot soldiers were relatively well-paid, despite their arrears which intermittently caused trouble, compared to what they—or their social equals—would have been earning in civilian life.

If the republican establishment had an inner core, it was in the army and the Congregational churches. Many of the administrators with whom we have been concerned in the earlier chapters of this book were attached to this establishment, or served as its auxiliaries; at the same time they were subject to the socially redistributive effects of office. Alternatively, the army and the churches can be compared, by analogy and not at all exactly, to the ruling party in a modern one-party state. And in this respect it is pertinent to ask whether England was witnessing the emergence of an equivalent to what Milovan Djilas has called 'The New Class'. The answer must involve a large element of speculation, for the Restoration and its social consequences clearly put paid to the possibility.

It also raises other related issues about the social character and implications of the Commonwealth and Protectorate.[26] We have already considered how far republican influences persisted after 1660 in terms of institutions, methods of administration and the individuals employed, and we shall return to this in the concluding chapter. Here it need only be said that until 1660 the wealth being transferred through government would seem to have been both quantitatively and qualitatively more important than before 1640–2. But the possible long-term consequences of this remain a matter of conjecture, rather than of historical interpretation and understanding.

CHAPTER 6

CONCLUSION

Frequent references have been made in the preceding chapters to attempts at administrative reform and to demands, mainly from outside the government, for more far-reaching changes. These were not new themes, or in any way an invention of the republicans of these years. The need for such reform had been a frequent, not to say constant topic of complaint under the monarchy. There had been several attempts to control the taking of fees (and gratuities): near the end of Elizabeth's reign, twice in James's reign (1610–12 and 1623–4) and almost continuously under Charles I (from 1627 to 1640).[1] There is a marked similarity between some of the criticisms voiced in the 1621 Parliament, and made manifest on the 1627 royal commission, and some of the attempts at reform during the Interregnum. There is even a parallel between Wentworth's call for higher salaries and for greater probity amongst officials whilst exploiting his own position in the king's service to his personal advantage, and the later role of some who had helped hound him to his death, such as Sir Arthur Hesilrige and the younger Sir Henry Vane. The preoccupation of would-be reformers with a rather narrow range of problems, such as fees and procedure in Chancery and certain other courts, to the neglect of more fundamental structural changes, can again be paralleled. A proper understanding of a public service, based on qualifications for office, competitive entry and promotion, and entailing greater security of tenure together with retirement pensions, and remuneration by salaries alone, was still largely lacking. Some of the radical pamphleteers of the 1640s and 50s can be seen groping their way towards it.

How can we relate achievement to aspiration? Apart from wartime and post-war improvisations, the major changes in the institutional structure of central government were almost wholly negative or else provisional in character. Even the Compounding and Indemnity Committees and Commissions, or the Treasurers-at-War and Receivers-General of the assessment, with their respective staffs, can be regarded as *ad hoc* and temporary; only the Maintenance Trustees have a less makeshift air about them. Most of the changes intended to be lasting were of a more negative character: the abolition of prerogative courts and conciliar

326

government (1641), of the Court of Wards and Liveries (1646), of the royal household and all its branches, except the Office of Works and the Standing Wardrobes (in 1649). By contrast the restoration of the Duchy of Lancaster and the Exchequer, and of the Privy Seal and Signet Offices (1654–5) marked the end of the post-war period of improvisation. The virtual cessation of advance, compounding, sequestration, indemnity, land sales and obstructions (1653–5) was part of the same process. With the restored Commonwealth of 1659 there was a brief and partial return to the administrative machinery of 1643–53. But political events moved much too fast for anything like a firm or clear pattern to have emerged.

There is no evidence that John Pym (back in 1642–3) or his successors had ever intended to introduce permanent changes of a revolutionary character. If we examine the most radical of the Long Parliament's innovations: the excise, the weekly pay (later the monthly assessment), penal taxation, the Committee of Both Kingdoms—all have the characteristic stamp of pragmatism, of meeting a pressing need in a practical way, not of belonging to a comprehensive long-term blueprint for a new government. And, despite the different political forms of a Commonwealth, the same was true under the Rump. On the ecclesiastical side, by contrast, after the abolition of the episcopal hierarchy, the substitution of an erastian but unmistakably presbyterian church system was meant by some contemporaries to form part of an enduring new order.

In the terms and conditions of administrative service, considerable changes were undertaken, and much was achieved. More still was attempted; even so these changes were not nearly enough for the regime's radical critics. Some of the pamphleteers and others saw parliamentarian and then republican administration as signifying little more than the replacement of one domineering, exploiting 'establishment', or 'spoils-system' by another. Some of these critics, while denying the charge of anarchism brought against them, seem to have favoured dismantling the entire structure of central government, and having only local amateur personnel for administration, justice and finance. In the Levellers' case, this was a part of their general belief in a free Anglo-Saxon past, characterised—as they were persuaded—by a near-perfect local democracy. Others were more realistic, or should we say less hopeful, but wanted drastic pruning of all unnecessary and corrupt branches of central administration; they demanded a much simplified and reduced public service, on a strictly salaried basis, in some cases embodying election of officials and rotating tenure. The Leveller programme was particularly strong on the need for the complete separation of powers; the unenforced self-denying Ordinance of 1645 lay, like a ticking time-bomb, under the floor of the Long Parliament—as a perpetual reminder of the members' collective self-indulgence.

Whether the higher salaries, which were generally paid to officials in these years compared with those which were normal before 1640–2, induced or made it easier to enforce higher standards of administrative probity is more arguable. It has been suggested here that, by and large, this was so. Although corruption still existed, and some guilty men went unpunished, the conclusion seems inescapable that more was being done about it than had been under the monarchy.

In the personnel of central government too there was a massive change. The social composition of the office-holding body became strikingly less upper-class, and far more representative of the 'middling sort' (amongst whom we should include the parochial gentry and the urban 'pseudo-gentry').[2] This was true in the armed forces, in local government, in Parliament, as well as in the central administration. The sector least affected, alike as to men and measures, was the legal side of government: the common-law courts and (despite the 1655–8 changes) Chancery.

While the main responsibilities and activities of local government were little altered by the national upheavals of 1640–60, the impact of the central government and its policies upon the localities did change markedly. Taxation, the military presence, para-judicial machinery, and the ideological preoccupations of successive regimes were among the most obvious aspects of this. A large part of our difficulty here lies in trying to gauge how far the printed words—of newsbook editors, preachers and pamphleteers—may be regarded as representative of anything which we can meaningfully call 'public opinion'. Signs of psychological unbalance in some of the tract-writers should perhaps induce caution, unless their evidence can be corroborated from other sources; as is the case (e.g.) with the unpopularity of the excise and the extent of resistance to it. Royalist and Leveller propaganda too must be discounted as indicative of republican misrule, again unless independent documentation points the same way; this too is occasionally the case from the records of the committees and commissions themselves.

Whatever the reasons for its downfall, the English republic did not fail because of the inadequacy or incompetence of its officials. On the contrary, there were enough of sufficient ability, especially among the hundred who were selected for special study here, to have implemented more radical policies, if these had been called for by the political leadership, and then given consistent support.

The Commonwealth and the Protectorate can fairly be criticised as insufficiently radical, in that the whole period witnessed a failed or incompleted revolution.[3] This can be seen very clearly in the failure to implement wider and more sweeping measures of law reform. The harvest here was meagre indeed, measured against the effort expended. Cromwell's personal sincerity is not in doubt, but his effectiveness as a moderate reformer may well be questioned. Whether anyone else could or would have done better may, however, seem an idle question; it is arguable that only he could have sustained the English republic at all, even for the brief span which it did enjoy.

Historians will probably divide over the possibility of greater achievements in administrative reform according to their general interpretation of the period. Those who believe that from the defeat of the Levellers in 1647–9 there was an inevitable drift towards the Restoration in 1660 will be less concerned with aims of different groups and individuals between 1649 and 1659. This applies to administration as much as to the constitution. Those who see the Barebones Parliament as the high-watermark of puritan reforming zeal, and the return to the traditional order as a natural outcome of its failure and of Cromwell's subsequent disillusionment, may be a little more heedful of the possibilities open for various kinds of reform until December 1653, but are less likely to have as much interest in what happened, or might have happened, between then and May 1660.

It is perhaps more rewarding to measure achievement against aspiration, in relation to each of the main parties within the state and in the context of each successive regime.

If the conservative parliamentarians, or so-called presbyterians, who controlled Parliament in 1646–7 and again in 1648, had achieved a settlement with Charles I, presumably something like the constitutional arrangements of 1641 or 1660 would have taken effect. It is unlikely that much trace would then have remained of the Long Parliament's temporary administrative reforms: higher salaries, fewer fees and gratuities, fewer grants on life tenure, no reversions, less sinecurism. Or whether anything would have been left of its institutional and fiscal innovations: the excise, the assessment, government by committees. A pre-condition of any successful settlement along these lines would have been to get rid of the army, or at least to transfer it to Ireland; this would also have entailed the conciliation of ex-royalists and neutrals in the counties. In administrative terms such a settlement would have come nearer to the pre-war system than any arising out of other possible resolutions of the political deadlock. Yet, assuming the abolition of the Court of Wards to have been accepted by the King as permanent, the Crown would have lost a valuable source of patronage. The consequent loss of revenue from feudal dues might well have entailed continuing the excise, as it was indeed to do in 1660. Under the 1646 Newcastle Propositions there would have been a change of faces at the top, with parliamentary control over major appointments to be made on good-behaviour tenure, and, until the King's forced period of accepting a 'presbyterian' church had expired, some continuance of the ecclesiastical changes of 1641–5.

By contrast, let us suppose that Charles I had come to terms with the

army leaders and radical parliamentarians or Independents, on something like the terms of the 1647 Heads of Proposals. This would necessarily have been at the expense of the parliamentary 'presbyterian'
majority—and of the popular movement (the Levellers and their allies),
although not of all radical groups and policies. In constitutional terms,
if we beg the question of the King's sincerity, this settlement would have
resembled the Protectorate constitution of 1653–7. Such hypothetical
arrangements have also been compared, more loosely but not too fanci-
fully, with the monarch's position after the Glorious Revolution of 1688.
How far the administrative changes of 1642–6 would have continued in
operation might well have depended on other elements in the situation,
notably at whose expense such a settlement was effected and on what
basis of power it rested. Despite their pledge in the Heads of Proposals
(summer 1647) to replace the Excise, continuance of a modified version
of it and of a reduced Assessment (or of either one of them unreduced),
would have been essential while the army remained in being. And if a
positive mercantile policy, requiring a strong navy, had also been followed, this would have been all the more true. An end to penal taxation
of royalists and the cessation of land confiscations and sales, at least after
the disposal of the bishops' lands, would seem to have been a pre-
condition of any settlement with the King. But with a royalist-army
détente this might not necessarily have entailed the restoration of the old
order at the local level. In many ways Charles I would have done well,
as can be seen in retrospect, to have clinched agreement with the army on
the basis of something like the Heads of Proposals; despite the ferocious
opposition which they would have had to overcome, an alliance between
the King and Cromwell with Fairfax perhaps in some kind of titular role
as High Constable of England, might have provided the strongest
government of the century. But because of the predictable opposition
from ultra-royalists, high-episcopalians, presbyterians, and Levellers,
extraordinary powers would still have been needed. Further measures of
law reform within the existing legal system might well have been achieved,
once these had been dissociated in the minds of the King and his party
from radical social subversion. The tax-burden and the long-term future
of the army would probably have remained the most intractable issues,
unless sufficient trust had been re-established for Cromwell or Fairfax
to have anticipated the role of Monck in 1660–1. Even then, the innovations and reforms on the civil and fiscal sides of government would seem
unlikely to have completely disappeared.

To imagine a truly popular victory, for the army agitators and the
Levellers, either in 1647 or 1649, requires so many unreal assumptions
that its usefulness may well be questioned. But let us try to suspend dis-
belief for a moment. Revolutionaries who do not gain power tend to be
seen by posterity in a different light from those who do. No sudden

violent social revolution has yet established itself on a permanent basis without continued coercion, and it seems fair to suggest that if the Levellers had defeated the army leaders and then subjected King and Parliament to their will, they could not have avoided this. Such an outcome would in turn have resulted in the tougher and more ruthless among them coming out on top: Sexby and Wildman rather than Walwyn, perhaps Colonel Rainsborough and Cornet Thompson rather than Lilburne or even Overton.[4] Nor is it clear that they could have avoided repressing the even more radical social and economic aspirations of the propertyless, for whom Winstanley and the Diggers had potentially a far greater appeal. Amateur, unbureaucratic, decentralised government has seldom been the accompaniment, even less often the outcome, of successful popular revolution. What all this would have meant in administrative terms is even more speculative. By 1649 the Levellers' programme included the separation of powers, rotation in office, abolition of the excise, salaries instead of fees, further measures of law reform and other social ameliorations, the dismantling of a coercive state church, and an end to municipal exclusiveness and corporate monopolies. Generally it implied more decentralisation and weaker government than the Independents wanted. That this kind of policy would have proved compatible with a popular-cum-military dictatorship, seems—to say the least—highly unlikely. Penal taxation, forced land sales, heavy direct taxation on property would not easily have been avoided. Whether such a regime could have maintained itself without using the methods of terror and repression may be doubted, but this need not be argued here. More relevant is the question whether the decentralising policies to which the Levellers were committed would have proved practicable, and what administrative results these would have had.

It is altogether easier to imagine a more lasting settlement being achieved by the Rump of the Long Parliament at some stage between 1649 and 1653. It was likeliest, on the surface at least, after the defeat of the Commonwealth's internal and external enemies, from the autumn of 1651. Presumably it would have involved moderate or limited reform. Considering the Commonwealth's achievements and the means at its disposal, its failure seems the more poignant, and perhaps the more squalid. Here we have a government which toyed with numerous potentially far-reaching schemes but always within the limits of its own indefinite continuance in power. These reforms included the election and composition of future parliaments, aspects of the law, the church and the fiscal system, the control exercised by England over Scotland and Ireland, and external colonial and mercantile policies. Further administrative reforms, in the general direction of a fully salaried civil service, based on reasonable security of tenure and with offices no longer regarded as pieces of private property, were not merely a necessary adjunct to such a settlement, arguably they were within striking distance of achievement.

What went wrong? First, the Rump was operating within the limitations of an existing system. Thus, it was an open question whether, even if they wished, they could conciliate their erstwhile enemies the royalists and the presbyterians (the moderate parliamentarians of 1646–8) sufficiently to be able to restore normal conditions of law and government. And above all, whether they could do this and at the same time avoid a frontal collision with their own ostensible servants but perhaps in reality their masters—the army. The heavy naval expenditure required for the Dutch War (1652–3) was an added complication, although not perhaps an insuperable obstacle. But the contradiction between the trend of policy symbolised by the Act of General Pardon and Oblivion (of February 1652), and such features of their rule as the Engagement, penal taxation, land confiscations and forced sales, rule by committee and para-legal indemnity for their own servants and supporters, were deep and ultimately insoluble. Paradoxically, Cromwell himself was strongly for the Pardon and Oblivion policy and for the conciliation of as many people as possible outside the narrow republican fold; yet it was precisely the expense of the armed forces and the extraordinary position of the army as a kind of extra 'estate of the realm' which made that goal so desperately difficult to attain. It may therefore seem otiose to suggest that the Rump also failed because of the individual and collective failings of its members; but it would be unhistorical to omit this aspect of the case. Above all, apart from pressure from the army itself which sharpened in the autumn of 1651 and then mounted to a climax between August 1652 and April 1653, the rulers of the Commonwealth were not answerable to anyone. The Rump's combined use of legislative, executive and judicial power seems to have had the predictable effect of 'tending to corrupt'. This is evident in the proceedings against Lilburne at the beginning of 1652. Power tended to corrupt, too, in the most humdrum everyday fashion. The long-weekend habit delayed the completion of matters in hand; the lack of a standing steering committee or a proper parliamentary front bench to control business, caused important items to be taken up, pursued for a time and then laid aside, when something more immediately urgent or compelling cropped up. Far too much time was spent on trivialities, the details of royalist land confiscations and sales, and private measures of compensation for individual Members or their close allies such as the notorious Alderman Fowke.[5] Whether the Rumpers were corrupted in the sense of being systematically dishonest, or of seeking to perpetuate themselves in power in order to line their own pockets at the public expense, is, as we have seen, less easy to answer confidently.[6] That they were dilatory and apparently incapable of carrying through even moderate and piecemeal reforms to a successful conclusion, and that their own and their friends' interests were often put before those of the public good, seems beyond dispute. Conceivably an internal coup, or a shift of power within the Parliament and in its relations with the army, at some time between the beginning of 1649 and the spring of 1653, could have altered this. An important study of the Rump and its politics, now in progress, may help to answer such questions.[7]

In its brief duration of just over five months the Barebones seems to have tried to complete a great deal of what the Rump had failed to achieve in more than four years. This was related to its different religious emphasis, due to the Baptist-Millenarian section of its membership and the relatively stronger radical Congregationalist element as compared with the Rump. Hence more drastic measures were taken to reform the law as well as the ecclesiastical system. It remains unproved, however, that the radicals of the Barebones were anti-intellectual, or even anti-academic in the sense of wishing to destroy, rather than to reform, the universities.[8] Such charges were brought against them retrospectively by their enemies, in order to justify the coup which led to the 'resignation' of the Parliament and its speedy replacement by the Protectorate. But in so far as one can postulate regular majorities being found for consistent policies, a settlement under the Barebones would thus have had many similar features to one which the Rump might have achieved, together with a few closer to the Levellers' aims. A fully salaried administration and a reformed fiscal as well as legal system would have formed an essential part of such a settlement. In the recruitment of officials, it would probably have produced the apparent paradox of a narrower sectarian basis for entry to the public service combined with greater social egalitarianism. This may be less surprising if we relate it to the concept of a 'Party-State' as this has been seen in the twentieth century. A grave but perhaps only temporary difficulty was that the radicals' conversion to support for the Dutch War had committed them to very heavy naval expenditure. This would have meant continuing the Excise and, unless they succeeded in reducing the army very drastically, keeping the Assessment as well. Their belief that a great deal more money could be raised from further land sales was an illusion; such confiscations, together with the disposal of the remaining ex-Crown assets (palaces, forests, etc.) would have done little more than complete the glutting of an already saturated land market. As with the Levellers, one may fairly wonder whether minority rule, or any kind of government without acceptance by the majority of the traditional ruling class in the localities, would have proved compatible with decentralised administration or unbureaucratic methods.

The early part of the Protectorate witnessed a more strenuous attempt at moderate reform than any other phase of republican rule. The wave of reforming Ordinances, passed by the Protector and his Council from January to September 1654, were not original in conception; most of them drew upon measures which had been in progress or at least contemplation under the Rump or the Barebones. These involved the future of the administration in numerous minor ways. First, the repeal of the Engagement Act opened the State's service to non-republicans. The reform and reconstruction of Chancery carried more of the moderate law reformers' ideas into practice, or would have done so if it had been vigorously implemented. In the church, the use of the Approbation Commissioners (*alias* the Tryers) and of the Ejectors showed ecumenical puritanism finely balanced between centralisation and local autonomy. The confiscations and land sales were ended; so, in practice if not by legislation, was penal taxation; the special machinery outside the ordinary law courts, for indemnity, was allowed to lapse when it expired the following year. Meanwhile the restoration of the Exchequer and the Treasury, the Duchy of Lancaster and (in 1655) of the Signet and Privy Seals, re-opened a further range of posts to appointment by patent; although most of these were to be held during good behaviour, not for life, and without reversions, their holders were to receive larger stipends, and the fees which they would take were strictly limited. The completion of the conquest of Ireland, the forced union with Scotland, the ending of the Dutch War and the consequent reductions of the Assessment, coupled with the reinforcement of the Excise, indicated the remaining priorities of the new government. The constitutional basis of this settlement was the Instrument of Government. As has often been pointed out, the Instrument owed a good deal to the 1647 Heads of Proposals; in all probability Lambert was the co-author of both documents. But in one respect at least it had different administrative implications. The Heads had provided for a Council of State, but one whose powers were strictly defined in relation both to the monarch and future (reformed) parliaments. In the Instrument, by contrast, the Council's role was enlarged and its powers were increased. In practice, this required a strong and efficient central executive; and, moreover, one which was 'out of court' in the sense of being distinct from the Lord Protector's personal secretariat. Hence it was more difficult than it might otherwise have been for Cromwell's secretary, William Malyn, to encroach on the position of Thurloe, who remained Secretary of the Council (not yet becoming Secretary of State) but was almost immediately given a seat on it without being a Councillor.

One might suggest that things were set fair but for the irresponsible republicans and the irreconcilable presbyterians who formed the opposition in the first Protectorate Parliament (September 1654–January 1655). And from this one may go on to argue that the ruin of this promising basis for settlement was completed by the royalist rising and attendant conspiracies both cavalier and republican in 1655, since this in turn led Cromwell to the disastrous error of imposing the Major-Generals on the country. Politically there is much force in both these contentions. But below the surface the policies of 1654 left many of the knottiest problems untouched. Perhaps the most intractable was how to obtain constitutional sanction from any parliament that was freely elected (by seventeenth-century standards) for taxes to maintain such large armed forces. The sharpest issue was the future of the army in England. Should it be a permanent garrison against threats of either cavalier or republican subversion and foreign-backed royalist invasion, and at the same time provide the equivalent of a modern police force? If so, then how was this compatible with a return to traditional forms at the local level? Although the men at the top remained insistent on limiting recruitment into office to those who were 'well affected' to the government, their concept of loyalty was wider and more flexible than it had been under the Rump or the Barebones. Generally speaking, this meant that more ex-royalists, ex-presbyterians or men who had simply kept out of public life under the Commonwealth are to be found in the service of the Protectorate.

Cromwell's second Parliament saw the fall of the Major-Generals and the introduction of a new constitution aimed at making him king. In the end of course the Humble Petition and Advice had to be accepted without the kingship. In administrative terms this represented a return not so much to 1654 as to 1648, a thoroughgoing attempt at a 'monarchical' settlement combined with a far-reaching reconciliation of the traditional ruling class. But the basic problem of the army and taxation remained unsolved. The experiment can be said to have lasted until the fall of Richard Cromwell in the spring of 1659. In almost every way less radical than the attempted settlements of 1647–54, this one was distinctly more civilian in character. One major influence on the administration was the new degree of budgetary constraint. Instead of an army of a specified size and a navy as the Protector and his Council judged fit, with taxes as required in order to meet these commitments (Instrument, clause XXVII), the amount of money allowed for both was now fixed in the constitution and—wartime emergencies apart—the size of the forces had to be accommodated within these limits (Humble Petition, clause 7). By contrast, more money was allowed for the civil government. Both the December 1653 and the June 1657 protectoral constitutions anticipated the 1690s in setting aside a fixed amount for the Household and the civil service, in what was a 'civil list' in fact if not yet in name. Within this figure (£200,000 raised to £300,000 a year in 1657) increased allowance was soon made for the Protector's household, which might have been expected to operate on a larger scale in 1657 than it had in 1654. It was not until the reign of George III that the cost of the royal household was to be statutorily separated from the rest of the civil list. Again, the use of pensions, sinecures and government contracts to build up a court-party (of what were later to be called the King's friends) as the Protector was accused of doing in 1656–8 and his son in 1659, was still a live issue in the time of Burke and the younger Pitt. It was not the case therefore that in all respects the abortive 1657 settlement was backward-looking, but, unlike the potentially more radical settlements of the preceding years, it did not imply more thoroughgoing changes. Lambert's withdrawal from public life removed the most creative and tolerant of the moderate reformers. The men behind the new constitution included some with genuine reforming instincts (Broghill and, up to a point, Henry Cromwell). But, hamstrung by lack of funds, owing to the war with Spain, and obsessed by the problem of the succession, they had made no progress by the time of Cromwell's death. Nor is any kind of further impetus for reform evident under Richard Cromwell, and it is unclear what direction his government would have taken if it had survived longer.

On the surface, the renewed Commonwealth of May 1659 gave the Rump a genuine second chance. And we have seen that, at least in administrative matters, the republicans had learnt some lessons from 1649–53. Unfortunately for them, the circumstances were different and the second chance did not in fact allow them the same possibilities as the first had done. Above all their collision with the army, which had reinstalled them in the first place, now came to a head in five months instead of taking four-and-a-quarter years as it had done before. As has already been suggested, the successive regimes which followed, of October–December 1659 and December 1659–February 1660, were too short-lived for any consistent policies to become apparent with significant administrative implications. That is not to argue that the Restoration was yet inevitable; commonsense suggests that this was not so until the end of the Republic, in all but name, on 21 February 1660. To say that the restored Commonwealth of 1659–60 offered the same potential for a reformed republican type of settlement as its predecessors had done in 1649–53 therefore means very little.

The final, and only technically republican regime which might have imposed a settlement was in power from February to May 1660. The men now in control of the government represented an alliance between ex-parliamentarians of 1646–8 (most of whom had opposed the regicide and the subsequent republic), together with some ex-servants of the Protectorate, a few of whom had royalist pasts, such as Monck and Broghill, and a few nominal republicans who had welcomed Monck as a champion of civilian rule against the other Generals. In theory this coalition had the opportunity of restoring monarchy, House of Lords and episcopalian church on their own terms, with the attendant administrative consequences. But any implied analogy with the possibilities open in 1646–8 is artificial. With King and peers as well as bishops now seeking restoration, on paper the parliamentarians' bargaining power might seem to have been greater than that of their predecessors in the later 1640s. But in practice, their own disunity, the resilience of upper-class leadership in the counties and the strong anti-military reaction in the City, made the currents moving towards the King's return so strong, that such an opportunity of dictating terms proved illusory. Hence Charles II was restored on minimal terms, and those largely of his own making (as he stated them in the Declaration of Breda).

Whatever the implications of a conditional Restoration might have been for the administrative system and its officials, the one which actually took place gave the King and his closest advisers a free hand in this, as in other respects. Charles had plenty of moral commitments, and some political constraints on his freedom of action. Offices had to be shared out between his fellow exiles, faithful Cavaliers who had stayed at home, wartime and pre-Civil War claimants and royal creditors, and the ex-parliamentarians and ex-protectorians who had made his return possible. He came back substantially to the constitutional *status quo* of 1641. In addition, the Parliaments of 1660 and 1661 were to validate certain measures of the intervening years; these affected particularly the revenue system and the country's commercial and colonial alignments. The abolition of wardship and feudal dues, the establishment of the Excise as a permanency, the revised Customs enactments and the new Navigation Act between them helped to open the way to the institutional developments of the next thirty or forty years, with the growth in size and importance of the new central departments: Treasury, Admiralty, Board of Trade and Plantations. But as regards the terms of service, officials were once more the King's servants. For the first few years at least, they were often appointed on life tenure. Entry was once again to be due mainly to family and political patronage, patrimony or purchase. The taking of fees and gratuities was revived on its old basis, and was soon once more to become the object of parliamentary scrutiny. To be only slightly cynical, the royalist civil servants of the later Stuart era enjoyed both the higher salaries dating from the 1640s and 50s, and the other time-honoured advantages of holding office which had existed under the Old Administrative System before 1642.

On one view the Restoration delayed serious administrative reforms for 150 years, anyway until the 1780s, so that eventually they occurred in an utterly different social and economic as well as political context. England, by then Great Britain, had meanwhile been overtaken in bureaucratic development by Prussia, and possibly by other absolutist States. Moreover, within a decade of losing her American empire, Britain was to be fighting for her life against France, where the bureaucratic legacy of the Revolution offered within certain limits 'the career

337

open to talents'.[9] And in this context we find major reforms, such as the replacement of fees by salaries, being put through by politically unprogressive governments, like those of Perceval and Liverpool.

If we look at the republican collapse of 1659–60 and the Restoration from another point of view, it could be plausibly argued that the failure to give a higher priority to radical administrative reform was itself a contributory reason for this collapse. To press this case too far would be to succumb to the besetting sin of the specialist, that of exaggerating the importance of one's particular subject. For the implied alternatives are not entirely realistic ones; if one or other of the regimes between 1646 and 1659 had succeeded in reforming the administrative system of the country, then such a government would have been manifestly other than it was, and the entire complex of contingent circumstances would have operated differently. It is plausible to argue that, as Milton had already discerned, the Long Parliament had become incorrigible years before 1653, and that Cromwell and Ireton ought to have got rid of it altogether in the winter of 1648–9, and to have proceeded with elections on the basis of the Independent-Leveller compromise, in the Second Agreement of the People (of January 1649). The possible consequences of this, too, are a matter of guesswork. But on the basis of a non-regicidal but substantially republican settlement, it might have been easier to reconcile political preferences with administrative needs than was to prove the case in the decade which followed.

Many will think that the historian should concentrate on describing and explaining what did happen and avoid what might have been. Of course this is true, but it sometimes helps to elucidate what did happen by outlining alternative possibilities. For at the other extreme of the argument is total determinism: what happened happened and it could not have been otherwise, because the nature of a society is given, subject only to economic and technological changes (or others, according to whatever particular logic of determinism the case is based upon). On this view the political system and its bureaucratic apparatus are pre-determined functions of the kind of society to which they belong. And the limits of significant variation are very narrow, whether in constitutional or administrative terms. The defeat of the Levellers therefore was not in doubt; even the eventual restoration of monarchy, aristocracy and established church was fully consonant with the stage of social and economic development which the country had reached. Thus a gentry-middle-class-puritan republic becomes a near impossibility too; a Cromwellian protectorate a mere halfway house or stepping-stone between 1649 and 1660. What needs explaining then is not why the republic—either Commonwealth or Protectorate—failed to perpetuate itself, but how it could have come into existence at all, let alone have had the temerity to survive for eleven years. If it is to be taken seriously, this is in turn bringing the need for explanation back to the Civil War and its immediate aftermath. As was suggested in chapter 2, the exigencies of wartime improvisation and the political deadlock which followed military victory go far to explain the administrative structure of the years from 1646 to 1653 and the kind of men who operated it. The process of functional radicalisation represented by the new fiscal system, the use of committees and the New Model Army, were at least as important as the principles and programmes of such representative figures as John Pym and Henry Marten, Denzil Holles and the younger Henry Vane, Oliver Cromwell and the Rump's civilian leaders, or John Lambert and the Barebones radicals. Yet this book has been written in the belief that within the wide limits of the given, history is made by individuals and that administration and politics, bureaucracy and social structure, interact in a two-way relationship. Can anything more positive be said about the general nature and significance of republican government and the men who served it?

The relationship between bureaucracy and revolution is not, at first sight, an obvious one. Many, perhaps most, revolutions are initially anti-bureaucratic, in that grievances against the existing state machine and its personnel provide part of their driving force. Yet most of them end by producing an enlargement of that very state machine which they have set out to overthrow. On the whole, bureaucracies seem to have grown even faster in the aftermath of civil war and revolution than under any other conditions except those of modern 'total' war. The role of functionaries in a revolutionary situation is likewise ambiguous. Many political ideologists and social theorists, particularly of the extreme left, would deny that there could be a revolutionary bureaucrat; they would see it simply as a contradiction in terms. They might, however, be prepared to concede the converse, even if they refused to go the whole way with Milovan Djilas: namely, that revolutionaries can, perhaps all too easily, become bureaucratised.

But in real life the same men can often act differently in different capacities. As Treasurer of the Navy, commissioner and committee-man, the younger Sir Henry Vane was a bureaucrat; so, as Lieutenant of the Ordnance, was Major-General Thomas Harrison; so, as principal organiser of the Irish expedition in 1649, was Commissary-General Henry Ireton; so, as Compounding and Indemnity Commissioners, were Samuel Moyer and Arthur Squibb, the radical leaders in the Bare-bones. Yet if these men were not also 'revolutionaries', then to me at least the word has lost all meaning. Perhaps we have come to take it too much for granted that bureaucrats are, indeed ought to be, faceless men of limitless discretion and exclusively middle-of-the-road opinions. The combination in the same person of high practical ability and extreme views may be more familiar today in Peking (or Havana) than in the Western world. But to suppose that the two could not go together in the 1640s and 50s, is to lose sight of an important aspect of the English Revolution.

The tendencies for all revolutions, whatever their initial anti-bureaucratic, anti-'Court' motivation, themselves to become bureaucratised once they are successful has grown stronger in the last two hundred years. This is due to the impact of science on government and society, the problems of operating a modern economy, the greater social involvement of governments, and the size and complexity of modern armaments production. Although some improvement may fairly be hoped for in the last respect, on the other counts it is hard to imagine how things could well be otherwise, outside an anarchist Utopia.

Returning to the individuals involved in such situations, at one extreme is the bureaucrat who stands or falls with his political masters. The pre-revolutionary *ancien régime* of Charles I numbered many such men amongst the King's servants. A revolutionary regime too required the services of officials committed to its cause. John Milton and Henry Parker were actually more important as ideological spokesmen for the parliamentary, and later republican cause, than they were in their capacity as officials. By contrast, the elder Gualter Frost was less successful as a propaganda apologist, but more useful as a functionary. Among those who were excluded from office for life in 1660 were at least five men whom we should classify as administrators. And three others were actually attainted with the regicides. Going outside these categories, Captain George Bishop had become a Quaker, but remained otherwise as committed to the 'Good Old Cause' as his erstwhile chief Thomas Scot MP, who was to suffer on the scaffold, while Captain Adam Baynes was regarded with only less suspicion than those who had actually joined in the final, desperate republican rising of April 1660, led by his one-time patron General Lambert.

At the other extreme is the stereotype of the bureaucrat as the careerist ready to serve any government which will employ him, and concerned only to keep in with the rulers of the day. So expressed, this is an emotive classification; put more coolly, it might fit a few of those who survived in the administration throughout the 1640s and who worked their passage successfully in 1660. But it would seem a mis-description for men who had a genuine preference for one form of government over another, or who distinguished between some aspects of the regime's activities and others. William Jessop may be cited as one who reluctantly accepted the *de facto* situation of the years 1649–60. There were many others who changed their allegiance, from whatever motives, and with some of these no doubt calculating self-interest was uppermost: the most obvious case here is Pepys's first chief, the odious but extremely able

George Downing. At first sight it is easy to add those who appeared as witnesses in the state trials of 1660–2. But, as we have seen, this would be misleading as well as unfair.

And this should suggest a caution. In the context of seventeenth-century English history, taken as a whole, it may be that 'the State's servants' were important more for what they signified than for what they were. Taken collectively, their work and careers do indicate that a new kind of public service, in some ways a new administrative system, was coming into existence in republican England until its development was retarded, if not reversed, by the events of 1660. But if we consider its inception and development, the men who staffed it were perhaps more acted upon than acting, the products of historical change rather than its originators. Some of them would have known what we mean by ascribing to them a role as agents of a new order, even if their terminology would have been different from ours. For many others, this would have meant nothing. Their collective consciousness is of course impossible to measure, but some of the letters and other documents quoted in this book (and many more which I have drawn on in my text) suggest a reasonably high level of historical awareness among several of them. The ablest men in practical matters are by no means always the most reflective, and only a small minority will ever be conscious witnesses for posterity as to their own part in events, let alone the historical significance of such events.

Vice and virtue, ordinary human kindness and the reverse may not be easy to correlate with class, status or ideology. Yet the prevailing beliefs and values of a society provide limits within which the vast majority of people in a given historical situation will in practice operate. If it is considered normal to receive gratuities from members of the public who need to avail themselves of the services of government departments or courts of law, then almost all officials in such institutions will take them, and moral condemnation is hardly in order. In mid-seventeenth-century England men's attitudes towards the poor, the treatment of prisoners, dependants and inferiors generally, and their philanthropic outlook, may not have depended primarily on whether they were anglicans or puritans, royalists or parliamentarians, republicans or monarchists. But there were some issues on which these divergences would make a difference, and perhaps administrative attitudes should be included among these. The concept of serving the State or the public did imply a difference from that of serving the King. The Long Parliament's attitude towards fees, venality and corruption, for all the failings of some of its own members and some of its servants, did differ substantially from that of the royal government before the Civil War; this was not all double-talk and window-dressing. A few men slipped badly below these standards, like Lord Howard of Escrick or John Jackson; most looked after themselves first. But within the limits of their beliefs and outlook the parliamentarians were trying to operate more honestly and efficiently a system which was definitely more open to talent regardless of social background, given the right ideological ticket of entry. Thus to blame the governments of these years for not tackling the needs of those at the bottom of society more vigorously, or for not sympathising with the programmes of the extreme radicals, is indeed otiose. To estimate whether the rule of the Long Parliament and then of the republic was any more equitable than that of its predecessors we need to look closely at the new institutions and how they operated; at the public services which were also used by private citizens, such as the Post Office, and above all at the fiscal system. Were the rich as undertaxed as they had been before 1642? The answer must surely be No. The navy which won the first Dutch War of 1652–4 had plenty wrong with it, but it was a more efficient and— for the ordinary man in it—even marginally a less brutal service than the royal navy of pre-1642. Nor were all the committees which affected the everyday lives of ordinary people high-handed and tyrannical, corrupt and irresponsible at every turn. The fact that the Indemnity authorities by no means always found in favour of government officials and military personnel is a reminder of this. The new bureaucracy certainly existed. But it will not do to say that the vested interests of the old upper class had merely been replaced by those of a new establishment, whether it was a new class or a different stratum of the same one. The evidence of pamphlets and other contemporary literature on the bureaucracy has to be measured against the official record; and as we have seen, these categories are not entirely consistent in themselves. In so far as they clash, it is our task either to reconcile them or in some cases to suggest that one is more reliable than the other. And in assessing how far the different types of evidence support each other or conflict, we become better aware of the underlying problems. A revolutionary government, which marks a breach with constitutional legitimacy, has some distinctive preoccupations. It has to concern itself more about securing recognition from its subjects; at the same time, within the limits of its own nature and the interests of its supporters, it can sometimes undertake more radical innovations or at least piecemeal improvements. This may well cease to be so if the issue of its own authority becomes obsessive, and thereby creates pressures which distort the original intentions of its leaders and their followers.

With extraordinary prescience for a contemporary of Bismarck and Napoleon III rather than of Hitler and Stalin, S. R. Gardiner described the Engagement as having tended 'to create a state within the nation'. In this he may seem to have underrated the role of the army, which was analogous to that of a modern revolutionary movement, also that of the Congregationalist and Baptist churches. The special relationship of the army and the Sects with every government of these years was necessary to their very existence, but at the same time it effectively prevented rational reform in the direction of the national interest and the common good. There is sometimes no alternative to a narrow basis for power; but unless it can be rapidly and substantially broadened, great achievement— let alone permanence—is seldom to be built on such a foundation.

NOTES

Place of publication is London unless otherwise stated.

Chapter 1 Introduction

1 *The King's Servants: The Civil Service of Charles I, 1625–1642* (Routledge & Kegan Paul, 1961).
2 See T. F. Tout, *Chapters in the Administrative History of Mediaeval England* (Manchester, 1920–33) and his *Collected Papers* (Manchester, 1934).
3 L. Glow, articles in *Historical Journal*, Vol. 8 (1965), *English Historical Review*, Vol. 80 (1965), *Journal of British Studies*, Vol. 5 (1965).
4 D. E. Kennedy, articles in *E.H.R.*, Vol. 77 (1962), *Historical Studies: Australia & New Zealand*, Vol. 11 (1964).
5 Ian Roy, 'The Royalist Council of War, 1642–6', *Bulletin of the Institute of Historical Research*, Vol. 35 (1962); (ed.) *The Royalist Ordnance Papers 1642–1646*, Pt I (Oxon Rec. Soc., Vol. 43), Introduction.
6 A. M. Everitt, *The County Committee of Kent in the Civil War* (Univ. of Leicester, Dept of English local history, occasional papers, no. 9. Leicester, 1957), since re-published as chap. 5 of Alan Everitt, *The Community of Kent and the Great Rebellion, 1640–60* (Leicester, 1966); Everitt, *Suffolk and the Great Rebellion, 1640–1660* (Suffolk Rec. Soc. III, 1960), esp. Introduction Pt II and Section I; Everitt, 'The Local Community and the Great Rebellion', *Historical Association Pamphlets* (G.70, 1969); E. M. Ives (ed.), *The English Revolution, 1600–1660* (1968), chapters by Everitt, Pennington and Roots.
7 D. H. Pennington and I. A. Roots (eds), *The Committee at Stafford, 1643–1645, The Order Book of the Staffordshire County Committee* (Manchester, 1957), esp. Introduction pp. xxvi–li; Pennington, 'The Accounts of the Kingdom, 1642–9' in F. J. Fisher (ed.), *Essays in the Economic and Social History of Tudor and Stuart England in honour of R. H. Tawney* (Cambridge, 1961), pp. 182–203. Mr Pennington also has in hand a fuller-scale study of committees in the 1640s.
8 Maurice Ashley, *Financial and Commercial Policy under the Cromwellian Protectorate* (Oxford, 1934, reprinted London, 1962), pp. 8–11.
9 H. J. Habakkuk, 'Public Finance and the Sale of Confiscated Property during the Interregnum', *Economic History Review*, 2nd series, 15 (1962), pp. 70–88; 'Landowners and the Civil War', ibid., 18, no. i. *Essays in Economic History presented to Professor M. M. Postan* (1965), pp. 130–51; 'The Parliamentary Army and the Crown Lands', *Welsh*

History Review, Vol. 3, no. 4, special number presented to Professor David Williams (1967), pp. 403–26.

10 J. E. Farnell, 'The Navigation Act of 1651, The First Dutch War and the London Merchant Community', *Econ. H.R.*, 2nd series, 16 (1964), pp. 439–54; 'The Usurpation of Honest London Householders: Barebone's Parliament', *E.H.R.*, 82 (1967), pp. 24–46.

11 For example, by Dr Hammond of the University of British Columbia, on the navy in the 1650s; by Dr G. A. Harrison on royalist administration in the counties; by Dr B. Quintrell on county affairs in Essex; by Mr Blair Worden on the Rump; and by Professor Roots on the rule of the Major-Generals. There are numerous others, and I must ask forgiveness of those whose current work is not mentioned here. David Underdown's *Pride's Purge: Politics in the Puritan Revolution* (Oxford, 1971) appeared after this book was completed; it is a work of the highest quality and importance. I have made comments arising from it here and there, but I have not attempted further revision in the light of this or any other work published since 1970.

12 J. E. Neale, 'The Elizabethan Political Scene', *British Academy Ralegh Lecture for 1948*, esp. p. 23, reprinted in *Essays in Elizabethan History* (1958).

13 H. R. Trevor-Roper, *The Gentry, 1540–1640* (*Econ. H.R.* supplements, 1, 1953), pp. 42–4, 47–8; *Historical Essays* (1957); 'Cromwell and his Parliaments', in R. Pares and A. J. P. Taylor (eds), *Essays presented to Sir Lewis Namier* (1956), reprinted in Trevor-Roper, *Religion, The Reformation and Social Change* (1967).

14 G. R. Elton, *The Tudor Revolution in Government* (Cambridge, 1953), pp. 424–5. Since then Professor Elton has suggested that the later seventeenth century may have seen major institutional changes, such as the growth of the Treasury and the Admiralty (see esp. *Past and Present*, no. 29 (1964), pp. 43–4, 'The Tudor Revolution: A Reply').

15 C. Hill, *The Century of Revolution, 1603–1714* (Edinburgh, 1961), esp. pp. 224–5; compare Hill, *The English Revolution, 1640* (1940 and later eds). Some of the same ideas are also developed in Hill, *Intellectual Origins of the English Revolution* (Oxford, 1965), and in his *God's Englishman: Oliver Cromwell and the English Revolution* (1970).

16 Articles cited above, 'Public Finance', and 'Landowners and the Civil War'; J. Thirsk, 'The Sales of Royalist Land during the Interregnum', *Econ. H.R.*, 2nd series, 5 (1952), pp. 188–207; Thirsk, 'The Restoration Land Settlement', *Journal of Modern History*, Vol. 26 (1954).

17 C. Wilson, *England's Apprenticeship, 1603–1760* (1965), esp. pp. 361–2, and 'Taxation and the Decline of Empires, an Unfashionable Theme', in his *Economic History and the Historian: Collected Essays* (1969), pp. 114–27.

18 The literature on this is now vast. For introductions to the subject, see J. H. Hexter, 'Storm Over the Gentry', ch. 6 in his *Re-appraisals in History* (1961), and L. Stone (ed.), *Social Change and Revolution in England, 1540–1640* (Problems and Perspectives series, ed. H. Kearney, 1965).

19 See particularly David Underdown, 'The Independents Re-considered', *Journal of British Studies*, 3 (1964), pp. 57–84; and note 11 above.
20 See esp. L. Stone, 'Social Mobility in England, 1500–1700', *Past and Present*, no. 33 (1966), pp. 16–55; this should be related to his earlier article, 'The Educational Revolution in England, 1560–1640', ibid., 28 (1964), pp. 41–80, and his later one, 'Literacy and Education in England, 1640–1900', ibid., 42 (1969), pp. 69–139. For another view of the same topic, with which I find myself in closer agreement, see Alan Everitt, 'Social Mobility in early modern England', ibid., 33, pp. 56–73.
21 J. H. Plumb, *The Growth of Political Stability in England, 1675–1725* (1967); see also his article, 'The Growth of the Electorate in England from 1600 to 1715', *Past and Present*, 45 (1969), pp. 90–116.
22 J. P. Kenyon, *The Stuart Constitution, 1603–1688* (Cambridge, 1966), p. 192.
23 C. V. Wedgwood, *The King's Peace, 1637–1641* (1955); *The King's War, 1640–1647* (1958); *The Trial of Charles I* (1964), published in America as *A Coffin for King Charles*.
24 Especially M. Ashley, *The Greatness of Oliver Cromwell* (1957) and *Cromwell's Generals* (1954).
25 Besides the gentry controversy, the whole problem of whether or not there was a 'general crisis' in mid-seventeenth century Europe, and, if so, of what nature, is also to the point. See T. Aston (ed.), *Crisis in Europe, 1560–1660* (1965) for some of the articles reprinted from *Past and Present*; otherwise any good up-to-date bibliography for seventeenth-century European history is the best starting-point. J. H. M. Salmon, 'Venality of Office and Popular Sedition in 17th Century France: A Review of a Controversy', *Past and Present*, 37 (1967), pp. 21–43, is a convenient introduction to one major aspect.
26 See, for example, H. G. Skilling, *The Governments of Communist Eastern Europe* (New York, 1966).
27 In July 1969 a Colloquium was organised by Mrs Sutherland of Cambridge on 'The Reform of the Civil Service in the 19th Century'; the papers presented there embody some of the best current work in this field. Most of them have now been published in Gillian Sutherland (ed.), *Studies in the Growth of Nineteenth-Century Government* (1972). See also articles in the *Hist. J.*, I–III (1958–60), by Macdonough, Kitson Clark and Parris, and in *Past and Present*, 31 (1965), by Mrs Jennifer Hart, and in *Victoria Studies*, 9 (1966) and 13 (1970), by Valerie Cromwell and Gillian Sutherland. Important recent works in this field include H. Parris, *Constitutional Bureaucracy: the development of British central administration since the 18th century* (Minerva series, 1969); G. K. Fry, *Statesmen in Disguise . . . 1853–1966* (1969).
28 S. N. Eisenstadt, *The Political Systems of Empires* (Glencoe, Ill., 1963).
29 P. M. Blau, *Bureaucracy in Modern Society* (New York, 1956 and later eds). By contrast, despite its title having raised my hopes, I found less of direct value in J. La Palombara (ed.), *Bureaucracy and Political Development* (Princeton, 1963).
30 Vol. 2 (New York, 1968).

31 Martin Albrow, *Bureaucracy* (Key Concepts in Political Science, ed. L. B. Schapiro, 1970), also with the most recent (select) bibliography.

32 With the greatest respect to the distinguished authors mentioned in this chapter, I have learnt most from my colleagues and students in the third-year undergraduate history course at York, 'Bureaucracy and Social Structure', which ran from 1966 to 1971.

33 See L. A. Fallers, *Bantu Bureaucracy* (Chicago, 1956 and 1965); Lucy Mair, *Primitive Government* (Harmondsworth, 1962).

34 See the chapters by Keith Thomas and Alan Macfarlane in *Witchcraft Confessions and Accusations* (Association of Social Anthropologists Monographs, no. 9, 1970); also Keith Thomas, *Religion and the Decline of Magic* (1971), and Alan Macfarlane, *Witchcraft in Tudor and Stuart England* (1970), a revised version of his 1967 Oxford D.Phil. thesis, supervised by Thomas.

35 What I have in mind is a kind of sixteenth–seventeenth-century equivalent of G. C. Homans, *English Villagers of the Thirteenth Century* (Camb., Mass., 1941); although as far as I know uninfluenced by social anthropology, the Leicester University school of local history is the nearest we have to this, see e.g. W. G. Hoskins, *The Midland Peasant: the economic and social history of a Leicestershire village* (1957).

36 For the relationship between the historian and the world in which he lives, I know of nothing more suggestive in print than Hexter's essay, 'The Historian and His Day', ch. 1 in his *Re-appraisals*; see also the magisterial Preface to Vol. 10 of S. R. Gardiner's *History of England . . . 1603–1642* (1884; new ed. 1891). We could hardly expect Gardiner (1829–1902) to have read Troeltsch or Weber, but it is fascinating to speculate whether he had read Marx. For his view of class and class-conflict in history see also *The History of The Great Civil War, 1642–9*, Vol. I (2nd ed. 1888), pp. 13–14, 265–6.

Chapter 2 The institutional structure

i THE POLITICAL SETTING

1 Although Charles I was executed on 30 January 1649, there was no legislation to abolish the monarchy until 17 March (C. H. Firth and R. S. Rait (eds), *Acts and Ordinances of the Interregnum*, 3 vols (1911), II, 18–20), despite a declaration of the Commons on 7 February (*Commons Journals*, VI, 133). The Convention Parliament declared the government of the country to be by King, Lords and Commons again on 1 May 1660 (*C.J.*, VIII, 8).

2 The concept of 'settlement' and the quest for it is a constant theme from the end of the first Civil War to the eve of the Restoration. This is more fully treated in my Introduction and in some of the other chapters in Aylmer (ed.), *The Interregnum. The Quest for Settlement, 1646–1660*, Problems in Focus series (Macmillan, 1972).

3 See *C.J.*, VI, 306–7, 310, 320; Firth and Rait, *A. & O.*, II, 241-2, 319–20, 325–9; and Gardiner (ed.), *Constitutional Documents of the*

Puritan Revolution 1625–1660 (3rd ed., Oxford, 1906), p. 391; Kenyon, *Stuart Constitution*, pp. 341–2, for the Engagement.

4 See ch. 4 below.

5 Ample evidence for this can be found in *C.J.*, VII, 846–80.

ii THE CIVIL WAR AND ITS AFTERMATH: RULE BY COMMITTEE

1 In modern phraseology. To contemporaries the distinctions were between 'ministerial' and 'judicial' officers, and between law-making, justice and other functions of government.

2 See J. E. Neale, *The Elizabethan House of Commons* (1949), esp. pp. 371–9; W. Notestein, *The Winning of the Initiative by the House of Commons* (1924) and his posthumous *The House of Commons 1604–1610* (New Haven, 1971), ch. 6; D. H. Willson, *Privy Councillors in the House of Commons, 1604–1629* (Minneapolis, 1940), ch. 7; and many more recent authorities, e.g. Elton, *Tudor Constitution*, ch. 8, and Kenyon, *Stuart Constitution*, ch. 2. For more specialised studies, see W. A. Aikin and B. D. Henning (eds), *Conflict in Stuart England: essays in honour of Wallace Notestein* (1960), chapters by Elizabeth Read Foster on the Parliament of 1621 and by Mrs M. F. Keeler on 1640–1.

3 L. Glow, 'The Committee of Safety', *E.H.R.*, Vol. 80 (1965), 289–313; W. Notestein, 'The Establishment of the Committee of Both Kingdoms', *American Historical Review*, Vol. 16 (1912); J. H. Hexter, 'The Rise of the Independent Party', Harvard Ph.D. Thesis, 1936, chapters IV and V. (I am very grateful to Professor Hexter for allowing me to read a photocopy of his thesis, the latter part of which has never been published.)

4 *Calendar of the Proceedings of the Committee for Compounding*, 5 vols (1889–92), ed. Mrs M. A. E. Green, see esp. preface to Vols I and V; *Calendar of the Proceedings of the Committee for the Advance of Money*, 3 vols (1888), ed. Mrs Green, preface to Vol. I.

5 Public Record Office, State Papers Domestic, Interregnum, Sequestration, S.P. 20/1–10. Strictly this was a Committee for London and Westminster; later there was a Sequestration Appeals Committee for the whole country.

6 Familiar to readers of George Orwell's *1984* (1949).

7 The best account is still W. A. Shaw, *A History of the English Church during the Civil Wars and under the Commonwealth, 1640–60* (2 vols, 1900).

8 M. Oppenheim, *A History of the Administration of the Royal Navy from 1509 to 1660* (1896; repr. Ann Arbor, 1961); J. R. Powell and E. K. Timings (eds), *Documents relating to the Civil War*, Navy Rec. Soc., 105 (1963); A. C. Dewar, 'The Naval Administration of the Interregnum 1641–59', *Mariners' Mirror*, 12 (1926), pp. 406–30, is the clearest published account; there is also work in progress by Drs Kennedy (Camb. Ph.D.) and Hammond (Univ. Brit. Columbia thesis). See also below, section vii.

9 The clearest account is in the Introduction to Pennington and Roots, *Committee at Stafford*.

10 Or in a few cases for two or more neighbouring counties. Mr Pennington points out to me that two MPs were appointed to supervise the War Treasurers' account from the beginning of the war.

11 For an account and explanation of the relations between the Eastern Association and the committees of its member counties, see Everitt, *Suffolk in the Great Rebellion.*

12 The fullest recent account for one county is Everitt, *Community of Kent,* esp. ch. 5; see also Everitt, *Suffolk;* Pennington and Roots, *Committee at Stafford; Yorkshire Archaeological Soc., Rec. Ser.* 118 (Leeds, 1953), 'Miscellanea', VI, pp. 1–30, A. Raine (ed.) 'Proceedings of the Commonwealth Committee for York and the Ainsty' (the Ainsty was the territory west of York towards Tadcaster under the city's jurisdiction from the fifteenth to early nineteenth centuries); A. H. Dodd, *Studies in Stuart Wales* (Cardiff, 1952), ch. IV, 'Nerth y Committee'; C. H. Mayo (ed.), *The Minute Books of the Dorset Standing Committee 1646–1650* (Exeter, 1902), the text shows that the main business of this particular body was largely to do with sequestrations.

13 See G. E. Aylmer, ' "Place Bills" and the Separation of Powers: some 17th century origins of the "non-political" Civil Service', *Transactions of the Royal Historical Society,* 5th series, Vol. 15, pp. 45–69.

14 See Pennington, 'The Accounts of the Kingdom', in Fisher, *Essays.*

15 See Shaw, *English Church,* Vol. 2, ch. 4; also Firth and Rait, *A. & O.,* I, 879–83, 887–904. For the financial and economic aspects of land sales, see this ch., section iv, pp. 25–8 and ch. 5, vi, pp. 319–21.

16 See Aylmer, "Attempts at Administrative Reform, 1625–40', *E.H.R.,* 72 (1957), pp. 231–3.

17 See G. Scott Thomson, *Lords Lieutenants in the 16th century* (1923); W. R. Willcox, *Gloucestershire 1590–1640* (New Haven, 1940); T. G. Barnes, *Somerset 1625–40: a County's Government under the 'Personal Rule'* (1961); L. Boynton, *The Elizabethan Militia 1558–1638* (1967).

18 *Dictionary of National Biography,* 'John Pym'; J. H. Hexter, *The Reign of King Pym* (Camb., Mass., 1941); Aylmer, *King's Servants,* pp. 352–3, 450; there are numerous interesting references to Pym in C. Russell, *The Crisis of Parliaments ... 1509–1660* (Oxford, 1971).

19 W. H. Black (ed.), *Docquets of Letters Patent of Charles I at Oxford* (1836); Roy (ed.), *Royalist Ordnance Papers 1642–1646,* Pt 1, pp. 38–9.

20 Firth and Rait, *A. & O.,* II, 329–35; *Cal. Cttee. Compdg.,* pp. 170–2 (Jan.–Feb. 1650).

21 *Cal. Cttee. Compdg.,* p. 74 (Dec. 1647).

22 See D. Underdown, 'Party Management in the Recruiter Elections, 1645–1648', *E.H.R.* Vol. 83 (1968), pp. 249–50; the story may be pieced together from *Cal. Cttee. Compdg.,* Vol. I, pp. 173, 194, 209, 221–2, 226–7, 238, 250, 252, 259–60, 265–6, 281–2, 286, 288, 291, 298, 300, 303–7, 309–10, 311, 315, 319–20, 323, 345, 351, 353, 354–5, 358–9, 363, 365, 369, 381, 387, 390–1, 393, 395, 405–6, 410, 419, 427, 444, 446, 450–1, 452, 453–4, 501, 511, 515, 534, 594–6, 625, 627, 629–30, 631, 635–6, 638–9, 642, 645, 650–4, 659, 663–4, 827. Underdown's *Pride's Purge* also deals with this conflict.

23 See *Cal. Cttee. Compdg.*, I, 591. The Compounding Committee's Minute Books (not calendared separately from the fair-copy Order Books, which they largely duplicate) show the Commissioners' attendance (PRO, State Papers Domestic, Interregnum, Compounding, S.P. 23/36–7).

24 The Maintenance Trustees were appointed as early as May 1649 (*C.J.*, VI, 199); their powers were considerably extended in 1650, and again in 1654 (Firth and Rait, *A. & O.*, II, 142–8, 369–78, 1000–6). Their records begin, effectively, in 1652 (Lambeth Palace Library, MS. Commonwealth, V/1–, Day Books).

25 Firth and Rait, *A. & O.*, I, 936–8; for the Committee's first order book see PRO, State Papers Domestic, Interregnum, Indemnity, S.P. 24/1. A further Ordinance, specifically to protect the officers and soldiers of Parliament's armies, followed on 7 June (Firth and Rait, *A. & O.*, I, 953–4).

26 *C.J.*, VI, 443, 469–71.

27 The six were the younger Vane and Col. George Thomson (Councillors of State); Mr John Carew and Major Richard Salwey (ex-Councillors); Mr James Russell (also a Compounding and Indemnity Commissioner) and Mr John Langley (non-MPs). *C.J.*, VII, 225, 227, 228–9. None of the existing authorities, Oppenheim, *Administration of the Royal Navy* ..., or S. R. Gardiner and C. T. Atkinson (eds), *Letters and Papers relating to the First Anglo-Dutch War 1652–4* (Navy Rec. Soc., 6 vols, 1899–1930), make clear the distinction between this commission and the other committees and commissioners concerned with the navy; but see Atkinson in ibid., V (Vol. 41, 1912), pp. vii–viii.

28 E.g. for supplying the forces attacking the royalists in Jersey and the Isle of Man.

29 *Calendar of the State Papers Domestic, Interregnum, 1651*, preface and pp. 278–83.

30 Vane's illness may have been 'diplomatic'; he was an opponent of the Dutch war.

31 26–28 November 1651, case of Deputy Sergeant John King and Col. Richard Conquest (S.P. 24/10, fo. 62v–63).

32 *Cal. Cttee. Compdg.*, pp. 327–8.

33 Ibid., p. 452.

34 Ibid., pp. 504, 514, 519, 530.

35 Ibid., pp. 537–8, 541.

36 Ibid., pp. 627, 647.

37 A somewhat different body, see this ch., section ix.

38 E.g. *Cal. Cttee. Compdg.*, pp. 725–6, 730–1, 733.

39 Ibid., p. 656.

40 Ibid., pp. 740 and 744.

41 W. Reid, 'Commonwealth Supply Departments within the Tower, and the Committee of London Merchants', *The Guildhall Miscellany*, 2 (1966), pp. 319–52 (the MS. vol. is described as [Tower of London] Inventory no. I, 56; Mr Reid's excellent article has other valuable references for the Regulators and their work); see also Firth and Rait, *A. & O.*, I, 1257–60; *Cal. S.P. Dom., 1650*, p. 274, etc.; *C.J.*, VI, 169,

170, 203, 206, 401. For the Customs see this ch., section iv, pp. 24–9, and ch. 3, ix, pp. 160–2; for the navy (and Ordnance), section vii, pp. 39–41, and ch. 3, ix, pp. 155–60. Several of the individuals concerned are also discussed in ch. 4.

42 It may also be that I have grown more adept at identifying the obscurer functionaries, but, this subjective factor apart, there are certainly more of them. See ch. 4, s. ii, pp. 172–4 for a fuller discussion of this.

iii THE CENTRAL EXECUTIVE

1 See *King's Servants*, ch. 2, s. ii. Readers should remember that the name is not a contemporary one, but a twentieth-century historian's label of convenience.

2 *Cal. S.P. Dom., 1648–9.* I have done less work on the MS. sources before 1649; this may well need revision.

3 See this ch., section vii, pp. 40–1 (navy).

4 See this ch., section vii, pp. 39–40 (army).

5 E. R. Turner, *Privy Council of England, 1603–1784*, 2 vols (Baltimore, 1927); Aylmer, *King's Servants*, pp. 19–22. The original sources are available as follows: *Acts of the Privy Council, 1629–30, 1630–31* (1960–4); PRO, P.C. 2/41–7, Privy Council Registers 1631–7, on micro-cards; *Privy Council Registers preserved in the P.R.O. Reproduced in Facsimile*, 12 vols, 1637–45 (1967–8).

6 *King's Servants*, pp. 358–9.

7 Except, it appears, on the King's side.

8 See Glow, art. cit., *E.H.R.*, vol. 80; Turner, *Privy Council 1603–1784* and his *Cabinet Council of England 1622–1784*, 2 vols (Baltimore, 1930). Both these authors are disappointing on this aspect, but *Cal. S.P. Dom., 1641–3, 1644, 1645–7* enables one to reconstruct—in outline—what was happening.

9 His eldest son and three other Frosts held subordinate positions by the early 1650s. See ch. 4, s. v, pp. 254–6 and notes 64–7 for full sources.

10 See *Cal. S.P. Dom., 1643–7*, and PRO, Cals of S.P. Foreign (unpublished), for the addressees of letters. Weckherlin was the Committee of Both Kingdoms' secretary for foreign affairs; the Committee decided to set aside part of every Thursday for such matters (*Cal. S.P. Dom., 1644*, pp. 17, 34, 95, 167, 175, 189, 202).

11 *Lords Journals*, VI, 252, 376; *C.J.*, III, 367–8; *The Humble Narrative of Oliver Fleming Knight*, repr. in *Somers Tracts*, 3rd collection, II (1751), 232–40.

12 See J. C. Hemmeon, *The History of the British Post Office* (Camb., Mass., 1912), ch. II, pp. 17–21, 192–3; H. Robinson, *The British Post Office: A History* (Princeton, 1948); *King's Servants*, ch. 6, pp. 369–71.

13 *DNB* 'Robert Rich', 'Edmund Prideaux'; other sources as above; also H. Joyce, *The History of the Post Office* (1893), pp. 21–3.

14 On this see J. Frank, *The Beginnings of the English Newspaper 1620–1660* (Camb., Mass., 1961), an authoritative and comprehensive account.

15 Some of the developments from the re-affirmation of Prideaux's appointment in March 1650 can be traced in the following: *Cal. S.P. Dom., 1650*, pp. 53, 56; PRO, State Papers Domestic, Interregnum, S.P. 18/16/47, 90, 91; *Cal. S.P. Dom., 1651–2*, pp. 189, 505, 509–10; S.P. 18/25/19; *Cal. S.P. Dom., 1652–3*, pp. 109–11, 446, 455; S.P. 18/37/939 a and b (MS. refs will be cited when the originals add anything of substance to what is printed in the *Calendars*); see also British Museum, Additional MS. 22,546, fo. 109–123v. His successor was appointed on 30 June 1653.

16 See Aylmer, 'Place Bills . . .' *T.R.H.S.*, 1965, pp. 53–4, n. 3.

17 For the number of Rumpers see D. Brunton and D. H. Pennington, *Members of the Long Parliament* (1954), ch. 3; G. Yule, *The Independents in the English Civil War* (Camb., 1958); Underdown, art. cit., *Journal of British Studies*, Vol. 3; also Underdown, *Pride's Purge*, ch. 8 and Appendix A.

18 The ballot was first proposed for the election of four additional members to the second Council, in February 1650 (*C.J.*, VI, 363–9); in February 1651 all were balloted for (ibid., 530–3).

19 *C.J.*, VII, 36–7.

20 Besides sources already cited, see F. M. G. Higham, née Evans, *The Principal Secretary of State, a Survey of the Office from 1558 to 1680* (Manchester, 1923), ch. 6.

21 His previous posts had been as chief Solicitor to the Sequestration Committee in 1645 (PRO, S.P. 20/1, iii), and as Judge of the sheriff's court of London (*DNB*). He now became Chancellor of the Duchy and Chief Justice of Chester.

22 In the sense of being against the rule of a single person, not only that of a crowned head.

23 Literally, 1,269 out of 1,314 sittings, February 1649–April 1653 (*Cal. S.P. Dom., 1649–53*, Prefaces).

24 The Council's orders and proceedings are printed with the other State Papers Domestic in Mrs Green's *Calendars* for 1649 on. To understand the different categories of Council records, it is necessary to consult the PRO *List & Index* series, xliii, *State Papers (revised)*. I have sampled parts of both the rough and fair-copy series of order books (PRO, State Papers Domestic, Interregnum, Council of State, S.P. 25/1– and S.P. 25/62–). Mrs Green's attendance lists ('Prefs' in *Cals S.P. Dom.*) are taken from the former; almost all her transcriptions and summaries are from the latter and from the letter-books (S.P. 25/94–). Points of procedure and provenance of documents apart, there is little to be gleaned from the originals which is not in the *Calendars*.

25 Since only three were on the first (1649–50) and not also on the second (1650–2) Council, this in effect meant new men.

26 See Z. S. Fink, *The Classical Republicans* (Evanston, Ill., 1945 and 1962), index 'ballot' and 'rotation'; and F. Raab, *The English Face of Machiavelli* (1964), chapters 5 and 6.

27 For the Council of State committees see *Cal. S.P. Dom.* for 1649–53; for the Trade Council, Firth and Rait, *A. & O.*, II, 403–6; *C.J.*, VII, 21; *Cal. S.P. Dom., 1651–2*, pp. 87–8.

28 This aspect of the War's causation has not been pursued by other historians. See S. R. Gardiner, *History of the Commonwealth and Protectorate* (3 vols and 1 chapter, 1894–1903; 4 vols 1903), chapters xx–xxii; C. H. Wilson, *Profit and Power* (1958); Farnell, art. cit., *Econ. H.R.*, new series, Vol. 16; also V. A. Rowe, *Sir Henry Vane the Younger* (1970).

29 *Cal. S.P. Dom., 1651*, p. 170; *C.J.*, VI, 568. See also ch. 3, i, pp. 68–9.

30 This dragged on terribly. See below, chapters 3 and 4.

31 Historians differ in their assessment of Thurloe's political importance. It is arguable that he was never, except by default, a policy-maker even when he was Secretary of State and a full member of the Council in 1657–9. The question becomes one of semantics—and personality: when and to what extent is a permanent under-secretary a policy-maker today, or the Secretary to the Cabinet (the latter less than the former, one can only surmise), or university registrars or bursars in relation to vice-chancellors and academic staff?

iv REVENUE AND FINANCE

1 The practical dependence of Parliament on the City of London has been stressed by historians, particularly by Mr D. H. Pennington in an unpublished B.B.C. talk on R. H. Tawney's *Business and Politics under James I: Lionel Cranfield as merchant and minister* (Cambridge, 1958).

2 See *King's Servants*, ch. 6, esp. Table 49.

3 Pennington, loc. cit.; this would also fit with Robert Ashton's argument in *The Crown and Money Market* (Oxford, 1960) especially ch. 3, and in Fisher (ed.), *Essays*, ch. 3, 'Charles I and the City'.

4 See Aylmer, *King's Servants*, pp. 34–7, 182–203, and 'The Officers of the Exchequer 1625–42' in Fisher (ed.), *Essays*.

5 Aylmer, *King's Servants*, pp. 405, 419–20. Pye was accused of treasonable correspondence with the enemy at least once. Mrs Menna Prestwich (in her study, *Cranfield: Politics and Profits under the Early Stuarts* (Oxford, 1966)) has suggested that I was too kind to him. I think she is probably right, but by Lord-Treasurer Juxon's time Pye had perhaps improved since his early days under Buckingham.

6 See Pennington and Roots, *Committee at Stafford*, Introduction.

7 See *Cal. S.P. Dom., 1649–50*, Preface.

8 E.g. *C.J.*, VII, 159–60.

9 See this ch., section ix, pp. 47, 50.

10 The other three were Francis Allen, Denis Bond, and John Downes.

11 The records of the Committee and the Commissioners both survive only in fragmentary form (PRO, Commonwealth Exchequer Papers, S.P. 28/260 etc.); some men, e.g. Holland and Downes, were on both. Signatures of Vane, who was on the Revenue Committee but was not a Treasury Inspections Commissioner, and others show some members of the Revenue Committee still acting after 20 April 1653; Vane did not, however, continue to act as an Admiralty and Navy Commissioner.

12 This can be clearly seen from the surviving records of the Army Committee: e.g. PRO, S.P. 28/58 *et seq.*, December 1648– .

13 See Habakkuk, art. cit., *Econ. H.R.* (1962), a masterly analysis which supersedes all previous authorities; and ch. 5, vi, pp. 319–21.

14 As its title suggests, Ashley's valuable study, *Financial and Commercial Policy under the Protectorate* (Oxford, 1934, repr. 1962) only really begins in 1653; some of his totals need revision in the light of Habakkuk's article.

15 PRO, Exchequer, Declared Accounts, E.351/653. The figures are: receipts from customs and subsidies in London £195,327. 16s. 0½d., and in all £272,189. 5s. 0¾d.; salaries (excluding the Commissioners' own allowances and extraordinary expenses) for London £17,047. 19s. 10d., and in all £28,534. 7s. 6d.

16 See ch. 3, ix, pp. 160–2.

17 For this see G. D. Ramsay, 'The Smugglers' Trade: a Neglected Aspect of English Commercial Development', *T.R.H.S.*, 5th series, 2 (1952), and Neville Williams, *Contraband Cargoes: Seven Centuries of Smuggling* (1959), ch. 3. Neither deals specifically with the years 1649–60.

18 For example, on the account for the three years Sept. 1650–Sept. 1653 the total out-payments on money raised under the 'Grand Ordinance' of 11 Sept. 1643 were £996,477, of which £87,929 went in poundage, salaries, expenses, etc., or just under 9 per cent (PRO, Declared Accounts, E.351/1296).

V THE LAW AND THE COURTS

1 The law reform movement of these decades still lacks a comprehensive history. The most useful modern works (in order of publication) are: R. Robinson, 'Anticipations under the Commonwealth of changes in the Law', in E. Freund *et al.* (eds), *Select Essays in Anglo-American Legal History*, I (Boston, 1907), 467–91 (but taken from *Papers Read before the Juridical Society*, III (n.d. but ? 1869–70), 567–601); J. F. Stephen, *History of the Criminal Law of England*, I (1883), ch. 11, s. ii; Goldwin Smith, 'The Reform of the Laws of England, 1640–1660', *University of Toronto Quarterly*, 10 (1940–1), 469–81; G. B. Nourse, 'Law Reform under the Commonwealth and Protectorate', *Law Quarterly Review*, Vol. 75 (1959), 512–29; S. E. Prall, 'Chancery Reform and the Puritan Revolution', *The American Journal of Legal History*, 6 (1962), 28–44; Mary Cotterell, 'Interregnum Law Reform: the Hale Commission of 1652', *E.H.R.*, 83 (1968), 689–704; D. Veall, *The Popular Movement for Law Reform 1640–1660* (Oxford, 1970).

2 See W. K. Jordan, *Men of Substance* (Chicago, 1942), ch. 3. Professor Jordan did not find it easy to relate Robinson's administrative activities and his writings to each other.

3 See ch. 4, vi, p. 276.

4 *DNB*; Wedgwood, *Trial of Charles I.*

5 G. H. Sabine (ed.), *The Works of Gerrard Winstanley* (Ithaca, New York, 1941) is the most comprehensive collection.

6 See C. Hill, 'The Norman Yoke' in *Puritanism and Revolution* (1958), ch. 3, pp. 50–122; also J. G. A. Pocock, *The Ancient Constitution and the Feudal Law* (Cambridge, 1957), esp. chapters 2 and 6.

7 E.g. Hugh Peter. See R. P. Stearns, *Strenuous Puritan* (Urbana, Ill., 1954), and esp. Peter's *Good Work for a Good Magistrate* (1651).

8 See W. Lamont, *Godly Rule* (1969), and P. Toon (ed.), *Puritans, the Millennium and the future of Israel* (1969).

9 *History of the Rebellion*, Bk XVI, section 89.

10 *DNB*, 'Vane'; M. A. Judson, *The Political Thought of Sir Henry Vane the Younger* (Philadelphia, 1969); also Rowe, *Vane*.

11 E.g. Orlando Bridgeman, Heneage Finch, Geoffrey Palmer. See Brunton and Pennington, *Members*, p. 5.

12 See *King's Servants*, ch. 6, s. viii, for political allegiance in different branches of the government from 1642 on.

13 See this ch., sections ii and iv, pp. 10, 12, 24–9.

14 Even the law reform movement is hard to study adequately without some general notion of what the business of the courts was like and how they conducted it. It is hard to establish even which courts were the slowest, most expensive and least satisfactory for litigants without this evidence.

15 The six who agreed to continue were Henry Rolle (Chief Justice of Upper Bench), Oliver St John (Chief Justice of Common Pleas), John Wild (Chief Baron), Philip Jermyn (Upper Bench), Peter Phesant (Common Pleas), and Thomas Gates (Baron). Those who refused were Edward Atkyns (Baron), Sir Francis Bacon (Upper Bench), Sir Thomas Bedingfield (Common Pleas), Samuel Browne (Upper Bench), Richard Cresheld (Common Pleas) and Sir Thomas Trevor (Baron). Phesant and Gates died within a short time, while Atkyns soon accepted re-appointment (in Common Pleas).

16 High Courts of Justice were set up to try Hamilton and others, February 1649; for East Anglia 1650–1; to try the Rev. Love and other conspirators 1650. But a court martial was used against the earl of Derby and others after the invasion of 1651 (Firth and Rait, *A. & O.*, II, 364–7, 407–8, 419, 492–3; *C.J.*, VI, 131). It is puzzling why this method was not used against Lilburne at either of his trials (in 1649 and 1653). Perhaps ordinary judges and jurors were expected to be less well disposed towards the Leveller leader than committed parliamentarians would be, perhaps too he was not seen as an 'enemy of the State' like royalist invaders and conspirators. Here the English republicans compare favourably—in humanity and legal correctness at least—with modern revolutionaries.

17 See T. G. Barnes, 'Due Process and Slow Process in the late Tudor-early Stuart Star Chamber', *American Journal of Legal History*, 6 (1962); *King's Servants*, pp. 48–9, drawing heavily upon H. E. I. Phillipps, 'The last years of the Court of Star Chamber, 1630–1641', *T.R.H.S.*, 4th series, 21 (1938); Kenyon, *Stuart Constitution*, ch. 3, iii. Professor Barnes is preparing a major work on the Court of Star Chamber.

18 See Marjorie Blatcher, 'The Writ of Latitat', in S. T. Bindoff, J. Hurstfield, C. H. Williams (eds), *Government and Society in Elizabethan England: Essays presented to Sir John Neale* (1961).

19 See W. J. Jones, *The Elizabethan Court of Chancery* (Oxford, 1967),

which renders out of date much of what I wrote earlier about Chancery in relation to the Common Law courts; unfortunately there is little as good for the major courts in the seventeenth century, but for the 1670s and 80s see D. E. C. Yale (ed.), *Lord Nottingham's Chancery Cases* (Selden Soc., Vols 73 and 79, 1957 for 1954 and 1962 for 1961).

20 See ch. 3, ii, pp. 90–3.

21 Gardiner, *History of England ... 1603–42*, ch. xxxv; *DNB*, 'Francis Bacon', and 'John Williams'.

22 *Memorials*, esp. for 8 February 1649. The 1853 ed. (Oxford, 4 vols) should if possible be used, although the 1682 folio edition is easier to come by. I am grateful to Miss Ruth Spalding for help with the dates of Whitelocke's writings.

23 *Cal. S.P. Dom., 1649–50*, p. 410; *C.J.*, VI, 38–9, 230, 231.

24 I am grateful to Dr Ailwyn Ruddock for helpful suggestions on printed sources for the Court of Admiralty. See also PRO, *Lists and Indexes*, Vol. 18, *List of Admiralty Records*, Vol. 1 (1904); W. Senior, 'Judges of the High Court of Admiralty', *Mariners' Mirror*, 13 (1927).

25 Firth and Rait, *A. & O.*, II, 75–8; *C.J.*, VII, 264; *Cal. S.P. Dom., 1651–2*, pp. 348, 372–3, 375, 387.

26 See British Record Society, *Index Library*, Vol. 54 (1925), T. M. Blagg and J. S. Moir (eds), 'Index of Wills proved in the P.C.C. ...', Vol. VII, 1653–1656', pp. xiv–xvi. Brent had various little-known 'surrogates' or deputies under him.

27 *DNB*, 'Oldisworth'; Jordan, *Men of Substance*, ch. 2.

28 *Cal. S.P. Dom., 1653–4*, p. 280.

29 See this ch., section viii, pp. 42, 44.

30 See ch. 5, iv, pp. 305–17 for a discussion based on surviving sessional records.

vi IRELAND AND SCOTLAND

1 *King's Servants* citations e.g. of Boyle, Loftus, Mountnorris, Radcliffe, Wandesford, Wentworth.

2 Wentworth was made Lord Lieutenant only in 1639, on the eve of his departure from Ireland.

3 Despite, or because of, his prominence in the events of November 1648 to January 1649, Ireton had failed to get elected to the first Council of State. Instead he took an active part in the House and formed its chief liaison with the army, February–July 1649.

4 These are listed by Edmund Ludlow (*Memoirs*, ed. C. H. Firth, 2 vols, Oxford, 1894, I, 261).

5 See this section, pp. 37–8.

6 See ch. 3, v, pp. 110–11, for the relative size of these stipends. For sketches of those involved, as well as *DNB*, and C. H. Firth and G. Davies, *Regimental History of Cromwell's Army*, 2 vols (Oxford, 1940), see Ashley, *Cromwell's Generals*, and two older works, C. E. Lucas Phillips, *Cromwell's Captains* (1938) and W. H. Dawson, *Cromwell's Understudy: the Life and Times of General John Lambert and the Rise and Fall of the Protectorate* (1938).

7 See J. P. Prendergast, *The Cromwellian Settlement of Ireland* (3rd ed., Dublin, 1922), Appendix V, for names and amounts; also K. S. Bottigheimer, *English Money and Irish Lands* (Oxford, 1971).

8 For the relevant legislation see Firth and Rait, *A. & O.*, II, 598–603 (the Act for Settling Ireland, Aug. 1652, also in Gardiner, *Constitutional Docs*), 722–53 (the Act for the Satisfaction of the Adventurers, Sept. 1653); R. Dunlop (ed.), *Ireland under the Commonwealth*, 2 vols (Manchester, 1913) has the fullest collection of the relevant documents.

9 J. Davies, 'A Discovery of the true causes why Ireland was never brought under obedience to the Crown of England' in H. Morley (ed.), *Ireland under Elizabeth and James I* (1870 and other editions).

10 Wedgwood, *The King's War*, is good on this; W. L. Mathieson, *Politics and Religion: A Study in Scottish History from the Reformation to the Revolution*, 2 vols (Glasgow, 1902), remains the clearest and fullest published account from the Scottish side; see the forthcoming book, based on a Glasgow Ph.D. (1970), by D. Stevenson.

11 Besides Gardiner, *Great Civil War*, the best account in print is still Mathieson, *Politics and Religion*.

12 *C.J.*, VII, 14, 47.

13 *C.J.*, VII, 30; *Cal. S.P. Dom., 1651*, pp. 71, 177, 236–7, 489–90; *1651–2*, p. 210.

14 The best accounts of Anglo-Scottish relations are again in Mathieson, *Politics and Religion*, and H. R. Trevor-Roper, 'Scotland and the Puritan Revolution', in *Historical Essays 1600–1750 presented to David Ogg*, ed. H. E. Bell and R. L. Ollard (1963), or in Trevor-Roper, *Religion, the Reformation and Social Change* (1967); the best modern history of Scotland is G. Donaldson, *Scotland: James V to James VII* (Edinburgh, 1965). None of these has much on the administrative side. See also C. S. Terry (ed.), *The Cromwellian Union*, and C. H. Firth (ed.), *Scotland and the Commonwealth* (Scottish History Soc., Vols 40 and 18, 1902 and 1895) for valuable extracts with explanatory notes.

vii THE ARMED FORCES AND OTHER DEPARTMENTS

1 Captain John Mason, 1586–1635 (*DNB; Acts of the Privy Council*, vols for *1625–9*, etc.).

2 *King's Servants*, pp. 391–2.

3 The point is made by Professor G. R. Elton, in his *Tudor Revolution in Government* (Cambridge, 1953), pp. 421–2.

4 See I. Roy, 'The Royalist Council of War 1642–6', art. cit., *Bull. Inst. Hist. Res.* 35 (1962). It is to be hoped that more of Dr Roy's work on royalist military organisation will soon be published.

5 See Aylmer, 'Attempts at administrative reform 1625–40', *E.H.R.*, 72 (1957), pp. 240–6.

6 It is a source of potential confusion that there was a post of Lieut.-General of the Ordnance (or Artillery), in the (Field) Army, held from 1646 to 1651/2 by Thomas Hammond; the Lieutenant of the Ordnance was the 'Presbyterian' Sir Walter Erle until 1648/9, and then the regicide

Thomas Harrison 1650–2. Hammond appears not to have been replaced, although Monck was Lieutenant-General of the Ordnance for the Army in Scotland (1650/1 to early 1652), and Broghill the same in Ireland (1649–51). Because Hammond was never a regimental officer he is not in Firth and Davies, *Regimental Hist.*; the *DNB* is somewhat muddled on the Hammonds. Thomas was the uncle of Cromwell's 'cousin Robin', Colonel Robert Hammond, and the brother of Henry, the Anglican divine. Back in 1647–8, Fairfax's committee of field officers for recommending appointments had suggested him as Lieutenant of the Ordnance instead of Erle—the post which Harrison actually got (Worcester College, Oxford, Clarke MSS., LXVI, fo. 18; *C.J.*, VI, 121, 226, 436; VII, 126, 217, 240; PRO S.P. 28/253A, 259, showing that Hammond had been invalided out of the service by autumn 1651).

7 Herefordshire Record Office, Foley MSS.; *Cal. S.P. Dom.* refs *1649–50* to *1651–2*.

8 See *King's Servants*, p. 367.

9 *C.J.*, VI, 401; VII, 124–6, April 1650 and April 1652.

10 According to Oppenheim, *Administration of Royal Navy*, p. 361, the Ordnance in 1653 'became a department of the Admiralty'. I cannot find that the sources support this.

11 See PRO, S.P. 18/11/84, 98 (for items in the controversy, November 1650).

12 Aylmer, 'Attempts', *E.H.R.*, 72 (1957), pp. 234–40; Oppenheim, *Admin. of R.N.*, pp. 279–301.

13 See this ch., section iii, p. 18, section v, p. 33.

14 See the many vivid and outspoken letters from Captain Nehemiah Bourne in *Cal. S.P. Dom., 1652–3 et seq.*; and contrast his position at Harwich, as a Commissioner, with that of Captain Henry Hatsell at Plymouth, who was merely an Agent.

15 See section ii, p. 348, note 8 for references.

16 On the Royal Navy since 1914, see C. N. Parkinson, *Parkinson's Law* (ed. Harmondsworth, 1965), pp. 16–18. Beneath the humour there is a real point, as with all good satire.

17 See this ch., section ii, p. 14.

18 See, for instance, Richard Salwey's letters in *Cal. S.P. Dom., 1652–3*.

19 Not as decisively as they might have done, because the Barebones Parliament failed to pay and re-equip the fleet promptly enough for the blockade to be maintained through the autumn of 1653. Despite English losses and the economic ill-effects of the war, especially in eastern England, the interruption of Dutch seaborne trade had continued much longer, internal convulsion or collapse must have followed, anyway in Holland and Zeeland. The contrast with the Second and Third Anglo-Dutch Wars of 1664–7 and 1672–4 is remarkable.

20 This may seem fanciful applied to Colonel Pride and his merchant partners (who held the contract from 1650), but see ch. 4, s. i, p. 168.

21 For the scale of activities in the later seventeenth century see D. C. Coleman, 'Naval Dockyards under the Later Stuarts', *Econ. H.R.*, new series, 6 (1953), pp. 134–55. Nothing for the 1650s can hope to rival J.

Ehrman's massive and masterly *The Navy in the War of William III, 1689–97* (Cambridge, 1953); see esp. chapters 7 and 13.

22 See refs to Wade in *Cal. S.P. Dom.* Dr G. F. Hammersley of the University of Edinburgh has been collecting material on this for many years.

23 For its earlier history see the encyclopaedic work of H. M. Colvin and others, *The King's Works*, medieval vols only so far.

24 Whether or not this included the 'double cube' room at Wilton; Jones's patron, the 4th Earl of Pembroke sat on the Council of State, February 1649 to February 1650; his son, the 5th Earl, was on it in 1651–2. Both were in the Rump. The 4th Earl obtained a seat after the abolition of the House of Lords; his son and heir already had one. On Jones's building and designs, the best account is now Sir John Summerson, *Inigo Jones* (Harmondsworth, 1966), where the authentic Jonesian oeuvre is much reduced, Wilton House being excluded!

25 Also in the Commonwealth's employment was an artist of comparable stature in a different medium: see ch. 4, p. 173, on Samuel Cooper.

26 *C.J.*, VI, 138, 305; *Cal. S.P. Dom., 1649–50*, pp. 503, 549; *1651*, pp. 231–4, 280, 460–1, 487–9; *1651–2*, pp. 260–3; *1652–3*, pp. 69–70; S.P. 18/3/114, 5/13, 9/3, 42, 15/62, 69 (I have cited the original State Papers only where these add something substantial to what is printed in the Calendars).

27 See ch. 3, vi, pp. 123–4.

viii 1653: THE ENTR'ACTE

1 See Mrs Mary Cotterell's excellent article on this body and its work (*E.H.R.*, 83, 1968).

2 But they were to be allowed to take the usual probate fees—an apparently retrograde step (*C.J.*, VII, 279, 286; Firth and Rait, *A. & O.*, II, 702–3, 824; see also Blagg and Moir, 'Index of Wills 1653–1656', pp. xvi–xviii.

3 *Cal. SP. Dom., 1652–3*, p. 342.

4 On this see ch. 4, ss. iii and iv, Tables 24 and 40, pp. 194, 207.

5 A. Woolrych, 'The Calling of Barebones' Parliament', *E.H.R.*, 80 (1965), pp. 492–513.

6 Other titles are the Nominated Parliament, the Little Parliament, the Parliament of the Saints, and—at the time, revealingly—'the Supreme Power', but the contemporary nickname (from Praise-God Barbon, one of the London representatives in it), has stuck, and it is pedantic to use any other.

7 *C.J.*, VII, 281, Tellers for the Ayes Sir William Roberts and Colonel Sydenham, for the Noes Sir Gilbert Pickering and Mr Carew, 6 July.

8 Compare H. R. Trevor-Roper, 'Cromwell and his Parliaments', reprinted in *Religion, Reformation and Social Change* (1967) with Woolrych, art. cit., and Woolrych, 'Oliver Cromwell and the Rule of the Saints', in R. H. Parry (ed.), *The English Civil War and After 1642–1658* (1970), pp. 59–77.

9 *C.J.*, VII, 296, 335.

10 See this ch., section v, pp. 29-30.

11 Major-Generals Disbrowe and Harrison, Sir Anthony Ashley Cooper, Samuel Moyer.

12 Firth and Rait, *A. & O.*, II, 753-64; for discussions of this topic back in 1649, see *C.J.*, VI, 161, 276, 323, 325-6, 327.

13 Ibid., 715-18.

14 See G. F. A. Best, *Temporal Pillars* (Cambridge, 1964), on the modern Commissioners. I do not think that the parellel is far-fetched. On the Trustees see this chapter, section ii, p. 13 also ch. 4, v, pp. 267-70.

15 In which even contemporaries indulged, under different names. See the list in Gardiner, *Commonwealth and Protectorate*, ch. xxviii, taken from a contemporary pamphlet.

16 See ch. 4, ss. iii-iv, Tables 24, 40, pp. 194, 207.

17 In addition to the authorities already cited, see G. D. Heath, 'Making the Instrument of Government', *Journal of British Studies*, 6 (1967), pp. 15-34.

ix ADMINISTRATION UNDER THE PROTECTORATE

1 Clauses III, XXV-VII, XXX-II, XXXIV, XXXIX-XLII of the Instrument have administrative implications. See Firth and Rait, *A. & O.* II, 813-22; Gardiner, *Constitutional Documents*, pp. 405-17; Kenyon, *Stuart Constitution*, no. 94.

2 See C. Hill, *Century of Revolution*, esp. pp. 133, 135, 141-4.

3 See Mrs Green, *Cal. Cttee. Compdg.*, Vol. I, Preface, and Vol. V, Introduction.

4 PRO, S.P. 24/16 and 25.

5 Shaw, *English Church*, Vol. 2, ch. IV; Firth and Rait, *A. & O.*, II, 855-8.

6 Under the Instrument, clauses XXXV-VIII.

7 Shaw, *English Church*, Vol. 2, ch. IV; Firth and Rait, *A. & O.*, II, 968-90.

8 To which even Mrs Green tended to subscribe in her prefaces to the various series of *Calendars*, already cited.

9 See section viii, p. 45, and ch. 4, ss. iii and iv, pp. 194-5, 207.

10 Compare Gardiner, *Commonwealth and Protectorate*, ch. xxxiv (Vol. II of 1897 ed., p. 477), with M. Roberts, 'Cromwell and the Baltic', *E.H.R.*, 76 (1961), pp. 402-46, and other authorities. The best of the Protector's biographers (Firth, Ashley, Hill) have reminded us that the Cromwell of 1658 was sadly altered from the Cromwell of 1654, as supreme power and failing health took this inevitable toll.

11 See ch. 3, s. ii, pp. 90-3.

12 See *King's Servants*, pp. 37-8, 63, 195, 432, and Aylmer, 'Officers of the Exchequer', in Fisher (ed.) *Essays*, pp. 167-8.

13 In their full panoply this was from 1655 rather than 1653-4.

14 See R. B. Pugh, 'The Patent Rolls of the Interregnum . . .', *Bull. Inst. Hist. Res.*, 23 (1950); *Guide to the Contents of the Public Record Office*, Vol. I, *Legal Records*, etc. (1963), p. 22.

15 PRO, Chancery, Crown Office, Entry Book of Commissioners, 1653-60,

C. 181/6; Chancery, Admission Roll, 1655–6, C. 216/3; Crown Office, Docquet Book 1643–60, Index 4213; Exchequer of Receipt, Enrolment Book, Pells, 1654–60, E. 403/2523; Deputy-Keeper of the Public Records, *5th Report*, Appendix II, pp. 246–77, Privy Seal Books, Pells, 1655–60 (corresponding to E. 403/2608, in which there is some additional matter not printed there); BM, Add. MS. 4184, Register of the Signet, 1654–60; Stowe MS. 497, Register of Letters Patent in the Treasury of Exchequer, 1654–9.

16 Again no full records have survived; its organisation and personnel have to be inferred from other sources, notably from the lists of those who were to receive mourning cloth and walk in Oliver Cromwell's funeral procession, October–November 1658 (J. T. Rutt (ed.), *The* (Parliamentary) *Diary of Thomas Burton* (4 vols, 1828), II, 518–29; PRO, S.P. 18/182/89–90).

17 Given in Gardiner, *Constitutional Docs*, pp. 427–47.

18 See *DNB*; he is not to be confused with the pro-Comwellian recruiter MP Colonel Thomas Birch.

19 See Ashley, *Fin. and Comm. Pol.*, p. 43, n. 1, for different versions of the report.

20 Even then only by counting lunar not calendar months, for which he was denounced by his opponents.

21 The first set of orders, of August, seem to have been regarded as unsatisfactory, and had little effect (Gardiner, *Commonwealth and Protectorate*, ch. XL).

22 When the appearance of D. W. Rannie, 'The Cromwellian Major-Generals', *E.H.R.*, 10 (1895), and Gardiner's *History*, made it difficult, except by wilful ignorance, to adhere to the older view; since then note also J. Berry and S. G. Lee, *A Cromwellian Major General* (Oxford, 1938). But there is room for a full-scale study (which, happily, Professor Ivan Roots is undertaking); see meanwhile Roots, 'Swordsmen and Decimators—Cromwell's Major-Generals', in Parry (ed.), *English Civil War and After*, pp. 78–92.

23 Some of these were, of course, ordinances and acts passed since March 1642 and therefore not recognised by royalists as legally binding; others passed since December 1648 were not recognised by some Presbyterian parliamentarians either; the ordinances of the Protector and his council were regarded as invalid by some militant republicans. This is not what is meant by 'outside the law' here.

24 See Barnes, *Somerset 1625–40*, ch. 1, esp. pp. 4–5, 13–14.

25 See ch. 5, s. iv, pp. 312–14, and notes 51–6.

26 See ch. 5, s. iv for fuller treatment of the interaction between central and local government.

27 E.g. Everitt, *Community of Kent*, pp. 294–5, quoting an eloquent letter from Major-General Thos. Kelsey, printed (almost *in extenso*) in *Cal. S.P. Dom., 1656–7*, pp. 87–8.

28 Generals Fleetwood, Lambert, Disbrowe, and Skippon (retired but essentially a military type), and Cols Sydenham and Philip Jones (a 'garrison' Colonel only): at most six out of fifteen in 1654–7, not 'largely'

Generals as Hill says (*God's Englishman*, p. 183). Montague was an ex-army officer but not 'of the Army'.

29 *DNB*; W. H. Dawson, *Cromwell's Understudy* (1938); M. Ashley, *Cromwell's Generals* (1954).

30 The evidence for when and why Lambert changed his line probably does not exist; one is driven back on hunch and character-reading.

31 For Assessment purposes, a year had twelve calendar months, but the army establishment was reckoned on a four-week lunar month (thirteen to the year), hence an almost chronic shortfall.

32 See Ashley, *Fin. & Comm. Pol.*, ch. 8, for a clear account.

33 See Ashley again, *Fin. & Comm. Pol.*, chapters 10 and 14; also Habakkuk, art. cit. 'Public Finance', and C. H. Firth, *The Last Years of the Protectorate 1656–1658* (2 vols, 1909). G. Davies, *The Restoration of Charles II 1658–1660* (San Marino, Cal., 1956) takes up in September 1658 but is less satisfactory on this aspect.

34 BM, Lansdowne MSS. 821–3 contain many letters to Henry Cromwell, 1655–9, which are not printed in *Thurloe State Papers* (7 vols, 1742) or elsewhere, though some are quoted in Firth's *Last Years*. See also R. W. Ramsey, *Henry Cromwell* (1933).

35 For Lambert see section vi, p. 35.

36 PRO, Index 4213; *Thurloe St. P.*, VII, 423–5, *et seq.*

37 W. Knowler, *Letters and Dispatches of the earle of Strafforde* (2 vols, Dublin, 1739); Sheffield Central Library, Wentworth-Woodhouse MSS., Strafford Papers, esp. vols. 1, 3–8, 10–19, 20(b), 24–5.

38 From April 1654; see Table 3, p. 38.

39 For whom see *DNB*; T. O. Ranger, 'Richard Boyle and the making of an Irish fortune, 1588–1614', *Irish Historical Studies*, X (1957); H. F. Kearney, *Strafford in Ireland* (Manchester, 1959); Wedgwood, *Strafford: a revaluation* (1961); Aylmer, *King's Servants*; T. O. Ranger, 'Strafford in Ireland: a revaluation', *Past and Present*, 19 (1961), esp. pp. 38–41, 43–4 and refs p. 45.

40 See Trevor-Roper, 'Scotland and the Puritan Revolution' in *Religion, Reformation and Social Change*. Monck's attitude can be worked out from his letters in *Thurloe St. P.*, II–VII, and Firth (ed.), *Scotland and the Protectorate 1654–1659* (Scott. Hist. Soc., 31, 1899).

41 This was William Boteler, Major-General for Bedfordshire, Huntingdon, Northants and Rutland. See P. H. Hardacre, 'William Boteler: A Cromwellian Oligarch', *Huntingdon Library Quarterly*, 11 (1947–8), 1–11; Firth and Davies, *Regimental Hist.*, and letters in *Thurloe St. P.*, III and IV.

42 See A. H. Woolrych, 'The Good Old Cause and the Fall of the Protectorate', *Cambridge Hist. J.*, 13 (1957). The fullest account is in G. Davies, *The Restoration*, chapters IV and V.

43 See ch. 3, s. i, pp. 70–82, s. ii, pp. 85–7.

44 See ch. 4, pp. 194, 207.

X FROM RESTORED COMMONWEALTH TO RESTORED MONARCHY
   (1659–60)

1 In Lambert's case only until 1657.
2 E.g. on the Council of State and/or as Major-Generals.
3 As Councillor and Comptroller. His colonelcy had been honorary since 1651, though he remained commander of the Cardiff castle garrison.
4 Sequestration and compounding were particularly heavy in parts of Wales during the years 1645–50, giving ample scope for abuse. See ch. 3, s. ix, 'Bribery', pp. 150–5.
5 *C.J.*, VII, 656, 663, 666, 684.
6 See *C.J.*, VII, 649, *et seq.*
7 Firth and Rait, *A. & O.*, II, 1342–3, 1347–9.
8 Ibid., 1299–1304.
9 Including, be it noted, some of the ablest: Vane, Salwey and Whitelocke.
10 They could at least have abstained from making payments or assignments in favour of themselves which had previously been vetoed by Parliament —as John Blackwell apparently did! (*C.J.*, VII, 831–3).
11 Four weeks after it was first restored in May 1659 the House had voted that its own dissolution should not be later than 7 May 1660, an uncanny echo of the 1651 vote for a 1654 dissolution but on a shortened time scale (*C.J.*, VII, 674, 6 June).
12 The burden of Professor Underdown's argument is that 'Rumper' is not a meaningful political classification; from Dec. 1648 he descries three main categories of future Rumpers: Revolutionaries, Conformists and Abstainers (D. Underdown, *Pride's Purge*, ch. VIII).
13 See chapters 5 and 6.
14 See *C.J.*, VII, 661, 671–2, 689, 731, 744, 758, 794. They were a little more 'self-denying' among themselves, presents of venison for Councillors of State being about as far as they went in collective self-indulgence! (*Cal. S.P. Dom.*, *1658–3*, *passim.*, and Bodleian Library, Rawlinson MS. C. 179, Register of the Council 19 May–10 Aug. 1659.)

Chapter 3   The terms of service

i   ENTRY AND APPOINTMENT

1 For the comparison with England 20–25 years earlier see Aylmer, *The King's Servants*, chapters 3 and 4; for a very general comparison with other parts of Europe, mainly France, see ibid., ch. 7, ii.
2 H. Cary (ed.), *Memorials of the Great Civil War in England from 1646 to 1652* ... 2 vols (1842), II, 46–7 (from Bodl. Tanner MSS.); also in W. C. Abbott, *Writings and Speeches of Oliver Cromwell*, 4 vols (Cambridge, Mass., 1937–48), I, 671–2.
3 PRO, E.351/653; A.O. 1/605/57, Customs Accounts; *Cal. S.P. Dom., 1656–7*, p. 211; Deputy Keeper, *5th Rept.*, App. II, p. 264.
4 Firth and Rait, *A. & O.*, I, 879–83, 887–904.
5 Colonel Robert Mainwaring (d. Sept. 1652); not to be confused with

Colonel Randall Mainwaring senior, Comptroller for the sale of royalists' lands, 1651–2 (d. Oct.–Nov. 1652).

6 Henry Robinson, for whom see *DNB*; Jordan, *Men of Substance*, ch. III; Firth and Rait, *A. & O.*, II, 168–91; and ch. 4, section v, pp. 225–6.

7 See this chapter, section iii, pp. 99–100.

8 As the Rump styled its legislation from February 1649 on, to emphasise the formal sovereignty of the Commons.

9 Firth and Rait, *A. & O.*, II, 168–91.

10 Ibid., 358–62, 11 March 1650.

11 For Chidley see ch. 5, s. ii, pp. 293–4, and note 48.

12 See e.g. Firth and Rait, *A. & O.*, II, 148–51, Commissioners appointed to give relief on articles of war (that is, according to various surrender agreements), to appoint a Registrar; ibid., 160–8, Trustees for sale of the late King's and part of royal family's goods, to appoint a clerk register and other offices; ibid., 520–45, Trustees for sale of lands of royalists forfeited for treason, to appoint Surveyors, Counsel Learned in the Law, and other officers (except the Registrar, who was named in the Act); ibid., 623–52, the third such Act for land sales for treason, appoints three men to the post of Registrar-Accountant (the redoubtable Mainwaring being dead).

13 See *King's Servants*, pp. 69–74, for examples of this.

14 See this chapter, ss. viii and ix, pp. 129–67 for further discussion of this.

15 And not to be confused with Colonel John Birch of Weobley, Herefordshire, also of Lancashire origin and also a recruiter but 'secluded' from 6 December 1648 to 21 February 1660.

16 *Cal. Cttee. Compdg.*, I, p. 178, 26 February 1650.

17 Ibid., p. 200, 19 April 1650.

18 See *DNB*; M. F. Keeler, *The Long Parliament 1640–41* (Philadelphia, 1954); Valerie Pearl, *London and the Outbreak of the Puritan Revolution 1625–1643* (Oxford, 1961).

19 See Firth and Rait, *A. & O.*, II, 105.

20 *Cal. Cttee. Compdg.*, p. 204, 26 April 1650.

21 Ibid., pp. 173, 194. See ch. 2, s. i, pp. 12–13.

22 *Cal. Cttee. Compdg.*, p. 275.

23 Ibid., pp. 408, 419, 12 February 1651.

24 Ibid., p. 428, 27 March 1651. There may have been an agent for each of the three Ridings, or at least this may have been what was proposed, so perhaps these nominations were not in direct rivalry.

25 Ibid., p. 437, 29 April 1651; ibid., pp. 524, 529, January 1652.

26 Ibid., pp. 478, 481, 486.

27 In 1650 he was trying to sue the erstwhile parliamentarian tax collectors in Lancashire, who had at one stage imprisoned him; they then sought the protection of the Indemnity Committee (PRO, S.P. 24/6–7).

28 *Cal. Cttee. Compdg.*, p. 584.

29 PRO, S.P. 18/25/61 (omitted from summary in *Cal. S.P. Dom.*), 15 November 1652. For the family connections, see A. P. Newton, *The Colonising Activities of the English Puritans* (New Haven, 1914), pp. 71–2, 119–21. It is not clear whether the Major was yet a candidate for

the Admiralty and Navy Commissionership to which he was appointed in 1653.

30 See *King's Servants*, ch. 3, pp. 144–6.

31 Gardiner, *Constitutional Docs*, pp. 155–6; Kenyon, *Stuart Constitution*, pp. 222–3.

32 Gardiner, ibid., pp. 267–71; Kenyon, ibid., pp. 263–6.

33 Gardiner, ibid., p. 391; Kenyon, ibid., pp. 341–2.

34 See chapter 2, section vii, p. 41, and note 26.

35 Abbott, *Writings and Speeches*, IV, App. III, p. 947, supplementing Vol. II, p. 394, n. 47, MS. from the Gribbel collection, Philadelphia. The recipient appears to be unknown, but is addressed as 'My Deare Friend'; note the interesting assumption that Vane too may have been cool towards the Engagement.

36 See ch. 2, section ii, p. 11.

37 PRO, S.P. 28/258, 23 November 1649.

38 S.P. 28/259, 5 November 1652.

39 S.P. 28/258, 23 October 1649, to Matthew Valentine.

40 Ibid., 19 October 1649, from Luke Robinson, Charles Fleetwood, Nathaniel Rich and Cornelius Holland.

41 Ibid., 22 December 1649, to Messrs Broad and Maddison. The name was normally spelt Tandy.

42 Ibid., 24 December 1649; for Tandy, see also pp. 142–3 and 231–2.

43 Tandy was accused of taking excessive fees and bribes in January 1652/3 too (*C.J.*, VII, 250–1).

44 S.P. 28/258, Sir Henry Mildmay, Alderman Isaac Pennington, Messrs Lascelles, Garland, Nelthorpe, Sir William Allanson, 26 January 1650.

45 S.P. 28/258 to the Committee, Whitehall, 30 October 1649, in Bradshaw's characteristic holograph, of 'court-hand' origin but 'secretary' in appearance. See section iv, note 24.

46 Unfortunately there were all too many John Bradshaws in North Cheshire and the surrounding region during the seventeenth century, and it is difficult to be sure that one has the right man.

47 Perhaps Richard Moore, future Compounding Commissioner, or John Moore the regicide MP for Liverpool. Identification is impossible.

48 I assume this is Captain Edmund Chillington, alias Chillenden, ex-Leveller and lay preacher.

49 Conceivably Edward Freeman, Attorney-General for South-West Wales but probably some more obscure under-officer.

50 S.P. 28/258, 16 November 1649, from London Bridge to Messrs Greensmith and Robinson.

51 Ibid., from Cant' (? Canterbury), 4 December 1649.

52 Ibid., 30 November 1649.

53 See *DNB*; and M. Ashley, *John Wildman Plotter and Postmaster* (1947).

54 S.P. 28/258, 20 November 1649 to Mr Nicholas Bond at his lodgings in Somerset House.

55 Ibid., to Mr N. Bond and Mr T. Richardson, 19 January 1650.

56 Ibid., to his friend Auditor Wilcox, 18 January 1650.

57 Ibid., to the Committee, from the Rolls, 1 February 1650.

58 Ibid., 19 October 1649.

59 PRO, State Papers Additional, S.P. 46/95, fo. 155, 156, July 1649.

60 S.P. 18/3/21i and 21, 16 and 20 October 1649.

61 S.P. 18/23/16 (and *Cal. S.P. Dom., 1651–2*, p. 127).

62 BM, Add. MS. 22,546, fo. 90, about a naval appointment, Feb. 1653.

63 See s. ii, p. 95.

64 S.P. 46/95, fo. 238, 240.

65 See *King's Servants*, ch. 3, ii.

66 George Vyne succeeded Christopher in another Exchequer post, that of Deputy Chamberlain, on the latter's death in 1655.

67 See ch. 2, s. ii, p. 16, and note 41.

68 See above, p. 59; Firth and Rait, *A. & O.*, II, 85, 97.

69 S.P. 18/11/103, 115. Some men were surveyors for capitular lands in more than one diocese, or for the same cathedral in two places. I have in this way slightly reduced the total obtained simply by counting the numbers of names; I have also cross-checked one list against the other. The 127 is a firm total; the figures for clerks, messengers and others are approximate.

70 See S. J. Madge, *The Domesday of Crown Lands* (1938); E. G. R. Taylor, 'The Surveyor', *Econ. H.R.*, 1st series, XVII (1947); S. C. Newton, 'Parliamentary Surveys', *History*, 53 (1968), pp. 51–4.

71 E.g. Henry Newman of Chewstoke, Somerset, in petitioning for a messenger's place in 1649 had a certificate from James Temple MP as to his intelligence work in the south-east of England, from Colonel Alexander Popham on his service in the west country and from Sir William Waller and Colonels Edward Popham and Thomas Wroth, Lord Fairfax, and Colonels Robert Blake and Thomas Ceeley in more general terms! (S.P. 18/26/83 and 83i, n.d., 1649).

72 E. A. Kracke, junior, *Civil Service in Early Sung China 960–1067* (Cambridge, Mass., 1953).

73 See ch. 2, section ii, p. 23.

74 *DNB*, for both; D. Nicholas, *Mr Secretary Nicholas* (1955); Aylmer, *King's Servants*; A. Bryant, *Samuel Pepys, The Man in the Making* (Cambridge, 1933).

75 *C.J.*, VI, 568; *Cal. S.P. Dom., 1651*, p. 170.

76 *Thurloe St. P.*, I, 205–6.

77 *Cal. S.P. Dom., 1650*, p. 374; *Cal. Cttee. Compdg.*, pp. 393, 465, 603, 658; Abbott, *Writings and Speeches*, II, 358, 387, 577 n., gives some, but not all, of these references.

78 S.P. 18/40/26.

79 S.P. 28/260, 13 July 1653.

80 William Trigg, to Maddison at his house in Channel Row, Westminster, 25 June 1653 (S.P. 28/260).

81 Firth and Rait, *A. & O.*, II, 783–812.

82 See ch. 2, s. viii, pp. 42–5.

83 *Milton State Papers*, ed. J. Nickolls (1743), pp. 85–6.

84 See ch. 4, s. v, p. 221.

85 See Shaw, *Hist. Engl. Church*, Vol. 2; also T. Richards, *A History of the*

Puritan Movement in Wales from ... 1639 to ... 1653 (1920), and G. F. Nuttall, *Welsh Saints 1640–1660* (Cardiff, 1957).

86 *Cal. S.P. Dom., 1653–4*, pp. 73, 84; *1660–1*, p. 47; PRO, S.P. 24/10, fo. 65v, 106v, 121v; Bodl., Rawl. MS. A xl, fo. 467; he was also at odds with one William Jones over the same office; see also ch. 4, s. v, pp. 265–6.

87 See ch. 2, s. vii, pp. 42–5 on this.

88 E.g. those of Coytmor as Admiralty Secretary, and of Arthur Squibb junior and Samuel Moyer as Compounding Commissioners.

89 See Farnell, art. cit., *E.H.R.*, 79 (1967). Without being able to accept all of Mr Farnell's classifications, I am happy to acknowledge a fellow worker in the field.

90 See ch. 4, ss. iii–iv, pp. 174–209.

91 See ch. 2, s. ix, pp. 45–54.

92 See Burton, *Parliamentary Diary*, II, 159–61. Denis Bond reminded Speaker Widdrington: 'In the Long Parliament ... what contests, discontents, and high animosities there were about matters of this nature'.

93 Firth and Rait, *A. & O.*, II, 1223–34.

94 *Thurloe St. P.*, III, 614–15 (from MS. vol. xxviii, p. 116).

95 The Clerkship of the Ordnance, not necessarily a military man's office. See refs to Edward Sherburne in *King's Servants*, pp. 79–80, 156–8, 291.

96 *Thurloe St. P.*, V, 13 (MS. xxxviii, 305). The style mentioned refers to the candidate's Latin, which Cudworth praised lengthily.

97 Firth and Davies, *Regimental History*, pp. 474–6.

98 *Thurloe St. P.*, IV, 222.

99 Not to be confused with his father, Sir Richard Saltonstall, the returned Lieutenant Governor of Massachusetts, also active until his death in 1658.

100 *Thurloe St. P.*, IV, 597–8 (MS. xxxvi, 357).

101 Ibid., IV, 659 (MS. xxvi, 703). Carrickfergus, 29 March 1656.

102 Ibid., V, 46–7 (MS. Earl of Shelburne).

103 Ibid., V, 155 (MS. Jos. Jekyll, esqre).

104 E.g. Major-General Packer on behalf of a widow to keep the office of Post-Master at Waltham Cross, 17 July 1656 (ibid., V, 222); Sir William Lockhart for a Mr Percivalle, migrating from Scotland to England in search of employment, 7 September 1656 (ibid., 352); Richard Bradshaw, Agent at Hamburg and the ex-Lord President's nephew, for a Bohemian, Elias Stransius, 3 September 1656 (ibid., 381); Henry Cromwell, that the present Deputy Governor of Beaumaris Castle, North Wales, may succeed the nominal Governor being lately dead, 19 November 1656 (ibid., 611); Monck recommending Mr John Harper as Attorney-General for Scotland, 6 January 1656 (ibid., 769); and for his brother-in-law Dr Thomas Clarges to succeed Mr Hopkins as Commissioner of the Admiralty and Navy, 19 March 1657 (ibid., VI, 126); Lockhart again for his own brothers, 7/17 June 1657 (ibid., 337–8); Henry Cromwell for Lieutenant-Colonel Baynes, father of an Irish preacher, to be a London buildings' Commissioner, 24 June 1657 (ibid., 367–8); Lockhart for his secretary Mr Swyft to be employed about the new Other House as a clerk, 16/26 December 1657 (ibid., 682); Samuel Morland, to succeed Denis Bond as Clerk of the Pells, 31 August 1658 (ibid., VII,

367); M. or N. Vernatti, for a place under Thurloe himself, 27 Feb. 1654 (Bodl., Rawl. MS. A, x, fo. 391); the officers of Major-General Worsley's regiment for Lieutenant Edward Moore to be Post Master of St Alban's, n.d. ? May 1655 (ibid., xxvi, fo. 18); John Lisle, Lord Commissioner of the Great Seal, for a privy seal clerkship for the bearer, 20 June 1655 (ibid., xxvii, fo. 469); Major General Goffe, for a Customs' Waiter's place for Nathaniel Whitfield, brother-in-law of Samuel Disbrowe, clerk of the Scottish Council, 22 April 1656 (ibid., 609); P. Rogers for some legal office, 2 August 1655 (ibid., xxix, fo. 60); Baron of the Exchequer Edward Atkyns for Mr Arderne, attorney in the office of pleas there, for favour, i.e. advancement, 30 January 1655 (ibid., xxxiv, fo. 965); Colonel Carter for the Receivership of North Wales, n.d. ? January 1657 (ibid., xlvi, fo. 287); St John for Mr Giles, son-in-law of Lady Barrington, to be admitted to the office of Pleas in the Court of Common Bench, 19 February 1655 (ibid., xxxv, fo. 171).

105 *Thurloe St. P.*, VI, 126–7.
106 Ibid., 438, 457.
107 Ibid., VI, 461–2.
108 See *DNB*.
109 BM, Lans. MS. 821, fo. 360.
110 Fleetwood to Henry Cromwell, ibid., fo. 16, 32, 42, 66, 152, 190, 196, 206, 244; Lans. MS. 822, fo. 39, 274.
111 *N.B.* In noting these and the applications to Thurloe (see above), I have tried to exclude those to do with obtaining military and church appointments, or with the payment of arrears, making of land grants, etc., and to limit my examples to appeals for civil office.
112 See BM, Lans. MS. 821, fo. 109, 160; MS. 822, fo. 136. Richard Cromwell was a Trade Commissioner (unpaid) from 1655, a Privy Councillor (paid) from 1657, Chancellor of Oxford University from 1658. He was also a Hampshire JP, militia commissioner, etc.
113 See ch. 4, s. v., pp. 264–5.
114 PRO, S.P. 46/117, fo. 71, 72a, 1655.
115 BM, Lans. MS. 822, fo. 162; and Noell to Henry Cromwell, ibid., fo. 164.
116 The original is in Bodl., Rawl. MS. A.189, fo. 383–406 (from the Pepysian MSS.); it is printed in E. MacLysaght, *Irish Life in the Seventeenth century* (2nd ed., Cork, 1950), App., pp. 417–46. The transcription is accurate except that pounds have been read instead of shillings throughout, making the cost of litigation as stated by Cook twenty times more outrageous than it no doubt was.
117 *Cal. S.P. Dom., 1658–9*, pp. 305–6, from East Greenwich, March 1659.
118 I.e. 1649–53 and 1654–9; I exclude for this purpose both the period April–December 1653 and the restored Commonwealth of 1659–60.
119 There are exceptions here. See s. ii, pp. 90–3, on the Chancery Ordinance of 1654 and its enforcement in 1655.
120 I owe this suggestion to Dr Christopher Hill.
121 S.P. 46/97, fo. 143, n.d. (? 1654).
122 E.g. for Roger Gillingham, gent., Solicitor in Chancery and lately clerk to Dr Bennet, one of the Masters there, for the office of Register under

the Masters or something comparable; petition accompanied by testimonial signed by 13 judges and other lawyers, including the Attorney-General and Bennet himself, 2 September 1654 (S.P. 18/76/44 and 44i).

123 E.g. Abbott, *Writings and Speeches*, III, 515–16, 575, to Admiral Penn, on behalf of his nephew Whetstone, 1654–5. The second letter rebukes Penn for not putting out his own relative in order to make the Protector's his lieutenant! Whetstone later proved a most unsatisfactory officer (*Cal. S.P. Dom., 1658–9*, pp. 156, 161, 339, etc.).

124 E.g. Charles Longland (Agent at Leghorn) sent the Protector a barbary mare via Thurloe, 1657 (*Thurloe St. P.*, VI, 201, 268, 407).

125 Major-General Worsley suggesting an alternative Duchy Judge to Fell, June 1656 (*Thurloe St. P.*, IV, 423–4); Major-General Robert Lilburne, an examiner in the Court at Durham, February 1656 (ibid., 499).

126 See ch. 6, pp. 326–39.

127 S.P. 46/97, fo. 140–1. Petition n.d. [1654]; date of reversion 5 August 1641. For Bere, see Evans, *Secretary of State*, pp. 155, 162; *Cal. S.P. Dom., 1645–7*, p. 500; *Cal. Cttee. Advc. Mon.*, p. 1187.

128 See this ch., s. ii, pp. 88–90.

129 *Cal. Cttee. Compdg.*, pp. 685–6, T. Robinson, June 1654; also p. 687.

130 See K. R. Swart, *Sale of Offices in the 17th Century* (The Hague, 1949); H. R. Trevor-Roper, 'The Gentry, 1540–1640', *Econ. Hist. Soc. Suppt. I* (1953), esp. pp. 26–30; and Aylmer, *King's Servants*, ch. 4, s. iv.

131 Firth and Rait, *A. & O.*, I, 644–5; *Somers Tracts*, Series i, Vol. I (1748 ed.), 'Several Draughts of Acts . . .' (printed by order of parliament, 12 July 1653), pp. 508–9, 'The Draught of an Act against the Sale of Offices'; *C.J.*, VII; 340.

132 *C.J.*, VI, 432, 440–1, 442, 444, 462.

133 *C.J.*, VII, 126.

134 *C.J.*, VI, 261–2; *Cal. S.P. Dom., 1649–50*, p. 233.

135 *Cal. S.P. Dom., 1660–1*, p. 180.

136 *C.J.*, VI, 603, July 1651. Humphrey Salwey MP was the father of the better-known Major Richard Salwey MP, an ally of the Younger Vane.

137 S.P. 18/73/35, to the Lord Protector, referred to the Council, 31 March 1654.

138 Deputy Major-General in East Anglia, 1655–6.

139 S.P. 18/131/20 (and *Cal. S.P. Dom., 1656–7*, p. 288), referred to Council 2 December, order made 4 December.

140 *Cal. S.P. Dom., 1660–1*, p. 100, 7 May 1660.

141 Ibid., 101–2.

142 H. E. Bell, *An Introduction to the History and Records of the Court of Wards and Liveries* (Cambridge, 1953), pp. 160–1, 192; Aylmer, *King's Servants*, p. 242.

143 See Edmund Ludlow, *Memoirs*, II, 97–8.

144 See ch. 2, s. x, pp. 54–7.

145 Firth and Rait, *A. & O.*, II, 1299–1304.

146 *Cal. S.P. Dom., 1660–1*, p. 244.

147 Keeler, *Long Parliament*, pp. 268–9; P. Laslett, 'Masham of Otes: the rise and fall of an English family', *History Today*, III (1953), 535–43. Both Mashams had been Rump MPs; the younger accepted a Treasury

Commissionership in 1654, as his family alleged afterwards, solely through financial necessity. For the Common Pleas office, see Bodl., Rawl. MS, A. xxxiv, fo. 171.

148 *Cal. S.P. Dom., 1660–1*, pp. 47, 55, refs to two different circuits. The latter is the same office in which Coytmor had been interested earlier; but this was not the one to which the reversion had allegedly been bought.

149 Hist. MSS. Comm., *5th Report*, Appendix, Sutherland Papers, p. 146; for his appointment, PRO E. 403/2523.

150 See this ch., s. ii, p. 95.

151 As we shall see in considering the question of tenure, and how and why men could be and were removed from office: s. ii, pp. 82–96, also more generally in chapters 5 and 6.

152 Quoted in many books on Cromwell, most recently in C. Hill, *God's Englishman*, pp. 64–68.

ii TENURE

1 *King's Servants*, ch. 3, s. iii.
2 *C.J.*, VII, 122.
3 Firth and Rait, *A. & O.*, II, 382–3.
4 Ibid., 422–3.
5 Ibid., I, 717–22.
6 S.P. 24/5–8, 10–12, order-books of the committee and then the commissioners for indemnity.
7 Firth and Rait, *A. & O.*, I, 1009, 1023–5.
8 Ibid., I, 1045–6.
9 Ibid., II, 620–1.
10 Ibid., 830–1.
11 See ch. 2, s. ii, pp. 13–14.
12 This was the implied argument of some Leveller and other radical pamphlets, but it was not in a more formal sense part of the Leveller 'platform'.
13 S.P. 46/95, fo. 368, n.d. [? 1649–50].
14 S.P. 18/17/8, 31 January 1651. At the foot is noted and deleted, apparently at the time, 'a good conclusion'. The *Swiftsure*'s captain at this time was Thomas Davis (R. C. Anderson, *A List of English Naval Captains, 1642–1660*, The Society for Nautical Research, Occasional Publications, no. 8 (1964), pp. 9, 42).
15 Worcester College, Oxford, Clarke Papers, MS. 181, Box 2, 1653/4— again a tale of immorality, swearing, irreligion, etc., as well as of gross neglect and abuse. Presumably written to Monck as General-at-Sea.
16 See ch. 2, s. ii, p. 16, and references given there.
17 At some date unspecified, but presumably either when the 3rd Earl of Pembroke was Lord Steward or the 4th Earl was Lord Chamberlain, i.e. between 1626 and 1641.
18 S.P. 18/15/11, February 1651.
19 *Cal. S.P. Dom., 1660–1*, pp. 360, 499. The younger George had replaced his father in the Under House-Keepership as early as Dec. 1647 (*Cal. S.P. Dom., 1645–7*, p. 582).

20 By contrast with this, in December 1653 the Protector proclaimed the continuance of all existing holders in their offices, until it was ordered otherwise (R. Steele (ed.), *Bibliotheca Lindesiana*, V, *A Bibliography of Tudor and Stuart Royal Proclamations*, Vol. 1, *England and Wales* (Oxford, 1910), p. 365, no. 3023).

21 Bodl., Tanner MS. 52, fo. 13, 21 May 1653. All those who subscribed the recent petition from the City for Parliament's recall were likewise to be dismissed, rather different to merely refusing to recognise, or serve, the new government.

22 S.P. 46/96, fo. 1.

23 See Aylmer, art. in *Bull. Inst. Hist. Res.*, 31 (1958), pp. 58–67.

24 *C.J.*, VI, 432 (June 1650), 488 (October); VII, 138 (June 1652), 226 (December).

25 *C.J.*, VII, 70.

26 S.P. 25/69, fo. 284–5, 13 June (supplementing *Cal. S.P. Dom., 1652–3*, p. 405). The members were Major-Generals Disbrowe and Harrison, Colonels Tomlinson and John Jones and Mr Moyer; the lawyer was Mr Fountaine, who had been put on to the Hale Committee by a vote of 28–16 in the Rump (*C.J.*, VII, 74), and formally pardoned of all earlier charges of delinquency 14 months later (ibid., 168).

27 See Appendix 1, pp. 436–7 for the full text.

28 Depending, of course, on the age and health of the grantee.

29 PRO, Index 4213; see above ch. 2, s. vi, p. 35.

30 Ibid., the terminal date was 24 June 1658.

31 PRO, E. 403/2523.

32 Ibid.

33 BM, Add. MS. 4184, nos 4 and 6.

34 For the systematic reduction of life tenure in offices after 1667–8, see J. C. Sainty, 'A Reform in the Tenure of Offices during the Reign of Charles II', *Bull. Inst. Hist. Res.*, 41 (1968), 150–71.

35 S.P. 18/153/7i, and *Cal. S.P. Dom., 1656–7*, pp. 228–9.

36 *King's Servants*, pp. 125, 466.

37 S.P. 18/123/56.

38 See ch. 2, s. ix, p. 47 and n. 15, for a list of these.

39 S.P. 18/70/97, and 97i–iv. See also *Cal. S.P. Dom., 1654*, pp. 135–6. For Willis's royalism, see also *Cal. Cttee. Advc. Mon.*, p. 612.

40 PRO, Patent Roll Index, 1655, Pt 3, no. 18; *Cal. S.P. Dom., 1658–9*, pp. 127, 370, 373; *1659–60*, pp. 29, 33; *1660–1*, p. 74. For Taylor see J. Burke, *History of the Commoners of England*, 4 vols (1833–8), III, 108; J. & J. A. Venn, *Alumni Cantabrigienses*, Part 1, iv. 207; Gardiner, *Commonwealth and Protectorate*, ch. 28, n. 'A Catalogue of the names of the Members of the last Parliament' (1654) where he is listed as a radical and not as a supporter of 'the Godly learned Ministry and the Universities'; his will shows that he was a friend of the influential congregationalist minister, George Cockaine (Prerogative Court of Canterbury, 1684, 155 Hare; *DNB*, 'George Cokayne' (*sic*)).

41 For Sir Thomas see Keeler, *Long Parliament*, pp. 234–6; Aylmer, *King's Servants*, pp. 92, 320, 339, etc. Since the pre-Civil War holder,

Sir Lawrence Washington (d. 1643) was also a royalist, the chronology is a little puzzling; one of the many reversions which Jermyn got for his sons was to the Keepership of books and orders in Chancery, possibly the same office (T. Rymer and R. Sanderson (eds), *Foedera*, XX (1736), 306, 17 July 1638).

42 Sir Thomas's younger son, Henry Jermyn was, of course, a very active Cavalier, the confidant and later reputedly the secret second husband of Queen Henrietta Maria.

43 S.P. 18/95/3 and *Cal. S.P. Dom., 1655*, p. 63.

44 See this ch., s. iii, p. 96.

45 Although both Corbet and Goodwin were in Ireland much of the time (see *DNB*, 'Miles Corbet'; Ludlow, *Memoirs*; Dunlop, *Ireland under the Commonwealth*).

46 G. W. Sanders, *Orders of the High Court of Chancery* . . . (Vol. I in two parts, 1845), pp. 288–9.

47 See pp. 42, 85, 163. The vote was 43–15, 3 June 1659 (*C.J.*, VII, 671).

48 *DNB*, 'Tyrrell'. Bradshaw was a very sick man by then; he died in November (*DNB*) or on 31 October according to one source (Richard Smyth, *Obituary* (Camden Society, XLIV, 1849), p. 51).

49 Sanders, *Orders*, pp. 289, 290–1; for Long's case, see also Hist. MSS. Comm., *7th Report*, Appendix, House of Lords Papers, pp. 79–80, 85.

50 Unlike many of them, he is noted in the *DNB*, though the article does not give much account of his administrative career; see pp. 256–8.

51 PRO, S.P. 46/99, fo. 123, 124. Scobell acted as Corbet's deputy from about 1649 (*Cal. S.P. Dom., 1648–9*, p. 129; S.P. 18/23/79); he was the brother-in-law of Jasper Edwards the senior Deputy Registrar, as opposed to Registrar's deputy (!), and left him £5 in his will when he died later in 1660 (P.C.C., 256 Nabbs).

52 For the text see Sanders, *Orders*, pp. 254–72, or Firth and Rait, *A. & O.*, II, 949–67.

53 Sanders, *Orders*, pp. 222–44; G. K. Fortescue (ed.), *Catalogue of the Thomason Tracts* (2 vols, 1908), I, 775.

54 Ibid., pp. 249, 253.

55 Sections I, II, LXVII; for the Six Clerks see Aylmer, *King's Servants*, and Jones, *Elizabethan Chancery*.

56 Bodl., MS. Carte 74, no. 50. I am grateful to Mr J. P. Cooper for giving me a transcript of this document. On 1 May the Commissioners and the Master reported to the Lord President their continued unhappiness at the Ordinance and unwillingness to act under it during the following law term (S.P. 25/26, fo. 57 or *Cal. S.P. Dom., 1655*, p. 152).

57 B. Whitelocke, *Memorials* (folio 1682), pp. 601–8 (quotation from p. 603a).

58 S.P. 18/99/20, received 12 April 1655; ibid./21, read 5 July and referred to the Treasury Commissioners (who, as from August, included the ex-Lords Commissioners of the Great Seal, Whitelocke and Widdrington; the outcome is not known).

59 Firth and Rait, *A. & O.*, II, 1131–42. Of the actual effect of the Ordinance on litigation and other Chancery business, we know next to nothing,

the want of work such as that of Professor W. J. Jones for the earlier
and of Professor D. E. C. Yale for the later period being acutely felt.
Mr Cooper has suggested to me that the vague promise to join in the
work of reformation, made at the end of the Humble Petition and
Advice (Gardiner, *Constitutional Docs*, p. 458) may refer to the future of
Chancery after the Ordinance had lapsed.

60 Sanders, *Orders*, pp. 275–6.
61 Ibid., pp. 277–8.
62 Ibid., pp. 282–3.
63 Ibid., p. 284.
64 Ibid., pp. 285–6, 16 May 1659, pp. 286–7, 21 and 30 May.
65 Ibid., p. 305, 22 May 1661.
66 Ibid., p. 291, House of Lords, 3 May 1660. Another version is in
   Huntingdonshire Record Office, Manchester Papers, M.32/5/25 (I am
   grateful to Mr Conrad Russell for giving me a copy of this); Eltonhead's
   appointment as Master in Ordinary dated from 1646–7 (*Thurloe St. P.*,
   I, 85).
67 J. P. Prendergast, *The Cromwellian Settlement of England* (Dublin, 1875),
   pp. 129–30 n., on the clerkship to the revenue commissioners at Wexford,
   July 1654.
68 PRO, S.P. 18/189/56, signed by General-at-Sea Edward Montague and
   Colonels Edward Salmon and John Clerke, 23 March 1657/8.
69 S.P. 18/190/15, signed by Clerke, Salmon and Colonel Thomas Kelsey
   (ex-Major-General for Kent and Surrey), 8 April 1658.
70 Ibid./9, to the Admiralty Commissioners, n.d. received 3 April.
71 See Gardiner, *Commonwealth and Protectorate*, ch. 39.
72 Bodl., Rawl. MS. A, xxvii, fo. 493, n.d. (June 1655).
73 PRO, Admiralty 2/1730, 17 (62), 19B (64B), May 1657. The outcome is
   unclear; Anderson, *List of Naval Captains*, shows that three out of the
   six Masters-Attendants in 1655–6 held seagoing commands at some
   time between 1642 and 1660.
74 Sir Thomas Hardres, *Reports of Cases Adjudged in the Court of Exchequer
   …* (1655–1660 and to 21 Charles II) (folio 1693), p. 130.
75 For Cromwell's relations with Colchester and the forced alteration of
   its charter see J. H. Round, 'Colchester during the Commonwealth',
   E.H.R., 15 (1900) correcting Gardiner, *Commonwealth and Protectorate*,
   ch. 43; also B. L. K. Henderson, 'Commonwealth Charters', *T.R.H.S.*,
   3rd series, VI (1912).
76 William Styles, *Modern Reports* (21 Charles I—1655) (folio, 1658), pp.
   452–3. Barnardiston apparently solved the problem by dying at the end
   of the year (Abbott, *Writings and Speeches*, IV, 38); confusingly, a man of
   the same name was made Steward of all courts leet and baron forfeited
   by Essex recusants the following May (BM, Add. MS. 4184, no. 183).

iii DEPUTIES, PLURALISTS AND ABSENTEES

1 *King's Servants*, ch. 3, s. iv.
2 For example the elderly Humphrey Salwey was authorised to execute

his Exchequer Remembrancership by deputy in 1651, but only during Parliament's pleasure (*C.J.*, VI, 603). See s. i, p. 79, and section i, n. 136.

3 See ch. 2, s. ii, p. 11.

4 Once George Mynne's office (see *King's Servants*, esp. pp. 117–21).

5 PRO, Chancery depositions, C. 3/431/37 (file torn and incomplete); E. 351/1676–7, 1680; A. O. 1/1375/127, Declared Accounts, Hanaper. For Allanson, see also Keeler, *Long Parliament*, pp. 83–4.

6 Gardiner, *Hist. England* ... *1603–42*, VIII, 194; H. F. Kearney, *Strafford in Ireland 1633–41* (Manchester, 1959), pp. 71–2; C. V. Wedgwood, *Thomas Wentworth earl of Strafford 1593–1641: a revaluation* (1961), pp. 202–3, 208.

7 For Nicholas Loftus see *Cal. Cttee. Compdg.*, pp. 47, 798; PRO, E. 351/1295 (as payee on the 1647–50 Excise account); for Henry Aldritch see S.P. 28/259; *Cal. S.P. Dom.*, *1650*, pp. 93–4, 448.

8 *Cal. S.P. Dom.*, *1654*, p. 241.

9 This point is made by Lambert's biographer (Dawson, *Cromwell's Understudy*, p. 202, n. 1).

10 S.P. 18/73/35. See this ch., s. i, p. 79.

11 Meaning the sifter or selector of spice imports; a civic, not a Customs, post apparently.

12 Styles, *Modern Reports*, p. 357, the Mayor and Commonalty of London versus Hatton, Michaelmas 1652; Hardres, *Reports of cases in the ... Exchequer*, pp. 46–9, Jones and Clark, Hilary 1655–Easter 1656.

13 PRO, E. 403/2523, but see n. 2 above, on Salwey.

14 E. 403/2608.

15 See ch. 2, s. v, pp. 29–33.

16 On this exceptionally valuable office and its holders see Trevor-Roper, *The Gentry*, pp. 10–11; Aylmer, *King's Servants*, pp. 305–8; L. Stone, *The Crisis of the Aristocracy 1558–1641* (Oxford, 1965), pp. 103, 113, 444–5.

17 For Drake see Keeler, *Long Parliament*, pp. 159–60; for Trevor see *DNB*.

18 See s. i, p. 81, and n. 147.

19 See *King's Servants*, esp. ch. 4, ii.

20 PRO, S.P. 18/38/72; E. 403/2523; Firth and Rait, *A. & O.*, II, 170.

21 See s. ii, pp. 90–3. s. LIV of the Ordinance forbade the execution of the Register's office by deputy, and prescribed four co-Registrars instead.

22 S.P. 18/23/79. See s. ii, pp. 89–90, and n. 50.

23 S.P. 28/258, letters, 21 March 1649, 4 July 1650, 26 September 1650; S.P. 46/95, fo. 262, 2 April 1650.

24 BM, Stowe MS. 185, fo. 86. For wise women, see K. Thomas, *Religion and the Decline of Magic* (1971), chapters 7 and 8.

25 For a fuller discussion of Jessop and his career, see ch. 4, s. v, pp. 234–8.

26 For Jackson, see s. ix, pp. 141–3.

27 For this office see G. R. Elton, 'War in the Receipt', in Bindoff, *et al.*, *Government and Society in Elizabethan England*; and Aylmer, *King's Servants*, index 'Bingley', 'Pye', 'Receipt'.

28 S.P. 46/97, fo. 181–2, verso (commas added)—presumably post-1660

but n.d., and handwriting not noticeably later than is usual for mid-seventeenth century.

29 PRO, S.P. 23/36, fo. 121.
30 See for example the sources in n. 23 above, and *Thurloe St. P.*, IV, 597–8.

iv CONDITIONS OF WORK AND EMPLOYMENT

1 A. Raine (ed.), 'Proceedings of the Commonwealth Committee for York and the Ainsty' in *Yorks. Archaelog. Soc., rec. ser.*, 118 for 1951 (1953). *Miscellanea* VI, p. 26. The reference is to the Solemn League and Covenant of 1643.
2 Ibid., p. 1.
3 PRO, S.P. 28/269, Revenue Cttee. Papers, examples from 1645–50.
4 Firth and Rait, *A. & O.*, II, 75–8.
5 Ibid., pp. 213–35.
6 Anon., *The Book of Oaths, and the severall forms thereof, both Antient and Modern*. BM, E.1129. Thomason's date, 13 February 1648/9.
7 *A Collection of Divers Orders & Rules, Heretofore established for the making & passing Entries in the Customs-House, as well for Merchandise, as for Goods from Port to Port within this Nation.* Published by order of the Commissioners of the Customs, 1650, Small octavo, 25 pp. Worcester College, Oxford, XX. B.3.10. It does not appear to survive in George Thomason's collection.
8 Firth and Rait, *A. & O.*, II, 940–1.
9 Ibid., pp. 1016–19.
10 Ibid., pp. 213–35.
11 Ibid., pp. 949–67, s. XLI.
12 *A Collection of such of the Orders heretofore used in Chauncery as the Lords Commissioners for the Great Seal of England have thought fit to ordain and publish for reforming of Abuses* ... BM, E.1377(4), 7 November 1649; repr. in Sanders, *Orders*, I, pp. 222–44.
13 But excluding the Barons of the Exchequer.
14 *Rules and Orders for the Court of Common Pleas.* BM, E.821(5). Michaelmas Term 1654, dated December; *Rules and Orders for the court of the Upper Bench*, ibid., (6), Michaelmas Term 1654. The two pamphlets are largely similar, the criminal side of King's (alias Upper) Bench being omitted; perhaps because of preoccupations with Chancery, none of the modern studies of the law reform movement mentions them.
15 Firth and Rait, *A. & O.*, II, 1007–13.
16 S.P. 28/260, individual items un-numbered.
17 S.P. 28/258.
18 Ibid.
19 Ibid., 19 November 1649.
20 Firth and Rait, *A. & O.*, II, 282–5.
21 PRO, Minute Books of the Committee for Compounding, S.P. 23/36, fo. 270.
22 See e.g. *Cal. S.P. Dom., 1649–50*, pp. 144–5.
23 Firth and Rait, *A. & O.*, II, 455–6.

24 Good examples of his holograph are in S.P. 28/258 cited s. i, n. 45; S.P. 46/95, fo. 281, on a paper by Marchamont Nedham, June 1650; Hofman and Freeman, *Catalogue 19, English Historical Manuscripts*, (1967) no. 6. Although it is technically what would be called 'secretary hand', few if any secretaries, in private or public service, were writing like that by the 1640s–50s.

25 H. Jenkinson, 'English Current Writing and Early Printing', *Trans. Bibliographical Soc.*, XIII (1916 for 1913–15).

26 E.g. printed forms for tax returns and soldiers' debentures.

27 See ch. 2, s. iv, pp. 24–9.

28 See pp. 25, 27, 47.

29 See Pennington, 'Accounts of the Kingdom' in Fisher (ed.), *Essays*.

30 See above, pp. 62–6.

31 Firth and Rait, *A. & O.*, I, 1169–74.

32 Ibid., II, 168–91.

33 The sources are somewhat confusing, made more so by the failure of many correspondents to make clear which Accounts Committee (civil or army) they are addressing (see PRO, S.P. 28/258; 259; 260; 263A (i) paper book of orders 1649–56).

34 S.P. 28/258, n.d. (1650 from internal evidence).

35 Who seem temporarily to have superseded the civil Accounts Committee of 1649–59 (Firth and Rait, *A. & O.*, II, 765–7, 768–72).

36 It is not clear whether or not they sent it.

37 See pp. 12, 13.

38 BM, Stowe MS. 185, fo. 35, Robert Castell to the fee-farm Trustees from Dutchy Court, 24 November 1653; fo. 42–3, their reply to this, n.d. and unsigned.

39 PRO, S.P. 26/8 contains some of their records; the main sales were of course over well before this. For fee-farm sales, see E. 315/139, 140; for Crown lands generally, Madge, *Domesday*.

40 PRO, E. 315/139, fo. 153v.

41 Its records form PRO, S.P. 20/vols 1–10, uncalendared.

42 Burton, *Diary*, IV, 425–6, 464, April 1659.

V OFFICERS' PAY

1 See *King's Servants*, ch. 4, for a survey, 1625–42.

2 In order to avoid confusion with the other kind of fees (for which see pp. 113–20), I shall call these salaries, or occasionally 'stipendiary fees'.

3 Firth and Rait, *A. & O.*, I, 27–9, 29–30.

4 Ibid., I, 887–904.

5 Ibid., 928–35.

6 As elsewhere, the Barebones pushed on with this faster than the Rump had done (e.g. *C.J.*, VII, 327, 359).

7 Firth and Rait, *A. & O.*, I, 1169–70.

8 Ibid., 1257–60.

9 See this section, p. 114.

10 Firth and Rait, *A. & O.*, I, 1086–8.

11 Ibid., II, 88–9.
12 Ibid., 168–91.
13 Ibid., 213–35.
14 Ibid., 282–5.
15 Ibid., 403–6.
16 Ibid., 358–62, 412–19.
17 Ibid., 498–500, 614–18.
18 Ibid., 623–52. Colonel Randall Mainwaring, Comptroller for the treason land sales, who also died in 1652, was succeeded by his son, also Randall. See this ch., s. i, p. 59.
19 Ibid., 720–2.
20 Ibid., 1000–6.
21 Ibid., 1412–15.
22 S.P. 28/253A, two separate items.
23 On 'Poundage', see this section, pp. 111–13.
24 For further discussion see s. vii, pp. 125–9.
25 Not quite. Andrew Marvell, MP for Hull 1661–78, is often cited as the last instance, but Thomas King was suing the borough of Harwich for unpaid wages in 1680 (see Sanders, *Orders in Chancery*, I, 353, 356).
26 See Aylmer, 'Place Bills and the Separation of Powers', *T.R.H.S.* (1965).
27 See s. vi, pp. 121–5.
28 Worcester College, Clarke MSS., Vol. 43, paginated from the back as shelved, fo. 1–4, Army Establishment November 1652 or October 1651, both dates given in different places; see also fo. 54 (annual rates are calculated on the basis of a 23-day lunar month). For the Protectorate, see also S.P. 18/99/43, 92; 101/121; 155/92; S.P. 25/78, fo. 426–7, 848–54. I cannot reconcile these figures with those given in Firth, *Cromwell's Army* (3rd ed., 1921), p. 188.
29 This is evident from Firth and Davies, *Regimental History*, as well as from the Clarke MSS., and other primary sources.
30 Oppenheim, *Administration of R.N.*, p. 360; PRO, E. 351/2293 (and *Cal. S.P. Dom.* refs). The rates given for captains were those in force from early 1653.
31 See ss. viii–ix, pp. 129–67. For all this, compare Underdown, *Pride's Purge*.
32 That is, excluding very short adjournments. This was longer than most parliamentary sessions under the later Stuarts.
33 Later a Household dignitary.
34 Not to be confused with Major-General Charles Worsley (d. 1656).
35 Later a General-at-Sea and a Colonel.
36 The payments to Councillors were often heavily in arrears (E.351/594, Jessop's account as Treasurer); it is significant that they were paid out of the Protector's contingency fund, not their own. See also *Thurloe St. P.*, III, 581.
37 Bodl., Rawl. MS. C. 179, pp. 65, 69, 74, 82, 93, 106, 330.
38 Ibid., pp. 151, 176–7.
39 See *King's Servants*, ch. 4, s. i, pp. 166–7.
40 Burton, *Parliamentary Diary*, IV, 364.
41 *Cal. S.P. Dom., 1653–4*, pp. 318, 341. A year later it was cut to £1,500,

but with the extra £100 (or 0.1 per cent) beginning at £700,000 (ibid., *1654*, p. 414; *1655*, p. 1); (in 1656 or 7 he apparently got it raised to £200 for every £100,000 above £700,000 (ibid., *1655–6*, p. 292; *1656–7*, pp. 138–9). See Table 42, p. 249.

42 Firth and Rait, *A. & O.*, II, 63–5.
43 Ibid., 75–8.
44 Ibid., 96.
45 Ibid., 160–8.
46 Ibid., 168–91.
47 Ibid., 329–35.
48 Ibid., 429–39.
49 Ibid., 456–90.
50 Ibid., 498–500, 583–8, 614–18, 520–45.
51 PRO, Exchequer, Augmentation Office, Miscellaneous, E. 315/139, fo. 18v, 19v. The calculation of one-thirtieth of 2*d.* on £90,978 is mine, but another reference (ibid., fo. 162) suggests a total poundage of 3*d.*, so perhaps one should multiply these figures by 1½. Later, the total poundage due, at 3*d.*, was given as £3,523. 14*s.* 1½*d.*; of the £117. 8*s.* 8*d.* (one-thirtieth of this) due, each person involved had received £80. 9*s.* 1*d.* and was still owed £36. 19*s.* 7*d.*, in February 1651 (ibid., fo. 157).
52 Some idea of the frequency of the Trustees' meetings can be formed from the order book cited in the previous reference.
53 See note 51 above.
54 Firth and Rait, *A. & O.*, II, 753–64.
55 Ibid., II, 839–42.
56 Ibid., 845–53, 954; see PRO, E.351/653–7, Declared Accounts Customs, 1652–7.
57 Firth and Rait, *A. & O.*, II, 1223–34.
58 Ibid., 1412–15.
59 PRO, S.P. 28/99, papers of the Army Committee, fo. 414–15, 417.
60 S.P. 46/117, fo. 199, 1655–6. At 4*s.* per man-year, 250 annual contributors would have equalled the salary which he proposed for himself.
61 See e.g. the elaborate Naval Victualling contract of November 1650 (S.P. 18/11/106); the ordnance contracts for cannon and shot (Herefordshire R.O., Foley Papers on deposit from Stoke Edith, Browne-Foley MSS.); the account of Charles Whalley, Agent at Chester for supplying the forces in Ireland (BM, Stowe MS. 185, fo. 100–2, 104–5); clothing contract for the Irish army, December 1653 (PRO, S.P. 28/98, fo. 41).
62 This arose from the Humble Petition's attempt to provide a sufficient, constant annual revenue from customs and excise alone, without an assessment or a land tax. An act of 26 June 1657 (Firth and Rait, *A. & O.*, II, 1268–9) gave power to the parliamentary committee to arrange the customs and excise farms for up to seven years; no member of the committee was to be a farmer; no farmer a trader in the same commodities for which he farmed the duties. See C. H. Firth (ed.), *The Clarke Papers* (4 vols, Camden Society, new series, 49, 54, 61, 62, 1891, 1894, 1899, 1901), III, 114, for news of the supposed deal (July 1657). Noell farmed the Salt and Soap excises, the Scottish excise and

the duties on exported sea-coal and (though only for 5½ months in 1655) the excise of drapery, linen and silk. His annual turnover ran into several £10,000s; if the rate of profit was 1s. in the £, or 5 per cent, he cannot have been making less than £2,500 a year on this and probably much more.

63 See R. Ashton, *Crown and Money Market* (Oxford, 1961).

64 *C.J.*, VII, 634–5, 637, 638, 676, 691, 694, 702–3, 739, 744–5, 761, 783, 790, 793–4. In this respect, at least, there was marked continuity between the last Protectorate Parliament and the restored Rump of the Long Parliament.

65 See below, chapters 5 and 6; also Ashley, *Financial and Commercial Policy*, and E. Hughes, *Studies in Administration and Finance* (Manchester, 1934).

66 Aylmer, *King's Servants*, ch. 4, ss. i–ii.

67 Examples of large salaries conditional on no fees being taken are: the Committee to audit the accounts of the Army, July–August 1648, £300 p.a. for each of its five members (Firth and Rait, *A. & O.*, I, 1169–70); the two Prest Auditors, £500 a year [each, presumably], September 1649 (*C.J.*, VI, 296); and of fees being restricted as a condition of payment: the Clerk, Under-Clerk and Sergeant of the House, £500, £200 and £500 p.a. respectively, August 1649 (*C.J.*, VI, 287–8; for the Barebones' schedule see S.P. 18/38/101—the chief profit was presumably on private bill legislation).

68 See below, pp. 120, 283–97.

69 Firth and Rait, *A. & O.*, I, 717–22.

70 Ibid., II, 88–9.

71 Ibid., 148–51. This referred to royalists who had surrendered conditionally, most often on terms arranged by the commanders in the field.

72 *Cal. Cttee. Compdg.*, pp. 311–12.

73 Firth and Rait, *A. & O.* II, 447–9, 920, 926.

74 Ibid., 1178.

75 Meaning colleague, probably.

76 BM, Stowe MS. 185, fo. 223–224v; MS. 184, fo. 171–2.

77 The Ordinances where one might expect to find them mentioned are those for Essex's appointment as Captain-General, July 1642 (Firth and Rait, *A. & O.*, I, 14–16), the 'New Model' Ordinance, February 1645 (ibid., 614–26), and the extension of the Commander-in-Chief's power to appoint junior officers direct, March 1645 (ibid., 653). Firth does not mention such fees in his discussion of military commissions (*Cromwell's Army*, pp. 48–55).

78 Worcester College, Clarke Papers, MS. CXVII, fo. 3–29, 32–45. Some lieut.-colonels and colonels paid £1, others £2; captains from 7s. 6d. to £1. 4s. od.

79 S.P. 28/269, 9 August, in Sussex.

80 *Cal. Cttee. Compdg.*, pp. 490, 494, October 1651, from Yorks.

81 *C.J.*, VI, 488, 520.

82 S.P. 24/29, unnumbered items.

83 *Cal. Cttee. Compdg.*, pp. 431, 433–4.

84 Firth and Rait, *A. & O.*, II, 429–39.
85 Ibid., 918–21.
86 S.P. 18/11/68–79.
87 S.P. 18/23/57–75, lists of fees taken in Exchequer offices, February 1651/2; ibid., /77–105, the same for Chancery, February 1651/2.
88 Ibid., /128, Thomas Parker, 19 March 1651/2.
89 Compare Firth and Rait, *A. & O.*, II, 702–3 and *C.J.*, VII, 279; see ch. 2, s. viii, p. 42.
90 S.P. 18/101/100 ii, n.d., calendared under November 1655 (*Cal. S.P. Dom., 1655–6*, p. 4). The top left-hand corner is torn off, but the subject and almost all the figures are perfectly clear.
91 From the British Record Society, *Index Library*, Vols 54 and 61 (1925 and 1936) 'P.C.C. Wills, VII, 1653–6', ed. T. M. Blagg and J. S. Moir, and 'VIII, 1657–60', ed. Blagg.
92 S.P. 18/123/24, and 25 (for which see *Cal. S.P. Dom., 1655–6*, pp. 107–9). On 9 June 1653 the Council had ordered the Probate Judges to report on suitable fees for their subordinates and to recommend how the money received should be handled (*Cal. S.P. Dom., 1652–3*, p. 395); but it seems unlikely that it was this order which resulted in the fee-table cited above (see n. 90), unless it is seriously misdated in the *Calendar*.
93 Firth and Rait, *A. & O.*, II, 824; *Cal. S.P. Dom., 1654*, p. 343. Their salary was £300 p.a. each; Charles George Cocke, also a Judge of Admiralty (1653–9), appears not to have been paid as a Probate Judge until 1657 (*Cal. S.P. Dom., 1656–7*, p. 374).
94 *Cal. S.P. Dom., 1655–6*, pp. 107–9, 9 June 1656 (and in Blagg and Moir, 'P.C.C. Wills, 1653–6', p. xx).
95 See E. W. Cohen, *The Growth of the British Civil Service 1780–1939* (1941), pp. 40, 45, 57–8.
96 S.P. 46/96, fo. 99 (verso. The receipt is in fact dated 13 April 1652).
97 S.P. 25/77, fo. 242–7 and 301–2 (*Cal. S.P. Dom., 1656–7*, p. 47, for 31 July 1656, is in this case not quite correct, a rare mistake by the editor, Mrs Green).
98 See this ch., s. ii, pp. 90–3.
99 Firth and Rait, *A. & O.*, II, 964–7, esp. LXV and LXVI.
100 See this s., pp. 115–16, n. 87.
101 A writ issuing a commission. See T. Blount, *Nomo-Lexikon: A Law Dictionary* . . . (2nd ed., fol., 1691); G. Jacob, *A New Law Dictionary* . . . (3rd ed., fol., 1736).
102 See this ch., s. ii, pp. 88–90, and notes 41–51.
103 Bodl., Rawl. MS. A. xxviii, fo. 718, 23 July.
104 PRO, Chancery, C.82/2251, nos 14 and 15; see also E.403/2523, fo. 67–9.
105 The 1650 schedule relates to the Deputy Chamberlains in the Receipt whose fees came exclusively from tallies and had at that date wholly ceased for seven years (S.P. 18/11/69, signed Thomas Fauconberge); the 1655–6 schedules are for the Chamberlains themselves, including their fees on tallies (E. 403/2523, n.d. S.P. 46/97, fol. 181–2, regrant to Scipio le Squire, 3 November 1655).
106 S.P. 18/23/98; E. 403/2523. (A draft is also in S.P. 46/99, fo. 54.)

107 S.P. 18/100/131.
108 Consisting of its most aristocratic members: an earl, a courtesy viscount (who was the eldest son of an earl), and a baronet.
109 S.P. 18/102/42, 18 December 1655.
110 S.P. 25/76, fo. 422–4. See also E. 403/2523, 11 July 1656, no salary is mentioned; and for the Signet Clerks see ibid., 9 January 1656/7.
111 H. B. Wheatley (ed.), *The Diary of Samuel Pepys*, 8 vols (1893–9), I, pp. 164, 192, 196–7, 200, 203, 206–7, 208, 275, 292. The new text ed. by R. Latham and W. Matthews should now, of course, be preferred.
112 See ch. 2, s. ix, pp. 45–54.
113 For example Anon. [H. Peter], *Long Parliament—Work*, BM, E. 985(23), 9 June 1659; *A Declaration and Proclamation of the Army of God*, ibid., 26, 9 June.
114 See ch. 2, s. x, pp. 54–7, and ch. 6, p. 336.
115 See this ch., ss. viii–ix, pp. 129–67.
116 *King's Servants*, ch. 4, s. i.
117 R. Vaughan, *The Protectorate of Oliver Cromwell and the State of Europe* ... (2 vols, 1839), II, p. 390, 5 August 1654.
118 The son of the well-known pamphleteer and social theorist.
119 See Firth and Rait, *A. & O.*, refs cited earlier in this section.
120 *Cal. Cttee. Compdg.*, p. 614.

vi ARREARS

1 S.P. 25/35/120–7 (*Cal. S.P. Dom., 1651–2*, pp. xxiv, 341, 512–13); S.P. 18/37/163 petition by G. F. junior, and 164 Philip Jones's report on same, 29 June 1653; also p. 255.
2 *Cal. S.P. Dom., 1655–6*, p. 180 (S.P. 25/92, fo. 336).
3 S.P. 18/70/59–60.
4 Bodl., Rawl. MS. A. xiv, fo. 114.
5 This can be traced in several of the Declared Accounts (PRO, E.351 and A.O.1).
6 S.P. 25/77, fo. 663–4 (and see *Cal. S.P. Dom., 1656–7*, p. 256, no. 32). Payments were owing from 25 March 1655 to 24 June 1656.
7 S.P. 18/157/110 i and iii (*Cal. S.P. Dom., 1656–7*, pp. 170–1).
8 Bodl., Rawl. MS. A lix, fo. 59, 61; *Cal. S.P. Dom., 1657–8*, pp. 251, 367; *1658–9*, p. 39; *1660–1*, p. 56; S.P. 18/179/27, 180/152, 152 i–ii.
9 Bodl., Rawl. MS. A xxxviii, fo. 487. There seem to have been two possible men of this name: one a ship's steward, the other a merchant who served on a Hospitals Committee in 1653 (*Cal. S.P. Dom., 1652–3*, p. 525; *1653–4*, pp. 40, 562; *1654*, p. 462; *1656–7*, p. 582; *1658–9*, p. 558).
10 S.P. 46/128, fo. 174.
11 See S.P. 28/58–9, 91–2, 98–9, Army Committee warrants and other papers, sampled for 1650, 1653, and 1653–4.
12 S.P. 28/58, fo. 120.
13 On this subject see Habakkuk, art. cit., in *Welsh Hist. Rev.*, 3 (1967).
14 Again, the clearest account is by Habakkuk, art. cit. in *Econ. H.R.*, n.s. 15 (1962).

15 S.P. 18/67/40, 69/68, 73/34 and 34i, 73/90, 76/17–20, 96/47, 123/39, 158/100, 179/68; for attention paid to this matter in the Rump, see *C.J.*, VI, 264, 496–7, July 1649 and November 1650—in the latter case some of its own members being involved!

16 Bodl., Rawl. MS. A. xxxiv, fo. 575, n.d. (? January 1656).

17 S.P. 18/131/20 and *Cal. S.P. Dom., 1656–7*, pp. 181, 188.

18 Bodl., Rawl. MS. A. xlvi, fo. 217.

19 See sections viii and ix, pp. 129–67.

20 The Discovery Commissioners' minute-book was sold at Sotheby's in 1967 and fortunately bought by the British Museum; it is now Additional MS. 54,198.

vii THE VALUE OF OFFICES

1 See ch. 4.

2 See *King's Servants*, ch. 4, iii.

3 *Cal. S.P. Dom., 1660–61*, p. 333.

4 Ibid., p. 446.

5 *Thurloe St. P.*, VI, 366. But was this £2,000 in pounds sterling or pounds Scots? If sterling, then it was worth £24,000 p.a. Scots, which seems unlikely; if Scots, then only £167 p.a. sterling, which is modest enough. For Johnston's own estimates, see *Scottish Hist. Soc.*, 3rd series, Vol. 34 (1940), 'Diary of Sir Archibald Johnston of Warriston, III, 1655–60', Appendix pp. 187–9. He asserted that his gross takings were £4,601. 9s. 10d. and his net profit for the two years June 1657–June 1659 was £1,801. 9s. 10d.; earlier in the same paper Johnston said that in 1650 his places as Clerk Register, Councillor, and Lord Judge of Session and of Exchequer were together worth £1,000 sterling p.a. So it seems unlikely that the Clerk Registership alone was worth c. £900 at the latter date (or half the £1,801 mentioned above); again a twelfth of this, or only £75 p.a. sterling, is clearly too little. Setting this puzzle aside, Johnston clearly regarded the tariff from men taking subordinate clerkships as the main profit of the office. See also his paper of November 1654 (Bodl., Rawl. MS. A xx, fo. 165).

6 *Thurloe St. P.*, VI, p. 436.

7 Ibid., VII, 470; see also his complaint the following February (ibid., 624).

8 Ibid., VII, 367, 470–1.

9 Ibid., VII, 492.

10 Bodl., Rawl. MS. A xxxvii, fo. 609.

11 Ibid., xlii, fo. 359.

12 Bodl., Rawl. MS. A xlii, fo. 345. The combination of pay as Major-General, Councillor, and officer in two (or more) regiments, points to Lambert, as perhaps does the lavish household expenditure. None of the other possibles (Disbrowe, Fleetwood, Skippon) fits these requirements so well.

13 Ibid., xxxvi, fo. 397–424. The total owing should be £321. 5s. 0d. according to my addition of the items on the receipts' side.

14 Ibid., fo. 671; for his will see Brit. Rec. Soc., *Index Library*, Vol. 61,

'P.C.C. Wills, vol. VIII, 1657–1660', p. 341. Another envoy to Sweden, Daniel Lisle, in 1654, had been allowed a round sum of £600 (Bodl., Rawl. MS. A xxvii, fo. 153).

15 Ibid., xxvii, fo. 439.

16 See *Thurloe St. P.*, *passim*, for his letters 1653–9; several for 1649–53 and 1659–60 are in *Cal. S.P. Dom.*; others are in PRO, State Papers Foreign, S.P. 82/7–9, Hamburg and North Germany, and among the Ffarington Papers, now in the Lancs. Record Office (see Hist. MSS. Comm., *6th Report*, Appendix, pp. 426–34). Much of this correspondence is taken up with a long series of disputes with other officers of the Merchant Adventurers, for whom the Hamburg resident also acted.

17 Bodl., Rawl. MS. A lxii, fo. 83–4, 94–5, 87, 89, 91.

viii THE USE AND MISUSE OF OFFICE FOR THE ADVANTAGE OF
OFFICIALS

1 In fairness to Professor Trevor-Roper who first emphasised its significance —and with acknowledgment to some of my earlier critics—this aspect is certainly underplayed in *The King's Servants*. Compare J. Hurstfield, *The Queen's Wards* (1958), chapters 10, 11, 16.

2 S.P. 18/128/72.

3 S.P. 46/97, fo. 148–9, 28 February 1654/5.

4 S.P. 18/97/9, 3 May 1655 (*Cal. S.P. Dom., 1655*, p. 150).

5 For Greene see s. ix, pp. 142–3.

6 For Thorpe's purchases see *Cal. Cttee. Compdg.*, index, 'Colonel Robert Thorpe'; for his downfall *Cal. S.P. Dom., 1653–4*, pp. 259, 262, 444; *1654*, pp. 150, 151, 273, 416–17; *1655*, pp. 41–2, 134–5. For forged debentures, see s. ix, pp. 141–3.

7 S.P. 46/95, fo. 135.

8 Ibid., fo. 287.

9 S.P. 28/258, March 1649/50.

10 S.P. 28/259.

11 Ibid., February 1650/1.

12 See J. P. Cooper, 'The Fortune of Thomas Wentworth, Earl of Strafford', *Econ. H.R.*, n.s. 11 (1958), pp. 233–4; Aylmer, *King's Servants*, ch. 4, pp. 167–8.

13 S.P. 18/17/71.

14 MS. torn here.

15 PRO, S.P. 46/117, fo. 55, Edward Hopkins, from the Navy Office, to Francis Willoughby, Navy Commissioner, at Clarendon Park, Wilts, 29 May 1655.

16 PRO, Admiralty 2/1730, fo. 145B (new pagination 190B), Admiralty to Treasury Commissioners, 1 May 1658, acknowledging their letter of 16 March with a copy of Cooper's petition enclosed, signed Clerke, Kelsey and Salmon.

17 For references to other Navy Commissioners, see Index, 'Bourne, Nehemiah' and 'Pett, Peter'; they are all included in the 100 selected officials, analysed in ch. 4, s. iv, below.

18 *Thurloe St. P.*, VI, 201. Further references to the barbary mare can be found in his letters of 18 May and 27 July (ibid., 268, 407).

19 Bodl., Rawl. MS. A. xxix, fo. 49, from Raby Castle, County Durham.

20 Ibid., A lxi, fo. 102, n.d. (1657).

21 Ibid., A xxxiii, fo. 425; xliii, fo. 53 and 73.

22 See pp. 147–50.

23 Bodl., Rawl. MS. A xxxiv, fo. 785, n.d. but signed.

24 Ibid., A lxii, fo. 147.

25 See P. H. Hardacre, *The Royalists during the Puritan Revolution* (The Hague, 1956), pp. 72, 107; *DNB*; Gardiner, *Commonwealth and Protectorate*, end of ch. 27. More material about the case can be traced via the indexes of the *Calendars* and other standard series.

26 Petition, BM 669, f. 19/37.

27 Ibid./60, December 1654.

28 S.P. 46/96, fo. 136, 165, 167, 170.

29 *Truths Triumph over treacherous dealing: or, the innocency of Captain John Bernard* (8 pp. octavo, 30 July 1657), Bodl. Pamphlet 104. Whether William Malyn was in fact recommended to Cromwell by Berry is not known. Another man of this name was a Captain in Cromwell's regiment, in which Berry had previously served. Firth and Davies (*Regimental History*, pp. 73 and 75, n. 2) identify the two William Malyns. But this one remained the Protector's secretary after the Captain's dismissal, for political opposition, in February 1658, and was also in office under Richard Cromwell (see ch. 4, s. v, pp. 264–5, and n. 81).

30 See *Every mans Right: or, Englands Perspective Glass* (1646) and *The Levellers Vindication or, A Tragicall Story* (1649).

31 *Times Present Mercy, and Englands Western Justice* (1647).

32 See pp. 162–4. For other broadside attacks on him see BM 669, f. 10/33, perhaps by Lilburne, 30 August 1645; /40, 'A Declaration and Appeale to all the free-born people of the Kingdom in general . . .' November 1645; 669, f. 14/52, 57, 62, 1649 (pro-Frese and anti-Lenthall). For Bernard, Frese and other such pamphleteers, see also ch. 5, s. ii, pp. 283–97.

ix CORRUPTION

1 If I understand him correctly, this seems to be the argument of Prof. Joel Hurstfield in his paper 'Political Corruption in Modern England: The Historian's Problem', in *History*, 52 (1967), pp. 16–34. But see his earlier article 'Corruption and reform under Edward VI and Mary: the example of Wardship', *E.H.R.*, 68 (1953), pp. 22–36, where he appears to allow for considerably more variation from one era to another; for a 'middle' attitude see Hurstfield, *The Queen's Wards* (1958), ch. 10, 'Corruption'.

2 Prestwich, *Cranfield*, pp. 8, 211. The same author employs the terms 'fungus', 'green bay trees' and 'rust' as alternative figures of speech (ibid., pp. 2, 10, 206, 389).

3 The context is the Arian resistance to Athanasius at the Council of

Milan: *Decline and Fall*, ed. J. B. Bury, 7 vols (1897), Vol. 2, ch. xxi, p. 372.

4 Firth and Rait, *A. & O.*, II, 213–35.

5 Venables' attempted use of the able young Mancunian, Charles Worsley, to warn the Protector, together with his assertion that the Rev. Eaton (the minister of Dukinfield, Cheshire), could serve as a witness supports Firth's hypothesis that the deplorable Jackson was himself a Lancastrian (C. H. Firth (ed.), *The Narrative of General Venables* ... (Royal Historical Society. Camden new series Vol. 60, 1900), pp. 28–9, 32–4, 92–3, 134). However, I would suggest that he was a Londoner, from Surrey, related by marriage to the Langham family (see pp. 161–2; Harl. Soc., XVII, *Visitations of London 1633–1635*, Pt II, p. 45).

6 Hist. MSS. Comm., *Leyborn-Popham*, pp. 166–7.

7 Ibid.

8 See pp. 12, 27–8.

9 *Cal. S.P. Dom.*, *1655*, p. 122 (and S.P. 18/96/25i); *1657–58*, pp. 141–2, 351; PRO E.403/2608, no. 213; St John D. Seymour, *The Puritans in Ireland, 1647–1661* (Oxford, 1912 and 1969), pp. 171–2, 177, 221. See also section iii.

10 The development of the forged debentures case (or cases) can be followed from BM, Stowe MS. 184, fo. 232; PRO, S.P. 18/24/101–2; Styles, *Modern Reports*, pp. 343–4; *C.J.*, VI, pp. 356, 390; VII, pp. 138, 236; *Cal. S.P. Dom.*, *1651*, p. 535; *1651–2*, pp. 93, 436, 535; *1652–3*, pp. 130, 333, 378–9; *1654*, pp. 340–1, 378–9, 381, 411–12, 412, 415, 419; *1655*, pp. 2–13, 17–19, 62, 119, 147, 334, 385–6; *1655–6*, pp. 99, 212; Abbott, *Writings and Speeches*, III, 541 n., 557–8, 563. The story closes without honour among thieves, Fugill and Granger being engaged in bitter mutual denunciations—each trying to get off by blaming the other; my own impression is that Granger was the tougher, if not also the more dishonest of the two. I have enjoyed discussing the case and its implications with Mr H. J. Habakkuk, Principal of Jesus College, Oxford, from whose understanding of the economic aspects of the land sales I have profited greatly. But he should not be held responsible for the opinions expressed here, nor for any mistakes. Only one fact is certain: we do not have the whole story, and perhaps by now we never will. For John Jackson, eliminating others of the same name, see also PRO, E.351/306, 1295–6; S.P. 24/5, fo. 146, 155; Firth and Rait, *A. & O.*, I, pp. 383, 1138; *Cal. S.P. Dom.*, *1649–50*, pp. 51, 348, 539, 566; *1650*, pp. 51, 402, 541, 566; *1651*, pp. 288, 589; *1651–2*, pp. 110–11, 463, 473, 590, 619–21; *1652–3*, pp. 328, 491–2; *1653–4*, pp. 92, 350; *1654*, pp. 361, 379; *1655–6*, p. 388; *The Publick Intelligencer*, 23–30 May 1659; Hist. MSS. Comm., *Leyborn-Popham*, p. 166. And for post-Restoration refs to Forged Debentures, see *Cal. S.P. Dom.*, *1661–2*, p. 600; *1676–7*, pp. 494–6; *Cal. Treas. Bks*, 5, I, *1676–9*, p. 322.

11 PRO, Admiralty 2/1730, fo. 197 B, 242 B.

12 PRO, S.P. 18/35/53, to the Admiralty and Navy Commissioners, 7 April 1653.

13 Ibid., 39/86, Hutchinson, Willoughby & Hopkins to the Commissioners, 27th August 1653.

14 Ibid., 169/28, fo. 53, Navy to Admiralty Commissioners, 6 July 1657. Some of the difficulties to which this order gave rise can be followed in ibid., 172/127, 189/14, 190/25, 28, 191/104, Oct. 1657–Apr. 1658.

15 Ibid., 171/56, from the Admiralty to the Navy Commissioners, 17 September 1657.

16 See S.P. 28/253A, 258–60.

17 Firth and Rait, *A. & O.*, I, 936–8, 1119–20; also for instances see S.P. 24/1–8, 10–17, Indemnity Order Books 1647–55.

18 *C.J.*, VI, 8, 11, 360; *Cal. S.P. Dom., 1649–50*, pp. 144, 470–1; *1651–2*, pp. 2, 6; S.P. 46/95, fo. 165, 218, 220–8, 284; S.P. 28/258, 259. For Clotworthy see also *DNB*; Brunton and Pennington, *Members*; Keeler, *Long Parliament*; Kearney, *Strafford in Ireland*, and other modern works.

19 See pp. 24, 27, 38–9.

20 Usually written Bressie or Bracy.

21 Firth, *Scotland and the Commonwealth*, pp. 111 (corrected from Clarke MS. XLIII, from back of vol. as shelved, fo. 5v–6), 114–19; Dawson, *Cromwell's Understudy*, p. 153 and n. 2; Firth, *Scotland and the Protectorate*, pp. 200–2; *Thurloe St. P.*, IV, 221; V, 490; VI, 816, 822, 828; VII, 194–5, 224; *Cal. S.P. Dom., 1657–8*, pp. 320, 330–1, 332, 356, 370–1; ibid., *1658–9*, pp. 2, 12, 17, 78, 126, 129, 373; H.M.C., *Leyborn-Popham*, pp. 117, 119, 178; Will P.C.C. 165 Nabbs.; Worcester College, MS. Clarke XXX, fo. 57, 20 March 1658, 86, 1 May; LXXXVI, Robert Lilburne's Letter-Book 1652–3, fo. 155, 19 Dec. 1653; L, Monck's Order Book 1654–7, fo. 138, 30 October 1659; LI, the same, 1657–9, fo. 45–60, Accounts and accompanying statements, 1658.

22 S.P. 46/81, fo. 46.

23 G. Sikes, *Life and Death of Sir H. Vane* (1662), pp. 97–8; Firth in *DNB*, XX, 126–29 (original ed. vol. 58).

24 M. Oppenheim, *E.H.R.*, 9 (1894), pp. 486–8, n. 52. Miss Violet A. Rowe, who completed a London Ph.D. thesis on Vane some years ago, agrees with Oppenheim on this (letter to the author, 1965); see also now her book, *Sir Henry Vane the Younger* (1970), Appendix D, p. 270.

25 S.P. 28/270; S.P. 28/350/10.

26 *Life and Death of Sir Henry Vane*, p. 97.

27 See *DNB*; Oppenheim, in *E.H.R.*, 9, 486–8, n. 52; *C.J.*, VI, 432, 440–4, 482; also pp. 40–1, 248–9.

28 With Oppenheim, loc. cit.

29 Sikes, *Life and Death of Vane*, pp. 97–8.

30 R. Howell, *Newcastle-upon-Tyne and the Puritan Revolution* (Oxford, 1967), esp. pp. 191–4, 346.

31 Bodl., Rawl. MS. B.239, nos 110, 531, 559, 612. The nominal purchases total £19,890. 13s. 0½d. For the significance of these 'sales', see Habakkuk, art. cit., *Econ. H.R.*, n.s. 15 (1962).

32 S.P. 28/258.

33 Ibid. /260.

34 Burton, *Parliamentary Diary*, II, 423–4, 2 February 1658.

35 Howell, *Newcastle*, pp. 192–3; Pauline Gregg, *Free-born John* (1961), pp. 309–11, 392.

36 The proceedings can be followed in *C.J.*, VII, 55, 64, 71–3, 75, 117. The best commentaries are in Gardiner, *Commonwealth and Protectorate*, ch. XVIII, and Gregg, *Free-born John*, loc. cit.

37 Beyond all hope of legibility, even under an ultra-violet lamp.

38 S.P. 23/36, fo. 250, 250v, 252v, 255, 260v, 261v (12 December, quoted here). (Earlier references, the previous March, are on fo. 152 and 162v; I have not transcribed the shorthand parts of these entries, which I cannot decipher.)

39 *C.J.*, VII, 682, 751, 760; Firth and Rait, *A. & O.*, II, p. cvi.

40 *Thurloe St. P.*, V, 229, 234, 19 and 21 July 1656.

41 John Fry and Gregory Clement respectively (*DNB*; Brunton and Pennington, *Members*).

42 *DNB*, 'Edward (Lord) Howard (of Escrick)' (*c.* 1595–1675); G.E.C., *Complete Peerage*; *C.J.*, VI, 451, 469, 470, 570, 590–1, 591–2, 600, 605–6, 618; *Cal. Cttee. Compdg.*, p. 427; *Cal. Cttee. Advc. Mon.*, p. 76.

43 *C.J.*, VI, 598, 604; Firth and Rait, *A. & O.*, II, pp. 522, 592, 639, 1346; S.P. 18/71/97i; *Cal. S.P. Dom.*, *1657–8*, p. 171.

44 *C.J.*, VII, 251, 257, 277, January–April 1653.

45 *Cal. Cttee. Compdg.*, pp. 390–1, 426, 432, 436, 437, 446, 477–8, 517, 679, 681, 684, 686, 735; also Bodl., Tanner MS. 55, fo. 110, Edward Winslow to the Speaker, 7 January 1652. For Bray and Cheesman, see Cary, *Memorials of the Great Civil War*, II, 141–8; Firth, *Clarke Papers*, I, 411–12 n.; Firth and Davies, *Regimental History*, pp. 457–9, 608; Fortescue, *Thomason Catalogue*, II, index, 'Bray', 'Cheesman' and 'Chisman'.

46 *Cal. Cttee. Compdg.*, pp. 512–13, 517; see *DNB*, 'Philip Jones'; *C.J.*, VII, 656, 663, 666, 684; *Articles of Impeachment* . . ., 18 May 1659, BM E.983 (31).

47 *Cal. Cttee. Compdg.*, Index and Vol. I *passim*; for Somerset, see ch. 2, s. ii, pp. 12–13, and this ch., s. i, p. 60.

48 When Charles I issued his Commissions of Array, attempting to regain control of the county militias from Parliament's nominees.

49 Three of the original seven were still acting to the end of December 1653, but on the 28th only one of them is recorded as having been present; of the three newcomers, one had been Examiner from 1650 to 1653 and so was also involved in the case.

50 *Cal. Cttee. Compdg.*, pp. 2606–10, supplemented by entries in S.P. 23/36–37 *Cal. Cttee. Advc. Mon.*, pp. 671–2; *A Catalogue of the Lords, Knights and Gentlemen that have compounded for their Estates* (1655), p. 114 (*C.J.*, VI and VII entries are duplicated in the *Calendars*); Le Neve, *Pedigrees of Knight created* . . . (Chas. II to Wm. III) (Harleian Soc., viii, 1873), p. 18.

51 See W. Lilly, *History of his Life and Time* in *The Lives of Elias Ashmole and William Lilly* . . . (1774), pp. 131–2; Firth, *Clarke Papers*, II, p. vii; *Cal. S.P. Dom.*, *1649–50*, p. 215; Worcester College, MS. Clarke 181, Box 1, letter of 26 June 1649. See also ch. 4, s. v, pp. 263–4 and n. 80.

52 Worcester College, Clarke MS. XIX, fo. 45v, Leith, 30 June 1651.

53 Worcester College, Clarke MS. XIX, fo. 26–7.

54 Ibid., fo. 36v, 21 June, 1651.

55 *Admin. of Royal Navy*, pp. 353–4.

56 S.P. 18/16/115, Thomas Symons, 27 November 1651.

57 S.P. 18/16/119, 124 iii (Phineas Pett signs twice, but it may be two men with similar handwritings), November 1651.

58 *Cal. S.P. Dom., 1651–2*, pp. 65, 70, 127–8 (S.P. 18/23/16–36); also BM, Add. MS. 22,546, esp. fo. 50–57v; *C.J.*, VII, 69–70.

59 S.P. 18/23/16.

60 Ibid., 17, 17a, 18.

61 Ibid., 19, 20; see also ibid. /36a, proofs against Holborne, n.d.

62 Ibid. /21.

63 See pp. 16, 84.

64 S.P. 18/23/22.

65 Ibid. /23

66 Ibid. /23a.

67 Ibid. /24–9.

68 Ibid. /30, 30a.

69 Ibid. /31–35a.

70 Ibid. /36.

71 Bodl., Rawl. MS. A xi, fo. 116, from Chatham, 6 February 1654.

72 S.P. 18/33/104, 24 February 1653.

73 See G. R. Smith, 'Royalist Secret Agents at Dover during the Commonwealth', *Historical Studies: Australia and New Zealand*, 12 (1967).

74 S.P. 46/95, fo. 187, 188, 199, 202, 204, 210 (apparent forgery of Henry Marten's signature in support of one candidate), 212, November–December 1649.

75 *C.J.*, VI, 523, 526, 528, 529, 554, 562, 563; *Cal. S.P. Dom., 1649–50*, pp. 63, 412; *1650*, pp. 101, 228, 251, 255, 256, 284, 299, 359, 387, 393, 399, 434–5; *1651*, p. 118; Hist. MSS. Comm., 77, *De L'Isle and Dudley*, VI, pp. 443, 460, 487. Sidney's biographers (A. C. Ewald, *The Life and Times . . .* 2 vols (1873); *DNB*, etc.) seem at an utter loss to explain this affair; Mr Smith does not mention it (see n. 73 above). See also p. 296 and ch. 5, ii, n. 64.

76 S.P. 46/117, fo. 276, 284; *Cal. S.P. Dom., 1656–7*, p. 413.

77 *Cal. S.P. Dom., 1658–9*, pp. 431, 439, 456, 27 July, 31 August, 5 October 1658.

78 Ibid., p. 457, 7 October; p. 459, 15 and 28 October.

79 Ibid., p. 461, 28 October 1658.

80 See Ramsey, 'The Smugglers' Trade', *T.R.H.S.*, 5th series, 2; and Williams, *Contraband Cargoes*.

81 S.P. 24/10, fo. 174, April 1652.

82 Sir T. Hardres, *Report of Cases . . .* (1693), pp. 137–47, Hil. Term 1658.

83 For Harvey, see M. Noble, *The Lives of the English Regicides*; *DNB*; A. B. Beaven, *Aldermen of London* (2 vols, 1908); Ashley, *Financial and Commercial Policy*, pp. 53, 102; Brunton and Pennington, *Members*; Yule, *Independents*, p. 101; Bodl., Rawl. MS. B239, nos 3, 236, 347; *C.J.*, VI, 193. For the customs affair in 1655–6, see *Clarke Papers*, III, 61; *Thurloe St. P.*, IV, 222; *Cal. S.P. Dom., 1655–6*, pp. 8–9, 16–17, 34,

37–8, 55, 63, 66, 71, 76, 78, 92, 119, 129, 136, 137, 164, 169, 242–3, 273, 286, 292, 295, 328–9, 352–3; *1656–7*, p. 59; Abbott, *Writings and Speeches*, IV, 17; PRO, E351/653–6, Declared Accounts, Customs, 1652–6.

84 PRO, E.134/1656–7, Hilary Term no. 6, file of three documents delivered to the Barons of Exchequer, 4 February, the third being depositions by five witnesses on 2 February: E.403/2608, Privy Seal Book Pells 1655–60, p. 139.

85 See ch. 5, ss. ii–iii, pp. 284, 287 and 299–300.

86 Sanders, *Orders*, I, pp. 214–16, 318–22, 1646/7 and 1666.

87 For instance Sir John Barrington, son and heir of an eminent puritan-parliamentarian of the 1620s–40s, spent part of 1653 in the Fleet (see BM, Egerton MS. 2648, Barrington Papers, Vol. V, fo. 205, 218, 225). *A List of all the Prisoners in the Upper Bench Prison ... 3 May 1653 Delivered in by Sir John Lenthall ...* 12 May 1653, BM E.213(8), includes about eight peers and 25 knights, although most presumably in practice enjoyed semi-liberty, on some equivalent of daily parole.

88 See e.g. *The Oeconomy of the Fleete; or an apologeticall answeare of Alexander Harris (late Warden there) unto xix articles sett forth against him by the prisoners*, ed. A. Jessopp (Camden Soc. new series 25, 1879), the main text is *c.* 1621; also R. B. Pugh, *Imprisonment in medieval England* (Cambridge, 1968), esp. chapters VIII and XV. There is a list of no less than 21 London prisons made in July 1644 (*Cal. Cttee. Compdg.*, Vol. I, p. 7).

89 For some of these see ch. 5, s. ii; others as already cited.

90 *C.J.*, VI, p. 487.

91 Ibid., VII, pp. 249–50.

92 Ibid., pp. 293, 297, 302–4, 304, 30 July, 8 and 17 August 1653.

93 *Cal. S.P. Dom.*, *1653–4*, pp. 370, 399–400; ibid., *1655*, pp. 131–3.

94 E.g. indemnity cases to which Lenthall was a party (S.P. 24/8, 10, 12, 13, 1650–3).

95 *The Case of Sir John Lenthall Knt., Marshall of the Upper-Bench Prison, Humbly presented to those in Authority, and to all Rational and indifferent men* (1653? August). Bodl. Godwin Pamphlets 644/8. He also published, in the following year, *The Representation of the Case of Sir John Lenthall, Knight, in his late Sufferings ...* 43 pp. [1654], BM, G.1040. This covered much of the same ground but took the story forward into 1654; it included a brisk counter-attack on Frese, who was 'imployed in some place about the Excise Office' but had been put out of it after being convicted of bribery and deceiving the State (p. 37, which should be p. 41).

96 Worcester College, Clarke MS. XXVII, fo. 143; PRO, S.P. 25/122 list of Council committees, 1655–6, fo. 2.

97 Clarke, MS. XXVIII, fo. 83v, 123v; *C.J.*, VII, 433, 440, 468, 471.

98 Clarke, M.S. XXIX, fo. 114.

99 Burton, *Parliamentary Diary*, IV, 403–12, III, 448–9.

100 Such as the Dover case already cited.

101 *C.J.*, VII, 250–1; Hist. MSS. Comm., *7th Report*, App., pp. 88n, 90, 91–2; *Cal. S.P. Dom.*, *1655–6*, p. 386; *1660–1*, p. 374. The Trustees

were empowered to appoint their clerk and to allow him poundage on sales. One of the Trustees was John Belchamp—an alternative spelling, and so conceivably a relative (Firth and Rait, *A. & O.*, II, 160–8).

102 See C. G. Weibull, *Freden i Roskilde* (Malmo, 1958), pp. 89–90, quoted in M. Roberts, 'Cromwell and the Baltic', *E.H.R.*, 77 (1961), p. 423, n. 5. According to my calculations this was equal to about 6,700 Dutch rix-dollars, or about 20,000 gilders, which was the equivalent of about £1,800 (see N. W. Posthumus, *Inquiry into the History of Prices in Holland*, I (Leiden, 1946), pp. LIV–V, 585, 592; C. R. Boxer, *The Dutch Seaborne Empire* (1965), Appendix III, p. 304. I am grateful to my colleague Dr D. W. Jones for help with the exchange-rates).

103 See E. Jenks (ed.), 'Some Correspondence between Thurloe and Meadowes', *E.H.R.*, 7 (1892), pp. 732–4.

104 Vaughan, *Protectorate of Oliver Cromwell*, II, 465. Parts in square brackets added by Vaughan.

105 Ibid., p. 470.

106 He does not seem to have told Thurloe about it, but he did record having had to present his own horse and sword to the Swedish monarch (*Thurloe St. P.*, VI, pp. 838–9, 2 March 1658). For additional refs see Weibull, *Freden*; Roberts, art. cit.; Firth, *Last Years*, chapters X and XVI. Meadowes's own *Narrative of the ... war between Sweden and Denmark* (London, 1677) is not revealing. The best biographical notes are in *DNB* and Venn, *Al. Cant.*, III, 171.

107 *C.J.*, VI, 103, 391, 451–3, 469.

108 Ibid., pp. 595, 618, 2 July, 8 August.

109 Ibid., VII, 64, 8 January.

110 The best account is still Firth's in *DNB*. See also ch. 4, s. v, pp. 258–60.

111 *Thurloe St. P.*, IV, 30, 13 September 1655; see also Ethel B. Sainsbury (ed.), *Cal. Court Minutes of the East India Co., 1650–54* (Oxford, 1916), pp. ix–x (note), 42–3, 211–12, and Index.

112 *Thurloe St. P.*, VII, 623–4. The information, recorded by Thurloe himself, came from a public-house conversation on about 17 February.

113 Ibid., VI, 425; see also Firth, *Clarke Papers*, III, 114, for a newsletter describing the same scheme.

114 *Cal. S.P. Dom., 1657–8*, p. 94 *et seq.*

115 Burton, *Parliamentary Diary*, IV, 139–43, 394–401, 415–20.

116 Bodl., Rawl. MS. A lxiv, fo. 237; A lxvi, fo. 162, A lxvii, fo. 60, 232, 235–7; *Thurloe St. P.*, VII, 807.

117 *Thurloe St. P.*, V, 581–2, 11 November 1656; 610–11, 29 November; Bodl., Rawl. MS. A xxxvii, fo. 228, n.d.; lvii, fo. 53, ? 1657–8; fo. 139–40, 141–2, n.d. (? 1657); more letters from Bampfield to Thurloe and others are in the Rawlinson MSS. and in PRO, S.P. 78/113–14, State Papers Foreign France, 1657–8. *DNB*, 'John [*sic*] Bampfield' is unhelpful on this, as is *Colonel Joseph Bampfeilds Apologie, Written by himselfe and printed at his desire* ([Holland] 1685), BM, C. 71.d.35).

118 This judgement is not to imply that Thurloe was a complete mediocrity or a mere hack: his letters, I think, disprove that.

119 In about 1952.

120 See ch. 4, ss. iii–vi, pp. 174–281 and ch. 5, s. vi, pp. 318–25. In this respect it will be clear that I am nearer to Mrs Prestwich than to Professor Hurstfield; it would be nice to be nearest to Gibbon. As far as I know, the only comparative study of corruption by a historian is J. van Klaveren, 'Die historische Erscheinung der Korruption. ...', *Vierteljahrschrift für Sozial- und Wirtschaftsgeschichte*, 44–6 (1957–9). The author is an expert on Dutch trade and colonisation in the East Indies; some of his generalisations on France and England are less well-founded. There have been numerous books and articles on corruption by political scientists and sociologists in the last ten years.

Chapter 4 Social biography

i PURPOSE AND METHOD

1 Including collectors and receivers, but not local sub-committee members and farmers, unless they were on a stipendiary or percentage rather than a rental basis for pay.

2 Nor are those of the Barebones (1653) and the three Protectorate Parliaments (1654–9) as such.

3 See pp. 172, 173, for a further discussion of this.

4 Notably Sir Herbert Butterfield, for whose work I have the highest respect. See, however, his *George III and the Historians* (1957).

5 Also known to historians of the ancient world as 'prosopography'. For a full discussion, see now L. Stone, 'Prosopography', *Daedalus*, Winter 1971, *Historical Studies Today*, pp. 46–79.

6 *The Structure of Politics at the Accession of George III* (1929) and *England in the age of the American Revolution: Pitt and Newcastle* (1930).

7 *The History of Parliament: The House of Commons 1754–1790*, 3 vols (1964), ed. J. Brooke, is in this respect a fitting memorial to Namier's work, but it is not, despite Mr Brooke's excellent introductory survey (also published as *The House of Commons 1754–1790*, Oxford paperbacks, 1969), an overall parliamentary, let alone political history of the period, and could not be when two-thirds of it is, of deliberate intention, a dictionary of members and constituencies.

8 See his essays, notably 'History' in *Avenues of History* (1952) and 'Human Nature and Politics' in *Personalities and Powers* (1955). See J. P. Cooper's review of Julia Namier, *Lewis Namier* (in *The Listener*, 1 July 1971, pp. 22–3) for his emphasis on war and revolution, rather than ideas, as the agents of fundamental change.

9 See E. J. Hobsbawm, 'Where are British Historians going?' in the *Marxist Quarterly*, 2 (1955), pp. 14–26, though the argument is carefully qualified in a footnote.

10 See ch. 1, p. 1.

11 See above n. 7. Further sections of the History are now also published and forthcoming: *1715–54* (1971), ed. R. Sedgwick, *1559–1601*, ed. Sir John Neale, etc.

12 M. F. Keeler, *The Long Parliament 1640–1641* (Philadelphia, 1954).

13 I am very grateful to my friend and colleague, Professor Gwyn A. Williams, for helping me to clarify these two distinct uses of tables.

14 With the greatest respect to Professor Geoffrey Elton of Cambridge, he seems to confuse these two charges in his excellent *Practice of History* (1967), pp. 33–4 (and paperback ed., 1969, pp. 49–50), where he criticises me along with others.

15 See section v, pp. 209–76, and notes 18–113.

ii SOURCES AND CHOICE OF SAMPLE

1 These include, it must be remembered, the records of many of the committees and commissions, especially for 1649–53, and some for 1649–60.

2 C. H. Firth and R. S. Rait (eds), *Acts and Ordinances of the Interregnum*, 3 vols (1911). Vol. 3 has a very full and 95 per cent accurate index of names.

3 Of Lords and Commons to 1648/9 and then, naturally, of the Commons only.

4 *Thomas Burton's Parliamentary Diary*, ed. J. T. Rutt, 4 vols (1828), covers the parliaments of 1656–8 and 1659; Vol. 1 also includes Guibon Goddard's diary for the first Protectorate Parliament of 1654–5. There are no extant diaries for the Rump, the Barebones or the restored Rump (of 1659–60).

5 Above all in J. Birch (ed.), *Thurloe State Papers* (7 vols, 1742).

6 See for instance R. A. Fisher and F. Yates, *Statistical Tables* (1943) and M. H. Quenouille, *Introductory Statistics* (1950), ch. 6, sections 1–2. I am grateful to Professor Mark Williamson, Biology Dept, University of York, for guiding me to these.

7 *King's Servants*, ch. 5, pp. 255 and 270 (and n. 1).

8 Anti-Protectorate republicans are, however, represented by Edmund Ludlow, and Rumpers of the second rank by Thomas Pury and the Elder Vane.

9 That is, a subjective choice by the author and not a sample.

10 See ch. 2, ii, p. 13.

11 Including John Thurloe himself, Cromwell's Secretary of State but a key administrator rather than a political leader, especially in his capacity as Secretary to the Council of State in 1652–3.

12 And of some schools.

13 From 1902. It now contains over 100 volumes, is complete for a dozen English counties and covers parts of over twenty others. There are considerable differences in treatment between counties completed before 1914 and those in progress since the 1950s.

14 Notably in the *Harleian Society* publications, some volumes in the *Chetham* and *Surtees* and other local *Societies* series and a few published separately in the nineteenth century by J. Foster, T. Phillipps, W. L. Fenwick and others.

15 These were still in Somerset House until 1969; they are now in the Public Record Office.

16 This is a subjective judgment naturally, but Samuel Cooper is surely at least Nicholas Hilliard's equal. The only other possible Samuel Cooper whom I have identified, alive and adult, in London during the 1650s was a member of the Fishmongers' Company. And he may have emigrated to Ireland where, as an 'Adventurer' he was entitled to a land grant (London Guildhall MSS. 5574/1, 5587/1, records of the Fishmongers' Co.; Bottigheimer, *English Money and Irish Lands*, Appendix A, no. 345, Appendix B, no. 2244; *Cal. S.P. Ireland, 1647-60*, p. 473; Ibid., *Adventurers*, p. 354). Either he, or the miniaturist, or a third, otherwise unknown Samuel Cooper was one of the Commissioners for sick and wounded seamen and for hospitals, 1653-60; the same one was probably also the Paymaster of St Thomas's hospital in the mid-1660s.

17 He was Comptroller of the Pipe in the Upper Exchequer, 1655-60.

18 Editor of *Historical Collections* (8 vols, 1659-1701); these cover the years 1618-49.

19 Professor Charles E. Ward, the fullest and most authoritative of Dryden's biographers, has argued at length (in his *Life of John Dryden* (Chapel Hill, 1961), pp. 16-19 and 326) that the John Driden, alias Dryden, who was on the staff of the Council of State and in the service of Sir Gilbert Pickering, one of Cromwell's councillors under the Protectorate, was not the poet. He maintains that there were at least two other J.D.s around at that time, but does not show why either of them was a more likely official than the future Stuart Laureate. Considering Dryden's stanzas on the death of Oliver, his father's appointment to a senior London Customs post in 1654, and his close connection with Pickering, I submit—with all respect to Professor Ward's excellent biography—that a kind of 'Occam's razor' is applicable here. It seems to me more unlikely that another J.D. received black cloth to walk in procession with John Milton and Andrew Marvell than that the poet did so. See also James M. Osborn, *John Dryden: Some Biographical Facts and Problems* (New York, 1940), pp. 168-70, who does accept the identification.

20 All three were at Cambridge.

21 The best biography is now W. A. Parker, *John Milton*, 2 vols (Oxford, 1967), but D. Masson, *Life and Times of John Milton* (rev. ed., 6 vols, 1871-81, index vol. 1894) is still of great value. Other works are legion; notably the long introductions to each volume of the current Yale complete edition of Milton's *Prose Works*.

22 The best critical study is now J. M. Wallace, *Destiny his choice: the Loyalism of Andrew Marvell* (Cambridge, 1968); for biography still consult B. Légouis, *Andrew Marvell* (2nd ed. Oxford, 1968). On *de factoism*, see Q. Skinner, articles in *Historical Journal*, VIII (1965), IX (1966), etc., and chapter in Aylmer (ed.) *The Interregnum* (1972).

23 Of the many critical works, L. T. Bredvold, *The Intellectual Milieu of John Dryden* (Ann Arbor, 1934; and paperback ed., 1956) seems to me among the most perceptive.

iii SOCIAL ANALYSIS: THE SAMPLE OF 200

1 Some of these are extremely short and should perhaps be called 'entries' rather than 'accounts'.
2 For a historian who conveys vividly the extraordinary richness of human types in a small pre-industrial society, see A. L. Rowse, *The England of Elizabeth* (1950). To agree with Dr Rowse on this score and to admire his portrait of Elizabethan England is not to share his other prejudices— nor to sentimentalise over what was in many respects a brutal, coarse, unjust and cruel society at the same time as it was a remarkable polity and civilisation.
3 See this section, pp. 190–2.
4 In his article, 'Social Mobility in England 1500–1700', *Past and Present*, 33 (1966).
5 On this see P. Laslett (ed.), *Filmer's Patriarcha and other writings* (Oxford, 1948), Introduction.
6 Notably Mr Laslett himself and his colleagues Dr E. A. Wrigley and Dr R. Schofield.
7 E.g. for Wales and for English counties where there are no reliable Heralds' Visitation records extant for the 1620s and 30s. I have not used the MS. visitations in the College of Arms.

According to the law of arms as administered by the heralds, use of the title Esquire was limited to (1) the heirs male of noblemen's sons, and their descendants; (2) the heirs male of knights (and presumably baronets); (3) the eldest sons of gentlemen who had themselves already been accepted as Esquires by the College of Arms, on a hereditary claim; (4) certain *ex officio* categories, such as sheriffs, JPs, some royal officials, and barristers. Holders of university doctorates were also reckoned as equivalent to Esquires. In theory, a title of Esq. arising from (4) was not heritable until three successive generations had enjoyed it by right of holding office (or the equivalent). In practice, the early Stuart heraldic visitations, when taken in conjunction with other primary sources, show that acceptance of a man's life-style, wealth and reputation could override genealogical and armorial niceties.

The title of Gentleman, the lowest rank in the gentry, was in theory restricted to those entitled to wear coat armour who did not qualify as Esquires. Again, the precise criteria were partly hereditary (heirs male of Esquires) and partly *ex officio* (holders of minor offices and MAs). The lower borderline for the title of Gent. was particularly ambiguous and controversial. By the 1630s the prefix 'Mr', originally an abbreviation for both Master and Mister, had usually come to signify Mister; this was sometimes used virtually as an alternative to Gent., as if the two were synonymous. In some counties, however, gentlemen who had been 'disclaimed' by the heralds, that is held not to be armigerous and banned from calling themselves Gentlemen, may have called themselves, or have been called, Mr instead. The term was also applied in some towns to civic worthies who had no pretensions to armorial gentility. The distinction may have become more meaningful again with the revival of heraldic visitations after 1660; the 1640s–50s provided the most favourable conditions for equating Gent. and Mr, or at least for blurring the distinction between them.

As far as the sources permit, and subject to minor revisions indicated above, I have tried to be consistent with my own earlier criteria (*King's Servants*, pp. 259–63; for a fuller discussion see Aylmer, 'Caste, Ordre (ou Statut) et Classe dans les premiers temps de l'Angleterre moderne', in R. Mousnier (ed.), *Problèmes de stratification sociale* (Paris, 1968). I am grateful to audiences in Paris, Oxford, Cambridge and York for helping me to clarify some of the points in this paper.)

8 As recently as 1963, however, a distinguished visiting Soviet historian said at a conference in London that 'the onus is on you to prove that the English Civil War was not a class struggle'!

9 A. M. Everitt, *The County Committee of Kent in the Civil War* (Dept of English Local History, University of Leicester, Occasional Papers no. 9, 1957, pp. 21–30); L. Stone, 'Social Mobility in England, 1500–1700', *Past and Present*, 33 (1966), p. 18.

10 L. Stone, 'The Inflation of Honours', *Past and Present*, 14 (1958), and Stone, *The Crisis of the Aristocracy 1558–1641* (Oxford, 1965), ch. III.

11 I have no reason to suppose that the authors cited above would wish to dissent from this.

12 See W. G. Hoskins, 'Estates of the Caroline Gentry', in *Devonshire Studies*, ed. Hoskins and H. P. R. Finberg (1952), pp. 334–65.

13 From my own researches, hitherto unpublished, and Mr M. Faraday's edition of the 1663 Herefordshire Militia Assessments (Royal Hist. Soc., Camden series, 1972).

14 Based on a small collective research project undertaken at Manchester by Mr D. H. Pennington, Dr Brian Manning and myself in the years 1960–2, with the kind support of Professor A. Goodwin, to study the Dorset gentry on the eve of the Civil War.

15 See J. T. Cliffe, *The Yorkshire Gentry from the Reformation to the Civil War* (1969), ch. 1.

16 Everitt, *Community of Kent*, ch. 2.

17 In theory, yeomen were freeholders. In practice by this time many were primarily tenants. Non-yeomen tenant-farmers would be styled Goodmen if they were substantial husbandmen.

18 For yeomen see Mildred Campbell, *The English Yeomen under Elizabeth and the Stuarts* (New Haven, 1942); Joan Thirsk, *English Peasant Farming* (1957); W. G. Hoskins, *Provincial England* (1963), ch. VIII; *The Agrarian History of England and Wales*, Vol. 4 (Cambridge, 1967), ed. J. Thirsk, ch. V, G. Batho, 'Landlords in England', pp. 301–6.

19 See *New English Dictionary* (Oxford).

20 A. Everitt, 'Social Mobility in early modern England', *Past and Present*, 33 (1966), pp. 70–2.

21 Excluding yeomen and other plebeian freeholders, of course.

22 Which by then, of course, included the parliamentarian structure of County Committees; see ch. 2, ii, pp. 10–11, and n. 12.

23 Everitt, *The Community of Kent and the Great Rebellion* (Leicester, 1966).

24 'The Local Community and the Great Rebellion', *Historical Association*, General Series, no. 70 (1969).

25 A. Everitt, 'Suffolk and the Great Rebellion, 1640–1660', *Suffolk Rec. Soc.*, III (1960), esp. pp. 11–21. I have not had an opportunity to consult Dr C. Holmes's recent Cambridge Ph.D. thesis on the New Model Army; what is stated in the text here may need modification.

26 *King's Servants*, pp. 265–7 and tables 17 and 18.

27 *King's Servants*, p. 266.

28 Ibid.

29 An alternative division of the country would be to put Rutland, Northants and Bucks (plus eastern Wilts and Dorset) with the east and south-east, since an approximate axis Grimsby–Weymouth is sometimes taken as a notional dividing line by historical geographers and economic historians; even then the preponderance of S. and E. over N. and W. would not be overwhelming.

30 See ch. 3, s. i, and this section, pp. 190–3.

31 See section iv, p. 202.

32 I have used *The New England Genealogical and Historical Register* and H. F. Waters, *Genealogical Gleanings*, but more could undoubtedly have been done here. I have not counted a spell in New England during adult life as 'colonial origins': one member of the sample would qualify on this basis.

33 The total number of known instances of origins is virtually the same for the 1649–60 sample as for that of 1625–42 (204–205).

34 See this section, p. 192.

35 Namely the discarding of the classification 'secondary areas and interests' as opposed to multiple instances.

36 See pp. 194–6, 207–8, Tables 24–6, 40–1.

37 In this connection, it is arguable (see also n. 29 above) that Bucks, Essex and Herts belong with the south-east, and not with the midlands or the east.

38 Although the invaluable check-list given by Mrs Phyllis Jacobs in *Bull. Inst. Hist. Res.*, 37 (1964), pp. 185–232, together with P. J. Wallis, *Histories of Old Schools: A Revised List for England and Wales* (Newcastle, 1966), enables one to look for particular schools and individuals wherever this is feasible.

39 Some of these are discussed by L. Stone in 'The Educational Revolution in England, 1560–1640', *Past and Present*, 28 (1964), pp. 47–51, 57–68, and by Joan Simon in 'The Social Origins of Cambridge Students, 1603–1640', ibid., 26 (1963), pp. 58–67.

40 A formidable task! Some college admissions are in print and can be used as a cross-check on Foster's *Alumni Oxonienses*, and Venn's *Alumni Cantabrigienses*, where appropriate. Andrew Clark's ed. of the *Register of the University of Oxford*, Vol. ii, *1571–1622* (4 pts, Oxford Hist. Soc., Vols 10, 11, 12, 14. 1887–9) is much more reliable than Foster; but having no published continuation after 1622 is of no use for men born after the early 1600s. Unlike Foster, or the much more scholarly and reliable Venn, Clark does not purport to give biographical entries.

41 I am grateful to the Librarian, Mr Breem, for allowing me to work on this typescript in the Library of the Inner Temple.

42 *Middle Temple Admission Register*, ed. H. A. C. Sturgess (3 vols, 1949); *Records of Lincoln's Inn*, Vol. i, ed. W. P. Baildon (1896); J. Foster (ed.), *Gray's Inn Admission Reg.* (1889).

43 I am grateful to Dr A. E. J. Hollaender, the Guildhall Librarian, for help over these, and to Professor Lawrence Stone for an earlier suggestion about bibliography.

44 This fits in well with Professor Stone's argument in his 'Educational Revolution', art. cit., and in his *Crisis of the Aristocracy 1558–1641* (Oxford, 1965).

45 Writing schools are very neglected in most social and educational histories of the period, but see Ambrose Heal, *The English Writing-Masters and their Copy-Books, 1570–1800* (Cambridge, 1931, repr. Hildesheim, 1962), esp. pp. xxii, xxx–ii, and Appendix I; J. Simon, *Education and Society in Tudor England* (Cambridge, 1966), ch. XV, esp. pp. 369–83.

46 And which I fear that I may myself have propagated in talks and lectures on this subject.

47 See ch. 2, esp. sections i–iii, pp. 8–24.

48 See this section, pp. 194–5.

49 See ch. 3, section i, pp. 58–82.

50 See *King's Servants*, ch. 6, sections i and viii. Even this is a slight over-simplification, but by and large it holds.

51 I am here going against the opinion of Mr Pennington, who has done more work than I have on the committees of the 1640s.

52 Relating to Clerkships, etc., but not to Judges' places.

53 That is, excluding the common law judges and officials on the revenue side of the Exchequer but including the staffs of the Scottish and Irish courts from 1653–5 on.

54 See *King's Servants*, ch. 3, pp. 69–96; ch. 5, pp. 274–7. Here, as in my earlier researches, I am indebted to Professor Sir John Neale both for his general emphasis on the importance of Patrons and 'Clientage' in later sixteenth-century England, and for a pointed question which he asked me about the officials of Charles I, a good many years ago.

55 See p. 175, Tables 5 and 6.

56 See this section, p. 195.

57 See pp. 175–80.

58 See Table 13.

59 The records for the purchasers of bishops' lands are relatively accessible; I have also worked through some of the relevant series for Crown lands and fee-farm rents and for buyers of sequestered royalist estates. Limited use of the Close Rolls for 1648–9 added little for private purchases by sample members.

60 Notably J. P. Prendergast, *The Cromwellian Settlement of Ireland* (3rd ed., 1922), App. V, and K. Bottigheimer, *English Money and Irish Lands* (Oxford, 1971).

61 For this thesis, see C. Hill, *Puritanism and Revolution* (1958), ch. 5; *The*

Century of Revolution (Edinburgh, 1961), pp. 145–54; *Reformation to Industrial Revolution: A Social and Economic History of Britain 1530–1780* (1967), pp. 116–18; and against it, H. J. Habakkuk, 'Landowners and the Civil War', *Econ. H.R.*, 2nd series, 18 (1965), and 'The Parliamentary Army and the Crown Lands', *Welsh History Review*, 3 (1967); and J. Thirsk, articles in *Econ. H.R.*, n.s. 5 (1952) and *Journal Modern History*, 26 (1954). There is, of course, a more extensive literature and documentation than this; further studies are needed before it can be said that Habakkuk and Thirsk have totally rebutted Hill (and older authorities).

62 On this see ch. 2, section ix, pp. 45–54.

63 This is certainly a point for Christopher Hill against his critics, but it is not the same thing as an inevitable step towards the Restoration.

64 I have used *Cal. S.P. Dom.* for 1660–70 and *Cal. Treasury Bks*, Vols I–III; also printed works on the army and navy. The main omission is the royal household, but fewer ex-republicans and Cromwellians would be found there.

65 Will, Prerogative Court of Canterbury, 1660, 193 Nabbs (these register books of wills are now in the PRO). The witnesses were his son-in-law Nicholas Bragge, an ex-teller of the Exchequer, and John Humphrey, a frequent commissioner and committee man of the 1650s.

66 The main proponent of this view again is Dr Hill.

67 That is, 152 out of 200 (see Table 25).

68 See section iv, pp. 207–8, and Table 41.

69 See some of the individual case-studies in section v.

iv SOCIAL ANALYSIS: THE 100 SELECTED OFFICIALS

1 That is, men who were primarily political, military or naval leaders, or judges, or aristocratic councillors and officers.

2 Firth and Rait, *Acts and Ordinances*; *Cal. S.P. Dom.*; *Commons Journals*; *Thurloe State Papers*—to go no further afield.

3 The evidence adduced by P. Styles in 'The Social Structure of Kineton Hundred in the reign of Charles II', *Trans. and Proceedings of the Birmingham Archaeological Soc.*, 78 (1962), pp. 96–117, is of particular interest on the recovery of sharper status definitions. But one cannot be sure that any one region is typical of the whole country.

4 Robert Coytmor, for whom see section v, pp. 265–6.

5 As was the case with Sir William Petty, according to Aubrey (*Brief Lives*, ed. A. Clark (Oxford, 1898), II, 143).

6 *Past and Present*, 33 (1966), art. cit.

7 W. L. Sachse, 'The Migration of New Englanders to England, 1640–1660', *Am. Hist. Rev.*, 53 (1947–8), pp. 251–78, and *The Colonial American in Britain* (Madison, Wisconsin, 1956).

8 Namely: Samuel Bartlett, Adam Baynes, George Bishop, Robert Blackburne, John Blackwell junior, Henry Broad, William Clarke, Edward Cosen, Robert Coytmor, Richard Creed, Martin Dallison, Richard Deane junior, Gualter Frost senior and junior, Richard Hutchinson, William Jessop, John Maidstone, Robert Mainwaring, Martin Noell,

Clement Oxenbridge, Edward Roberts, Samuel Sandford, Henry Scobell, Richard Sherwyn, Arthur Squibb junior, James Standish, George Thom(p)son, Thomas Turner, Nathaniel Waterhouse, William Webb, Richard Wilcox, Francis Willoughby, Benjamin Worsley.

9 As could have been inferred from ch. 2.
10 E.g. Milton as Latin Secretary and John Maidstone as the Protector's cofferer.
11 George Foxcroft, John Jackson and George Bilton. Peter Pett was also accused of improper practices: see ch. 3, ix, pp. 157–9.

v SOME CASE HISTORIES

1 See the wonderfully perceptive remarks by Richard Cobb in *A Second Identity* (1969), Introduction, pp. 43–9.
2 See *King's Servants*, ch. 2, pp. 156–8, ch. 5, section iii, ch. 6, section vi, for the use of some such materials; also Aylmer, 'Officers of the Exchequer', in Fisher (ed.), *Essays*, pp. 171–8.
3 As well as Pepys and Evelyn, there are memoirs, diaries or contemporary lives of Elias Ashmole, William Dugdale, Stephen Fox, Francis and Roger North, John Pottinger, Sir John Reresby, Sir William Temple, Edmund Warcup and others. For some of these problems, see P. Delany, *British Autobiography in the 17th century* (1969), although he does not discuss officials as such. For further references, see W. Matthews, *British Diaries* (Berkeley, Cal., 1950) and *British Autobiographies* (Berkeley, 1955; repr. Hamden, Conn., 1968).
4 See Delany, *British Autobiography*, chapters 3–6.
5 *Memoirs*, ed. C. H. Firth, 2 vols (Oxford, 1894) is the best edition.
6 *Memorials of the English Affairs* (either 1682 or 1731 folio; the 4-vol. Oxford (1853) ed. is the best, but still unsatisfactory).
7 Miss Ruth Spalding, to whom I am grateful for her account of the Whitelocke MSS.
8 Now BM, Add. MS. 53,726.
9 *Milton on Himself*, ed. J. S. Diekhoff (New York, 1965).
10 *Poems and Letters*, ed. H. M. Margoliouth (Oxford, 2 vols, 1927, repr. 1952), Vol. 2.
11 *King's Servants*, pp. 85–6; C. Dalton, *History of the Wrays of Glentworth* (Aberdeen, 1881), II, 113–15.
12 *A Dying Father's Last Legacy* . . . (1660).
13 *Memoirs, Letters, and Speeches of A. A. Cooper, earl of Shaftesbury*, ed. W. D. Christie (1859).
14 The full text is in Hist. MSS. Comm., ser. 77, *De L'Isle and Dudley Papers*, VI (1966), *1626–98*, pp. 559–624.
15 Ibid., esp. pp. 455–7, 472–3, 475, 477, 487–8, 499, 502–3, 523–31; P.C.C. 1698, 78 Last.
16 After the early death of his wife, Dorothy née Percy, he never married again but had at least three natural daughters by two London ladies, Grace and Jane Pensac. He provided generously for mothers and children alike (Will).

17 The sequence of names was not alphabetical after Berners.

18 In the 200 sample and the 100 selection. Sources: Harl. Soc., XV, *Visitations of London 1633-5*, I, 68; Foster, *Gray's Inn Reg.*, p. 161 (partly erroneous); Noble, *Regicides*, I, 90. It is not clear whether Noble ascribes this moderating influence to his first wife, née Coton, or his second, Abigail Keighley, by whom he was survived; J. Waylen, *The House of Cromwell and the story of Dunkirk* (1880), 87; Firth and Rait, *A. & O.*, I, 268, 970, 1011, 1087, 1246, 1254, II, 303, 310, 382-3, 581-2, 588-90, 702-3, 783, 809, 824; *Cal. S.P. Dom., 1648-9*, p. 174; *Cal. Cttee. Compdg.*, p. 591; PRO, S.P. 24/12, fo. 114, 24/23-4; *Cal. S.P. Dom., 1660-1*, p. 451; *C.J.*, VII, 74, 617; Bodl., Tanner MSS., Vols 51-2; Rawlinson, C. 179; PRO, C. 181/6; Index 4213; E. 403/2523; P.C.C. 141 Juxon; In *Catalogi Codicum Manuscriptorum Bodleianae* (Oxford, 1843), *Pars Quarta, Codices T. Tanneri*, the addressee of the 1653-9 correspondence is wrongly given as Sir John Hobart of Norfolk; see C. H. Firth in *E.H.R.*, 7 (1892), pp. 102-10. Some of his letters to John Hobart in 1642 are actually signed 'Jo. Berners', and not 'J.B.' (Bodl., Tanner MSS. 63 and 66).

19 In selection, not sample. Sources: *Cal. S.P. Dom., 1645-7*, p. 110; *1650*, p. 526; *1651-2*, p. 34; *Cal. S.P. Ire. Adventurers, 1642-59*, p. 86; Firth and Rait, *A. & O.*, I, 487, 842, II, 382-3, 588-90; *Cal. Cttee. Compdg.*, pp. 172, 745; PRO, S.P. 46/81, fo. 226, 230, and 99, fo. 79; *Guildhall Miscell.*, II, 326, 330; PRO, E. 351/439: *To His Excellency ... The Humble Representation of several Aldermen ... and other Citizens of London ...* n.d. (May 1653), BM, 669, f. 17(8); Hist. MSS. Comm., *Leyborn-Popham*, p. 168; Bodl., Rawl. MS. B. 239, no. 455; J. C. Whitebrook (ed.), *London Citizens in 1651* (1910), pp. 5-10; C. E. Surman (ed.), *Register-Books of the 4th Classis in the Province of London, 1646-59* (Harl. Soc. reg. ser., 82-3, 1952-3), pp. 3, 8-36, 150; P.C.C. 87 Laud. He is to be distinguished from the London surgeon James Molins (Whitebrook, loc. cit.; Harl. Soc., lxvi, *Grantees of Arms*, p. 173, ? grant to his father James M., surgeon, 1614), and from the two minor gentry W.M.s of Dorset and Oxon respectively (Foster, *Al. Ox.*, I, 1019; Clark, *Reg. of Oxford*, II, 306, 317; *Mid. Temp. A.R.*, I, 78, 83; Harl. Soc., v, *Visn. Oxon*, 233; lxiv, *Hants*, 121-2; cv-vi, *Wilts*, 131)—both being too old for our man.

20 In selection. Sources: *DNB*, notice of his grandfather also deals with his father and notes him briefly (giving his dates as 1627-98); Keeler, *Long Parliament*, p. 279, for Ric. M. sr.; Firth and Rait, *A. & O.*, I, 126-II, 1448, *passim*, for Samuel; *Gray's Inn Adm. Reg.*, p. 241; Firth and Rait, *A. & O.*, II, 382-3, 588-90; PRO, E. 403/2523; Index 4213; S.P. 46/99, fo. 79; *Cal. Cttee. Compdg.*, p. 745; Hist. MSS. Comm., *Leyborn-Popham*, p. 168. He was not the R.M. who came from Salop but moved to Hants and was a parliamentarian there (Harl. Soc. lxiv, *Visn. Hants*, 28-9; xxix, *Salop*, Pt 2, 366; xliii, *Surrey*, 196; *Cal. Cttee. Compdg.*, p. 54; Firth and Rait, *A. & O.*, I, 335, 450, 540, 696, *et seq.*); nor the R.M. who died intestate in St Clement Danes in 1660 (P.C.C. 161 Laud; Prob. Act. Bk 1660, p. 193) who was probably a cousin of the

Hants commissioner. I am grateful to the Shropshire County Record Office for further information about Moore and his family.

21 In selection. Sources: Firth and Rait, *A. & O.*, I, 9, 802, 914, 1007, 1057, 1129, 1246, 1259, 1261, II, 302, 364-7, 382-3, 588-90, 702-3, 824; *The Publick Intelligencer*, for 16-23 May 1659; *Cal. S.P. Dom.*, *1650*, p. 307; *1651-2*, pp. 501-2; *1652-3*, pp. 355, 376; *1653-4*, p. 368; *Cal. Cttee. Compdg.*, pp. 8, 745; *Cal. Cttee. Advc. Mon.*, p. 27; Bodl., Rawl. B. 239, nos 426, 516, 566; PRO, E. 351/439, 653, C. 181/6, S.P. 46/99, fo. 75; *C.J.*, VII, 74, 617; H. N. Brailsford, *The Levellers and the English Revolution* (1962), pp. 611, 622 n.; Trevor-Roper, 'Cromwell and his Parliaments', in Pares and Taylor (eds), *Essays presented to Namier*, p. 26 n. 3; Prendergast, *Cromwellian Settlement*, App. V, nos 213, 1210; J. Ward, *Lives of the Professors of Gresham's College* (1740), p. xv; Hist. MSS. Comm., *7th Rept.*, Appendix H. of Lords MSS., p. 71; *Leeds, etc.*, p. 3; P.C.C. 96 Drax; P. Morant, *History . . . of . . . Essex* (2nd ed., Chelmsford, 1816), I, 256; J. and J. B. Burke, *Extinct Baronetcies* (1838), p. 378; Mercers' Company Records, Apprenticeships 1624-5, Freedoms 1633. Later entries show an apprentice to Moyer (1642) and his own sons becoming free (1668 and 1669).

22 In selection. Sources: *Gray's Inn Adm. Reg.*, p. 229; Firth and Rait, *A. & O.*, I, 5, 105, 164, 795, 872, 889, 1007, 1042, 1191, 1259, 1261; II, 302, 382-3, 588-90, 855-8, 899; *Cal. S.P. Dom.*, *1644-5*, p. 347; *1649-50*, p. 20 (unless this was the Jas R., future under-clerk of the Council: see *Thurloe St. P.*, VI, 591; PRO, S.P. 18/182/90); ibid., *1652-3*, pp. 354, 393; *C.J.*, VII, 228; *Humble Representation*; PRO, E. 351/439, 653; C. 181/6; Bodl., Rawl. B. 239, nos 119, 226; *Cal. Cttee. Compdg.*, p. 542; T. K. Rabb, *Investment and Empire* (Cambridge, Mass., 1968), p. 369 (too old for our man); P.C.C., Administrations 1655, fo. 47. For the Danish business see *Thurloe St. P.*, II, 456. Drapers' Company Records, and P. Boyd, *Roll of the Drapers' Company of England* (1934); Pearl, *London*, App. II, pp. 324-5; D. L. Kirby, 'The Radicals of St. Stephen's, Coleman St., London, 1624-1642', *Guildhall Miscellany*, III (1970), pp. 110-11.

23 In selection. Sources: H. H. London and G. D. Squibb, 'A Dorset King of Arms: Arthur Squibb, Clarenceux, 1646-1650', *Dorset Natural History & Archaeological Soc.*, Vol. 68, pp. 58-65, App. I, fig. p. 64; *Thurloe St. P.*, I, 289, VI, 185; H.M.C., *9th Rept.*, App. ii, p. 44a; P.C.C., 299 Brent (Powell), 206 May (John Squibb), 363 and 378 Alchin (Arthur the elder), 50 Bath (our Arthur); *Cal. S.P. Dom.*, *1645-7*, p. 428; *1649-50*, p. 280; *1654*, p. 272; *1655*, pp. 193-5; *1661-2*, p. 369; *Cal. Cttee. Compdg.*, pp. 525, 745; PRO, C. 181/6; S.P. 23/36-7; S.P. 28/269; S.P. 26/8; E. 351/453, 439; Firth and Rait, *A. & O.*, II, 303, 382-3, 830; *C.J.*, VI, 335; Trevor-Roper, 'Cromwell and his Parliaments', loc. cit.; R. Latham and W. Matthews (eds), *The Diary of Samuel Pepys* (1970–), Vol. 1, *1660*, pp. 31, 49.

24 In selection. Sources: *DNB*; W. Sterry-Cooper, *Edward Winslow* (Birmingham, 1953); Waters, *Genealog. Gleanings*, I, ii, 179; Rabb, *Investment and Empire*, p. 406; Firth and Rait, *A. & O.*, II, 382-3, 830,

839, 899; *Thurloe St. P.*, II, 456, III, 249–52, 352, IV, 28; *Clarke Papers*, III, 6–7; PRO, E. 403/2523; Pat. Roll Indexes, 1655, Pt 4, no. 59; *Cal. Cttee. Compdg.*, p. 724; *Cal. S.P. Dom.*, *1651–2*, p. 184; *1652–3*, p. 607; P.C.C. 377 Aylett; *A Humble Representation* (May 1653).

25 In selection. Sources: Venn, *Al. Cant.*, I, 292; *Mid. Temp. Adm. Reg.*, I, 139; Firth and Rait, *A. & O.*, II, 283, 619, 830, 839; *Cal. S.P. Dom.*, *1650*, p. 81; *1653–4*, p. 8, 427; *1655–6*, pp. 252–4; *1656–7*, p. 595; *Cal. Cttee. Compdg.*, p. 215; *Cal. Cttee. Advc. Mon.*, p. 81; *Clarke Papers*, III, 69; *Thurloe St. P.*, III, 558–9, 744; PRO, S.P. 24/8, fo. 84; S.P. 24/29; C. 181/6; E. 403/2523; E. 351/439; Index 4213; *A Narrative of the late Parliament* (1657); P.C.C., 343 Ruthen. He is to be distinguished from various other Edward Careys, from Devon (Harl. Soc., vi, 51), Somerset (Harl. Soc., xi, 20) and Staffs (Harl. Soc., xiii, 45, and Foster, *Al. Oxon.*, I, 246).

26 In selection. Sources: Keeler, *Long Parliament*, pp. 368–9, esp. n. 21 (on his father); Brunton and Pennington, *Members of Long Parliament*, pp. 130, 220, 243; Firth and Rait, *A. & O.*, II, 75, 830, 839, 1040, 1087; *Cal. S.P. Dom.*, *1650*, p. 503; *1655–6*, pp. 14, 16, 189, 215; *1656–7*, p. 536; *1657–8*, pp. 401, 403, 407, 414, 420, 427, 436, 541; *1658–9*, p. 435; *1660–1*, pp. 369, 492; *Cal. Treas. Bks*, III, *1669–1672*; *Thurloe St. P.*, III, 662–3; PRO, A.O. 1/605/56; E. 403/2523; S.P. 25/69, fo. 15; Index 4213; BM, Add. MS., 4184, no. 114; Add. (Sloane) 3931, fo. 7 *et seq.*; Inner Temple Adms., typescript, I, 336; *Visn. Devon* (Harl. Soc., vi), 292–3; P.C.C. 13 Dyke; W. H. Upton, *Upton Family Records* (1893), esp. pp. 8–9, 36–8, 59, 65, 83, 432 (a clearer and more accurate compilation than many family histories).

27 In selection. See also ch. 3, i, pp. 69–70. Sources: *Visitations of London* (Harl. Soc., xv and xvii), I, 294, II, 302, 352 (for the London mercer); *Lincoln's Inn Adm. Reg.*, I, 125 (if he was of Carmarthenshire origin and born as early as 1582–3); *Milton St. P.*, ed. J. Nickolls, pp. 85–6; Firth and Rait, *A. & O.*, I, 970, 1087, 1136, II, 304, 343, 830, 839, 973, 1074, 1328; PRO, E. 403/2523; Patent Roll Index, Pt 4, no. 59; Index 4213; Bodl., MS. Carte 74, p. 286 v; J. A. Bradney, *History of Monmouthshire* (1904–32), III, 101; IV, 289; D. F. McKenzie, *Stationers' Company Apprentices*, *1605–40* (Charlottesville, Va., 1961), nos 1417, 2751–5; *Strena Vavasorencis, A New Years-Gift for the Welsh Itinerants* ... 30 January 1654. BM, E. 727 (14), p. 6.

28 In selection, not sample. Sources: 'The Private Chronology of Denis Bond, Esq. 1636 and 1640' (1919 typescript of 1828 MS. copy. Dorset County Museum); *Cal. S.P. Dom.*, *1641–3*, pp. 415, 483; *1644–5*, pp. 65, 172, 177; *1645–7*, pp. 247–8; *1651*, p. 447; *1651–2*, pp. 245, 274, 295, 506; *1652–3*, p. 415; *1654*, pp. 127–8; *1655*, p. 249; *1655–6*, pp. 61, 92, 135, 386; *1656–7*, p. 514; *1657–8*, pp. 59, 78, 81; *Cal. Cttee. Advc. Mon.*, p. 35; Firth and Rait, *A. & O.*, I, 1101, 1169–70; II, 277; *C.J.*, VI, 497; *L.J.*, VIII, 24–5; PRO, S.P. 25/78, fo. 409; S.P. 26/8; S.P. 28/258–9; S.P. 24/5, fo. 65, 68, 84, 134, 164; S.P. 24/7 fo. 155, 165; Bodl., Rawl. MS., B. 239, no. 290; P.C.C. 21 and 136 Pye.

29 In selection. Sources: Foster, *Al Oxon.*, I, 184; Inner Temple Adms.,

t.s., I, 297; *Grantees of Arms* (Harl. Soc., lxvi), p. 34; *Cal. S.P. Dom.,*
1641–3, pp. 404, 458; *1644*, p. 362; *1644–5*, pp. 168–70, 206–7, 264;
1645–7, pp. 483–4; *1649–50*, p. 415; *1655*, p. 178; Firth and Rait,
A. & O., I, 1169–70; II, 277; *L.J.*, X, 131; Hist. MS. Comm., *7th Rept.*
App., House of Lords Papers, p. 16; PRO, S.P. 28/258, 259, 260, 269;
BM, Add. MS. 4,184, no. 76.

30 In selection. Sources: T. C. Dale (ed.), *Inhabitants of London in 1638*
(Soc. of Genealogists, 1931), p. 181; D. V. Glass (ed.), *Inhabitants of
London within the Walls in 1695* (London Rec. Soc., Vol. 2), p. 128; *Cal.
S.P. Dom., 1641–3*, p. 197; Frank, *English Newspaper*, p. 311; *Cal. S.P.
Dom., 1644–5*, p. 584; *1652–3*, pp. 157, 415, 455; *1654*, p. 287; *1655–6*,
pp. 30, 299–300; *Cal. Cttee. Compdg.*, p. 745; Firth and Rait, *A. & O.*,
I, 802, II, 277; *C.J.*, VII, 739; Prendergast, *Cromwellian Settlement*,
App. V, no. 844; Bottigheimer, *Irish Lands*, Apps. A and B; Hist. MSS.
Comm., *Portland*, I, 227; PRO, S.P. 28/58–60; S.P. 25/69, fo. 6–7;
78, fo. 409; S.P. 46/99, fo. 79; P.C.C. 114 Hyde. The publisher and
printer Greensmith was born about 1608, the son of a London merchant-
taylor, apprenticed in 1626 and free of the Stationers' Company in 1635
(McKenzie, *Stationers' Apprentices*, nos 617, 665; Guildhall Library,
Children's Registers of Christ's Hospital, Vol. 1, fo. 396; H. R. Plomer,
Dictionary of Printers and Booksellers 1640–1667 (1907), p. 86); another
John Greensmith, son of a Nottinghamshire farmer, was apprenticed
to a London haberdasher in 1629 and free of that Company in 1639
(Haberdashers' Company, Apprenticeship and Freedom records). I
have not identified the tobacconist for certain with either of these.

31 In selection. Sources: *Cal. S.P. Dom., 1644*, p. 362; *1644–5*, pp. 168–70;
1648–9, p. 33; *1652–3*, p. 415; *1655–6*, p. 179; *Cal. Cttee. Compdg.*, pp. 5,
467; Firth and Rait, *A. & O.*, I, 1169–70, II, 277; *L.J.*, X, 131; Hist.
MSS. Comm., *7th Rept.*, pp. 16, 75; Hist. MSS. Comm., *Beaufort, etc.*
(Hulton Papers), p. 176; *C.J.*, VII, 326, 337; PRO, S.P. 25/78, fo. 409;
S.P. 28/258–60; *Visitation of Leicestershire in 1619* (Harl. Soc., ii), p. 135;
P.C.C. 111 Juxon; Prendergast, *Cromwellian Settlement*, App. V, no. 841;
Bottigheimer, *Irish Lands*, App. A. Possible Richard Wilcoxes were
apprenticed in the Haberdashers', Merchant-Taylors' and Vintners' Cos
too. The daughter of the elder of two possible Haberdashers (appr.
1615; free 1622) in 1635 married Justinian Pagitt, son of a Baron of the
Exchequer and himself a future legal officer-holder under the Republic
(Haberdashers' records; Merchant-Taylors' MSS., Apprentices, I, fo. 48v;
Vintners' Co., MS. AP/1; C. H. Josten (ed.), *Elias Ashmole, 1617–1692*
(Oxford, 1966), II, 319 and n. 7).

32 In selection. Sources: *DNB*; W. K. Jordan, *Men of Substance* (Chicago,
1942), pp. 38–66; *Visns. of London 1633–5*, II (Harl. Soc., xvii), 204;
Cal. S.P. Dom., 1649–50, p. 44; *1651*, p. 467; *1652–3*, pp. 367–8, 450;
1654, p. 287; *1655–6*, p. 126; *1658–9*, p. 211; Firth and Rait, *A. & O.*,
II, 277; *C.J.*, VII, 426, VII, 327, 483–4, 711, 758; PRO, S.P. 26/8,
28/260; Bodl., Rawl. MS., A lvi, fo. 156.

33 In selection. Sources: *The Scriveners' Company Common Paper*, ed.
F. W. Steer (London Record Society, Vol. 4), pp. 115, 119, 120, 121,

126; *Cal. S.P. Dom., 1641–3*, p. 441; *Cal. Cttee. Advc. Mon.*, pp. 13, 25–6, 37, 77, 78, 111; PRO, E. 351/439, 2523; A.O. 1/15/301; S.P. 24/29; *Grantees of Arms* (Harl. Soc., lxvi), p. 70; P.C.C. 635 Wootton.

34 Not to be confused with the much more important office of (the King's) Attorney of the Court of Wards.

35 In sample and selection. Sources: Venn, *Al. Cant.*, II, 11; *Notes and Queries*, 1st series, V, 545–6; *Gray's Inn Adm. Reg.*, p. 197; *Mid. Temple Adm. Reg.*, I, 130; *DNB*, 'Sir John D.'; *Corrections and Additions to the DNB, 1923–1963* (Boston, 1966), 'Sir John D.'; Noble, *Regicides*, I, p. xli; H. E. Bell, *History and Records of the Court of Wards and Liveries* (Cambridge, 1953); *C.J.*, V, 663–4, VI, 98, 108, 112, 223, 267, 287, 288, 292, VII, 375, 424, 476, 706, VIII, 224–5; Deputy Keeper of the Public Records, *5th Report*, App. II, p. 260; Firth and Rait, *A. & O.*, II, 529–30; *Cal. S.P. Dom., 1653–4*, p. 282; Hist. MS. Comm., *7th Report*, App., pp. 41, 43; *Cal. Cttee. Advc. Mon.*, pp. 60–1, 62; *Cal. Cttee. Compdg.*, p. 777; PRO, E. 315/139, fo. 14v; E. 351/438, 439; C. 181/6; Burton, *Parl. Diary*, I, 266, II, 316–18, 336–7, 348–50, III, 5; S.P. 24/8, fo. 84; S.P. 26/8; S.P. 28/286.

36 In sample, not selection. Sources: *Visitation of Dorset* (Harl. Soc., xx); J. Hutchins, *Hist. of Dorset*, 3rd ed. (4 vols, 1861–70), II, 692, IV, 323–4; P.C.C. 161 and 175 Twisse (brother and father), 126 Berkeley (Francis Meverell); PRO, S.P. 28/253A, 259, 350/8; S.P. 46/81, fo. 5; *Cal. S.P. Dom., 1656–7*, p. 128; R. Milnes Walker, 'Francis Glisson and his Capsule', *Annals of the Royal College of Surgeons*, 38 (1966), esp. pp. 7–15; BM, Sloane MSS. 2251, 3315.

37 In sample, not selection. Sources: *DNB*, and *Dictionary of Welsh Biography* (English ed. 1959), 'John J.'; J. R. Woodhead, *The Rulers of London, 1660–1689* (1965), p. 100; *Cal. S.P. Dom., 1625–49, Addenda*, p. 632; *1655–6*, pp. 116, 213, 320, 393; *1656–7*, p. 350; *1657–8*, pp. 84, 240; *C.J.*, VII, 618; Burton, *Parl. Diary*, IV, 224; J. Mayer (ed.), 'Inedited Letters . . .', *Trans. Hist. Soc. Lancs. and Cheshire*, n.s., I (1861), pp. 189, 221–3, 227–30; PRO, S.P. 46/102, fo. 49; Bodl., Rawl. MS. B. 239, nos 172, 600; P.C.C. 155 Dyke.

38 In sample and selection. Sources: W. D. Cooper, 'The Oxenbridges of Brede Place, Sussex and Boston, Mass.', *Sussex Archaeological Collections*, xii (1860), 203–20; Dale, *Inhabitants of London*, p. 41; *Mid. Temple Adm. Reg.*, I, 184; Inner Temple Adms. t.s., II, 15; *Cal. Cttee. Advc. Mon.*, pp. 406, 578; *Cal. Cttee. Compdg.*, 1268, 2166; Joyce, *Hist. of Post Office*, pp. 29, 31–2; Hemmeon, *History of British Post Office*, pp. 193–4; *Cal. S.P. Dom., 1651–2*, pp. 45, 151, 456; *1653–4*, pp. 372–3; *1654*, pp. 20–5, 349; *1660–1*, p. 409; *1665–6*, p. 179; Bodl., Carte MS. 74, fo. 119; Rawl. MS. A, lxiv, fo. 237, xxviii, no. 122, Rawl. MS., B. 243, fo. 9, 10a, 10b; PRO, E. 351/2293; *C.J.*, VII, 631, 633; Burton, *Parl. Diary*, IV, 382.

39 Sources: *Visitations of London 1633–5* (Harl. Soc., xvii), II, 146; *Gray's Inn Adm. Reg.*, p. 240; Rymer and Sanderson, *Foedera*, XX, 161–3, 340–1; *Cal. S.P. Dom., 1636–7*, p. 162; Firth and Rait, *A. & O.*, I, 169, II, 669; *Cal. S.P. Dom., 1650*, pp. 88, 467; *1651*, p. 16; *1651–2*, p. 361;

PRO, S.P. 18/16/130 ii; S.P. 24/29; S.P. 28/253A, 258; S.P. 46/95, fo. 262; P.C.C., Administrations 1659, fo. 151, 152.

40 In sample, not selection. Sources: Foster, *Al. Oxon.*, I, 1455; Thomas Edwards, *Third Part of the Gangraena* (1646), pp. 54–9; *Cal. S.P. Ire.*, *Adventurers, 1642–59*, pp. 9, 95, 343, 344; Bottigheimer, *Irish Lands*, App. B; *Cal. Cttee. Compdg.*, p. 665; *Cal. S.P. Dom.*, *1655*, pp. 11, 122; *1655–6*, pp. 84–6, 290; *1656–7*, pp. 26, 46, 355; *1657–8*, pp. 141–2, 351; *1658–9*, p. 196; *Cal. S.P. Ire.*, *1647–60*, pp. 673, 685; Dep. Keeper, *5th Report*, II, 271; Firth and Rait, *A. & O.*, II, 651, 767; *C.J.*, VII, 184, 250–1; PRO, E. 403/2608, p. 213; E. 351/439; S.P. 28/258, 259; S.P. 18/96/25; Seymour, *Puritans in Ireland*, pp. 171–2, 177, 221; M. H. Nicolson (ed.), *Conway Letters . . . 1642–1684* (1930), pp. 120, 159, 161, 261, 262; E. MacLysaght, *Supplement to Irish Families* (Dublin, 1964), p. 119. See also ch. 3, sections i, iii, ix.

41 In selection. Sources: *DNB*; G. Isham, 'Adam Baynes of Leeds and Holdenby', *Northants Past and Present*, II (1956), pp. 138–46; Firth and Davies, *Regimental History*, pp. 255–7; J. Y. Akerman (ed.), *Letters from Roundhead Officers . . .* (Edinburgh, 1856); *Proceedings of the Soc. of Antiquaries*, II (1849–53); ibid., III (1853–6); *Tait's Edinburgh Mag.*, 17 (1850), 18 (1851); BM, Add. MSS. 21,417–27 (the complete collection from which the three preceding items print selections); Firth and Rait, *A. & O.*, II, 297, 835, 851; *Cal. S.P. Dom.*, *1651*, p. 335; *1654*, p. 343; *1655–6*, p. 64; *1657–8*, pp. 282, 334; *The Publick Intelligencer*, 23–30 May 1659; PRO, Index 4213; S.P. 24/10, fo. 99v, 124; S.P. 28/286; Joan Wake (ed.), *Quarter Sessions Records Northants.* (*1630, 1657, 1658*), Northants. Rec. Soc., I, 251; R. Thoresby, *Ducatus Leodiensis* (1715), pp. 101–7; *Yorkshire Pedigrees* (Harl. Soc., xciv), p. 141; *Grantees of Arms* (Harl. Soc., lxvi), p. 18; P.C.C., 74 Duke.

42 In selection, not sample. Sources, *Parish Register of St Mary's Stafford* (Staffs. Parish Register Rec. Soc.); Newton, *Colonising Activities of the English Puritans*, pp. 62–3, 318; *Dugdale's Visitation of Lancs. 1664*, Pt 2 (Chetham Soc., lxxxv, 1872), p. 159; *Gray's Inn Adm. Reg.*, p. 294; Bottigheimer, *Irish Lands*, App. B.; BM, Add. MS. 4,184, no. 187; Add. MS. 10,615; Stowe 184; Add. 46,190, esp. fo. 190–3 (from which my quotations are taken); Bodl., Carte MS. 63, fo. 630–1, 636; Noble, *Regicides*, I, xli; *Cal. S.P. Dom.*, *1649–50*, p. 13; *1650*, pp. 61, 450; *1651–2*, p. 15; *1652–3*, p. 415; *1654*, p. 48; *1655*, p. 128; *1655–6*, pp. 14, 35, 311; *1656–7*, p. 291; *1657–8*, pp. 38, 84; *1660–1*, p. 176; *C.J.*, VI, 11–12; VIII, 1, 184, 239, 245; *L.J.*, VII, 604; *Thurloe St. P.*, VII, 809, 812; Firth and Rait, *A. & O.*, I, 797, 874, 1191; II, 283; PRO, Ind. 4213; C. 181/6; S.P. 18/183/72; S.P. 28/350(4); E. 351/594, his account as Protector's Treasurer, 1653–59, passed 1663 (Jessop paid in a deficit of £20 to clear a turnover of £52,500-odd); Bodl., Rawl. MS. A ii, 134–40; *Clarke Papers*, I, 9; Latham and Matthews, *Diary of Samuel Pepys*, Vol. 2, *1661*, p. 32 and n. 3; Wheatley, *Diary of Samuel Pepys*, VIII, 268, 279; Lancs. R.O., Hulton Muniments, DD Hu 22/1, 24/1, 45/1, 46/1–22, 47/1–141, 48/3, 7; 49/13; 53/21–32, 83; 55/13, 14; 56/3, 6. He is to be distinguished from the W.J. who invested in the Bermudas in 1620

(Rabb, *Investment and Empire*, p. 324); from W.J. of Broom Hall, Sheffield (1610–41) who was educated at Magadalene College, Cambridge, and the Middle Temple (Burke, *Commoners*, ii, 251–2; Venn, *Al. Cant.*, II, 475; *Mid. Temp. Adm. Reg.*, I, 121; C. Clay (ed.), *Dugdale's Visitation of Yorks.* (Exeter, 1907), II, 94–7); and from a W.J. who was living at Braintree, Essex, in 1681 (inf. Essex R.O.). This is far from an exhaustive list of references. I am grateful to Mr Christopher Thompson who is writing a book on the Earl of Warwick, and to the County Archivists of Essex, Lancashire and Staffordshire, for their help.

43 In sample, not selection. Sources: M. E. Lucy, *Biography of the Lucy family of Charlecote* (1862), pp. 33–7; Alice Burnham, alias Fairfax–Lucy, *Charlecote and the Lucys* (Oxford 1958), pp. 150–6, 160–2, 320 (a delightful account which, like the preceding item, unfortunately confuses our man with his uncle, Sir Richard, and totally overlooks his administrative career); Brunton and Pennington, *Members of the Long Parliament*, pp. 224, 236; G.E.C., *Baronetage*, I, 113–14; *Gray's Inn Adm. Reg.*, p. 262; *Visn. Warwicks, 1682–3* (Harl. Soc., lxii), p. 94; Firth and Rait, *A. & O.*, I, 1094, II, 1244, 308, 311, 704, 835, 828–9, 1403; *Cal. S.P. Dom., 1654*, p. 343; *1655*, pp. 155, 178; *1655–6*, p. 320; *1656–7*, p. 374; *1657–8*, p. 334; PRO, E.403/2523; C. 181/6; P.C.C. 39 Bath.

44 In sample, not selection. Sources: *Visns London* (Harl. Soc., xvii), II, 204; Jordan, *Men of Substance*, Pedigree fig. p. 38, p. 51; Pennington and Roots, *Committee at Stafford*, pp. 106, 159, 186, 317; *Cal. S.P. Dom., 1651*, pp. 49–50; *1652–3*, pp. 109–11; Hist. MSS. Comm., *Leyborn-Popham*, pp. 73, 100; *C.J.*, VI, 230–1, VII, 814; Firth and Rait, *A. & O.*, II, 522, 591–8, 639; PRO, S.P. 18/101/167; C. 181/6; *Thurloe St. P.*, VII, 747; Bodl., Rawl. MS. C 179, p. 235; National Register of Archives, no. 5723, photostats of Willcocks MSS. (from which my quotations are taken); Mercers' Co. records, William s. of Wm. R. senior, free by patrimony 1633; Drapers' Co. records, William s. of Wm. R., free by patrimony 1649; Guildhall MS. 11,593/1, fo. 121, a W.R. free of the Grocers' Co., taking apprentices 1641–2; P.C.C., 2 Sadler, will of W. Robinson, cit. and mercer, 1635; 522 Ruthven, of W.R. of Inner Temple, Esq., 1657; 149 Mico, will made 1665, pr. 1666 of Wm. br. of Henry; Inner Temple Adms., t.s., I, p. 460 (fo. 644 of MS.), Wm. R., s. of Wm., barrister, Esq., adm. June 1637; P. Toon (ed.), *Correspondence of John Owen (1616–1683)* (1970), pp. 156–7. With the greatest respect, I think that Professor Jordan was wrong to identify the elder Inner Temple William, who was Registrar of Affidavits in Chancery, with the father of Henry Robinson (Jordan, *Men of Substance*, p. 50; Foster, *Al. Oxon.*, I, 1269; *Students admitted to the Inner Temple*, p. 169). The sources cited here will indicate some of the problems involved in trying to identify the William of the 1649 letters.

45 In selection, not sample. Sources: *Cal. S.P. Dom., 1651*, p. 488; *1653–4*, Preface; *1654*, p. 343; *1655–6*, p. 14; Firth and Rait, *A. & O.*, II, 812–13, 828–9, 851–3; Hist. MSS. Comm., *7th Report*, App., p. 89; Shaw, *Church*, II, 555; PRO, Ind. 4213; C. 181/6; S.P. 28/59, fo. 188; E. 351/655; P.C.C., 147 Reeve. Beaven (*Aldermen of London*, I, 60, 317,

II, 78) identifies the John Stone who d. 1678 (will P.C.C. 147 Reeve, not 117 as Beaven says) with the 1650 Master of the Merchant-Taylors' Co., who paid a £200 fine to get off being Alderman for Bridge ward in 1651. This J.S. had been apprenticed in 1597/8 and became free of the Merchant-Taylors' Co. in 1604/5 (Merchant-Taylors' Co. MS. Apprentices, 1593-7, II, fo. 94; 19th-cent. Lists of Freemen). On this reckoning, he was therefore about 72 when elected to the Council of State in 1653 and died at about 97, yet leaving two children under age, no grandchildren and a wife young enough to remarry by 1681 (will of his son, J.S., P.C.C. 173 North), which seems most unlikely. The number of possible John Stones in London can be gauged from *Visns of London* (Harl. Soc., xvii), II, 265, 266, 267; Burke, *Landed Gentry* (1937 ed.), p. 2165; Dale, *Inhabitants . . . 1638*, index refs; Venn. *Al. Cant.*, iv, 168, etc. For the merchant-taylor see also Firth and Rait, *A. & O.*, II, 81-104, 105, 302; Shaw, *Church*, II, 555; Rabb, *Investment and Empire*, p. 384. The Captain and Councillor of State seems more likely (if he was an ex-apprentice at all) to be the son of Matthew Stone, late Citizen and Haberdasher, whose master was Alderman John Warner, Grocer, 1640 (Guildhall MS. 11,593/1, fo. 107v). If he became free in 1648, this would explain his entering the administrative scene only in 1649.

46 In sample and selection. Sources: Goldsmiths' Co., Apprentices, I, fo. 313; PRO, E. 351/1295; A.O. 1/1601/52; A.O. 1/891/7, 9; Firth and Rait, *A. & O.*, II, 1436; *Cal. S.P. Dom., 1649-50*, p. 549; *1658-9*, p. 211; *1660-1*, pp. 11, 106, 317; *Cal. Cttee. Compdg.*, p. 130; *C.J.*, VII, 327, 329; Josten, *Elias Ashmole*, II, 776-7, 789-90, 797-9, 801; P.C.C. 44 Duke. For Vyner see *DNB*; Beaven, *Aldermen*; and Ashley, *Financial and Commercial Policy*.

47 See ch. 2, s. iv, pp. 24-8.

48 In selection, not sample. Sources: Dale, *Inhabitants . . . 1638*, p. 182; W. L. F. Nuttall, 'Governor John Blackwell: His Life in England and Ireland', *Penna. Mag. of Hist. and Biog.*, 88 (1964), pp. 121-41; Firth and Davies, *Regimental Hist.*, pp. 200-2; Beaven, *Aldermen*, II, 78, 88, 90, 187; *C.J.*, VI, 23, 117, 132, 188, 300, 497; VII, 258-9; Firth and Rait, *A. & O.*, I, 887-904, 1113, II, 310, 688-90; *Cal. S.P. Dom., 1644*, 109, 155; *1625-49, Addenda*, p. 688; *1645-7*, pp. 376, 574, 576; *1651*, p. 86; *1654*, pp. 127-8; *1655*, pp. 249, 303; *1655-6*, pp. 86, 119, 147, 156; *1657-8*, pp. 370-1; *1658-9*, p. 253; E. Peacock (ed.), *Army Lists of Roundheads and Cavaliers* (2nd edn. 1874), p. 100; PRO, C. 181/6; E. 403/2523, p. 223; E. 101/676/51; E. 351/306; S.P. 18/38/72; S.P. 28/286; S.P. 26/8; *Thurloe St. P.*, II, 356, IV, 765-6 (from which the last quotation is taken); Bodl., Rawl. MS., A xxxiv, fo. 259, xiii, 104, 112, xxvii, 295-6; B. ccxxxix, nos 9, 331, 473, 496; P.C.C. 41 Wootton; Bottigheimer, *Irish Lands*, Apps. A and B; Prendergast, *Cromwellian Settlement*, App. V, no. 521; Woodhead, *Rulers of London*, p. 382; *Le Neve's Knights* (Harl. Soc., viii), 459; *Stats. Realm*, 12 Car. II, c XI, s. xlii; Ludlow, *Memoirs*, II, 61; Noble, *Regicides*, I, xli; Dunlop, *Ireland under the Commonwealth*, II, 358-9 and n.; *Narrative of the late Parlt.* (1657); *City Spectacles* (1647); *Cal. S.P. Ire., 1660-2*, pp. 67, 101, 204,

NOTES TO PAGES 246–250

227, 270–1, 400, 433–6; *1663–5*, pp. 257, 271, 336, 426, 645; C. M. Andrews, *The Colonial Period of American History* (4 vols, New Haven, 1934–8), III, 308 n. 3, 308–11; B. Bailyn, *New England Merchants* (Camb., Mass., 1955, repr. New York, 1964), pp. 184–7; S. M. Janney, *Life of Penn* (Philadelphia, 1851), pp. 351–2 (from which the Penn quotation comes).

49 His name is spelt Cosen, Cosin, Cosyn, Cosyns, Cozens, Cousins, Couzins etc. He seems normally to have signed himself Cosen or Cosyn.

50 Vane was Cofferer of the Household from 1625 to 1632, Comptroller 1632–1639, and then Treasurer 1639–41.

51 In selection, not in sample. Sources: T. F. Fenwick and W. C. Metcalfe, *Visn. of Glos. 1682–3*, pp. 48–9; *Grantees of Arms* (Harl. Soc., lxvi), p. 63; *Cal. S.P. Dom., 1641–3*, p. 52; *1644*, p. 235; *1645–7*, pp. 58, 84, 106, 125, 167, 202; *1650*, p. 39; *1660–1*, p. 8; PRO, S.P. 18/70/74, ii, 38/72; S.P. 28/269; 350/10; *Scotland under the Protectorate*, pp. 385–91; *The Mystery of the Good Old Cause* (1660); P.C.C. 55 Dyke.

52 See ch. 2, section iii, p. 18, and ch. 3, sections i and ix, pp. 78–9, 145–7.

53 See also ch. 3, v, p. 111.

54 The ex-Navy Treasurer and returned New Englander must not be confused with the Richard Hutchinson, father and son, of Mile End Green (Stepney) and the City, who were also extremely wealthy, with massive East India Company investments (see P.C.C. 174 Pett, for the father; 129 North, for his wife; and Woodhead, *Rulers of London*, p. 95, for the son, who died intestate just before his father in 1699). A further complication is provided by the Richard Hutchinson who was appointed joint or sole Paymaster of the Navy, that is as a subordinate to the Treasurer, in November 1668, and still appears to have been acting in 1671, certainly so in December 1670. As the ex-Treasurer's will was proved 11 April 1670, this cannot be he; it may be one of the Mile End Richards. I have not pursued this further (Pepys, *Diary*, ed. Wheatley, VIII, 139 and n., 256, 260; *Cal. S.P. Dom., 1668–9*, pp. 351, 620; *1670*, and *Adds. 1661–70*, pp. 563, 638; *1671*, pp. 34, 97–8, 481; *Cal. Treas. Bks, 1672–5*, p. 661).

55 In selection, not sample. Sources: Anon., 'Memoir of Governor Hutchinson', *New England Historical and Genealogical Register*, I (1847), 297–310, esp. pp. 297–9; P. O. Hutchinson, *Diary and Letters of His Excellency Thomas Hutchinson . . .* II (1886), 456–62; Waters, *Genealog. Gleanings*, II, 1266; G.E.C., *Compl. Peerage*, 'Donoughmore'; Bailyn, *New England Merchants*, p. 94; Prendergast, *Cromwellian Settlement*, App. V, nos 825, 1306; Bottigheimer, *Irish Lands*, Apps. A and B; *Cal. S.P. Dom., 1644–5*, p. 632; *1648–9*, p. 355; *1652–3*, pp. 265, 464; *1653–4*, pp. 318, 341; *1654*, p. 414; *1655*, p. 1; *1655–6*, pp. 24, 44, 292; *1656–7*, p. 96; *1657–8*, pp. 123, 138–9, 373; *Cal. Cttee. Advc. Mon.*, p. 34; Firth and Rait, *A. & O.*, I, 330, 484, 989, 1129, 1259, II, 233, 753–4; *C.J.*, VI, 482, 547, VII, 612; *The Mystery of the Good Old Cause* (1660); PRO, E. 351/439, 2289–96; S.P. 18/35/53, 103/72–3, 157/50; S.P. 24/10, fo. 5v, 8, 43v, 69, 126; 13, fo. 53v, 77–v; S.P. 28/253A; C. 181/6; Bodl., Rawl. MS B 239, no. 76; P.C.C. 47 Penn; Lincolnshire Record Office (information kindly supplied); *Samuel Pepys Naval Minutes*, ed. J. R.

Tanner (Navy Rec. Soc., 60, 1926), p. 252; J. Nicholl, *Some Account of the Worshipful Company of Ironmongers* (1851), pp. 288, 431, 433.

56 Thomas Vyner, Edward Backwell, and perhaps already John Banks, may all have been wealthier than Noell but their relations with the government were less intimate and involved.

57 In selection, not sample. Sources: E. Hughes, *Studies in administration and finance 1558–1825* (Manchester, 1934), pp. 132–5; Ashley, *Financial and Commercial Policy, passim*; Beaven, *Aldermen*, I, 6, 317, II, 87, 186; *Scriveners' Comm. Pap.* (London Rec. Soc., IV), pp. 59, 117, 120, 121, 122; T. Fuller, *Worthies*, ed. P. A. Nuttall (1840), III, 139; W. A. Shaw, *The Knights of England* (2 vols, 1906), II, 237, 241; Le Neve, *Knights* (Harl. Soc., viii), 160; *C.J.*, VI, 34; *Thurloe St. P.*, II, 543, III, 453–4, VI, 714, VII, 554; Firth and Rait, *A. & O.*, I, 1057, 1129; *Cal. S.P. Dom., 1654*, p. 258; *1655*, p. 36; *1655–6*, pp. 2, 6, 44; *1656–7*, p. 136; *1657–8*, pp. 159, 206, 221, 370, 514; *1658–9*, pp. 107, 110, 112, 113; PRO, C. 181/6; E. 351/1296; E. 403/2523; S.P. 25/78, fo. 363; Bodl., Rawl. MS. A, lxiv, fo. 237, xvii, 415–24; BM, Add. MS. 4,184, no. 14; *Cal. S.P. Col., Am. and W.I., 1574–1660*, pp. 348–468, *passim*; *Clarke Papers*, III, 114; P.C.C. 120 Hyde; BM, Lans. MSS. 821–3; Josten, *Ashmole*, ii, 731–2 n. 6; Farnell, *Econ. H.R.*, 2nd series, XVI, 453 n. 2; Latham and Matthews (eds), *Pepys Diary*, III, *1662*, 189–90, 190n. Neither Ashley nor Farnell gives a source for the statement that Noell and Thurloe were brothers-in-law, and I have not been able to trace the connection.

58 He was no relation of Lewis (or Lewes) Roberts, Londoner and economic theorist, for whom see *Visns of London* (Harl. Soc., xvii), II, 202, and *DNB*.

59 See *DNB*; I. Morgan, *Prince Charles's Puritan Chaplain* (1957), pp. 32–3; C. Hill, *Puritanism and Revolution* (1958), ch. 8.

60 In selection, not sample. Sources: Burke, *Extinct Baronetcies*, pp. 446–7; *Visns London* (Harl. Soc., xv), I, 32; *Middlesex Pedigrees* (Harl. Soc., lxv), 166; Venn, *Al. Cant.*, iii, 467; *DNB* (a somewhat inadequate account); Firth and Rait, *A. & O.*, I, 93, *et seq.*, under Middlesex; I, 887–904; II, 303, 581–2, 702–3, 824, 828–9, 851–3; *C.J.*, VII, 74; *Cal. S.P. Dom., 1641–3*, p. 417; *1652–3*, p. 398; *1654*, p. 343; *1655–6*, p. 14; *1656–7*, p. 47; *1657–8*, p. 320; *1660–1*, pp. 334, 428; PRO, E. 403/2523; C. 161/6; Ind. 4213; S.P. 26/8; S.P. 25/77, fo. 246–7, 301–2 (correcting the *Calendar*); *Clarke Papers*, III, 51; Bodl., Rawl. MS., B239, no. 356; P.C.C. 142 Laud.

61 In selection, not sample. Sources: *Dugdale's Visn. of Lancs.* (Chetham Soc., lxxxviii, 1873), Pt 3, p. 253; Foster, *Al. Oxon.*, 1311 (incompatible with the Dugdale pedigree); Firth and Rait, *A. & O.*, I, 973, 1091; II, 307; PRO, E. 351/1295; A.O. 1/891/7 and 9; S.P. 18/159–60; Mercers' Co. records; Boyd, *Drapers*; Salop R.O. (information kindly supplied); P.C.C. 162 Pett.

62 See *King's Servants*, pp. 308, 311–13, 380–1; *DNB*; now also Prestwich, *Cranfield, passim*, esp. pp. 488–9, n. 3. See ch. 2, section iv, n. 5.

63 In selection, not sample. Sources: *Cal. Cttee. Advc. Mon.*, pp. 91–2,

110; *Cal. Cttee. Compdg.*, p. 233; *Cal. S.P. Dom., 1652–3*, pp. 388, 454; *1656–7*, pp. 310–11; *1657–8*, p. 94; *1658–9*, p. 358; *C.J.*, VI, 511; VII, 604; Burton, *Parl. Diary*, III, 307; Firth and Rait, *A. & O.*, II, 839; *Thurloe St. P.*, VII, 601; *Cal. Treas. Bks, 1660–7, 1667–8, 1669–72, passim*; *1681–5*, App. II, p. 1630; Pepys, *Diary*, ed. Wheatley, IV, 313, 315, 378, VIII, 18; *Wilts Archaeological Magazine*, IV, 72, 80, 104–5; PRO, S.P. 28/350/10; S.P. 46/98, fo. 135, 143; C. 181/6; E. 351/439; S.O. 1/15/301; P.C.C. 78 Dycer. S. B. Baxter, *The Development of the Treasury 1660–1702* (1957), pp. 146–9, gives a full and sympathetic account of Sherwyn's career after 1660, but overlooks his early connections with Pye (from 1643–4 at least: S.P. 28/350/10) and the religious commitment shown in his will.

64 For the Barnardistons of Suffolk and their role in public events, see *DNB*; Newton, *Colonising Activities of English Puritans*, pp. 127–8; Brunton and Pennington, *Members*, pp. 69–74; Keeler, *Long Parliament*, pp. 96–7; Everitt, *Suffolk and the Great Rebellion*, pp. 16–17. Thomas Barnardiston, Comptroller of the Mint 1649–60, is in both the sample and the selection on which sections iii and iv of this chapter are based. Another possible connection is through the Bourchier family of Stambridge, Essex, who were related by marriage to a Suffolk family of Frost as well as to Oliver Cromwell.

65 In selection, not sample. Sources: P. Boyd, 'Suffolk Marriages', typescript, Soc. of Genealogists; Guildhall MS. 5576/1, G.F. [senior], free of Fishmongers' Co. by redemption, by order of the Lord Mayor and Aldermen, 30 May; MS. 5587/1, free 22 June 1643; R. Baker, *Chronicle* (1670 folio ed.), p. 492; G. Burnet, *History of his own Times* (3rd ed. 1766), I, 36–7, and Burnet, *Hist. own Time*, I, *Reign of Charles II*, ed. O. Airy (Oxford, 1897), I, 42, corrected by Gardiner, *Hist. Eng.*, IX, 178, n. 1; Anon. [J. Denniston] (ed.), *The Coltness Collections 1608–1840* (Maitland Club, Vol. 58, 1842), 'The Denham Memoir', Pt II, ch. I, 'Of Sir James Stewart of Kirkfield and Cultness', pp. 19–20 and f.n. 'b'; Venn, *Al. Cant.*, II, 182 (see Burke, *Landed Gentry*, 1937 ed., for a Suffolk family but no seventeenth-century Walter; see *Visn. of Yorks.* (Harl. Soc., xvi), 130 for a Walter Frost but too early; see *Cal. Cttee. Compdg.*, pp. 739–40 for the royalist suspect); J. Hogan (ed.), *Letters and Papers relating to the Irish Rebellion . . . 1642–6* (Irish MSS. Comm., 1936), pp. 161–3, 166–7; *Cal. S.P. Dom. 1644*, pp. 46, 70 *et seq.*; *1649–50*, pp. 221, 11, 106, 227, 189, 255, 233, 316, 264, 469–70, 590; *1651*, p. 411; *1651–2*, pp. 41, 198, 201, 232, 341, 426, 512–13; *1652–3*, pp. 155, 202; *1655–6*, p. 247; *1656–7*, pp. 240–1; *C.J.*, VI, 143; Firth and Rait, *A. & O.*, I, 1011; *A Briefe Relation*, Oct. 1649–Oct. 1650; *A Declaration of some proceedings of Lt. Col. John Lilburne*, Feb. 1647/8; J. Frank, *The Levellers* (Camb., Mass., 1955, repr. N.Y. 1969), pp. 148, 165; Frank, *English Newspaper*, pp. 200–4, 347; J. B. Williams, *Beginnings of Engl. Journalism* (Cambridge, 1911), p. 122; *Mercurius Elencticus*, no. 27, Oct.–Nov. 1649; PRO, S.P. 18/35/120–7, 37/163; S.P. 46/95, fo. 264; Hughes, *Patentee Officers in Ireland 1173–1826* (Irish MSS. Comm. 1960), p. 54; P.C.C. Administrations 1652, fo. 129.

66 See ch. 3, i, pp. 68–9.

67 In selection, not sample. Sources: See footnote 65 above, on his father; George Atwell, *The Faithfull Surveyor* ... (Cambridge, 1662, but first ed. was 1658; see D. G. Wing, *Short Title Catalogue* ... *1641–1700* (3 vols, N.Y. 1945–51), A. 4163), p. 81; E. G. R. Taylor, *Mathematical Practitioners of Tudor and Stuart England* (Cambridge, 1954), 'Works', no. 237; *Cal. S.P. Dom.*, *1648–9*, pp. 58, 290, 291; *1649–50*, pp. 11, 255, 539; *1651*, pp. 53, 542; *1651–2*, pp. 42, 199, 224, 328, 514; *1652–3*, pp. 246, 314; *1653–4*, pp. 74, 386–7, 458; *1655*, pp. 127, 273; *1655–6*, pp. 34–5, 26, 180; *1658–9*, p. 367; Firth and Rait, *A. & O.*, I, 1102, 1117; PRO, S.P. 18/95/90, 102/80–169, 125/78–105, 128/90.i; Bodl., Rawl. MS. A. 259, p. 145.

68 See ch. 3, section iii, pp. 88–90.

69 See ch. 3, section v, pp. 107–11, for comparable salaries.

70 In selection, not sample. Sources: Burke, *Landed Gentry*, a Somerset family but no seventeenth-century Henry; *Grantees of Arms* (Harl. Soc., lxvi), p. 224; a John S. of Plymouth, 1629; Prendergast, *Cromwellian Settlement*, App. V, no. 670; Bottigheimer, *Irish Lands*, App. A; Clement Walker, *History of Independency*, Part II (1649), p. 254; *Cal. S.P. Dom.*, *1641–3*, p. 456; *1625–49, Addenda*, p. 663; *1648–9*, p. 129; *1654*, p. 322; *1655*, pp. 128, 231; *1655–6*, p. 311; *1656–7*, pp. 156, 310–11; *1657–8*, pp. 268, 272–3; *1658–9*, pp. 204, 357; *1659 60*, p. 28; *C.J.*, VI, 111, 209, 287; Burton, *Parl. Diary*, I, p. xx, II, 316, 336, 348–50, 403–4; *Clarke Papers*, III, 132, 133–4, n. 1; PRO, S.P. 18/38/72, 183/72; S.P. 46/99, fo. 123; *C.J.*, VII, 365, 581, 587, 590; E. 403/2523; Ind. 4213; C. 181/6; F. Peck, *Desiderata Curiosa* (1779), 491–2, 494–9; Shaw, *Church*, II, 517; A. G. Matthews, *Calamy Revised* (Oxford, 1934), for J. Rowe and S. Wood; P.C.C. 256 Nabbs.

71 See ch. 3, section i, pp. 68–9.

72 As has already been shown; see ch. 3, section ix, pp. 165–7.

73 In selection, not sample. Sources: *DNB* (very thin on the personal side); *Lincoln's Inn Adm. Reg.*, I, 253; Venn, *Al. Cant.*, iv, 239; *Thurloe St. P.*, I, xi, xix, 205–6; II, 94; III, 640; IV, 409; V, 46–7, 475; VI, 628; VII, 559, 574, 785–8, 788, 807, 826, 888, 895, 897–8, 914–15, 915; Bodl., Rawl. MSS., A, i, 131; ii, 134–40; xxix, 444; xxxix, 452; xl, 279; lvi, 23; B, 239, nos 1, 487, 549; *Cal. Cttee. Compdg.*, pp. 393, 465, 603, 658; *Cal. S.P. Dom.*, *1650*, p. 374; *1651*, p. 170; *1651–2*, pp. 198, 199, 203, 213, 223; *1652–3*, p. 335; *1653–4*, pp. 14, 89, 201, 205, 458; *1655*, pp. 128, 138–9, 240; *1656–7*, p. 370; *1657–8*, p. 81; *1658–9*, pp. 196, 234, 254, 259, 333, 340, 342–3; *1660–1*, p. 207; *L.J.*, XI, 120; PRO, C. 181/6; S.P. 24/4, fo. 95; Dep. Kpr., *5th Report*, II, 277; N. Walker and T. Cradock, *History of Wisbech and the Fens* (1849); P.C.C. 36 Hene. I am extremely grateful to Mr Conrad Russell for the two 1637 references, from Russell MSS., Woburn, and PRO, Index 9990.

74 In selection, not sample. Sources: *DNB*; J. Aubrey, *Brief Lives* (ed. A. Clarke), II, 207–8; Frank, *English Newspaper*, pp. 73–4, 82–4, 99, 136, 202–3, 237–8; *C.J.*, III, 170, 202, VI, 1, 432, 471, VII, 74; Foster, *Al. Oxon.*, I, 1290; *Cal. S.P. Dom.*, *1641–3*, p. 417; R. Bell (ed.), *Memorials*

of Civil War . . . Fairfax Correspondence, I (1849), 17–19; Hist. MSS. Comm., *Portland*, II, 147, 151, 164–5; *Cal. S.P. Dom., 1654*, p. 203; *1655*, p. 150; *1656–7*, pp. 203, 268; *1657–8*, pp. 142–3, 198; *Cal. Cttee. Compdg.*, p. 130; Firth and Rait, *A. & O.*, II, 702–3, 824; *Thurloe St. P.*, VII, 826; PRO, S.P. 18/182/90, S.P. 26/8; S.P. 46/97, fo. 148–9; BM, Add. MS. 4184, no. 1; Ludlow, *Memoirs*, II, 495; Hist. MSS. Comm., *Buccleuch-Montagu*, I, 311; *Northumberland County History*, V (1899), p. 381; Hist. MSS. Comm., *Various*, I, 17–18 (R.'s letters to Berwick corporation as MP and Recorder); he also acted as agent in London for Newcastle corporation (information kindly supplied by Northumberland Record Office); Josten, *Ashmole*, IV, 1658–9 (letter from Sir Thomas Herbert to A., 1680, hoping for continuation of *Historical Collections* from 1640 to 1648); *Cal. Treas. Bks*, I, 1660–7, pp. 215–16, 645.

75 In so far as the exact dating is important, Thomason obtained his copy of the first edition of the *Observations* on 2 July 1642 (Fortescue, *Thomason Catalogue*, I, 130) and Parker was appointed Secretary to the Earl of Essex's army on the 12th (*L.J.*, V, 206, 208).

76 In selection, not sample. Sources: *DNB*; Jordan, *Men of Substance*, ch. II, esp. pp. 29–37; *Cal. S.P. Dom., 1649–50*, pp. 34, 158, 238, 364; *1652–3*, p. 108; *C.J.*, III, 313, 677, 687–8; IV, 187; VII, 268; Bodl., Tanner MS. 56, fo. 91–92v; *L.J.*, VIII, 121, 147; Hist. MSS. Comm., *6th Report*, House of Lords Papers, pp. 95, 97; Abbott, *Writings and Speeches*, II, 85; L. Glow, 'The Committee of Safety', *E.H.R.*, 80 (1965), 291 n. 8.

77 Although he may have been admitted to the Inner Temple in November 1646, as W.C. of London, Gent., at the special instance of John Merefield, Esq., Bencher (Inner Temple Admissions, t.s. I, 491, quoting fo. 719 of original MS.).

78 In selection, not sample. Sources: *DNB*; Firth, Introduction to *Clarke Papers*, esp. Vols I and II; II, 224, 227–8; E. S. de Beer, note on Clarke in *DNB Corrigenda*; Noble, *Regicides*, I, xli, II, 206–7; Cary, *Memorials*, II, 332; Hist. MSS. Comm., *Leyborn-Popham*, pp. 102, 104, 105, 194, 259–89; Dunlop, *Ireland under Commonwealth*, I, 214 n.; PRO, E. 351/306; Worcester College, Clarke MSS.; P.C.C. 95 Mico.

79 In sample, not selection. Sources; *Cal. S.P. Dom., 1650*, p. 576; *1651*, pp. 536, 575; Nickolls, *Milton St. P.*, pp. 131–2; *Thurloe St. P.*, IV, 526–30; Hist. MSS. Comm., *Leyborn-Popham*, p. 122; Hughes, *Patentee Officers in Ireland*, p. 81, quoting R. Lascelles, *Liber Munerum Publicorum Hiberniae* (1852), II, 83 (appointment to Clerkship of Council in Ireland, Sept. 1661, in fact a reversion. See below); BM, Stowe MS. 194, fo. 157, appointment as Secretary-at-War, Ireland, 12 Feb. 1660/1 (again not taken up in person); *Cal. S.P. Dom., 1661–2*, pp. 288, 491, 560, 583; *1665–6*, pp. 438, 441, 448; *1666–7*, p. 204; *1667*, p. 243; *1672*, p. 531 (showing that he was the nephew of Sir Paul Davys, one time Irish Secretary and Clerk of the Council in Ireland, a fact which may explain Locke's original appointment); *1672–3*, pp. 315, 435 (Locke drops out, as a reversioner to the Irish Council Clerkship, in favour of another member of the Davys family); *1673–5*, pp. 82–3, 247 (complaining of

Locke's execution of the Irish Secretaryship-at-War *in absentia*); *1683*, pp. 306, 334, 419; *DNB*, 'William Blathwayt'. The three Matthew Lockes can be distinguished in *Cal. Treas. Bks, 1660–7*, pp. 51, 421, 565, 709; the administrator and the musician are noted correctly in Latham and Matthews, *Diary of Samuel Pepys*, I, 51n. and 63n. For the scrivener and republican customs officer, see also *Scriveners' Common Paper* (London Rec. Soc., IV), p. 116, 1635; *High Court of Admiralty Examinations 1637–8* (Anglo-American Foundation, II, 1932), no. 155, M.L. of St Olave's Hart St, writer, *aet.* 26 as a witness in 1637; PRO, Declared Accts, Customs, E. 351/653; A.O. 1/605/56; *Cal. Treas. Bks, 1667–8*, pp. 62, 132, 209; P.C.C. 19 Coke, a Matthew Locke of Shoe Lane, London, Gent., will made Mar. 1666, proved February 1669, shows connections both with scriveners and with Hull. For the musician, see *DNB*; E. J. Dent, *Musica Britannica XXII–III* (1971–2), ii; Dent, *Foundations of English Opera* (Cambridge, 1928), pp. 84–5; P. A. Scholes, *The Puritans and Music* (Oxford, 1934), pp. 131, 190, and fig. p. 206. I am extremely grateful to Dr Peter Aston of the Music Dept, University of York, for his help with Locke, the composer.

80 In sample, not selection. Sources: PRO, S.P. 28/41 *et seq.* (Warrants of Army Cttee and C. in C., 1646); *Cal. S.P. Dom., 1649–50*, p. 215; W. Lilly, *Life*, p. 91; J. Oldmixon, *History of the Stuarts* (1730), p. 483; Hist. MSS. Comm., *Leyborn-Popham*, pp. 8–9 (letter to Clarke, quoted in text); Abbott, *Cromwell*, II, 85–6; Worcester Coll., Clarke MS. 181, Box 1, letter of 26 June 1649; *Perfect Occurrences*, 22–29 June 1649; P.C.C. 165 Grey and 42 Bowyer; parish register transcripts of Appleton-le-Street, North Riding, Borthwick Institute, York.

81 In selection, not sample. Sources: Firth and Davies, *Regimental Hist.*, 73, 75, index; D. Underdown, 'Cromwell and the officers February 1658', *E.H.R.*, 83 (1968), pp. 101–7; Abbott, *Writings and Speeches of Oliver Cromwell*, Vols ii–iv, *passim*; Thurloe St. P., II, 224, III, 237–8, IV, 501, VII, 39; *Cal. S.P. Dom., 1650*, pp. 214, 589; *1654*, pp. 20–5; *1656–7*, p. 150; *1660–1*, p. 471; Nickolls, *Milton St. P.*, 143–4; Burton, *Parl. Diary*, II, 523; M. Noble, *House of Cromwell* (2 vols, Birmingham, 1787), I, 458; BM, Lans. MS. 821, fo. 50; P.C.C. 114 Pye (wills of Elizabeth Maylin and of Elizabeth Maling, both proved September 1673, the latter referring to £100 owed to her by the widow of William Maling); Boyd, *Drapers' Records*, and *Drapers' Roll* (William, s. of Thomas M., of Saffron Walden, Essex, appr. to Wm. Rowe for 7 years, 1616); P.C.C. 374 Wootton (the nuncupative will of W.M. junior of Saffron Walden, making his father, W.M. senior his residual heir and executor, and leaving 10s.—intriguingly—to the latter's maid, Alice Thurloe); G. R. Sitwell, *The Hurts of Haldworth* (1930), Pedigree IX, pp. 150–1 (a minor gentry family of Rotherham, Yorks, but no William of the right date). I am grateful to Mr R. A. Malyn of Stratton Audley, Oxfordshire, for helpful suggestions about his family ancestry.

82 In selection, not sample. Sources: *Cal. S.P. Dom., 1625–49, Addenda*, p. 644; *1641–3*, pp. 139 *et seq.*; *1649–50*, pp. 36–7, 395, 433, 452; *1651–2*, pp. 358, 376; *1652–3*, p. 509; PRO, S.P. 18/2/103, 3/109, 45/19; S.P.

24/10 fo. 65v, 106v, 121v; S.P. 23/36, fo. 307v; S.P. 46/114, fo. 180; Firth and Rait, *A. & O.*, I, 978, 1183; *L.J.*, VII, 604; *C.J.*, VI, 342; *Cal. S.P. Dom.*, *1654*, p. 483; *1655*, p. 514; *1660–1*, p. 47; Bodl., Rawl. MS. A xl, fo. 467; Noble, *Regicides*, I, xl; Foster, *Al. Oxon.*, I, 343; Inner Temple Adms. t.s., II, 59; L. Dwnn, *Visns. of Wales*, ed. Meyrick, II, 165–6.

83 In selection, not sample. Sources: *Cal. S.P. Dom.*, *1641–3*, p. 557; *1651–2*, *passim*; *1652–3*, p. 515; *1653–4*, p. 342; *1657–8*, pp. 218, 290; *1653–9*, pp. 170, 251, 313; *1660–1*, pp. 307, 378; PRO, S.P. 18/35/163, 103/72–3, 42/159; E. 351/2296; E. 351/653; S.P. 46/122, fo. 105 B; *L.J.*, X, 548; BM, Egerton MS. 2978, fo. 270; *Hunter's Pedigrees* (Harl. Soc., xxxviii), p. 769; *Lancs. Visns* (Chetham Soc., lxxxiv), 36; *Miscellanea Genealogica et Heraldica*, n.s., ii, 78; Glass, *Inhabitants of London ... 1695* (L.R.S., 2), p. 30; P.C.C. 30 Bath (= a Derbyshire gent. of Lincs. origins, 1680; and so most unlikely to be our man); Latham and Matthews *Diary of Samuel Pepys*, I, 263; Wheatley, *Pepys Diary*, III, 314–18, VIII, 184, 247–8; *Cal. Treas. Bks, 1667–8*, pp. 77, 145, 158. For his brother James, Customs official in Plymouth, still living there 1675, see also E. 351/653, etc.; information kindly supplied by Plymouth Library; for the Blackburne family of Richmond, Yorks., see North Riding Record Office, 2A2 109 (I am grateful to the County Archivist for this reference); *Hunter's Pedigrees* (Harl. Soc., xxxviii), p. 769; Mercers' Co., apprenticeship records, 1647 (Robert, s. of Robert B. of Richmond, Gent., and so too young). For other possible London apprentices see McKenzie, *Stationers' Apprentices*, no. 2768 (s. of a Glos Gent., free 1625—possible); Guildhall MSS. 5576/1, 5587/1, Fishmongers' Co. (free 1646 and so too young); Merchant-Taylors' Co. Records, Freeman's Lists (free by patrimony of his father William, merchant-taylor, 1638—a distinct possibility).

84 In sample, and selection. Sources: *Cal. S.P. Dom.*, *1641–3*, p. 555; *1645–7*, p. 510; *1649–50*, pp. 120, 170; *1651*, p. 199; *1655*, p. 414; *1660–1*, pp. 175, 308; *C.J.*, VII, 478; PRO, S.P. 18/103/72–3; Bottigheimer, *Irish Lands*, App. B; P.C.C. 10 Cottle (brief, strongly if conventionally Calvinist. Sole heir = wife, Elizabeth; she being already dead, administration is granted to sons Moses and Aaron); J. Strype (ed.), John Stow, *A Survey of London* (2 vols, 1720), II, App. i, p. 90 (M.I. in Deptford church to his son John, a naval officer (1645 or 7–1672)); Latham and Matthews, *Diary of Samuel Pepys*, I, 183–4, 189; II, 54; III, 137; Wheatley, *Pepys Diary*, IV, 246, 268, 332; V, 199–200; VI, 145, 169, 309–12; VIII, 112–113; E. S. de Beer (ed.), *The Diary of John Evelyn* (6 vols, Oxford, 1955), III, 622 and n. Note numerous other Thomas Turners, e.g. Venn, *Al. Cant.*, iv, 277 and *Visitations of Essex* (Harl. Soc., xiii), I, 509 (ibid., xiv), II, 612; *Visitations of Middlesex 1663*, ed. Foster, p. 90; *Visitations of London 1633–5* (Harl. Soc., xvii), II, 301; *Visitations of Bedfs.* (Harl. Soc., xix), 147.

85 See ch. 2, sections ii, viii, ix, pp. 13, 44–6.

86 For whom see *King's Servants*, esp. pp. 291–4.

87 He must be carefully distinguished from his namesake—no close relative

—Sir John Thoroughgood of Clerkenwell, Middlesex, and Billingbere, Berks. (d. 1657), who had been secretary to the 3rd Earl of Pembroke in the 1620s, and was also a parliamentarian committee man and commissioner for his two counties.

88 Other Trustees included Edward Cressett, a London alderman; Richard Sydenham, one of the famous Dorset brothers from Wynford Eagle; and Edward Hopkins, returned New Englander and Navy Commissioner (in the selection of 100).

89 London, duodecimo, 1665. Sigs. A1–4 + 160 pp.

90 See T. Birch, *Life of Henry Prince of Wales* (1760), pp. 329–30; N. E. McClure (ed.), *The Letters of John Chamberlain* (Philadelphia, 1939), I, 345, 395; Hist. MSS. Comm., *Salisbury (Hatfield)*, XX, *1608* (1968), pp. 63, 362. He was promoting the marriage of the Princess Elizabeth and Frederick of the Palatinate.

91 Meautys was the author's brother-in-law; his master, Finch, was one of Charles I's most hated ministers, although he was only Chief Justice in 1635.

92 Her husband was a prominent London merchant, related to Charles I's lord treasurer, the future archbishop William Juxon (see *Cal. Cttee. Advc. Mon.*, p. 838; Dale, *Inhabitants of London*, MS. p. 308).

93 The famous James Ussher, d. 1656 (see *DNB* and other authorities); he was held in high esteem by Cromwell and other leading puritans. Ussher's Calvinist yet ecumenical Protestantism would have appealed to Thoroughgood (see e.g. his *Body of Divinitie, or the summe and substance of Christian Religion*, 4th ed., 1653).

94 Of whom I know nothing, but his employers were not puritans or parliamentarians. The first Earl of Elgin, cr. 1633, d. 1663, married, secondly, the widow of Henry Vere, Earl of Oxford (G.E.C., *Complete Peerage*).

95 The same applies.

96 Probably Robert Harris of Gloucester (1581–1658), Visitor of the University of Oxford (1647–8) and President of Trinity, a presbyterian Puritan who was accused of pluralism (see *DNB*).

97 Possibly of the same family as the immortal Reginald Scot, earliest and greatest English sceptic on witchcraft and introducer of brewing with hops, but there were several Kent gentry families named Scot(t)—see Everitt, *Community of Kent*, index.

98 For the Howlands see *Cal. Cttee. Advc. Mon*, index.

99 The well-known Huguenot refugee, Pierre du Moulin senior, father of the pamphleteer and secret agent of the 1650s–70s (see *DNB*; K. Haley, *William III and the English Opposition 1672–74* (Oxford, 1953), pp. 12–14).

100 Presumably Samuel Crooke (1574–1649), chaplain to the East India Co. and a parliamentarian-puritan (see Venn, *Al. Cant.*, I, i, 424).

101 In selection, not sample. Sources: P.C.C. 132 Dycer (The will of the other Sir John Thoroughgood, P.C.C. 234 Ruthen, is more characteristically republican; his stepson was the political theorist Henry Nevill, and he was also friendly with Josias Berners, Thomas Chaloner

and James Harrington); Firth and Rait, *A. & O., passim*; Shaw, *English Church*, II, 223, etc.; Lambeth Palace Library, Augmentation Order Books (information kindly supplied by Mr E. G. W. Bill, the Librarian); *Visitations of Essex*, II, (Harl. Soc., xiv), 608; *Visitation of Norfolk ... 1664 ...*, II (Harl. Soc., lxxxvi), 219–20; *Visitation of Middlesex ... 1663* (ed. J. Foster), p. 65.

102 See particularly F. A. Yates, *Giordano Bruno and the Hermetic Tradition* (1964); also D. P. Walker, *Spiritual and Demonic Magic from Ficino to Campanella* (1958).

103 There is evidence of trouble with Petty back in 1647, probably as a rival projector.

104 In selection, not sample. Sources: C. M. Andrews, *British Committees, Commissions and Councils of Trade and Plantations, 1622–1675* (Johns Hopkins Univ. Studies in Historical and Political Science, 26, nos 1–3, Baltimore, 1908), esp. ch. 2 and App. IV; Andrews, *Colonial Period of American History*, IV, 41n., 58–60; R. W. K. Hinton, *The Eastland Trade and the Common weal in the 17th century* (Cambridge, 1959), pp. 90–4, 154, App. B, pp. 203–19; J. B. Whitmore, 'Dr. Worsley being dead', *Notes and Queries*, Vol. 185 (28 Aug. 1943), pp. 123–8, taking up John Evelyn's erroneous belief that Worsley died in 1673 rather than resigning, but also sketching his entire career; de Beer, *Diary of John Evelyn*, III, p. 603 and n. 1, 628 and n. 3; R. P. Bieber, 'The Plantation Councils of 1670–4', *E.H.R.*, 40 (1925), pp. 93–106, esp. 100 and n. 3, for the earlier modern correction of Evelyn; Marie Boas Hall, *Robert Boyle and 17th-century Chemistry* (Cambridge, 1958), p. 23, n. 2, criticises Whitmore rather fiercely but adds little new; J. E. Farnell, 'The Navigation Act of 1651, the First Dutch War and the London Merchant Community', *Econ. H.R.*, 2nd series, 16 (1964), 441; Hill, *Intellectual Origins*, p. 109 n. 3; K. Haley, *Life of the first earl of Shaftesbury* (Oxford, 1968), p. 260; J. P. Cooper, 'Economic Regulation and the Cloth Industry in seventeenth-century England', *T.R.H.S.*, 5th series, 20 (1970), pp. 88–91. The additional source refs on which my account is based are as follows: Firth and Rait, *A. & O.*, II, 406; *Cal. S.P. Dom., 1652–3*, pp. 272, 395; Dunlop, *Ireland under the Commonwealth*, I, pp. cxlii–iii; II, 418n.; *Harl. Soc.*, xcii, 'London Visitation Pedigrees, 1664', p. 154; Hist. MSS. Comm., *Ormonde*, new series, II, pp. 256, 284; BM, Lans. MS. 821, fo. 852–3, a letter to Henry Cromwell written from London in March 1656/7, apologising for his long delay in returning to Ireland owing to the continued disputes about the distribution of Irish lands between Adventurers and members of the army, written in a beautifully regular neo-Carolingian minuscule hand; *Calendar of the Clarendon State Papers*, Vol. V, ed. F. J. Routledge (Oxford, 1970), p. 154; T. Birch (ed.), *The Works of the Hon. Robert Boyle* (7 vols, 1772), VI, pp. 40, 76, 77, 78–83, 85, 93, 94, 98, 107, 127, 129; R. C. Winthrop (ed.), *Correspondence of Hartlib ... with Governor Winthrop ... 1661–1672* (Boston, repr. from the Mass. Hist. Soc. Proceedings, 1878), pp. 12, 13–14; *Catalogus Librorum ... Doctoris Beniaminis Worsley ... to be auctioned on 13 May* (1678. BM, 11906 e. 5 and C. 120.c.2(5))—by any

standards a remarkable collection for a man in Worsley's position to have built up, although two other collections for sale are listed without distinction of ownership in the same booklet. I am grateful to Mr C. Webster of Corpus Christi College, Oxford, for providing me with a list of references from the Hartlib MSS., Sheffield Univ. Library, to Mr J. P. Cooper for lending me copies of some of these as well as for other help with Worsley, and to Professor W. H. G. Armytage for making it possible for me to look at others. But omissions or errors concerning Worsley are my own.

105 As tends to be done by Dr Christopher Hill in his *Intellectual Origins*, loc. cit., and *God's Englishman*, pp. 130–1.

106 Besides the works by Andrews, Haley, Hill, Hinton, Farnell and others, already cited, see also Aylmer (ed.), *The Interregnum* (1972), ch. 5; J. P. Cooper, 'Social and Economic Policies under the Commonwealth'.

107 See Frank, *English Newspaper*, pp. 53, 309; P. G. Morrison, *Index to Wing's S.T.C.* (Charlottesville, Va., 1953), p. 32.

108 New Councils were elected in February 1649, February 1650, February 1651, November 1651, November 1652; each appointed its own committees.

109 See D. Underdown, *Royalist Conspiracy in England 1649–1660* (New Haven, Conn., 1960), ch. 4, and for Bishop p. 21.

110 Bristol Record Office, information (for which I am extremely grateful to the Archivist, Miss Ralph); McKenzie, *Stationers' Apprentices*, Pt I, no. 193; Plomer, *Dictionary of Printers & Booksellers*, pp. 24, 193; E. Arber (ed.), *Transcript of Stationers' Co. Registers 1554–1640* (repr. N.Y. 1950), III, 686; G. E. B. Eyre and C. R. Rivington (eds), *Transcript ... 1640–1708*, I (1913, and N.Y. 1950), entries for 1644–5; Fortescue, *Catalogue Thomason Tracts*, Vol. II, index, 'Bishop'; *Cal. S.P. Dom.*, *1641–3*, pp. 563, 566; ibid., *1644*, pp. 561–2; *1649–50*, pp. 149, 443–4, 453; *1650*, pp. 400, 443, 461; *1651*, pp. 11, 33, 49; *1651–2*, pp. 39, 374; *1653–4*, pp. 14, 133–4, 143; *1660–1*, pp. 359–60; PRO, S.P. 18/128/90i; A. S. P. Woodhouse (ed.), *Puritanism and Liberty* (1938 and 1950), pp. 81, 107; *Bristol Rec. Soc.*, Vol. 17 (1952), 'Merchant Venturers of Bristol', pp. 30, 32, 46; ibid., 13 (1948), 'Deposition Books', II, '1650–54', pp. 6–7, 123; *Thurloe St. P.*, III, pp. 153–4, 161, 165, 171–2, 177–8, 242, 268; VI, pp. 829–32; Bodl., Rawl. MS. A xxvi, 296; Tanner MS. 55, fo. 26v; Firth and Davies, *Regimental History*, p. 603; H. Barbour, *Quakers in Puritan England* (New Haven, Conn., 1964), pp. 148 n. 69, 199–202; George Bishop, *A Book of Warnings ... To the King and his Parliament ...* (1661), *New England Judged ...* (1661); Bristol Rec. Office, Friends' MSS., Men's Meeting Minute Book, 1667–86; J. Latimer, *Annals of Bristol in the 17th century* (Bristol, 1900), pp. 349–50.

111 Norman H. Mackenzie, 'Sir Thomas Herbert of Tintern: A Parliamentary "Royalist" ', *Bull. Inst. Hist. Res.*, 29 (1956), pp. 32–86. All references are from this article unless specified otherwise. The *DNB* entry is quite inadequate.

112 Dunlop, *Ireland under the Commonwealth*, Vol. I, p. 162 n., II, pp. 335,

416, 485–6, 285 n.; Firth and Rait, *A. & O.*, II, pp. 603–12; PRO Admiralty, 2/1729, fo. 176 (new pagination 203); S.P. 46/98, fo. 71; Firth and Davies, *Regimental History*, II, p. 427; Hist. MSS. Comm., *Buccleuch-Montague*, III, p. 419; *Montague of Beaulieu*, p. 165; some additional refs from *Cal. S.P. Dom.*, and *Thurloe St. P.* Mr Mackenzie was not primarily interested in Herbert's Irish career during the 1650s.

113 Other sources used here, not all of which are cited by Mr Mackenzie, include: Bradney, *Hist. of Monmouthshire*, Vol. II, pp. 248–51; *Harl. Soc.*, xciv, 'Yorks Pedigrees', p. 3; Venn, *Al. Cant.*, Pt I, Vol. ii, p. 357 (correcting Foster, *Al. Oxon.*, I, 696); Borthwick Institute, York, Prerogative Court of York, Wills Vol. 59, fo. 256v–257v (his will); D. Bush, *English Literature in the Earlier Seventeenth Century* (Oxford, 1945), bibliography, Pt VI, 'Individual Authors', p. 549; F. W. B. Yorke, 'The House and the Herberts . . .' (typescript York City Library, 1953); T. W. French, 'The Herbert House, York', *Yorks. Archaeolog. Jnl*, 39 (1956–8), 343–55; Josten, *Ashmole*, i, 238; iv, 1657–60, 1664–5.

vi CONCLUSION: A COLLECTIVE PORTRAIT

1 W. L. Sachse, art. cit., *Am. Hist. Rev.*, 53 (1947–8); see also Sachse, *Colonial American in Britain*.

2 A Somerset gentleman (1628/30–1673/4), for whom see R. W. Ramsey, *Cromwell's Family Circle* (1930), chapters IV–VI, pp. 118–170; for his purchase of the First Remembrancership of the Exchequer in 1658, see Hist. MSS. Comm., *5th Report*, Appendix, Sutherland Papers, p. 146, and for the grant PRO, E. 403/2523, and ch. 3, i, ii, pp. 81, 95.

3 Reading had been an official of Charles I's unpopular Incorporation of the London suburbs and their tradesmen in 1636–41 (see N. G. Brett-James, *Growth of Stuart London* (1935), pp. 230, 236–7, 239, 284; Pearl, *London and the Outbreak of the Puritan Revolution*, p. 37). In the 1640s and early 50s he was particularly active in connection with London sequestrations and compositions (see *Cal. Cttee. Compdg.*, and *Cal. Cttee. Advc. Mon.*, indexes).

Sheppard (in sample not selection) had practised law in Gloucestershire, although he was not a barrister; he became the main spokesman of limited law reform under the Protectorate and was rewarded with one or two minor legal appointments (see *DNB*; supplemented by additional refs in *Cal. S.P. Dom.*; Firth and Rait, *A. & O.*; *Thurloe St. P.*; *Visitation of Glos. 1682–3*, ed. W. C. Metcalfe, p. 167; W. R. J. Williams, *Hist. of the Great Sessions in Wales* . . . (Brecon, 1899), pp. 59–66). An Oxford B.Litt. thesis by Mr M. R. Whitaker, on the social policies of the Protectorate is also likely to throw new light on Sheppard's career.

Beck, a Gloucestershire man too, is a more obscure, also more radical figure. Trained at Lincoln's Inn, but likewise not called to the bar, he was acting as a solicitor to Parliament's committee for the advance of money by September 1643, and climbed steadily, to become a Visitor of the University of Oxford in 1647, and Solicitor to the Council of State and then to the Protector's Council during the 1650s; he was particularly concerned with Irish accounts around 1648–50 (*Lincoln's Inn Adm. Reg.*, I, 218; other refs to him come from *Cal. S.P. Dom., Cal. Cttee. Advc. Mon., Commons Journals*, Firth and Rait, *A. & O.*, and *Thurloe St. P.*; see also *Cal. Treas. Bks, 1660–67*, p. 202; he bought, or was given in settlement of a debt, a wood belonging to the bishopric of Worcester, worth £241, in March 1648: Bodl., Rawl. MS. B 239, no. 135).

4 Some of these have already been described, or mentioned in passing. Several are in the *DNB*, others in W. Munk, *The Roll of the Royal College of Physicians of London* (3 vols, 1878) and R. W. Innes-Smith, *English Graduates at the University of Leiden* ... (1932). Of those mentioned here, Waterhouse was the brother of Cromwell's Steward, and Wright brother of a Navy Commissioner.

5 Their employments were spread across the Universities, the Mint, the Channel Islands, the Excise, the government of Ireland, army musters and diplomacy.

6 Edward Dendy, in 200 sample and 100 selection; Cryer of the High Court of Justice 1649; Sergeant-at-Arms to the Council 1649–60.

7 Andrew Broughton, co-Clerk of the High Court of Justice; Clerk of the Crown in Upper Bench, 1649–60.

8 John Phelps, co-Clerk of the HCJ; Assistant Clerk of the Parliaments (House of Commons), 1649–53 and 1659–60. Unlike the other two he was to be spared his life by the Attainder Act, but like Broughton and Dendy he escaped abroad.

9 John Blackwell, in 100 selection: see section v, pp. 242–6, and n. 48. He had the added distinction of having acted as paymaster for the Jan. 1649 High Court of Justice, and its successor for the trial of Hamilton and Company in Feb.–Mar. (*C.J.*, VI, 117, 132).

10 Richard Deane, in 100 selection: see ch. 4, section v, p. 244. He had been brought into the central executive as a Council Clerk by the Generals in 1659 and was acting for Fleetwood and Lambert in November (Bodl., Rawl. MS. C179, p. 2; *The Publick Intelligencer*, 16–23 May 1659; Firth, *Clarke Papers*, IV, 105).

11 William Burton, Admiralty and Navy Commissioner 1653–4; in charge under the Navy Commissioners at Great Yarmouth *c.* 1655–8; a radical in the Barebones; Major-General Disbrowe's son-in-law (Firth and Rait, *A. & O.*, II, 708–11, 812–13; *Cal. S.P. Dom., 1649–1659*, indexes, *passim*; C. T. Atkinson (ed.), *Letters and Papers relating to the First Dutch War*, Vol. VI (Navy Rec. Soc., Vol. 66, 1930), index wrongly distinguishes two W.B.s; *A Catalogue of the Last Parliament*, June 1654. BM, 669 f.19(3); G. F. Nuttall, *Visible Saints* (Oxford, 1957), p. 150). I am at a loss to explain why Burton was picked out for inclusion among the 20; there would seem to have been several other likelier candidates.

12 Richard Keble or Keeble, Lord Commissioner of the Great Seal, 1649–54; President of the High Court of Justice for royalist conspirators, 1651; one of the most politically committed of the Judges (*DNB*; *Cal. S.P. Dom.*; *C.J.*, VI, 92, 165–6, 569).

13 John Ireton, in 200 sample; Excise Commissioner 1656–8; Lord Mayor

1658–9; besides being Henry Ireton's brother his real offence was to have been one of the leading republicans in London, who had opposed the return to monarchy in 1660 (*DNB*; Beaven, *Aldermen of London*, II, 78, 184, etc.; Woodhead, *Rulers of London*, p. 96; R. W. Ramsey, *Henry Ireton* (1949), pp. 4, 47, 159, 206).

14 See R. Holborne, *The reading in Lincolne's Inne Feb. 28, 1641, upon the Statute of 25 E.3 Cap. 2 . . .* (Oxford, 1642); E. Coke, *The Third Part of the Institutes of the Laws of England: concerning High Treason, and other Pleas of the Crown, and Criminall Causes* (1644), chapters 1, 3, 101; M. Hale, *Historia Placitorum Coronae: The History of the Pleas of the Crown* (ed. S. Emlyn, 2 vols, 1736), I, chapters x–xxxviii, pp. 58–377, II, ch. xxxvii, p. 282; W. Holdsworth, *History of English Law*, Vol. IV (1945 ed.), 492–500, 523–4; VI (1937 ed.), 168–70, 232–4, 399–400; VIII (1937 ed.), 307–24; S. Rezneck, 'The trial of treason in Tudor England', in *Essays in honour of C. H. McIlwain* (Cambridge, Mass., 1936); L. B. Smith, 'English Treason Trials and Confessions in the sixteenth century', *Jnl of the History of Ideas*, 15 (1954). C. Russell, 'The Theory of Treason in the Trial of Strafford', *E.H.R.*, 80 (1965); G. R. Elton, 'The Law of Treason in the early Reformation', *Historical Jnl*, 11 (1968); L. M. Hill, 'The Two-Witness Rule in English Treason Trials: Some Comments on the Emergence of Procedural Law', *American Jnl of Legal History*, 12 (1968). For the actual conduct of the Regicides' trials, see W. Cobbett (ed.), *State Trials*, Vol. 3, or F. Hargrave (ed.), *State Trials*, Vol. 2. Sir Edward Coke is sometimes thought of as a prolix author, but on the law of treason and related matters, he is positively succinct compared to Sir Matthew Hale.

15 PRO, S.P. 18/100/72, the Remonstrance of Richard Nonnelly to the Army Committee, 31 Aug. 1655. He was also spelt Nunelly (see Hargrave, *State Trials*, 2 (1776), p. 307 *et seq.*; *Cal. Cttee. Advc. Mon.*, p. 1502).

16 See, e.g., D. Ogg, *England under Charles II* (Oxford, 1934); A. Browning, *Danby*, 3 vols (Edinburgh, 1944–51); Clarendon, *Continuation of his own Life* (Oxford, 1759); *Cal. S.P. Dom.*, vols for 1660s–70s; *Cal. Treas. Bks* for 1660s–70s; Pepys, *Diary* and *Naval Minutes*; Evelyn, *Diary*, ed. de Beer; Josten (ed.), *Elias Ashmole*, etc.

17 Trevor-Roper, *The Gentry*, pp. 15–16.

18 My list of houses and their builders for the 1640s and 50s is based on N. Pevsner, *The Buildings of England* (Harmondsworth, 1951–); Royal Commission on Historical Monuments, *Reports* esp. used where published for counties not yet covered by Professor Pevsner and his collaborators; L.C.C., and now G.L.C., *Survey of London* (1900–); H. M. Colvin, *A Biographical Dictionary of English Architects 1660–1840* (1954); J. Summerson, *Architecture in Britain 1530–1830* (Pelican Hist. of Art, Harmondsworth, 3rd rev. ed., 1958); M. Whinney and O. Millar, *English Art 1625–1714* (Oxford Hist. of English Art, 1957). I have also consulted the older works by J. A. Gotch and H. A. Tipping, and some of the earlier county histories and the *Victoria County History*. I am extremely grateful to Dr A. A. Tait of the Dept of Fine Art, Univ. of

Glasgow, for his help; he very kindly looked through my list and suggested several additions. His own forthcoming work, *England and Italian Architecture 1600–1660*, will include a valuable new treatment of the decade 1650–60. I am well aware that my own work in this field is amateurish and impressionistic; more systematic study of the sources would seem unlikely, however, to alter radically the conclusions reached here.

19 See J. Ehrman, *The Navy in the War of William III 1689–1697* (Cambridge, 1953), chapters VII and XIII, for an excellent account of this.
20 See M. Raphael, *Pensions and Public Servants: A Study of the Origins of the British System* (Paris and The Hague, 1964).
21 For the reform in the tenure of offices under Charles II, see Mr J. C. Sainty's article, *Bull. Inst. Hist. Res.*, 41 (1968), cited in ch. 3, ii.
22 See for example nos xxxvii–xl in A. L. Cross (ed.), *Eighteenth-century Documents relating to the Royal Forests, the Sheriffs and Smuggling Selected from the Shelburne MSS. in the William L. Clements Library* (Ann Arbor, Michigan, 1928), for the continuing concern to recruit properly qualified personnel from the 1680s to the 1710s.
23 P. G. M. Dickson, *The Financial Revolution in England A Study of the Development of Public Credit, 1688–1756* (1967), pp. 42, 342.
24 W. R. Ward, *The English Land Tax in the Eighteenth Century* (1953), esp. ch. I.

Chapter 5   The Impact of the regime

i INTRODUCTION

1 PRO, State Papers Interregnum, Indemnity, S.P. 24/1–8, 10–17, Committee's and Commissioners' Order Books, 1647–55; 23–25, Commissioners' Minute Books, 1652–5; 29, Misc. Papers; 30–87, Papers of Cases (arranged alphabetically by plaintiffs' or complainants' surnames). See section iii, pp. 299–302.
2 E. S. de Beer (ed.), *The Diary of John Evelyn* (6 vols, Oxford, 1955).
3 R. Baxter, *Reliquiae Baxterianae*, ed. M. Sylvester (1696).

ii THE PAMPHLET EVIDENCE

1 BM, E. 1186(1), p. 9.
2 *The Humble Representation of Severall Aldermen . . . and other Citizens of London . . .* (BM, 669 f.17(8)).
3 BM, E. 574(15), 21 Sept.; Bodleian shelfmark Godwin pamphlet 1371(7), pp. 5–7, items IV, XII, XIII. It is cited in W. Haller and G. Davies (eds), *Leveller Tracts 1647–53* (New York, 1944), p. 30, but no modern reprint exists.
4 *To the Supreme Authority, the Parliament of the Commonwealth . . . The Humble Petition of divers constant Adherers to this Parliament, & faithfull Assertors of the Fundamentall Lawes and Liberties of the Commonwealth.* BM, 669 f.16(54) dated 29 June 1652, item 11.

5 BM, E. 673(10), 7 August 1652, 43 pp., comprising 53 points, 10 additional proposals and a postscript. The pamphlet may in practice have been the work of a single author; it purports to be a collective work.

6 *A Perfect Diurnall of . . . the Armies*, no. 4.

7 Ibid., no. 13, 4–11 March 1649/50.

8 Ibid., no. 3, 28 December 1649.

9 *The Works of the Hon. Robt. Boyle*, ed. J. Birch (7 vols, 1772), VI, 40.

10 BM, E. 624(7), esp. items 2, 16 and 17. It even advocates life peerages six years before the Humble Petition and Advice (item 15)!

11 *A Declaration of the Armie to His Excellency the Lord General Cromwell, For the Dissolving of this present Parliament, and chusing of a new Representative* BM, E. 673(13), 20 August 1652. The authors' general attitude is symbolised by their describing the army as 'the Academy of Europe; or, an Army of Saints' (p. 8).

12 *To the Supreme Authority the Parliament of the Commonwealth of England. The humble petition of the Officers of the Army.* BM, 669 f.16(62) single sheet. 14 August 1652, esp. items IV, VIII, IX.

13 On law reform, see ch. 2, section v, pp. 29–30, and ch. 3, section ii, p. 90.

14 See *C.J.*, VII, 321, 325, 333, 334, 347, 351, 355, and Anon., *A True Narrative of the Cause and Manner of the Dissolution of the late Parliament Upon the 12 of December 1653 By a Member of the House then present at that Transaction.* BM, E. 724(11), 12 Dec. 1653 (answered in E. 725(20)); Bodl., Godwin Pamphlet 1371 (24), 1653. It seems to be largely due to the accident of L.D.'s *An Exact Relation* having been reprinted in the eighteenth century that it is so much better known than *A True Narrative*, in some ways a more detailed and circumstantial account.

15 In March 1649 a committee was made responsible for greater equity in the apportionments of the monthly total between different localities, and three months of the current six months' assessment was ordered to be in the form of a rate at so much in the pound (*C.J.*, VI, 159, 170, 173); the lack of equity in the apportionments was again committed in December 1651 (*C.J.*, VII, 151). A pound-rate was never implemented, unless by the Assessment Commissioners in some localities.

16 The problem of apportioning the Assessment continued to exercise Parliament during the Protectorate (see *C.J.*, VII, 392, 414; Burton, *Parliamentary Diary*, I, pp. ci–ii, for 1654–5; *C.J.*, VII, 554, 555–6; Burton, *Parliamentary Diary*, II, 207–19, 224–8, 229–37, 245–7, for 1657).

17 See Woodhouse, *Puritanism and Liberty*, Pt 2, pp. 125–78.

18 BM, E. 720(1), 1654, corrected by Thomason to 20 November 1653. The author's bibliography, for the 'Humane Learning' section (on pp. 177–80) includes Bacon's *Advancement of Learning*, so he was not exclusively clericalist and academically reactionary; he wanted new universities, too, as well as old (p. 171).

19 Edmund Ludlow, writing admittedly a good many years later, refers to 'the court interest' in the 1654 elections and to 'the court-party' in the parliament which followed (*Memoirs*, ed. Firth, I, 388, 390).

20 See chapter 3, section ii, pp. 90–3.

21 BM, 669 f.19(4), one large sheet, dated by Thomason 29 June.

22 *To the Parliament of the Commonwealth ... The humble Petition of divers of the Inhabitants of the North Riding ...; in the behalf of themselves and the well affected of the Nation*, read in Parliament 23 December 1656, presented by George Lord Eure. BM, 669 f.20(44), 10 January 1656/7.

23 *Made by a Member of Parliament lawfully chosen, but secluded illegally by my Lord Protector.* BM, E. 891(3), 27 October 1656.

24 *With an Account of the Places of Profit, Salaries, and Advantages which they* [the MPs] *hold and receive under the present Power ...*, repr. in *Harleian Miscellany*, ed. W. Oldys and T. Park, III (1809), 449–69.

25 *Of the late Parliament* [so-called] *...*, ibid., 470–89.

26 London, 1658. BM, E. 1583(2), Thomason's date 21 November 1657. See esp. ch. V, pp. 175–9.

27 Although the terms are not used in as fully developed a form as might be supposed by the unwary. The original 1659 version (Anon., *A True and Impartiall Narrative of the most material Debates and Passages in the late Parliament*. BM, E. 985(25), 9 June 1659) uses the phrase 'Court' and 'Court Party', but not 'the Country' or 'the Country Party', whereas the 1680 version ([S. Bethel], *A Brief Narrative of ... the most material Debates and Passages in that pretended Parliament ... called by Richard Cromwell*, appended to *The Interest of Princes and States* (1680), BM, 523 b.l., pp. 331–54) has 'the Country Party' inserted, sometimes in place of 'the Commonwealthsmen' or 'those that were for a Commonwealth' in the 1659 text.

28 See ch. 2, section x, pp. 54–7.

29 Notably Fleetwood, Disbrowe, and the soon-restored Lambert.

30 In Lambert's case only to 1657, but he remained a government pensioner even in opposition, 1657–9.

31 See *A Seasonable Question soberly Proposed, Argued and Resolved.* BM, E. 988(14), 24 June 1659; *Twenty Four Queries touching the Parliament and Army.* BM, E. 785(8) [12 June] 1659; *A Secret Word to the Wise ...* BM, 986(6), [13 June], etc.

32 John Canne, *A Seasonable Word to the Parliament-Men.* BM, E. 983(1), [10 May] 1659, pp. 2–3.

33 See *Articles of Impeachment of ... crimes ... committed by Col. Philip Jones ... read in Parliament 18 May 1659.* BM, E. 983(31).

34 *The Publick Intelligencer*, no. 176, 9–16 May 1659 (BM, E. 762/12), pp. 424–5.

35 *Mercurius Politicus*, no. 569, 26 May–2 June 1659 (ibid., 17), pp. 473–4.

36 On 6 June (*Mercur. Polit.* 570, BM, E. 766(1); *C.J.*, VII, 674).

37 BM, E. 985(23), 9 June 1659.

38 E.g. William Covel, Gent., *A Declaration Unto the Parliament, Council of State, and Army, shewing impartially the Causes of the Peoples Tumults, Madness, and Confusions ... With the Method of a Commonwealth.* London, 1659. Bodl. Godwin Pamphlet 1372 (8), and (somewhat less radical) [William Sprigge], *A Modest Plea for An Equal Common-Wealth Against Monarchy ...* Sept. 1659. BM, 1802(1) and E. 999(11).

39 W.W. [Wm. Wither], Gent., *Proposals to the Officers of the Army, and to the City of London for the taking off all Excise, Taxes, and Custom* ... London, 1659. BM, E. 1013(11); Bodl., Wood 526(5).

40 See Anon., *Offices and Places of Trust not to be Bought or Sold, or given to insufficient persons Discovered in a sober and Peaceable Letter*. London, 1660. Bodl., Wood 526(8). I am grateful to Mr Keith Thomas for this reference.

41 Roger Coke, Esq., *A Detection of the Court and State of England*, 3rd ed., 1697, pp. 363, 404–5 (in Vol. 2, which is bound and paginated with Vol. 1 in this edition). The author was the grandson of the famous Chief Justice, and describes his own travails as a Norfolk cavalier. Some of his narrative is suspect, being marked by a determination to prove that Monck was a strong crypto-royalist throughout the 1650s.

42 See ch. 2, section ii, pp. 14–17.

43 A broadside, 18 November 1655. BM, 669 f.20(18).

44 See *Visitation of London, 1633–5* (Harl. Soc., XV), I, 125; Andrewes Burrell, Gent., *A Briefe Declaration. Discovering Plainely the true Causes why the great Levell of FENNS ... have been drowned and made unfruitfull for many years past AND As briefly how they may be drained, and preserved from Inundation in the times to come*. 1642. BM, E. 148/18); *Exceptions Against Sir Cornelius Vermuyden's Discourse For the Draining Of the great Fennes, etc*. 1642. BM, ibid. (22); *To the Parliament The Humble Remonstrance of Andrewes Burrell, for a Reformation of England's Navie*. BM, E. 335(6). n.d. [May 1646]; *The Answer of the Commissioners of the Navie, To a scandalous pamphlet published by Mr Andrewes Burrell*, London, 1646, in which he is described as a 'sometime servant in the Navie' who is now in search of a job. His naval service was intermittent (Firth and Rait, *A. & O.*, I, 392; *Cal. S.P. Dom., 1648–9*, p. 377; *1651–2*, pp. 20–1, 158–9); his will suggests a man in very reduced circumstances (P.C.C. 30 Reeve, made 1663, pr. 1678).

45 See *The King's Servants*, pp. 90, 107, 122.

46 For Walker see *DNB* and his writings, chiefly *The History of Independency* in 4 parts, 1661 (the most complete 1-vol. ed.); for the Ushership, *The Case between Clement Walker, Esq and Humphrey Edwards truley stated* and *The Case of Mrs Mary Walker* ... BM, 669 f.15(39–40); for Edwards, *DNB*, and G. Yule, *The Independents in the English Civil War* (Cambridge, 1958), App. A, p. 95.

47 *A Brief Vindication of William Jervis, Gent. Against the Scandalous Aspersions of John Hodder Gent. By Way of a Narrative*. n.d. [1653]. BM, 669 f.17(1).

48 Samuel Chidley, *The Dissembling Scot Set forth in his Coulours or a Vindication of Lt. Col. John Lilburne and others*. BM, E. 652(13), dated 1 February 1652[/3], pp. 10–14; see also Aylmer, 'Gentlemen Levellers?', *Past & Present*, 49 (1970), pp. 123–4 and n. 13, and Anon., 'Samuel Chidley, Philanthropist and Iconoclast', *Trans. Congregational Hist. Soc.*, V (1911–12), 92–9. Chidley himself had been named as a suspect in the forged debentures scandal (S.P. 18/24/101, Aug. 1652).

49 Note particularly the attacks on Sir John Lenthall, the Speaker's brother

and Keeper of the Marshalsea, the prison of King's Bench. See ch. 3, ix, pp. 162–4.

50 *A Whip for the Marshalls Court, and their Officers. The Petition of Robert Robins Gent. to the House of Commons. Against the Abuses practised in the Marshal's Court* (etc.). n.d. [?1647]. Worcester College Library, shelf-mark AA.S.4; the same or another ed., BM, E. 475(27), 7 Dec. 1648.

51 *C.J.*, VI, 599; *Cal. Cttee. Compdg.*, pp. 400–1; for Say, see *DNB*. In 1651 he was also on the Council of State (*Cal. S.P. Dom.*, 1651, p. xxxv and *passim*).

52 See ch. 3, viii, p. 139. His publications are as follows: A *Declaration and Appeale to all the freeborne people of the Kingdom in general.* November 1645. BM, 669 f.10(40); *Everymans Right: or, England's Perspective Glasse* ... BM, E. 340(2), 5 June 1646; *Times Present Mercy, and Englands Western Justice* ... Bodl., Vet. A3.e.368, 1647; *Why Not? Eight Queries, made to the Parliament, from the People of England, in 1649.* BM, 619 f.14(67), Thomason's date 22 Aug.; *A Second Why Not or Eight Queries*, ibid. (72), 3 September; *The Levellers Vindication or A Tragicall Story* ... BM, E. 573(8), 11 September 1649; *A True and Faithfull Advice to the Army* ... Worcester College, AA.8, 13(39), May 1650; *A Moderate Inspection into the Corruption of the pratique part of the common Law of England*, BM, E. 882(4), 17 June 1656; and *The Out-Cry and Just Appeale of the Inslaved People of England.* BM, E. 983 (17), 18 May 1659. Not all Frese's works are equally autobiographical; his Leveller sympathies seem incidental rather than fundamental to his role as a pamphleteer.

53 See ch. 3, ix, pp. 149–50.

54 I refer particularly to M. A. Gibb, *John Lilburne The Leveller: A Christian Democrat* (1947), and Pauline Gregg, *Freeborn John: A Biography of John Lilburne* (1961).

55 See G. H. Sabine (ed.), *Works of Gerrard Winstanley* (Ithaca, New York, 1941); *DNB Corrigenda*; Aylmer, '*England's Spirit Unfoulded* ... A Newly Discovered Pamphlet by Gerrard Winstanley', *Past and Present*, 40 (1968); Keith Thomas, 'Another Digger Broadside' and 'The Date of Gerrard Winstanley's *Fire in the Bush*', ibid., 42 (1969).

56 See *DNB* and *The Works of that Grave and Learned Lawyer Judge Jenkins* ... 1648. BM, E. 1154(2), pp. 75–86, '*The Armies Indemnity* ...'

57 W. Prynne, *A Declaration and Protestation against the new Tax and Extortion of Excise in general and for Hops in particular.* Oct. 1654. BM, E. 813(16).

58 *England's Spirit Unfoulded.* (See n. 55 above.)

59 See *The Upright Man's Vindication: Or, An Epistle writ by John Lilburne, Gent.* ... BM, E. 708(22), 5 August 1653, p. 29.

60 See *DNB*; Nuttall, *Visible Saints*, p. 151 n. 1; P. Zagorin, *Political Thought in the English Revolution* (1954), p. 83; Anon., *Rights of the Kingdom; Or, Customs of our Ancestors.* BM, E. 561(3), 22 January 1648/9.

61 *A Declaration or Testimony given by Captain Robert Norwood ... 21 April 1651. Together with several his answers ... after his excommunication*

... BM, E. 632(1), 9 June 1651; *A Brief Discourse made by Capt. Ro. Norwood on ... the 28 of January 1651[/2] in the Upper-Bench at Westminster.* BM, E. 652(11), 1 February 1651/2; *Proposals for Propagation of the Gospel, Offered to the Parliament.* BM, E. 656(21), 20 March 1651/2; *A Pathway unto England's Perfect Settlement; And its Centre and Foundation of Rest and Peace* ... BM, E. 702(16), 27 June 1653; *An Additional Discourse Relating unto a Treatise lately published by Capt. Ro. Norwood intituled A Pathway ... with a Brief Answer to Mr John Spittlehouse.* BM, E. 708(9), 2 August 1653. He attacked Spittlehouse's *First Addresses to H.E. the Lord General* ... for its biblical literalism and neo-Judaism, e.g. over the death penalty for petty theft which Norwood opposed, denying that this was part of the original (and so fundamental) laws of England.

62 London, [May] 1653. BM, E. 697(21); Bodl. 4° L.91 Jur.

63 *Advice, sent in a letter From an Elder Brother, to a Younger.* BM, E. 838(8), 12 May 1655. He now pinned his remaining hopes to the Ordinance reforming Chancery of 22 August 1654 (pp. 7–8), for which see ch. 3, ii, pp. 90–3. He seems to have egarded the Courts of Upper and Common Bench as acceptably reformed (p. 8); in this he was a law reformer, not a revolutionary.

64 *For every individuall Member of the Honourable House of Commons* ... 8 August 1649. BM, E. 568(19); S.P. 24/4, fo. 8v–9, 12, 28, 10 August and 26 July. That all was not well at Dover is suggested by Algernon Sidney's removal from the Governorship in 1650. Mr G. R. Smith has argued that the Clerk of the Passages there (who incidentally had the same surname as the Mayor accused by Burt) was a crypto-royalist throughout the 1650s (G. R. Smith, 'Royalist secret agents at Dover during the Commonwealth', *Historical Studies: Australia and New Zealand* 12 (1967), pp. 477–90); see ch. 3, section ix, pp. 159–60, nn. 73, 75.

65 See ch. 3, section viii, pp. 137–8.

66 For suggestive historical parallels, see R. Hofstadter, *The Paranoid Style in American Politics and Other Essays* (1966), ch. 1. To believe that the Levellers were a 'front organisation' for the Society of Jesus was indeed a delusion worthy of the John Birch Society!

67 *Mr Tillam's Account Examined, or, A Brief Reply to his Unchristian Account of some passages of Providence. By a friend to Truth* ... (1657). Bodleian Pamphlet C 104(16).

iii THE OFFICIAL RECORD: COMMITTEES AND COURTS OF LAW

1 Birch published them in 1742; Thurloe's collections contain little before 1652; he died in 1668.

2 See ch. 4, section v, p. 260, and n. 74.

3 PRO, S.P. 28.

4 See ch. 3, section ix, pp. 149–50.

5 See Fortescue, *Cat. Thomason Tracts*, II, 562–4 (index, 'Excise') and compare the number of entries under 'Commissioners for Composition', 'Royalists', 'Sequestration', etc.

6 Ashley, *Financial and Commercial Policy*, pp. 63–4.

7 Worcester College, Clarke MS. XVII (unfolio'd), 4 and 14 Dec. 1649.

8 Helen Stocks and W. H. Stevenson (eds), *Records of the Borough of Leicester ... 1603–1688* (Cambridge, 1923), pp. 396 (1650/1), 454–5 (1659). The latter of these cases coincides with the attack on Thurloe over the farmers of the beer excise in the London area (see ch. 3, section ix, p. 166).

9 These generalisations about excise cases are drawn from S.P. 24/1–8 and 10–16. There is no subject index of the cases in these volumes; my point about geographical distribution is based on over 70 identified cases.

10 S.P. 24/12, fo. 26, 114v–115; 15, fo. 81v (quoted), 174-v, 206v.

11 S.P. 24/14, fo. 38v. See also Firth and Davies, *Regimental History*, p. xxvi, and ch. 3, section ix, p. 152, and n. 46.

12 These remarks about assessment cases are again based on S.P. 24/1–8, 10–17, *passim*; disputes between landlord and tenant, over liability for assessment on rent, form easily the largest single category.

13 *The Committee-Man Curried. A Comedy presented to the View of All Men*. BM, E. 398(21), 16 July 1647, and *The Second Part*, E. 401(40), 14 August; note also *The Committee-Man's Last Will and Testament*, BM, 669 f.11(73), 2 September 1647.

14 S.P. 24/4–8, 10–15. The cases involve both exports (cloth, wool, butter) and imports (dye stuffs, cards, tobacco, wine). For the Bristol case see S.P. 24/15, fo. 157v–158, November 1653.

15 G. Parsloe (ed.), *The Minute Book of Bedford Corporation* (Bedfordshire Hist. Rec. Soc., 26, 1949), pp. 10–11; see also pp. ix, xxxii; S.P. 24/4, fo. 43v–44, 85 and S.P. 24/49, 'Samuell Gibbs'.

16 S.P. 24/13, fo. 155, case from Worcestershire, May 1653.

17 S.P. 24/12, fo. 22v, 48; 13, fo. 53v–54, 101v; 15, fo. 28v.

18 I have done no more than dip into the unprinted records of the common-law courts (Upper and Common Bench and Exchequer) for these years; what follows is based on printed sources only. Adequate PRO Calendars or Indexes so far cover only some Chancery series and scarcely any of the other court records.

19 Hardres, *Reports of Cases*, pp. 137–47.

20 See ch. 3, section ix, pp. 160–2.

21 Styles, *Narrationes Modernae, or, Modern Reports*, p. 338.

22 Ibid., pp. 457–8.

23 Ibid., pp. 452–3; see ch. 3, section ii, p. 95.

24 Ibid., pp. 32–3, 35–6, 42–3.

25 Ibid., pp. 415–16. For Streater, see *DNB*; Firth and Davies, *Regimental History*, pp. 415–17; Fortescue, *Cat. of Thomason Tracts*, index; Wing, *S.T.C.*; *C.J.*, VII, 754; Plomer, *Dictionary of Printers and Booksellers*, p. 173; Eyre and Rivington, *Stationers' Co. Transcripts*, I, 233, 247, 317.

26 Anon. [John Clayton], *Reports and Pleas of Assizes at Yorke* (London, duodec., 1651), p. 130, no. 232.

27 Ibid., pp. 141–2, no. 257.

28 For Rainsborough, see E. Peacock, 'Notes on the Life of Thomas

Rainborowe . . .' *Archaeologia*, 46 (1877); *DNB*; Firth and Davies, *Regimental History*; H. R. Williamson, *Four Stuart Portraits* (1949), pp. 109–42, 151–3.

29 [Robert Siderfin], *Le Second Part de les Reports . . . Estreact plusieurs Cases comme ils Estoyent Argue and Adjudgees en la Court del Upper Bench En les Ans 1657, 1658 and 1659* (folio, London, 1684), pp. 17–19, 36–7, 81–4, 137–43.

iv   IN THE LOCALITIES

1 *Bedfordshire Hist. Rec. Soc.*, 18 (1936), pp. 1–42, G. H. Fowler (ed.), 'The Civil War Papers of Sir William Boteler, 1642–55', no. 97.

2 Or to their equivalent, the Judges arriving with Commissions of Oyer and Terminer, or of Gaol Delivery.

3 The distinction is made clear in Charles I's (1629) charter granted to the borough of Dorchester. The JPs for the town, who were to comprise the Mayor, the immediate ex-Mayor, the Recorder, the Bailiffs and one of the Capital Burgesses, were given the same powers to inquire into felonies, etc. as the county Justices, but they were not to determine cases involving murder, treason, felony or other matters for which the penalty would be loss of life or limb (C. H. Mayo (ed.), *The Municipal Records of the Borough of Dorchester, Dorset* (Exeter, 1908), pp. 56–60, esp. p. 58). Alternatively, there is the practical substitution of lesser penalties, without the abandonment or curtailment of jurisdiction. In 1650 the Grimsby magistrates ordered a whipping until the prisoner's back was bloody, for the theft of a sheep, which (unless it was a beast of unusually little worth) ought by law to have carried the death penalty (Hist. MSS. Comm., 37, *14th Report*, App. VIII, *MSS. of Lincoln, etc.*, p. 283).

4 *Bedfs. County Recs*, II (n.d.), 'Notes and Extracts from the County Recs, being a Cal. of Vol. I of the Sessions Minute Books 1651 to 1660', p. 24.

5 *Herts. County Recs*, V (1928), W. le Hardy (ed.), 'Calendar to the Sessions Books and Sessions Minute Books . . . of the County of Hertford 1649 to 1657', pp. 455–6, 497, 499, 500, 502; ibid., VI (1930), '1658 to 1700', p. 2.

6 1603–25, 73.6 p.a. av.; 1625–49 but 5 years incomplete, 33.9 and the 10 heaviest years av. 45; 1649–59, 40.27, figures including executions for Treason, and by *peine forte et dure* for refusing to plead (J. C. Jeaffreson (ed.), *Middlesex County Records*, III, *1 Charles I to 18 Charles II* (Middlesex County Rec. Soc. 1888), pp. xvii–xix).

7 Ibid., p. xxii.

8 The first such indictment is found in January 21 Car. I (1645/6); thereafter they become frequent (ibid., pp. 180, 239, etc.).

9 Ibid., pp. 186–7.

10 Ibid., p. 102. The Recognizances totalled £80, May 1648.

11 Ibid., p. 104.

12 Ibid., p. 189.

13 E.g. a widow of Stepney bound over in 1656 to answer for words uttered

by her apprentice against the Protector and Chief Justice Glyn (ibid., p. 252).

14 The sentence is not clear (ibid., p. 261, August 1657).

15 Ibid., p. 265.

16 Ibid., p. 277.

17 Ibid., pp. 215–16. It is not clear that the court even saw the offending text.

18 *Norfolk Rec. Soc.*, 26 (1955), D. E. Howell James (ed.), *Norfolk Quarter Session Order Book 1650–1657*, no. 377, 1652.

19 Ibid., nos 709, 741, 1655.

20 Ibid., no. 768, 1655.

21 *Warwickshire County Records*, III (1937), S. C. Ratcliff and H. C. Johnson (eds), 'Quarter Session Order Book 1650–1657', p. 88.

22 Ibid., VI (1941), 'Quarter Sessions Indictment Book, . . . 1631 to . . . 1674', p. 105.

23 Anything which I could say here is rendered obsolete by the appearance of Keith Thomas's *Religion and the Decline of Magic* (1971), chapters 14–18, to which any interested reader is referred.

24 *Hist. MSS. Comm., Reports on MSS. in various Collections*, I (1901), pp. 65–176, County of Wilts (17th-century records).

25 Ibid., p. 124.

26 Ibid., pp. 132–3.

27 *North Riding Rec. Soc.*, V–VI (1887–8), J. C. Atkinson (ed.), 'Quarter Session Records'.

28 The standard account remains E. M. Leonard, *The Early History of English Poor Relief* (Cambridge, 1900, repr. London 1965), an excellent monograph but desperately in need of revision.

29 See G. R. Elton, 'An Early Tudor Poor Law', *Econ. H.R.*, 2nd series, VI (1953), 55–67, and 'State planning in Early Tudor England', ibid., XIII (1961), 433–9; see also Elton, 'Reform by Statute: Thomas Starkey's *Dialogue* and Thomas Cromwell's Policy', The Ralegh Lecture on History 1968 (*Procs Brit. Acad., LIV*), pp. 174–6.

30 W. K. Jordan, *Philanthropy in England 1480–1660* (1959), esp. ch. V; see also Barnes, *Somerset 1625–1640*, ch. VII; C. V. Wedgwood, *Strafford: a revaluation* (1961), pp. 97–9, 102, 120, and J. P. Cooper, 'The Fortune of Thomas Wentworth, Earl of Strafford', *Econ. H.R.*, 2nd series, XI (1958), 227–48. See also W. Notestein, *The English People on the Eve of Colonisation 1603–1630* (1954), chapters 18, 20.

31 Margaret James, *Social Problems and Policy during the Puritan Revolution 1640–1660* (1930, and repr. 1966), esp. ch. VI, 'The Relief of the Poor'; E. M. Hampson, *The Treatment of Poverty in Cambridgeshire 1597–1834* (Cambridge, 1934).

32 A. L. Beier, 'Poor Law in Warwickshire, 1630–1660', *Past and Present*, 35 (1966), pp. 77–100.

33 For a graphic portrayal of high prices from Essex, see *The Diary of the Rev. Ralph Josselin*, ed. E. Hockliffe (Camden 3rd series, XV, 1908), pp. 42, 45, 46, 59, 61, 63, 64–6, 69–70, 78, 84, 94. Josselin has recently been the subject of a brilliant study by Alan Macfarlane, a pioneering work of

historical anthropology: *The Family Life of Ralph Josselin* (Cambridge, 1970).

34 In addition to those already cited, see B. C. Redwood (ed.), 'Quarter Sessions Records (Order Book) 1642–9', *Sussex Rec. Soc.*, Vol. 54 (1954); S. C. Ratcliff and H. C. Johnson (eds), 'Quarter Session Order Book ... 1637–1650', *Warwickshire County Recs*, II (1936).

35 See Mayo, *Records of Dorchester*; Hist. MSS. Comm., 73, *Rept. on Recs of City of Exeter* (1966); Helen Stocks and W. H. Stevenson (eds), *Recs of the Borough of Leicester ... 1603–1688* (Cambridge, 1923); Howell, *Newcastle and the Puritan Revolution*, pp. 314–19; J. M. Guilding (ed.), *Reading Recs. Diary of the Corporation*, Vol. IV, *Charles I and Commonwealth (1641–1654)* (1896); M. Weinstock (ed.), *Weymouth and Melcombe Regis Minute Book 1625–1660* (Dorset Rec. Soc., I, 1964); Joyce W. Fowkes, 'The Minute Book of the York Court of Quarter Sessions, 1638–1662', *Yorks. Archaeolog. Jnl*, 41 (1963–6), 449–54.

36 Firth and Rait, *A. & O.*, I, 1042–5.

37 Ibid., II, 104–10, May 1649.

38 Unless from counties and towns whose records exist in MS. only for these years and which I have not consulted.

39 See *C.J.*, VI, 137, 160, 161, 167–8, 201, 226, 322, 351, 374, 416, 481, 535; VII, 104, 127, 129, 190, 212, 258. Except for short intervals of crisis, sittings were from Tuesdays to Fridays inclusive most of the time from the summer of 1649 on.

40 *C.J.*, VII, 296, 358.

41 Firth and Rait, *A. & O.*, II.

42 Elizabeth Melling (ed.), 'The Poor', *Kentish Sources*, IV (Maidstone, 1964), pp. 20–22, 51.

43 For Norfolk, n. 18 above; Joan Wake (ed.) with introduction by S. A. Peyton, 'Quarter Sessions Records of the County of Northampton ... (1630, 1657, 1658)', *Northants Rec. Soc., Publications*, I (1924 for 1920–2) —of particular interest because the redoubtable Adam Baynes was an active Justice there in 1657–8; Dorothy L. Powell and Hilary Jenkinson, 'Surrey Quarter Sessions Order Book and Sessions Rolls, 1659–1661', *Surrey Rec. Soc.*, Vol. 13, no. 35 (1934)—together with Ratcliff and Johnson on Warwickshire, and S. A. Peyton on Lincolnshire later in the century, this has the most valuable introduction of all these volumes.

44 The usual names for middlemen in corn and livestock respectively.

45 Innkeepers' prices, of oats and hay for visitors' horses, were fixed by the Dorchester JPs in 1658 (Mayo, *Recs of Dorchester*, p. 674). Action on grain prices can also be found in Cheshire and Wiltshire (I am grateful to Mr J. P. Cooper for this information).

46 The standard authorities here are still R. H. Tawney, 'The Assessment of Wages in England by the Justices of the Peace', *Vierteljahrschrift für Sozial- und Wirtschaftsgeschichte*, XI (1913), pp. 307–37 and 533–64; R. K. Kelsall, *Wage Regulation under the Statute of Artificers* (1938). W. E. Minchinton (ed.), *Wage Assessment in Pre-Industrial England* (1972), table II, pp. 20–1, strengthens my point in the text, showing an exceptionally large number of assessments from the 1650s.

47 See M. G. Davies, *The Enforcement of English Apprenticeship ... 1563–1642* (Camb., Mass., 1956), and the much older study, still valuable for its use of town records, O. J. Dunlop, *English Apprenticeship and Child Labour: A History* ... (1912), esp. chapters VI–VII.

48 *Cal. S.P. Dom., 1655*, pp. 296, 344, 390; the latter are reprinted in Kenyon, *Stuart Const.*, pp. 348–50. For other references see ch. 2, ix, pp. 48–9, and nn. 21–2.

49 *Thurloe St. P.*, IV, 197, 241; and as Berry implied when he wrote on 12 January 1656 to Thurloe, 'I am now at last become civell, and have taken my place among such magistrates in the quarter sessions at Sallop' (ibid., 413); Disbrowe, by contrast, although he had other complaints and suggestions, does not seem to have been troubled by the distinction between the powers of the special Commission for securing the peace and those of the ordinary Commission of the Peace (see his letters, *Thurloe St. P.*, IV, 300–520, *passim*).

50 T. B. Macaulay, *History of England*, ch. II, Everyman ed. (1906 and repr.), Vol. I, p. 129.

51 *Thurloe St. P.*, IV, 450. A newsletter writer referred to the suppression of 30 or 40 in some individual corporations (cities or towns), even of over 60 in others; taking this together with their enforcement of the Poor Laws, he wrote of the Major-Generals, 'Wee hope for an extra-ordinary reformation speedily from them' (Worcester College, Clarke MS. XXVII, fo. 163v–164, from Westminster to William Clarke in Scotland, 2 February 1656). For Worsley's work, see now J. S. Morrill, 'The Government of Cheshire during the Civil Wars and Interregnum', Oxford D.Phil., 1971.

52 Lancs. Record Office, Quarter Sessions Petitions (transcripts), 21/22; 31/6; 96/23.

53 Ibid., DDF/2437(QSV/11/1–2), Minutes of the JPs at the Sheriff's Table ... (1577–1693), transcript by Mr Sharpe France.

54 Ibid., transcript, p. 7.

55 *Norfolk Rec. Soc.*, XXVI, nos 857, 868, 879.

56 Ibid.; *Herts. County Recs*, V, 480–1. There may well be other cases, which I have failed to track down, of orders being issued when a Major-General or his deputy was present. Gardiner (*Commonwealth and Protectorate*, Vol. III (1901 ed.), ch. 42, pp. 248–50) cites contemporary newspaper reports of anti-alehouse measures in Warwickshire, Shropshire and Middlesex.

57 He belonged to the Worsley family of Platt Hall, now the Manchester City Costume Museum, and was no known relation either of the Yorkshire Worsleys or of Benjamin Worsley.

58 See Parsloe (ed.), *Bedford Minute Book*; Mayo (ed.), *Municipal Recs of Dorchester*; Stocks (ed.), *Recs of Leicester*; Howell, *Newcastle*, pp. 277–81; Hist. MSS. Comm., 31, *13th Report*, App. IV, *Rye and Hereford Corporations, etc.*; Hist. MSS. Comm., 55, *Reports on Various Collections*, IV (Salisbury); Weinstock (ed.), *Weymouth Minute Book*; *Yorks. Archaeolog. Jnl*, 41 (York). I have also used Barbara M. Wilson, 'The Government of York 1580–1660', Univ. of York M.Phil. Thesis (1967),

and the *Victoria County History* for York, Hull and some other towns. It seems fair to say that, while a great deal of interesting and important work on urban history is now in progress, there are few good town-histories which treat the period 1640–60 both in detail and within a longer chronological context.

59 *Hist. MSS. Comm., Rye, Hereford, etc.*, pp. 217–18. The whole letter is printed below, by permission of the Secretary of the Royal Commission and the Comptroller of Crown Copyright H.M.S.O., in Appendix 2.

60 *Hist. MSS. Comm.*, 73, *City of Exeter*, pp. 212–13.

61 For the Messengers see Aylmer, 'Attempts at Administrative Reform 1625–40', *E.H.R.*, 72 (1957), pp. 248–50; *King's Servants*, pp. 67, 463. For the Council in the Marches, see Penry Williams, *The Council in the Marches, of Wales under Elizabeth I* (Cardiff, 1958), and more particularly his two articles, 'The Activity of the Council in the Marches under the Early Stuarts', *Welsh Hist. Rev.*, 1 (1961), pp. 133–60, and 'The Attack on the Council in the Marches, 1603–1642', *Trans. of the Hon. Soc. of Cymmrodorion* for 1961, Pt 1, pp. 1–22.

62 'Notes and Extracts from the County Records . . . Vol. I of the Sessions Minute Books. 1651 to 1660', *Bedfs. County Records*, II (n.d.). See also the excellent article, P. H. Hardacre, 'William Boteler: A Cromwellian Oligarch', *Huntington Library Quarterly*, II (1947–8).

63 O. L. Dick (ed.), *Aubrey's Brief Lives* (paperback ed., 1962), p. 347. His father, also Silas, is in the 200 sample (ch. 4, section iii) as a commissioner and trustee.

64 See e.g. Everitt, *Community of Kent*; Mary Coate, *Cornwall in the Great Civil War and Interregnum* (Oxford, 1953, and repr. Truro, 1963).

65 *Thurloe St. P.*, IV, 402.

66 Ibid., 393. The dashes between 'broad' and 'ministers' are in the original of Berry's letter (Bodl., Rawl. MS. A xxxiv, p. 217).

67 Not that I suppose Professor Everitt or others who have written so well on the local communities of seventeenth-century England in recent years to have this intention, or themselves to share this viewpoint. But the danger of such an assumption is there and should be resisted. To use another terminology, the Country is not *ex officio* in the right, nor the Court always in the wrong.

V ADMINISTRATION AND SOCIAL STRUCTURE

1 See W. A. L. Vincent, *The State and School Education 1640–1660 in England and Wales* (1950); C. Hill, 'Propagating the Gospel', in H. E. Bell and R. L. Ollard (eds), *Historical Essays 1600–1750 presented to David Ogg* (1963), p. 54; C. Webster (ed.), *Samuel Hartlib and the Advancement of Learning* (Cambridge, 1970), esp. the Introduction and the Bibliography. On writing schools see ch. 4, section iii, p. 185 and n. 45.

2 First mooted, like so many other Cromwellian measures, by the Rump (*C.J.*, VI, 410, 589, May 1650–June 1651).

3 The latest study is H. Kearney, *Scholars and Gentlemen: Universities and Society in pre-industrial Britain 1500–1700* (1970), ch. VII, 'The Crom-

wellian Decade'; see also M. H. Curtis, *Oxford and Cambridge in Transition 1558–1642* (Oxford, 1958), and C. Hill, *Intellectual Origins of the English Revolution* (Oxford, 1965), Appendix.

4 Even allowing for any continued fall in the value of money. The original authority for this appears to be C. H. Firth, *A Commentary on Macaulay's History of England* (1937), pp. 120–1, probably in turn based upon the writings of Charles D'Avenant (1656–1714); see his 'Essay upon Ways and Means' and 'Discourses on the Public Revenues'.

vi GOVERNMENT AND SOCIETY: FISCAL AND ECONOMIC RELATIONS

1 Having suggested some tentative estimates for the 1630s (*The King's Servants*, pp. 248–9, 331–3), I have been alarmed to find them quoted almost as if they were established facts, and do not, therefore, propose to attempt the same thing for the 1650s.

2 See Maurice Ashley's *Financial and Commercial Policy under the Cromwellian Protectorate* (Oxford, 1934, and London 1962), chapters 4–9.

3 See PRO, Declared Accounts, E. 351/438, account of the Treasurers for the money raised on these acts, of 1651–3. By contrast £604,934 was raised through 'doubling'. See also Habakkuk, art. cit., *Econ. H.R.*, 2nd series, 15 (1962).

4 PRO, Declared Accounts, Audit Office, A.O. 1/15/301, account of Waring & Herring for 1643–54; Declared Accounts, E. 351/439, account of Sherwyn & Leech, 1653–5; E. 351/592, account of the same as Treasurers to the Commissioners for the Advance of Money, 1653–4; see also *Cal. Cttee. Compdg.*, Vol. V, Introduction by Mrs M. A. E. Green, pp. xxxi–ii.

5 That is of the Treasurers to the Committee at Haberdashers' Hall. See *Cal. Cttee. Advc. Mon.*, Vol. I, p. xxii, for some fragmentary financial statements.

6 E.g. the report made from the Ways and Means Committee in September 1650 (*C.J.*, VI, 461–3, 464). Others are cited by Ashley, *Financial and Commercial Policy*, pp. 41 n. 4, 43 n. 1.

7 The great majority are among the Declared Accounts of the Exchequer: PRO E. 351/ (parchment originals) and A.O. 1/ (Audit Office paper copies).

8 E.g. E. 351/1295, the account of the Excise Commissioners for 1647–50.

9 PRO E. 401/1402–6, 1930–2 and E. 405/289, 390–1. The weekly 'Remains', or statements from the Exchequer of Receipt for 1655–9 are in the State Papers, as follows: S.P. 46/97/fo. 84, S.P. 28/333 (1st bundle), S.P. 18/102/170–82, S.P. 28/333 (2nd bundle), S.P. 18/131A, S.P. 18/156/115–52, S.P. 28/333 (3rd bundle), S.P. 18/183/149–50, S.P. 46/99, fo. 25, S.P. 18/201/52–7.

10 *Fin. & Comm. Pol.*, p. 96. I am afraid that I cannot reconcile the totals given there for 'Revenues Paid into the Exchequer' with the figures in his Appendix A, pp. 184–5, 'Yields of Taxes'.

11 He calculated expenditure to have averaged rather under £2½ million p.a., giving an average annual deficit on these figures of £973,000.

12 PRO, E. 351/304–7; A.O. 1/47/1, E. 101/676/51; Ashley, *Fin. & Comm. Pol.*, ch. 8.

13 PRO, E. 351/653–7; Ashley, *Fin & Comm. Pol.*, ch. 6.

14 PRO, E. 351/1295–7; A.O. 1/890/4, 5, 7, 9; Ashley, *Fin. & Comm. Pol.*, ch. 7.

15 PRO, E. 101/604/26, 28 (Alienations); E. 351/1960 (Duchy of Lancs.); A.O. 1/1216/87 (First Fruits and Tenths); E. 351/1676–80 (Hanaper); E. 101/125/3 (London Buildings); A.O. 1/1601/52, 1629/234 (Mint); E. 351/517 (Prisage of Wine); Ashley, *Fin. & Comm. Pol.*, ch. 9 and Appendix A.

16 See *Cal. Cttee. Advc. Money*, Vol. 1, Introduction and General Series; PRO, E. 351/592.

17 PRO, A.O. 1/15/301; E. 351/439.

18 PRO, E. 351/453; Bodl., Rawl. MS. B 239 (Bishops' lands); PRO, E. 351/603 (Crown lands); A.O. 1/367/2 (Capitular lands); E. 351/602 (Fee-farm rents); E. 351/604 (Royal forests); E. 351/438 (Royalist lands, forfeited for Treason); Habakkuk, art. cit., 'Public Finance', *Econ. H.R.*, 2nd series, 15, table 1, p. 87.

19 *Bedfs. Historical Rec. Soc.*, 18 (1936), (1), 'The Civil War Papers of Sir William Boteler, 1642–1655', ed. G. H. Fowler, Appendix.

20 D. A. Johnson and D. A. Vaisey (eds), *Staffordshire and the Great Rebellion* (Staffs County Council, county records committee, n.d. [1964–5]), nos 27, 29, 30.

21 *Observations on the Life and Death of King Charles*, in F. Maseres (ed.), *Select Tracts* (1825), I, 155.

22 C. Wilson, *Economic History and the Historian* (1969), ch. 7, 'Taxation and the Decline of Empires', pp. 119–20; J. U. Nef, *Industry and Government in France and England 1540–1640* (repr. Ithaca, New York, 1957), p. 128.

23 *The King's Servants*, pp. 246, 248. The figures suggested were within the range £250,000–400,000 a year; the Crown's revenues rose during the 1630s from about £600,000 to nearly £900,000 p.a. (ibid., p. 64).

24 See ch. 3, section v, pp. 120–1, for some discussion of this, also sections vii–viii.

25 As some other historians have suggested, including the authorities on the Court of Wards—Professor Hurstfield and Mr M. J. Hawkins—and Professors Stone and Trevor-Roper. They may well be right.

26 Compare for instance the emphasis given here with that in Christopher Hill's recent book, *God's Englishman: Oliver Cromwell and the English Revolution* (1970).

Chapter 6 Conclusion

1 See *The King's Servants*, ch. 4, ii, and Aylmer, 'Attempts at Administrative Reform, 1625–40', *E.H.R.*, 72 (1957); also Jean S. Wilson, 'Sir Henry Spelman and the Royal Commission on Fees', in *Studies presented to Sir Hilary Jenkinson* (1957), pp. 456–70, and Aylmer, 'Charles I's

Commission on Fees, 1627–40', *Bull. Inst. Hist. Res.*, 31 (1958), pp. 58–67. On the Jacobean period note particularly R. H. Tawney, *Business and Politics* (Cambridge, 1958); Joel Hurstfield, *The Queen's Wards* (1958), ch. 15; and Menna Prestwich, *Lionel Cranfield* (Oxford, 1966); work is in progress by Dr P. R. Seddon of the University of Nottingham on other aspects.

2 As described by Professor Alan Everitt in his recent writings.

3 As is argued most notably by Dr Christopher Hill.

4 As I suggested in a review of H. N. Brailsford's remarkable posthumous work, *The Levellers and the English Revolution*, ed. C. Hill (1962)—see *E.H.R.*, 78 (1963), pp. 173–4, and as Christopher Hill, interestingly, now appears to accept—see *God's Englishman* (1970), p. 207.

5 For John Fowke, see *DNB*; Beaven, *Aldermen*, I, 277, II, 66, 181; *C.J.*, VI–VII; Firth and Rait, *A. & O.*; Pearl, *London and the outbreak of the Puritan Revolution*, esp. pp. 316–20; *Cal. S.P. Dom.*, *1651–2*, pp. 416, 455; *1652–3*, p. 205; Bodl., Rawl. MS. B 239, no. 254. He was Comptroller for the sale of episcopal and capitular lands, as well as a Trustee for the same, Comptroller to the Obstructions Committee, law reform commissioner and a probate judge, but he was removed from the customs commission in 1645, for alleged dishonesty.

6 See esp. ch. 3, sections viii–ix, pp. 130–6, 145–50, 151, 165.

7 By Mr Blair Worden of Pembroke College, Cambridge.

8 As is apparently accepted by Professor Hugh Kearney in his *Gentlemen and Scholars: Universities and Society in pre-industrial Britain, 1500–1700* (1970), pp. 119–20.

9 See C. H. Church, 'The Social Basis of the French Central Bureaucracy under the Directory 1795–99', *Past and Present*, 36 (1967), pp. 59–72, for a preliminary survey, very stimulating for comparative purposes with republican England, also relevant for a comparison with Britain around 1800.

APPENDIX 1

The Method (and style) of issuing Instruments under the Great Seal, n.d.
[*?December 1653*]
(S.P. 18/42/5)

All originall warrants from the King were signed on the topp over the first line in the beginning of the line as followeth Charles R. Our pleasure is, That you prepare a bill fitt for our Signature containing A grant, etc. A proclamacon. etc. A pardon etc. as the nature of the buissines warranted required. etc. and was closed thus. And for soe doeing this shall be yor. warrant, Given at Our Court at Whitehall the   day of   1653: and was directed as followeth vizt. To our trusty and wellbeloved Sr. Jo. Bankes Knt. or Attorney Genll. or thus To our Attorney Generall or to our Sollicitor Genll. or to either of them. or thus To Oliver St. John Esqr. or. Sollicitor Generall. The bill being prepared in parchmt. by the Attorney Genll. was signed by him under the end of the bill in this manner vizt. Excr. by Oliver St. John: and also under the Dockett vizt. under the Bill also on the left side thereof. and the manner of the Docketts was as on the other side. [verso] May it please yor. Matie. This contayneth yor. Maties. grant of the office of etc. to A.B. Esqr. during his life, Together with the fee of etc. And is donne by warrant under yor. Maties. signe Manuall. Ol. St. John 1° December 1653 The Attorney alwayes put a date to the Bill when it passed his hand. The Bill thus prepared and signed by the Attorney Genll. was or ought alwayes to have byn brought to one of the Secretaryes of State, and by him tendred to the King to be signed for wch. Mr. Secretaryes fee was 5 li and to his Clerke xl s. The King signed on the top of the Bill, over the beginning of the first line. The Bills then alwayes began thus. vizt. Charles R. Rex etc. Omnibus ad quos etc. Sciatis qd. Nos de grā nēā spīāli certa scientia et meru natu vr̄is: etc. & were signed as above. After the King had signed the Bill tendered to him by Mr. Secretary. The party prosecutor thereof came to the [next page] Secretary for it, and himselfe carried it to the Signet office. where the Bill was transcribed, with a direc̄c̄on to the Ld. Privy Seale, and the originall remaynes wth. the Clerke of the Signet: and the transcript was againe brought to Mr. Secretary to be sealed. And then that under Seale, was delivered to the party prosecuteing and by him delivered to the Clerke of the Privy Seale. who kept the transcript from the Signet for his warrt. and transcribed anew & directed it to the Ld. Keeper and put it under the privy seale. That privy seale, the party prosecuteing tooke himselfe and carried to the Ld. Keepers Seale-

436

bearer who, imediately carried it to the Ld. Keeper, and the Lord Keeper at the bottom of the transcript under the privy seale wrote upon it thus Recepi: 2° die Decembr. 1653 Littleton This recepi, was the warrant for the date of the Pattent, and it alwayes bore that date, according to the Act of Parliamt. The party prosecuting then tooke the Privy Seale back with the Teste thus entred upon it, and delivered it to the Clerke of the Pattents in Chancery, who ingrossed it for the Greate Seale. [verso] All Bills for the Kings Signe Manuall were made up after this manner, and if the buissiness was of hast, or not to be passed under the Signet and Privy Seale. then Mr. Secretary with his owne hand. or one by his appointment. for none else might presume to doe it, but the King himselfe wrote theis words followeing on the top of the outside of the Bill. vizt. and signed them. thus vizt. after it was first signed within in the head of the Bill as before. Charles R. Our pleasure is, that this bill passe by imediate warrant. The bill itselfe then was carried imediately to the Ld. Keeper who made his recepi upon it, and soe it was ingrossed by the Clerke of the Pattents, as if it had byn the Privy Seale.

APPENDIX 2

Rye under the Commonwealth

(From Historical MSS Commission, 31, *13th Report*, Appendix IV, *Loder-Symonds, etc.* (including Corporations of Rye, Hastings, and Hereford), pp. 217–18).

1651, November 20—The Mayor and Jurats of Rye to Colonel Morley, Mr John Fagge, and Mr William Hay.

'Upon severall complaints of the poore tradsmen of this towne unto us made that many of the disbanded souldiers and other strangers did sett upp and exercisse publike trades and callinges, to there great prejudice and apparent ruine, and desiringe redresse therein and withall being acquainted that divers of the said disbanded souldiers and strangers had wives and children which are like to bee a sudden and great charge to this place which is already so poore that the inhabitants are very much oppressed in beareinge the charge thereof (as also by the souldiers quarteringe in private houses, forcibly against the minds of the inhabitants) for remedy whereunto we did proceed according to law and the priviledges of this Corporation for our own conservation, that we fall not into an irrecoverable mischiefe, in manner followinge:—Firste, we have received into and permitted all such souldiers which were, now or at any tyme heretofore have beene disbanded, having formerly either beene borne or belonging to this place, to sett up and exercise their severall trades and callinges therein. 2ly Wee have permitted all such disbanded souldiers which have married wives of this place also to sett up and exercise their severall trades and callinges therein. 3ly Wee doe permitt and suffer many disbanded souldiers and others as also those which are in present service to worke as journymen under master workemen of this towne. Now upon the desires aforesaid we have proceeded with all such which are not comprehended in these severall qualifications aforesaid in this legall order. First, we gave them tymly warning to desist the publique exercise of there callinges and depart this place and goe to there severall places of birth or last abode, there to use there severall trades, according to Act of Parliament in that case made and provided. 2ly After an expedient space of tyme expired, fynding them soe farre from observinge this order that they did not only stay but contempuously in there behaviour did abuse the Governors and Government of this place, whereupon we directed our warrante to the Constables for the apprehendinge and committinge to prison of some of them for their misdemeanors aforesaid, in the prosecution of which we have found great opposition by Captain Farley (as we conceive by Captain Fissenden's instigation) who did rescue one of these, so committed, from our Officers as they were carrying him to prison under pretence that he was listed under him. Whereupon we desired a meetinge, and accordingly had, where wee desired of Captain Farly to know whether hee and the rest under committment were listed or not, whereupon hee ingenuously confessed that they were not, only he sayd he had promised Captain Fissenden to list sixe of his men next muster, but he did not know the names of them, only one of them he said he promised to list at the tyme above said, which is not the man soe rescued but one Dearinge, a man of evill behaviour and greatly prejudiciall to the poore tradesmen of this place whereby the course of justice is obstructed and the souldiers imboldened to despise and contemne all Government and ministers thereof. Of all which proceedinges we thought fitt to give you a true, full, and naked narrative thereof that you may be rightly informed of the premisses. Wee fearinge it may be presented to you in another dresse.

The premises considered we are in a sore and deplorable condition, poverty and misery cometh upon us like a armed man and wee are obstructed in the use of the remedy the law provided for the prevention thereof.

Wee therefore humbly begge your Honors would be pleased to take this our sad condition into your serious and speedy considerations (some of you being members of this opprest Corporation and so cannot but sympathize in our misery) and some way or other free us (who cannot as free men lye under soe great bondage) from our aforesaid obstructions, that we may freely execute the law committed to us by this present power on those that are offenders and contemne the Ministers thereof'.

[1651] 'Visible causes threaening the destruction and ruin of this town if not prevented'.

The causes may be summed up as the increase of alehouses and brewers, allowing strangers, pedlars and chapmen to sell their wares privately instead of in the market place, and suffering strangers to remain in the town until they become by law inhabitants, and thus in course of time a parish charge.

INDEX

Absentee(s), Absenteeism, *see* Officials
Accountants, 105, 114, 160; dishonest, 144–6
Accounts, Accounting: arrears in, 144; under the Council, 239; demanded, 287; fraudulent or careless, 140, 144–6, 161; offices connected with, 205; rendered, 319; settling, or taking, 12, 273; skill in, 62, 74, 223; of treasurers and commissioners, 122
Accounts, Army, or military: Committee for taking, 99, 103, 105, 107, 108, 144, 219, 224; Auditor, 222, 224–5; members 222, 223, 225; staff, 107, 108; sub-committee, 147
Accounts Commissioner(s), 43, 64
Accounts of the Kingdom, then of the Commonwealth: Commissioners or Committee for taking, 11, 26–7, 31, 98, 105–6, 108–9, 114, 144, 145, 147, 319; approaches to, 62–6, 131, 147–8, 231; clerk(s), 103, 229; committee to choose, 224; co-Treasurers, 103, 105; dispute in, 102–3; location, 105–6; members, 99, 102–3, 220, 221–6, 232, 236, 241, 252; Messenger, 114; offices and staff, 63–6, 69, 83, 108–9; papers, 62–6, 131, 147–8, 298–9; procedure, 103; Registrar or Secretary, 64, 98–9, 229, 231, 232; Registrar-Accountant, 63; secretary, 105
Accounts and Public Debts Committee, 105
Ackworth, John, 160
Act(s) of Parliament, 76, 91, 95, 96, 108, 361 (*see also* Legislation; Ordinances; Parliamentary Enactment; Poor Laws; Recusancy Laws); for Accounts Committee, 103, 105; Adultery, 49, 306, 307; Anti-vagrancy 310; Artificers (1563) 311; of Attainder,

419; Blasphemy, 295, 307, 315; on Catholic recusants, 114, 164; on conditions of work, 102; Cottages (1589), 310–11; on Customs (1660), 337; Engagement, 62, 83, 334; Excise, 29, 82–3, 101, 108, 140, (1660) 337; fees in, 114; of General Pardon and Oblivion, 83, 88, 273, 332; incapacitating from office, 84; Indemnity, 46, 55, 80, 83, 299; for land sales, 108, 112, 113, 151, 294; London building, 70–1; for London Corporation for poor, 310; Marriages, 44; Monthly Assessment, 28, 112, 124; Navigation, 270, 272, (1660) 337; Pardon and Oblivion (1660), 259, 277; for passing accounts, 114; for probate judges, 116; on revenue farms, 378; for sale of Crown lands, 59; for sale of royalist lands, 27; Settlement (1662), 310; for settlement of Ireland, 36; for subsidies and Poll-taxes, 26; Test (1673), 271; Treason (Edward III), 304; for use of English, 104; validating ordinances, 91–2; against venality (Edward VI), 78, 81; of voluntary dissolution, 95
Adderley, Rev. William, 157–9
Administration; and administrators, 1, 2, 3, 5; central, 41–2, 50; civil, 55, 279, 324; costs, 29, 40; different branches, 205; history not pathology, 167; and machinery of justice, 302; members, defined, 168; middle ranks, 210, 255; of Parliament, 204; republican, and Administrative System of English Republic, 17, 23, 29, 46, 57, 341–2 (*see also* Government; Offices; Officials; Republic); and social structure, 317–18
Administrative attitudes, 341
Administrative history, 282

Administrative reform, 16, 52, 77, 92, 101, 120, 285–90, 326–9, 331–2, 333–4, 337–8, 343
Administrators (*see also* Officials): and Establishment, 324; of middle rank, 172, 244; of Protectorate, 318; religious zeal among, 70; sample, 174–97; selection, 197–209
Admiral, The, 240
Admiral(s) (*see also* Blake; Deane; Generals-at-Sea; Monck; Montague; Penn; Popham): pay, 110
Admiralty, (High) Court, 33; co-Registrar, 260; Judges, 40
Admiralty: Chamber, 129; Commission, 40; Commissioners, 76, 77, 93, 132; Committee (of Council of State), 15, 18, 40–1, 157, 168, 265–6, and appointments, 67, 83, Secretaries, 40–1, 99, 235, 236, 265–6, reference to, 136; office, 237, 337, Secretary, 89, 107
Admiralty and Navy Commissioners, 14, 25, 40–1, 90, 159, 216, 241; and petitions, 122; Secretary, 99, 265, 266–7
Adultery, 150 (*see also* Acts)
Advance of Money, 13, 25–8, 319, 321, 324, 327 (*see also* Fifth and Twentieth; Harberdashers' Hall); Commissioners for, 153 (*see also* Compounding Commissioners); offices for, 205; Committee for, 10, 12, 15, 26, 150, 224, 226 (*see also* Haberdashers' Hall); Accountant to, 226; records, 298; Treasurer, 227
Adventurers, *see* Ireland; Merchant
Advowsons, 44, 45, 217
Africa, 5, 264
African, *see* Royal Africa(n) Company
Agents, British, abroad, 19, 127, 129, 261; alleged corruption, 164–5 (*see also* Army; Foreign; Wine)
Agreement of the People, 83; Second, 338
Ainsty, the, 349
Albrow, M., 4
Aldermen, *see* London; Officials, status
Aldritch, Henry, 96
Aldworth, Richard, MP, 157
Alehouses, Alehouse-keepers, 49, 84, 307, 312–14, 431
Alexander, Sir Walter, 274

Alienations (of land), revenue, 27
Alienations Office, 27, 44; Commissionership in, 80
Allanson, Sir William, MP, 96
Allen, Francis, MP (Treasury Inspection Commissioner), 353
Almshouses, 309
Ambassadors, British, abroad, 19 (*see also* Agents; Diplomatic offices; Envoys)
Ambassadors extraordinary, 258
Ambassadors (of foreign States), 15
America, 337 (*see also* Colonies; New England; Virginia)
American colonial circles and interests, 244
Americans, colonial, 184 (*see also* New Englanders)
Anabaptist(s), *see* Baptist(s)
Anglican(s), 48, 283, 296, 308, 341 (*see also* Episcopalians)
Anglo-Irish, *see* Old English
Anglo-Scottish relations, 255 (*see also* Scotland)
Anthropologists, Anthropology, 4, 429–30
Anti-Levellers Antidote . . ., 284
Antilles, *see* West Indies
Antiquarian research, 101
Appeal from Chancery, An, 296
Appeale From the Court to the Country, An, 289
Appointment(s): academic, 62; by Act of Parliament, 95; and entry (to office), 42, 44, 47, 54, 57, 58–67, 68–75, 76, 77–8, 81, 83, 190–3, 204, 337; by patent, 76, 83, 84–5, 87, 91, 97, 334; protectoral, 119–20; protectoral invalidated, 80; and re-appointments, 55, 232; recommendations for, 60 (*see also* Patronage); rights, 59, 69, 70–1, 76, 78, 82, 90
Apprentice(s), Apprenticeship, Apprenticing, 309, 311, 315 (*see also* London; Officials); indemnity cases concerning, 301–2; legislation, 301; records, 173, 184, 189
Approbation Commissioners, *see* Tryers
Argyll, Archibald Campbell, 8th Earl and 1st Marquis of, 36–7
Aristocracy, *see* Peer(s); Peerage
Armagh, *see* Ussher

Armed Forces, *see* Army; Navy; State
Armigerous, *see* Gentry; Officials, status; Titles
Armoury and Stores offices, 16
Arms: grants, 234, 246; law, 394; Office, or College of, staff, 86
Army, Armies, 13–14, 18, 20, 28, 43, 48, 50, 52–3, 55, 83, 103, 110, 288, 316, 322, 324, 329, 330, 332, 333, 335–6, 342–3 (*see also* Accounts; Generals; Maimed Soldiers; Military); administration, 38–9; Agents, 126, 233; Agitators, 330; captains, *see* Army officers; colonels, *see* Army leaders, etc.; Army officers; Commissary for, 222; Commissioners to, 275; ex-apprentices, 301–2; and the Excise, 299; ex-soldiers, parliamentarian, 309, 310, 315; and Free Quarter, 314–15; Gentleman of Ordnance in, 241; grievances, 302 (*see also* Indemnity; Army pay, arrears); leaders; *also* Commanders; High Command; authorities, 42, 53, 54, 56, 109, 136, 155, 159–60, 171, 225, 290, 330–1; Millenarians in, 287; Monck's, 291; musters, 419; New Model, 109, 339; Northern Brigade, 233; pay (and Establishment pay), 287, 324, 362, 377; arrears, 59, 122, 123, 141, 240, 287, 319, 320, 324; payments to, 321; radical(s), 304; in Scotland and Ireland, 28, 34–7, 50, 52, 96, 123, (Agent for) 126; scandals and abuses, 155–6; Scoutmaster-General, 100; Secretariat, 33, 155; service in, by officials, 89, 233, 243; soldiers, 316; soldiery, abuses against, 141
Army Committee(s), 14, 18, 25, 43, 100, 141, 240, 301; Clerk, 226; members, 99, 233–4, 238
Army Council, or General Council (of officers), 18, 42, 160, 224, 231; Secretaries, 260–3, 265
Army officers, 13–14, 42–4, 49, 53, 55–6, 110, 278, 279, 287, 315, 316 (*see also* Army Council; Army Leaders; Generals); as civil officials, 168; Committee, 231; in Ireland, 51; as patrons or sponsors, 67; petition, 287; rates of pay, 110; republican, 264; and soldiers, 103
Arrears (*see* Army, pay; Pay); Com-

missioners for, 234
Arrests, fees for, 118–19, 285
Articles of War, 156; Commissioners for indemnity or relief on, 114, 230, (Registrar to) 231; surrender on, 364
Artists, 171
Ashe, John, MP, 13, 60
Ashley, M., 2, 4, 320
Ashmole, Elias, 242, 399
Ashton, R., 113
Aske, Richard (Judge of Upper Bench), 94
Assembly; of Divines, 306; of Settlers, 245
Assessment Commissioners and Committees, 10, 46, 124, 268–9, 301, 311–12
Assessment, Committee on equity in apportioning, 422
Assessment, the Monthly, 10, 24, 26, 28, 29, 50, 125, 281, 305, 311, 320, 323, 327, 330, 333–4, 362 (*see also* Act(s); Bills); arrears, 113; assignments out of, 123; attacks on, 314, 321; cuts in, 288; indemnity cases concerning, 300–1; local staffs for, 112, 241, 301; Receivers-General, *see* War Treasurers; on rents, 427; total yield, 321; Treasurers, 112
Assizes (half-yearly), 31, 56, 305; Judges, 303, 304
Association(s), *see* Eastern Association; Northern Association, Committee; Southern Association, Committee
Atheism, 308
Atkyns, Edward, 355, 368
Attorney-General, the, 304 (*see also* Prideaux)
Attorneys, 102
Aubrey, John, 316
Augier, Réné, 19
Autobiographies, 173, 209–10, 399
Ayscue, Admiral Sir George, 146

Backwell, Edward, 409
Bacon, Francis, 31, 32, 422
Bacon, Sir Francis, 355
Bailiffs, 285
Baines, *see* Baynes
Baker, Clement, 99, 114

demnity suits concerning, 301; in London, 162, 214, 264; officials and staff, 16, 101, 168, 303; record books, 67; scandals and abuses, 160–2; Searchership(s), 87; Secretary to Commissioners, 99, 266; Solicitor to Commissioners, 266; waiter's place in, 126

Customs (duties or revenues), 24 26, 28–9, 101, 113, 123, 124, 320, 323, 337; arrears, 234; giant farm proposed, 166; total yield, 321

Customs, preservation, or improvement of, Commissioners for, 233

Dallison, or Dallyson, Martyn, or Martin, 398; career, 226–8
Dallison, Martyn, jun., 227
Danvers, Lady, 135
Darnell, Sir John, 228
Darnell, Ralph, 278; career, 228
Davies, G., 243
Davies, Sir John, 36
Davys, Sir Paul, 412
Dawson family, 233
Dawson, Martha, 233
'Dead Pay', 125, 155
Dean, Forest of, 39, 41, 273
Deane, Col Richard (Major-General; General-at-Sea), 38, 244, 262
Deane, Capt. Richard (Treasurer-at-War; Receiver-General of Assessment), 99, 244, 277, 398, 419
Dean(s) and Chapter(s) (or capitular) lands, revenues, 240, 268
Dean(s) and Chapter(s) (or capitular) lands, sale, 12, 240; Committee, 164; Contractors, 112, 211, 216, 230, 252; numbers of staff, 67–8; Registrar, 108, 114, 257; Surveyors, 67–8, 164; Treasurers, 112; Trustees, 67
Death, dates of, see Officials
Death penalty, 144, 307, 428
Debentures (for arrears of army pay), 59, 123, 141, 233, 278; forged, 64, 130, 141–3, 232, 424; Receiver, 293
Debt: Committee on prisoners for, 139; law, 162; prisoners, 44, 139, 162, 270, 294
Debt(s), public, 28, 319, 320 (see also Accounts; Officials)
Debts, sequestered, 300
Decimation Tax, 49, 312, 319
Delinquency, 14, 153–4
Delinquents, 12, 134; procrastination by, 155
Delinquents' lands, 27–8, 79 (see also Royalist(s))
Dendy, Edward (Sergeant-at-Arms), 163, 277, 278, 419
Denmark, 129, 165, 216
Departments (of state, or government), 17, 341 (see also Courts; Office(s)); location, 104
Deptford (Kent), dockyard, 157; store keepership, 267
Deputies, see Officials; Sergeant; Sheriffs; War, Treasurers-at-
Deputy Lieutenants, 11, 251, 311
Derby, Earl of, 355
Derby House Committee, 9, 10, 17, 18, 21; examinations, 256; Secretary, 255
Derbyshire, 312
Devereux, see Essex
Devereux family, 237
Devereux, George, MP, 240
Devonshire, 135, 179; officials from, 184, 185, 220; sequestration, 152
Dictionary of American Biography, 250
Dictionary of National Biography, 171, 174, 197, 212, 218, 242, 250, 256, 260
Diggers, the, 30, 291, 295, 331
Diplomacy, 21 (see also Foreign affairs)
Diplomatic offices, or posts, 205, 419
Diplomats, 276 (see also Agents; Ambassadors; Envoys; Secret Emissary)
Disbrowe, John (Major-General), 43, 48, 50, 53, 312, 360, 361, 371, 423; and law reform, 90; local office, 86; as Major-General, 431; as Protectorate councillor, 111
Disbrowe, Samuel, 368
'Discoveries' (also concealments), 15, 125, 229; Commissioners for, 134, 219
Dismissal, see Office(s)
Distraints, 300
Divines, see Assembly; Clergy; Congregational(ists); Minister(s); Presbyterian(s)
Djilas, M., 4, 324, 339
Dockyards (naval), 40–1, 125 (see also Chatham; Deptford; Portsmouth;

361; creatures of, 152; as garrison colonel, 110; regiment, 300
Jonson, Ben, 227
Jordan, W. K., 99, 225, 226, 261, 309, 318
Journalism, 260
Journalists and newswriters, 20, 21
Journals: Parliamentary, 172, 319; private, 173
Judaism, neo-, 426
Judge-Advocate, of the Army, 38, 297
Judges, 31, 56, 59, 82, 83, 85, 95, 96, 291, 304–5 (*see also* Assizes; Chancery; Common Pleas; Equity; Exchequer; Upper Bench; Wills); salaries, 123, 289
Jury, 97
Justices of the Peace, 33, 49, 137, 179, 278, 305–6, 311–12, 314; officials as, 233–4
Juxon, Mr John, 269
Juxon, Mrs, 269
Juxon, William, Archbishop, 33, 415

Keeble, or Keble, Richard, 277, 419
Keeler, M. F., 170
Kellam, Richard, 66
Kelsey, Thomas, 361
Kennedy, D. E., 2
Kensington (Middx.), 224, 268
Kent, 39, 179, 180, 217, 247, 310; Excise officials, indemnity case in, 299–300; officials from, 184, 201; property, 213; rising, 84
Kentish: gentlemen, 65, 131; petitions, 157
Kenyon, J. P., 4
Kineton, (War.), 270
King of Arms, *see* Norroy
King, Gregory, 322, 324
King, John, 350
King, the, 7, 8, 9, 12, 17, 36, 148, 235–6 (*see also* Charles I); Commissioners to negotiate with, 266; grants by, 86; service under, 341
King, Thomas, MP, 377
King's friends, 336; goods, *see* Movables; quarters, in Civil War, 214, 224; Servants, the, 6–7, 9, 337 (*see also*

Charles I; Great Officers; Officials, of 1625–42); service, 62
King's Bench, Court of, 31–2 (*see also* Upper Bench); Chief Clerk, 97–8; Judges, 303; prison, *see* Marshalsea
Kingship, 49, 295; abolition, 31
Kingston, Lord, 244
Kinneill (Scotland), 145
Kinsala (Ireland), 240
Kirke, Stephen, 153
Knight Harbinger, 245
Knightly, Sir Richard, 152
Knight Marshal, 294
Knight(s), 389 (*see also* Gentry families; Officials, status)

Labourer, 302
Lambert, John (Major-General), 35, 43, 47, 52, 53, 55, 56, 171, 212, 262, 278, 334, 339, 340, 361, 363, 382, 423; and Barebones Parliament, 70; daughter, 244; forces, in the North, 137, 233; and Ireland, 35; as Major-General of North, 48, 51, 97; as patron or sponsor, 63–4, 231, 233–4; and Protectorate, 49–50, 53, 234, 336, 362; as Protectorate councillor, 111; and reform, 288, 334; and Restoration, 234; and Scotland, 36–8
Lambertian, 215, 234
Lambeth, 134
Lancashire, 15, 237, 313, 314, 364; excise, 253; offices, 131; officials from, 253; Sequestration commissioners, 15, 61; sequestration committee, agents, 60; sequestration disputes, 152
Lancaster, Duchy of, 322, 327, 334; court and jurisdiction, 27, 44, 47; fees, 114; House, 105; revenues, 27
Land revenues, 24; Receiver-General, 101, 122
Land sales, 3, 11, 12, 25, 26, 27–8, 125, 194, 232, 319–20, 327, 330–4; commissioners, 104; committees, 26; offices connected with, 205–6, 257; Registrar-Accountant, 226; total yield, 321; Treasurers, 11, 27; Trustees, 27, 104
Land surveyors, *see* Surveyors
Land tax, 281, 291

Maynard, John, MP, 280
Meadowes, Philip (envoy to Denmark and to Sweden), 165, 276
Meautys, John, 269
Meautys, Thomas, 268
Medals, 41
Medical, *see* Doctors; Officials, status
Members of Parliament, or MPs, also Rumpers, 20, 23, 34, 53, 56–7, 59, 168, 278 (*see also* Five Members; Secluded Members); and accounts, 131, 349; approaches to, 165; attack on, 284; of Barebones, 296; and Chancery offices, 88–9; civilian, 243; as commissioners, 14, 25–7, 107; on committees, 10, 19; compensation, 332; cost, 323; as Councillors, 20–1; and deputies, 96; dilatoriness, 310; ex-Rumper, 273; financial position, 110; group biography, 169, 170; income and estates, 109; letter to, 296; as officials, 24, 27, 32, 109, 243, 244, 252; as patrons or sponsors, 60–4, 66; or politicians, 171; privilege, 151, 160; under Protectorate, 111; purged, 8, 9; quorum, 236; recruiter, 292; the Rump, 10, 392; as Scottish Councillors, 52; self-indulgence, 327; as sheriffs and accountants, 113–14; in 1659–60, 54–7; social background, 179; wages, 109; weekly allowance, 109
Membership of Parliament, exclusion from, 151
Memento For the People . . ., *A*, 289
Menial servant(s), 169, 248
Mercer, 247
Mercers' Company, 215, 225, 229, 240
Merchant Adventurer(s), 216, 220, 383; Secretary, 261
Merchants and traders, 197, 302 (*see also* London; Officials, status); accounts, 167; as administrators, 16; as committee-members, 50; of Dublin, 36; Muscovy, 139; and mercantile connections, 264; as officials, 215, 221; and shippers, 101
Messengers, 21, 106, 114, 120, 163; ex-Messenger, 278; of the Chamber, 316
Michels, R., 4
Mickleton, Christopher, 134
Mico, a merchant, 160

Middlemen, 430
Middlesex, 306, 431; commissions and committees, 211, 251, 268–9; excise farm, 166, 307; justices, or magistrates, 238, 306; officials from, 184, 185, 201, 210, 226, 251; property, 212, 252; Sequestration Committee, 106
Middleton, Henry, as patron or sponsor, 66
Middleton, Hugh, 65
Middle Temple, the, 187–8, 203, 219, 228
'Middling sort', the, 282
Midlands, the, 396; officials from, 183–6, 202–3; east, 179; west, 39, 185
Midwives, 101
Mildmay, Sir Henry, MP, 130; as patron or sponsor, 66
Milford Haven (Pembrokeshire), 240
Militia, the, 10, 11, 48–9, 239, 312; Committees, 10, 15, 46, 311–12 (*see also* London)
Mill, Col John, 137–8
Millenarian(s), 30, 44, 69, 218, 287, 333 (*see also* Fifth Monarchists)
Military, *see* Army: administration, 205; commissions, fees, 115, 379; commissions, loss, 156; Junto, 244; regime (of autumn 1659), 56, 120
Milton, John (Latin Secretary), 21, 23, 171, 173–4, 210, 279, 291, 338, 340, 399
Minister(s), 46, 113, 279, 315 (*see also* Clergy); impoverished, 254, 270; non-puritan, 10 (*see also* Scandalous Ministers Committee); puritan, 10 (*see also* Plundered Ministers Committee); stipends, 268
Ministry, the, 45, 279, 288, 295 (*see also* Church)
Mint, the, 322; administration, 41; Assay-Master, 242; Chief Graver, 86; Committee, 10; Master, 27, 41; offices, 205; officials and staff, 41, 86, 242, 419; resignations, 62; revenue, 27 (*see also* Revenues, minor); Warden, 27, 41
Minute Book(s), 16, 22, 149, 298
Mobility, *see* Officials, geographical origins and destinations; Social mobility
Molins, James, surgeon, 400
Molins, Molyns, or Mullins, William

Sunderland, Robert Spencer, Earl of, 167
Surat, posts at, 166
'Sureties'; for those bailed out, 142; on entering office, 101, 124
Surgeons, 276; army, 38; City of York, 101
Surrender, see Articles of War
Surrey, 295, 310; Excise farm and farmers, 166, 307; officials from, 185, 214, 217, 222, 242; property, 241
Surveyors of lands to be sold or confiscated, 67–8, 164, 271, 366
Sussex, 309, 312; property, 224
Swearing, 102, 308
Sweden, 58, 127, 165; King of, 390
Switzerland, envoy in, 120
Syddall, Matthew (Assistant Prize Cashier), 143
Sydenham, Richard, 415
Sydenham, Thomas, 173, 276
Sydenham, Col William, MP (Treasury Commissioner), 50, 359, 361; as garrison colonel, 110; as Protectorate councillor, 111

Tandy, Napper, 232
Tandy, Philip, alias Tendy, 63–4; career, 231–2; charges against, 142–3
Tany, Mr, 295
Tawney, R. H., 1, 167, 170
Tax(es), Taxation, 3, 11, 56, 283, 316, 324, 331, 342; Agents, 254, 301; burden, 286, 287, 319–23, 330–1, 335; cuts, 122; farming, 251; local, 311; penal, 10–12, 48, 151, 295, 319, 327, 330, 332, 334; reform, 288, 289, 331; returns, 179; yield, 433; (see also Advance of Money, Assessment; Compositions; Decimation tax; London, building; Poll-taxes; Subsidies; Weekly pay)
Taylor, A. J. P., 323
Taylor, John, 157–9
Taylor, Nathaniel, 88
Taylor, Silas, sen. (Commissioner and Trustee), 432
Taylor, Silas, jun., 316
Teachers, 44 (see also Dons; School(s))
Teesdale Forest (Co. Durham), 134

Tellers (in Parliament), 43, 359
Tellers, see Exchequer, Lower
Temple, the (London), 130
Temple family, 261
Temple, Sir William, 399
Tendy, see Tandy
Tenure, see Office(s)
Terms of Service see Officials
Terrill, or Tyrrell, Thomas, 89
Tests, see Engagement; Loyalty oaths and tests; Protestation; Solemn League and Covenant
Testimonials, 58, 68, 77
Thames, river, 102, 104; Ballastage, 237; shore, 214
Thirsk, J., 3
Thomas, Isay, MP, 240
Thomason, George, 135, 138, 412; quoted, 243
Thomason Tracts, 172, 299
Thompson, or Thomson, Col George, MP, 157, 399; as Admiralty and Navy Commissioner, 350
Thompson, Cornet (James), 331
Thompson, or Thomson, Maurice, 264
Thomson, William, 158
Thoroughgood, or Thorowgood, Sir John; career, 267–70; The King of Terrors Silenced, 269
Thoroughgood, or Thorowgood, Sir John, 415
Thorpe, Col, 130
Thorpe, Judge Francis, MP, 304
Thurloe, John (Secretary of the Council of State; Secretary of State), 21, 46, 53, 97, 121, 265, 280, 306, 334, 392; allegations against 165–7, 427; appointment, 23, 68, 256; approaches to, 71–2, 72–3, 74–5, 77, 94, 118, 122, 126, 132–5, 367–8; career, 258–60; earnings, 126; and excise, 166; family connections, 72–4, 220; health, 259–60; and Henry Cromwell, 75; information to, 274; knowledge of alleged bribe, 165; letter(s) from, 245–6, 258; letters and reports to, 71, 75, 145, 150, 158–9, 167, 312, 313, 317, 431; papers, 71, 127, 134, 165, 298; as patron or sponsor, 72, 73–4, 253, 259; as Postmaster-General, 74, 166–7, 230; present for wife, 166; probity, 165–7; promotion, 68–9; as Protectorate

I 3